PRIME TIME
The Life of
EDWARD R. MURROW

At Glen Arden Farm, Pawling, New York

Prime Time
The Life of
EDWARD R. MURROW

by ALEXANDER KENDRICK

LITTLE, BROWN AND COMPANY · BOSTON · TORONTO

LIBRARY OF CONGRESS CATALOG CARD NO. 78-83740

Second Printing

The author and the publishers wish to thank Alfred A. Knopf Incorporated for permission to reprint excerpts from *In Search of Light: The Broadcasts of Edward R. Murrow 1938–1961,* edited and with an Introduction by Edward Bliss, Jr. © Copyright 1967 by the Estate of Edward R. Murrow.

Published simultaneously in Canada
by Little, Brown & Company (Canada) Limited

PRINTED IN THE UNITED STATES OF AMERICA

Contents

Picture Credits

Ed Clark, *Life* magazine © Time Inc.: frontispiece and page
451 (bottom)
CBS: pages 21, 22 (both), 58 (all), 63, 170, 185, 229 (top),
237, 245, 296 (both), 315, 336 (all), 345, 353, 356,
357, 361 (both), 366 (both), 370 (both), 385, 394
(both), 443, and 444
Bob Gomel, *Life* magazine © Time Inc.: page 23
Madame Yevonde: page 118 (both)
Wide World Photos: page 186
Vogue Studio Photograph by Sylvia Redding: page 287 (top)
Photo by Loren Smith: page 287 (bottom)
Yoichi Okamoto: pages 501 and 502

Illustrations

PRIME TIME
The Life of
EDWARD R. MURROW

I

"To give the public what it wants"

COMMUNICATION is not to be confused with communications, Ed Murrow would say. He did not believe that the medium is the message. Murrow himself has been called a great communicator; certainly he left the deepest of impresses on the broadest of media. But though he was conscious of the potential of technological innovations, many of which he and his colleagues introduced to radio and television, he wondered with Thoreau whether Maine had anything to say to Texas, or, later, as director of the United States Information Agency, whether this country had anything to say to the rest of the world.

He was sure they did have, and should have. He believed that the medium made it possible to convey and interpret the message, but that there had to be a message to start with, that in the beginning was the Word. Otherwise, he said, "all you have is a lot of wires and lights in a box."

From the electronic revolution which the United States has undergone in the past two decades, Murrow and McLuhan drew contrary conclusions. The statement that television is a tactile rather than a visual, much less a rational experience, is an invitation to accept and be complacent, as the real merges into the unreal. Murrow regarded television as a sound-equipped mirror held behind American society, reflecting its good and its bad, both only too real. He affixed to the electronic mirror a magnifying lens and a powerful focusing searchlight. Not the medium but the society was the message.

He understood, however, that communication was not a one-way street. In his CBS office hung a quotation from Thoreau: "It takes two to speak the truth — one to speak and another to hear."

Murrow's independent, imaginative and incisive reporting helped radio and television to become important journalistic media, instead of only channels of entertainment or advertising. After his radio war reporting and that of his staff had made him internationally known, his *See It Now* television documentaries set the standard for all networks. Against the pressures of the commercial environment, which sought to keep news and public affairs as conformist and "noncontroversial" as the rest of television, these programs shook up America by questioning, arousing and stimulating, the true fulfillment of the medium's potential. They were on the side of history, perhaps of the angels.

Yet Murrow was not a crusader in the accepted dogmatic sense. He acknowledged himself to be part of the honorable tradition of muckraking, but the muckrakers were not ideologues. Lincoln Steffens, who was one of them, described them as more interested in exposure than in analysis. They dealt not so much in objective or subjective as in what might be called corrective journalism. Murrow always regarded himself as a reporter rather than an analyst, but he was more. He was a disturber of the peace and a collector of injustices. Radio and television are by their very nature ephemeral. He endowed them with a sense of permanent substance by giving them a purpose.

Murrow's searchlight has gradually faded. His reflecting magnifying mirror has on too many occasions, in television news and documentary, become a distorting one, as in a boardwalk fun palace. Indeed it might be properly asked, how much does the mirroring of confusion and complexity itself enhance that confusion and complexity?

The technical devices — the coaxial cable, microwave relays, videotape, communications satellites, interconnection, community antenna and cable television, color — have continued to develop, but the tone of the medium has become a bland one, and its message is not marked urgent.

Nearly a century after Thoreau asked, "What if Maine has nothing to say to Texas?" John A. Schneider, taking office as the first "broadcasting group" vice president of the Columbia Broadcasting System — signifying that the radio-television network had branched out, or "diversified," into other, nonbroadcasting ventures which diffused its original undertaking — remarked on the imminence of "an instant communications capability, worldwide."

But, he added, "As to what we are going to say to the world when we have their attention, I'm not certain yet. That's the thing that worries me. We are thinking about it. We have respect for it. I don't have any solution to it quite yet . . . It's rather frightening, though, to think we'll be able, maybe, to talk to everybody in the world. Now all we've got to do is to decide what we're going to say."

One of the things the CBS executive decided would not be said, on his network at least, was the live, unedited, cautionary words about the Vietnam War by former Ambassador George F. Kennan before the Senate Foreign Relations Committee. A rerun of the *I Love Lucy* comedy series was shown instead, and the president of CBS News, Fred W. Friendly, resigned, as his collaborator in television's most notable news partnership, Ed Murrow, had left broadcasting some years before, with a feeling not only of nonfulfillment but of frustration and indeed despair.

It did not take too long for Schneider to get his answer as to what America would decide to say to the world. In March 1967 the first picture ever transmitted by two connected earth satellites was sent instantaneously from Honolulu to London, a distance of eighty-five hundred miles. It showed Swedish Crown Prince Carl Gustaf gazing raptly at a bikini-clad co-ed on the beach at Waikiki. Except for such occasions as the Churchill funeral, or the Olympic Games, satellite global transmission has produced little of the immediacy or participation that had once been proclaimed, nor has it risen much above the level of the instant newsreel. And yet because television has always been at its best in live coverage, even this glimpse of the potential has made the day-to-day contrivances of the medium seem more drab than ever.

American television is now in its third decade as a mass broadcasting instrument. What is missing from its programming today is the vital ingredient of yesterday, its promise. Despite its relative youth, the medium has aged prematurely, and one of the symptoms of its senescence is lack of a sense of aim, apart from the one frequently expressed within the industry that "people would rather look at something, no matter what, than at nothing."

At a dinner in 1959 for his friend J. Robert Oppenheimer, Murrow heard the physicist say, "Communication is what makes us men." In Murrow's own last public speech in October 1964, receiving a Family of Man Award, the broadcaster amplified the theme: "The speed of communications is wondrous to behold. It is also true that speed can multiply the distribution of information that we know to be untrue. The most sophisticated satellite has no conscience. The newest computer can merely compound, at speed, the oldest problem in the relations between human beings, and in the end the communicator will be confronted with the old problem, of what to say and how to say it."

Murrow was always conscious that television's power for good was no greater than its power for evil. Following the night in 1954 when his career came to its high plateau, and the medium reached the peak of its effectiveness — the night he permitted Senator Joseph McCarthy to undo himself — Murrow remarked that television could as easily be used to elevate a dictator as to topple a demagogue.

He believed television was weighted on the good side, but only for so long as it could distinguish between good and bad. For one thing, he thought it offered too little opportunity for the expression of minority views, though later, it was true, urban racial explosions would force minority views onto the screen.

Murrow believed with Jefferson that an informed public will make its own best decisions if given the facts on which to judge. He felt that television did not demand enough of its audience. He himself appealed to the courage, decency and fair play in people. He was able, like Churchill, a man with whom he was much taken, to lift people out of themselves.

But he had learned that in television, many of the individual local stations were not honestly involved in the life of their communities, nor reflected it, even when they presented what was unavoidable in the way of public affairs. He was particularly vexed by the failure of the broadcasting medium to take positions in public matters, as the printed medium did.

As has been so often remarked, the heart of the problem is the basic cross purpose between radio-television as an agency for the sale of commercial products, and radio-television as a belt for the transmission of ideas. There are those in the industry who believe broadcasting can move men, and even some who believe it could move mountains, but they are outnumbered by those who believe all it has to do is move goods.

Radio ⸱gan as a noncommercial enterprise, or at least as one limited to the mercantile idea that interesting programs put on by the manufacturers of radio sets would induce people to buy the sets in order to hear more such interesting programs. Said Secretary of Commerce Herbert Hoover in 1922: "It is inconceivable that we should allow so great a possibility for service, for news, for entertainment, for education, for vital commercial purposes, to be drowned in advertising chatter."

Again Hoover declared: "Radio communication is not to be considered merely a business carried on for private gain, for private advertising, or for entertainment to the curious. It is a public concern impressed with the public trust, to be considered primarily from the standpoint of the public interest." He saw it as a glorified kind of public utility.

The two radio pioneers David Sarnoff and Merlin H. Aylesworth, of NBC, also regarded the medium as one for education and entertainment, rather than advertising. Numerous proposals were made for financing it — appreciative listeners sending money directly to speakers and entertainers; public-spirited citizens sending funds to stations; coin-operated boxes attached to receivers; and Government subsidy. But listeners, who in 1922 represented three million American homes as the number of stations increased from thirty to two hundred in a single year, were already accustomed to getting their radio programs free. It was too late to change matters, and commercial sponsorship was deemed the only way out. Even so, Secretary Hoover opposed direct advertising. He thought sponsors should offer programs as a public service and say so in introducing them, but that there should be no commercial interruptions. "There must be no national regret that we have parted with so great a national asset," he said, meaning the allotment of the public airwaves to private companies.

But starting with its first commercial in 1922 for a New York City real estate development, radio had soon become the longest and largest set of billboards ever known, and when its impact was diminished and it continued as what has been called "audible wallpaper," television took over without more than the barest pretensions of public service. If only for technological reasons, which were considerable, serious news and public affairs programming had a long and difficult television gestation period, and some believe it was born deformed.

For even though, as at CBS, the news division may be the only one in the corporate structure not required to operate on a profit-and-loss basis, television news and public affairs are bound to be peripheral to the main body of programming, much more so than in radio. Expansion or development of news and public affairs programs has been against the entrenched interests of the entertainment and advertising people, who yield any time reluctantly, again, perhaps because the stakes are considerably higher than was true in radio. Profits may not always be achieved by news programs, but this does not mean that profits are not avidly sought. As corporatism has increased in television, news has come to be increasingly regarded as simply another commercial product rather than a public service. Whether it is allowed to exceed its budget or not is less important than the fact that the news department, too, is adjudged a success or failure largely by its audience ratings, i.e., its commercial value.

The expectation that news can and should be profitable is based, even if unconsciously, on the belief that it need not be controversial in a way which makes advertisers afraid to risk sponsoring it, as they sometimes did with Murrow-Friendly programs. There are cases today where a network itself has suggested to sponsors that they withdraw from news and public affairs programs to which they were committed, to spare their sensibilities in the event of ensuing controversy.

The Federal Communications Commission, created not only for the technical task of allocating radio frequencies and later television channels, but also because presumably broadcasting is much too serious a matter to be entrusted to the broadcasters, has, as so often happens with regulatory agencies, come to identify itself with the interests of the industry it was intended to regulate. There are exceptions, like the one attendant upon the 1968 Democratic National Convention in Chicago, when widespread criticism of television coverage led the FCC to adopt a posture of censorship also.

But over the years, at least until the time of writing, not only has no television license ever been lost for failure to provide adequate public service programming, but the FCC has had no effective system of holding stations to their pledged obligations.

It may be remarked in passing, as typical of the relationship of FCC members to the networks, that the broadcasting industry's most outspoken critic in the Federal Government, the FCC chairman who found television to be "a vast wasteland," subsequently became legal counsel in Chicago for a television network. Other governmental critics of commercial broadcasting practices, including numerous FCC commissioners, have also found happiness with the networks.

The game, of course, is played with a good deal in the pot. The value of a broadcasting license is considerable. In 1964, for instance, a television station in Pittsburgh was sold for $20,600,000. Its tangible assets were $3,-800,000. Its "good will," or more accurately its FCC license, was thus worth $16,800,000.

"A television license is a license to print money," once remarked Lord Thomson of Fleet, the international communications tycoon.

Television is the greatest advertising medium ever known, with its turnover of $3 billion a year, and CBS was for years the world's single largest advertising outlet, though in 1968 the claim was disputed by NBC.

Television's present state of affluent barrenness is not entirely a matter of concentrating on money-making, however. Murrow, who for long regarded the American commercial radio-television system as "potentially" — a significant qualification — "the best and freest yet devised," ascribed television's failure to do its public duty to overcommercialism, and the subordination of creative and analytical talent to technology.

Criticizing television for being commercial may be like criticizing lions for eating Christians. One of the most frequent defenses of television commercialism is the phrase, "It's the nature of the beast." Another familiar answer to the charge that television is not good enough is that it is better than it might have been, considering its cash nexus, though this might be less an answer than a begging of the question.

But other factors besides money are involved. One is corporatism as such, the gigantic growth of what were originally small enterprises. When he held the television screen, or the radio microphone, many thought Ed Murrow personified CBS, and in a sense he did, in matters of public obligation and conscience. Some may have even thought he was bigger than CBS.

Though he often appeared to be so, and autonomous to boot, the plain fact is he could not have done what he did as a broadcaster without CBS encouragement, facilities, money and general mood of enlightened self-interest. He could not have done it on NBC, which then did not have the wholehearted CBS attitude toward news and public affairs, and he could never have done it on the lesser broadcasting organizations.

In an industry given to rule by committee, he was always an individual. He did what he thought had to be done on the air, and worried about the consequences later. He had no tolerance of governmental and other forces opposed to free broadcasting, forces which a corporation had to take into account. He resisted the influences that sought conformity in thought and popular and easy answers. There may be comfort in conformity, but there is also a great and perverse satisfaction in rejecting it. In that sense Murrow was perverse, and perverseness found widespread response.

Within the company, he had immediate access to the chairman, William S. Paley, and more than that, Paley's personal friendship and understanding. Until a few years ago, the CBS News correspondents and executives were on familiar terms with members of their board and their corporation officers. The news and public affairs division was a badge of honor, proudly worn by the network.

This kind of relationship, paralleling that of many good newspapers and magazines, has now been lost in the corporate labyrinth. The corporate structure, like the human body, rejects irritants. CBS, in Murrow's prime, was a single entity, dedicated only to broadcasting, run by a board, a president and a few officers. Now it is made up of seventeen corporate divisions, with numerous sections and areas, has more than a hundred vice presidents, and has diversified its interests widely.

As its stockholders were proudly told in 1967, from an Eastern seaboard radio network of sixteen stations in 1927, CBS had grown into a worldwide communications enterprise, distributing services and products in a hundred countries. From its original base in broadcasting it had expanded into phonograph records, film syndication, record and stereo "clubs," musical instruments, toys, and "educational services."

It does research and development not only in communications but in military and space technology. It has acquired a major league baseball team and two publishing houses, and has invested in a Broadway musical and in community antenna television. It has radio and television affiliates in Canada, Mexico, Antigua, Bermuda, Puerto Rico, the Virgin Islands and Guam, in addition to those in the continental United States.

This process of horizontal expansion, called takeover in Britain, has now also become a corporate pattern in the United States, where it is known as conglomeration.

One reason given for CBS unwillingness to broadcast some programs in the past, such as the Senate hearing on Vietnam which resulted in Fred Friendly's resignation, was that the network depended more on its direct broadcasting revenue than, for example, the rival NBC, which is merely part of a much larger corporate enterprise, RCA. Thus CBS would suffer more proportionately by preempting commercial time to show unsponsored public affairs events. The CBS diversification of interests, assets

and profits might lead a corporation lawyer to argue that this will free it
of dependency on broadcasting revenue alone, and thus enable it to broadcast more public affairs programs. But can it really be thought so? Whatever the merits of "conglomerates" in other areas — and there is considerable controversy, for they seem generally to be aimed at improving stock
market positions rather than commodities or service — it can risk being
said that in broadcasting, conglomeration will be to the detriment of public service rendered. This is not only because of the new interests, apart
from broadcasting, acquired by corporate boards, but because of the
absentee ownership local radio and television stations must suffer from if
they pass into alien hands.

This kind of diversification, motivated by the accumulation of profits,
may be inevitable in modern corporate practice. Yet despite diversification, CBS fortunes have been shown to rise or fall with network television.
Instead of concentrating on that, as it used to do, it has gone afield into
investment finance, like so many other American corporations. In 1969, it
decided to increase its common stock from 30 million to 50 million shares
for the purpose of "future acquisitions."

Corporatism has had other effects. It has created a situation in which a
company like CBS is not only competitive against other broadcasting
companies, but competitive within itself. The CBS radio network is a commercial rival of the CBS television network. The television network,
which serves 187 individual stations, competes with the five stations
owned and operated by CBS itself, and they can earn more by rejecting
network programs in favor of their own local ones. CBS News, a corporate
division, sells its product to the radio and television networks, but it must
lease their facilities and use their personnel in order to create it.

This corporate intricacy has fragmented authority, and helped remove
or dilute the burden of responsibility for what goes out on the air. Seldom
is anyone required to press buttons in broadcasting anymore. Having
been preset, they now in a sense press themselves.

Diversification is a two-way street. If all the networks have gone into
fields of alien corn, so too have other American corporations, representing
all sorts of remote interests, come into broadcasting.

The CBS television network's most successful comedy star, Lucille Ball,
who was an independent agent and producer, as well as actress, is now
owned by Gulf & Western Corporation, which began in auto parts. It
now possesses Miss Ball's Desilu Productions, Paramount Pictures, and
Famous Players Canadian, with other holdings in radio, television, wired
music and movie theaters, in addition to zinc and sugar.

The NBC radio-television network has always been a subsidiary of the
Radio Corporation of America, which is a worldwide commercial communications organization but also manufactures radio and television sets.

Its sales in 1967 totaled $3 billion. NBC has also diversified, into golf clubs and paper pulp, and has taken over an outstanding publishing house which had previously absorbed two others.

The third network, ABC, has long been identified with movie interests, and it would have merged with International Telephone and Telegraph, the largest communications and communications-manufacturing system, if it had not been forced to give up the plan because of concern that it would be contrary to the public interest — not for economic reasons, but lest it be prejudicial to the fair and adequate presentation of news.

For ITT has sizable interests in forty countries, including some ruled by military dictatorships. Would an ABC television documentary on one of these countries be inhibited by such interests? Would it even be undertaken? ITT owns a finance company. Could ABC do a candid program on credit and interest rates? ITT set up the Dewline warning system, the Moscow "hot line," and NATO and SHAPE communications. What effect might this have on ABC's thoughts about East-West detente? ITT derives 40 percent of its domestic income, 25 percent of its total income, from United States defense and space contracts. Thus the ABC broadcasting networks would financially have become an important component of the defense establishment.

ITT obviously did not view matters in this light. For it, ABC may have been simply a "diversification," a way of increasing revenue. When its absorption of a broadcasting system failed, it took over a vending machine company instead. It also owns a car rental company, a home construction company, a baking company and a hotel chain. ABC, the third network, would have become a small cog in a large industrial-financial complex. Its broadcasting function could only have been impaired.

The big networks are not alone in straying from broadcasting. Two lesser radio groups own an airline each. One of them, RKO-General, also controls the operation of 125 theaters and community antenna television facilities in twenty-nine cities, and has been sued by the Justice Department under the antitrust laws.

Profit-making, gigantism, multiple corporatism, and even monopoly status, which is what the television networks are sometimes charged with, are not only economic but social phenomena. They make television not merely a communications medium but also an industry. But in its broadcasting activities it does not have the same inhibitions, limitations and correctives as other industries.

Warped values cannot be recalled, as warped automobile doors are, or defective steering wheels. Television's quality has nothing to do with its success; in fact, a good argument could be made to justify lack of quality. Television is carried on without the normal business risk of failure. Once a broadcasting license has been granted it is virtually never revoked, and certainly not for breach of the contract that stipulates a small amount of public service. The financial side of the industry has its ups and downs, there are good seasons and off seasons in the sale of advertising time, and thus in revenue, but the steady upward progression of profits is a foregone conclusion. Television actually does have a license to print money.

But the television industry is more than a fortunate sector of the free enterprise system. Because it deals in ideas and images, as well as in cosmetics and cigarettes, it is wittingly or unwittingly an instrument of the Establishment, that complex of governmental, political, economic and psychological forces that, even when some enlightenment intrudes, is dedicated to the preservation of the status quo, or what Madison Avenue and the White House basement alike call "the mix."

The historical Establishment view of the citizen is a narrow one, as target, as consumer, as statistic, but hardly ever as participant in decision-making. Television, too, normally talks to people as consumers, in the context of Veblen's "pecuniary culture."

In terms of modern economics, overcommercialism and profit-seeking are a much too simple explanation of things, however. Television's profits, whatever their size and whether they go up or down, are incidental to its function of stimulating the demand for goods, thus keeping the consumer economy expanding. It is not required for television to be a marketplace of ideas, only a marketplace.

As magazines like the *Saturday Evening Post* are killed off, television becomes even more important as an advertising medium. Mass communications move mass-produced goods into mass consumption. As has been pointed out, television does not sell goods directly, much less sell programs to audiences. What it does is sell audiences to the sponsors, and its need therefore is for more and more audiences.

In the larger game of "national product," no matter what its nature — as a measurement of power, of economic growth which cannot be left to the risks of a free competition in quality — television profits are secondary to this institutional role.

It can be argued, and is, that the interests of the Establishment and the public interest are therefore identical, and that television serves both. But a nation does not live by singing commercials alone.

Moreover broadcasting has imposed upon American society what in the supreme civic sense may be a fatal contradiction. The extension of communication should be an extension of democracy. Yet while the participatory base of democracy has been broadening, the ownership and control of the means of communication have narrowed.

It could be said indeed that far from being an expression of majority desire, as the networks say, television programs are the imposition of a social minority on the majority, the minority consisting of the fifty top advertisers, the three networks, and a dozen or so advertising agencies. It is what they think public taste is and demands that governs the nature of broadcasting. As a British critic has put it, "Which came first, the program or the taste for it?"

In the corporate intricacy of broadcasting, the men who make the decisions as to what the public shall see, the program executives, are nameless managers, like most of those in industry. Who can identify the CBS West Coast vice president any more than the General Motors vice president for sales?

Once the program schedules have been decided upon, many months in advance, they are "locked in," and become virtually sacrosanct, though meanwhile the earth may be shaking about them. What television does best is its extended and often poignant, indeed harrowing coverage of such historic events as the assassinations of John F. Kennedy, Martin Luther King and Robert F. Kennedy — to which, some critics believe, it also contributed by its unrestrained daily portrayal of violence on the home screen. But some broadcasting executives have complained because this kind of coverage is done by the suspension of commercial time, and the consequent loss of revenue. There is almost a feeling of resentment at the interruption of normal business, not only on Madison Avenue but in Wall Street, where broadcasting stocks are often not recommended by brokers because public service reduces profits and dividends. Indeed it is one of the great truths of broadcasting that when they are at their best as communications media, radio and television are injuring themselves as profit-making corporations.

Establishment influence is not always so overt or pecuniary. It may be worth at least a footnote that the president of one network has served as chairman of the RAND Corporation, that Government-supported "think tank" which some regard as an annex of the Pentagon. The same man has been head of the Committee on Information Policy, which looks over the shoulder of the Government's propaganda activities. The chairman of a network board has also been the chairman of a presidential Commission on Resources. In 1961 top executives of both CBS and NBC were consulted by Vice President Lyndon Johnson, in his capacity as chairman of the Space Council, and they recommended greatly accelerated spending on a space program. The recommendation spurred President Kennedy, though he may not have needed much spurring, to proclaim that the United States would get a man to the moon "in this decade."

These can be classified as public, and some indeed as patriotic assignments which could not be refused, but they also illustrate the meshing of the supposedly independent public communications function with the Government's machinery.

The same meshing has taken place in even more substantive ways, that is, between the Government and the parent corporations of some broadcasters, in terms of defense contracts. The RKO-General broadcasting group is owned by General Tire and Rubber, which also owns Aerojet General, manufacturer of the Polaris missile. Group W radio stations are owned by Westinghouse Electric, a defense contractor, as is the Radio Corporation of America, which owns NBC.

But even without any financial interest in defense, television would depend nakedly on the Government for its existence. Unlike other communications media, its stations are directly licensed by the Federal power, and frequently the networks themselves are threatened with licensing. They are never allowed to forget their dependence by Government agencies and Congressmen.

Not only can the President, by virtue of his office, command television to his own purposes, which may be partisan and political as well as presidential, but the administration as a whole can use television at will in any public controversy — as it notably did in the case of Vietnam policy — by offering Cabinet members to network panel and interview programs. This makes legitimate news, of course, but it is also "managed" news.

It is perhaps just a sign of the times that Lyndon B. Johnson was in fact the first "television President" in more than the political sense, for his personal, not inconsiderable fortune was derived from broadcasting. He acquired a radio station while a Congressman, added a television station after he entered the Senate and became Democratic whip, and a second Texas television outlet when he became majority leader. As Vice President and President, though nominally his broadcasting interests were put in "trust," he further expanded them, with the help of favorable FCC rulings against competitors. The Johnson television station in Austin, the state capital, exemplified the monopolistic nature of broadcasting in so many American cities. Without competition, it could select from the offerings of all three networks those programs which it decided the citizens of Austin should see and hear. When cable television entered upon the scene, as competition, the Johnson interests absorbed it by investing in it.

Apart from the free radio and television time given most of the legislators by their local stations, there has always been a similar special relationship between Congress and the broadcasting industry. In the 90th Congress it was estimated that twenty-five members had direct or family-related interests in television or radio.

Some such interested parties have served on committees dealing with broadcasting, indeed the chairman of a committee holding hearings on industry practices was himself a television station owner. His investigation eventually faded away. In New York State a broadcasting corporation with no fewer than five Congressmen holding interest in it was given an FCC license precisely because their presence, in the eyes of the Federal agency, endowed the company with "civic participation."

No one knows how many congressional lawyers have radio-television clients — Mr. Johnson's friend and adviser Clark Clifford had one of the biggest when he became Secretary of Defense — but the House of Representatives in 1964 actually passed a bill by a wide margin prohibiting the FCC from imposing any limitation on the number or frequency of television commercials. The only limitation is the one self-imposed by the industry, and it is obviously based on what the traffic will bear. It should cause no surprise that more money is earned by members of the Screen Actors Guild from television commercials than from any other source, including their appearances on television entertainment programs, or in Hollywood movie roles.

Even though the networks have frequently been accused of trying to monopolize the resources of television — among others, the charge has been made by Congressmen who either hold television interests themselves or represent them — an even more blatant kind of monopoly operates in many American communities.

There are some five hundred commercial television stations in the United States and three hundred of these are without competition in their local communities. The owner of one of these, who in some cases also owns the town's only newspaper, often has the choice of two or even three networks in making his programs. Obeying the dictum of "giving the people what they want," or what he thinks they want, the choice is invariably of entertainment, situation comedy, panel games and pap.

The competition of ideas that Murrow and others believed should be radio-television's stock-in-trade has to a large extent been abandoned. Chain ownership of both newspapers and radio-television stations, and frequently of both together, has become increasingly common. Nearly half of America's 1700 or so daily newspapers are owned by combines, about 30 percent of the AM and FM radio stations, and almost three-quarters of all commercial television stations. Newspaper publishers in 1967 held interests in a third of the regular-channel commercial television stations, and there were newspaper-television monopolies in twenty-seven American cities. More than half the 4200 AM and 1800 FM stations had newspaper connections.

When competitive enterprises, in the form of cable-TV companies, seek to relay other programs or even originate them locally, they are either fought bitterly by the established and in a sense protected interests — the issue becomes "pay TV" versus "free TV" — or as so often happens, simply bought out, becoming a part of the monopoly themselves.

The lowest common level of television practice is the local network affiliate, the station which keeps printing money; the man in the South who, as Murrow and Friendly discovered, would not run a program about Marian Anderson because she was a Negro, or acknowledge that there may be racial trouble in his own community; who has decided that his audience is not really interested in Washington or Europe, or even in controversy around the corner from the station. This has changed somewhat recently under new community pressures.

Affiliates represent not only commercial but political stakes in a community, which may not be representative of the community as a whole, or consonant with its best interests. Too often television is spoken of in monolithic terms, and as a social force it may well be, but the networks are after all made up of individual local stations, and though networks and affiliates are mutually dependent, their outlooks and motivations are not always the same.

When Congressmen, who may themselves own shares or holdings in local stations, support those stations in an outcry against network "monopoly," they are usually opposing higher standards, low as network standards may be, than they themselves can or want to offer. They also make more money that way.

The local affiliates of the networks prefer to stand pat on the regularly scheduled programs — in 1968 this meant an old movie every night of the week from one network or another — rather than disrupt them with special news or documentary broadcasts. It is often difficult for networks to get local "acceptance" of special programs even of the utmost urgency, and some public affairs programs have indeed had to be canceled or postponed for lack of "acceptance."

The CBS television network has some 250 local outlets but for public service programs an acceptance of ninety is average. The others show old movies or reruns of old television programs. Most rarely are any public service programs of local origin shown, and then usually on network owned and operated stations, which are not strictly affiliates.

Ideology or inertia may play a role in nonacceptance, but many public affairs programs from the networks carry a smaller "price tag" or no price tag at all — no commercial sponsorship — and therefore local stations receive less revenue from them. Affiliates oppose more network news because they receive only 50 percent of the profit from the advertising involved, while local news programs, of course, net them the full 100 percent.

Whatever other reason might have existed for CBS to refuse to carry "live" the Senate Foreign Relations Committee hearings on Vietnam, the most important may well have been the attitude of the local affiliates.

In the nine-day period during which the committee hearings were held, and President Johnson flew to Honolulu for a war strategy conference to capture his own headlines, affiliates of the three television networks rejected 30 percent of all news and public affairs programs offered them. On the Sunday after the hearings only 42 percent of CBS affiliates and 30 percent of NBC affiliates showed the networks' Vietnam "specials." During the nine-day period twenty-seven news and public affairs programs were fed out by the two networks. Of the two hundred-odd stations on each network, only fourteen CBS affiliates and only twenty NBC affiliates accepted all of them. Even Ambassador Kennan's appearance before the Senate committee, carried by NBC with extravagant self-praise after CBS blacked it out, was not shown on twenty-four NBC affiliates.

The demand of the affiliates for more mass-appeal programs, with the threat of replacing network offerings by their own canned fare, forms one arm of the pincers within which network programmers operate, the other arm being the demand of the stockholders for more dividends. And off and on, Congress enters the picture, breathing hotly down the networks' necks in the name of "the public interest," which usually turns out to mean the interests of the local affiliates.

A notable example of these combined pressures was the national drubbing given the two big television networks for their coverage of the 1968 Democratic National Convention, with its climax coming not in the nominations in the convention hall, but in the clash between Chicago police and youth demonstrators outside the convention hotel and in the park across the street.

Not only Congressmen, FCC members and "law and order" advocates accused the networks of not "telling it like it is," but a great deal of criticism came from the networks' own affiliates, which obviously do support their local police though their nightsticks be thick or thin.

The networks were accused of telling only part of the story by the mayor of Chicago, who had deliberately made it difficult to tell the story at all. They were said to have "sensationalized" events, though the events would have seemed to be fairly sensational in themselves.

Though clearly part of a national refusal to face facts — by putting the blame for events on television, which showed the events — the public clamor and the demands for investigation were a boon to the networks. It was ironic indeed that television should have been taken to task for what it could not escape doing, for what came to it naturally, when the significant thing about the 1968 campaign was television's failure to provide sufficient depth, background, or interpretation, in a historical situation. Some Americans saw the theory of democratic choice atrophied in 1968, and that after a President had been compelled to give up renomination because of widespread disapproval, and the course of American foreign policy modified. Yet virtually the only way in which politics was presented, during the campaign, apart from snippets in daily news programs and unrevealing Sunday afternoon panels, was in paid radio and television advertising by the rival candidates. And not merely a saturation of short "spot" commercials, but whole packaged hours of personality projection, staged "forums," and glossed-over issues. Aided and abetted by Congress, the networks did not even have to present "debates" of the 1960 Nixon-Kennedy stripe.

Thus the outcry against television for doing its duty at Chicago, while a tribute to its potential as a public instrument, may at the same time have constituted evidence of its failure to do its duty for so long. The public had forgotten what television was for, and what it used to be.

The networks might also have welcomed the Chicago uproar for the opportunity it gave them to perceive a peril to the First Amendment.

Government control of any information medium can be represented as a threat to freedom of expression. But the networks have cried wolf many times before, and have too often stigmatized as "thought control" the attempts to get them to redeem their public service obligations. They have equated freedom of speech with freedom from criticism. They long refused to take the First Amendment issue to a court test, for the very real fear of losing the case. After Chicago, CBS and NBC did challenge the Federal Communications Commission's "fairness doctrine" on constitutional grounds, in a case before the Supreme Court, and did lose. The tribunal upheld the FCC doctrine and ruled that "it is the right of the viewers and listeners, not the right of the broadcasters, which is paramount."

Assuredly it is not consonant with democratic development that, by threat if nothing worse, congressional critics, politicians, a Federal agency, and local station owners, in the name of "the public interest," should try so desperately to make television even more irrelevant than it usually is.

Perhaps this is a further payment in coin for television's own deficiencies. There is nothing novel in the fact that networks should be subject to pressures. What is distressing, as Murrow found out in his time, is that they should so often yield to them.

Nor are pressures confined to commercial broadcasting. The educational network, too, found twenty-five of its 120 stations refusing to show the first program of its keenly anticipated, foundation-financed Public Broadcast Laboratory because it was "controversial," that is, devoted to the racial problem. The same kind of disaffection by local affiliates has been expressed to the NET educational network as to CBS and NBC. Some of it is sectional in origin, the Midwest and South versus the East, and some is political.

The principal criticism by the affiliates is that the network holds views which are "too liberal" and takes attitudes out of keeping with their own, and presumably those of their communities. "Educational" would seem to have a very narrow definition in noncommercial broadcasting.

Like the commercial networks, the educational television network was virtually AWOL during the 1968 campaign. It, at least, could plead lack of funds.

One of television's original promises was that it could be, not merely with the times and of the times, but frequently ahead of the times. The Murrow-Friendly partnership on CBS, for instance, regularly presented programs about national and international situations, problems and possibilities which the average viewer thereby became aware of for the first time. Thus they prepared him for events that might affect his life and well-being.

In a sense, these programs "made" news by anticipating rather than following the headlines, and at the same time they helped shape opinion toward it. *See It Now* producers did not have to read the *New York Times*, as is so often the case with news producers these days, not only to provide a story but to guarantee its acceptability, to the corporate boards which now rule the news divisions. Very few of the Murrow-Friendly reports had to be "legitimatized" by prior publication.

Even at its most routine, television serves to provide information as well as entertainment. But it also has, or should have, the power to aid insight, add to perception, and educate. The essayist E. B. White has put it this way:

"I think TV should be the visual counterpart of the literary essay, should arouse our dreams, satisfy our hunger for beauty, take us on journeys, enable us to participate in events, present great drama and music, explore the sea and the sky and the woods and the hills.

"It should be our Lyceum, our Chautauqua, our Minsky's and our Camelot. It should restate and clarify the social dilemma and the political pickle. Once in a while it does, and you get a quick glimpse of its potential."

How far television has fallen short is best measured in the field of news documentary, which in Murrow's time, week after week, presented illumination and a sense of wonder and participation in the burning issues of the times — civil rights, atomic fallout, American foreign policy, the processes of government.

During a two-month period in 1967, by contrast, the three commercial networks had three "prime time" documentaries, *An Essay on Women, The Royal Palaces of Britain,* and *Thoroughbred,* a stud-farm chronicle. In the same period newspapers and magazines dealt in depth with the fall of Congressman Adam Clayton Powell, the row about the Manchester book on the assassination of President Kennedy, the conviction of Bobby Baker, the President's former protégé, and the dispute about new Federal safety rules for auto manufacturers. Even prior publication in the *New York Times* provided no warranty for such stories on television. They were kissed off with brief daily reports on the evening newscasts.

Even *Variety,* the Bible of show business, which yields to no one in its appreciation of P. T. Barnum, had to ask: "Why feed a tour of Westminster in prime time when attention in the United States is focused on whether Hanoi will come to the peace table?" It is true the networks, during the same period, covered the fatal fire in the Apollo space capsule in a way which mere newspapers could not hope to compete with, but not much depth of perception or brilliance of insight was needed.

In the spring of 1968, one of the judges for the Emmy awards for television news documentaries summed up the two full days devoted to viewing the twenty-one entries of four proud networks, three commercial and one educational.

The four awards went to reports on the Detroit riots, Africa, Vietnam, and Ronald Reagan.

"Yet for all the Vietnam films, the riots, the politics, how little we had seen of the world in twenty-two hours," he noted. "There was nothing about American or foreign education, nothing about de Gaulle or France, nothing about Franco's Spain, about gold and money, Cuba and South America, the Communist bloc, Sino-Russian relations, nothing about drugs and sex. Everything was made with a high degree of technical competence; nothing was boring; but how little we had learned, how infrequently I had been moved."

In the actual presentation of the Emmy awards, nationally telecast, "all the attention went to those situation comedies and comic hours and dreary dramatic hours that television really cares about." Awards, like ratings and program credits, are what television lives on. They compensate for lack of substance.

Though Murrow and Friendly in their time won more awards than anyone else, they once wrote a speech — never delivered but strongly felt — arguing that such ceremonies were in fact a "racket" and so numerous as to be meaningless. "It is possible there are more national awards than there are network television programs," they said, adding that the most important act of television courage would be to refuse such "honors." As president of CBS News, Friendly later would refuse his network's participation in the Emmy awards for news, but after he left it resumed. As for Murrow, he always believed that "the only real award is public confidence."

Most of today's regular news documentaries and "specials" are what is called "soft," such as "portraits" of popular singers, or "biographies" of

Murrow and microphone

With Norman Thomas, the perennial Socialist candidate for President

General Omar Bradley, a radio guest

Murrow and Friendly, the "team" that brought television news of age

movie stars made by the film studios themselves, or "essays" on pop art and other pop phenomena. Even otherwise serious news programs are often narrated by stage or screen actors.

None of these can be objected to as such, under the head of entertainment or perhaps even enlightenment, but the point is that they are presented as "news" and occupy the extremely scarce "news hours," to the detriment of more pertinent public matters. As for being in any way specials, the term is apparently used in a supermarket sense.

Television cannot escape reacting to overwhelming events, such as the war in Vietnam or antidraft demonstrations or campus strikes, but this is usually done on an "instant" basis. The networks race to be first on the air with their old footage brought out of the files, and their studio discussions by "experts." But this "actualité," as the French call it, without adequate preparation or editorial view, is a long way from the careful, measured documentary method that *See It Now* employed.

Moreover the television line between news and entertainment, between public affairs and show business, has become blurred, by politicians on late-night programs with popular "personalities," Senators narrating epic patriotic cantatas, mayors with their own chat programs, political comments on comedy programs — even by the "press" interview programs of Sunday afternoon, which are controlled by never asking the unaskable of the Secretary of State or a four-star general.

Even in daily news programs, which have brought the violence of war and urban riots into the American living room at cocktail hour, the impact has been dissipated. In 1966 the CBS pictures showing the Marines in Vietnam setting fire to peasants' huts with cigarette lighters caused nationwide furore and roused the Pentagon to charge television reporters with virtual treason. In 1968 the piling-up of Viet Cong bodies, Dachau-fashion, and their airborne disposal as refuse, evoked no measurable public response and raised no questions for the Pentagon to answer. The nightly news "pill" may be like the other pill which prevents conception.

For television engenders a vicarious participation in events but not an actual one; indeed the vicarious participation may satisfy enough to stultify and replace the actual.

How much television's nightly presentation of battle scenes from Vietnam had to do with the unpopularity of that war is arguable. It undoubtedly trivialized the war by making it part of the ordinarily superficial treatment of news, sandwiched between commercials. Even on a CBS special, *Christmas in Vietnam*, which showed an American child praying for her soldier father, this scene was followed by two commercials, for a mouthwash and a brassiere.

In a way, the reality of the Vietnam War was washed out, perhaps, by being equated with the fantasy of most other television programming.

If anything, the battlefield pictures may have hardened viewers instead of shocking them, by their regularity and matter-of-factness.

Moreover, pictures are by no means the whole story. Television news depends on them, but pictures represent moments of impact, and those moments may not be representative of the whole. Life is not constituted by points of impact, but by slowly evolving processes. An English observer has remarked that the function of television reporters should be to "make watching as difficult as reading," to demand as much of a viewer as a newspaper or book demands of a reader.

Most television news producers, intent on pictures, believe that spoken words are a mere accompaniment and should not "fight the picture." But the true function of words, as Murrow knew and practiced it, is to distract from the picture by giving it a further dimension, by qualifying and complicating.

Murrow stayed clear of the presentation of "hard news" on television because he evidently perceived its shortcomings and pitfalls.

His more considered weekly programs were designed to expose the viewer to the realities of American life, but to do so purposefully. Street riots and battle scenes may be real enough, but they carry no meaning unless it is supplied by something besides the camera eye.

The 1968–1969 television season began with only one regularly scheduled hour per week of news and public affairs programming, out of all the hours filled by the three commercial networks. It was on CBS and a pale memory of *See It Now*, for it was primarily devoted to "soft" subjects and magazine material. It is always possible to show news specials, and many are produced in a season, especially to take the place of a commercial program which may not have done very well in the ratings. But television is no longer ahead of the news, as *See It Now* was, dealing with trends, indulging in premonitions, exploring the woods and the hills of ideas. Instead, and only when it must, television follows the news. It is the prisoner of events, not so much concerned with news analysis as psychoanalysis.

Obviously times have changed, and Ed Murrow, as he was the first to admit, was lucky to be where he was when he was. In his life and career, the time and place always seemed to adhere.

There were the Anschluss and Munich crises before the Second World War, and they can be said to have created the new journalistic dimension. There was the war itself, which stretched the dimension to its broadest limits, as it moved from the drama of a crowded island under heavy bombardment to sweeping battle across the face of Europe, and the emergence of an altered continent and society. There was the Joe McCarthy era after the war, the time of the Bomb and of the cold war, of Korea and America's assumed global role.

Murrow's career in broadcasting spanned the period from 1935 to 1961, anxious, troubled, disoriented times — "years of crisis," as his year-end round-table radio-television discussions with CBS foreign and national correspondents called them. "It seems incredible," one couple wrote him in 1949, "that while we have been listening to you, our children have gone through their teens, have married, have made us grandparents — and we are still listening." And presumably they continued to listen for twelve years more, and their grandchildren began to.

Largely due to Murrow and the men he found and brought to it, CBS in the field of news and public affairs during those decades was constantly a center of public controversy, a target of criticism, and a source of civic enlightenment and involvement. The other networks were more prosaic, played it safer, and were more taken for granted. More came to be expected of CBS, and often in those days it delivered. People actually talked, in office building elevators and subway trains, about programs they had seen or heard the night before. All that is gone.

But it is at any rate a commentary on the history and essence of television that its outstanding figure thus far is not a laboratory scientist, developing color or videotape, or tinkering with satellites; not a network executive, devising new formats, decreeing "trends" or buying up old movies; not a board chairman, making speeches about public service and informing stockholders of increased dividends; not an advertising salesman, or a producer of commercials, or a market research analyst, or even an entertainer — though these make up the warp and woof of the communications fabric — but it is Ed Murrow.

Apart from what he gave his audiences, who hung on his every word — often as vehement in their disapproval as they were voluble in their approval — his influence on his colleagues and all others in radio-television news is a continuing monument.

Consciously and unconsciously, his standards and values have been adopted by the best of them. They have rated themselves against him, and measured themselves by his work. There is no commentator now who will not agree that whatever he is privileged to say on the air is in large part due to Murrow.

It was not his specific attitude on any question that gave him his authority and credit. He often tended to take a conservative view. But his general attitude of open-mindedness, which is the core of liberalism, influenced the people who worked with him and the CBS way of handling the news, raising the level of reporting and heightening the climate of inquiry. The "Murrow style" became, and to some degree still remains, the CBS style.

It may be unfair to judge television by the best it can do, for even in Murrow's time the best was but a small part of the whole. *See It Now*, even as only a half-hour a week, and other programs like it, compensated for the endless hours of studio audience programs, quiz shows, and family comedies with built-in laugh tracks that packed in the viewers and made the money. It was this artificed acceptance world that Murrow was never really part of, though the commercial nature of the medium made him not only a recognizable public figure but a highly paid one.

He was not a cynic. His earnest upbringing saw to that. But he was considerable of a skeptic, as he himself would have phrased it, or, as his colleague William L. Shirer called him, "a skeptical idealist."

A story Murrow told frequently, when discussing television, was of his youthful logging-camp surveying days. He went out with an older man, the timber cruiser, a quiet, dour type, and the rain of the Olympic National Forest poured down and poured, and soaked them through. They came to a shed in a clearing and took shelter, sopping wet. The surveyor reached into his pocket.

Slowly, clump by sodden clump, he pulled from it the pulpy mass of a breakfast cereal he had been carrying in a small packet. He munched it silently and solemnly, bit by bit in his fingers, and then he said, "Son, I tell you, this here raisin bran is much overadvertised." It became Murrow's own attitude to a large part of the world around him.

Controversy was the inevitable outcome of the Murrow brand of electronic journalism. Friendly relished controversy for its own sake. "That's the nature of television," he said. Murrow was the one who defined the purpose of controversy and believed its function was not only to provoke but to illuminate. The focusing searchlight affixed to the mirror made his kind of television truly the window on the world he felt it was designed to be, and took it out of the shadow realm of parlor games, soap opera, idle chatter, synthetic personalities and old movies.

With some qualification, for in television the one often overlaps the other, Friendly provided the techniques and Murrow the thought processes. They did not always agree on what should be said, but they accommodated each other's ideas in exploring the how and why of things, and together they penetrated the consciousness and sometimes the consciences of their audiences.

Gradually the Murrow-Friendly window on the real world has been shrunk to a peephole. By 1965, less than fifteen years after *See It Now* had first burst on the home screen, the issue-attentive species of television news documentary had virtually vanished. Controversy, with its pros and cons, had given way to compatibility. A vew of life had become "a slice of life." The treatment of public questions was subjective, instead of objective. As one CBS News president described it in 1967, the orientation was "from inside looking out."

It was enough merely to turn the cameras on, without worrying about the focus or lighting. The sharp, shrewd editing of film that enabled a Murrow-Friendly program to make point after point was replaced by a kind of cinéma vérité that substituted impressions for points. The dissecting table became a psychoanalyst's couch. People with problems, or victims of conditions, were encouraged to talk about them endlessly, but hardly ever was it considered what might be done about the problems or conditions.

If *See It Now* was engaged in the business of presenting "the little picture," the new soft-line public affairs program offered the little, little picture, a variant of the late, late show. Its approach to such realities as tenement life, homosexuals, hippies and marijuana — and these were among its favorite subjects — was that it didn't matter very much how social problems — or rather phenomena, for problems is a pejorative word — looked to Congress, the welfare department, the sociologist, or the man in the street, to run the old gamut of television documentary. What mattered was the individual involved with the problem-phenomenon. As for the viewer, he became voyeur.

Thus emotion replaced editorial perspective. Old-style, or Murrow-Friendly, documentaries dealt with cause and effect, and tried to show the circumstances which produced the consequences. The new wave offers the viewer a sensory experience rather than balanced judgment. It would make the medium not only the message, but the massage.

Even the immediate transmission of an occurring event, which is television's forte, often becomes a sensory rather than a cogitative experience if the raw camera alone is given sway, without the exercise of sufficient human editorial judgment or appraisal.

The controversy over television coverage of the 1968 Chicago convention echoed that of the Detroit insurrection a year before when many viewers called Station WXYZ-TV to demand that it "stop the riot right now." They did not accuse the station of staging the disturbances but evidently did feel that if television did not show the pictures, they would not be occurring.

This kind of fantasy could be applied to the Vietnam War, black militancy, college rebellions, drug abuses and other aspects of American society.

Another television branch of what is now regarded as public affairs embraces such largely pictorial series as *The Saga of Western Man, The World of Animals, Great Explorations*. These are proper, often fascinating programs. They would provide a valid supplement to news documentary. Instead they are the substitute for it.

Gauguin in Tahiti, the re-creation of the voyages of Ulysses, or essays on women, doors and bridges — even driving, voting and science tests — merely underline the fact that commercial television has failed to treat adequately such questions as the Vietnam War, America's policy in Asia, pacifism, the worldwide traffic in arms, Church versus State, the right of dissent, the police use of force, congressional ethics, the New Economics, stock market speculation, or a dozen other important matters which would have been standard operating procedure for Murrow and Friendly with *See It Now* and *CBS Reports.* In the 1968 election year, the electoral system itself, obviously in crisis, was discussed in no serious way on any network.

In the entertainment areas of television, as apart from news and public affairs, the argument is made by the men responsible for programming that they cannot compel the audience to change its tastes by force-feeding.

They point out that such social-minded series as *East Side, West Side* (the cases of a social worker); *Slattery's People* (a state legislator's problems); *That Was the Week That Was* (satire); and *The Defenders* (issues before the bar and the nature of justice) were all developed and offered by the networks and, except for *The Defenders*, all of them failed to interest the public, as shown by the ratings.

This, in the end, is what television always gets back to. The networks hold that the public wants nothing more than domestic or situation comedy because superior drama deals with realities and disturbing ideas. Yet when the networks do occasionally put on original contemporary plays — recalling the days of *Studio One* and *Playhouse 90*, except that then they were presented weekly and now they are exceedingly rare specials — they run for two hours or more and command top ratings. Even the old movies frequently present more meaningful drama than the hackneyed regular television programs.

That political comment and even controversy in 1968, an election year, should have had to be made to such a large extent in the form of wisecracks and throwaway gags on popular comedy programs, and that only through the censorship screen of the program practices department, is a sobering fact with which to celebrate television's chronological coming-of-age. For such didoes are usually uninformed, venomous and based on personalities rather than issues.

It may be true that, according to the ratings, the combined audience in New York City of the three commercial networks for the Security Council sessions on the eve of the June 1967 Arab-Israeli war was less than that for an Alfred Hitchcock movie rerun on a local independent station, and that many complaints were received by the networks over the cancellation of their regular fodder. But this does not eliminate the responsibility of the networks to provide programs of minority as well as majority interest, instead of giving grants to an educational station to do so, as CBS has done. Indeed, in a basic way, television practice brings into dispute some of the premises of democracy, with respect to minorities and majorities.

Thus Britain's Pilkington committee report in 1960, which recommended additional channels for both the noncommercial BBC and commercial ITV, noted that " 'what the public wants' is what individuals want. Some tastes and needs are shared with virtually everybody, but most are shared with different minorities. A service which caters only for majorities can never satisfy all, or even most of the needs of any individual."

If viewers were thought of as a mass audience, said the report, they would be offered only the ordinary and commonplace and "kept unaware of what lies behind the average of experience."

"In time they may come to like only what they know. But it will always be true that, had they been offered a wider range from which to choose, they might have chosen otherwise, and with greater enjoyment."

The report summed up: " 'To give the public what it wants' is a misleading phrase. It appears to be an appeal to democratic principle but is in fact patronizing and arrogant, in that it claims to know what the public is, but defines it as no more than the mass audience, and limits its choice to the average of experience."

In 1968 Britain went through a massive television shakeup, as channels were reallocated and new commercial broadcasting companies came into being to replace some that had been judged to have failed in their duties to the public. It is inconceivable that such a thing could happen in the United States.

In passing it was noted that under the pressure of competition by commercial television, which began in 1954, and in the quest for mass audience ratings, the noncommercial BBC had appreciably lowered the high standards and lost the illuminating purpose of Lord Reith.

Financially and in terms of ratings there was nothing wrong with British television when it was so drastically overhauled. The American ailment from which it suffered was a deeper one. But not long before the upheaval an FCC commissioner ridiculed critics of American television by attributing to them the principle, "If it works, it must need fixing."

Yet for all its dedication to giving people "what they want," television has come to find its biggest problem is not in getting people to watch, but in getting them to care. The medium no longer transmits public excitement, as the Kennedy-Nixon debates did, or the *See It Now* program on the Radulovich case, or *CBS Reports* on the Polaris missile, or even Murrow's other programs, the celebrity-visiting *Person to Person* and the global conversation piece *Small World.*

People no longer seem to anticipate television programs with any particular zest or talk about them afterward. Every Monday the newspapers dutifully record all the Sunday public affairs television programs, but as with most newspaper headlines, they provide information, perhaps, but not insight. Even *Town Meeting of the World*, the first real use of satellite television for other than spot news, has palled and faded away.

In Britain, which instituted television as a public trust, administered by a public corporation and supported by viewer license fees rather than advertising (until the BBC was supplemented by commercial ITV), the public affairs portfolio in Harold Macmillan's cabinet was held by William Deeds, M.P., who said of television that it "has within its power to decide what kind of people we become. Nothing less."

There might be some dispute about cause and effect, or the chicken and the egg, but it is clear that television's widespread influence has raised important questions not only of public policy but of individual conscience. Since television is, in the statutory sense at least, intended to serve "the public interest, convenience and necessity," the individual in broadcasting may increasingly face the question, which began to be posed to Murrow, whether he owes his true loyalty to the company by which he is paid, or to the faceless and often inert and uncaring public he nominally owes allegiance to. Sometimes the two interests can be reconciled. But suppose they cannot be? How does one stay within the ruling establishment without being part of it? Is it better to work for improvement within the existing framework, or to go outside it?

Murrow was confronted by these questions when the quiz show scandals had brought television to ignominy, and its dehumanized corporatism had made it a kind of Golem. For a long while he believed it was possible to improve commercial television from within, indeed from the top down, and his most important public pronouncement on the subject, his Chicago speech to the Radio and Television News Directors Association in October 1958, was dedicated to that end.

Murrow's view of television's responsibility contrasted with the preponderate view in the industry, attributed to David Sarnoff, though he later denied saying it, that "we're in the same position as a plumber laying a pipe. We're not responsible for what goes through the pipe."

After the McCarthy broadcast, which provoked nationwide controversy, Murrow remarked to his friend David Lilienthal that the networks had "power, great power, but no responsibility."

"I get credit for courage in putting on the McCarthy show," he said. "That illustrates what I mean. That should have been a decision of the

network, of CBS itself, and a deliberate part of its editorial policy, for
which it would be held accountable.

"The networks say we are only conduits, pipes; they might better say
sewers. We carry whatever anyone wants to transmit to the country, for a
charge, and that is the extent of our responsibility. But that is power without responsibility."

The discouraging response received from the industry to the Chicago
speech — "Mr. Murrow does not, of course, speak for CBS," said the
company's president — impelled the broadcaster to look outside the commercial networks for succor. He was active in the movement advocating
a so-called "fourth network" — which has now taken form as Public Television — and was indeed offered the post of editor-in-chief of a new public
service network, under foundation auspices. Instead, when the time came
to leave broadcasting — which was after prospects for improvement from
within had noticeably failed to appear — he went into the Federal Government, as director of the United States Information Agency.

As for Friendly, he departed from CBS five years after Murrow, and
less than a year after his former associate's death, to some extent because
of Murrow's belief that the independence of the news operation must at
all costs be preserved.

Corporate reorganization had ended the free access to the top CBS
level that the CBS news director had always enjoyed, by interposing another administrative echelon between them. Though John Schneider's decision not to have live cameras at the Senate Foreign Relations Committee
hearings in February 1966 precipitated Friendly's withdrawal, the fact that
editorial decisions had been taken out of his hand caused it.

Ironically, by resigning to protest the subordination of news in the
corporate structure, as he saw it, Friendly merely further lowered the
status of news and public affairs and handed them over more completely
to corporatism.

In this controversy it was pointed out that the cost of preempting regular programs to make way for the Senate hearings was given as $175,000,
and the question was asked whether Schneider's decision might have
been otherwise if the cost had been only $175.

But there was much more involved in the argument. Indeed, the whole
order of priorities of public affairs broadcasting had changed markedly
between the time of the Murrow-Friendly partnership and Friendly's assumption of the helm of CBS News.

In the days of *See It Now* the primary concern, as between producer
and network, had to do with programs, the choice of subjects, the treatment, and in a sense, the message. But by 1966 the principal issue had
become the availability of air time. As has been so often pointed out, a

network or a radio or television station cannot add hours to the day, as newspapers or magazines add pages to their editions.

The fight for "prime time," as it is called — the network period between 7 and 11 P.M. — has always been part of television, as of radio before it, but it has come to be only a horological expression, instead of one with a connotation of merit or quality. It no longer mattered, in television's new small world of public affairs, what a particular program was about, or how it was handled, but whether it would get on the air at all against the competition of more profitable entertainment programs.

Indeed as the networks had grown bigger and more impersonal, as corporatism and diversification both increased, their preoccupation had come to be less with broadcasting itself, it seemed, and more with their public relationship to, and influence upon, other and frequently highly technical aspects of the complex American society. The problem was no longer that of providing election returns, for instance, as quickly and efficiently as possible, but whether the returns from one state should be given before the polls closed in another state, thus allegedly helping people make up their minds. Or whether the electronic extrapolation of early returns into the confident calling of final election results justified the abortion of the traditional process of really counting the votes.

It came to seem less important what communications satellites should do than to whom they should belong. Equal time for political candidates outweighed the necessities of a full and continuing examination of political issues. More time was spent in debating what form public television should take than how it was to compensate, if only in small part, for the neglect of duty of commercial television.

After he left CBS Friendly went into public television, as TV consultant for the Ford Foundation and a moving spirit behind the Public Broadcasting Laboratory. The road to a "fourth network" had been cleared by Murrow.

Whatever it may have done to news and public affairs programming at CBS, Friendly's departure also removed the competitive pressure that had done so much to spur the respective CBS and NBC news divisions into public service, despite the corporate indifference surrounding them. Regular public affairs scheduling has all but vanished at both big networks, as their 1968–1969 program listings showed.

As more sets are switched off in the evenings, some critics have gone so far as to call commercial television merely a form of air pollution.

Certainly, in the area of news and public affairs, it could come within Disraeli's description of his parliamentary opposition, as "a range of exhausted volcanoes." They may rumble occasionally, and sometimes even give off sparks, but buried in their ashes lie the artifacts, the cultural utensils, and the petrified human bodies that were seized by the lava and overwhelmed.

In his speech at Chicago, Murrow advised the broadcasting industry to look forward by looking back at its best, to keep at least a rear-view mirror functioning. It was not merely because he himself, in that golden age, had been the keeper of the conscience, but because the keeping had increasingly come to be of the privy purse instead.

A month before Murrow died the CBS stockholders were told by their board chairman that news coverage of unscheduled events — such as the Churchill funeral, the space "shoots," and civil rights demonstrations — had raised programming costs and thereby reduced earnings by six cents a share. The quintessence of the medium was thereby given its true corporate valuation, a negative one.

Under the stockholders' baleful scrutiny, William S. Paley was reported to have deplored the fact that CBS had ever "gone public," that is, offered its shares for sale, and to have said that it could have done better the things he wanted to do if it had remained a privately held enterprise. Even if this had been possible, in the century of the common stock, it may be doubted, since the society is television's message, whether the results could have been much different.

The day Ed Murrow died he was paid high tribute by many of those who had, in effect, driven him out of broadcasting. It was lip service, as it would continue to be, at dedication ceremonies, awards in his name, and other memorials.

The day he died, CBS Television interrupted its regular afternoon soap opera to make the announcement. On CBS Radio the news of his death, reportedly from lung cancer, was followed by a cigarette commercial.

II

"The terror is right here in this room"

THE EVENING of March 9, 1954, was called Good Tuesday by one editorial observer, television's "finest hour" (or more accurately, half-hour) by numerous others, and by the *New York Times* the occasion on which "broadcasting recaptured its soul."

It was the evening Edward R. Murrow, on his weekly program *See It Now*, presented the nation's most successful and most feared demagogue, Senator Joseph R. McCarthy, as his own executioner, in full view of tens of millions of enthralled Americans.

By the simple but devastating method of merely showing the Senator in action on various typical occasions, the filmed program had a direct and powerful cumulative effect that outdid any kind of printed or spoken appraisal, though it did not shrink from such an appraisal itself. It illustrated the force of the still relatively new medium of visual broadcasting, its dangers as well as its promises. It indicated the ironic retribution that could be exacted by mass publicity against one of its own creations.

More than anything else, perhaps, it demonstrated the unique position Murrow held, not only as the leading practitioner of the broadcasting art, but through it as a public figure in his own right — at the age of forty-six — who could challenge the man the President himself, the Secretary of State, and many others in the American Establishment either would or could not challenge. And he did so at the height of McCarthy's sway.

Murrow, who had made his mark by introducing the new brand of journalism by radio in the European crises before the war, who during the war had exemplified not only reporting at its most vivid but also the convictions behind the reporting, had effected the difficult transition from radio to television with the provocative program *See It Now*. It doomed the newsreel concept of mere pictorialism and made people aware that the camera could find meaning as well as action.

At the same time his other television program, *Person to Person*, a weekly "visit" to the home of some well-known person or "personality," had given Murrow a different and more diffused audience and a broader popular base for the prestige required to take on McCarthy, an undoubted idol to a large part of that same mass audience.

Murrow was moreover still the most listened-to and respected radio broadcaster of the time, with his nightly fifteen-minute program of news and comment, based on wide acquaintance with the makers of news, and on equally wide perspectives.

The two television programs were the top and bottom panes of the window on the world that Murrow had opened, for he regarded the medium as not only a means of communication but also a means of transportation for the viewer. Three months earlier he had scored a notable success by taking his *See It Now* camera crews to America's distant and difficult war front for the second time, and filming Christmas in Korea, reporting from "a foxhole in the ground surrounded by sandbags."

But before that, and after it, he had also grappled with the problems of the Age of Suspicion that the Korean War had piled on top of the cold war, and that the atom bomb, the Berlin airlift, the trial of the Rosenbergs, and the Alger Hiss case had intensified, enabling someone like McCarthy, who apparently had no real convictions of his own, to exploit and expand national fears.

Thus, five months prior to Murrow's encounter with McCarthy came *See It Now*'s report on the case of Lieutenant Milo Radulovich, Air Force Reserve, which Murrow regarded as an even more telling, more controversial and more courageous stand against the dangers of the time. And after the McCarthy broadcast came the story of Annie Lee Moss, which technically at least was a more adept use of the television medium, without the intrusion of a commentator to make its point about fair trial and due process.

It was the Radulovich case that made inevitable and set into motion the Murrow-McCarthy passage at arms, though the true roots of it went back to Murrow's boyhood and upbringing; his experiences in Nazified Europe and wartime England; his beliefs in the inviolability of free government, free speech and free thought; and two incidents which made what is generically known as McCarthyism a personal matter for him.

One of these incidents was the attack made on him by the Hearst press, later echoed by McCarthy, for his participation twenty years before in student exchange with foreign countries, including the Soviet Union. The other was the death, by fall or leap from a New York skyscraper, of a friend, a former State Department official, whose name had been brought into the Alger Hiss case.

Moreover, in the broadcasting industry itself, the Age of Suspicion had taken form in the wholesale listing of "controversial" performers and producers, depriving them of employment, on insinuations made by individuals and organizations which, despite lack of any other standing, were regarded as possessing power to alienate both sponsors and viewers from the networks. It was Murrow's belief that the networks had shamefully failed to resist such pressures, and thus helped make McCarthyism possible.

The Radulovich case symbolized the McCarthy era, for it was a classical case of guilt by association.

On the evening of October 20, 1953, *See It Now* told the story. Murrow reported that a young lieutenant in the Air Force Reserve, a senior at the University of Michigan after eight years active duty in the Air Force, had been classified as a security risk under Air Force Regulation 36–52, because of his close association with "Communists or Communist sympathizers." This association was, in fact, with his father and his sister, who read "subversive" newspapers and engaged in "questionable" activities, by Air Force standards, although there was no question about Lieutenant Radulovich's own "loyalty." When he refused to resign, an Air Force board was given the case and recommended his severance.

Radulovich, describing himself as a realist, raised the question: if the Air Force wouldn't have him, as a "security risk," who else would when it came time to find a job?

The board of three colonels which heard the case, based on eight allegations involving Radulovich's sister and four involving his father, ruled against the lieutenant even though the Air Force produced not a single witness, did not give the specifications of the allegations, and in fact kept the supposed evidence in an envelope that was never opened at the hearing. It also refused to say where the allegations came from.

See It Now presented interviews with a cross-section of the citizenry of Dexter, Michigan, Radulovich's hometown, the consensus being that they would not want to be held responsible for the views and actions of their relatives, and that if this could happen to Radulovich it could happen to any one of them. It turned out also that the "subversive" newspaper Radulovich's father read was a Serbian-language one that was pro-Tito.

This was five years after Tito had broken with the Russians and Yugoslavia had been expelled from the Cominform, to receive aid and comfort from the West.

Radulovich's sister also appeared on the program, to proclaim that her political beliefs were her own affair, and that whatever they might be, they had nothing to do with Milo and he had nothing to do with them.

The lieutenant's own position was that blood is thicker than anonymous accusations, and he said he would not end normal "association" with his father and sister, much less denounce them, as the Air Force board had suggested he do. He also said he would not resign quietly, as he also could have done, in order to avoid the issue. As *See It Now* viewed it, the issue was his right to a fair trial on the basis of openly presented and cross-examinable evidence.

After providing the facts in the case and noting the difference between a security risk and a loyalty risk — a difference which many Americans still did not grasp — Murrow concluded that "whatever happens in this whole area of the relationship between the individual and the state, we will do it ourselves. It cannot be blamed upon Malenkov or Mao Tse-tung, or even our allies. And it seems to us that that is a subject that should be argued about endlessly."

If not the subject, the program assuredly was. For it was in a sense an editorial, an unknown genus on television, though strictly speaking it might be called advocacy by reporting. In the broadcasting industry this fact stirred up as much commotion as the contents. One reviewer noted it was probably the first time a major network and an important sponsor had consented to a program taking a vigorous editorial stand in a matter of national significance.

It was further pointed out that most television documentaries were indignant over matters about which there was no argument — like the famous editorial stand against man-eating sharks — and that in any case they were presented after the dust had settled. But Murrow and Friendly had rejected this "illusory and often self-deceptive approach" for a "bold bit of enlightened crusading" that "offered help when it counted."

Actually the network had no hand in the Radulovich program except to provide the air time for its showing. Its consent was a technical matter. *See It Now* was an autonomous operation, tangential to the network news department but not responsible to it. The decision to explore the Radulovich case was Murrow's own. It had not been reported in the Eastern metropolitan press or on the wires of the news agencies, but had been noted in Detroit, and Murrow had the daily habit of reading many out-of-town newspapers.

Both CBS and the *See It Now* sponsor refused to publicize the program, and Murrow and Friendly used $1500 of their own money to buy an ad in the *New York Times*. It was signed by them and made no mention of CBS, merely announcing the local television channel. It was the kind of thing, in short, that emphasized Murrow's extraterritorial status and helped sow the first seeds of corporate apprehension and doubt, not mitigated by the success of the program.

For the Radulovich program brought praise from many quarters, including those inhabited by the executives of the two rival networks. One television critic wrote Murrow that he was the young lieutenant's Zola.

Much more to the point, the program compelled reappraisal of the Radulovich case by the Secretary of the Air Force. Five weeks later the

Secretary appeared on *See It Now* to say that, on second thought, the lieutenant was not a security risk, that his association with his sister was not a vital matter for the Air Force, and that his father's newspaper reading did not really peril the nation's safety.

There could be no doubt that if Murrow had not made the Radulovich case public, nothing like that would have happened. The program also demonstrated a salient feature of many of Murrow's radio and television news broadcasts — that they reached across the nation into local communities where issues originated, held those issues up for examination in the national limelight, and then handed them back to the communities, if not always resolved, at least illuminated.

This was true again in *See It Now*'s next cause célèbre, even before the happy ending of the Radulovich case. In November it presented *An Argument in Indianapolis,* which showed the American Legion of that city, opposed to the formation of a chapter of the American Civil Liberties Union, using its influence to prevent the ACLU from exercising the traditional American privilege of hiring a hall. The chapter was finally given refuge in a Roman Catholic church.

Murrow and Friendly used their cameras to cut back and forth between American Legion and ACLU meetings held the same evening, in separate halls, thus providing a running debate on a question of constitutional rights. It was a highly effective use of the television medium. Not only the antagonists but the juxtaposition of their arguments spoke for themselves. The Legion passed an anti-ACLU resolution, the ACLU reiterated its intention of defending civil rights cases, and all Murrow had to do before saying his familiar "Good night and good luck" was to note that "Indianapolis is still there, and the controversy is everywhere." No further editorial was required.

Variety, in its review of the medium for 1953, called the Radulovich program easily the most important single contribution of the year. "Even if it had not had the stunning result of returning him to duty, it would still stand as historic."

That and the argument in Indianapolis, said *Variety*, made television better in 1953 than it had been in 1952, though *I Love Lucy, Dragnet,* Groucho Marx and Ed Sullivan had continued to dominate the home screen.

1953 was also the year of the television "spectacular," as it was called, meaning the broadcasting of such events as the New Orleans Mardi Gras parade, the presidential inaugural ball, and the atomic blast at Yucca Flat, Nevada. But the true spectacular, in terms of the medium's influence on national affairs, was the Radulovich broadcast. McCarthyism had been given a setback. Now McCarthy himself stood dead ahead.

Wisconsin's Republican junior Senator had gained some notoriety and indeed power since the February evening in Wheeling, West Virginia, in 1950, before the Ohio County Republican Women's Club, when he began brandishing supposed secret documents and charging that Communists were employed by the State Department.

Even before his anti-Communist "crusade" thus began, Joseph R. McCarthy had inaugurated the methods by which he and the era named for him have come to be known. In 1949 the man, misleadingly elected as "Tail Gunner Joe" by a constituency that included many of German origin, had used sweeping unsupported statements, hypotheses presented as facts, accusations of lying by witnesses, conversion of a congressional hearing into a trial, and attacks on the integrity of other Senators — all in order to indict the United States Army for torture, in the so-called Malmedy Massacre case.

Near that village in Belgium, in December 1944, eighty-six identified and perhaps seventy other American prisoners of war had been killed by the First SS Panzer Regiment, "Hitler's Own," during the Battle of the Bulge. Two years later seventy-three men of the SS regiment were tried at Dachau by an American military court and convicted of war crimes, forty-three of them receiving death sentences, which were never carried out.

The SS men, in turn, charged that they had been tortured, and McCarthy, attaching himself to a Senate Armed Forces subcommittee in 1949, pleaded their case because, he said, he was opposed to lynch law.

The subcommittee rejected the cruelty charges though it did find the Dachau trial had been an overhasty procedure. Despite his rebuff, which may have given him the deep-seated grudge against the Army that was evident later on, McCarthy had established himself as something more than the ordinary freshman Senator. He confirmed this fact shortly thereafter when he rose in Wheeling to assert that "205 Communists" were "working and making policy" in the State Department and were known to the Secretary to be conscious Soviet agents. It was a month after the conviction of Alger Hiss, the former State Department official, nominally for perjury but implicitly for betraying confidential information.

At various times thereafter McCarthy used various figures, ranging from 205 down to 57, in his State Department accusations. It was not the numbers that were important, but their effect.

McCarthy waxed in Washington, as well as in the newspaper headlines, not only because it was the period of the atom bomb, the cold war, the Korean War and the Soviet spies, but also because the Truman administration had been labeled by its critics an administration of "mink coats, deep freezes, cronies and five-percenters," as a result of some minor scandals. And McCarthy could always be relied on by the generally anti-Truman press for anti-Truman dicta.

During the last two years of the Truman administration and the first two years of the Eisenhower presidency, no important decisions were made in Washington without taking McCarthy into account. There were some opposing voices in the Senate. Margaret Chase Smith, in 1950, had made her Declaration of Conscience, and a few other Senators signed it.

But in the 1950 midterm elections some Senators critical of McCarthy lost their seats, and this dampened such intramural criticism. Moreover the Wisconsin Senator enjoyed wide approbation throughout the country. By the time he had accused both the Truman and Eisenhower administrations of treason, and called General George C. Marshall "a man steeped in falsehood," an opinion poll reported that 50 percent of Americans held a favorable, and only 29 percent an unfavorable opinion of him.

In passing it might be said that Murrow regarded General Marshall as the greatest living American, and he was visibly angered by McCarthy's attack. The Marshall matter came up in a *See It Now* television interview with Truman a few months before Murrow's momentous McCarthy broadcast. McCarthy, the former President said, was not "fit to shine General Marshall's shoes." Murrow signed off the program with a sardonic reference to the "shoeshine boy."

In any case, by 1953, recognizing that though McCarthy was a maverick he was a powerful one, the Republican campaign leadership consciously adopted his issue of "communism in government," meaning of course in the previous Democratic administration. It was reckoned as one way of stemming any Democratic resurgence in the 1954 congressional elections.

So, after the 1953 local elections, Eisenhower's Attorney General, Herbert Brownell, in a speech in Chicago said to be "cleared" by the White House, figuratively waved secret FBI files about and charged that Truman as President had promoted a Soviet spy to high office. He referred to the late Assistant Secretary of the Treasury, Harry Dexter White, who had been called a member of a Communist group in Washington during the war, in the plethora of accusations, revelations and confessions in and around the Alger Hiss case in 1948.

As Brownell spoke, a Senate committee aide was drafting a letter to FBI Director J. Edgar Hoover accusing the nuclear physicist J. Robert Oppenheimer of having been "more probably than not" a Soviet agent, and this charge, too, would become part of the McCarthy era.

Former President Truman appeared on radio and television to answer Attorney General Brownell, and said that he had left White in his high position as vice president of the International Monetary Fund, despite adverse FBI reports, to aid the bureau's continuing inquiry into the White case. Truman also made the countercharge that the Eisenhower administration had, "for political advantage, embraced McCarthyism." He said

McCarthy himself was unimportant, but defined McCarthyism as "corruption of the truth, abandonment of our historical devotion to fair play, and of due process of law. It is the use of the Big Lie and the unfounded accusation against any citizen, in the name of Americanism and security. It is the rise to power of the demagogue who lives on untruth; it is the spread of fear and the destruction of faith at every level of our society."

That the demagogue had indeed risen to power the television networks quickly confirmed, by giving McCarthy air time to answer Truman, under the industry's "fairness" doctrine. This was once defined by Murrow, quoting Winston Churchill, as the willingness "to give Jesus and Judas equal time."

McCarthy, the Republican, used his time to attack the Republican Eisenhower administration for being "soft on communism," as the phrase went. He thus further distressed the soldier-President, already distressed by the attacks on Truman, a fellow member of the Presidents' Club. Eisenhower had said that "Communists in government" should not be a 1954 campaign issue, hoping that it would somehow blow away since, as he put it, he had no intention of "getting down into the gutter with that fellow," McCarthy.

But meanwhile Eisenhower's Attorney General and his nominal subordinate J. Edgar Hoover had testified before the Senate Internal Security subcommittee on the suddenly reopened White case, and Hoover denied that he had ever recommended that a loyalty suspect be kept in Government office in order that he might be further watched, though this indeed seems to have been fairly common FBI practice.

Murrow broadcast a comment on the White case. "The question is not whether Brownell is right, or Truman is right, or whether Harry Dexter White was a spy. We are being asked to make up our minds without access to evidence. And if that should become our habit, then our heritage is in danger."

As part of its regular coverage of the Washington scene, and for possible use on its weekly broadcast, Murrow's *See It Now* program was filming the Jenner subcommittee hearings, where the White case had come up. Outside the Senate caucus room Murrow's reporter, Joe Wershba, was hailed by Don Surine, a cashiered FBI agent who had become McCarthy's staff investigator.

"Hey, Joe, what's this Radwich junk you putting out?" Surine asked, in obvious reference to the previous month's Radulovich program. Then, added McCarthy's man, "What would you say if I told you Murrow was on the Soviet payroll in 1934?"

From his briefcase Surine showed Wershba a photostat of the front page of the *Pittsburgh Sun-Telegraph*, a Hearst newspaper, of nearly nineteen years before. It was about the Institute of International Education, of which Murrow had been assistant director for three years before he joined CBS in 1935. The *Sun-Telegraph* headline read, "American Professors, Trained by Soviet, Teach in U.S. Schools," and the story referred to a summer seminar at Moscow University which the IIE, as the primary American organization devoted to student exchange, had sponsored in 1934 and 1935.

Hearst's principal target in the story was Professor George S. Counts of Columbia University, who had been critical of the Hearst empire and its finances — the Lord of San Simeon had paid the nation's largest income tax in 1935 — but it also mentioned John Dewey and other prominent educators who were members of the IIE advisory board.

Surine told Wershba that, as the article stated, the Moscow seminar was arranged through VOKS, the Soviet agency for cultural relations with foreign countries, and he deduced that this made Murrow part of a "Moscow conspiracy." The ex-FBI agent said he was not calling Murrow a Communist but an anti-anti-Communist, which he regarded as equally dangerous, and he uttered a favorite McCarthy committee aphorism: "If it walks like a duck and talks like a duck, it must be a duck."

Surine added a final touch. "It's a terrible shame, Murrow's brother being a general in the Air Force." The broadcaster's oldest brother Lacey was indeed a brigadier general, and another general and a colonel had been sent by the Air Force to "talk" to Murrow when he was preparing the Radulovich program, and try to convince him not to do it.

Surine's implication, as Wershba gathered it, was that if Murrow remained quiet on such matters as "this Radwich junk," nothing would be said about his past "Communist affiliations." It was a proposition that made McCarthyism a vital personal matter, as well as a professional one, for the broadcaster.

The reference of his connection with the IIE, of which he was still a trustee, may have recalled to Murrow the story of his good friend, the IIE's director, Laurence Duggan. For the latter had also been a friend of Noel Field, Frederick Vanderbilt Field, Henry H. Collins, Jr., and others named by such recanted Communists as Whittaker Chambers, Ruth Bentley and Hede Massing, in connection with an alleged Communist apparatus in wartime Washington.

Duggan had been in the State Department for fourteen years and had risen to become head of the Latin-American Division, actively pursuing the Roosevelt administration's Good Neighbor policy and the formation of the Organization of American States. After a brief spell with the United Nations Relief and Rehabilitation Agency after the war, he had succeeded his father, Dr. Stephen Duggan, as director of the institute.

Murrow had been the elder Duggan's assistant for three years, two decades before, and the widely known educator was a preceptor who had had a strong influence on him. Murrow was also a member of the IIE committee of trustees which chose the younger Duggan as director, and had known him well for eighteen years, being taken by both his intellect and his charm.

As IIE director, Larry Duggan widened the institute's ideas of cultural exchange beyond the merely "educational" to include businessmen, labor leaders, and artists and musicians. He made the IIE board of trustees more representative of the American population. The institute also became the screening agent for the entire student program under the Fulbright Act.

On the murky evening of December 20, 1948, Laurence Duggan fell or jumped from the institute's sixteenth-floor offices at 45th Street and Fifth Avenue, in New York. He was forty-three years old and left a wife and four children. A few days before, Alger Hiss had been indicted for perjury as a result of Whittaker Chambers's accusation that he had been a Soviet spy. Duggan himself had been questioned by FBI agents ten days before, among many others. Chambers was later to deny that he had ever accused Duggan of actually being a Communist.

A few hours after Duggan's death, indeed at midnight the same day, a subcommittee of the House Un-American Activities Committee was summoned into special session by its acting chairman, Representative Karl Mundt.

The meeting consisted of two men, Mundt and Representative Richard M. Nixon, later to become Eisenhower's Vice President and in 1968 elected President. They told reporters that according to secret testimony given before their committee, Whittaker Chambers had nine years before named Duggan as one of six State Department officials who had given him information. But the next day Chambers himself said he had not even known Duggan nor received anything from him. The committee's "revelation" was repudiated by some of its own members, and after the committee had received scathing editorial criticism, Nixon withdrew his previous remarks and said that Duggan's name had been "cleared." The Justice Department issued a statement calling Duggan a loyal American citizen, and said an FBI investigation had produced no evidence of any connection with the Communist Party or espionage.

Duggan's former State Department associates Cordell Hull, Sumner Welles, and Francis B. Sayre also rendered him testimonial. Welles, the former Under-Secretary, called Duggan's detractors "unscrupulous slanderers." The day before Christmas the *New York Herald-Tribune* carried a poem, "The Black Day," by Archibald MacLeish, in memory of Laurence Duggan. It began: "God help that country where informers thrive! Where slander flourishes and lies contrive."

Duggan's family revealed that Laurence's three insurance policies had all been paid in full, in fact in double indemnity for accidental death, and that he had no motive for committing suicide and had not done so.

It could not be disputed, however, that the Hiss-Chambers miasma had enveloped Duggan, and that it had in one way or another contributed to his death.

Murrow, on the day after Duggan's death, did a radio broadcast on the case. On the basis of no evidence, he declared, "a dead man's character is being destroyed in some of the public prints. Some of the headlines that I have seen might as well have read 'Spy Takes Life' — and the police have no evidence to show that he jumped rather than fell. The members of the committee who have done this thing upon such slight and wholly discredited testimony may now consult their actions and their consciences." At the same time the "secret witness" Mundt and Nixon had cited, the professional anti-Communist Isaac Don Levine, denied he had implied Duggan had ever received anything from Chambers, and assailed Mundt for saying so and Mundt and Nixon for "breach of faith."

The sponsors of Murrow's radio program, a soup company, objected to his remarks on Duggan, on the ground that they editorialized and "carried a torch." Murrow replied that his contract gave him the sole right to exercise news judgment on his program.

He also sent a memorandum to the CBS chairman, William S. Paley, proposing a half-hour radio documentary, *The Duggan Story*, suggested, he said, "with complete conviction of success," using the voices of the participants "in this fantastic story." It would be wholly factual, he said, with no editorial opinion, would have a great impact on the public mind and "reflect great credit upon CBS." The proposal was not taken up.

Duggan's father, who had become director emeritus of the institute, wrote Murrow to thank him for defending Larry's honor "when he could no longer defend himself." He expressed hope that the House Un-American Activities Committee could be abolished, and felt that at any rate Larry's death would result in some improvement in congressional committee hearings. It was a hope which remains unfulfilled.

As it happened, Laurence Duggan left behind an almost completed book manuscript on the subject nearest his heart, hemisphere cooperation. Published posthumously, his last public utterance was a plea for recognition of the new economic and truly social forces at work in Latin America, unlike the many personal and palace "revolutions" of the past. He spoke against authoritarianism of any hue, red or black, and for an inter-American system supplementing, but not substituting for the United Nations.

America's role in the hemisphere, as Duggan saw it, was to help it diversify economically and encourage industrialization, land reform and trade union organization. Nor did he believe the Roosevelt Good Neighbor policy was any longer enough, because it paid no heed to economics. His recommendations foreshadowed what would in the Kennedy administration emerge as the Alliance for Progress. It was hardly a revolutionary program, and perhaps not even a realistic one, against the continuing tradition of military dictatorship and economic stratification.

The Duggan case never died, despite the exoneration. His name continued to be mentioned in the confessionals of the ex-Communists. Whittaker Chambers's book, published in 1952, was still being widely read when in 1953 McCarthy's investigator threw at Murrow the charge of "complicity" with the Communists, through his IIE connection two decades before.

When Joe Wershba brought him Surine's photostat of the 1935 newspaper clipping, Murrow reddened slightly. "So that's what they've got," he said. He was ill that day with a cold, and looked drawn. But he mused about McCarthy and his influence on the news media. "I haven't even been able to talk about the whole problem of American relations with Communist China," he said.

A few days before, also talking of McCarthy, he had said to another colleague, "The only thing that counts is the right to know, to speak, to think — that, and the sanctity of the courts. Otherwise it's not America."

He asked Wershba to put down a full account of the encounter with Surine. Next day he was better. The furrows had smoothed out. The cold and the pallor were gone. "The question now is when do I go against these guys," he said.

Murrow was named television's "most outstanding personality" in that winter's Emmy awards, and *See It Now* the best program of "news or sports," both of which he considered rather dusty compliments. Dr. Nathan Pusey, president of Harvard University, appeared on *Person to Person* in February, and although the educator was under attack by McCarthy for "harboring Communists on the Harvard faculty," he and Murrow consciously stayed clear of any discussion of McCarthyism or academic freedom. This emphasized the difference between the two weekly Murrow programs. *Person to Person* was entertainment, not public affairs, though it presented public figures. Still, Dr. Pusey's very appearance on the Murrow program, while under McCarthy's fire, made a point. And there were no inhibitions about subject matter where *See It Now* was concerned.

The question of timing for the planned McCarthy program was fundamental. Each week saw new developments and a further widening of the Senator's scope. After the inconclusive hearings in the Harry Dexter White case McCarthy and his Subcommittee on Investigations had taken on the Army, charging Communist "espionage" at the Fort Monmouth, New Jersey, signal center, where radar work was going on against the danger of atomic attack. McCarthy also found "Communist influence" in the case of an Army dentist, Captain Irving Peress, a finding subsequently determined to be without foundation.

Peress, a draftee, had invoked the Fifth Amendment during a routine loyalty investigation and his dismissal had been recommended. Meanwhile, awaiting honorable discharge, and Army paper work being what it was, he had also been automatically promoted to major, among seven thousand doctors and dentists promoted en masse under new legislation. McCarthy made "Who promoted Peress?" his theme in his examination of Brigadier General Ralph W. Zwicker, a combat hero, the commandant at Camp Kilmer, New Jersey.

This browbeating session, shown on television, took place February 18, 1954, and brought objections from Army Secretary Robert T. Stevens, who defended his department and his officers. McCarthy then produced the Annie Lee Moss case, charging that a "Soviet agent" had been at large in the War Department code room in the Pentagon.

Each week *See It Now*'s contemplated McCarthy program was revised to take account of such new developments. Each week the film editors would finish their task of updating and ask "Do we go?" Friendly would consult Murrow and then say, "No, let's hold for another week." They were doing the timing with a sense of calculated risk. For McCarthy could strike first, as he often did. Or *See It Now* could choose a week when some sudden major happening somewhere in the world might overshadow the McCarthy broadcast.

It was not true, of course, that Murrow was a lone crusader, or indeed, as he saw it, a crusader at all. McCarthy was opposed by many in public life, who did not hesitate to speak. There was Senator Herbert Lehman. There was Senator William Benton, who stepped outside his congressional immunity to charge misconduct, demand expulsion, and provoke a two-million-dollar libel suit, later dropped.

Many in the news media also opposed McCarthy, like Walter Lippmann, the Alsop brothers and the cartoonist Herblock. Because of them, indeed, McCarthy called the *Washington Post* "the Washington edition of the *Daily Worker*," and called the *New York Times* the Communist daily's "uptown edition." Several newspaper groups and the Luce magazines also criticized the methods of the Wisconsin Senator, and the columnist Drew Pearson played a notable opposition role. Radio commentators like Elmer Davis, Quincy Howe and Edward P. Morgan spoke up.

But most of the American press throve on the sensationalism McCarthy fed it and panted for more. Even those papers opposing him on their editorial pages gave their front pages to the unsubstantiated charges Mc-

Carthy continued to produce. This was defended as "objective" reporting.

The academic community had faltered under attack, which was followed by alumni pressures. The labor unions, the White House, the State Department and most of the American Establishment had taken McCarthyism lying down. Hollywood, after the case of the "Unfriendly Ten," had retreated into self-censorship and blacklisting.

It was left for the most unlikely of all champions, commercial television, to step forward and pick up the gauntlet — unlikely because that industry had also indulged in wide-scale blacklisting to ingratiate itself with sponsors and display its "patriotism." CBS, which attracted creative and imaginative, hence unconventional talent, and had earned a reputation for forthrightness from the wartime and postwar news broadcasts of Murrow and his staff, was a special target for McCarthyism and had made special efforts to purge itself. It introduced its own "loyalty oath," the only network to do so, and dismissed some employees.

CBS contracts contained a "morality" clause which allowed for their cancellation if its broad and somewhat vague provisions were not observed.

"You will at all times act with due regard for public morals and conventions.

"If at any time you shall have done, or do, any act or thing which shall be an offense involving moral turpitude under Federal, state or local laws, or which might tend to bring you into public disrepute, contempt, scandal or ridicule, or which might tend to offend the community or any organized group thereof, or which might tend to reflect unfavorably upon us . . . the sponsors, if any, or their advertising agencies, if any, or injure the success of the program," then the contract could be declared null and void.

Because of such network sensitivity toward offending "the community or any organized group thereof," it was believed by many at the time that Murrow and Friendly had presented CBS with an unwelcome fait accompli in the McCarthy program.

As Friendly recalled it, however, "the company" was notified five days before the McCarthy program was shown, though he added he was not certain whether the news ever reached the executive floor, where sat the chairman of the board, William S. Paley, and the CBS president, Frank Stanton. Actually, as Murrow ended the previous week's *See It Now* broadcast he had declared that the next one would deal with the prevailing climate of "unreasoning fear."

One CBS news executive, informed of Murrow's decision to "go" with the McCarthy half-hour, was quoted as saying, "If that's what you intend to do, then this conversation never took place, and I know nothing about it."

Stanton's recollection was that it was not until 4:30 P.M. that Tuesday afternoon, six hours before air time, that he was told what Murrow and Friendly would be showing that evening.

The two producers offered to let him see the completed version of the film but he demurred, on the ground that even if he had any suggestions to make, it was too late to do anything about them. Stanton was somewhat taken aback to learn of a program which he could not remember as being discussed in editorial conferences. It was true, however, that that morning's *New York Times* had carried an advertisement of the McCarthy program, again paid for by Murrow and Friendly themselves from prize money, after CBS had refused.

Stanton's only comment was, "If you attack McCarthy, make sure you offer him equal time to reply."

It was advice that Murrow had already received and acted upon. For whoever else at CBS knew, did not know, or professed not to know about the McCarthy program, Bill Paley was fully aware and fully approved. The board chairman and Murrow had a strong personal relationship, founded in the war, and often, as the corporation grew and the medium became more complex, the broadcaster acted as if Paley were separate and distinct from the CBS hierarchy.

He had kept Paley informed of the progress of the McCarthy project, and the chairman, a personal friend also of the President whose administration was being challenged by McCarthy, heartily supported it. On the day before the scheduled broadcast, Murrow came to Paley's office to tell him that the program might cause a row, and Paley, always conscious of the FCC and its rulings, advised him to make sure McCarthy was offered equal time to reply.

Paley was not aware of what Murrow intended to say — in fact, he did not see the program even when it was broadcast next evening — but he felt that a strong editorial stand would transgress upon the CBS traditional position of objectivity in public affairs.

Nevertheless the next morning Paley telephoned Murrow to say, "I'll be with you tonight, Ed, and I'll be with you tomorrow as well." And during the clamor and controversy the broadcast would provoke, Paley and Murrow, as the former remembered it fifteen years later, "were never closer."

Even beyond Paley's support, the key to the McCarthy broadcast lay in the fact that *See It Now* was virtually autonomous, and Murrow and Friendly were obviously held to possess both judgment and responsibility. The program regularly went on the air without advance notice to Paley and Stanton of its specific contents.

The moment for the McCarthy broadcast had finally been decided on that previous weekend.

On Saturday, March 6, Adlai Stevenson warned against McCarthyism in a speech carried on television by CBS and on radio by NBC. The Democratic nominee of 1952 acted against the counsel of his own party advisers, who believed it better to remain silent now that the Wisconsin Senator had begun to attack the Republican administration. Indeed McCarthy would soon charge "twenty-one years of treason" instead of only twenty. But Stevenson felt it was no time to be playing partisan politics.

McCarthy was fishing off the Florida Keys when Stevenson spoke in Miami. The Senator came to shore and demanded air time to answer, thus confronting the two networks with a sizable problem. Lenient as they had been about granting time before, if they agreed now they would in effect be recognizing McCarthy de facto as the Republican spokesman, as Stevenson was de jure the Democratic one.

The day after the Stevenson speech, Murrow was as usual in the *See It Now* projection room, in flannel shirt and his favorite red suspenders, for Sunday was the day that Tuesday's program was normally finally edited, and some thought given to the required narration.

The tentative decision to show the McCarthy program that Tuesday had been made the week before, but since *See It Now* was kept flexible enough to accommodate other news developments to the last possible moment, indeed change subjects entirely, it was not until now that the "locking-in" process was begun.

Murrow asked to see the revised McCarthy footage again, as he did every week. Aside he said to Friendly, "I've been thinking over a lifetime and I've made up my mind." The film was shown. It had no narration, only the separate sequences of McCarthy in action.

Murrow asked the small *See It Now* group whether the program would be effective. The editors said yes, but the reporters said no. One of the latter explained that the film itself was "neutral," that it would encourage McCarthy's supporters by showing them their hero in full cry, but at the same time would give McCarthy opponents no comfort that anything could be done about McCarthyism. Indeed since the opinion polls showed McCarthy's popularity to be rising, his appearance on a national television program in prime time might enhance it even more.

Murrow shook his head impatiently and pointed to the darkened screen. "The terror is right here in this room," he said. It was clear, as it had been from the first, that not the McCarthy pictures but the Murrow narration would be the touchstone of the program. Someone in the room asked him what he proposed to say.

"No one man can terrorize a whole nation unless we are all his accomplices," he replied. He thought a moment, then added, "If none of us ever read a book that was 'dangerous,' had a friend who was 'different,' or joined an organization that advocated 'change,' we would all be just the kind of people Joe McCarthy wants."

It was the first time he had ever preached to the staff, but they did not seem to mind. Murrow knew fully what he intended to do, and what reaction it would provoke. He went around the room, asking the individual reporters and editors about anything in their own lives that might not stand up before the expected onslaught of the McCarthyites. Again, given the circumstances, the staff did not seem to mind.

A girl film-cutter asked whether the White House might not do something about McCarthy. "The White House is not going to do, and not going to say one god-damned thing," he answered. It was the first time anyone there had ever heard him swear before women.

Murrow stood up, his brows more knitted than usual, and with no trace of his customary Sunday good humor. "Ladies and gentlemen, thank you. We go with this Tuesday night."

As they walked out Friendly remarked, "This is going to be a tough one to do." Murrow answered, "They're all going to be tough after this."

On Monday McCarthy came to New York to press his request for broadcast time against Stevenson. But the Republican National chairman, Leonard Hall, apprehensive lest McCarthy attack the Eisenhower administration again, announced that Vice President Richard Nixon would be heard instead, on behalf of the Republican National Committee.

McCarthy fumed for the benefit of the reporters and cameramen who were as always trailing him about. When told that several FCC commissioners felt the networks to be within their rights in yielding time to the Republican Party rather than to him personally, he said ominously, "The networks will grant me time, or learn what the law is."

At CBS that Monday Murrow was writing the script to be spoken by him against the McCarthy film.

Usually, with *See It Now* programs, Friendly prepared a draft narration on the basis of the final editing, and Murrow amended, corrected and rewrote it. This time Murrow took over completely, dictating every word, reading, correcting and then redictating. "Give me short active words," he said to an assistant assigned to collect excerpts from newspaper editorials on McCarthy. His own words were also short and active.

On the floor of the Senate that afternoon, Flanders of Vermont became the first Republican to attack McCarthy there in four years, or since Margaret Chase Smith had issued her Declaration of Conscience. Flanders said the Wisconsin Senator was trying to set up a "one-man party, McCarthyism," and scoffed at McCarthy's "war dance" that, he said, had produced "the scalp of a pink Army dentist."

On Tuesday evening at 10:30 P.M., from *See It Now*'s Studio 41 in the Grand Central Terminal building, the McCarthy program was broadcast. There was tension in the control room. A film projector had broken down and was repaired with only seconds to spare. Some difficult technical problems emerged, as the program moved from Murrow live in the studio, to film of various kinds, to radio tape without pictures, back to Murrow on the live camera, then to video tape, to more film, and again to Murrow.

In the pre-air rehearsal the program seemed more forceful to those in the control room than the actual aired version, which was a bit jumpy, perhaps from nervousness. Still, it hit millions of American homes with overpowering simultaneous impact.

The camera opened on an unusually grim and purposeful Murrow. He took the unaccustomed step of reading directly from a script, to insure that he was saying exactly what he wanted to say, and he admitted the controversial nature of anything that had to do with McCarthy.

"The line between investigating and persecuting is a very fine one," Murrow noted, "and the junior Senator from Wisconsin has stepped over it repeatedly."

The film that followed showed McCarthy in action. There was the brave McCarthy, vowing "to call them as I see them, regardless of who happens to be President." There was the stern McCarthy, challenging President Eisenhower's disinclination to make communism an election issue by making it one. There was the self-righteous McCarthy, with a tear in his eye, touched by the faith of assembled followers, and complaining of persecution. There was the avenging McCarthy, harassing General Zwicker during the Peress hearings. There was the inexorable McCarthy, cross-examining Reed Harris, deputy administrator of the International Information Administration, as the United States Information Agency was then known.

McCarthy had investigated the Government's information activities the year before, to the extent of sending his assistants Cohn and Schine on their astonishing ten-day tour of American overseas libraries. The information agency, with its subsidiary Voice of America, which McCarthy labeled "the Voice of Moscow," was so demoralized that it would not be able fully to regain its position and prestige until, as it happened, Murrow took over its directorship in 1961, after he had left broadcasting.

The Reed Harris excerpt on *See It Now* showed the deaf McCarthy, also, for no matter what the witness said in his defense, and it was a good deal, McCarthy continued as if he had heard nothing. The film also showed the malicious McCarthy, chuckling during an anti-Stevenson speech in the 1952 campaign as he made his mock slip of the tongue, "Alger — I mean Adlai."

Murrow accused McCarthy of half-truth, and pointed out that his investigations had been protected by senatorial immunity. He also demonstrated the falsity of McCarthy's assertion, made twice during the Reed Harris hearing, that the American Civil Liberties Union had been listed as a "subversive front" by the Department of Justice. Indeed, as a generous though anonymous contributor to the ACLU himself, he may have taken particular relish in doing so.

That evening marked the first time on American television that McCarthy's citations had ever been refuted by the recital of the true facts in each case.

When the film had finished, Murrow made his own challenge, in the summation he had so carefully written.

"We will not be driven by fear into an age of unreason, if we dig deep into our own history and our doctrine and remember that we are not descended from fearful men, not from men who feared to write, to speak, to associate, and to defend causes which were for the moment unpopular.

"This is no time for men who oppose Senator McCarthy's methods to keep silent. We can deny our heritage and our history, but we cannot escape responsibility for the result. There is no way for a citizen of a republic to abdicate his responsibilities."

Murrow spoke his words over McCarthy's head, over the heads of all the combatants on the crowded political battlefield, to the people. And as he concluded the broadcast with his Shakespearian verdict, "Cassius was right. The fault, dear Brutus, is not in our stars but in ourselves. Good night and good luck," there was a drawing of breath across the nation. Millions of Americans had been waiting for someone to say, steadily and dispassionately, what Murrow had just said.

In New York, as the program ended, a CBS colleague, Don Hollenbeck, came on the air with the regular 11 P.M. news and said, "I want to associate myself with every word just spoken by Ed Murrow." Three months later Hollenbeck would commit suicide, after a continuing series of attacks upon him by a Hearst newspaper columnist, as one of Murrow's "pinkos."

Though in the public mind Murrow was forever to be the broadcaster who had "stood up to" McCarthy, he himself did not feel the program was to any large degree responsible for McCarthy's downfall, which he attributed to the Wisconsinite's attacks on other Senators — "the club" — in the days that lay ahead. Many other Americans, however, felt that McCarthy's eventual censure by the Senate was merely ratification of the censure delivered that night on television.

What he did the Senator may have done to himself, as he would do again in the Army-McCarthy hearings that followed, but television showed him doing it. The *See It Now* broadcast helped persuade people that he was not invincible or immune, and put him on the defensive. Whether it changed many made-up minds among the public is uncertain, but apparently it did influence Senators and others who had hitherto tolerated McCarthy, and who possessed the power to do something about him.

Indeed it was the evidence of television's dominion which most disturbed Murrow about the McCarthy broadcast and perhaps contributed to his unwillingness to take any credit for it. He felt that it had to be made, but he was aware that by using television against a single individual he might have set a precedent that could some day be employed to damage or dishonor free government.

"Is it not possible," he asked, "that an infectious smile, eyes that seem remarkable for the depths of their sincerity, a cultivated air of authority, may attract a huge television audience, regardless of the violence that may be done to truth or objectivity?"

Some critics, who could not be considered pro-McCarthy, nevertheless thought the McCarthy broadcast was a misuse of the medium, and that it was not a factual "report," for instead of being merely an impartial judge's summing-up without directing the jury, it was the summation of a "hanging judge."

As he made clear, Murrow was cognizant of the implications of what he had done, but if public opinion had been manipulated in order to counteract a previous manipulation, if it had taken two wrongs to make a right, the feeling of most Americans seemed to be that the power of television for good had been impressively demonstrated.

The immediate response to the program was overwhelming, and though Murrow received some hostile comment, accusing him of "helping the forces that have weakened America, injured free enterprise, and favored unions, immigrants and minorities" — a stock phrase from an organized postcard-writing campaign — the general reaction was not only favorable but highly approving. The day after the broadcast CBS reported the largest spontaneous response it had ever received to any program, 12,348 comments, fifteen-to-one in Murrow's favor. The sponsors also received four thousand letters, most of them favorable, but the sponsoring company's president admitted to his stockholders he was "concerned" about the controversy with McCarthy. At a CBS board of directors meeting, the reaction Murrow got, he said, was, "Good show. Sorry you did it."

The day after the broadcast, Murrow lunched at his club, the Century, with his old friend, the radio dramatist Norman Corwin, and Corwin reported they were stopped by strangers shaking Murrow's hand and pronouncing blessings on him. At the Century, fellow club members greeted him warmly, including the naturalist Henry Fairfield Osborn. But the eminent scientist wanted to ask him a scientific question. He was the only person there, or perhaps in all New York, who did not know there had been a McCarthy program.

It was still the same the next day, when a visiting BBC friend, Frank Gillard, lunched with Murrow at the Century. "As we walked in Ed was recognized, and from every corner of that club members came crowding around him, thanking him, congratulating him, eager to grasp his hand in gratitude . . . After lunch we walked up Fifth Avenue; it was a rash thing to have done. Of course he was instantly recognized. First our own pavement was jammed with people who were determined to give him the hero's treatment, and then Fifth Avenue traffic was brought practically to a standstill as the news of his presence spread, and men and women came rushing across the road in all directions. It was a most moving experience for him, and though he took it modestly, he clearly found great satisfaction in such a demonstration of support and approval."

Murrow received messages of commendation from George Meany, president of the American Federation of Labor; Mrs. Hubert H. Humphrey, wife of the Minnesota Senator, Congressman Adam Clayton Powell, of Harlem; Reinhold Niebuhr, the theologian; Irwin Edman, the philosopher; Walter White, of the National Association for the Advancement of Colored People; Senator Herbert Lehman, and Myrna Loy, the actress, among others.

A note from a BBC official in London, where the McCarthy program had been shown with equally stunning effect, said: "It's salutary for those of us who prefer public service to commercial television, to see an occasion when only under a non-public service system was it possible for the right step to be taken."

Perhaps the most heartfelt response to the program came from within the American "non-public service" television industry itself. Film-cutters, electricians, cameramen, producers, writers, makeup men and researchers sent collective messages.

The program, many of them said, had restored their faith in the medium, and had reconciled them to working at what had often seemed a fruitless, even if well-paid, endeavor. "You have made me proud and happy to work for CBS," several letters said.

Murrow's response to the commendations he received was that "it's a sad state of affairs when people think I'm courageous to do this." As he looked back at it some years later he said: "The timing was right and the instrument powerful. We did it fairly well, with a degree of restraint and credibility. There was a great conspiracy of silence at that time. When there is such a conspiracy and somebody makes a loud noise, it attracts all the attention."

The encounter with McCarthy had barely begun, however. For some reason the Senator did not comment on the program the same night, though in the past he had shown himself a master of timing and reply, with an awareness of newspaper deadlines and radio-television air times, and he could immediately have offset the program by either direct or diversionary means, if he wished. His staff said he went to bed early that evening and didn't even see the broadcast, which may seem unlikely.

On Wednesday, the day after the broadcast, President Eisenhower at a news conference passed off a question about McCarthyism with his customary obliqueness. On Thursday McCarthy reappeared in public in the Senate caucus room to conduct the hearing in the case of Annie Lee Moss. He seemed unusually absorbed and quiet.

Mrs. Moss was a middle-aged Negro woman who McCarthy said was a Communist Party member, and as such represented a danger to national security because she was employed in the Pentagon code room. As the hearing began, McCarthy said he was less interested in her than in the superiors who had given her the job.

The latest hearing was part of his developing campaign against the Army, and "Who transferred Annie Lee Moss to the code room?" replaced "Who promoted Peress?" as the Senator's burning question.

Mrs. Moss testified that she merely mechanically operated the machine that sent and received code messages, and had no knowledge of the contents of such messages, in fact she had never been inside the code room proper.

Also, she said, she had never been a member of a Communist club, as charged, or attended meetings or subscribed to the *Daily Worker*. When asked by Senator Stuart Symington, "Did you ever hear of Karl Marx?" she said, "Who's that?"

At the conclusion of the hearing, when it had been established that Mrs. Moss's accuser, a woman undercover agent for the FBI, had never met her but only knew her name from a list of dues-paying Communists, and that there were at least three Annie Lee Mosses in Washington, Senator Symington said that if she did not get her job back from the Army, he would see to it she got another one. She was eventually restored to duty when the Pentagon found she was not "actually subversive or disloyal to the United States."

McCarthy questioned the witness absentmindedly and soon left the hearing, citing a previous engagement. It was with the friendly radio broadcaster Fulton Lewis, Jr. On Lewis's program that evening McCarthy made his first rejoinder to Murrow, produced the 1935 Hearst newspaper clipping, and charged that the broadcaster had aided the Communist cause by sending American teachers to a Moscow University summer seminar.

McCarthy also said, in answer to Lewis's question, that he had not seen the Murrow broadcast. "I never listen to the extreme left-wing, bleeding heart elements of radio and TV."

A few months earlier, though before the Radulovich case, McCarthy had been quoted as wishing every radio and television commentator "was as fair as Murrow."

Fifteen minutes after the Senator's broadcast, Murrow, on his own nightly radio news program, reported McCarthy's remarks. He had steeled himself for the McCarthy attack, but his voice broke briefly as he spoke of it. About McCarthy's characterization of him, he said, "I may be a bleeding heart, being not quite sure of what it means. As for being left-wing, that is political shorthand, but if the Senator means I am somewhat to the left of his position and of Louis XIV, he is correct."

The same evening the Army released its report charging that McCarthy and his committee counsel, Roy M. Cohn, had used improper pressures in seeking to win favors for their protégé, G. David Schine, scion of a leading hotel empire, who had become a reluctant Army private.

This was to lead directly to the Army-McCarthy hearings, which in turn led to McCarthy's censure. But through all the months and proceedings that followed, devolving about matters of procedure — such as McCarthy's famous "point of order" — about the play of personalities, political partisanship, public behavior, and the honor of that exclusive club, the Senate of the United States, it was only the Murrow broadcast that had faced the fundamental issue, the threat to free government and to a free society.

Murrow's position thus differed from that of the "anti-Communist left" and of many liberals, whose criticism was that McCarthy was scattering his shots, missing his targets, and ridiculing what they believed in, by behaving in unseemly fashion in his pursuit of it. They were the people who strained at McCarthy but swallowed McCarran. They were repelled by McCarthy as the "scourge of communism," but hailed him as a "public educator" in its dangers.

Thus, a 1954 account sponsored by the American Committee for Cultural Freedom, presumably a CIA-financed organization like its counterparts abroad, accepted an internal Communist threat as well as an external one — it said they were indistinguishable — and demanded only that it "be handled in a systematic and thoroughgoing way." It regarded McCarthy as "not effective enough," and his anticommunism as neither "authentic" nor "responsible," nor, one might add, "respectable." It denied that a witch-hunt was taking place because "witches, after all, never existed, but Soviet agents are unfortunately all too real." Even stout defenders of the Senator, like William F. Buckley, Jr., and L. Brent Bozell, complained that he confused the anti-Communist cause by his "exaggerations," such as turning "fellow traveller" into "Communist," and "alleged pro-Communist" into "pro-Communist."

Such distinctions were lost on Murrow. While "anti-Communist liberals," many of whom were former Communists themselves, accepted McCarthy's

purpose if not his performance, the broadcaster's reaction was that of an old-fashioned constitutional liberal, who noted that McCarthy never presented any real evidence of past or present Communist Party membership or activity by any of the persons he named. Murrow's position was that "accusation is not proof," and that "conviction depends on evidence and due process of law."

Though he accepted the possibility of a Soviet military move in Europe, most likely for Berlin, and had no illusions about what happened when a Communist regime took over — as in the 1948 coup in Czechoslovakia in which his warmhearted friend Foreign Minister Jan Masaryk had mysteriously died — Murrow did not believe, despite the Soviet spy cases, that wholesale Communist subversion was at work in the United States.

Nor did he think that a clear enough line was being drawn between dissent and disloyalty. Most of all he felt that when the "enemy" was described as not only Communists but "pro-Communists, fellow travellers, spies and Communist agents," in the words of the American Committee for Cultural Freedom, it was inevitable that communism would be confused with "liberalism, socialism, or some other democratic philosophy and program," a confusion which the same committee officially deplored.

With respect to the Alger Hiss case, which had put "a generation on trial," as a British observer saw it, Murrow had declared in a radio broadcast after the verdict: "The conviction of Mr. Hiss does not prove that the New Deal was Communist-led or inspired any more than the scandals of Mr. Harding's regime proved that all Republicans were crooks. Let politicians make such capital of conviction as they can. Other politicians would have tried to benefit by acquittal."

He saw it as important that in the Hiss case, though it would "haunt the halls of American jurisprudence for years to come," the judicial process had been preserved. He did not feel that was true about McCarthy's activities. Moreover the Hiss verdict was "subject to appeal," while many of McCarthy's victims had been able to find no such recourse.

Murrow had opened his McCarthy broadcast by offering the Senator time for a reply. That weekend McCarthy accepted, and proposed a proxy, his journalistic admirer from Yale, William F. Buckley, Jr. But Murrow insisted that the reply be made personally. Meanwhile the time McCarthy had demanded from the networks to answer Stevenson had been filled by Vice President Nixon, who spent it trying to woo McCarthy back to party regularity. Murrow and Friendly were apprehensive lest the Vice President go so far in this quest as to attack them and their program. He stopped short of that.

However another member of the Eisenhower Cabinet, Secretary of the Treasury George Humphrey, that week appeared as a guest on Murrow's

Millions of Americans watched Senator Joe McCarthy strike back at Murrow, n "equal time" on See It Now, *but Murrow had the last word, the counter-ebuttal to McCarthy*

other program, *Person to Person*, after refusing an offer of postponement if he regarded an amiable tête-à-tête with Murrow at that particular time as embarrassing. Obviously, if Humphrey had begged off it would have been taken as another example of administration appeasement of McCarthy.

The other guest on *Person to Person*, Brigadier General David Sarnoff, who had often tried to lure Murrow away from CBS to his own rival NBC, praised Murrow's role in broadcasting. He did not mention Mc-Carthy directly, but on that evening the meaning of his words was not lost upon the much wider audience than *See It Now*'s that was commanded by *Person to Person*.

McCarthy's formal reply to Murrow was scheduled for April 6. The week after the original McCarthy broadcast, challenging McCarthy again, *See It Now* on March 16 presented a program devoted to the Annie Lee Moss hearing. This time no commentary by Murrow was needed. The sound cameras made their own findings, as they lingered on McCarthy's empty seat after he had left, and showed proceedings obviously based on hearsay, without corroboration. The Democratic minority members of the committee emphasized this fact. Murrow concluded: "You will notice that neither Senator McClellan, nor Senator Symington, nor this reporter know or claim that Mrs. Moss was or is not a Communist. Their claim was simply that she had the right to meet her accusers face to face." The program ended by showing President Eisenhower speaking also of due process of law and of the American right "to meet your accuser face to face."

Four years later, when it was reported by the Subversive Activities Control Board that Annie Lee Moss had indeed been a member of the Communist Party, Murrow's position would remain what it had been at the time of the hearing — that the question was not so much whether Annie Lee Moss was a Communist as whether a hearing based on anonymous information, without the right of personal confrontation or cross-examination, was in violation of her rights as an American citizen.

The Moss program produced another spate of public response, to add to the continuing reverberations in streets and homes, newspapers and magazines, on radio and television, which had made the Murrow-McCarthy encounter a national spectacle. Again the favorable comments far outweighed the unfavorable, though the latter had developed into a flood of similarly worded and often anonymous postcards. Many of them were addressed to "Red" Murrow. Eight-year-old Casey Murrow was taunted at school with his father's "communism," though the school was regarded as a select institution. This time President Eisenhower, asked what he thought of McCarthy's charges against Murrow, gallantly replied that though he had known the broadcaster as a friend in wartime, he would not care to comment on his "personality or loyalty."

At the White House photographers' banquet a few days later Murrow, surrounded by a crowd, felt an arm around his shoulder, and a hand rubbed his back. "Just feeling to see if any of the knives are still sticking out, Ed," said the President puckishly. Murrow turned away also with a quip, taken from the broadcasting studio. "Now over to you, Mr. President," he said.

At the annual dinner of the Overseas Press Club, as Secretary of State Dulles prepared to speak, 1500 people rose to their feet, not in the Secretary's honor, but to give Murrow an ovation when he entered the room. On that occasion he received an award for his previous year's work.

When Murrow encountered Albert Einstein at another dinner, the physicist greeted him, "Aha, a fighting man!"

Since the McCarthy program had gone out under their imprimatur, so to speak, the sponsors became involved in the controversy. The Aluminum Company of America's association with *See It Now* had, in ways that only Madison Avenue can calculate, changed its popular image from that of a virtual monopoly constantly being pursued by the Government, into one of public service. The Radulovich program even made ALCOA "radical" instead of "reactionary" to many. It also presented the corporation with an immediate hot potato, for one of ALCOA's biggest customers was the Air Force. But all it said to Murrow and Friendly was, "You do the programs, we'll make the aluminum."

The McCarthy potato was even hotter. As a result of the program, ALCOA received both praise for its courage, though it had nothing to do with the contents, and threats of boycott from McCarthy partisans.

The Senator himself sent a telegram attacking ALCOA directors if they intended to continue using "tax money" to sustain Murrow, meaning money spent on institutional advertising instead of going for taxes. Implied, as usual, was an investigation of some sort. ALCOA wavered but finally stood firm. A year later, however, it would drop its sponsorship of *See It Now* in another controversial situation, though the ostensible reason would be to sell "pots and pans" instead of mere good will.

Besides the telegram, ALCOA had some differences with McCarthy about who was to pay for his filmed reply to Murrow. The Senator asked the corporation for $7500 to cover costs. ALCOA, which paid for the air time of the program but not for any of its production, passed the bill to Murrow. He said he refused to pay to have McCarthy defame him, and turned it over to CBS. The network finally paid $6336 and Murrow was openly annoyed.

For one thing, he regarded it as a McCarthy bid for public sympathy.

Moreover the Senator was receiving $1500 a lecture for many lectures, thus ranking with Mrs. Roosevelt and John Gunther at the top of the women's club circuit. And of course he had to pay nothing for the half-hour of prime broadcast time on which he finally made his reply. It had been written for him by his friend and admirer, the Hearst columnist George Sokolsky, also presumably at no cost.

"Murrow is a symbol, the leader and the cleverest of the jackal pack which is always found at the throat of anyone who dares to expose individual Communists and traitors," the Senator began.

He repeated the charge that Murrow "sponsored a Communist school in Moscow," and that by its selection of American students and teachers to attend the summer sessions at Moscow University, the Institute of International Education "acted for the Russian espionage and propaganda organization known as VOKS," to "do a job which would normally be done by the Russian secret police."

McCarthy went on to say that Harold J. Laski, the Labor Party theoretician, with whom Murrow had made wartime broadcasts from London, and whom the Senator identified as "admittedly the greatest Communist propagandist of our time in England," had dedicated to Murrow his book *Reflections on the Revolution of Our Time*. He neglected to add that the gesture was in appreciation for the Battle of Britain broadcasts. Indeed the book, which advised European Socialists to reject postwar unity with the Communists, had been denounced as counterrevolutionary in 1946 by the Soviet propaganda chief Alexandrov.

Laski's dedication was in fact a dual one, "with appreciation" to Murrow and to Lanham Titchener, one of their wartime censors at the BBC, who later became a Foreign Service official.

"Our country owes an immense debt to Mr. Edward R. Murrow," Laski wrote. "Day and night since before the war began he has done everything that courage and integrity can do to make events in this country a living reality to his fellow citizens of the United States. I am only one of the many Englishmen who have found in his faith and trust in our people a new power to endure and hope."

The date was November 1942, a time when "Tail Gunner Joe" was leaving for his Marine Corps desk job in the South Pacific.

Although it was not very effectively delivered, and the makeup and lighting were amateurish and garish, McCarthy's considered reply to Murrow was an archetypal example of the Senator's methods and style.

He "connected" the broadcaster with the Russian secret police, Soviet espionage, known Communists, the American Communist Party, the *Daily Worker*, the IWW, and with Owen Lattimore whom McCarthy had previously called the "top Russian spy." It was all done by innuendo.

The Senator also spoke about Communists "in high places" who con-

A lesson from J. Robert Oppenheimer, at the Institute for Advanced Study, Princeton

nived "to turn over all of our Chinese friends to the Russians." He pointed out that only thirty-seven years before "there was not a single foot of ground on the face of the globe under the domination or control of the Communists," but now more than one-third the earth's area and 800 million people were in Communist hands. He implied that Edward R. Murrow was to blame for it all.

But as usual, McCarthy was using one occasion to springboard into another. He shifted his ground from Murrow to make broad new political charges. The hydrogen bomb, announced a week before, had been delayed for eighteen months, he declared, because of Communist influence, if not indeed by "traitors in our government." A few months later J. Robert Oppenheimer, a man who had done much to bring the A-bomb about but had opposed an H-bomb "crash program," would lose his security clearance, and Murrow would present him on *See It Now*.

McCarthy's new attack on Murrow brought a statement from CBS, subscribing to his "integrity and responsibility" as "a broadcaster and as a loyal American." The company indeed had engaged a former judge as special counsel to support Murrow in whatever situation might arise, and he had put the broadcaster and members of the *See It Now* staff through hours, even days of intensive examination of minute details of their past lives. With the help of a friend and associate of college and post-college days, Chester Williams, Murrow went back more than twenty years to his term as president of the National Student Federation, for possible Communist and fellow traveller influence in that organization that McCarthy might make use of against him. It was all a humiliating procedure, or would have been in any other time.

But what was regarded generally as "CBS's finest hour" was also the beginning of a new sensitivity in Murrow's relations with and position in the network. Despite the outpouring of public thanks and gratitude, and the undeniable support of Paley and Stanton, there may have been a growing consensus within the board of directors — of which Murrow was a member — that the network should not engage in strong partisanship on basic issues, even though it was partisanship on behalf of democratic ends. The overwhelming public approval of Murrow vis-à-vis McCarthy delayed any evidence of restraint. But the corporate psychological pattern may have been set, even if only subconsciously, against the man who was "bigger than the network."

At the time, however, the corporation basked in public esteem, not only on the side of the public good, but fortuitously of the Establishment. Bill Paley provided not only legal but moral support to Murrow, in the tense month between the original *See It Now* program and McCarthy's reply.

When it was over, Murrow called the board chairman to thank him.

"There's a saying they have in North Carolina and I'll repeat it. You're the kind of man I'd go hunting with," he declared.

Murrow also consulted with Paley on what to say at the news conference forced upon him by McCarthy's latest insinuations. "How can you reply to such things without dignifying them?" he asked. "There's one thing you can say," the board chairman suggested. Murrow jotted it down.

When he faced the press he said it, in a way that is still remembered and quoted. "Who has helped the Communist cause and who has served his country better, Senator McCarthy or I? I would like to be remembered by the answer to that question."

In his sur-rebuttal, Murrow called McCarthy's charges against the Institute for International Education false, and spoke of its origin in 1919 as a student exchange organization to improve American relations with foreign countries. Indeed, though he did not say so, the first students and teachers brought to the United States by the IIE in 1921 were five hundred refugees from Russia's Bolshevik Revolution.

He noted that IIE student exchange was largely financed by the Carnegie Corporation and the Rockefeller Fund, and that his fellow trustees of IIE included Secretary of State Dulles, Milton Eisenhower, Dr. Ralph O. Bunche of the United Nations, and Dean Virginia Gildersleeve of Barnard College. In 1932–1935, when he was assistant director, IIE's National Advisory Council included such educators as John Dewey and George S. Counts of Columbia University, Robert M. Hutchins of Chicago, Frank P. Graham and Howard W. Odlum of the University of North Carolina, Harry Woodburn Chase of New York University, Hallie Flanagan of Vassar, and William Allan Neilson of Smith.

It was not that Murrow expected any of this to impress McCarthy, but he was not speaking to McCarthy any more than McCarthy had been speaking to him.

As for the Moscow University seminar, Murrow explained that, shortly after this country's diplomatic recognition of the Soviet Union, the university had in 1934 organized an Anglo-American Institute for summer sessions. IIE acted as the American sponsor, as it did for similar summer courses in Britain, France and even Nazi Germany. For it had been Stephen Duggan's view, and Murrow's, that political relations between countries should not hamper educational exchange.

Though small groups of American and Soviet students had been exchanged for some years, despite the absence of official relations between the two countries, and hundreds of American engineers went to the Soviet Union to help the Five-Year Plan, the 1934 Soviet offer was regarded as something of a bonanza in American academic life. Before the Stalin purges set in, and on the crest of a Soviet construction wave that included such projects as the Moscow subway and the Dnieper Dam, it came at a time when the Soviet Union was more open and friendly to foreigners, more receptive to outside ideas and influences, than perhaps any time since.

Murrow's superior, Professor Duggan, had visited the Soviet Union himself in 1925 and talked with Lunacharsky, the Commissar of Education, and even Trotsky, then Commissar of Trade, about the possibilities of exchange. In 1934 he was suddenly invited by the Soviet government to organize a summer session at the University of Moscow. He discussed the idea with other American educators and found widespread enthusiasm for it.

What was envisaged was courses given in English by Soviet professors, on the changes in education, art and literature in the country wrought by the Bolsheviks. Obviously it would not be an objective curriculum. But there was more than enough teaching back home in America to balance it.

Murrow explained that he was a member of the twenty-four-person IIE national advisory council, all of whom had been chosen by the institute itself and "none by VOKS or any other Soviet agency," and that they had in turn supervised the selection of two hundred Americans to attend Moscow University for six summer weeks in 1934. They came from sixty universities and colleges in the United States, and the only contact they had with VOKS was in its provision of living and travel facilities inside the Soviet Union, since that was its ordained function.

The 1934 seminar was accounted successful, and the IIE agreed to sponsor a similar session the following summer. But in 1935, as two hundred Americans and thirty Britons arrived in Leningrad, the Soviet government abruptly canceled the project, and instead provided sightseeing tours around the country for most of the students and teachers.

Duggan, then in London, asked Ambassador Ivan Maisky to find out what had gone wrong, and Maisky cabled Moscow but received no answer. Back in the United States, Duggan queried Ambassador Troyanovsky but received no information. He then wrote to Moscow University himself, without result.

No reason was ever given for the sudden reversal, but the secret internal struggle which had surfaced with the Kirov assassination in Leningrad in December 1934 was obviously a factor, and it led to Stalin's purges, a wave of Soviet distrust of foreigners and foreign ideas, and espionage and treason trials that were in their own way a preview of McCarthyism.

In any event the IIE, after the cancellation, severed any connection with Moscow University. After the war, when it tried again to arrange for American students to go to Russia, at the request of the State Department, it was called by the Russians "the center of international propaganda for American reaction." Trustee Dulles was called "one of the most violent of the warmongers," and Trustee Murrow "the reactionary radio commentator."

None of these facts had been allowed to interfere with the indictment of Murrow and the institute drawn up by Sokolsky and read by Mc-Carthy. And it may seem unlikely now, with scores of American students regularly studying at Moscow University, with scholarships, grants, fellowships and endowments available around the world, that such an incident as McCarthy's attack could have occurred as recently as 1954.

Murrow, as he answered McCarthy, stated what at that late date should not have had to be stated. "I believed eighteen years ago, and I believe today, that mature American graduate students and professors can engage in conversation and controversy, the clash of ideas with Communists, anywhere under peaceful conditions, without being contaminated or converted.

"To deny this would be to admit that in the realm of ideas, faith and conviction, the Communist cause, dogma and doctrine is stronger than our own. This reporter declines to admit that, but remains uncertain as to Senator McCarthy's position on this matter."

Though McCarthy had used the time given him to reply to Murrow for opening up other matters, notably that of Oppenheimer, he had become too embroiled with the Army to go on any further himself with any of them. Two weeks after his appearance on *See It Now*, he was on nationwide television again, and thirty million Americans were watching the Army-McCarthy hearings.

They lasted thirty-six days, occupied television for 187 hours, and reduced McCarthy from a threat to a travesty, or possibly, as some of his more devoted followers thought, a tragedy. They were climaxed by Attorney Joseph Welch's line, "Until this moment, Senator, I think I never gauged your cruelty or your recklessness," after McCarthy had tried to stigmatize a young lawyer in Welch's office who had nothing to do with the case.

The defense attorney went on. "If it were in my power to forgive you for your reckless cruelty, I would do so. I like to think I'm a gentle man, but your forgiveness will have to come from someone other than me." Any playwright could have envied such a curtain.

Fred Friendly, mulling over the CBS refusal to broadcast a Senate Vietnam hearing years later, has raised the question whether the Army-McCarthy hearings, historic as they were, would be broadcast if they had taken place in 1966 instead of 1954. Actually, though they captivated the nation, they could not have been regarded as saturation coverage even then. Only the small Dumont "partial network," now extinct, carried them every day coast to coast. The equally small ABC network, which had less commercial time to lose than the other two, carried them every day but only as far as Denver. NBC gave up its routine daytime fare for only a few days to broadcast the hearings coast to coast, then decided there was not enough "public interest" in them and went back to its soap operas.

And CBS, in 1954 as in 1966, did not carry them live at all, but showed recorded excerpts in the evenings, on the ground that it did not wish to duplicate other networks' programs — as if a newspaper would omit the leading news story of the day simply because another paper printed it. Or CBS may have felt that it had already, through Murrow, done its share in the matter of the People versus Joseph McCarthy.

For Murrow had also made numerous broadcasts on his nightly radio program about McCarthy and his methods, dating back in fact to the time of the Wheeling speech. On the eve of the new year 1952, he broadcast to the Senator an "oral postcard" of season's greetings, reading, "Look before you leap; the pool may be empty."

Discussing the Senator's investigation of the Voice of America, he noted that the only important thing about that or any other broadcasting operation "is what comes out of the loudspeaker," and not "the arguments, the personal jealousies, the differences in news judgment that are inevitably involved in the preparation of any broadcast," and that the McCarthy committee had concentrated on, in its hunt for "Communist influence."

About McCarthy's attack on the Army in the Peress case, Murrow said two weeks before the *See It Now* television program, "What is at issue is whether a Senator is to delve into interdepartmental matters, goad subordinates into criticism of their superiors, taint them with insinuations of Communist sympathies, and impugn their judgment and integrity to the demoralization of the department. This is not the way Senate investigations are supposed, or entitled to function. They have a proper and important role in our system of government. This is not the role."

During the Army-McCarthy hearings he called the Senator's "Loyal American Underground" of Federal employees — who fed him information, often from secret files — "a private Gestapo," and he saw McCarthy's defiance of the President on this matter the basic constitutional issue raised by McCarthyism: "Who is going to run the government of this country?"

Murrow made a wry comment about Joseph Welch's reaction to McCarthy's attack on his young associate, Fred Fisher. "It is safe to assume, I think, that had Mr. Welch never heard of Mr. Fisher, his emotion, his anger would have been considerably less. It seems to this reporter that there is a widespread tendency on the part of all human beings to believe that because a thing happens to a stranger, or to someone far away, it doesn't happen at all.

"The muscles of moral indignation become flabby when those who are being damaged, either in their bodies or in their reputations, are re-mote or unknown."

As a result of the Army hearings, nightclub comics for the first time began to imitate McCarthy. "Point of order!" and "Mr. Chairman! Mr. Chairman!" became wisecracks. Mass publicity, which had helped cre-ate him, now helped to destroy McCarthy.

His censure by more than two-thirds of the Senate in December ef-fectively ended his career, and he died two and a half years later. Shortly before his death, the Senator sought out Murrow at a party in Washington, threw an arm around his shoulder, and grinned. "No hard feelings, Ed?" Murrow broke away.

McCarthy never gave Murrow much credit for what had happened to him, thus sharing Murrow's own view. McCarthy blamed the Eisenhower "palace guard" and deserters from his own ranks.

When McCarthy died in 1957 the Senate majority leader, Lyndon B. Johnson, eulogized him somewhat beyond the pro forma necessities. "Joe McCarthy had strength, he had great courage, he had daring. There was a quality about the man which compelled respect and even liking from his strongest adversaries."

Even though McCarthy was gone, "hounded to death by those who would not forget and would not forgive," as George Sokolsky saw it, his heritage would remain. And the United States, in its global role, would continue in one degree or another the anti-Communist basis of its foreign policy. McCarthy's downfall, in fact, coincided with the little-remarked ac-tion of President Eisenhower in writing to the obscure President of a far-away and dubiously legal state called South Vietnam, to pledge American aid. Murrow, in a radio broadcast about the 1954 Geneva Conference, which was almost blacked out by the Army-McCarthy hearings, foresaw American armed intervention in Vietnam.

Murrow received the 1954 Freedom House award for his McCarthy program and the obvious public service it had rendered — winning out against German Chancellor Konrad Adenauer as the recipient — but a few weeks later he learned that in the Army Counter-Intelligence school near Baltimore, in lectures intended to disclose the "deep penetration of communism in American life," he was being cited as a member of three Communist-front organizations, and as having written for Communist newspapers. Yet as the Army-McCarthy hearings began, he had been lec-turing on international affairs at the United States Military Academy at West Point. And the next time he applied for a new passport, he en-countered dossier trouble. McCarthyism was by no means dead.

Murrow's most considered appraisal of the McCarthy era, and the role of the mass media in it, was made five years later in his Guildhall speech in London, when he was starting a sabbatical year that not long afterward would be followed by his own disappointed departure from broadcasting. He said of McCarthy:

"His weapon was fear. He was a politically unsophisticated man with a flair for publicity, and he was powerfully aided by the silence of timid men who feared to be the subject of his unfounded accusations. He polluted the channels of communication, and every radio and television network, every newspaper and magazine publisher who did not speak out against him, contributed to his evil work and must share responsibility for what he did, not only to our fellow citizens but to our self-respect . . .

"The timidity of television in dealing with this man when he was spreading fear throughout the land is not something to which this art of communication can ever point with pride. Nor should it be allowed to forget it."

It may be more clearly seen now than then — now when television has been able to influence and often create happenings, such as antidraft demonstrations; when it brings war into the living room, and conveys impressions and moods about the state of the Union; when as between politicians and their constituents it is difficult to tell which acts and which is acted upon — that it was public opinion, informed by television, that judged McCarthy in 1954.

Television was a kind of X-ray that showed the malignancy inside the body politic. But unlike the role it played in the Kefauver anticrime hearings of 1951, when it first impinged itself upon the public consciousness by linking nineteen Eastern cities; unlike its role in the 1952 nominating conventions and presidential campaign, when it was still an observer — now for the first time it had been a political instrument, actually changing the course of events. Noticeable in the Army-McCarthy hearings was the open appeal, in direct address, to the television audience, rather than the Senate caucus room.

This new power was to be confirmed in the 1960 political campaign and the Kennedy-Nixon television debates which many believe turned its scales.

Television, still relatively new in 1954, enjoyed its golden age then in more ways than one. In drama as well as in news, it was establishing new levels of mass communication and participation, imparting a sense of worthwhileness, originality, above all unpredictability. It had not yet become mired, though it was beginning to be, in formula Western, mystery and comedy series, in routine violence, in quiz games and panel shows — in the mere consumption of time as against its utilization.

Yet despite the qualitative changes, television of the Sixties has possessed the same quintessence as television of the Fifties. The immediacy of an unfolding event on television overshadows its meaning. Unlike historic retrospect, the camera has no zoom lens for cause, and no range finder for effect. Its focus is not universal. It is everything in itself at a fixed moment in time.

Whatever may have come after and for whatever reasons, it was not doubted, by the millions of Americans who witnessed their encounter, that it was Ed Murrow and the medium who vanquished Joe McCarthy and the medium.

Television applied its own ruthless test to McCarthy, as to any other performer. His ratings had dropped. He was through.

III

"You must hoe to the end of the row"

EGBERT ROSCOE MURROW was born at a time when life in America, as in the rest of the world, was beginning to get complicated. They were still "the good old days" in 1908, still remote from thought of war and relatively free of internal strife and suspicion, and though the muckrakers had inked in the form and features of the "malefactors of great wealth" President Theodore Roosevelt inveighed against, innocence prevailed and another baseball season was always starting.

The nation was embarking on "a raft with Taft," on the advice of the Republican campaign song, seeking a harbor of "peace and tranquility" after seven strident years of the activist in the White House, who believed in "the strenuous life" for the Government as well as for himself. Promising a breathing spell from "more laws, always more laws," "Good Old Bill" Taft and his running mate "Sunny Jim" Sherman easily won election over the Great Commoner, William Jennings Bryan, his third and last defeat.

North Carolina, of course, voted Democratic like the rest of the South, but in Guilford County, where there were many Quakers, there were also many Republican votes, including those of Joshua Stanley Murrow, a well-off farmer and former state senator, and his son Roscoe. Guilford, always known for its independence of mind, also, and perhaps for that very reason, seemed always to be divided against itself — Whigs versus Tories in the revolutionary period, Unionists versus secessionists in the Civil War, high tariff versus low tariff supporters in the Era of the Trusts.

The new President, like the old, would distinguish between "good" and "bad" trusts. His Supreme Court would order not only the Standard Oil Company to be "dissolved," but also the Tobacco Trust, which from the ducal seat of James Buchanan Duke in Durham controlled three-quarters of the entire American tobacco industry. Guilford County, which lay in the fertile Piedmont country between the two great tobacco towns of Winston-Salem and Durham, knew the decision would change nothing. Nobody was indicted, fined or sent to jail for violating the antitrust laws. Roosevelt and Taft were not opposed to the political and economic system. They were merely trying to save it from itself.

Taft's raft was rather wobbly, however. Beneath the tranquil waters ran the deep swift currents of the New Nationalism, as T.R. called it. The decades of European immigration had spilled the Old World's get across the continent. There was still unemployment after the 1907 Panic, and unrest and dissatisfaction were stirring.

The head of Princeton University, speaking in North Carolina, thought he knew the reason. "Nothing has spread Socialistic feeling in this country more than the use of the automobile," declared Woodrow Wilson, meaning that this new status symbol was also the symbol of disparity between rich and poor.

As the youngest of the three sons of Roscoe and Ethel Murrow was born on April 25, 1908, on Polecat Creek, in the Center Community of Friends outside Greensboro, Guilford's county seat, Henry Ford had emerged to stem the Socialist tide by starting production of his cheap Model-T, for $850.

Wilbur Wright had flown seventy-five miles in 113 minutes, and he and his brother had won a War Department contract insuring the future of aviation.

The first American skyscraper, the forty-seven-story Singer Building, had opened in New York. The first motion picture Greensboro had ever seen, a few months before, was so popular that now there were four movie houses in the town. And the United States Navy, the Great White Fleet of sixteen battleships, was showing the American flag on a fourteen-month voyage around the world, and especially to the Japanese, who had become perhaps too exhilarated by their victory over the Russian empire.

Under the first Roosevelt and his predecessor McKinley the United States had extended its Manifest Destiny beyond its own natural frontiers — "national purpose" had replaced "national destiny" as the motivating force — and had acquired the Hawaiian Islands, occupied the Philippines, controlled Cuba, seized the Panama Canal Zone, and was engaging in Dollar Diplomacy everywhere. Taft himself, America's first viceroy, had served as governor of the Philippines, and as Roosevelt's Secretary of War became provisional governor of Cuba.

But the domestic frontier was not quite filled in, and the Pacific Northwest had become its new outpost. The former Oregon country was calling settlers, not only from the East and South but from Europe. The logging camps and sawmills of Washington State, it was said, were run by "Swede power," and Roscoe and Ethel Murrow, on Polecat Creek, received cheerful letters from their cousins, the Cobles, who had settled on Puget Sound and found the climate pleasant and the opportunities plentiful. Moreover, in May 1909, seven hundred thousand acres of Government land would be opened to settlement in Washington, Idaho and Montana, and homesteads would again be available.

Roscoe and Ethel Murrow had two other sons, Lacey Van Buren, aged four, and Dewey Joshua, aged two, when Egbert was born. They owned a 160-acre farm which Roscoe had received from his father when he was twenty-one, and later he worked for and bought another 160-acre tract from his parent.

The Piedmont, between the Tidewater and the Blue Ridge, was a natural stopping place for the wave of migration which came from the original colonial settlements further north. The Murrow ancestry reflected the ethnic and cultural composition of Guilford County, settled by the Germans, the Scotch Irish and the English Quakers, between 1750 and 1800. But the Quaker breed was predominant in Guilford, and the Murrows had become pillars of the Society of Friends in the Center Community.

Ed Murrow, who had little interest in genealogies, once remarked offhandedly that his family had been established in the New World by "a couple of Scotch Irish who jumped overboard." There was more to it than that. They presumably came from Ulster, where the name at one time was evidently spelled Murrugh, and may have arrived in Pennsylvania by way of Nantucket.

Whether they were Quakers, as so many Scotch Irish became, before they went south or after they arrived there, they were part of the second surge of migration that came into North Carolina starting with 1770, via the Great Philadelphia Wagon Road. This ran from the Schuylkill, outside Penn's town, to the Susquehanna and then turned south along the Blue Ridge.

John Murrow, with a wife who, it was said, was half Cherokee Indian, established the new family foothold right on the Philadelphia Road — a remount station, lodging house and tavern for travellers. He prospered selling rum, and soon was able to buy farmland.

The Center Community in Guilford, so called because it was halfway between the New Garden and Pleasant Garden Quaker settlements, south of Greensboro, had been established in 1757 on the rich red Piedmont soil, which originally was "covered with wild pea vines," but soon was converted into thriving farmland by the Quakers. It was called "prairie land" because grain grew there best, and flocks of sheep could graze everywhere, but the rolling countryside, abounding in wooded areas and nurtured by creeks, with a wide variety of wild flowers — Guilford's flora were known to naturalists all around the world — and an abundance of birds and small game, gave the county a character which endures into this industrial age.

It was Joshua Stanley Murrow, born in 1851, who elevated the family's sights above yeomanry, honorable though that estate might be, and gave it a horizon extending even beyond Greensboro. He had come into 750 acres of farmland, but his chief interest was politics.

The Murrows had been Whigs from revolutionary days. They were Unionists and favored the abolition of slavery, and since they were also Quakers the Civil War, though hateful, did not create the traumatic tragedies so many North Carolina families went through — the neighboring Coltranes, for instance, who were divided over slavery and secession. Guilford County had voted overwhelmingly against secession and for the Union in 1861, but when President Lincoln asked North Carolina for troops to support the Union, the state chose to secede rather than fight its sister states. Most of the Quakers retained their antisecession feelings.

Family divisions in Guilford, as elsewhere, were not only political but religious, and many Quakers became Methodist instead, for the Southern Methodists approved of slavery, unlike their Northern brethren. Religious change was undertaken not only by some of the Coltranes but also the prominent Lambs.

Joshua Murrow, after the war, plunged into the politics of the Reconstruction, married Roella, of the sundered Coltranes, when he was twenty-seven, rode about the county to become a familiar figure in the crossroads stores, the political forums of their time, and when he was thirty-six was elected a Republican state senator and served two years. He was credited with the legislative arrangement by which, in exchange for his support for the establishment of the State Agricultural and Mechanical College, now the University of North Carolina, Guilford County received a "similar but equal" Negro university, now the large and prestigious Agricultural and Technical College at Greensboro.

Joshua and Roella Murrow had two children, Grace and Roscoe, the latter named for the man the North Carolina state legislator for some reason most admired, New York's United States Senator, Roscoe Conkling. They also adopted Edgar Murrow, the infant son of Joshua's brother Shuble when the child's mother died.

As the new twentieth century began, Roscoe Murrow married Ethel Lamb from the adjoining farm, who had been teaching county school in the small community on the hill above Polecat Creek.

Unlike the Murrows, who came from the lowland Scots transplanted into Ulster, the Lambs represented the other Scots strain in North Carolina's settlement, the Highlanders who had left after "Bonnie Prince Charlie's" failure. The Lamb progenitors were Finley Stewart and his wife Prudence Shaw, who came to the United States in 1755. They landed

in New York, lived briefly in Pennsylvania, then settled in the Alamance
Church section of Guilford County. Not far away, at Guilford courthouse
in 1781, Cornwallis's Pyrrhic victory over Nat Greene would lead to
his surrender seven months later at Yorktown.

Finley Stewart took part in the American Revolution and for his war
services was granted 640 acres of land by Governor Caswell. Thereafter
he industriously increased his land holdings and chattels, which included
numerous slaves. Unlike the Quakers, he had no objections to slave-
holding.

From the Stewarts, via the McAdoos, came the Cobles. George Coble
and Judith Hanner were married in 1828 and had nine children. One of
them, Isabelle, married George Van Buren Lamb and had five children.
It was their eldest daughter Ethel who was Ed Murrow's mother.

Murrows and Lambs alike were farmers, and Ethel became a Quaker.
But George Van Buren Lamb had been one of those who favored the
South and secession, and had fought in the Civil War on the Confederate
side from its first day to its last.

The family legend was that he had been on Stonewall Jackson's staff,
and indeed caught the redoubtable leader in his arms when he was mor-
tally wounded by fire from his own side after Chancellorsville. Van Lamb's
military record needed no such embellishment.

He was a volunteer who received battlefield promotion from sergeant
to captain of I Company of the 22d North Carolina Regiment — the
"Davis Guards" — saw continuous action with that heavily engaged,
much-casualtied and much-cited unit, and was himself wounded four
times, carrying a musketball to his grave. The "Davis Guards" fought at
Manassas, Seven Pines, Second Manassas, Harpers Ferry, Shepherdstown,
Gettysburg — they took part in the attack on Cemetery Hill — Spotsyl-
vania, Cold Harbor, Petersburg, and were at Appomattox for the surrender.

Captain Lamb may have been present when Stonewall Jackson was
wounded by fire from the nervous rifles of the 18th North Carolina.

But more to the point may be the fact that at Chancellorsville the 22d
North Carolina, taking part in Jackson's flank attack on Hooker, had suffered the severest losses in its combative history.

At any rate Ethel Lamb Murrow was entitled to be designated Daughter of the United Confederacy, as well as Daughter of the American Revolution, though she never exercised either option, and profoundly scorned
such matters.

The best the Murrow side could offer in the way of a war record was
Roscoe's. The large easygoing man who was Ed's father enlisted in the
Spanish-American War, but a boyhood injury below the eye incapacitated

him, though he was kept on in camp in a noncombat role. In any case, North Carolina troops saw no action in the short war, and spent it bivouacked outside Jacksonville. The First North Carolina Regiment was sent to Havana after the war, the first United States troops to enter the city and be hailed as liberators. But Roscoe Murrow was not among them. When his second son was born, however, he named him Dewey after the victor of Manila Bay, who was his particular hero.

Back from the war, Roscoe Murrow married and applied himself to farming. His cousin Edgar, who was also his adopted brother, recalled that he was "the workingest man" he ever knew, possessed of "the finest hands with a turning plow." But his heart may not have been in farming as fully as his hands were. Edgar thought that after his time away from home in the army, Roscoe was restless and always "looking away, wanting to go."

In North Carolina in 1900 the average farm covered a hundred acres — that was the size of the Lamb farm — though the plantations of the Tidewater region were of course much larger. Roscoe Murrow's 320 acres were not only unusual, but productive. Land in the area was selling at twelve to twenty-five dollars, even up to forty dollars an acre.

But he did not seem to make much of a go of it. The corn and hay crops brought about six hundred dollars a year, provided there was no drought.

The house, situated in a hollow on the bank of shaded Polecat Creek, was a small one, not to be compared for instance with the spacious white frame dwelling not far away on the same winding stream, where Dr. Porter's son William had been born, later to be known as O. Henry.

But the Murrow home was comfortable both outside, being entirely surrounded by a wide porch, and inside, where a huge fireplace took up a whole wall of the main room. The house was made of yellow poplar and black walnut logs, from the trees which sheltered it, and it had a "punching floor," made of logs which had been planed off.

The fireplace was the source not only of heat, for all the cooking was done there, and not only of light, but also of some inner comfort. Roscoe would sit there, his feet propped up to the fire, sometimes reading the Bible, sometimes silently looking at the flames, when his exceedingly active sons would let him.

The third boy was born without much ceremony. Late that Friday evening Roscoe Murrow came over to his father's house with the news that the baby was on its way, and woke up the thirteen-year-old Edgar to send him for the doctor. It was a five-mile horseback trip to the Pleasant Garden Community, and when Edgar arrived the doctor had gone out to attend another delivery. When he finally found him and they got back to Polecat Creek at four o'clock Saturday morning, the baby had preceded them, delivered by its grandmother Roella, and was in fine voice. "It was Ed Murrow's first broadcast," Edgar said.

On that Friday evening, in Greensboro, thoughtful citizens had attended a lecture at the public library to see Professor W. C. A. Hammel of Normal College demonstrate wireless telegraphy by sending a message to an adjoining room. Also, some members of the second-year class of the A. & M. College for the Colored Race, which Joshua Murrow had legislated into being, were "on strike" against what they considered unfair grading, and had been expelled.

In the wider world the nation's press was calling on President Roosevelt to "spank" a Castro, the president of Venezuela, who had confiscated American property, and the United States was sending a gunboat. Secretary of War Taft was successfully lining up delegates for the Republican National Convention. Winston Churchill had been defeated for Parliament at Manchester. The New York to Paris auto race, via Siberia, was in its seventy-ninth day, and men were in revolt against women's huge "Merry Widow" hats, which had dominated the Easter Sunday scene while blotting out most of the view.

The Murrows, after their third child's birth, did not remain long in the house on Polecat Creek. They decided to move to higher ground, on the other tract of land Roscoe owned, and he built a new and larger house there.

Ed Murrow's earliest recollections were of trapping rabbits, eating watermelon, and listening to Grandfather Van Lamb, who had a long white beard and was regarded by everyone as a "charmer," tell long and intricate stories of the Civil War. The boy acquired an interest in history.

Sometimes his Uncle Vance, his mother's brother, a horse trader in Richmond, visited them and strummed the guitar, singing "Little Yaller Gal, Won't You Come Out Tonight?"

His mother also sang, and she needed no accompaniment. She knew "The Baggage Car Ahead" and all the verses of "The Cowboy's Lament," and many hymnlike ditties, her favorite being "You Must Hoe to the End of the Row." It was a precept she followed for herself, and instilled into her three boys.

Perhaps to make it sound more touching — and there was a definite dramatic streak on the Lamb side of the family — Ed Murrow in later life would remark with nostalgic fortitude upon the tribulations of a North Carolina tenant farmer on forty acres of poor land. But Roscoe Murrow was no tenant. He owned his own land, which came to eight times forty acres, and he would sell it after he moved West.

Indeed, to all the numerous young cousins, the Murrows, Lambs, Coltranes, Dicks and Hodgins, "Aunt Ethel's" house was the most pleasant and certainly the most generous in the community. There was always something to eat there — Mrs. Murrow was renowned for her meat pies and her biscuits — and they were always welcome. If it rained, or became too late to go home, Aunt Ethel laid a row of pallets in the room under the roof, and they would whisper and giggle in the darkness.

Life in the Center Community was plain and spare. The Murrows had enough food from their farm, and for others as well, but the staple diet for many was cornbread and molasses, sometimes three times a day. Occasionally there were candy pullings for the children, possum hunts and even fiddlers' conventions, but the more usual memories were those of long days at school and in the field of red soil which turned to thick deep mud in the winter and spring, miring the wagons; and of many silent hours sitting starchly in Friends' meeting, reflecting upon the Inward Light.

Ed Murrow's cousin Louise never saw an automobile until after the Murrows had left for Washington State, when she was past five, so it is possible the Murrow boys did not either. Greensboro was only a few miles away, but it took all day to get there by horse and buggy, and there was no real reason for going. And there was always too much that had to be done at home.

Ethel Murrow was tiny alongside her tall two-hundred-pound husband — "she never weighed more than ninety-eight pounds sopping wet," Ed would say, exaggerating slightly — and she was of a bustling nervous disposition by contrast with her husband's imperturbability. She fretted constantly, worried every time one of the boys strayed away for long — "I'll never see sonny again," she kept repeating — and had apprehensions about accidents and her health, and frequent premonitions of undefined catastrophe. She suffered from asthma, which Ed may have inherited in the form of bronchial weakness.

Roscoe Murrow seemed to live for the particular day alone. He forgot about yesterday immediately, never harbored a grudge or recrimination, and thought he should not be concerned about tomorrow until it arrived, by which time he might not have to be. With all his contented disposition, however, he was a man of resolve, and once his mind was fixed, it was said, not even torture could change it.

Both father and mother, though roughhewn in a roughhewn environment, were gentle in instinct and lived their whole life through with affection toward each other, which the boys remembered.

Ethel Lamb Murrow, unlike the "dark Murrows," had light hair and sharp and intent blue eyes, the beacons of the strict discipline she enforced upon her sons. She ruled by copy-book maxim, and hoped that Egbert, the youngest, would become a preacher.

The three boys worked hard at farm chores — in later life Ed Mur-

First day of school. Egbert, LEFT, *was too young to go, but insisted on having a book. Lacey,* CENTER; *Dewey,* RIGHT

row often said that not working made him feel "miserable" and that he had never been "equipped to have fun" — and when one of them did "wrong," usually consisting of some manifestation of sibling rivalry, she punished all three, thus displaying no favoritism.

Though he lived in North Carolina past the age of five and always considered himself a Tar Heel from Guilford County — whence Dolley Madison, O. Henry and Speaker Joe Cannon also came, while Andrew Jackson briefly practiced law there — and frequently found it convenient in later life to be regarded as a Southerner, especially by Senators and Congressmen, Egbert Murrow was obviously too young to be whistling Dixie when the family moved West. Only his oldest brother Lacey, who was nine at the time, retained a Southern accent.

Mother and father never lost their Southern intonations, but in Ethel Lamb Murrow's speech the striking characteristic was what her son Dewey called its Spenserian quality. It was expressive, often poetic, the kind of English spoken in the Elizabethan times, which still survives in isolated cultural pockets in the South. The exact choice of words and their precise use, inverted phrases like "this I believe," and verb forms like "I'd not" and "it pleasures me," which Ed Murrow, broadcaster, used on and off the air, came directly from his mother. The two other boys also used such speech patterns, colorful and perhaps even archaic, all through their lives.

The Murrow family decided to go West for several reasons which boiled down to one, namely that Mrs. Murrow's cousin, Terry Eli Coble, who had moved to Skagit County, Washington, made resettlement sound promising. Besides, there was Mrs. Murrow's health, which demanded a softer climate, as well as the fact that though a farmer by inheritance, Roscoe Murrow was apparently not a farmer by temperament.

In 1913 the family traveled West by train, spending the crop money and what an auction of their chattels had brought them. They sat up for six nights in the day coach, eating from two wicker baskets packed with food, and stopping off in San Francisco to visit Chinatown. Their destination was Blanchard, a small farming and sawmill community on Puget Sound, about seventy miles north of Seattle and thirty below the Canadian border. Blanchard was where the Cobles lived.

It was not yet a final move. Settling in a new country, far from the Murrow tribe and the numerous descendants of Finley Stewart, required more thinking over. Roscoe Murrow was undecided about scraping the tar from his heels, and went back to Polecat Creek a year later to have another look. Moreover Ethel's asthma had not cleared up in the West, where it rained more often than not.

After the visit, however, they decided that Guilford County was no longer big enough for them and settled in Washington for good. Even so, Roscoe did not sell his farm for several years, and it was not until 1920 that his cousin Edgar took over the first 160-acre tract and not until 1926 the second.

For a while the Murrows lived in Blanchard in a tent, pitched alongside the Coble house, which was already being shared by their cousins. Finally they found a house of their own, and at the same time Roscoe Murrow, having tried his hand as an agricultural laborer and disliking it, acquired a new calling. He went to work on the big saw at the Hazel Mill, and then as brakeman on the lumber camp railroad of the Samish Bay Logging Company. Soon he became a locomotive engineer, one of the proletarian aristocracy of the lumber industry. Explaining his father's nature as "simple and direct," not at all reflective, Ed Murrow in later years recalled that "when he was asked how he was, he always replied he was 'still on the rails and on the payroll.' "

Blanchard, situated on the Samish Flats alongside blue Puget Sound, was flanked inland by the tall slopes of Blanchard Mountain, covered with Douglas fir, cedar and hemlock, where the logging operations took place. From them a timber road led down to a railroad siding, and the logs were rolled down to be loaded.

The town, with its sawmill and its lumberjack boardinghouses and dormitories, was surrounded by small produce farms — since developed into one of the richest pea-producing areas of the country — and on these farms but principally for the Cobles and the Lawsons — George Lawson had married Alice Coble — the three Murrow boys worked for hire, to augment the family income. They pitched hay, weeded beets, hoed corn, milked cows and mowed lawns.

The life was hard but not without its fun. There was plenty of opportunity for fishing and hunting, but although they were on tidewater Egbert never learned to swim, and explained later that he had not really had the time. All the boys became good shots, bagging rabbit, duck and pheasant, not for mere pleasure, however, so much as for profit. They were ingenious in finding ways to earn money, and Egbert embarked on his first financial venture at the age of nine by buying three piglets, raising them, and selling them for a profit of six dollars.

Because of Mrs. Murrow's firm discipline and constant supervision — she believed it was "better to wear out than to rust out" — the ideal was to combine work with the more enjoyable sporting activities. The boys would not go out to shoot duck, as their school friends did, but they would shoot a few on the way to milk cows. They set muskrat traps as part of farm chores. They received ten cents for each duck sold, and the shells cost five cents, so while the margin of profit was plain, they could not afford to miss very often.

Dewey when he was fourteen earned money by playing baseball for one of the sawmill teams. He even played once on Sunday, but was so overcome with remorse when he remembered this was against his mother's law that he never desecrated the Sabbath again, at least in that fashion.

The boys also learned to handle horses, and later tractors, and sold those skills also to nearby farmers. Dewey drove a farm wagon when he was nine and operated the first mechanical milker in the county when he was twelve.

There was school, of course, in a two-room shack with two teachers and twenty-five other pupils, but it was only part of the day-long routine activity and by no means the most important, since there were so many chores outside the schoolroom.

Egbert liked school, or rather the idea of going to it, for when he was not yet old enough to attend, and his two brothers were departing with their spelling books under their arms, he insisted on having a book of his own and going with them, at least to the door. The insistence took his usual form of raising a row about it, and his brothers bestowed on him the neo-biblical nickname "Eber Blowhard," shortened to "Blow."

The name was confirmed for the whole town when, in the little Methodist church, the six-year-old Egbert fell asleep during the sermon, and then awoke with a start and a loud bawl. About the same time he made his first recorded public speech. At a parent-teacher meeting to which his mother took him, when the chairman called for further business, he rose and reported, "We sold a wabbit."

A photograph was taken on that first day of school, showing the three boys in knee pants and caps, in front of the Coble house. Egbert, with his commandeered book clutched in his hand, was a squat little boy, firkin-shaped, with a round face and a determined chin, thrust downward.

This facial expression, later to become lean instead of round, remained with him all his life for special dire occasions, both on the television screen and off. Some would call it his doomsday look.

From the first, also, the youngest and loudest Murrow had a kind of mordant grin, which later came to be described as sardonic. As the youngest he had the privilege, as he explained it, of hollering the loudest, and he took full advantage of it when he was whipped, or as he soon came to learn, to prevent being whipped. The anticipatory noise he made enabled him to avoid the worst by causing his mother to say, "Egbert, hush. What will the neighbors think?"

When he did get to school Egbert was only a fair student, having trouble with spelling and arithmetic, as he would continue to do in adulthood.

His real early education, indeed, was at home and had nothing to do with the alphabet. The teacher, their mother, was intent on imparting to the three boys what she so obviously was strongly possessed by, a sense

Dewey, Lacey and Ed

Early days on the Last Frontier. Ed, with knife, and his brother Dewey, out hunting

of responsibility. She was a Quaker, but the only church in Blanchard was Methodist, so she went there. The result, at home, was an amalgam of sternness and forbearance.

She ran a Bible-reading house, a chapter each evening, and the boys were made to do their share of it on Sundays. Grace was said before every meal, and she prayed a good deal besides, though the boys were not impressed and were inclined to regard it as some of her dramatics. Once Dewey accused her of lack of faith, arguing that if she really believed in the power of prayer she would not always be anticipating disaster.

She would not permit any work on Sunday, nor any play either, and would not allow the boys to go to the movies on that day, or on many another.

She forbade card-playing in her house also, though if visitors chose to indulge when they called for an evening she would overlook it, and she forbade smoking though she knew that the boys, like all the boys in town, stole a few puffs now and then. She warned against the evils of tobacco all her life, but once in North Carolina on her father's birthday — his white beard was flecked by tobacco stains — when the boys asked her what they could get him with the dime they had received for a skinned rabbit, she suggested a plug of the famous local honey-flavored twist. She was opposed to it, but she had come to accept it, as she would Ed's relentless habit of cigarette chain-smoking, which he took up seriously in college.

Mrs. Murrow dressed plainly, even drably, and always wore a shawl, Quaker-fashion. She lived frugally and sparingly, and taught the boys to. She also taught them not to lie, cheat or steal, but perhaps even more she drilled into them a sense of respect, not only for other people's property and persons, but for their opinions. Her ideal was tight control of one's self combined with tolerance for others and nonintrusion upon their affairs. In her own life she carried the nonintrusion principle to the extent of denying herself the normal parental privilege of sharing her children's joys and honors. She would not attend weddings and other family occasions, and would not visit her children. They came to see her, and it was only with reluctance that any of them could persuade her even to go for a drive with him. When she did agree, she would find a concrete purpose, such as to look for bric-a-brac.

With the feeling of tolerance for others that she taught her sons went a cherishing of their own identities, and a regard for their own things, especially their own land.

All of them grew up with what Dewey called "an appreciation of real estate" — in the natural, not legal sense; not as property, but as land — a love of the outdoors, and an affinity with the processes of nature. When he attended college, financing himself by working summers in logging camps, Ed would manage to put enough aside to buy a small parcel of land on the installment plan. He always wanted ground he could possess.

Mrs. Murrow also tried to teach her sons not to scrap among themselves and to keep the peace, and though she was frequently defeated by the natural mischief-making of boys aged two years apart, she had the last word. When the scuffling, wrestling and punching reached its peak she halted it and sent the aggrieved party, so far as she could determine, out to cut a good-sized switch, which she then used upon the culprit. If from brotherly compassion he brought back a light switch, she would let him have a taste of it and send him back for a heavier one. When she could not decide who was in the wrong, which was usually the case, all three boys received equal punishment. And when they had to be spanked she did it at once and got it over with, without waiting for the father to come home.

But in the major matters of her sons' lives, like choosing what they wanted to be and going where they wanted to go, the strict disciplinarian gave them their own full discretion.

For all her iron, the mother was essentially shy, a trait which Ed Murrow, the public figure who knew Presidents and prime ministers, inherited to some degree and would never lose. She was moreover reserved and formal in her dealings with other people. She always called them Mr. and Mrs. and never used first names.

The relationship between parents and sons was summed up by Dewey. "They branded us with their own consciences," he said.

The mother was the dominant factor in the household, obviously, but if the more easygoing father stood by, it was as a kind of family supreme court, to uphold the constitutionality of the mother's precepts and to make sure they were not violated.

The boys often thought themselves unduly restricted by their mother. On the other hand, they reasoned, how many mothers would have allowed an eight- or ten-year-old to go off on his own with a shotgun?

Later they would decide that what they primarily felt in her was a sense of martyrdom. She gave them the impression of always being on trial and enduring ordeal, in the broad terms of *Pilgrim's Progress*, even if, as on many occasions, she had to create the ordeal for herself. She had a large capacity for enjoyment of life, but knowingly denied it to herself.

And with her dramatics, Ed frequently said, the stage lost one of the great actresses of the century when she became a housewife. He came by some of her theatrical endowment and was not averse in later life to playing up to her, one actor to another, especially in his letters.

His mother, for instance, was a tolerable cook, Southern style, and he was fond of her biscuits, and fatback and turnip greens. But as he grew up and became increasingly indifferent to anything that might be set before him, he masked his lack of appetite with extravagant praise of her efforts. Once he wrote his parents from the *Île de France*, "This ship is famed as having the best food in the Atlantic, but they can't touch Mom's cooking." Even on the *Île de France*, however, what he usually ate would be scrambled eggs.

But not very much acting was required for Murrow's appreciation, all through his life, of the way in which the traits of manhood had been formed.

Thirty years later, during the war, he would write his parents: "Whatever we have made of ourselves is due to the fundamental training we received at home. The shortcomings are our own. I could quote you learned men of science to prove that point but you know it as well as I do.

"It might be that not all of your boys will come out of this business [all three were in the war, in one way or another]. Probably they will, but if they don't you must take some pride in the fact that you sent them out with as good mental and moral equipment as three boys ever had.

"It could be that one of your boys could bring sorrow and shame to you by some voluntary act, but if one should be hit he will act as he was taught to act as a small boy, and he will bring no shame upon the name.

"The point of all this . . . is just to tell you that small boys don't really ever grow up. They never escape from their early training and when the going is tough they return to a few fundamentals, drilled into them between the ages of six and ten. Although I still maintain that Pop walloped me harder than necessary when I dropped that chicken coop on Lacey, or maybe it was Dewey. Anyway I'd probably be a better man if he had licked me more just for exercise . . . I'll sure wipe the floor with him when I come home again. The house will shake when I pin his shoulders to the floor."

The reference was to the wrestling that had gone on, as a nightly pastime, between Roscoe Murrow and his sons. When he came home from his day on the logging locomotive he took them on, one by one, on the kitchen floor while the mother, as Ed recalled, "used to fly around in the background wringing her hands and telling us to stop." When they were in the late teens and even their twenties, home from college, the father was still usually able to throw them.

Of the three boys Egbert, the youngest, was also the most daring, if only to outdo the others in their fierce natural rivalry. Then, as in later life, he often did things just for the sake of doing them, or as he might have thought, because they had to be done. On one occasion he put his right forefinger into a cider press, on Dewey's dare, and then could not snatch it out in time. He carried a twisted finger into adulthood.

A scar on his forehead was another boyhood award for boldness. This came about when a neighbor boy with a new air rifle boasted about his proficiency and Egbert challenged him to prove it. From the protection of a wall, the youngest Murrow kept poking his head out and taunting the marksman to hit him. The boy finally did, with a BB shot squarely between the eyes. Egbert bled profusely and howled loudly, the more so when his mother whipped him into the bargain for frightening her.

Another forehead scar came from falling head first into a drainage ditch. The boys had salvaged from the town junk heap a bicycle with no seat or pedals, only frame and wheels. Dewey tied Egbert to the frame with a piece of rope and sent the wheels on their way. Egbert could see the drainage ditch coming and knew what was going to happen. He kept shouting loudly, but it did no good.

With Egbert's audacity and loudness went a hot temper. He frequently flared up against his older and stronger brothers, but his outbursts were shortlived, and though he took them with him into adulthood and often seethed visibly at major annoyances, he would be able later to turn his anger into long freezing silences. A friend who knew him from his first broadcasting days and was associated with his career once said, "He had a devil inside him somewhere, making him do unpredictable things."

The Murrow boys got an early glimpse of the world outside their own household when, soon after they had settled in Blanchard, they saw a neighbor's son swinging on a creaking gate. From the swinger's mother inside the house, repeated at intervals, came the command, "Leo, get off that gate." Leo continued swinging. Finally his mother shouted, "Get off that gate or I'll knock your block off," and came out. Leo continued swinging. His mother went in again. Leo's block remained intact. To the three young Murrows, who knew that their blocks would have been forfeit if they had disobeyed their mother, it was the revelation of other ways, in other homes.

The outside world had other fascinations. In Puget Sound lay Samish Island, which had been connected with the mainland by a causeway, and over this the boys and girls of Blanchard drove on picnics and hayrides. The interurban trolley ran through Blanchard also, on the way from Seattle to Bellingham, and occasionally, when they had no more pressing use for the dimes they collected for ducks and rabbits, the Murrow boys would ride along a scenic coastline, with the view of snowcapped Mount Olympus, nearly eight thousand feet high, across the sound.

They played about the town's logging camp and Egbert found a favorite resting place above the sluice. Years later, at the peak of his broadcasting career, he was to tell a hometown friend he would give it all up "to sit on the dike at Blanchard with a gun, waiting for a duck to fly by." He was a tall, thin boy with an easy grin, and though his clothes were often hand-me-downs and fit him something like Huck Finn's, somehow he seemed always debonair.

The Great Northern Railroad ran through Blanchard and hauled away to Seattle or Bellingham the logs brought to the siding by Roscoe Murrow's locomotive from the timber-cutting site. When Dewey was old enough he became his father's brakeman. And Egbert, at fourteen, went into the logging camp himself, to work summers as a whistle punk and donkey-engine fireman.

In Blanchard, where the bulk of the population consisted of the six hundred men who worked at the Hazel Mill, and their families, there was, besides the school and the church, Hinkston's general store. It had on display four kinds of penny candy, so the Murrow boys could for four cents sample everything available, and decide what they liked best. It was a fulfillment without confusion that modern youth, with a superabundance of choice, probably could not appreciate.

Blanchard was able to remain a relatively untroubled community, though situated in a center of industrial strife and violence, because it was a permanent settlement with a resident working population, further stabilized by the Samish Flats farms surrounding it. Occasionally an IWW organizer would come to town, but the "Wobblies" found no foothold there for their One Big Union, as they did in the transient logging camps along Puget Sound and on the Olympic Peninsula across it.

But the labor turbulence that swept through the Pacific Northwest before, during and after the First World War had at least emotional repercussions in Blanchard and must have made its impression on Ed Murrow as he himself became, if only in the summer, one of the "working stiffs" the Industrial Workers of the World addressed themselves to.

There was for instance the Everett "massacre" on the "Bloody Sunday" of November 5, 1916, two days before the reelection of Woodrow Wilson because he had "kept us out of war." On the dock of the Puget Sound city, which was also on the interurban trolley only forty miles from Blanchard, five hundred deputies lined up and opened fire on a boatload of IWW members and sympathizers, as they landed from the excursion steamer *Verona* from Seattle.

They had come to Everett to demonstrate on behalf of free speech and assembly, as they saw it, though their larger aims were frankly revolutionary — "abolish the wage system" — and their descent on Everett followed a period of mass arrests, beatings and "deportations," as the result of trying to organize the migrants, itinerants and transients who made up the bulk of the Northwest's labor population.

The volley from the dock was met by some scattered gunfire from the steamer, and the result of a ten-minute exchange was five IWW martyrs, with thirty-two others wounded, and two slain deputies, with sixteen wounded.

The two-month trial of the first of 174 IWW men charged with unlawful conspiracy as a result of the Everett "massacre" — one of the great trials in American labor history — was still in progress when the United States entered the European war in April 1917. It ended with a not guilty verdict for Thomas Tracey and through him the IWW, and it inevitably resulted in a broad and successful organizing campaign for One Big Union, as well as an industrywide lumber strike for the eight-hour day.

American entry into the war changed the nature of the labor conflict. The IWW, which had been organizing in the Northwest since 1912, continued to talk revolution but its immediate objectives were simpler and more readily understood — better wages, shorter hours and improved working conditions.

The Northwest depression of 1914–1916, moreover, had laid off thousands of the migrant workers who in 1910 had constituted a full third of the entire American labor force, and included lumberjacks, construction workers, miners and farm laborers, living mostly in camps. Many of them were new immigrants who had come from Europe in the human tide that swept the American shore between 1890 and 1910.

Remarking on the transient nature of such labor, one lumberman explained that it took three crews to keep a logging camp running — "one coming, one working, one going."

The Murrows, who had left the Tobacco Trust behind them in North Carolina, found the Lumber Trust regnant in the state of Washington. For the opening of the "last frontier" had long since ceased to be a matter of individual enterprise and courage. It was being done by the corporations, including the lumber companies.

To save valuable natural resources, the Federal Government had adopted the policy of conservation and withdrawn sixteen million acres of land from public settlement, as national forests. But this was at the expense of the latecomers, still pushing across the continent, as the Murrows had, seeking ground to settle on. Instead of homesteads they found wage employment. Instead of property owners, many of the new arrivals became migrant labor.

So the IWW had fertile ground for its organizational efforts. Even though it was a marginal movement, never representing more than five percent of trade unionism in the country, it had a kind of romanticism about it and an underdog vitality that gave it influence far beyond its numbers. The repressive measures taken against it by the sheriffs' deputies and vigilantes of the timber country increased sympathy for it in many quarters, notably in the Puget Sound area.

The Federal Government's Special Commission on Industrial Relations reported in 1917 that the suppression of free speech carried out by the forces of "law and order" . . . "strikes at the very foundation of government. It is axiomatic that a government which can be maintained by the suppression of criticism should not be maintained. Furthermore, it is the lesson of history that attempts to suppress ideas result only in their more rapid propagation."

Egbert Murrow, seated in the Blanchard grammar school — it had three rooms by then — was nine years old at the time these words were widely published in the Northwest. It is doubtful if he read or understood them then. But they were part of the tradition he grew up in, and was to live by.

Whatever victories the IWW won before the United States entered the war were wiped out by the war. American entry ended the Northwest's depression and created a boom. Lumber was in great demand. Prices soared from $16 to $116 per thousand feet in a few days. Spruce was required for airplane fuselages, at $1200 per thousand feet, and the rain-swept Pacific slope was the greatest single source of spruce.

But loggers' wages did not go up at the same pace as lumbermen's prices, and long hours and bad working conditions still prevailed. So the Great Lumber Strike of 1917 was called by the IWW, ten thousand men laid down their tools, and most of the sympathy the Wobblies had enjoyed was dissipated. The strike was regarded as treasonable. Moreover the revolutionary situation in Russia had become more acute, and the IWW was depicted as the American branch of worldwide Bolshevism.

Again there were mass arrests and beatings of IWW members. The strike was lost when the Army itself took over logging operations and sent "spruce soldiers" into the forests and even built a "spruce railway" to step up the production of airplane lumber.

The Government's assumption of control remedied many of the conditions the IWW had struck against, but the vindication was an ironic one. In September the Department of Justice raided forty-eight IWW halls throughout the country, and 165 IWW leaders were indicted in the Illinois Federal court for antiwar conspiracy and sabotage.

The trial of 101 of them, which began in Chicago on April 1, 1918, lasted five months and all were found guilty and received long prison terms, though they were later amnestied by President Harding. During the war, one observer noted, "to kill a Wobbly was more patriotic than to kill a German."

Even after the war anti-IWW raids and attacks continued, such as the lynching of Wesley Everest, an IWW member, in his Army uniform on Armistice Day 1919, after the American Legion, parading with gas pipes and rubber hoses, attacked an IWW hall in Centralia, Washington, and was met by gunfire. Egbert Murrow was eleven years old when a state-wide wave of violence followed the Centralia incident, and hundreds of IWW members were arrested. Eleven were tried and found guilty of murder because four of the Legionnaires who attacked the union hall had also been killed.

Despite such difficulties, however, the One Big Union idea was not entirely extinguished in the Puget Sound area after the Armistice. The big cities of Seattle and Tacoma were subjected to organizing drives, some big industries were tied up by strikes, and in 1919 even a general strike was called in Seattle.

But by the time Egbert Murrow entered the woods as a summertime whistle punk in 1922, at the age of fourteen, the IWW had almost expended itself as a labor force. It remained more prudent to carry a red card than not to, because there were still many zealous Wobblies in the camps, and it was certainly true that a red card was effective insurance against being thrown off a freight train — some railroad brakemen regarded it as good as a regular passenger ticket — but the militancy, the leadership and the romanticism of the One Big Union movement had been dissipated. Its memories remained, however.

Four decades later one of Murrow's most powerful television documentaries, *Harvest of Shame*, revealing the plight of migrant farm labor, was in one sense an evidence of the psychological impression left by his boyhood recollections.

It would not be the only heritage of his work in the woods. Senator Joe McCarthy, striking back at Murrow after the *See It Now* television program that challenged his power, declared among other charges that the broadcaster had been a card-carrying member of the IWW. Murrow denied it, and indeed he was never an actual member, but once he acknowledged that he "might" have carried a red card for "protection." And no doubt with some small vestige of romanticism.

Another related facet of life in the Northwest was communalism. The Puget Sound Cooperative Colony, one of the more ambitious and enterprising Utopias, had faded at the turn of the century after reaching a membership of two thousand throughout the state of Washington. But some of its relics of settlement remained and its materialistic ideals — free land, water and light; no taxes, rent or interest — survived if only as wistful longings. Moreover the colony's social objectives of an eight-hour day and abolition of the wage system were embodied in the IWW philosophy, and the Wobblies attracted many of the same kinds of free souls who had earlier been drawn to the communal way of life.

At Blanchard, as Egbert Murrow grew up, a community popularly called the Colony — its formal name was Equality — existed without exactly flourishing, on sloping farmland just outside the town. It numbered sixty men and women and it was not very good propaganda for social experiment, for it finally broke up in mundane quarreling over the apportionment of shares, and in trying to arrive at rules satisfactory to everyone. Some of the colonists smashed the windows of others.

Still, as an idea at least, communalism was present in the youngest Murrow's boyhood. He was exposed also, whether consciously or not, to the generally progressive politics that set the social patterns in the Pacific Northwest. Washington State had introduced the direct primary in 1907 and women's suffrage in 1909, while the banner year of 1911 — the same year in which Lloyd George in England instituted the beginnings of the welfare state — brought to Washington an eight-hour day for women, a food and drug act, and the initiative, referendum and recall.

Civics as such, however, played no important role in Egbert Murrow's high school career, nor did any other strictly academic pursuit, for that matter. The high school was at Edison, four miles from Blanchard, and when he entered it in 1922 Dewey was two classes ahead of him, a junior, while Lacey had finished and had gone to the other end of the state, away from home, to attend Washington State College.

Egbert and Dewey could go to school part way by interurban trolley, but usually they walked, until the time came when the school board provided a makeshift bus, fitting a wooden coach body to a Model-T chassis. Dewey, as a senior, was the first driver of the bus, making a fifteen-mile sweep of the countryside, picking up his schoolmates in the morning and letting them off in the afternoon. When Dewey left home, also for Washington State College, Egbert took over the wheel for his last two years. It was another way of earning income, for there was less time now for shooting ducks.

The town of Edison had been named for the Wizard of Menlo Park, and in 1923 when Dewey was advertising manager of the school's yearbook — naturally called *The Mazda* — he wrote Edison soliciting the customary "Compliments of a Friend" paid notice. Alas, replied Edison, he had no money.

In the little high school, with its faculty of five and in 1923 a student body of eleven seniors including Dewey, fifteen juniors, fifteen sophomores including Egbert, and fourteen freshmen — all about equally divided between boys and girls — the Murrow brothers were the leaders in extracurricular activity, though in the classroom their grades were not remarkable.

Both were in the school orchestra, with Egbert playing the ukulele, a popular instrument of the day requiring no musical ability, and Dewey the banjo-ukulele. Both were on the baseball team, where Egbert was right-handed when only a single hand was required — in this case for pitching — but when both hands were needed, for batting, he became

Growing up in Washington State.
RIGHT: *Ed and friend, 1924. The*
"E" is for Edison High. BELOW: *He*
always had a flair for clothes

left-handed like his mother. In the same way, later, he would become a
left-handed golfer.

Both boys were also in the school glee club, Egbert already singing
bass, or what passed for it, at the age of fifteen, while Dewey was second
tenor. In 1923, in the school's first operetta *In Old Louisiana*, Egbert
played the Marquis de la Tour and sang a solo. The following year he
was a soloist in *The Bells of Beaujolais*.

In the winter Dewey and Egbert played on the basketball team, called
the Edison High Spark Plugs, and in 1925, with Egbert as a forward, it
won the Skagit County championship. In one game during the season
the star forward was knocked out in a collision with an opposing guard,
and awoke to the sound of applause. Dazedly he thought he must have
scored a goal while unconscious, but the cheers were for the coach, who
was carrying him off the court over his shoulder.

That year, as a senior, Egbert was also president of his class and of the
entire student body.

It was in debating, however, that he found his deepest satisfaction.
The grandson of Joshua Stanley Murrow, the crossroads grocery politician,
on the one side and of Van Lamb, the dashing yarn-spinner, on the other
had a natural bent for it, quite clearly, and he was aided by his English
teacher, Ruth Lawson.

Outside of class he was also a great arguer. The juvenile "Eber Blowhard" had become a serious teen-ager who night after night was at the
Coble house confabulating with his elders. The subject did not matter,
nor the side taken. Egbert talked so well indeed that a farmer-neighbor
said he wanted him to preach at his funeral, and the boy promised.
When the neighbor died, Egbert did speak. His mother was especially
proud. She still wanted him to enter the ministry.

The school debating team, consisting of Egbert and three girls, won
the northwest Washington championship, taking the affirmative in the question, "Resolved, the United States should enter the World Court." When
Dewey, who had also been on the debating team before Egbert, left school
for college, as class valedictorian he "willed" his "gift of speech" to his
younger brother. In the class will of 1925 Egbert Murrow was recorded
as leaving "his unsurpassable gift of elocution to anyone needing the
same." He was also named "the boy who had done most for the school,"
though with no specifications given, and in the composite word portrait
of "A Perfect High School Boy," printed in *Mazda* for 1925, others were
cited for scholarship, wit and manners, but he was cited for "charm."

Under his class-book photograph, showing a smiling boy with prominent
ears, was inscribed the description, "A man in the world's new fashion
planted, that hath a mint of phrases in his brain."

A bright future was seen by his classmates for the thin, energetic, curly-haired boy. It was forecast in the class prophecy that on May 2, 1965, forty years on, Egbert Murrow would "speak on social reform."

He would then be, it was predicted, "professor of social science at the University of Washington." For Edison in 1925 this was a broad vista, as Murrow was graduated in a class with six other boys and four girls, under the class motto, "Impossible is un-American." The class flower was the gold dust.

In addition to his classroom studies and numerous extracurricular activities, Egbert had driven the school bus before and after school for two years. It had no self-starter and no antifreeze fluid, and its thirty-mile daily round included eleven unguarded rail crossings, a fact which troubled his mother considerably. Once he ran over a dog, which as he recalled troubled him considerably.

All this left little time for shooting, and some of the ducks Egbert brought down were out of season, which meant he was constantly eluding the law, in the person of Sheriff Tip Conn. He seemed to have no trouble doing so, nor any compunction.

One weekend, in season, he agreed to go pheasant shooting with a neighboring farmboy. Instead, as he discovered, he had to pitch hay for hire that day. He took his shotgun to the field with him, and on the way home bagged three birds while the other boy, shooting all day, got none. Murrow later remembered the incident as symbolic of his career. His conscience, or his mother, had compelled him to pitch hay. His luck enabled him to get three pheasant anyway. It was a combination, conscience and luck, that would recur many times.

As Egbert finished high school in 1925 his oldest brother Lacey had completed his four years at Washington State College and was joining the State Highway Department, while Dewey had finished his sophomore term. The way lay open, in classroom, on campus and in fraternity house, for the youngest Murrow to follow in their footsteps.

But Egbert thought he would like to go to the University of Virginia instead. It may have been because American history was his favorite subject in high school. It may have been because the Virginia–North Carolina country was his native soil.

To go to an Eastern college would cost money, and there was not too much of it available in the household of Roscoe Murrow, logging-locomotive engineer. Lacey, now earning a salary, thought he might be able to help out his brother financially, but Egbert decided to take a year between high school and college to earn his own money. He went to the Olympic Peninsula, and into the woods for a whole year.

The decision was made a family one by Roscoe Murrow. That placid man had been prodded by his wife into dislike of a new superintendent, whom he himself had nothing against but whom Ethel Lamb Murrow for some reason could not abide. Despite her vaunted tolerance, she kept shaking her head and muttering uncomplimentary remarks about him. Roscoe said nothing, but on the job one day, as the superintendent approached, he felled him without a word. "What will become of us and the boys?" his wife asked, on second thought, when he came home and revealed what had happened.

But news had reached Blanchard that the big lumbering firm of Bloedel-Donovan had begun logging operations on the far slope of the Olympic Peninsula. Once again the Murrow family went west, this time about as far as they could go without actually wading into the Pacific Ocean. A hundred miles west of Seattle, they moved into a company house at Beaver Camp, on Beaver Lake near the town of Forks, and both father and youngest son went into the still primeval rain forest.

Egbert was the only one of the three boys still at home, as the family entered another phase of its existence. Lacey, on the state payroll in the capital, was thinking of a political career. Dewey had decided he had had enough agriculture at college, and after a few weeks of his junior year dropped out to go prospecting for emeralds in South America.

For Egbert, seventeen-year-old high school graduate who liked the outdoors, the peninsula was overwhelming evidence of the grandeur of nature. Above the rain forest rose white-tipped peaks, and between them lay Alpine valleys. Icy streams, fed by melting snow, filled crystal lakes on the bosoms of the giant glaciers. Lake Crescent, which in the Nineties had been the end of the logging trail from Forks, was credited with the bluest water "anywhere," because of its depth, the reflected blue sky and the minerals it contained. It was, too, the only known home of the Beardslee trout, which weighed up to thirty pounds and was renowned for its fighting qualities. Over Lake Crescent stood Storm King Mountain, 4500 feet high, a game refuge.

On Mount Olympus, visible from any part of the peninsula and far beyond, grew columbine, dogtooth violets and Indian pipes. In the national forest roamed herds of deer and elk. Ptarmigan, grouse and pheasant were abundant, but, it had to be admitted, there were bear and cougar, too.

Before Alaska and Hawaii entered the Union, Clallam County, Washington, was the westernmost part of the westernmost American state. No stretch of it was far from salt water, since it was bounded on one side by the ocean and on another by the Strait of Juan de Fuca, across which lies Vancouver Island and Canada.

At the extreme northwest corner of the state lived the Makah or "canoe" Indians, and along the ocean coast were numerous Indian villages, fishing shacks, lighthouses, logging locations and trading posts. From Forks, the last "civilized" settlement, one road led to the most forlorn spot of the American mainland, Destruction Island, a black rock used as a Coast Guard station.

When the Murrows came to the peninsula, conditions in the lumber industry had improved considerably over those which had led to the IWW strike less than a decade before. At Forks, so named because it stood near the juncture of three rivers, in lush meadowland between towering spruce and fir forests, the tents and bunkhouses of yore had given way to family dwellings, boardinghouses, a dining hall, dormitory building, club, church, school, stores, and a locomotive roundhouse, which was the elder Murrow's province.

Egbert, finding his name embarrassing in a rough logging camp, now preferred to be called simply Ed, and had moved upward from whistle punk on a steam donkey engine, charged with signaling the successive steps in the timber-felling process, to become a compassman and assistant to a "timber cruiser."

Before logging changed into a mechanized forest-products industry, its various functions were not only a matter of individual skills, but were jealously guarded by their possessors. Forest engineers planned the roads into the woods and devised the methods of moving the logs out. Foresters, who had to keep in mind future "crops," decided when to cut, and where to plant new trees. Fellers cut the trees down and had to know where to let them fall. Buckers cut the tree trunks after they fell, and sawed logs into proper lengths for hauling to the mills.

But the timber cruiser was the elite of lumberjacks. He did not participate in the actual felling or hauling. He worked ahead of the logging, estimating the amount, kind and quality of lumber that could be taken out of a specified area, and he was guided in his movements and measurements by his compassman.

"You map from one section corner to another, which is a mile. My job was to gauge this distance by pacing it," as Ed Murrow recalled it twenty-five years later. "The country was very rough, but accuracy was important in making a map. The first time I paced a mile, down into streams and over hills, I hit the section corner within fifty feet of where I said it would be. It gave me a great sense of achievement because it was something I'd done completely by myself."

The timber cruiser and his compassman roamed about in the woods, camped on the banks of streams, found time to fish, and explored hemlock groves. It was an experience that completely pleasured Ed Murrow. Moreover the timber cruisers, who were often independent agents working for professional fees for either buyer or seller of timber, were better educated and sometimes even highly literate men. The young student, who used to argue of evenings in the Coble house, now spent even longer evenings around campfires, again talking endlessly, and listening, too.

Though living conditions were far better than in 1917, men were still tough in the logging camps in 1926 and even took pride in the injuries they received and the pain they felt. To the rugged and untutored French-Canadians, Poles, Scandinavians, Germans and Scots who made up the work force, a college boy was a curiosity. They had respect for his literacy, indeed a clerkship was the dream of many a rough timber hand.

But the college boy had to show his mettle, too. Since danger was always present and accidents occurred on a large scale, caused by trees, logs and earth slides — and the suddenly falling high branches called "widow makers" — the opportunity came often enough, even if it meant merely being unmoved by the sight of crushed bones and shattered flesh.

As living conditions became more refined at Forks and other settlements in the West End of the Peninsula, logging operations had, under the same banner of progress, become bigger, more mechanized and more destructive. In the earlier cutting, at the turn of the century, horses were taken into the forests to bring the timber out, and as the logs were dragged along the ground, they scraped only a few trees bordering the greased skid-road. Only the best trees were taken. Small trees were left behind, and new seedlings were planted.

But in the Twenties high-lead logging was introduced. Cables and pulleys were slung from the tops of the tallest trees, or spars, and with the power supplied by a steam donkey engine, the daily output was raised from the ten thousand to twenty thousand feet of logs produced by horse teams, to seventy-five thousand and even one hundred thousand feet per engine.

Huge logs were yanked from the woods rapidly and roughly, shearing everything down before them as they moved. No green timber was left standing, and the debris piled high. Since only the best-grade logs were commercially desired, "clear cut" logging, as it was called, meant vast waste and spoilage. This might have been tolerable on a limited scale, but the widespread devastation of large operations was by the Thirties to leave the beautiful peninsula scarred by desecrated hillsides bearing the shattered remains of forests.

To get the logs out from the West End the lumber company built its own railroad to Sekiu, on Clallam Bay, where they were slid into the water from Roscoe Murrow's train and towed as huge rafts along the Juan de Fuca Strait to the company's two big sawmills at Bellingham, on Puget Sound. In the other direction the railroad line was extended to Sappho. And how in the world did a rough-and-tumble lumber camp in the middle of the woods come to be called after a Greek poetess?

At least Bloedel-Donovan, as it went into the high hills where Douglas fir stood three hundred feet high after having taken eighty years to mature, could plead local enterprise for its reduction of the forests. It had bought its Clallam County acreage from absentee owners, housed in Grand Rapids, Michigan, and in its two decades of logging on the peninsula it was to bring out four billion feet of lumber by the end of the Second World War. In the peak year of 1928, five hundred men had steady employment, accounting for three hundred million feet, and in the summer one of the five hundred would be Ed Murrow.

Beaver was now his home address when, having given up the idea of the University of Virginia, he registered as a freshman for the 1926–1927 year at Washington State College, in Pullman, in the southeast corner of the state. It was to Beaver and the small company house that he returned on visits and nominal vacations. Beaver was largely a Polish settlement, and polkas, mazurkas and other such dances enlivened the customary Saturday night revels, in the town hall. And Prohibition or not, whiskey in kegs somehow found its way in by packhorse, further to lubricate the proceedings. Even in Forks, the trading center of a large area, packing was in the Twenties still the only way to get supplies to settlers in the Hoh River country.

The young compassman had saved enough for at least a year at college, and Lacey would help besides. The new freshman entered as Egbert R. Murrow, enrolled in business administration, and because he could not imagine things otherwise, began to work by washing dishes in a sorority house. As a sophomore he would advance to waiting on table.

His roommate and closest friend at college was Edward J. Lehan, who had come to Pullman from nearby Spokane and Gonzaga College, the most notable alumnus of which was Bing Crosby, the crooner. Lehan also had an itch for show business, and though he too was enrolled in business administration and would become a lawyer, when he learned what Washington State had to offer the stagestruck, he changed his enrollment after the first semester. The other Ed, Murrow, followed suit. For both, the major college interest became speech.

For Murrow what Washington State had to offer, apart from a dramatic society of near professional quality and an excellent debating team, was the first collegiate course in radio broadcasting given anywhere in the country. It was called community drama, in order to qualify it as an academic course, and it was taught by Maynard Lee Daggy, a well-known lecturer and author of books on public speaking. Professor Daggy, a small, sprightly man, was one of the two major formative influences at college on Murrow's life and career.

The other, and most important, was that rare jewel, a dedicated, understanding and effective teacher. She was Ida Lou Anderson, who had been crippled from the age of nine by infantile paralysis, and who held in her

Home from college

small twisted body a love of learning, and a zeal not so much for perfection as for steady betterment — "she demanded not excellence so much as integrity," Murrow recalled — that communicated itself irresistibly to her students.

Ida Lou Anderson was only eight years older than Ed Murrow. She herself had been graduated from Washington State as a speech major only two years before he arrived there — her education had been interrupted and delayed by the long illness spent in hospitals and sanatoria — and she was an instructor in the speech department when he changed his enrollment in the middle of his freshman year.

It was she who after his mother had most to do with what he would become. She was a voluminous reader of poetry, and imparted to him the value she put upon the meditations of Marcus Aurelius, who would be for him, as for her, a counselor. He adopted for himself the Stoic philosophy:

"If thou workest at that which is before thee, following right reason seriously, vigorously, calmly, without allowing anything else to distract thee, but keeping thy divine part pure, as if thou shouldst be bound to give it back immediately; if thou holdest to this, expecting nothing, fearing nothing, but satisfied with thy present activity according to nature, and with heroic truth in every word and sound which thou utterest, thou wilt live happy. And there is no man who is able to prevent this."

Ed Murrow, the broadcaster, would become to many a symbol of "heroic truth in every word and sound." The college student's favorite advice from the philosopher-king was, and always remained, "to live not one's life as though one had a thousand years, but live each day as the last." He would put it into practice during the war. Some of his friends would see it as a death wish. Marcus Aurelius knew better.

Many years after college the broadcaster was asked by an interviewer, "If you weren't yourself, who would you like to be?" He answered, "Marcus Aurelius, a great mind and a good man."

Apart from the richness of her own intellectual life, gained from wide reading and, despite her crippled condition, from wide travel, Miss Anderson's outstanding quality as a teacher evidently sprang from two not always related possessions. One was her critical ability with respect to the technical requirements of good speech, diction and presence. The other was her concern for, and involvement in the personal as well as the classroom problems of her pupils.

They sought her advice, and her frank appraisal both of their potentialities and their limitations. They not only erased the usual ten-minute pause between classes by thronging about her desk with their questions, but visited her in droves and for hours at the family home in nearby Colfax.

They wrote her letters in bales, during vacations and long after they had left school. It may have been the relatively small difference in their ages that led them to accept her as she offered herself, on their own level, but there was also her infinite patience, sympathy and enthusiasm.

She was a transplanted Southerner also — she had been taken west from Tennessee at the age of three — and Ed Murrow was her favorite pupil and would become her best-known one. It was she who, during the war, when he spoke from the bombarded but defiant metropolis, suggested that his opening phrase, "This is London," sounded too hurried and not consonant with the thoughtful pace of history. He changed it. "This . . . is London," with its measured pause and impact, became his famous identification mark.

At the time she was listening to his every broadcast, made the more vivid because she was beginning to lose her eyesight, was unable to read but had to be read to, had left the classroom, and would die a year later.

Shortly before her death she would sum up his overseas broadcasting in a letter to his mother. She noted the routine nature of most European war broadcasts, mired in casualty and other figures, and wrote: "What pleases me about Ed is that he gives us a little of that, plus his personal observations, from which he usually draws some thought that is bigger than the observation itself. His delivery seems excellent to me. He would have to be feeling pretty well or he could not be speaking as he does."

Miss Anderson, at Murrow's request, made numerous comments on his broadcasts, enabling him to improve them. She may have been the country's first radio critic. For she was a student at Washington State when its pioneer campus radio station KWSC made its first broadcast in 1922 and she became instructor and adviser to the students associated with it, many of whom went on to become successful broadcasting figures. Murrow is remembered by one college friend as having done an occasional sports broadcast for the campus station.

Ida Lou Anderson's students repaid her with devotion, and Ed Murrow was one of the most devoted. He not only attended every class she gave but escorted her to the college plays, when he himself was not in the cast, looking down protectively from his six-foot height as he led her on his arm down the aisle to her seat. Such occasions symbolized her triumph over adversity. For despite her double curvature of the spine, she had as a student in the same hall won every declamation contest she entered, and become the leading campus actress. Her first role, in which the crippled girl was cast as a crippled girl, gave her confidence, but then she went on with considerable artistry to play various character and even romantic parts.

She was Murrow's declamation coach and dramatics adviser, and she turned a natural debater and broadcaster into a serious, skilled and polished one. She also gave him an example of courage which he never forgot.

The relationship was a tender one. It also had a poignant aspect. Even after Murrow had left school, the brightest luminary of his class, and begun his career in public affairs, writing to her frequently, she still felt Pygmalion-like that he belonged to her. When he told her he was to be married she was upset and opposed the idea. He wrote at length explaining that it would make no difference between them, but she was never truly reconciled.

He also wrote to Janet Brewster, his wife-to-be, about Ida Lou. "She is very much a part of my life and always will be, but in a way that is hard to understand . . . She taught me to love good books, good music, gave me the only sense of values I have, caused me to stop drinking myself to death." He was dramatizing, as young fiancés do.

"I've talked over in letters every decision. She knows me better than any person in the world. The part of me that is decent, that wants to do something, be something, is the part she created. She taught me to speak. She taught me one must have more than a good bluff to really live.

"I owe the ability to live to her, and to her you owe the things you like in me. She calls me her masterpiece."

In his freshman year at college Egbert, as he was still officially listed, escorted his absent brother Dewey's girl, Donna Jean Trumbull, to campus social functions. He did not dance himself — he was not good at it and besides his mother had frowned on it — but he saw to it that Donna Jean's card was always filled. And his ballroom attendance added to the campus popularity he was already finding.

For although he was a slightly better than average student, particularly in speech courses, classroom work seemed to be only incidental to all the other things in which he was involved. He and Ed Lehan were quickly pledged to Kappa Sigma, the oldest and considered the best fraternity on campus — unlike the Eastern custom, fraternity membership came in the freshman year — and they lived with forty other boys in the big rambling house which dominated Fraternity Row.

Washington State took its campus politics seriously. No "non-Greek," that is, nonmember of a Greek letter fraternity, could achieve campus leadership, and Murrow, who seemed to have an instinct for such things, was impressed by the fact. He would become president of his class and president of the student association because in both cases he was the candidate of Kappa Sigma, the biggest and strongest house. In return for their support of Murrow, other fraternities were allowed by the Kappa Sigs to fill other student posts.

When he became engaged in the international student movement, Murrow would frequently argue about college fraternities with European students, and stoutly defend them. Once he was asked how they had benefited him. "They taught me table manners," he replied. It was not intended as a jest.

During his freshman year Murrow began the heavy smoking he would continue until the end of his life, and after it and another summer in the Olympic Peninsula logging camps, he changed his name from Egbert to Edward. There continued to be some confusion about it. In his sophomore year the college yearbook listed him in three ways. He was Egbert, in Kappa Sigma. He was Edward in the school play, *Craig's Wife* — he played the part of the husband. And he was Ed, master of the class executive committee and sergeant-at-arms. By his senior year it was all straightened out.

His mother, whom he saw during the summer, took note of the change. "I think Egbert is not happy with his name. If I had known how it looked when written out, I wouldn't have given it to him. It didn't look pretty." Moreover she usually called him "Sonny," anyway.

By his sophomore year Ed Murrow was becoming the complete man-about-campus. The country boy had smoothed down his curls, begun to be a modish dresser, and was functioning as actor, politician, social arranger and military cadet. He liked the intensive drilling of the ROTC, continued with it voluntarily after the first two compulsory years, and received his consistently best marks in military training.

He and Ed Lehan also served as waiters at the Kappa Delta sorority house, but it was not his métier — he frequently spilled things on the sisters — though he enjoyed what seemed to him to be the unusually frank conversation that went on.

His own fraternity life took a good deal of his time. As an officer of the Kappa Sigma chapter he consulted with the alumnus adviser on other boys' problems — drinking was the principal one — and made frequent visits to the chapter house at the University of Idaho nine miles away, where, it was rumored by other fraternities, a whiskey still was being operated in defiance of the Prohibition law. For whatever reason, the traffic across the state line between the two Kappa Sig chapters was a heavy one.

Though his marks as a sophomore were largely B's and C's, his roommate Ed Lehan remembered his "photographic mind." He did not recall that they "opened more than a dozen textbooks" between them, though Murrow read all sorts of nonrequired volumes. But "he could sit through classes all week and never take a note. On Friday night he could give the professors' lectures almost verbatim."

Dewey came back from South America and he and Donna Jean were soon to be married, giving Ed even more time for his extracurricular interests. These did not include athletics. At high school he had played baseball and basketball, but in college military training early every morning and three afternoons a week took the place of sports. And student politics was almost a full-time career in itself.

As a junior Murrow held his own in the classroom, with A's in three speech courses and in military training, and B's in history and sociology. But he had also become class president, served on the prom committee, represented his college in ex tempore oratory at the Pacific Forensic League, placing third; was one of the three cadet lieutenants in the ROTC, commanding Company C, and served on the committee for the annual military ball. As the college yearbook *Chinook* reported the latter occasion, "The bright blaze of flags from every nation contrasted with the metallic glint of machine guns, transforming the new gymnasium into a maze of militarism."

He also appeared in two more college plays, as the "sensitive, poetic" hero in Channing Pollock's *The Enemy*, and as a waiter in Molnar's *The Swan*. Ed Lehan and Hermine Duthie — it was whispered on campus that she and Murrow were "secretly engaged" — also played in *The Enemy*, and all three were chosen that year for the National Collegiate Players, the honorary dramatic society.

The summer between his junior and senior years was for the first time not spent in lumberjacking. Instead he took part in the six-weeks ROTC encampment at Fort George Wright, near Spokane, and returned to college as the cadet colonel and indeed the biggest man on campus. He was not only president of the student body, numbering 2800, but also head of the Pacific Student Presidents Association.

When he went to the National Student Federation convention at Stanford University as a delegate in 1929, he was elected its president, too, even though he came from what was regarded as a "cow college."

Moreover he had decided that he liked that sort of thing, student meetings, politicking, argument over issues — even if no more important than convention voting procedure, or whether auditor courses in colleges should be unrestricted — the rubbing of shoulders with other young people from all parts of the country, identification with the pursuit of "education," and travel. The student movement was not only national but international. It was even worth considering as a serious career.

Ed Murrow's senior year at college was indeed a golden one. The Wall Street crash of October 1929 punctuated it, and introduced the Great Depression. But in the Pullman hills on which the campus, like Rome, was built, the outside world did not intrude much. There were proms and other social functions, boy-and-girl strolls through Tanglewood in the evenings, bull sessions at the Kappa Sig house, the bachelors' shacks at Sleepy Hollow where bathtub gin was available, picnics in the

Moscow Mountains, and Sunday afternoon excursions downtown to Maiden Lane, to the movies and a drugstore soda afterward.

In class he finished with A's in speech and military training though he received only a B in the famous course in radio broadcasting, and as for political science, barely a C.

Outside of class he had no time for dramatics or oratory in his final year because of his student activities which, according to the yearbook *Chinook* were achieving "international prominence for himself and his college."

The yearbook attributed his success to "an A-plus personality, together with a level head, and the ability to see clearly into the problems confronting the college students of the present day."

But time did remain for his military pursuits. He was not only cadet colonel, regularly reviewing his troops — they wore surplus World War One uniforms — but an instructor in machine gun. He mastered "command voice," as it was called in the ROTC course. He was named the captain of Scabbard and Blade, the honorary military society, and he led the grand march at that year's military ball, attended by the governor. However, in the ROTC march at graduation he tripped over his saber.

There may have been something symbolic about it. For he received a second lieutenant's commission in the Inactive Reserve, and if in 1930 there had been any way of utilizing such a status, some of his classmates would not have been surprised, student movement or no student movement, if he had embarked on a professional soldier's career.

At graduation on June 2, 1930, when he received the diploma of a Bachelor of Arts in Speech, he was also Phi Beta Kappa and a member of two other scholastic honorary societies, though his highest mark was the unofficial A-plus awarded him by *Chinook* for "personality."

With his success in oratory and drama, and his student movement activity, he had clearly established the direction in which he was going. All through school he had never been interested in the written word, except as a reader, but in the spoken. He never wrote essays, plays or stories, like his classmates, nor even many letters, and he toiled through term papers and theses. But always he acted, debated and orated. He was a poor speller and had atrocious handwriting. Later he would dictate his notable broadcasts. They were meant to be spoken, not read. But it would be amazing how well so many of them would read also.

When Ed Murrow, having made his mark as the nation's outstanding broadcaster, was serving as USIA director and returned in 1962 to Washington State University, as it had become, to receive its Distinguished Alumnus Award, he looked back over more than three decades and spoke about his college years.

"A man is the product of his education, his work, his travel, his reading, all his experience. But first among these is education. It was here that I found the contagious spark that is curiosity, the ravenous excitement that devours ideas, the emanating wisdom that hopefully opens the pathway of logic, bypassing fancy and leading to fact."

A college friend of his, recalling the serious young graduate, summed up Murrow's four years thus: "He didn't mind being told he was in error, but he did mind being told that what he thought was not important."

In June 1930 the United States and Europe were moving through depression to despond. The world into which the president of the National Student Federation, a Bachelor of Arts in Speech, was stepping — a world of breadlines, closing factories, relief rolls and sharpening ideological conflict — could hardly be called a cheerful, welcoming one.

IV

"A sort of revolving seminar"

B ANKS were closing throughout the United States, the stock market had touched new lows, wheat, cotton and corn prices were dropping and unemployment was rising when, just out of college, Ed Murrow came to New York in June 1930 as president of the National Student Federation of America. He had assets of forty dollars and a few debts. His job was an unpaid one but it carried a living allowance of twenty-five dollars a week, and he had decided to continue with it full-time because, for one thing, there were not too many other jobs available, as the depression began to settle in, and because he hoped it would lead to something broader in what he now accepted as his chosen field of "education."

As he noted later, he had embarked on two of the best years of his life. The federation, an organization of student body officers, was less than five years old, an outgrowth of the Intercollegiate World Court Congress which had met at Princeton in December 1925 — the following month the United States refused to join the court except on its own unacceptable terms — and it was vague about its objectives, except that American students, like students in other countries, should "get together," both nationally and internationally. In 1927 it had actually sent four groups of fourteen American students each as a "delegation" to the Soviet Union for travel and study.

From a one-room basement office on midtown Madison Avenue, opposite the baronial bulk of the Pierpont Morgan library, the president of the federation busied himself with cheap tours to Europe for American undergraduates, and with visits to the United States by debating teams from Oxford and Cambridge.

That summer he received in New York fourteen foreign students from Britain, Austria, Italy, Sweden, Switzerland, Poland and South Africa, and saw them off on a three weeks' tour of America. He himself then embarked for a similar tour of Europe, working his way over as a sort of shipboard monitor. On this, his first trip abroad, he lived in youth hostels and visited student organizations in Britain, France, Germany, Holland and Belgium.

The purpose of the journey was to attend a congress of the Confédération Internationale des Étudiants, in Brussels, and the purpose of those who sent him was to demonstrate to European students that American students were not as feckless and frivolous as they seemed to believe. Ed Murrow was their case in point.

At the New York office, when he arrived there, Murrow had found, acting as secretary, Chester S. Williams, a thoughtful young Minnesotan, made more so by suffering from poliomyelitis. Just graduated from the University of California, Williams had helped elect Murrow to the NSFA presidency six months before, at the annual convention, at Stanford University. He had heard the representative from Washington State College make a speech deploring exactly what Europeans felt about American students, that they were "too provincial, overly concerned with fraternities, football and fun, and too unconcerned with the wider world." Murrow wanted the federation to change that, and Chet Williams wanted to help him.

Apart from its election of Murrow, the convention was notable in NSFA annals because the Stanford University psychology department tested all the delegates from 109 colleges for their executive ability. Murrow reported the findings — fifty-seven introverts, eight extroverts, and seventy-six ambiverts — and explained that the last-named type made the best executives. He was, of course, among them.

Another Murrow supporter at the Stanford convention, Martha Biehle, from Wellesley, had heard from English friends that the international students' confederation badly needed leadership. Murrow, she thought, was the obvious man for that also.

Martha Biehle was now also working at the federation's national office in New York, an unpaid volunteer, and she and Chet Williams, at dinner in a downtown speakeasy, prepared Murrow for the Brussels meeting.

When he got there he made a speech calling for the admission of German students to the international organization, because the sins of their fathers in the First World War could not be attributed to them. The European students were enthusiastic about Murrow, but less so about taking in the Germans. The motion was defeated, and the American declined the presidency.

In London, in 1930, the Five-Power Conference on disarmament had been held, and from it had originated transatlantic news broadcasting, though the graduate of Washington State's radio course may not have been aware of it. In Germany the last Allied troops were departing the

Rhineland, leaving it a demilitarized zone, and the Nazi Party, denouncing the Versailles Treaty, was rapidly gaining strength. In elections two months later it would win 107 parliamentary seats.

For Murrow his trip to Europe was the beginning of an ever-widening circle of acquaintanceship on the Continent, and an ever-present awareness of European political problems.

The NSFA was part of an international students' confederation which represented nearly forty countries. The English and Americans, less "political" than the Continentals, were more interested in cheap travel, cultural exchange, and the desire to "avoid war" by strengthening ties among youth. But at student congresses held in Prague, Rome, Budapest, and now Brussels, the young of the new nations that had emerged from the war were taking themselves as seriously as their elders at Geneva.

Some delegations were led by government youth functionaries professing to be students. European students were older than the Americans, and fervently nationalistic. At the congresses, Czechs and Poles argued over Teschen, Poles and Lithuanians over Vilna, Hungarians and Romanians over Transylvania, Poles and Germans over Danzig. Serbs argued with Croats, though they came from the same new country, Yugoslavia.

The Germans seemed to be the focal point of most student disputes, but not far behind them came the black-shirted Giovenezza from Fascist Italy. The Germans were never formally admitted to the confederation, which was created as an "Allied" institution, but they worked with it at a "practical" level.

This consisted of trying to obtain recognition of their "right" to represent the Volksdeutsch students of Austria and of Czechoslovakia's Sudetenland, exactly as Hitler would do in wider terms, including the military, in the Austrian Anschluss and the Munich agreement eight years later.

The Italians, at international congresses, proclaimed their equivalent of "student power," and within the confederation anti-Fascist elements set themselves up also. It was all a far cry from NSFA conventions discussing hazing, scholastic credits for glee club activity, and faculty influence on student government.

Despite the frictions generated by the rival nationalisms in the international student movement, it was the hope of many, especially the Anglo-Saxons, that these could be counteracted by emphasizing peace, cooperation, and understanding, even to the extent of what later came to be called appeasement. In England the student movement played a major role in creating the Peace Oath mood which held the country before Munich.

Murrow, aged twenty-two, thoroughly enjoyed his first trip abroad, though he was not much impressed by England, where the rain came down steadily and ruined his "boater" straw hat. After only a few weeks in Europe he came back much older and wiser, he thought.

He and Chet Williams found a one-room apartment together, in an old brownstone house around the corner from the office, and set up light housekeeping. Their combined income was $150 a month, of which $45 went for the rent. They played poker to decide who went down three flights for the milk on cold mornings, and played poker and held long discussions on dark evenings.

Their principal charge was to raise funds for the student cause, and Murrow visited many colleges and universities and made earnest speeches about Europe and education. In New York, in lieu of money contributions, they sometimes received invitations to the theater, opera, dinner, once even to Texas Guinan's nightclub. They gave office work to social-minded girl graduates, and not only were the modest salaries paid by grateful parents, unbeknownst to the girls, but the girls and their families held fund-raising functions for them.

The two young men also engaged in radio to advance and advertise the student movement. Williams had persuaded the Columbia Broadcasting System to put on a weekly program, called *University of the Air,* over thirty stations, and Murrow joined him in getting speakers for it, from college campuses and public life.

It was Murrow's first radio venture. Among those he persuaded to broadcast were Rabindranath Tagore, the Indian poet, and Albert Einstein, the latter from dockside as he arrived in New York by ship.

In the frequent serious discussions that took place in the office, at home with Chet Williams, and in the homes of others, Murrow was an ideal listener, thus encouraging those who were speaking to further discourse. He displayed the ability to seize upon and distill the thoughts of others, add a few dimensions of his own, and emerge with a forceful new synthesis or conclusion. This would be one of his outstanding traits in broadcasting. Once he told Williams, "I may appropriate ideas and use them, but that's what they're for. Who knows how ideas originate, anyway?"

The NSFA convention at the end of that year, when he was reelected president, was held at Atlanta. It is still remembered in that city as the first of its kind to be racially integrated there, or as a headwaiter recalled thirty years later, "the first time Negro students ever came in the front door of the Biltmore — and no trouble!"

The integration, though only a partial one, was managed by Murrow. He persuaded the Southern white delegates not to walk out, lest they besmirch the federation name "in the *New York Times,*" and he reminded the hotel that its convention contract compelled it to accommodate "all delegates," for it had never dreamed that some of the delegates could be black. There were a dozen of them, and they actually dined at the Atlanta Biltmore in 1930. The hotel refused to serve them directly, as a violation of the custom of the country, but agreed to let them sit at the table while the white students were served. The latter then passed their plates to the Negroes. The Negro waiters thought it all rollicking.

The Atlanta convention voted to end any bar to NSFA membership by reason of color or race.

The shoestring financing of the student federation came from the dues of its members in four hundred colleges, but guidance and advice came from the Institute of International Education, which was part of the Carnegie Endowment. The institute's director, Dr. Stephen Duggan, an internationally known educator with a spruce goatee, believed that "education is the only certain road to the attainment of world peace."

When he took visiting students and teachers from Europe and Latin America on the round of "places of educational interest" in New York, he usually stopped in at the whitewashed office of the student federation, with its travel posters, mimeograph machine, and donated rustic furniture, to chat with the tall, thin, thoughtful, cigarette-smoking president. Sometimes Murrow, with Chet Williams or "the girls" in the office, the unpaid volunteers Martha Biehle from Wellesley and Marjorie Marsden from Vassar, went to the institute offices a few blocks further uptown, to discuss their problems with Professor Duggan.

The Duggan-Murrow friendship would last twenty years, until the educator's death, and would lead the younger man into the broader endeavor he envisioned.

Murrow spoke frequently of taking further degrees at Columbia University's Teachers College, and said he wanted to remain "in education." At the federation office he was regarded as modest "in everything except the belief that, at twenty-two, he knew all about international affairs."

If not yet quite all, he kept adding to his knowledge of them. Again in the summer of 1931 he worked his way to Europe, and this time he drove with two others from Paris across central and eastern Europe to Bucharest. There Crown Prince Carol had just become king, and the international students' confederation was holding its congress.

The depression had begun to grip the Old World also. The Credit-Anstalt had failed in Vienna, Britain was leaving the gold standard, and the Smoot-Hawley high tariff in America was definitely reducing European trade. Even more threatening was the political uncertainty growing out of the economic. A Fascist coup was attempted in Austria, and Adolf Hitler formed an alliance with the old German Nationalists led by the businessman Hugenberg. In Asia overt aggression was beginning, with the Japanese move into Manchuria.

Ed Murrow at twenty-three, a long way from Beaver, Washington, was receiving his political education early and at first hand. In this respect he was regarded by the European students he met as quite untypical of

American students, though few of them had met very many American students as yet. The depression and the worsening political situation kept student exchange at a minimum.

But, as the federation president noted in his annual report that year, if the depression lasted long enough, it might end the "provincialism" of American students. Already, under the impact of events, they were finding interest in the larger world. In Europe meanwhile, he reported, there was increasing "jealousy, hatred, and intense nationalism" in the student groups.

At some international student meetings Murrow was the only American present. While arguing for an increasing political consciousness by American students at home, he found himself arguing against what he regarded as the subversion of student political activism in Europe. He believed education should be nonpolitical, and that internationalism, not nationalism, should be its aim. French, German, Hungarian and Polish students liked him — he was convivial yet soberly earnest — and thought him naïve.

Equally naïve at Bucharest, against the running tide of European nationalisms, was a Scotsman, Ivison Macadam, one of the founders of Britain's National Union of Students. He was considerably older than the others, and if he believed so intently in peace it was because he had served in the First World War, and commanded a British intervention unit at Archangel. Murrow had met him in New York, where Macadam helped NSFA organize its travel bureau, but as the Anglo-Saxon "idealists" at the congress they became firm friends, into the days of the Second World War.

From Bucharest, Murrow drove on to Constantinople, for his first glimpse of Asia across the Bosphorus, then returned home for more conferences. The first was that of the International Student Service, which sought to apply Christian principles to education, held at Mount Holyoke College, the girls' school at South Hadley, Massachusetts.

At the conference, a twenty-one-year-old Mount Holyoke sophomore looked down on the proceedings from the balcony. She was a leading student activist on the campus, but she could not take a more active part in the conference because she was suffering from ivy poisoning, and her face was covered with splotches of purple permanganate. Some of the foreign students called her the American Indian delegate, in war paint.

Janet Huntington Brewster, from Middletown, Connecticut, remembered that as she saw a large crowd, mostly women, swarming around a jaunty Ed Murrow, who was clearly enjoying himself, she thought the scene "repulsive." Three years later they would be married.

Murrow's roommate, Chet Williams, had already lost his bachelorhood, and moved out of their apartment. Murrow visited the newlyweds frequently. His wedding gift was a copy of a book by D. H. Lawrence, and he had inscribed it.

"With many happy memories of poker-playing days before Mr. Williams' departure from the ranks. Those who are to follow in your footsteps salute you." But he seemed in no hurry to follow. Instead he spoke of going around the world with a pack on his back, instead of the conventional suitcase.

To stretch his twenty-five dollars a week, he found even smaller quarters in Patchin Place, in Greenwich Village. Though that community, as it then was, in many ways represented opposition to the Coolidge-Hoover values which had come to grief in the depression, it was not for idealistic, much less for bohemian reasons that he moved there, but because it was cheap.

Economizing had become a national necessity. Britain's departure from the gold standard brought fears the United States might follow suit, and when the Bank of United States failed in New York that winter — many believed, because of its name, that this private institution was operated by the Government — it touched off something of a panic, as assets were liquidated, loans called, and collateral stocks and bonds sold off. Theaters were blacked out on Broadway and taxis stopped running. Unemployment reached the eight-million mark, affecting a quarter of the nation's families.

In this economic decline, radio came into its own as a form of entertainment and communication, helping alleviate the depressed frame of mind which accompanied the depressed state of business. Radio was the universal solvent, a forum, schoolroom, music hall, convalescent ward, companion and soothsayer.

Millions of people, who had lots of time on their hands and little money in their pockets, stayed at home around the radio set while other forms of amusement and pastime faded away.

Movies played to empty houses despite the introduction of double features and giveaway prizes. Parties were few and far between. On radio, besides comedy, drama, songs and news events, was offered the chance to win cash in slogan contests.

The national habit of regular mass radio listening, formed during the depression, would remain until television replaced it, and when times improved, offered the largest and most susceptible market of consumers in the history of buying and selling. Radio in the Thirties was not only the "poor man's theater," but, as the CBS vice president, Paul Kesten, remarked, "the only form of advertising that runs like a train, that people wait for, that becomes an event or institution in their lives."

Actually television had already started in 1931 and by the end of that year CBS was on the air forty-nine hours weekly. But even if television sets had been available, not many people could have afforded the squat box with its tiny screen, flecked by the "snow" of static. The first CBS television program, lasting forty-five minutes on July 21, 1931, was opened by New York's popular mayor, Jimmy Walker, and offered a series of musical turns. They included Kate Smith singing "When the Moon Comes Over the Mountain," the Boswell sisters singing "Heebie Jeebie Blues," and George Gershwin playing his own song "Liza" on the piano.

Ed Murrow was not looking at television. At the student federation's convention, held in Toledo that year, he again rebuked American students for their "political apathy and complacency," and declared conformism to be "an opiate to intellect." He called for "radical" individualism, though, as he explained, he was not avowing any particular radical cause.

The convention's major debate was on military training in colleges. The issue split the membership, many of whom saw military training as making war more acceptable, and the federation finally voted to oppose compulsory training, a kind of rebuke to its president who, after all, had been a cadet colonel himself and firmly believed in ROTC. By 1933, however, with Hitler come to power, the federation would have second thoughts and vote its endorsement of ROTC, while at the same time withdrawing from the International Confederation of Students as "too nationalistic."

After two years as president of the National Student Federation — which would eventually founder between pacifism and "patriotism" with the coming of the Second World War — Murrow "retired" and was elected an honorary director.

He was planning to take a course in educational administration, the "deans' course," at Teachers College, but instead stepped into another job, this one with a salary attached. Dr. Duggan, director of the Institute of International Education and the student federation's paternal adviser, had passed sixty but instead of contemplating retirement was looking for an assistant. Both Murrow and Chet Williams applied for the post, the latter at Murrow's suggestion. Murrow was chosen, while Williams went back to the West Coast, then joined the United States Office of Education.

The new job, like the old, demanded attendance at educational conferences of every variety, and the student federation, as usual, was holding its annual year-end convention, this time in New Orleans.

On his way to it the past president stopped off in North Carolina to do some Christmas shooting with his Murrow kinfolk, and reboarded the train one early morning in Greensboro. There, bound for the same convention, was the same fair-haired Mount Holyoke student who had viewed him with such repugnance from the balcony the year before. They had caught glimpses of each other at other student meetings since then, while holding their distance, and now they eyed each other and talked politely.

She began to revise her feelings about him. He did seem to know a good deal about Europe. He could sing American ballads and folk songs. He became dramatic as he related hunting stories, and no doubt, like Ivan Skovinsky Skovar, he could tell fortunes with cards. He was lanky, had what she thought were "lambent" brown eyes, and the luminous smile that he occasionally broke into was all the more emphasized by his habitual seriousness.

At New Orleans he asked her to breakfast at the hotel and ordered strawberries, though it was midwinter. As a New Englander she was impressed by the extravagance of that, in both senses of the word, and though she abhorred strawberries, this time she ate them. They were together constantly during the convention and when they parted he began to write to her as if they had grown up next door to each other.

For both, their interest in each other outweighed the convention proceedings, though Murrow successfully presented a resolution rebuking the American Government for forbidding foreign students, who had found political refuge in this country, from also earning a livelihood here. The convention rejected a resolution favoring the payment of football players through athletic scholarships. It was a no-nonsense organization.

Ed Murrow and Janet Brewster left the convention city on the same train — four years later another New Orleans convention would present them with the most important decision of their lives — and he got off at Nashville to start a campus tour for the institute.

He wrote her daily, ending his letters with the phrase "Love and luck," and calling her "my Hunka," apparently because of her part-Swedish ancestry. From a college convention at Atlantic City, where he spoke, he wrote that he was the only person there under forty-five. He was not yet twenty-five, although in order to seem more mature, when he applied for his new job he had added two years to his age, a fact which would cause confusion at various times later on.

He returned to New York to find a telegram from Seattle offering him the management of the Shanghai office of a Pacific Coast lumber company, at double his modest salary, but replied that he had other commitments. He meant not only the IIE but also J.H.B., whom he had now made up his mind to marry.

It was not an entirely propitious time for either education or marriage. During the 1932–1933 term, a third of a million children were out of school for lack of funds, and thus of teachers. Nearly two million people

ABOVE: *Janet Murrow*. BELOW: *Ed and Janet in a British 1937, or Ivor Novello, pose*

were "on the road" in America, including the "Okies." The Bonus Marchers had descended on Washington and finally been routed by the Army chief of staff, General MacArthur, and his aide, Major Eisenhower.

Back in Murrow's home state of Washington wooden nickels were issued by several communities, as a form of scrip, and the city of Seattle had gone over to widespread barter. The unemployed cut unsalable timber for fuel, dug unsalable potatoes, picked unsalable fruit and caught unsalable fish all of which they exchanged for the services of doctors, barbers, carpenters and cobblers.

As for international education, which was the institute's reason for existence, that was suffering from politics as well as economics. Adolf Hitler ruled in Germany. The Burning of the Books had taken place, and the great exodus of European scholarship had begun. Every ship brought new refugees.

Part of Murrow's job was to arrange radio broadcasts and other appearances by scholars, poets and educators — American as well as refugee European — and he served as intermediary between the radio networks and the educational world, in which he had become widely acquainted.

The new assistant director wrote on an imposing letterhead which listed such foreign connections as Deutscher Akademischer Austausch Dienst, Berlin; American Office for Educational and Intellectual Cooperation, Florence; Institut J. J. Rousseau, Geneva; American University Union, London; Junta para Ampliación de Estudios, Madrid; American University Union, Paris; Austro-American Institute, Vienna, and Swiss School Council, Zurich.

But he signed all letters in red ink, he told Janet, for that was what was being used in the office to draw up the institute's financial statements.

It was receiving hundreds of letters from students everywhere, asking for money, and from professors asking for work. Many came into the office every day inquiring about nonexistent teaching vacancies, and the young assistant director would hear anguished tales from eminent elderly educators.

Cables arrived. A student was seriously ill in Vienna, a British lecturer had canceled his engagements, the Paris office needed five hundred dollars for research. But the budgets of all the foreign offices were being drastically reduced.

The European political horizon was equally troubled. In March 1933, which was six years ahead of the actual events, Murrow wrote Janet: "If interested in the most likely springboard for the next European war, get out a map and find Danzig at the mouth of the Corridor. Last summer I flew up there from Berlin and spent a couple of days. The Polish munitions dump on the Westerplatte is bound to cause trouble, and it represents one of the many mistakes of the League, that august body that turned out to be merely an instrument of thinly veiled imperialism. It is shot through with intrigue, even in its cultural cooperation work."

He had added to his sensibility of international affairs by being elected to the Council on Foreign Relations, though as he explained it, he was thirty years junior to most of the membership and "they probably want me to do some dirty work for them!"

A few days later, "Things in Germany are causing us trouble, many people wanting to know if they should bring their sons and daughters home. So far we are sitting tight." He had been to the German con-sulate-general for dinner and "they are much worried." He also had made several radio broadcasts on education and CBS, he wrote Janet, had asked him to do a series on the network but "there simply isn't time to do all the things I'd like to."

It was not only consuls-general, but government ministers, ambassadors, scholars and other foreign notables he was meeting regularly now as part of his work, in addition to American educators, foundation directors and government officials. The small and cramped sixteenth-floor office of the institute at 45th Street and Fifth Avenue was a clearinghouse for intellectual problems which more often than not were also political, eco-nomic and diplomatic problems.

The assistant director supervised exchange scholarships, visited scores of universities, managed international collegiate debates, helped students to travel, studied the educational system of Mexico, wrote memoranda for the League of Nations and European ministries of education, joined Professor James T. Shotwell in writing a book, *Channels of International Cooperation*, and occasionally managed to shoot some weekend golf on Long Island.

He kept long hours and wrote about them to Janet, not in complaint but with a pride that, starting then and ever afterward, turned the physical fatigue to which he drove himself into a kind of accolade of self-satisfaction. He was always breaking off letters to "fall into bed" from tiredness, and he was beginning to have recurrent bouts of respiratory illness, although "I have never been sick in my life before."

If Murrow as the institute's assistant director was its energetic young man of all work, in meeting immediate concrete problems, its director was the "professor at large," as he once styled himself, who provided the background, experience and continuity for an intellectual venture, even adventure, of considerable significance.

Stephen Pierce Duggan, a product of the New York City public schools, who then went into the teaching of political science and government and graced the faculty of the City College of New York for thirty-five years, left at an age when most teachers would be thinking of retirement, to embark on an entirely new career in the practice, as contrasted with the mere preachment, of international cooperation. The Yankee who began by teaching the principles of American government in evening lectures to immigrants on New York's East Side ended by carrying the principles of world accommodation to the countries from which the immigrants came.

He lectured in London, Berlin, Vienna, Prague and Budapest. He visited Russia and China and helped formulate and advance the Good Neighbor policy for Latin America, which his son Laurence then carried on in the State Department.

Professor Duggan believed in world peace through education. He had founded the Institute of International Education in 1919 at the request of the Carnegie Endowment for International Peace, and would be its director until his retirement in 1946. He died in 1950, in his eightieth year.

It was long his view that whatever political relations existed between the United States and other countries, including no relations at all, educational relations should not be restricted. This had led him as early as 1925 to visit Moscow and seek educational exchange with the Soviet Union, which the United States had refused to recognize. His efforts in this direction, leading to the sponsorship of a summer school for Americans at Moscow University in 1934 and 1935, were to cause embarrassment to Murrow during his controversy with Senator Joe McCarthy two decades later.

In the Thirties Duggan and his assistant Murrow similarly believed that however much they might dislike what was happening in Nazi Germany, and despite the political feeling in the United States toward the Hitler Reich, educational exchange should be continued in order "to aid the restoration of more reasonable views."

The Nazis made it difficult, so much so that it was a cultural rescue operation, rather than one of cultural exchange, that in 1933 fused together the international idealism of Stephen Duggan, the energy of Ed Murrow, the good will of most Americans, and the practical self-interest of American colleges and universities, in the Emergency Committee in Aid of Displaced German Scholars.

Murrow, looking back, said it was "the most personally satisfying undertaking in which I have ever engaged, and contributed more to my knowledge of politics and international relations than any similar period in my life."

In March 1933, after Goebbels had become minister of public enlightenment and propaganda, dismissals began to take place from German universities and other cultural institutions. Not only Jews were affected but many "Aryan" scholars regarded as politically unreliable from the Nazi point of view. American educators were both perturbed and angered by what they regarded as a blow to academic traditions as well as a violation of free speech, and they hailed the formation of the committee by Professor Duggan. His assistant naturally became the committee's general factotum, report-writer and speechmaker.

Even before the emergency represented by conditions in Germany, Professor Duggan had introduced the idea of visiting professors to American universities, and one of them was Professor Harold J. Laski, of the London School of Economics, who thereby met the assistant director of the IIE as well. He and Murrow became good friends, a relationship reinforced by Laski's active interest in the "visiting professor" program for the distressed German scholars. Back in London, he saw to it that all the members of his prestigious school faculty contributed a percentage of their salaries every month to help their German colleagues.

Represented in the American emergency committee were the academic communities of Cornell, Columbia, CCNY, the Carnegie Institute of Technology, Bryn Mawr, Colorado, the University of California, Minnesota, Northwestern, Oberlin, Princeton, Harvard, Williams, Vanderbilt, Vassar, Smith, Stanford, Mount Holyoke, the California Institute of Technology, and the Rockefeller Institute.

Their purpose was to bring displaced scholars to the United States "irrespective of race, religion and political opinion," and place them in American colleges.

But because of the depression university revenues in the United States had been curtailed, and many teachers dropped. American universities could not be asked to provide posts and give stipends to foreign scholars while American scholars went without. So the money had to come from other sources. Moreover the committee had to limit its help to the older and more established scholars rather than younger men, who might be equally deserving but whose employment would also emphasize the plight of younger American scholars. It was estimated that five thousand American Ph.D.'s were unemployed.

The committee's funds, to be matched by grants from the Rockefeller Foundation, came from private donors, benefit concerts, such as by Heifetz and the Stradivarius Quartet; several small foundations, and the American Jewish Joint Distribution Committee. By January 1934, when the committee made its first report covering seven months, fifty-three German scholars had been received in the United States and placed in thirty-eight universities. They included the theologian Paul Tillich, the economist Otto Nathan, the mathematician Otto Szacz, the political scientist Karl Loewenstein, and the social psychologist Kurt Lewin. Eventually the transplanted scholars would include Martin Buber, Philipp Franck, Hans J. Morgenthau, Herbert Marcuse and Jacques Maritain. With Hitler's seizure of Czechoslovakia, the committee's name was changed to the Emergency Committee in Aid of Displaced Foreign Scholars.

Of the first twenty-four to arrive in the United States, eighteen were Jews, one a Gentile, and the religious adherence of five was unknown.

But as the rescue work went on the proportions changed and were more heavily weighted with Catholics and Protestants. The committee disclosed it had 1100 applications for aid in its files, of which more than two hundred came from "Aryans."

Other agencies were similarly active, both in the United States and in other countries, to succor musicians, artists and writers, as well as scholars. In the United States a University in Exile was formed at the New School for Social Research in New York City. But the Duggan-Murrow committee thought it better, more leavening perhaps, for the scholars to be distributed across the spectrum of American colleges, rather than be concentrated in one place and thus in a sense segregated. The colleges which got the eminent Europeans naturally agreed.

The committee's initial report, assailing the "new ideology" in Germany and Hitler's "New Order," was written by Murrow, who noted that the expulsion of Greek scholars from Byzantium in 1453 and their entry into Italy had hastened the Renaissance of humanism. He also recalled the Huguenot emigration from France to England, and the expulsion of the Jews from Spain in 1492. He was clearly history-oriented.

The committee's plan, as outlined by its assistant secretary, was to create honorary lectureships for the displaced scholars for one or two years, and certainly not permanently. But as the Nazi repression continued, and spread to other countries, and as war created a historical watershed for Europe, the scholars for the most part not only stayed permanently as valuable working parts of the American academic society, but many went into Government service directly, aiding in notable advances in astronautics, mathematics, atomic energy research, ballistics and climatology.

During the two years Murrow devoted to the committee's work, almost to the exclusion of all else — he received fifty letters a day from dismissed professors, interviewed twelve to fifteen persons daily, and carried on an endless telephone service — about a hundred German scholars were successfully reestablished in the United States. Eventually the number would be 288 within the committee's thirty-to-sixty-year age limit, and 47 others.

The religious affiliation of the scholars was definitely known in 177 cases. Eighty-two were Jewish and 95 were not. The latter included 55 Protestants, 39 Catholics, and one from the Eastern Orthodox church.

Murrow recalled the period as "a sort of revolving seminar," and said "the only good education I ever got . . . came from experience with these men." He found the exiles to be "less bitter than I expected, only sorry about what has happened to German culture." Their principal complaint, he jested, was that American buildings were overheated.

The committee's work was done in an interminable round of meetings, lunches and dinners; in speeches and appeals for funds, in reports, leaflets, draft plans and memoranda. Murrow wrote Janet that he was working so hard, the doctors were "threatening" him with a nervous breakdown. "I'm no boy wonder, but I've driven myself terribly in the past few years to get where I am."

A few days later he was brooding, after reading Spengler. "It's really a pretty rotten world, isn't it? No one can look at what is happening without realizing that civilization is disintegrating and there are no standards left. Everyone is lost and wandering in a thick fog . . . Sometimes I almost wish I'd never gone to college and kept working in the woods, getting drunk when I came to town once a month."

He told Janet he had sent her picture to his mother inscribed "This is the young lady I love." "She'll probably faint," he remarked. "I'm sure she expected me to remain a batchelor [he never could spell] or marry some-one out of a Broadway show."

In the summer of 1933 Janet, just graduated from Mount Holyoke, was taking courses in New Haven and planning to teach school in the fall, back in Middletown. He admonished her not to study too hard, because "there's too much living to do, and let's do it while we can."

He reported that his mother and father had approved of her, or at least of her picture, and that Mrs. Murrow had said "you don't look like a flapper." By now he was referring to "our secret" and forecasting that their marriage would "surprise everyone." He thought they should continue to live in Manhattan, while Janet took courses at Columbia and did "a bit of social work." "Then when little Edward comes along, we'll move out to Long Island and I'll commute."

He addressed his next letter, "Hello, Mrs. Edward R. Murrow," and said he was "practising to be a swell husband." He visited her on weekends, either in New Haven or in Middletown, though sometimes his work with the German scholars prevented it, and he refused a chance to go to Germany himself that year, in order to be with her. "Next time I go abroad you will be with me," he promised.

In September Janet went back to Middletown and began teaching English at the high school. Murrow had been busy with a list of student fellowships for the fall term, and he informed her that he had sent a telegram to his parents. "Your son Edward joyfully announces the acceptance of Miss Janet Huntington Brewster of a personal permanent fellowship, providing board, room and tuition, from next summer till death do us part."

They had agreed to be married the following year.

He was making speeches at dinners and conferences on the decline of democracy in education, meaning in Germany, and wrote an article defending the continuation of educational relations with the Nazi regime, while confessing he did not "care much for it." He wrote Janet, "Tomorrow our German students arrive. I hope the fools don't arrive in brown shirts!"

Murrow's experience with exchange students for the IIE, though he engaged in it enthusiastically, carried within it the seeds of later doubt about the ultimate worth of such programs.

Chinese students, for instance, who had been in the United States, became discontented with the standards and practices they found when they returned home, and in the Chiang Kai-shek regime, he felt, developed into national liabilities rather than assets. When he became director of the USIA twenty-five years later and faced the question of student exchange again, in terms of national policy, he thought it would be more useful, instead of bringing foreign students to the United States, for the United States to endow and establish teaching institutions in their own countries.

The institute also arranged for foreign lecturers to speak in the United States. There would be 150 that year, giving three thousand lectures. Murrow wrote a leaflet for them, warning against underestimating the knowledge and intelligence of American audiences, and added some advice. "Individuals of official standing in their own countries should remember that extreme caution in discussing controversial matters often gives the impression of evading issues, and failing to discuss with any frankness the real implications of the subject." He was for open controversies, openly arrived at.

The good news came that starting October 1 his salary would be raised to five thousand dollars a year. He moved from Greenwich Village to a new apartment, midtown again on the East Side, and he wrote Janet that a new committee had been formed to help medical men exiled from Germany.

He had become its secretary, for the extra money it brought — both of them were saving toward their marriage — and because "it means close working relations with some of the most influential men in the city . . . I do not propose to spend my entire life working at a salary of $5000 a year." Actually, for a twenty-five-year-old in the middle of the depression, pretending to be twenty-seven, it was a princely sum.

He did a fifteen-minute radio broadcast, and wrote Janet about the possibility of an added assignment from the Rockefeller Foundation to supervise all German fellowships in the United States. They had talked to him about it, but he thought he was considered "too radical, in the words of the vice president!"

He had always prided himself on being a gambler, and when the dollar was devalued and the institute lost six thousand dollars in its London and Paris offices by the lowered exchange rate, he told Janet that he had urged the office to buy fifty thousand dollars worth of sterling four months before. "They called me a gambler. We didn't do it, and now we are stuck."

He gave another radio talk, on education and democracy, this time over CBS, and confided that "if I can get the time, I want to try to really do some broadcasting."

With the new year 1934, which merely saw the depression spreading, he wrote Janet indignantly about "an economic system that damns some of us before we are born." Concerning a large formal dinner he was attending at the Waldorf for the first Soviet ambassador to the United States, Troyanovsky, he remarked about the proletarian occasion, "What a paradox, his speaking at a dinner at six dollars per head."

Glumly, and perhaps dramatically, he confessed, "I have no confidence in the future and little pride in the past, feel no responsibility for posterity."

Then, "I've been sitting here trying to figure out what the years may hold for us. We have no money, and I have no profession, and on top of all that I'm at heart a bum and vagabond and will always be that way. For a very few short years we should be happy, and then would come bitterness and thoughts of what might have been."

He soon recovered from the kind of apocalyptic gloom that would often beset him in the profession he did find. His name was "up in Washington for Commissioner of Immigration for the Port of New York," at a salary of $7500. He wasn't sure he wanted the post, but the mere consideration made him feel better about things, including the prospect of matrimony.

"Marriage has always been and still is an extremely serious business for me, but I have unlimited confidence in us. So many people stop growing and expanding when they are married. We shall be the kind of people whom people will look twice at when we are fifty — of whom our children may be proud. We shall make of our lives a real work of art."

He went on. "Above all else, there must be nothing cheap and nothing small in our lives. They must burn with a clear bright light. No matter what happens we will, like Cyrano, keep our white plume."

Their engagement was announced June 27.

The summer was a busy but fretful one. Again, he did not go to Europe, where in any case the worsening political situation not only impeded the institute's activities, but cast doubt on the future of international relations in general.

Civil strife had erupted between the authoritarian regime and the Socialists in Austria, and the famed workers' apartment houses had been shelled by the Dollfuss forces. And on June 30, in Berlin and Munich, Hitler carried out his purge of the storm troops, in exchange for the support of their rival, the new regular army.

It was not only Ernst Röhm and other Brownshirt leaders who were killed, however, accused of plotting against the Reich, but dissidents like Erich Klausener, leader of Catholic Action, and some of his followers.

Murrow was especially depressed by the shooting of Fritz Beck, "the best friend I had in Germany, and a harmless old fellow who ran the student hostel in Munich." A few days later he told Janet, "The director of our Berlin office is in a concentration camp, and the Russian summer school may blow up at any time!

"I think we are going to stop all our German work and that means plenty of trouble. The fellow Probst, leader of the Catholic Youth Organization, was a very good friend of mine. He was shot 'while trying to escape.' "

The Russian summer school at Moscow University, sponsored by the institute, was only one of ninety-six such foreign sessions and seminars sponsored during Murrow's tenure, the chief of which were the courses for foreigners at Berlin University and the Sorbonne in Paris. Apart from any political reasons, arising from anti-Soviet feeling in the United States and growing Soviet apprehensions of fascism in Europe, there were some practical conditions militating against the project.

"Our Moscow summer school is driving me mad," Murrow reported to Janet. "Cables from our man there saying the people were to be housed in a dormitory with six people in a room and three toilets and three showers for 140 students! Many of the students so-called are old-maid school teachers and I can imagine the hell that will be raised when they get there." But the 1934 session passed without any international incident provoked by inadequate lavatory facilities.

A month before their marriage Murrow asked Janet, "Do you want to go to Europe instead of going West?" for their wedding trip. He had been asked to represent the State Department at meetings of the High Commission for German Refugees in London. But it would mean "crowds, meetings, parties. It might not be good. I would like to be alone at least part of the time and get away from this refugee business." He decided against it. "There are years ahead of us for going to Europe, and I want to be able to show it to you."

Meanwhile Chancellor Dollfuss had been murdered by the Nazis in Vienna, but of more interest to most Americans seemed to be the fact that, three days earlier, John Dillinger was shot down by the FBI in Chicago.

Ed Murrow and Janet Brewster were married on a Saturday afternoon, October 27, 1934, at the Brewster home in Middletown. He was twenty-six, she had just passed twenty-four. Janet's mother, a staunch Episcopalian, wanted a church ceremony. But the young couple thought that would be extravagant in the middle of the depression. Furthermore, the bridegroom was not much of a churchgoer, preferring to play golf on

Sundays. There were no Murrows among the twenty-five persons at the wedding. Ed's mother, typically enough, said it would be unfair to go to his wedding since she had not gone to those of her two other sons.

Janet's father was a Congregationalist, and the Congregationalist Brewsters of New England went back even further in America than the Quaker Murrows and Lambs of North Carolina. But in contrast with the agrarian and populist tradition of the latter, the Brewsters belonged to the Yankee world of shrewd small-town merchant trade. The family seat had become Worthington, Massachusetts, after Deacon Jonathan Brewster, descended from Elder William Brewster of the *Mayflower*, moved there from Connecticut in 1777, while Jonathan's son Elisha was with Count Pulaski in the Revolution.

It was Elisha who joined the Brewsters with the Huntingtons by his marriage to Sarah Huntington, and it was Charles Huntington Brewster, Janet's father, who had joined them with a more recent European stock by marrying Jennie Johnson, daughter of Swedish immigrants. The family name was Swan, but the fourteen-year-old boy who passed through American immigration in the Eighties identified himself as August, John's son, and so he became. He came from a farm, but he went to work in the brownstone quarries of Connecticut, and married the daughter of a Swedish music teacher in Middletown.

There Charles Huntington Brewster of the *Mayflower* Brewsters had also settled. He was the grandson of the second Elisha, who had been a merchant in Worthington, born in 1809 and married to Sophronia Kingman. By perhaps apt coincidence, Janet's great-grandfather Elisha was, like Ed's grandfather Joshua, a practicing politician, a Whig, an Abolitionist, and after the Civil War a Republican. He was also a state senator, elected in 1871, after serving in the lower legislative house and as county commissioner. He later became a member of the Governor's Council.

Elisha's grandson, Charles Huntington Brewster, grew up together with that symbol of the new age, the automobile. Before Henry Ford produced the Model-T and the assembly line made Detroit the American industrial capital, motor cars were made by dozens of small local plants, some of which had formerly been carriage works. In one of these, the Knox Motor Company of Springfield, Massachusetts, Charles Brewster had the kind of job that mass production would make obsolete, and that had carried on the kind of personal service his storekeeper ancestors had represented.

He was the personable young man sent out by the factory, not only to break in a new car for the family which bought it, but perhaps even more important, to break in the family to its formidable new possession, representing a new way of life. He actually lived with the family, for a week or more, in the delicate adjustment period from horse, or even foot, to machine.

The Knox factory in 1897 had introduced the first air-cooled or "water-less" engine in its three-wheeler, and in 1901 a gasoline runabout, "Made in America for Americans," which sold for $750 and got 180 miles on the six gallons of fuel it carried. Knox also made touring cars, landaulettes, sportabouts (with single and double rumble seats), and later it specialized in commercial vehicles, before it closed down in 1914. But its pride and joy was its Model-M limousine of 1909, with elaborate fittings, goatskin upholstery, and storm curtains. The Model-M cost six thousand dollars and adjustment to it was obviously required, supervised by Charles Brewster.

After cars no longer presented psychological problems, he became a salesman of them and was doing very well at it, in Middletown, when the depression arrived. He had continued to pay his help despite the lack of orders. That was another reason the Murrow-Brewster wedding was a small, quiet, home affair.

Janet had been certified as qualified in several subjects besides English for the new term at Middletown High School, but marriage ended her short teaching career. She might have become, however, the wife of a college president, for at that moment Murrow was offered the presidency of Rockford College, a small school for women in Illinois. But further investigation of his qualifications by the selection committee revealed that he was even younger than had been supposed — a week before he had confessed to Janet he had given the institute a wrong impression by two years — and the Rockford offer was withdrawn.

Instead the newlyweds went to the West Coast by car to see Ed's parents, traveling by way of North Carolina and his birthplace, and detouring into Mexico. With a valued passenger, he drove carefully, even slowly, fighting off the urge to speed which normally seized him behind the wheel of a car.

Mother Murrow was relieved to have confirmed her belief that Janet was "no flapper," the term itself being long out of date, and accepted her as "sensible." The young lady from Connecticut was, in point of fact, Murrow's temperamental opposite, and thus balanced, rounded out, and even smoothed out his own restless nature. She was slow-spoken, calm and deliberative, where he was incisive and often impulsive. Her equanimity, made up of a blend of humor and melancholy, contrasted with his mercurial moodiness. She had a wide streak of practicality, and a homespun candor which often outmatched his. She fully shared his curiosity about the world, his interest in public affairs, and his thirst for knowledge, but she would take with less wonderment than he and his family did the things that would happen to them in the life that lay ahead.

They returned to New York and a small apartment in the East 60's. Murrow continued with his speeches and meetings for the committee aiding German scholars. In Europe, Anglo-French diplomacy sought for a settlement with the New Germany, a second Locarno Pact of mutual assistance covering eastern Europe, as the original Locarno covered the West. But Hitler would have none of it, and instead repudiated the no-rearming clause of the Versailles Treaty and reviewed his new army. The British and French protested, but did no more.

Winston Churchill, opposing the policies of what passed for a national government in Britain, warned of the danger of war from Fascist expansion, both in Europe and in Asia, and said, "We have never been so defenseless as we are now."

But other speakers in a series of radio programs called *Whither Britain?* broadcast simultaneously by the BBC and CBS included Lloyd George, H. G. Wells, and Bernard Shaw, and they did not think war was likely, because mankind had come too far for that.

The British Oxford "oath" — "This House will in no circumstances fight for King or country" — had been put to the students in twenty-six American colleges by the National Student Federation, with the result that about half the eleven thousand votes cast opposed any war service whatever. Now further antiwar sentiment was being created by Senator Gerald Nye's committee investigating the munitions industry.

The congressional probe of the "merchants of death" symbolized American suspicion of Europe, the fear of entanglement in foreign wars, the desire for isolation, and the idealistic hope of peace. The hearings of the Nye committee, the general counsel for which was a young lawyer named Alger Hiss, overshadowed the efforts of another committee, headed by Bernard Baruch, to draft plans for an American mobilization, if and when necessary. Soon Congress would pass the American Neutrality Act.

The summer of 1935, a fateful one in Europe, was also a milestone for the newly married couple. Murrow, who had been doing occasional radio "talks" on education, and was a familiar figure at educational conferences, had become well acquainted with another conferencegoer, who in fact arranged such broadcasts. He was Fred Willis, a young Englishman, the "director of education" for the Columbia Broadcasting System, and an assistant to its president, William S. Paley.

Murrow had known Willis from student federation days and had helped him get prominent speakers for educational programs, through his campus connections. He continued to do this as assistant director of the institute.

Now a new job was being created at CBS and Willis suggested that Murrow call on Edward Klauber, the network vice president. He did, and emerged from the office as the CBS "director of talks," educational, religious and "special." He took the precaution this time of adding, not two but five years to his actual age, for if twenty-four had been too young for the assistant director of the Institute of International Education, twenty-seven was obviously too young, he thought, to hold an important executive post for a national radio network. No particular premium was put on youth in those days, and it was not until the war a few years later, with its dependence on young manhood, that he felt secure enough to straighten out his age.

The CBS job had first been offered to Raymond Gram Swing, who had won some reputation as a radio commentator, in Britain, during his long service there as an American newspaper correspondent. Back in this country, he became the American end of a weekly transatlantic program exchange — suggested by President Roosevelt to the BBC's director, Sir John Reith — and at the same time did a weekly talk on foreign affairs for the CBS *American School of the Air*. But something about his voice offended Ed Klauber, and Swing was offered and accepted the new post of "director of talks" instead. When he learned that he would not be able to broadcast, however, he changed his mind, and it went to Murrow. The latter agreed to refrain from broadcasting, and did not seem to mind.

Swing would become, in later years, not only a close friend of Murrow's and his associate at CBS, but one of the most honored of American broadcasters himself, both on the domestic networks and on the Voice of America's worldwide English-language programs. As for Murrow, when he succeeded to the kind of authority Klauber had, he made it a point to choose broadcasters not for their voices, but for their journalistic ability.

At the same time that Murrow joined the CBS network, so did another young man, from Ohio State University. He was Frank Stanton, who had been teaching there part-time while writing his Ph.D. thesis on industrial psychology. One of his conclusions was that advertising was more effective when heard than when read, and a radio network which earned its revenue from aural commercials would obviously be interested in it.

Stanton, of Yankee and Swiss-German stock, who also had worked his way through school and had been a leading campus figure at Ohio Wesleyan, in school politics, fraternity affairs and dramatics, came to CBS as a fifty-five-dollar-a-week research "specialist." This meant he was interested in radio "listenership," and proposed to measure it, dissect it, and analyze it for commercial as well as "scientific" ends. When television arrived, with its tremendous commercial possibilities, Stanton would find that advertising was most effective when seen and heard.

As they simultaneously began their broadcasting careers, the two young men represented, if not contrary, at least obverse facets of communications philosophy. Stanton sought to learn how audiences were constituted, what they liked, and what they wanted or thought they wanted, so that radio programs could be devised to attract and please them. Soon, with Paul Lazarsfeld, he was to develop an electric appliance called the Program Analyzer. A selected group of listeners would press a button to indicate their like or dislike of a program. No reason had to be offered.

Murrow believed that though it took two to communicate, "one to speak and another to hear," the most important element in radio was not the audience but the broadcaster and his content, and that what was said would find its own listeners.

It may have been inevitable that there would later be conflict between Murrow and Stanton, but in 1935 they were merely two bright newcomers at CBS. Their paths did not cross, except in the most casual way, and they were not conscious of representing anything except their own youthful ambitions.

There were then thirty million radio sets in use in the United States, and more than six hundred broadcasting stations, a hundred of them constituting the CBS network. Though it earned heavily from commercial programs — indeed it had taken the lead from NBC with Burns and Allen, Al Jolson, Eddie Cantor, Kate Smith, and Lum 'n' Abner — Bill Paley was proud of the fact that fully half his network's air time was sustaining, or nonsponsored. These programs included the radio drama of the *Mercury Theater*, the music of the New York Philharmonic Orchestra, *Capitol Cloakroom* and other interviews with Washington notables, and most of all, the *American School of the Air*.

Paley had thus in a sense recaptured radio "for the people" from some of the special interests which had been using it for their own purposes, such as political propaganda. Instead of any longer selling air time to politicians like Senator Huey Long, or to clerics who applied it to political ends like Reverend Charles E. Coughlin, Paley began radio discussions and debates under CBS auspices. That was why it was necessary to have a "director of talks," a title borrowed from the BBC.

Murrow's other post, "director of education," had similarly been created to meet the demands of the nation's educators, supported by labor and farm groups, for radio channels of their own. It was believed such channels could be operated on a nonprofit basis, with only enough advertising to cover their expenses. But even this would have been taken by the commercial broadcasters as an encroachment on their prerogatives. As a compromise, they offered free time on the commercial networks.

The CBS network had begun with what might be called enlightened self-interest. Eight years before, discovering that a radio program in Philadelphia had more than doubled the sales of the family-owned cigar company, Paley had formed a small financial consortium to buy the fledgling broadcasting system, with sixteen stations, for four hundred thousand dollars. He had two principal criteria. CBS would be devoted strictly to broadcasting, unlike NBC, which was a subsidiary of the Radio Corporation of America. And CBS would be conscious of more than profits. But that was in 1927.

Before Murrow took over his new job in September 1935, he and

Janet went to Europe on the trip he had long promised her. It was not a luxury crossing. They worked their way over as "social directors" on a Dutch liner, in charge of bingo and other pastimes, and Janet was seasick most of the time.

On this, his first visit to Europe in three years, Murrow was at the same time conducting his final round of calls for the IIE, and surveying the European scene for CBS in search of possible speakers — politicians, educators, writers, scientists and others who could make radio "talks." In a sense his new job was merely a logical extension of his old. It all came under the head of "education."

In London he met Cesar Saerchinger, CBS's European representative, who arranged the talks and "special events" broadcasts from overseas, and who by coincidence had been Raymond Swing's assistant in newspaper days. Murrow and Janet also visited the House of Lords to witness the ceremony of the Royal Assent. The American-born Lady Astor was heard telling two small schoolboys that the Lord Chancellor "looked like a pig with a wig on," and Janet noted that this was indeed true, but that Lady Astor was nevertheless "a slight showoff."

In Paris, at a sidewalk café, Ed bargained for a white fur rug with an Algerian vendor and brought the price down from 450 to 50 francs, "with no knowledge of French," in what was voted a superb performance by other café sitters. One evening he won a bottle of champagne throwing wooden balls at a street fair in Pigalle, and they took it to a university friend's house for dinner. They finished the evening and spent most of the night singing American and English ballads on the steps of Sacré Coeur.

But there was grimness, too. In Berlin, the focal point of their trip, the Nazis were in full command, on the tide of enthusiasm caused by the restoration of the Saar and Hitler's rearmament. In their hotel room the Murrows were visited surreptitiously by university professors and their wives, telling of academic repression and asking about American refuge. Hitler had destroyed German education as an affirmative force, and it was no longer the classroom but the Labor Service and then the armed services that were deemed the proper training for German youth.

Berlin was utterly depressing. "Too many swords and daggers, too many Heil Hitlers," Janet wrote her parents. An ordinary conversation was impossible, for it either became a lecture on national socialism, or fell into silence. It was "not like the old days Ed knew, of argument about politics, national and international, evening after evening." A few weeks later the Nuremberg Laws went into effect, outlawing Jews as citizens and classifying them only as "subjects."

In Holland, where they attended an ISS conference — the ISS had appealed to the institute for aid on behalf of 1500 to 1800 German students, unable to continue under Hitler — Murrow spoke on academic freedom in the United States, a country which at that moment seemed extremely far away.

No German delegate was present, for relations had been suspended by the Christian organization because of the Nazi treatment of professors. Janet wrote that Germany had become "a house divided" between the Nazis and those who opposed them, and that "probably before long Germany will be a military dictatorship."

How much the rising tide of nazism had to do with it, how much Soviet internal conditions, and how much the antagonism that the 1934 summer session had created in the United States — particularly in the Hearst newspapers, which had labeled it a "Communist propaganda school" — the Moscow University seminar which had failed to "blow up" in 1934 did so in 1935.

The Murrows were in western Europe when the abrupt cancellation occurred. Two hundred American students arriving in Leningrad were informed that Moscow University's English-speaking professors, who were to give the courses, had all been "commandeered" for government work. The students were given Intourist excursions about the Soviet Union instead.

As the younger Murrows were moving from one sphere to another, from universities to broadcasting, the older Murrows had made a change also. They left the Olympic Peninsula, where they had spent nine years, and moved back across Puget Sound to Bellingham, the lumber, shipyard and fishing center slightly north of Blanchard, where they had originally settled. Roscoe Murrow had given up timber railroading — although he was only in the midfifties his health had begun to fail — and after a trial at running a small motor camp in the Olympic Forest, he went to work in the Bellingham shipyard as a night watchman.

From the porch of their white frame house on Bellingham Bay, he could see the San Juan Islands and the Olympic Mountains.

When he suffered a paralytic stroke some years later, he would sit on the porch for hours looking through a telescope at the sunsets, and at a shoreline and slopes which had once been covered with thick forest and now stood bare as the result of intensive logging.

In New York, Ed Murrow was arranging broadcasts by former Secretary of State Henry L. Stimson, on the subject of neutrality; former President Hoover, attacking the New Deal; and from Europe, by Harold Nicolson, the British writer-diplomat, Prime Minister Mussolini of Italy, and the crown prince of Ethiopia, appealing for aid against Mussolini's aggression. He also had to decide when President Roosevelt was to be distinguished from Candidate Roosevelt, so that "equal time" could be granted, or not granted, to his opponents.

Distinction had to be made also, and it was not always possible to do so clearly, between "talks" on CBS and "special events." Was a Roosevelt fireside chat from the White House, for instance, a talk or a special event? It might make no difference whatever to the listener, but since Murrow was director of talks and Paul White was director of "public affairs and special events," it made considerable difference to the two young men, both jealous of their own provinces, and both extremely energetic.

Though White, also a six-footer, with bulldog features, had established a Columbia news service in 1933, with its own correspondents across the United States, this had been primarily a means of circumventing the refusal of the big news agencies to supply their wires to the radio stations, because of the objections of their clients, the newspapers.

But news broadcasting was still not being taken very seriously.

It was true that on CBS there were three news broadcasts a day, five minutes at noon and 4:30 P.M. and fifteen minutes at 11 P.M. Moreover White had introduced a conversational style in CBS news writing, in place of the formal, often stilted and frequently inverted newspaper language, and listeners liked that. But "news" in general consisted of either "talks" or "special events," and one inevitably infringed upon the other.

White professed to be pleased that Murrow had relieved him of some of his burdens, but he was not. Murrow, still pretending to be older than he actually was and thus older than White, tried to outdo, outdrink and out-tough his nominal superior. Frequently they would roll down to Times Square to have it out in a shooting gallery, always one of Murrow's favorite haunts. There was a good deal of horseplay and practical joking in the radio newsroom, though it was run in what some there regarded as the Prussian manner by the stern, pince-nezed Ed Klauber.

Beyond the seventeenth floor of 485 Madison Avenue the Murrow-White contention was not noticeable. Cesar Saerchinger, in London, obtained "talks" at Murrow's behest and arranged "special events" for White with equal aplomb. From Washington, Wells Church would put on the air Cabinet members' speeches, comments by Senators, presidential fireside chats, campaign oratory, debates, and ceremonial occasions, either as "talks" or as "special events" depending on whether Murrow or White had won that particular round.

Murrow was frequently in Washington himself and it was then that Bill Paley, who had an active interest in what his network was doing, especially in the field of public affairs, was first struck by his young talk director's zeal and undoubted skills. They saw each other often, and the business relationship began to develop into personal friendship.

For the most part, in making Washington arrangements, Murrow let "Ted" Church decide which Congressmen should be heard on which side of which public question, and this began an association between the two men which would lead to the most fruitful years of CBS News, when Murrow, as vice president in charge of news, then as the network's, indeed the nation's, top broadcaster, and Church as news director supervised a global staff and an authoritative brand of reporting and analysis that won the network unquestioned priority.

As director of talks Murrow also had to do with the much-lauded CBS *American School of the Air*, which utilized radio for direct education. Daily, from October through April, more than ninety stations relayed classroom programs in history, music, literature, science and even vocational guidance.

But the young administrator received his and the network's first real education in practical civics in the 1936 presidential election campaign between Franklin D. Roosevelt and Alf M. Landon. It was the first campaign to utilize radio on a nationwide basis, and the two parties allocated a total of two million dollars for broadcast time, despite the depression.

Murrow attended the two party conventions and the broadcasting of the proceedings mirrored the conflict in jurisdiction between him and Paul White, aggravated by White's habit of spending as much time in the convention hall "hospitality" lounges as in the broadcasting booth.

But the important broadcasting conflicts of the political year transcended the intramural. Because radio was so important in the campaign, the demands for air time for the rival candidates and their spokesmen became a matter of prime urgency, with pressures exerted from all sides and constant dispute. Murrow, who was learning that radio is a channel of power as well as of persuasion, was in the thick of it.

The controversy began when President Roosevelt decided to broadcast his State of the Union message to Congress, not at noon but for the first time as a fireside chat in the evening. He wanted the largest possible audience, and to talk, as usual, to the people above the heads of their legislators. Since he was a candidate for reelection as well as the chief executive fulfilling a constitutional duty, the Republicans not only asked equal time, but as the campaign went on and similar occasions arose, they charged that the networks were under the influence of the Democratic administration. This was the more deplorable, from their point of view, because 80 percent of the nation's press opposed Roosevelt's reelection.

But as radio meted out its favors with as even a hand as possible, considering that President Roosevelt never did distinguish himself from Candidate Roosevelt, not only were the Republicans given time to reply, but even within the Democratic Party the onetime "happy warrior," Al Smith, received full facilities as he denounced the New Deal at a dinner of the American Liberty League, formed by those Roosevelt called "economic royalists."

Indeed Murrow carried the principle of fairness to the point where, for the first time in broadcasting history, a Communist candidate was allowed to give a campaign speech. As pickets marched outside the CBS building, Earl Browder advocated a "farmer-labor" party "to defeat Wall Street." Though unmistakable conservatives, like the publisher David Lawrence, defended the CBS action — if only because Browder, he thought, was not much more opposed to Wall Street than some New Dealers were — it was taken more seriously by the advertising agencies which had come to dominate radio programming, and which were not accustomed to having their values scorned by way of their own chosen instrument.

It was the first of the large public controversies in which Ed Murrow would be involved, within the broadcasting industry and beyond it. As it turned out, Browder polled eighty thousand votes that year, but more symptomatic of the times was the fact that the right-wing Union Party, carrying the support of the demagogic Father Coughlin behind the candidacy of Representative William Lemke, polled ten times as heavily as the Communists.

Meanwhile Murrow had made his first CBS news broadcast, as distinct from his earlier talks on education as a guest. He had been fascinated by the professional ease and gift of ad-libbing possessed by Bob Trout, the network's news announcer and principal "special events" broadcaster, and frequently talked with him about speaking technique. Though the prepared radio talks had been thoroughly acceptable, Murrow, the actor-debater, felt he would never really be effective on the medium because the microphone was only an inanimate metallic object.

"No people!" he complained. He said he could speak only to a live audience.

Trout finally persuaded him that the microphone was not intended as an inert substitute for living people, and should not be declaimed to, or debated, but used casually as an instrument of communication, like a telephone.

Now the tutelage was put into effect. There had been a Christmas Eve party in the CBS newsroom, and when the time came for Trout's evening news program, Murrow took over the microphone instead and wrestled the script from him, with the explanation that Trout had enjoyed the party too well. He began reading the news.

Trout, a temperate man in every sense of the word, realized that Murrow was the one who had overindulged and waited for the concrete evidence of it, in the form of slurred words and fumbling phrases.

But Murrow never faltered. He marched through the news clearly and precisely, as if it had been made for him, and he for it.

This was exactly the case.

V

"Hello, America . . . Hitler is here"

THE most important decision in Ed Murrow's life was made in February 1937 when the young director of talks — he was not yet twenty-nine — attending the familiar annual meeting of the National Education Association in New Orleans, received a telephone call from Edward Klauber, the CBS news executive in New York, asking if he would like to become the CBS European director. The answer was yes.

Though the coming war may have played a part in Klauber's proposal, the principal factor was that in the intensive competition between CBS and its senior rival NBC for "special events" broadcasts, NBC had taken the lead in Europe, and CBS wanted to even the terms. Moreover Paul White would not be displeased that his own vigorous competitor would be three thousand miles away.

Indeed, though he very much wanted it, Murrow regarded the assignment to Europe as a probable setback in his career as a radio administrator, and felt that White would now have reason to expect the realization of his open ambition to become a network vice president, then as now the traditional goal on Madison Avenue.

Actually it was Murrow who would come back from Europe as a vice president, ending White's dream. So in later years he was able to look back on his European assignment as another example of "Murrow luck."

"That decision gave me an opportunity to watch Europe tearing up its maps," he said in retrospect, somewhat rhetorically, "to see and hear the last peacetime performance at Salzburg; Vienna cheering the arrival of the oppressors; dismemberment of Czechoslovakia by her sworn friends; then the full tide of war sweeping across Europe like a brown stain. It gave me the opportunity to know Britain in her darkest, and finest, hour."

At the time, however, though Germany's rearming and the march into the Rhineland had alarmed American as well as European diplomats, and the excesses of nazism and the virulence of anti-Semitism had shocked the population of the United States, the significance of a European war for this country was not widely appreciated, much less the chance of American involvement.

Coming out of the depression, with its self-centeredness, many Americans believed that a struggle between Europe's New Order and the old one was Europe's own affair. Moral revulsion against Hitler was strong, but not strong enough to outweigh the appeal of American neutrality.

In the world of journalism heightened tensions in Europe had brought preparations for possible hostilities, and American newspapers and agencies had augmented their staffs, as they would have done for any other large newsworthy event, like an earthquake or a flood. But radio was not yet an accepted part of the world of journalism, though it purveyed news of a sort on the periphery of its daily serials and musical programs.

Murrow was not being sent to Europe as a reporter — after all, he wasn't one — but as an arranger of "talks" and a supervisor of "events." Even if war came, he would merely get other people to expound upon the European situation, and would broadcast set occasions such as speeches, or ceremonies, or, who knew, perhaps even a little gunfire.

H. V. Kaltenborn, CBS's principal news "commentator" in New York, had been able to do just that in 1936, from the French side of the Spanish frontier, as he watched some of the fighting in the civil war.

The new job carried a small raise in pay, to eight thousand dollars, and when Murrow poked his head into the door to say good-bye, James Seward, assistant treasurer at CBS, offered to make sure that the extra money was safely deposited. For twenty-eight years until Murrow's death — and indeed after it, as executor — Jim Seward would serve as a financial and personal adviser, as the modest salary grew into an imposing one.

The position was sometimes a delicate one, as Seward himself rose at CBS to become a vice president of the corporation, but he saw no conflict of interest between Murrow and the company, and indeed at the time there was none. In any case, Seward represented neither of his two interests directly vis-à-vis the other, and the arrangement was never questioned by either side. On Madison Avenue he was sometimes referred to as "the CBS vice president in charge of Murrow."

As Murrow prepared to leave for Europe he was given a farewell luncheon, and the talk was not of news coverage but of the opportunity to "broaden Anglo-American understanding," at least in the world of entertainment. Said one network official, "Broadcasting has no role in international politics. The greatest service rendered by CBS to international understanding was the broadcast of the song of a nightingale from Kent" — an event which had indeed been voted "the most interesting broadcast of the year" 1932 by American radio editors.

Even if the radio industry had wanted to transmit news from Europe, its concept of such a function was much more limited than the facilities, the shortwave telephone, available to make transmission possible.

Radio news in the United States had begun only in 1920, when Egbert Murrow was still in grade school at Blanchard, with the Harding-Cox presidential election returns over Pittsburgh station KDKA, and the first radio reporters were the announcers who read the figures. But commentators like Kaltenborn and Lowell Thomas did not begin to broadcast regularly until the end of the decade, their function being to give not just the headlines but what might be called "the feel" of the news, with something of their own personalities injected into the presentation.

But the commentators were exceptions. Though it had developed its own news services and sources, radio for the most part was exactly in the business of providing headlines, with the announcer usually adding, "For further details consult your local newspaper."

On any larger scale, news was "dramatized" and even orchestrated, like everything else on radio. The most familiar regular program was the theatrical and often portentous *March of Time*. Real personages were portrayed by actors, without regard for their true personality, saying imagined lines. It was magnifique, but it was not responsible journalism.

Another typical weekly program, put on by the *Detroit News*, included orchestra music, a gypsy singer who explained folklore, a "political report" from Washington, dramatized versions of news events, and a master of ceremonies who would end the broadcast with a "hot flash," such as the ending of a local strike.

One 1937 weekly news program in New York was "for women." It had a newsroom atmosphere, that is to say, typewriters could be heard clacking and in the background was the rumble of the printing presses. Then, one by one, four feature writers would come into the editorial sanctum to report to the editor.

Another kind of news program was called a "reporter's notebook," a hodgepodge of trivia passing for information. News programming was merely another novelty of the kind radio constantly strove for, a form of "public service" like spelling bees, "good will courts," advice clinics and audience participation broadcasts. Man-in-the-street interviews were common, but regarded as highly dangerous, since all broadcasting was live and therefore to some degree uncontrolled. In New York once an irate citizen being interviewed on the sidewalk made a peevish remark about auto-driving tests. Not only did the State License Bureau protest, but the station apologized publicly and agreed to help apprehend the malcontent who had offended, and compel him to "prove it or apologize."

News broadcasting from overseas to the United States began in 1930 at the Five-Power Conference in London, to which CBS and NBC sent a commentator each from Washington. Their job was to introduce delegates, who would then give their own subjective and nationalistic versions of what was happening, but in "setting the scene" for these speakers the American radio men themselves reported on the conference. The emphasis was on who did what, without trying to explain why. But it was enough for the radio audience at home actually to hear King George V welcoming the delegates, or Secretary of State Stimson setting forth naval tonnage formulas, without inquiring about national motivations or what went on in the corridors. CBS did twenty-three broadcasts in the two months of the conference, but because of time differences and the network no-recording rule, they were heard in the off-peak hours and not by many people.

Frederick William Wile, the CBS man at the conference, was aided in corralling speakers by Cesar Saerchinger, then a London-based correspondent for the *Philadelphia Public Ledger* and *New York Post*, and when Wile left for home CBS decided it might be useful to have a resident European director and appointed Saerchinger to the first job of its kind. He held it for seven years until he was succeeded by Murrow. Not only was Saerchinger the impresario for the Kent nightingale, but for innumerable songfests, national holiday celebrations, sporting events, French wine festivals, the carnival at Nice and the Pickwick centenary.

There was opera from Moscow, Eamon de Valera marking St. Patrick's Day from Dublin, the Grand National from Aintree, Palm Sunday services from Jerusalem, Easter music from Rome, the tulip festival from Holland, and the four hundredth anniversary of Erasmus's death from Rotterdam. During 1936, while Murrow was director of talks, CBS presented 311 broadcasts from twenty-seven foreign countries, doubling the number of the preceding year, and proudly announced that it "frequently found it necessary to send representatives and commentators on swift voyages of thousands of miles."

For Americans, as heard over their radios, there seemed to be two histories of Europe in those days. One was the inexorable march of events toward war, with civil strife in Austria, upheaval in Germany, disunity in France and self-deception in England. The other was the march of American microphones from one foreign vaudeville act to another, in the name of "understanding." Dollfuss may have been murdered in Vienna but Toscanini was still conducting at Salzburg.

Saerchinger, and Murrow after him, were kept busier booking these bits of entertainment than in following political and economic developments, until the inevitable moment when culture was displaced by Kultur.

Saerchinger, for example, was in Frankfort arranging for the broadcast of the national Saengerfest when Chancellor Bruening was forced to resign in 1932, paving the way for the accession of Adolf Hitler a few months later. Saerchinger went to Munich and got Hitler to agree to a fifteen-minute broadcast to the United States for $1500. But CBS in New York told him to get back to the Saengerfest, explaining aloofly, "Unwant Hitler at any price."

During the Ethiopian War, though it received broadcasts from Addis Ababa by newspaper correspondents, CBS in New York deemed that just as important to its listeners as an appeal by Emperor Haile Selassie to "boycott the aggressor" was a concert of native instruments by Ethiopian tribesmen.

In America, too, "special events" had been somewhat on the trivial side. They included presidential speeches and election campaigns, true enough, the baseball World Series, and the Scopes "monkey trial" of 1925. Under the aegis of Paul White at CBS and A. A. Schechter at NBC, radio had broadcast the first arrival of the Graf Zeppelin over New York, and the disastrous fire at the Ohio State Penitentiary in which 320 convicts perished.

But too often "news" had consisted of stunts like the sizzle of frying eggs on a hot sidewalk, a parachute drop, a wedding ceremony on an airplane, the sound of the waves at Atlantic City, and Gertrude Ederle, the Channel swimmer, broadcasting while aquaplaning.

Murrow arrived in London to attend a royal coronation amid the repercussion of the destruction of Guernica by Nazi bombers in the Spanish civil war. But the latest great triumph of American radio had been NBC's broadcast of an international Singing Mouse Contest, with entries in the United States, Britain and Canada.

Still it was not only frivolous triviality that American listeners heard on radio from overseas. With Murrow as director of talks in New York, many notables of the day were brought to the CBS microphone in Europe. There were Viscount Cecil, the man whose Peace Ballot in 1935 more than anything else conveyed the British national mood; Prime Minister Ramsay MacDonald, Sir Norman Angell, John Maynard Keynes, Sir William Beveridge. There were John Masefield and H. G. Wells — Kipling and Barrie declined — G. K. Chesterton talking about Dickens on Christmas Day, and George Bernard Shaw's famous "little talk about Russia," which he had just visited, addressed to "you dear old boobs" in America. Even Gandhi and Trotsky, and Mussolini speaking in broken English were heard, and League of Nations debates.

One notable CBS broadcast, to instead of from Europe in 1934, came from Little America in the Antarctic, via Buenos Aires to New York, and was then relayed to Britain, where it was clearly heard over a distance of nine thousand miles.

Moreover there was no lack of radio news or commentary from Europe.

It simply was not being done by American radio reporters — there were none — but by well-known British and other European journalists, authors, politicians, and what are now called publicists.

In London such men as Vernon Bartlett, Stephen King-Hall, Gerald Barry and Sir Frederick Whyte made regular appearances on CBS, discussing politics and international relations. Thus, in the abdication crisis of 1936, American radio presented more exhaustive analysis, interpretation and comment on both sides of the question — which was of course constitutional rather than moral or sentimental — than anything that the discreet English press or radio could offer.

During the ten days of the crisis leading British figures in law, sociology, Parliament and academic life made eighty broadcasts of fifteen minutes each for the American networks, and CBS presented thirty-nine of these. As for the abdication itself, Saerchinger scored a notable "beat" by reporting it from the House of Commons before the prime minister read the royal message. "The king has abdicated," he said. "Here is Sir Frederick Whyte to speak to you about this momentous event."

All through the crisis, however, while Edward VIII was still king, it was NBC which had the superior coverage because its European representative, Fred Bate, was a personal friend of the monarch and a member of the set which revolved around him. Mrs. Bate danced with the king and once, from Fort Belvedere, the royal retreat, Bate called the BBC on behalf of His Majesty and asked the orchestra to play a favorite royal tune.

Such NBC entree was a principal reason Murrow was sent to London in 1937. It was after the abdication of Edward, and to attend the coronation of his brother George VI, that the new CBS European director and his wife sailed from New York in mid-April on the S. S. *Manhattan*. He was followed on the next ship by Paul White and Bob Trout, and after the ceremonies Murrow would remain in London. Harold Laski, who had been lecturing in the United States and whom he had known from his IIE days, was also on board the *Manhattan*, and they deepened their mutual respect for each other. It was a convivial crossing. Champagne cost three dollars a bottle, and Curt Roberts and his ensemble played Victor Herbert, Romberg and Friml at dinner.

The coronation, the first since 1910 and therefore the first ever broadcast — it was also the first worldwide radio program — was reported by six BBC announcers who in six hours of talk thoroughly negated their oft-repeated remark that the spectacle had left them speechless.

A large American audience heard what was called "the longest radio commercial on record," on behalf of the British empire. The American announcer, Bob Trout, introduced the British announcers for CBS. Ed

Murrow did not broadcast. That was not his job. He and Janet sat in the stand at Apsley House, Hyde Park Corner, and watched the procession go by.

When Murrow arrived in London he called on Sir John Reith, the tall, craggy and bushy-eyebrowed mixture of Scottish clansman and biblical evangelist who was head of the public corporation for broadcasting, the BBC, though soon to leave it.

As one dedicated radio man to another, the American newcomer informed Sir John that he intended to bring broadcasting "down to earth" by taking a microphone into country villages and London districts, and letting people speak. One of his first finds was a philosophical cabby named Herbert Hodge, or 'Erbert 'Odge, as his Cockney mates called him, a sort of English Mr. Dooley, who became something of a feature on CBS, remarking on affairs from a pub on Saturday nights.

It was a notable news story in Britain, reported by the entire press — perhaps as a slap at the BBC — that a live broadcast from a village pub should be heard throughout America but not in Britain itself. Murrow, on the transatlantic crossing, had confided to Laski his idea for such broadcasts, and the latter invited him to his weekend cottage at Little Barfield, in Essex. The doings at the Spread Eagle included dart-playing, badinage, and the singing of British and American popular tunes, and were heard from the Atlantic to the Pacific.

The technical arrangements and equipment for what were called "outside broadcasts" were made by BBC engineers, who thoroughly relished the job of helping to entertain America.

Murrow thus began a close personal relationship, as well as a corporate one, with British broadcasting in all its ranks that was to make him as well known and appreciated there as in his own country.

For one thing, he at once ended the impression in Britain and on the Continent, which NBC had tried to cultivate, that somehow the National Broadcasting Company was the official national American network, as the BBC was the British. In London, Murrow's NBC rival was Fred Bate, who had twenty-five years' European residence. He had come abroad as a painter, worked for American financial houses and industrial corporations in Europe — helping introduce the Model-A Ford into Spain — and after the First World War had served on the Dawes and Young reparations commissions. He had been with NBC since 1932, as Saerchinger's opposite number.

Bate was twenty-two years older than Murrow, and a mild-mannered, soft-spoken person. The young man from CBS was introduced to Bate by Saerchinger when they met in the BBC lobby, and evidently influenced by Saerchinger's account of the bitter local competition between the two networks, Murrow clenched his fist and challenged Bate to step outside and settle matters then and there.

Bate could not be sure whether Murrow was joking or not — he decided later he must have been, though it is by no means certain that he was — but he explained that the rivalry was not really that deadly; that the number of European singing societies and politicians was sufficient for both American networks; and that anyway he was too much older than Ed to fight him.

Murrow was properly abashed. The two men became fast friends and trustworthy colleagues, and when the circumstances of war made them both broadcasting reporters they covered many dangerous stories together, ignoring the fiercely competitive cables they both received from New York.

On one assignment which found them together in Paris Murrow was stricken with pneumonia, the first of numerous times, and was taken almost unconscious by Bate to the American Hospital, an incident which cemented their friendship. Bate recalled that Murrow awoke three days later in a barred and heavily padded room, and for a few minutes believed it was not a physical ailment that had brought him there. The only bed available at the time had been in the lunatic ward.

Though he was not formally trained in news, and lacked the customary long years in a city room or a Washington bureau, or even the benefit of a journalism school, Murrow had the prime requisites for news work. As an arranger of talks on public affairs, he obviously was concerned with pertinent developments in politics, education, science and the arts. His choice of speakers was in itself a news judgment. His experience at the Institute of International Education, demanding the ability to talk with people and make estimates of character, to negotiate with governments and institutions, to arrange ideas and impressions, and to write reports on what he saw and learned, had provided him with the indispensable tools of journalism.

Moreover, he had traveled in Europe and come to know people and political conditions there perceptively.

He was always conscious of his shortcomings in formal news practice. But he made sure that the men he brought into broadcasting did have extensive news background, and until the very end, when radio and television were producing indigenous news staffs without prior experience in the printed media, he always preferred the old-fashioned kind. Voice and appearance, the accepted criteria in electronic journalism, he regarded as not very important, though he himself possessed both in full measure.

A 1937 photograph taken on a typically wet London pavement, in front of a traffic sign pointing to Oxford Circus, shows Murrow as a serious-miened young man, in a wrinkled raincoat, wearing a double-breasted suit obviously from Savile Row, a rakish wide-brimmed hat, and black gloves, or rather glove, since the right hand was thrust into trouser pocket, with presumed insouciance.

Clothes indeed were an important part of his professional ensemble from the beginning. Immediately on arrival in London he acquired a morning suit, or striped trousers and a short black coat — "not swallowtails," Janet noted, for though he had wanted a cutaway, "after consideration [he] decided he'd get more wear out of the other."

Even after he had returned to America, his clothes would always come from Savile Row and be recognized as "English cut."

He took over the CBS offices in Langham Place, opposite BBC's Broadcasting House, from Cesar Saerchinger. When he entered he found a red-haired young lady at a desk with a pile of Bank of England notes before her, just paid out by Barclay's Bank downstairs. "I see you're in charge of the money," he said. "I hope you'll stay with me." Katherine Campbell did for twenty-three years, in London, in New York and in many other places as Murrow's confidential secretary, amanuensis, keeper of the keys, and paragon.

In London, though Fred Bate had the advantage of experience over Murrow, CBS and NBC at least had parity with regard to facilities, because of the equal-treatment policy of BBC, through which all blessings flowed. But in Germany, an increasingly important news area, NBC had the inside track by virtue of a contract with the official broadcasting agency DRG. In Vienna, similarly, where trouble was brewing, NBC was "exclusive" with Ravag, the Austrian state radio station.

European radio in 1937, because it consisted of a congeries of official government services without commercial taint, was also without the spur of efficiency, backward in technique, and not acutely conscious of timing, as American radio was. The BBC frequently had long intervals of silence between programs. French programs invariably began minutes late, while Austrian programs invariably ran much longer than scheduled.

In the broadcasting of live events in Europe, microphones were used "blind," that is, without earphones by which to hear the return circuit, and "go ahead" cues were given by hand signals from the engineers. With the frequent uncertainty of the radio signal across the Atlantic, plus the uncertainty of getting a landline signal from an "outside" location to the transmitter, all this gave overseas radio a haphazard quality in the United States. But that only added to its spontaneity, unpredictability and thus "magic."

Less enchanting was the fact that American radio men, who at home had only to call the telephone company for broadcast facilities, in Europe encountered government bureaucracies and civil service regulations, as well as work habits like long weekends and numerous holidays.

There was also a European protocol about getting in touch with people. The telephone was somehow beneath the dignity required. When Murrow first sought to reach Winston Churchill, the CBS secretary, Kay Campbell, was horrified to be asked to telephone him. The British custom was to write a note and get an answer in a few days, or else seek an appointment with the Member for Epping, as he then was, through the House of Commons information desk.

But Murrow told her to "ring through" to Churchill, at home if necessary — an even more shocking breach of convention — and received a quick, indeed eager personal response.

The future prime minister knew how important American interest was for Britain's future, and how valuable an acquaintance the enterprising young man from CBS could be.

As Murrow began his nine-year stay in Europe, arranging for other people to broadcast, the network's big name in radio news was that of Boake Carter, who despite a British accent and some British language mannerisms, had a wide American following. He was "controversial" because he had abandoned reporting for editorializing, and was especially outspoken in his criticism of the Roosevelt administration and of labor unions. Many listeners complained of his one-sidedness, though it was not unique on the air, and called on radio news to free itself of bias.

Hans van Kaltenborn, a veteran of many newspaper years, was also broadcasting for CBS in New York and regularly visiting Europe. In 1936 he had provided vivid radio reporting from the French-Spanish frontier. CBS in New York, as usual, was more interested in "events" than in history, and Saerchinger had been sent to Berlin to prepare for the Olympic Games when the Spanish civil war broke out. Kaltenborn, who had been traveling in Europe, broadcast virtually every day for five weeks from Hendaye, providing the first running commentary on the war — "like a football game," it was called, except that actual gunfire could be heard — and interviewing some of the participants who had crossed the border. Inside Spain, the networks did not bother to have their own men, and it was newspaper correspondents who did the broadcasting, under serious censorship handicaps.

In a previous civil war, in Austria two years before, the coverage was not by reporters at all. Chancellor Dollfuss broadcast his own version of his government's attack on the Social Democrats and the shelling of Vienna's famous municipal housing blocks. Dollfuss was not even introduced by a newsman, for John Gunther refused to undertake the task out of repugnance, but by an Austrian government spokesman.

After his border reporting Kaltenborn, until then an occasional broadcaster at fifty dollars a program, returned to New York for an incisive series of broadcasts critical of American nonintervention policy in Spain.

They not only established him as a regular "commentator," but contrary to most American views about Europe, raised the possibility of a more widespread war.

As Murrow took up his European post, the Spanish civil war and the Sino-Japanese War were the leading continuing news stories from abroad. Broadcasting from China, made notable by Floyd Gibbons at the time of the Manchurian "incident" in 1932, had been interrupted in 1937 when Japanese bombs blew up the main transmitter at Chenju, but was finally restored when Madam Chiang Kai-shek spoke for CBS from a temporary transmitter at Hankow, though barely audibly.

In London that summer Neville Chamberlain succeeded Stanley Baldwin as prime minister and, two whole years before the actual declaration of hostilities against Hitler, Murrow witnessed his first war scare, as the largest chain of movie houses began to drill all its employees for air-raid emergencies, and announced it would provide splinterproof bomb shelters for all its theaters. Such war preparations were considerably grimmer than his own, which had consisted of visiting the penny arcades near Leicester Square to practice his rifle-shooting.

The Murrows settled into a small furnished flat in Queen Anne Street, around the corner from the BBC — it was taken over from the Saerchingers, but Ed soon discovered that the bed of the five-foot–two-inch Cesar was much too small for him — and began to make a widening circle of British acquaintances. Janet, thinking of herself as a Connecticut Yankee at King George's Court, served baked ham and sweet potatoes at her first dinner party, American dishes which none of her guests had ever seen before.

Queen Anne Street was sedate, with its doctors' offices and red-brick town houses — gradually being occupied by insurance companies — and nearby was Wimpole Street, where the Barretts lived when Robert Browning came to visit. The BBC, moved from its original location on Savoy Hill near the Thames, was in a modern building at a point where Regent Street, coming up from Piccadilly Circus, curved past Nash's cone-spired All Souls Church into Portland Place, with its Adam houses and foreign embassies, for the last sweep to Regent's Park.

It was a comfortable and convenient section of the city in which to live, and life itself was comfortable, fascinating, and even amusing, not only for young American cousins but for many Britons. The shadows of war were perceptibly lengthening but the prevailing mood, except for a few Cassandras, was one of disbelief that it could actually happen. For this was the time during which "England slept," as it was described by both Winston Churchill and the future President of the United States, John F. Kennedy, whose father would become the American ambassador in London in 1938.

At the Oxford Union a large affirmative vote had been recorded at a debate on the resolution that "this House will not fight for King or country," and Lord Cecil's Peace Ballot had tabulated the votes of more than eleven million Englishmen against war, or more specifically, in favor of collective security under the League of Nations, in favor of arms reduction, the abolition of warplanes and an end to arms manufacture, but also in favor of international sanctions against any aggression.

Murrow found an England going through indecision and uncertainty, nearing the end of its imperial cavalcade, and with a social structure still based on class and replete with inequalities.

The "ruling circles" of the time were small and interlocking, representing the law, journalism, the Church, business, the landed gentry, the armed services and the pecrage. The "old school tie" was qualification enough for many jobs and directorships.

In the world of affairs Parliament was still the focal point of influence and prestige. Its part-time membership, grossly underpaid, either had to enjoy private income or earn additional income while legislating. Winston Churchill, for instance, lived handsomely not on his official salary but on his earnings as a writer and speaker.

The intellectual and political elite gathered in stately homes for long weekends, went to the dinner parties and soirees of fashionable hostesses like Lady Sybil Colefax, and met at the Carlton and other exclusive clubs in London's Mayfair, creating circles within ruling circles. Europeans, especially the blood-and-iron cult in Germany, could be pardoned for believing that English politics was made in the drawing room.

The new CBS European director found no difficulty in squaring all the circles. In a land where John Reith's BBC had pioneered in noble thoughts, as well as good English, any M.P. was only too pleased to be asked to broadcast to America, for the customary fee. Many M.P.'s indeed were also journalists, which made them even more pleased.

British journalism, like other institutions, had a class structure, and what was called in London "Fleet Street" — the reporters, subeditors and even specialized correspondents — did not enjoy the same standing as the "working press" in the United States. It was the publishers, the so-called "press lords"; the editors and editorial writers, the book reviewers, the columnists and the diplomatic correspondents who were not only kept aware of what was going on, but often were involved in it themselves.

Foreign correspondents found it easier to know and associate with such men than the British "working press" did, for foreignness removed the normal social and professional distinctions. Members of the foreign press corps and especially Americans — who had had their own accredited correspondents' association since 1919 — had privileged acquaintance with cabinet ministers, and perhaps more important, with the key departmental men in the Foreign Office. The Americans were accounted the image-makers for Britons abroad, and they certainly made it possible, by publicizing them, for M.P.'s and other British figures to be called to America for lecture tours, or be commissioned to write books.

An example of favored treatment received by American correspondents, including Murrow, was the famous off-the-record lunch with Neville Chamberlain, arranged by Lady Astor at Cliveden, when four months before the Munich crisis the prime minister frankly told of his plans for a European four-power pact excluding Russia, and said he favored Germany's annexation of the Sudetenland. He did not bother to tell his cabinet, much less the House of Commons, and when he was asked parliamentary questions on the basis of some American news reports he evaded them and would not answer.

Murrow, with easy admission into all sections of British society, made a great impression upon his boss Bill Paley, who was a frequent visitor to Europe and who found that government ministers and even broadcasting officials were more accessible through personal than through business channels, at dinner at the Connaught or in a "stately home" rather than an office in Whitehall. Even before the war, Murrow had begun to be the best-known American in London.

He would later recall, in a postwar broadcast to Britons, that on first acquaintance with England as a student in 1930, he had thought the country to be "a sort of museum piece, pleasant but small. You seemed slow, indifferent and exceedingly complacent — not important. I thought your streets narrow and mean, your tailors overadvertised, your climate unbearable, your class-consciousness offensive . . . Your young men seemed without vigor or purpose. I admired your history, doubted your future, and suspected that there was something that escaped me. Always there remained at the back of a youthful and undisciplined mind the suspicion that I might be wrong."

When he took up his post in London in 1937, he remembered, he was always asked by people in other countries whether the British had not become soft and decadent, and lost faith in their future. His answer, he said, was, "You may be right. There is evidence to support your view. But I have a suspicion you are wrong. Perhaps you misjudge those young men who are rather languid, and wear suede shoes, and resolve that they will fight not for King or country."

For though the British state of mind was still definitely a pacifistic one, there could be no doubt that the New Germany was creating some apprehension. Hitler had undone the results of the last war by rearming in violation of the Versailles Treaty. His hysterical speeches had cast into doubt such exercises in diplomacy as the Anglo-German naval treaty and the Locarno Pact, and his march into the demilitarized Rhineland indeed ended Locarno. His Axis partner Mussolini, despite their rivalry in Austria, had joined Hitler in providing arms and equipment, and later even troops, to the Fascist side in Spain.

In Britain, Charles Lindbergh, who was living there in his flight from publicity in America, was telling influential Britons that the Luftwaffe was invincible, there was no place to hide from such air power, and that Britain would be beaten and therefore should not fight. Lindbergh opposed the "Russian Reds" and the "decadent French," and saw no way for Britain except a choice between communism and fascism. There was no doubt about which he favored.

The British response to the growing Hitler threat was the policy of appeasement. They had already tried it out, in the Hoare-Laval Anglo-French plan for the dismemberment of Ethiopia in favor of Mussolini's new "Roman empire" in Africa. It had failed, partly because of public revulsion, but then economic sanctions against Italy also failed, for lack of enforcement, when Il Duce invaded Ethiopia. Similarly Britain and France enunciated their own policy of nonintervention when Germany and Italy aided Franco in Spain.

When Murrow arrived in London Britain was beginning to rearm, though reluctantly, and the Labor Opposition, which had previously voted against, now only abstained when arms appropriations were considered. Two weeks after he succeeded Baldwin as Conservative prime minister, Chamberlain announced the appeasement policy. Britain would be rearming, he said, but at the same time she would be trying to remove the causes of tension which made rearming necessary.

Many in Britain, particularly the influential Establishment newspapers, like *The Times*, regarded this as a realistic point of view, taking into account the country's state of unpreparedness. Rearmament was to be achieved in a five-year plan not to be completed until 1940, while Air Raid Precaution measures would not be completed until 1941. Therefore time had to be bought, and appeasement was the logical way to do it.

Moreover most Britons did not really believe that war could come again. Their opposition to Hitler was not based on fear that Germany would attack their "right little, tight little" island, whatever he might do in Europe, but on the fact that the Fuehrer was a "nasty piece of work," who cozened his own people. As Chamberlain took office Churchill said he was "astounded" at the optimism, confidence and complacency of Parliament and public opinion. But it was evident that with appeasement, Britain had at last found some sort of unity again, if only unity in false security.

The pipe-smoking Baldwin of the cartoonists was replaced by the umbrella-carrying Chamberlain of the cartoonists, while the Anglo-German Association held banquets at the Savoy, the members of the "Cliveden set" gathered at the Astors' near Maidenhead, and *The Times*,

Daily Mail and *Sunday Observer* called for an understanding of Hitler's legitimate, understandable, even laudable aims.

As the Murrows went about Europe that year, while Ed arranged talks on "the prospects of peace," they attended the ISS conference at Nice. The Germans walked out of the meeting, then returned. But, Janet noted, "their speeches made it only too clear that they and the democratic countries have absolutely nothing in common. Even discussion is impossible because there's no common starting point."

In September, American radio listeners heard Hitler and Mussolini speaking from their Berlin conference, and soon after, President Roosevelt at Chicago was denouncing war, "declared or undeclared," and demanding that the world "quarantine the aggressors." Though his remarks had to do primarily with Japan's victories in China, he was preparing public opinion for the change in sentiment from "keep away" to "can't keep out," as one observer put it, of the growing crisis in Europe.

And though most broadcasting from Europe continued to be of entertainment features — NBC scored a coup by "getting" the Salzburg Festival for another two years — Murrow had begun to build a CBS foreign news staff. His first recruit was William L. Shirer, a veteran of European reporting whose latest job had vanished with the sinking of the American news agency Universal Service. Shirer had been in Berlin for the three tense and important years since 1934, and the day his job blew up he received a telegram from Murrow in Salzburg, suggesting dinner at the Hotel Adlon.

Shirer's reporting was penetrating and his writing ability was graphic, but his voice was something else, as he had discovered in his first radio broadcast, made for CBS three months before on the shocked German reaction to the catastrophe that had befallen the airship *Hindenburg*. Shirer was extremely soft-spoken, in fact he sounded timorous and often tended to drone, though what he had to say was usually forthright enough and even bold.

When he met Murrow and discovered that this was not to be a "brain-picking session," as was customary when visiting correspondents came to town, he was dubious about the job that was offered, for it was conditioned on the acceptance of his voice by "our directors and numerous vice presidents in New York."

Since his primary job, like Murrow's, would not be to broadcast himself, but to get others to do so, while he stood by to introduce or interview, it would not seem to have mattered very much. In any case Murrow, who had his eye on the future, told the numerous vice presidents that he was hiring reporters, not announcers, thus establishing a principle that endured at CBS, even into television days, and did much to make the network so successful in news broadcasting.

Shirer would be based in Vienna, a city that both he and Murrow, the latter from his student federation days, knew well, the "city of dreams" that in its fast-approaching tragedy would also be for them the city of their professional destiny. The Vienna assignment, to American correspondents, meant covering all the Hapsburg succession states — Czechoslovakia, Hungary and Yugoslavia, as well as Austria — and Poland besides.

In Berlin Goebbels's propaganda ministry had repeatedly denied CBS requests to shortwave "special events" to the United States, and NBC, by virtue of its favored position, had scored a series of broadcasting triumphs. Its representative in Berlin was a former German correspondent in Washington, Dr. Max Jordan. Part of Shirer's mandate was to overcome NBC's broadcasting lead on the Continent, and especially in Germany.

He went to Vienna at Christmastime 1937, to "pick up" for the United States a program of carols sung by the children of the American colony, a typical CBS venture in "international understanding." He found the Austrian capital a depressing, disconsolate and divided city, with increasing Nazi influence at the top of all affairs, and increasing Socialist influence at the bottom, that is to say, underground. There was no question that this would be the focal point of Europe's next crisis, he decided, as he moved there, prepared to report upon it.

Even in its self-limited way, radio had begun to change the nature of news from abroad, as it had done at home. News, as provided by the newspapers, had been a record of what had already happened. But radio could transmit the event itself, or eyewitness accounts of it, even while it was happening, and soon reporters like Murrow and Shirer would not only be chronicling such events, but trying to explain and evaluate them.

For the two CBS men their hour came in February 1938 when Hitler set into motion the Austrian Anschluss that, like so many other things, he had vowed he never intended. He called the Austrian chancellor, Kurt Schuschnigg, to Berchtesgaden, and delivered an ultimatum under threat of invasion. He wanted the inclusion of the Nazi Seyss-Inquart in the cabinet, an amnesty for all Nazis in prison, and political restoration of the Nazi Party.

When Schuschnigg returned to Vienna the American chargé d'affaires there, John Cooper Wiley, reported to the State Department the chancellor's conviction that Hitler "undoubtedly is a madman with a mission, and in complete control of Germany." Wiley warned Washington that Hitler intended annexation despite any statements to the contrary.

In London, meanwhile, the British foreign secretary, Anthony Eden, had resigned from the Chamberlain government. It was partly a protest against appeasement, specifically against Chamberlain's initiation of negotiations with Mussolini for recognition of the Ethiopian conquest, without some Italian gesture like withdrawal from Spain. But Eden's action was also in protest at Chamberlain's increasing personal diplomacy, by the use of special emissaries. Chamberlain had sent Viscount Halifax to Berchtesgaden in November 1937 to hint to Hitler that some changes in Europe might be acceptable. Now Halifax replaced Eden as foreign secretary, and Halifax believed in Anglo-German rapprochement.

When the storm began to break in Vienna, Murrow and Shirer were as usual busy elsewhere with the enterprises that the entertainment-conscious network believed the entertainment-starved American people were clamoring for. In Rotterdam, Murrow had arranged for a broadcast from the maiden voyage of the liner *Niuew Amsterdam* by Shirer, while writing to Janet, "Things look bad in Austria. There's likely to be bloodshed there before long."

Then in Berlin, where he was joined by Shirer, he asked Herbert Hoover, visiting the German capital on a European "tour of inquiry," to make a radio report for CBS on his return home. Murrow and Shirer also tried to get communications facilities in Berlin, to break NBC's virtual monopoly, and Murrow proposed to CBS that it solicit a broadcast from Ribbentrop, the German ambassador to London, who had just been named foreign minister. But CBS "unwanted" Ribbentrop as it had "unwanted" Hitler. "Hope they get tough," Murrow remarked about the Germans and his negotiations with them. "It would please me to be thrown out of their pagan country."

From Berlin, Murrow had gone to Warsaw to arrange a Polish children's program for the CBS *American School of the Air,* while Shirer was sent to Yugoslavia to put on a chorus of miners' children for the same program.

Though Schuschnigg was trying to stave off Hitler's embrace, even to the extent of negotiating with the workers the Dollfuss regime had driven underground, and had ordered a plebiscite on Austrian independence, CBS had decided that the education of Americans would be better served by song from Slovenia than any on-the-spot reporting of European political realities.

It presented the biggest European crisis since the First World War, in headline style, through an announcer in the New York studio. "The Austrian tea kettle is likely to boil over any minute," he declared at 7:56 A.M. on the decisive day, Friday, March 11. "Angry Nazis are battling with the police in the streets of Innsbruck," was the word at 9:25 A.M.

Shirer had returned to Vienna that morning, by train from Ljubljana. The streets of the capital seemed normally drab and dispirited as he went immediately to the hospital where his wife Tess was seriously ill after a difficult childbirth.

That afternoon he went back to the hospital and on his way, at the Karlsplatz, saw two lone policemen dispersing a crowd of five hundred brown-shirted Austrian Nazis. But two hours later, as he returned from the hospital, large-sized Nazi mobs were surging from the Karlsplatz across the Ring, past the Opera and into the inner city where, as the police stood by with grins, they demonstrated and shouted "Sieg Heil!" saluting the portrait of Hitler that could be seen through the window of the German Tourist Bureau.

Schuschnigg had "postponed" his plebiscite and, except for the formalities, the onetime capital of the Hapsburgs had fallen to the successor of the Hohenzollerns.

Shirer heard Schuschnigg's broadcast farewell on the radio at the American legation, and later the announcement that Seyss-Inquart had become chancellor. Between interviews with bewildered members of the dispossessed government, who were already in hiding, he saw Nazi units that evening moving into the Austrian chancellery in the Ballhausplatz. He telephoned Murrow in Warsaw, but was unable to get through to him. At 11 P.M. he went to the radio station to broadcast to New York, and entered the building in the Johannesgasse past Nazi guards.

But there would be no more broadcasting from Vienna, Shirer was told, except via Berlin. Engineers tried repeatedly to make a connection with the German capital but failed, explaining that the lines had been tied up by the army. At 3 A.M. Shirer was told to leave, prodded by bayonets.

His troubles were not news to Bill Paley in New York. The CBS president, during one of his frequent visits to Europe, had come to know the head of the Austrian State Radio, and when he heard it might be difficult to get facilities from Vienna, he called his friend by telephone.

Paley was in bed with the flu and a 102-degree fever but he forgot them as he heard the anguished voice of the Austrian official say, "It is no longer in my control. The Germans are here," and then break down and weep openly.

Paley also knew that NBC enjoyed excellent relations with the Germans, through Max Jordan, who was in the confidence of some Nazi officials. He was afraid NBC would be able to broadcast from Vienna while CBS could not, and cast about for some way of trumping the NBC ace. "Why do we have to depend only on one microphone?" he asked the CBS engineers. "Can't we get several overseas reports in at the same time for the same program?" He was told it could not be done, or at least it never had been. "Well, let's try," he said.

When Shirer left the barred radio station it was 10 P.M. of the preceding evening in New York. The day's events had continued to be reported by the studio announcer, reading news agency bulletins — at 12:29 P.M. the postponement of the plebiscite; at 2:15 P.M. Schuschnigg's resignation; at 2:45 the crossing of the Austrian border by the first German units; at 3:43 the raising of the swastika flag over the Ballhausplatz.

Radio was able to bring the news into American homes earlier than the next morning's newspapers did, and perhaps more handily, but it was exactly the same news, it was fragmentary, and it was possessed neither of acute observation nor any particular insight. Indeed the valued news period at 11:15 P.M. was filled that evening, not by a CBS commentator but by a New York staff writer for the United Press. "What will be the result of this tense situation, we cannot say; we are reporters of occurrences, chroniclers of fact," he primly concluded.

At midnight the CBS announcer brought the day's chronicling to an end with a bulletin from Vienna: "The Nazis are now holding jubilation meetings throughout the country."

It was then 5 A.M. in Vienna and as Shirer returned home after his vain attempt to broadcast, the telephone call he had placed the evening before to Warsaw came through. It was Murrow. Shirer reported that broadcasting from Vienna had been suspended, and that even if it were to be resumed, it would be under Nazi censorship. Murrow, who had meanwhile talked to Paul White in New York, proposed that Shirer fly to London, to give the first uncensored eyewitness account of the Nazi putsch, while Ed himself would come to Vienna.

At Aspern airport Shirer tried vainly to get a seat on a plane to London. He offered one passenger after another a considerable sum for yielding a place, but all refused. Most of them were Jews, leaving Austria as the Nazis arrived. "I couldn't blame them," Shirer said. The American did manage to get a last-minute seat on the plane to Berlin instead, changed there for London, drove from Croydon directly to the BBC, and that evening did make the first report on the events in Vienna. Now radio was offering what the newspapers could not.

It was heard at 6:30 P.M. on Saturday. Five minutes earlier the New York announcer had reported Hitler on his way from Linz to Vienna by car, following his triumphant entry into the country of his birth. "I'm here tonight to report what I saw, not to give any personal opinions," Shirer declared, but he made it plain that Goebbels had lied when he proclaimed that "German Austria" had been "saved from chaos" caused by "violent Red disorders" in Vienna.

Shirer reported that when he flew out of Vienna that morning it already looked like any city in the Reich, bedecked with swastikas. He found Berlin three hours later similarly decorated and shouting the same slogan, "One Reich, one people, one leader." "And that's what they got, and as I said, very quickly, too," he finished. It was a concise and vivid account, and nobody was paying much attention to the timbre of his voice.

In Warsaw Murrow was encountering difficulty in getting to Vienna. "Rotten luck that I should be here when Austria broke," he had written Janet. There were no scheduled flights but finally he boarded a plane for

Berlin and there was able to charter a twenty-seven-passenger Lufthansa craft, to fly to the Danube on Sunday morning in solitary, and what may have seemed to the CBS accountants in New York extravagant, splendor. The cost was one thousand dollars.

In Vienna his primary concern, as for all radio men, was with the means of transmission. But the jubilant Nazis had opened the Vienna–New York circuit again, though it now went via Berlin and censorship had been imposed. That made broadcasting a delicate business, especially any attempt to talk about anti-Jewish and other excesses by the Nazi crowds.

That afternoon Paul White, in New York, called Shirer in London, the European coordinating point, and ordered an overseas "roundup" for I A.M. European time — a full half-hour of reporting from London, Paris, Rome, Berlin and Vienna. "Can you do it?" he wanted to know.

The engineers, and perhaps the lawyers, in New York had decided there were no technical or legal reasons why Bill Paley's idea of a multi-point instead of an individual point-to-point transmission could not be carried out. They now passed the burden to the men on the scene.

Until then only two such programs had been attempted in an entire year, and they were not news programs. The speakers were leading Europeans and the arrangements had to be made over a period of months, with frequent breakdowns and revisions.

Now the two young Americans, six hundred miles apart, had eight hours to provide a complete live broadcast involving five European capitals, that is to say, five separate transmitters and national work staffs.

Each transmission had to be so accurately timed as to come into New York ready for broadcast while the preceding transmission was still on the air. It had to be able to go on the air itself in its proper order, or before or after its scheduled order if a sudden emergency should interfere with one of the other circuits. This had to be done on a Sunday night, when government offices were closed and technical facilities reduced, and above all, at a time when the international crisis caused by Hitler's aggression scarcely made for normal operating conditions.

Murrow in Vienna and Shirer in London talked frequently to each other by telephone that evening and gradually put things together. They had friends everywhere on the Continent among American newspaper correspondents, and knew the various radio directors and chief engineers. Shirer summoned up Edgar Ansel Mowrer in Paris, Frank Gervasi in Rome, and Pierre Huss in Berlin, and spoke directly to the engineers of the French PTT and the broadcasting authorities in Berlin and Turin. Murrow had explained the requirements. Each reporter had to get to a shortwave transmitter in his country powerful enough to reach New York, or else use landlines to the nearest such transmitter.

During the next few uncertain hours New York serenely took everything for granted. White cabled the exact times for each capital to take the air, in the event that it was not able to hear the preceding portion of the program and New York's "go ahead" cue. The Rome and Berlin radio frequencies were cabled to New York. Permission was obtained from the news agencies concerned for their correspondents to broadcast for a rival means of news dissemination.

In London, Shirer located Murrow's friend, Ellen Wilkinson, M.P., enjoying an English weekend in the country, and she agreed to come in to the BBC to give a British reaction to the Vienna events.

Turin reported that Rome would not be able to set up a Gervasi "feed" in time for the broadcast, so the reporter would try a landline across the Swiss border to the Geneva transmitter. But that attempt failed also and finally Gervasi would have to read his story over the telephone to London, where it was transcribed for Shirer to read it, in turn, to New York.

In New York, Sunday had been a day of news alarums. The CBS network opened at the unusual hour of 6 A.M. with the announcement that special broadcasts were being arranged from European cities, and soon began flashing bulletins about German warplanes over Czechoslovakia, Hitler's progress toward Vienna, and the resignation of Austrian President Miklas.

At 8 P.M. in Studio 9, on the seventeenth floor of the CBS building, Bob Trout, identified as "the Voice of CBS News," took the microphone. "The program *St. Louis Blues* will not be heard tonight," he said. Instead there would be a special broadcast "which will include pickups direct from London, Paris and such other European capitals as at this late hour abroad have communications channels available." Even at air time it was not certain how much of the entire program would get through.

It was 1 A.M. in London and Shirer began on Trout's cue. In the next half-hour radio came into its own as a full-fledged news medium, the most immediate and forceful yet devised, reaching across three thousand miles of ocean and hundreds of miles of Europe in several directions, to bring a sense of history into the American home.

Overseas radio was no longer a mere phonograph. Shirer talked, not about Austria, which was past, but about Czechoslovakia, which was next, and wondered whether France and Britain would help her if she were attacked. Ellen Wilkinson reported that the Vienna putsch had "annoyed" Britons but that it had provoked curiosity rather than real concern, as just some more of Hitler's bad manners.

Mowrer in Paris and Huss in Berlin, both veteran American foreign correspondents, commented on the inevitable reaction in their capitals, disquiet in the one, "inspiration" in the other. Then Murrow came in from Vienna, making the first news broadcast in what was to become the most notable career in radio and television journalism.

Vienna, with its chestnut trees, concert halls, cafés, wine gardens, busy university — which he had known well — and many Beethoven sites, was filled with holiday crowds. "They lift the right arm a little higher here than in Berlin, and the Heil Hitler is said a little more loudly. There isn't a great deal of hilarity, but at the same time there doesn't seem to be much feeling of tension." Hitler's arrival had been delayed, he reported. Only later was it learned that the vaunted Wehrmacht had broken down on the road between Linz and Vienna.

After Murrow, United States Senator Lewis Schwellenbach in Washington — serving as a reporter, for CBS had no Washington correspondent as yet — provided that capital's reaction, which was one of interest more than immediate concern. It was Europe's affair.

The first "news roundup" ended exactly at 8:30 P.M. as scheduled. It had been a complete success, and made an indelible impression that Sunday evening throughout America, a multiple-city program more than matching the various datelines on a newspaper's front page. It would be a standard kind of news broadcast ever after, listened to while shaving in the morning, or at the breakfast table.

On Monday, March 14, Hitler finally entered Vienna, almost simultaneously with Prime Minister Chamberlain's report to Commons on the Anschluss, admitting that it was a blow to his appeasement policy. But he indicated that all that lay ahead was more appeasement.

At 3 P.M., from Vienna, Murrow was heard again. "Hello, America . . . Herr Hitler is now at the Imperial Hotel. Tomorrow there is to be a big parade and at that time he will probably make his major speech . . . Please don't think that everyone in Vienna was out to greet Herr Hitler today. There is tragedy as well as rejoicing in this city tonight."

Already his eye for pertinent detail was at work. He described the small unit of German soldiers, "obviously enjoying themselves," who were now quartered next door to the radio building. "They're sleeping on straw, and there are stacked rifles and iron helmets arranged neatly along the wall. They don't talk a great deal with the Viennese, but they're always courteous and they certainly give the impression of iron discipline."

For years afterward Murrow remembered the oranges that Nazi soldiers threw to the crowds in the Ringstrasse from their trucks. It would come to his mind most vividly after Pearl Harbor when, on leave in the United States, he saw oranges tossed to the crowds at a Bowl football game in Miami.

The second "radio tour of world capitals" that Monday night brought in Shirer from London with Philip Jordan, the British journalist, who said,

"Hitler is now the master of Austria because British foreign policy has been almost nonexistent for the last seven or eight years," and spoke of the need for defending Czechoslovakia. He was not a Chamberlain supporter.

From Paris, Kenneth Downs, of International News Service, reported that France would march if Hitler attacked Czechoslovakia, or at least France said so, which he described as "indeed news." From Berlin, Albion Ross, of the *New York Times*, reported that the annexation of Austria, despite the takeover of the gold reserve of the National Bank, "is not going to solve Germany's economic problem."

Murrow spoke from Vienna to say that the presence of Hitler, heavily guarded by SS men, had not brought much of a celebration. He looked forward to the Fuehrer's speech, due within a few hours from the Heldenplatz or Heroes' Square, in the Royal Palace enclosure.

From Rome, Gervasi again had to telephone his dispatch to London, for lack of Italian radio facilities, so that could not be accounted a living link with New York, though it provided a Rome dateline.

On Tuesday, March 15, Hitler made his speech before one hundred thousand people in the Heldenplatz and was heard at 5 A.M. in New York proclaiming "my new mission" for Austria, as "the strongest bulwark of the German nation and the Reich," and warning that "nobody will dare to interfere with the execution of this mission!" Thus he annexed Austria by proclamation, not awaiting the foreordained result of the plebiscite in April.

Two hours after the speech Murrow broadcast his impressions of it. "There are no halfway measures about this cheering," he said. "It's either wholehearted cheers, or complete silence." Now that the spectacle was over, Austria's future and the status of her citizens would be determined by the promulgation of decrees. Democracy, even though only the ersatz Austrian kind, had ended.

That evening, as Hitler left Vienna to return to Munich, CBS made its final crisis broadcast from the Reich's new "bulwark." Murrow talked with an Associated Press reporter about the rapid Nazification of the country.

Shirer returned from London to Vienna and was met by Murrow at the airport. They saw Nazi soldiers carrying out silver and other loot from the Rothschild palace, next to Shirer's apartment house. That evening, when they sought a café after dinner in the inner city, Murrow steered Shirer away from one of their favorite places. He had been there the evening before.

"A Jewish-looking man was standing at the bar," he said, "and after a while he took an old-fashioned razor from his pocket and slashed his throat."

Swiftly and surely, the Anschluss had been carried out. But it only accentuated and did not end the crisis in Europe. Wholesale arrests were made of Jews, who had constituted one-sixth the population of Vienna, and many were beaten and humiliated, thousands committing suicide. Mussolini, though outmaneuvered by Hitler in Austria — he had supported the Home Guard who were Schuschnigg's chief prop — graciously yielded to his Axis partner and called the annexation "inevitable" and "a national revolution."

Secretary of State Cordell Hull condemned the resort to force as an instrument of national policy, and Hitler told his Reichstag that with the Anschluss, Germany "again has become a world power."

As was its effect on future events in Europe, so the effect of the Anschluss on American radio news was weighty. It not only established the "roundup" as an exciting kind of "instant news" program, but as Murrow and Shirer continued afterward to broadcast regularly scheduled news analyses, it established the radio foreign correspondent as a new journalistic species.

It had also emphasized the fact that for all the broadcasting of the crisis week, only two of those who had given CBS its new distinction were CBS reporters, the others being borrowed from other news organizations. It was therefore obvious that radio had to develop its own news corps if it were to vie authentically with the print medium.

On the technical side, during the long broadcasting days of the crisis, CBS had achieved difficult connections throughout Europe, including one from Kaunas, Lithuania, without missing a single cue or losing a single second of air time, though some hookups had to be completed while the program was already in progress.

In later years all this would be routine procedure. In March 1938 it was regarded as miraculous, or at least, as Murrow saw it, "lucky."

But despite its emergence as a powerful news form, radio continued to be viewed in a different light by some of the network magnates. An NBC executive could still tell the United States Chamber of Commerce, "Radio is a show, and with its own technique has built illusions of reality for those in the seats before the proscenium of their loudspeakers."

There were already some fears of radio's new capability, expressed even by the architects of it. Addressing his stockholders, Bill Paley said, "Broadcasting . . . must forever be wholly, honestly and militantly nonpartisan. This is true not only in politics but in the whole realm of arguable ideas," Boake Carter to the contrary, apparently notwithstanding. "We must never have an editorial page . . . we must never try to further either side of any debatable question."

Yet as it had begun to prove in the Anschluss crisis and was about to demonstrate even more forcibly in the Munich crisis, radio — by its own nature, by merely presenting events as they occurred, and the factual but personalized accounts of its own reporters — was able to help make up people's minds for them, and to further one side of the biggest debatable question of the time, the rise of Nazi power.

This fact overshadowed the simple journalistic truth that for detail, depth and brilliance of reporting, the story of Vienna's immolation, Murrow's and radio news's first big assignment, did not substantively measure up to the work of some newspaper correspondents, especially the British, and patently not up to radio's later standards. These would develop gradually, with quantum jumps at Munich and during the Second World War. But the revelation came at Vienna.

With Austria annexed, the Germans controlled all the landlines from central Europe to the big Geneva and London transmitters, including those from Prague. In April, Shirer was in the Czech capital to supervise a broadcast by President Beneš and Alice Masaryk, daughter of the nation's founder, and instead of going via Geneva, as was customary, the transmission went through Berlin. The broadcast was about the International Red Cross, but Shirer had persuaded Beneš to say something about the German threat to his country, and at that point the signal faded and his words were lost.

The Germans denied they were responsible, but the Czechs decided it was time to speed up the building of their new transmitter, which would be powerful enough to reach New York directly. It was tested in July, and in August Shirer used it for an eyewitness account of a fighter plane crash a few yards away, during Czech army maneuvers. The engineers in New York complained that the plane crash caused "too much noise" for an "ideal" broadcast, but said the new circuit was fine. A few weeks later, during the Munich crisis, it was to be beleaguered Czechoslovakia's most important link with the outside world.

In western Europe, meanwhile, Murrow was visiting France's Maginot Line, to make the first broadcast ever permitted from the strategic and highly secret fortification that would be so easily enflanked two years later. He obtained authorization from Premier Daladier himself, and though there were military restrictions on the names of towns, the identity of regiments and the like, Murrow was able to describe eloquently the possibility of war.

Some at NBC, which was underemphasizing the prospects of war, thought Murrow was wrong to make such a broadcast because they felt it glorified the military prowess of one country against another, and compromised American neutrality.

For CBS, however, the principal effect of the Maginot Line broadcast was that it made the network even more unwelcome in Berlin and further strengthened NBC's preemptive arrangements with the state radio.

After the Anschluss, Murrow and Shirer, since Czechoslovakia was next on Hitler's timetable — Konrad Henlein, the Nazi leader in the Sudetenland, was in fact visiting London at the time and deciding that Britain would not defend the Czechs — proposed a daily broadcast from Prague, or at least a weekly one, but New York scoffed at the idea. As it turned out, Prague was soon to be on the air several times daily, and so were the other European points, over a long period, as the Czech crisis grew.

Shirer, unable to function in Nazi Vienna — which had become merely a German provincial city instead of a European capital — moved his headquarters to Geneva, but spent most of his time in Prague or Berlin.

If the Vienna events of March had put Murrow and CBS in the forefront of American news reporting, the Sudetenland and Munich events of September made them, in a sense, indispensable. For NBC, under its policy of deemphasis, minimized the Czech crisis until Prime Minister Chamberlain's visit to Hitler in Berchtesgaden proved the point, somewhat belatedly.

On Monday afternoon, September 12, from Nuremberg, both American networks broadcast Hitler's closing address to the Nazi Party congress. The German leader spoke of the Sudetenlanders as "our people exposed to the democratic hordes who threaten" them, namely the Czechs, and warned "this cannot go on." He had been demanding the "return" of the 3.5 million ethnic Germans, who were never part of Germany.

Though the frenzied cheers of "Sieg Heil!" and "Heil Hitler!" told their own story, NBC's presentation of the event was noncommittal, while for CBS Kaltenborn, in the New York studio, provided a nine-minute commentary pointing out the inflammatory passages and explaining their significance.

Four hours later the first CBS "roundup" of the crisis, an "international news broadcast," as it was announced, was presented. Murrow opened it from London, and was followed by an Associated Press correspondent in Berlin, Shirer in Prague, and a *Chicago Daily News* correspondent in Paris. Hitler's speech, reported Murrow with British understatement, had not decreased European tension, but the British had once again "demonstrated their ability to fly into a great calm at a time of crisis." The British government, he thought, would urge the Czechs "to do anything short of actually dismembering the country to prevent war." Or, as it turned out, including dismembering. A few days before, *The Times* of London, the once mighty Thunderer, which had become the reasoned voice of appeasement, publicly proposed that the Sudetenland be seceded to Hitler, in order to make Czechoslovakia "a more homogeneous state."

In the days that followed, Europe's most traumatic, the American networks operated on a twenty-four-hour basis to provide transatlantic news reports. Within a week CBS was carrying a dozen broadcasts from Europe every day, and NBC followed suit.

American listeners heard Mussolini speaking in Trieste, calling for a Sudeten plebiscite, and four hours later Czech Premier Milan Hodza, in Prague, rejecting a plebiscite. They heard the Archbishop of Canterbury praying for peace, and the next day Pope Pius XI. They heard Hitler again, at the Berlin Sportpalast, attacking Beneš personally, saying he had reached the "limits of our patience," and calling on Germans to "fall in behind me, man for man, woman for woman." They heard Chamberlain from Downing Street. "How horrible . . . incredible it is that we should be digging trenches and trying on gas masks here, because of a quarrel in a faraway country between people of whom we need know nothing."

On the Black Wednesday when war seemed inevitable they heard from the House of Commons how Chamberlain's report on his negotiations with Hitler had been dramatically interrupted by the arrival of the Fuehrer's invitation to a conference in Munich the next day.

Between the official utterances Murrow and his European staff supplied reports, analyses and interviews all around the clock. "Hello, America," they would begin. Once Murrow put on Jan Masaryk, the Czech minister in London, at 4 A.M. in what was later selected as the most notable "talk" of the radio year. Many in America wept as they heard it.

His small country, the diplomat said, had decided to resist "in full confidence that this time France and England will not forsake us." At Godesberg a few hours before, Chamberlain had received Hitler's repudiation of their previous understanding of a "peaceful settlement," and his new demands for immediate military occupation of the Sudetenland, with the obvious view of the destruction of the Czech state.

"My father was buried just a year ago," Masaryk told the people of his mother's country, America. "My unified nation is assembled around his simple village grave, firmly resolved to safeguard the principles he laid down for us, and we are convinced that truth, decency, freedom and love will triumph in the end. We shall defend it to our last breath.

"I tell you, Americans," he concluded. "Our powder is dry." But Chamberlain's and Daladier's was not.

Another Murrow guest, a British M.P., likened the Sudetenland to Northern Ireland and therefore favored its autonomy. Ed's taxi-driver friend Herbert Hodge reported British sympathy for the Czechs, but not at the cost of war. The British, like Candide, "just want to be left alone to grow their marigolds," he said.

Between September 12 and 30, when Chamberlain returned from Munich with "peace in our time," H. V. Kaltenborn lived and slept adjacent to Studio 9 at CBS. In eighteen days he made eighty-five extemporaneous broadcasts about the Czech crisis. He talked frequently with Murrow and the other reporters in Europe in what has come to be known as "two-way" broadcasting. There were fourteen "news roundups."

On some days the network opened at 5 A.M. and frequent bulletins interrupted regular news programs. There were newsroom jokes about bulletins that interrupted bulletins. CBS had its reporters everywhere, it seemed, though all but two of them were the correspondents of American newspapers and not CBS men.

But it was Murrow who as European chief was the pivotal figure, and the entire nation, clinging to earphones and entranced by loudspeakers, heard Kaltenborn saying again and again, "Calling Ed Murrow, calling Ed Murrow . . ."

By his clear voice, crisp tones and authoritative manner, the young man became a household name and personality. As was to be the case through his entire career, people who heard him felt they knew him. But he himself, as he remembered Bob Trout's guidance, never conjured up in his imagination any particular listener to address himself to, as other broadcasters said they did. He spoke only to the microphone.

Both at microphone and at desk, he was calm during the tense days, but fatigue, as it would do so many times, turned his features haggard and furrowed his thirty-year-old brow. He worked around the clock, dividing his time between the BBC studio and the CBS office across the street. By telephone with the continental capitals he arranged the broadcasts of the day ahead, as events moved. Meanwhile he had to make the rounds of his own news sources in Downing Street and the House of Commons.

During the Munich crisis Murrow made thirty-five broadcasts himself and arranged for 116 others from eighteen points in Europe.

This was history in the making, as the phrase goes, and adding to the thrill of it for American listeners was its live and spontaneous quality. In a radio era that now relies on its recording facilities, with news reports often made hours before or even overnight, the sputter, static and instantaneity of shortwave radio in the Thirties and Forties may have been forgotten.

In those days the networks followed the strict policy of no recordings. The live broadcasts came directly from the scene of distant events, sometimes the most unlikely places, with equally unlikely technical improvisation. Thus, as seventy-five news correspondents left Berlin for the second Chamberlain-Hitler meeting at Godesberg, Shirer made a live broadcast, interviewing some of them, from the platform of the Friedrichstrasse railroad station. Paul White wanted it done from the moving train, but even German technicians were not up to that yet, at such short notice.

The correspondents cautiously had not very much to say, but they said it in brisk trenchcoat fashion, and the broadcast was colorful and successful. It replaced the canceled program, *Let's Pretend.*

In Prague an open microphone gave CBS a news beat. As Maurice Hindus, of the *New York Herald-Tribune*, was ending a broadcast in the studio he was handed a message, which he promptly read. It was the Czech Government's communiqué telling Britain and France that, in spite of what Jan Masaryk had said, it was accepting the Munich diktat.

Frequently Americans got radio news from Europe which Europeans themselves did not hear. From his constituency at Stratford-upon-Avon, CBS carried a speech on the Munich crisis by Anthony Eden, who had resigned as foreign secretary.

The BBC, for its own peculiar reasons, did not broadcast the speech. But a newspaper item that Eden's words would be carried to America brought hundreds of calls from Britons to the CBS office in London inquiring whether there was any way they too could hear it. There was none, except by having one's own shortwave station capable of listening to a commercial frequency.

Live broadcasting from abroad had its problems also. An open microphone at the scene often missed an event because of altered schedules. Shirer was to broadcast Hitler's arrival at the Quirinal Palace in Rome one May evening and stood waiting on the roof of the royal stables, with the "cut through" from New York timed to the moment of the arrival of the carriage with the Fuehrer and the Italian king. But the horses galloped faster than anticipated.

By the time the microphone to New York was opened, Hitler had already driven into the palace, come out on a balcony and bowed to the crowd, then disappeared again. Shirer was able to improvise a past-tense account from notes taken during the day, but suddenly the light attached to the microphone went out and he was left in darkness. He tried to ad lib, but not very successfully, and saved the broadcast by waving to a technician to bring over one of the Fascist torches burning on the roof in honor of the Nazi guest.

In live broadcasting, unforeseen circumstances added both to the difficulties and, when these were overcome, to the satisfactions. Not only did light fail, but weather changed, radio signals faded, sunspots interfered. On three successive days in the Czech crisis, during the Nazi rioting in the Sudetenland and Chamberlain's visit to Berchtesgaden, sunspots blotted out the CBS broadcasts from Prague and Shirer's reports had to be cabled to New York and read in the studio.

So adept did the practice of overseas broadcasting become that if one circuit failed, a switch was made at once to another waiting one, or Murrow in London or Kaltenborn in New York would fill in time with spoken commentary, instead of resorting to the familiar domestic technique of returning to the studio or offering a "musical interlude."

As the Anschluss crisis established the European and later the "world news roundup," with separate reports from several cities abroad, so the Munich crisis established the news round table, in which correspondents in four or more cities, linked together by shortwave circuits and landlines, could carry on a spontaneous continuing conversation, instead of merely reading separate scripts. Thus questions could be raised from the United States which had not occurred to those in Europe, and could be answered.

The first round table, operated from Studio 9 in New York, linked that city with Washington, London and Paris. This technique is now also used in routine fashion, not only on radio, but by the use of communications satellites, on television. In 1938 it was impressive.

On the night of the Munich agreement, when Chamberlain and Daladier bowed to Hitler at Czechoslovakia's expense, Max Jordan in Munich, broadcasting from the Fuehrerhaus itself, by virtue of NBC's "good connections," had the text of the pact on the air nearly an hour before his CBS rival Shirer. But the edge had been taken off, for Murrow in London, listening to the Munich radio, was able to flash the first report of the signing to New York.

After this he went to the Czech legation and spent the rest of the night sitting with his friend Jan Masaryk. The usually jovial man was slumped in his chair. He knew it meant war and that his country was doomed, Murrow reported, but there was no bitterness in him and no defeat.

When Ed rose to go at dawn Masaryk pointed to a picture of Hitler and Mussolini in a magazine. "Don't worry," he said. "There will be dark days and many men will die, but there is a God and He will not let two such men rule Europe."

In his broadcasts, which had described the ditches dug, the sandbags and gas masks distributed, and the schoolchildren evacuated, Murrow reported the jubilation in London over the Munich agreement. But he decried the terms and said that the nettle of danger Chamberlain had tried to pluck was still there. While the British were talking about a knighthood for the prime minister and proposing him for the Nobel Peace Prize — the *Daily Mail* welcomed him back from Munich as "the Prince of Peace" — Murrow concluded that Hitler had "scored one of the greatest diplomatic triumphs in modern history."

Few voices were raised in Britain against the Munich agreement. One was Winston Churchill's, of course. Another was that of the left-wing Laborite D. N. Pritt, who openly criticized the pact while his party leadership remained silent. Pritt was given no forum in Britain, but Murrow brought him to the CBS microphone. The Briton seemed overwhelmed when the young American told him that no prepared script was necessary, not even notes, for the BBC, if it had allowed him to broadcast at all, would have required a full advance text and strict adherence to it.

"You can say anything you want," Murrow told the startled Pritt. Prophetically he said that Chamberlain, trying to avoid both war and dishonor, would end up by having both.

During the Munich crisis, from September 10 to 29, CBS on its 115 stations broadcast 151 shortwave pickups from Europe, and NBC 147. The coverage cost the large sum, for that time, of two hundred thousand dollars, more than for any other "single sequence of events."

Included were transmission costs — the average shortwave pickup came to five hundred dollars and transatlantic telephones were eight dollars a minute — fees for the newspaper correspondents who participated, translation and secretarial expenses, and rebates to sponsors whose regular programs were preempted or interrupted.

In exchange, it was judged, Murrow and his colleagues had established three clear advantages for radio over newspapers. They were ahead of the newspapers by hours. They reached millions of Americans in small towns who were not otherwise exposed to foreign news in their local papers. They "wrote their own headlines" by the selection of material, and the fact that there was no editor or other intermediary between them and their listeners.

They had also made it plain that radio could no longer be content as a nonprimary medium, in news. For radio had always been, in a sense, parasitic. Though direct in its impact, its talents and resources — actors, orchestras, speakers — came mainly from other arenas, and radio merely provided them with an added dimension.

In news its dependence had been on the correspondents of newspapers and magazines, whose broadcasting in turn depended on their willingness, their availability, and the consent of their employers. For a network they provided no mark of separate identity or of continuity. A correspondent could be heard once, and never again, or he might be replaced by someone else for several succeeding broadcasts. On the second night's CBS roundup in the Anschluss crisis two of the three guest reporters were different from those heard on the first night. Variety was not lacking, but consistency may have been.

Moreover the primary responsibility of newspapermen was to their newspapers. There was frequently a conflict of time or of assignment, and there came to be a feeling by employers that there was a conflict of interest in permitting the services of their reporters to a rival medium.

And while a man's voice was not in Murrow's judgment as important as his reportorial ability, the fact remained that a news report written to be read by the eye differs stylistically and in method of presentation from a report written to be spoken. It was evident that newspaper correspondents, however able, could not suffice for radio's purposes if radio proposed to continue as a news medium in its own right.

Not only had the Austrian and Czech crises established it as such, but in both instances radio had itself become a positive factor, speeding up events, producing reactions and counter-reactions, arousing public opinion. Radio introduced a new element into diplomacy by divesting it of some of its secrecy, for better or worse, and radio bulletins took the place of diplomatic telegrams between capitals, to some extent.

It was even believed by some that radio changed events by making unmistakable to the dictators the great desire for peace, and thus averting war in 1938. This seems an exaggeration. Hitler obviously exploited the desire for peace in order to make further demands and threats. And in the end war came anyway, a year later. But radio may indeed have helped postpone it.

Certainly, in those two crises, American radio provided more people with more information, faster and more accurately, than ever before in any international situation — far more than the people of any other country received, including information about their own country.

After Munich CBS took the unusual step of making a broadcast statement not only congratulating itself on its achievement — it had received many thousands of messages of thanks from listeners — but pledging itself to continue the kind of news broadcasting that provided "comprehension" as well as information. All usages and conventions had been broken and CBS hailed the arrival of radio "not merely as a disseminator of the news, but as a social power."

After Munich, Murrow and Shirer, the entire CBS news staff in Europe, become veteran broadcasters after only a few months, met in Paris to take stock. It was a gloomy rendezvous, not relieved by champagne or tramping the streets for hours at night, talking. They agreed that, despite Chamberlain's assurances, a war was likely after the next harvest, in August 1939, and that Poland would be Hitler's next victim, since he had already begun to talk about Danzig and the Polish Corridor.

They also decided that CBS had to have its own staff of radio reporters in Europe to cover the coming war, the more so since NBC, they had learned, was planning to employ so-called "big names" instead, like Churchill in London and former Foreign Minister Flandin in Paris. The radio reporters would have to be Americans, and thus as neutrals able to function from either side in a war. Some American newspapers had Britons and other Europeans among their continental correspondents.

By the time the conflict did come, CBS had staff correspondents in London, Paris, Berlin, Rome, Amsterdam, Helsinki and the Balkans, and more important, they were not mere makers of arrangements but re-

Shirer and Murrow, with local friend, at a Paris cafe before the fall of France

porters and broadcasters able to compete with, and in many cases outdo, the newspaper and wire agency men. They were working for and in their own medium, and the "Murrow boys," as they were to be known, growing with radio and entering television, left their distinctive stamp on every aspect of electronic communication.

In London the BBC, from which Murrow made his reports to the United States, was also not persuaded by Chamberlain's assurance of "peace in our time." It set up an emergency system at Broadcasting House, in the event of air attack, and built emergency studios in the sub-basement, equipped with gas masks, protected by sandbags, and provided with emergency power.

R. T. Clarke, the BBC home news editor, who had become one of Murrow's closest friends, was asked by the public corporation's board of governors to suggest what could be done to improve national morale. "The only thing that would strengthen morale is all the news, and nothing but the truth, no matter how horrible," he said in a famous reply.

After Munich also, though the "Cliveden set" still flourished, Winston Churchill, a back-bench Member of Parliament, took to inviting foreign journalists, businessmen and other professional travellers, as well as Foreign Office and army people, to his country home Chartwell. This was part of his private information system, which paralleled and often eclipsed the government's own. The representative of CBS, the American radio network which had done so well in the Munich crisis, was among those invited.

The diplomatic defeat at Munich and the blow to Britain's prestige, as well as the shock caused by the realization that bombs could be dropped on her cities, finally began to awaken the island kingdom. It was still hoped war could be averted and that Hitler would be satisfied with his gains, but his seizure of Czechoslovakia itself in March 1939, the logical consequence of Munich, made it apparent that he could no longer be bought off. Military conscription was introduced and 310,000 men were called up, though the government had promised there would never be a peacetime draft. The Labor Opposition in Parliament still voted against conscription. But by the time Prague fell to the Fuehrer, and Bohemia became a "protectorate," a million Air Raid Precaution workers had been mustered in Britain, air-raid shelters were ready for ten million people, forty million gas masks were available, and evacuation plans had been drawn up. Chamberlain amended his Munich phrase to "peace for a time."

The British were still not fully prepared in 1939 and their pledge of support to Poland, after the dismemberment of Czechoslovakia, was in many ways unrealistic — for example, it lacked the cooperation of the Soviet Union — but it was indicative that the mood had changed, and that the lesson of Munich had begun to be learned, though not yet in the full terms of collective security.

After Munich the Murrows returned briefly to New York, so that Ed could talk with Klauber, White and other CBS officials about the extended coverage that would be demanded by war. He was widely applauded at home for his broadcasts during the two 1938 crises. He made several speeches and in one of them, at Buffalo, declared, "Whether we like it or not, the answer to Europe's problems will be found, not in Europe, but right here in the United States."

The audience seemed puzzled. Even though war in Europe might be inevitable, the prevalent feeling still was that it had little to do with the United States, except as something to be watched, indeed literally eavesdropped upon, through the medium of entertainment and advertising that had so dramatically become also a medium of news communication.

A month after Munich, a Sunday night radio drama done in simulated news style, about an invasion from Mars — based on H. G. Well's novel *The War of the Worlds* — panicked a large part of the United States by using the news bulletin interruption technique, and the on-the-spot reporting and interviews the American public had become conditioned to during the European crises. It even re-created the atmospheric hum associated with a "live" overseas circuit.

It may have been post-Munich jitters. It may have been illustration of the fact that Americans had come to be dependent on radio for their "big news." It may also have been the first indication of radio's — now television's — power to blur the distinction between reality and fantasy.

VI

"London is burning, London is burning"

O N Saturday, August 24, 1940, as, before the radio sets in thirty million American homes, "this peaceful nation was settling down to an evening of relaxation" — in the words of one newspaper account — "into its midst, from another world, intruded the growling of air-raid sirens, the furtive movements of people taking cover, and dramatic descriptions of ARP contingents manning the defense of a city."

The Battle of Britain had begun. German planes were over blacked-out London. It was 11:30 P.M. by Big Ben. "This is Trafalgar Square," reported Ed Murrow. "The noise that you hear at this moment is the sound of the air-raid siren. A searchlight just burst into action, off in the distance, an immense single beam sweeping the sky above me now. People are walking along very quietly. We're just at the entrance of an air-raid shelter here, and I must move the cable over just a bit, so people can walk in."

America's living rooms heard antiaircraft guns in the background. In Trafalgar Square, Murrow moved from the steps of St. Martin-in-the-Fields and the entrance to the church crypt which had become a shelter, and sat on the edge of the sidewalk. He said nothing. His open microphone picked up the sound of unhurried footsteps. Directly above him, two men stopped to talk. One casually asked the other for a light. The sirens and guns kept working.

The memorable broadcast, one in the Saturday evening series called *London After Dark*, signalized the fact that after all the unbelievable events on the European continent, after Hitler's blitzkrieg in the East and his conquest in the West, after Dunkerque and the fall of France, Britain stood alone, face to face once more with history.

The supreme contemporary annalist of that encounter was the young man with the dark look and the creased forehead, whose measured cadence, "This . . . is London," and trenchant style brought to this country not only vivid firsthand reporting, not only sober political and social appraisal, but also the Donnean awareness that Britain was not really an island and that in her ordeal, whatever the outcome, the bell tolled for the United States also.

The young man who had come to London in 1937 as carefree and lighthearted as his restrained nature would allow him to be, with an absorbing job, an understanding wife and a facility for making friends, had by 1940 definitely taken upon his shoulders the cares of the world.

In April he had begun a new series of Sunday afternoon broadcasts, which allowed him to be a scrutator instead of merely a spectator of momentous events, but he was not sure how many he would be able to do from Britain. Like Churchill, he had been critical of the government's indecisiveness even after Munich.

"I'm getting pretty prejudiced as far as the British are concerned, and they have made it quite clear that they don't like some of the things I've said lately," he wrote his parents. "It may be that I shall be thrown out of this country before the war starts. Several people in high places have been giving me fatherly advice about it being in my own best interest to do talks favorable to this country."

If war did come, "don't worry about me. Janet will go to the country and I shall have the nicest and softest bombproof cellar you can imagine. I have no thought of dying for Columbia Broadcasting, nor for anyone else, if it comes to that. This business is a strain on the nerves, but there will be little actual danger, probably no more than there used to be from 'widow-makers' when I was in the woods!"

The war had come and in it Murrow, the broadcaster, found himself. During the Anschluss he had been thrown into a cataclysmic situation in Vienna, and though he and radio had acquitted themselves well, it was after all a brief and passing incident in the swift progress of events. During the Munich crisis, which splashed across the Continent, he had conveyed the mood, setting and action of the British portion of the overwhelming drama, but much of his time was spent administratively rather than editorially, making arrangements for the broadcasts by which the story was so relentlessly brought to the United States.

Now, laid out before his eyes, with no distractions, continuing day after day for many months, was the spectacle of a nation fighting with its back to the wall, not only as a state but as an aggregation of human beings. It was to be Murrow's distinction to make the story of the Battle of Britain and the London Blitz one of the fortitude of the human spirit, even more than of the senseless destructiveness of war.

No other accounts of the German air assault — and they were given additional forcefulness by being spoken accounts — so brought the reality of the conflict home to Americans, or so identified them with a cause that was becoming increasingly a common one.

Bernard Shaw, whom many of his countrymen regarded as their own devil's disciple, lived to see disproved the prophecy he had made in 1934.

"Great fleets of bombing planes over capital cities will cause them to raise the white flag immediately rather than suffer destruction," he had said. But London did not capitulate.

By the time the Battle of Britain began that August, Murrow was a seasoned reporter. He had achieved excellence as a communicator of "pure news," as his colleague in New York, Elmer Davis, put it. Like most radio newsmen, who had learned their trade painstakingly in another medium, Davis was "faintly scandalized" that such good reporting could be done by a man who never worked on a newspaper.

"The only objection that can be offered to Murrow's technique of reporting is that when an air raid is on, he has the habit of going out on the roof to see what is happening, or of driving around town in an open car to see what has been hit. That is a good way to get the news, but perhaps not the best way to make sure that you will go on getting it."

Murrow's Trafalgar Square broadcast, "live" and instantaneous as all broadcasts were, even from overseas, was made the more emphatic, as so many of his reports were, by its understatement. It was part of a half-hour program that moved about London that night, from one "hot" microphone to another, nine in all. After Murrow a BBC reporter at an antiaircraft post explained the operation of the air-raid warning system. Then two CBS correspondents were heard, for the network now had its own news staff in Europe. Larry LeSueur reported from an Air Raid Precaution or ARP station. A telephone was heard ringing and someone called out, "Stretcher party, one ambulance, one car to 114 High Street. Sector 220. Messenger, don't forget your helmet." From Hammersmith's famous plebeian Palais, Eric Sevareid reported that fifteen thousand people had gathered there for their regular Saturday night dancing party and that soldiers were taking off their boots and putting on dancing pumps provided by the management.

Sevareid, a young and sensitive North Dakotan, had come to Murrow's attention through his work in the Paris *Herald*, and had been hired away from the clutch of Hugh Baillie, the president of United Press, who also wanted him as the European war drew near. Sevareid, as with so many others chosen by Murrow, failed miserably in his "voice test" to New York, but reporting ability and insight prevailed, and the voice came around, too. By this time he was already a veteran of transatlantic radio.

The "personal history" journalist Vincent Sheean, perched on a balcony overlooking Piccadilly Circus, told of the Saturday night crowds below that had been scattered by the warning sirens.

J. B. Priestley, the British author who had become Britain's favorite broadcaster, concluded the program. He was in Whitehall, the focal point of government, looking at the Cenotaph, Britain's memorial to the dead of the First World War which was now taking on the added mournful burden of the Second. This "historic ground," he said, was now "the center of the hopes of free men everywhere. The heart of this great rock that's defying the dark tide of invasion that had destroyed freedom all over western Europe."

Priestley was more fustian than most Englishmen. But nothing could deny the stark effectiveness of the program. And it could only have been done by radio.

The attack that night was on the Thames Docks. After the broadcast Murrow and Sheean went to London Bridge and from there saw the red glow spreading along the river. They knew that London's hour was striking.

The Battle of Britain had begun a few weeks before, against the Channel coast, with its ports and convoys. But the European war was by then almost a year old. During that year overseas news by radio had flourished in the United States, as the rival networks competed for news bulletins and "firsts."

Murrow and the CBS European staff, which now included Thomas Grandin in Paris, had after Munich begun to report daily on the drift toward another world war. From Munich they had moved, like the politicians, through Hitler's seizure of Czechoslovakia and Mussolini's invasion of Albania, and through the Soviet-German nonaggression pact, the obvious signal for Hitler's attack upon Poland.

All this time CBS in New York was still looking at Europe as a source of radio entertainment also, and a week before war came, as children in London took part in a test evacuation, it ordered a program called *Europe Dances*, to be broadcast from London, Paris and Berlin cabarets. Murrow and Shirer were unable to convince the entertainment-as-usual executives that the program should not be done, that it would be something like the Masque of the Red Death. In the end they simply refused to do it.

The night before the Nazi-Soviet pact was signed, Kaltenborn, broadcasting from Paris, had disappointed CBS listeners by not telling them categorically, as Americans liked to be told, whether there would be war. But he made it clear that this time the French were resolved to fight, or at any rate to go to war, which would prove to be not quite the same thing.

From London, Murrow was equally sure that appeasement was over. The Conservative Party, he reported, was behind Prime Minister Chamberlain this time only if he stood firm. Murrow disagreed with some other Americans, in the London embassy as well as in news bureaus, that there would be another Munich. He did not share the belief of the American ambassador, father of a future President, that if war came the British would go down, and that therefore they should avoid war by any means possible.

From Berlin, Shirer reported the feeling that war was certain unless Hitler's demands on Poland were met — not only Danzig and the Corridor, but Posen and Silesia — though the same night the NBC correspondent, who had better Nazi sources, stated unequivocally there would be no war and "mediation" would triumph yet again. That same day, however, the German government announced food, textile and fuel rationing. It was Saturday, August 26, 1939.

The Chamberlain government, stiffened by the Churchill-Eden opposition, sent back its ambassador to Berlin, Sir Nevile Henderson, to reply to Hitler's demands.

Murrow broadcast: "I have a feeling that Englishmen are a little proud of themselves tonight. They believe that their government's reply was pretty tough, that the Lion has turned and that the retreat from Manchukuo, Abyssinia, Spain, and Czechoslovakia and Austria, has stopped. They are amazingly calm; they still employ understatement, and they are inclined to discuss the prospect of war with, oh, a casual 'bad show,' or 'if this is peace, give me a good war.' I have heard no one say, as many said last September, 'I hope Mr. Chamberlain can find a way out.' "

He spoke to his audience in the first person, a style then in vogue in radio, and reminded it that the question whether there would be a war was heightened by the question of what it would be fought for, and what the position of the United States would be.

"And now the last word that has reached London concerning tonight's development is that at the British embassy in Berlin all the luggage of the personnel and staff has been piled up in the hall. It is remarked here that the most prominent article in the heavy luggage was a folded umbrella, given pride of placement amongst all the other pieces of baggage."

The imminence of war in Europe fastened Americans to their radios at home, while Americans in Europe rushed for steamship sailings west. Murrow, Shirer and Grandin were broadcasting four and five times a day, from noon to four o'clock the next morning. Multiple hookups for radio round tables were made for the slightest reasons. Between August 22 and 29, CBS counted eighty-one shortwave pickups from Europe and NBC seventy-nine. On Sunday the twenty-seventh alone, CBS had nineteen and NBC seventeen.

Many broadcasts came in the middle of the night, American time. During the week before the war American radio reached a new peak in news broadcasting, exceeding that of Munich, and listeners heard Chamberlain, the peace appeal of Pope Pius XII, President Roosevelt, King Victor Emanuel, and Polish President Beck.

Based on what it had learned during Anschluss and Munich, CBS depended almost entirely on its own news staff, while NBC continued to employ newspaper correspondents, parliamentarians, and other public figures as broadcasters. The CBS "family group," the trade paper *Variety* reported, "gets closer to the human element, and they get to essentials quickly, interpret past and present as simply as possible for the ordinary listener."

Moreover, as CBS in New York opened its overseas circuits, its editors told the correspondents of the latest developments in Washington and elsewhere, so that they were more aware of the context of the news as they themselves broadcast. Since they could hear one another on the circuits, they could also refer to remarks made from the other capitals, thus supplying contrast as well as continuity.

Commenting on the various broadcasters, *Variety* said, "While less facile in speech than his colleagues, Murrow in London always gets close to the dramatic and human element and furnishes an account which is clear and to the point."

Other American listeners found no lack of facility in the speech from London. On August 31, the day before Hitler sent his troops into Poland, Murrow reported on the government's decision to begin evacuating schoolchildren and invalids from the city. "Poland should conclude from this decision that war is being regarded as inevitable." He quoted from the evacuation instructions with such full attention to personal details as to make American parents listening put themselves into the harrowed place of British parents.

Women and children were helping the men dig trenches in London's parks. "Those of you who are familiar with military terminology will understand what I mean when I say that in London last night the command seemed to be 'Stand steady.' Tonight it seems to be 'Prepare for action.' "

That last night before the attack on Poland, Shirer noted in Berlin that the population generally opposed war, and that official optimism was melting away. There was no evacuation, no sandbagging, but communications with other European cities were cut off. Berlin and London were not able to talk to each other.

That night, however, Murrow in London and Shirer in Berlin were able to converse, by way of New York, as they took part in a round table. It was another radio achievement and even during the war Murrow and Shirer would often link London and Berlin when no one else could do such a thing, though the censors in both capitals had to approve in advance the scripts of proposed conversations, to guard military secrets. What they could not censor was tone of voice and inflection, frequently telling more than was in the script. Neutral America was able to hear both sides of the war.

Because Kaltenborn had been in Europe that summer CBS employed

Elmer Davis, the scholarly but down-to-earth Hoosier, as a substitute for three weeks. He remained as a commentator for three years, became a national figure heard by twelve million persons as he broadcast nightly, and would leave only to become head of the Office of War Information.

On the night before the Nazis invaded Poland, indeed as their planes were warming up and their troops beginning to move for the predawn attacks, Kaltenborn was in the New York studio, just back from Europe. He had changed his mind. He confidently predicted that Britain would not fight for Poland, and there would be no war, hinting at more Munich-type appeasement.

The Wehrmacht crossed the Polish frontier, engaged in "counter-attack," as Dr. Goebbels called it, and the Polish government appealed to Britain and France for support. London and Paris sent separate ultimatums to Hitler announcing they would help the Poles unless he withdrew his troops.

Murrow reported that the slow movement of formal diplomacy might have created the impression that appeasement again was at work. "I suggest that it is hardly time to become impatient over the delayed outbreak of a war which may spread over the world like a dark stain of death and destruction. We shall have the answer soon enough. If war comes tomorrow or the next day, most folks here believe that it will be a long war, and it is the historical belief of Britishers that wars are won at the end, not at the beginning."

He also took occasion to state on the air, for the first time of many, the principles of news broadcasting in which he believed. He mentioned the impression of possible new appeasement that listeners might have gained elsewhere. "I have had my say concerning appeasement. I reported that I have seen no evidences of it for some time. I have also given you such facts as are available in London tonight. I have an old-fashioned belief that Americans like to make up their own minds on the basis of all available information. The conclusions you draw are your own affair. I have no desire to influence them, and shall leave such efforts to those who have more confidence in their own judgment than I have in mine."

Thus was stated an issue that had already risen in the United States, that was to endure for years — indeed, it still does — and that would cause sharp conflict inside and outside the broadcasting industry, the issue of freedom of expression, or as sometimes stated, editorializing on the air.

It was not as simple as Murrow's remarks seemed to imply, and he was the first to recognize that. Whether or not Americans could and did make up their own minds, "on the basis of all available information," there may be considerable difficulty in deciding what constitutes a fact, and the selection and presentation of facts by any reporter is in itself an editorial valuation, no matter to what extent objectivity might be sought.

The war had complicated the situation. In the three years between

Munich and Pearl Harbor the official American position of neutrality toward hostilities had too often and too easily become a radio position of neutrality with respect to all American policy, including a good deal of domestic. America First broadcasts, for example, opposing aid to Britain, would escape the network restrictions on political controversy by being offered, and accepted by the National Association of Broadcasters, as "nonpartisan."

Many difficulties lay ahead, in this matter of free expression, but as the war began Murrow for his part resolved the question as he would continue to do. While not stating conclusions, he reported events as he judged them, and thereby left an imprint on whatever conclusions his listeners chose to draw.

While Berlin was undergoing its first air-raid alarm and blackout, though the only warplanes in the European sky were the Luftwaffe's own, Hitler on September 2 was considering the Allied ultimatums. Murrow reported again the continuing rumors of appeasement. "Some people have told me tonight that they believe a big deal is being cooked up which will make Munich and the betrayal of Czechoslovakia look like a pleasant tea party. I find it difficult to accept this thesis. I don't know what's in the mind of the government but I do know that to Britishers their pledged word is important, and I should be very much surprised to see any government which betrayed that pledge remain long in office.

"Most observers here agree that this country is not in the mood to accept a temporary solution. And that's why I believe Britain in the end of the day will stand where she is pledged to stand, by the side of Poland, in a war that is now in progress . . .

"What prospects of peaceful solution the government may see is to me a mystery. You know their record. You know what action they've taken in the past, but on this occasion the little man in the bowler hat, the clerks, the bus drivers, and all the others who make up the so-called rank-and-file would be reckoned with. They seem to believe that they have been patient, that they have suffered insult and injury, and they certainly believe that this time they are going to solve this matter in some sort of permanent fashion."

That Saturday in the House of Commons as Chamberlain still temporized, the acting leader of the Labor Opposition, Arthur Greenwood, was greeted by the predominantly Conservative benches with the shout "You speak for England!" as he rose to press for a decision. As the war came, and continued, whoever spoke for England in England, and it was usually Winston Churchill, Ed Murrow was to be speaking for England to Americans. No crusading was necessary.

As he saw it, the facts spoke for themselves. The test of his broadcasts is that they were not only puissant and poignant at the time, when spoken, but that three decades later they retain their qualities of forthrightness, underemphasized compassion, and moral as well as political judgment, even in written form, even though the voice is lacking, with its fatigue, its dutiful alertness, and sometimes sadness. Nor is the voice altogether absent. The better-known war broadcasts are still heard on records and occasional retrospective radio programs.

On Sunday, September 3, the decision was no longer avoidable. As Big Ben struck the quarter-hour fifteen minutes after the British ultimatum had expired at 11 A.M., Chamberlain spoke over the BBC from Downing Street. Murrow followed him with a report to the United States from a studio in the sub-basement. He had not had time to write a script, and the newly materialized and nervous censor stood with a finger on the cut-off switch in case of any violation of "military secrets."

"Forty-five minutes ago the prime minister stated that a state of war existed between Britain and Germany. Air-raid instructions were immediately broadcast, and almost directly following that broadcast the air-raid warning sirens screamed through the quiet calm of this Sabbath morning. There were planes in the sky, whose, we couldn't be sure. Now we're sitting quite comfortably underground. We're told that the all-clear signal has been sounded in the streets but it's not yet been heard in this building.

"In a few minutes we shall hope to go up in the sunlight and see what has happened. It may have been only a rehearsal. London may not have been the objective — or may have been.

"I have just been informed that upstairs in the sunlight everything is normal; that cars are traveling through the streets, there are people walking in the streets, and taxis are cruising about as usual. The crowd outside Downing Street received the first news of war with a rousing cheer, and they heard that news through a radio in a car parked near Downing Street."

Barrage balloons had gone up that morning over Regent's Park, where Murrow, like many BBC men, walked for his daily exercise because it was so near Broadcasting House. In the park people were filling sandbags for the protection of the RAF balloon crews, and deep furrows of earth had been dug among the goldenrod and asters of that sunny late-summer day.

The air-raid alert, caused by a single French civilian plane arriving from across the Channel, dispersed the crowd in Downing Street and a similar crowd which had gathered outside Parliament for the expected special Sunday session. It also drove the congregation at St. Paul's into the crypt, where it received the Blessing after the interrupted morning service.

But it was not until November that the first German bomb fell on Britain, and that on a naval installation in the remote Shetlands. Since it was not immediately disclosed, it passed unnoted. Alarms and alerts were many but not until April 1940 was the first British civilian killed on British soil, in Orkney. What began now was the period which Senator Borah of Idaho called the phoney war, the British referred to as the Bore War and the Germans the Sitzkrieg.

For though Hitler was in a state of hostilities with Britain and France, he was concerned more immediately with the shelling of Warsaw and the partition of Poland, the latter in conjunction with the Russians. Murrow reported that the war in the West was likely to be fought in its early stages with pamphlets and radio, rather than bombs, even though on the very first day the British liner *Athenia* had been sunk with a sizable loss of life, one hundred Britons and twelve Americans.

With the declaration of war, Winston Churchill had entered the Chamberlain cabinet as First Lord of the Admiralty, so the first British setback was in his province. Anthony Eden, who had resigned before the Austrian Anschluss, also returned to the cabinet as Dominions Secretary.

Murrow worked at the BBC all night the first night, and would do so many more nights. His friend R. T. Clarke had opened the news editor's room on a twenty-four-hour basis and it was here the news of the *Athenia*'s sinking was received, followed by another air-raid warning which put sirens and police whistles into action at 3 A.M.

Murrow passed on the official first communiqué, that the RAF had "reconnoitred extensive areas of northern and western Germany. They flew unmolested and dropped six million leaflets in Germany." He reported on the internment of German and Austrian nationals in Britain, explaining that the citizens of the former Czechoslovakia were not being treated as enemies. He gave details of evacuation, rationing, and the home-front mobilization of ambulance drivers and stretcher-bearers, for civilian defense.

Then he struck more deeply. "It might be useful to request the services of a good sociologist, because if this business of repeated air alarms goes on the sociological result will be considerable. This is a class-conscious country. People live in the same small street or apartment building for years and never talk to each other. The man with a fine car, good clothes, and perhaps an unearned income doesn't generally fraternize with the tradesmen, day laborers and truck drivers. His fences are always up. He doesn't meet them as equals. He's surrounded with certain evidences of worldly wealth, calculated to keep others at a distance, but if he's caught in Piccadilly Circus when the siren sounds he may have a waitress stepping on his heels, and see before him the broad back of a day laborer as he goes underground.

"If the alarm sounds about four in the morning, as it did this morning, his dignity, reserve and authority may suffer when he arrives halfdressed and sleepy, minus his usual defenses and possessed of no more courage than those others who have arrived in a similar state. Someone, I think it was Marcus Aurelius, said something to the effect that 'death put Alexander of Macedon and his stable boy on a par.'

"Maybe I'm wrong. I'm not a very good sociologist, but I can tell you this from personal experience, that sirens would improve your knowledge of even your most intimate friend."

The young broadcaster's sociology was practical enough, and Marcus Aurelius, whom he much admired, was only one of the many authorities he would cite as he sowed his broadcasts with the allusions and homilies that helped give them their depth of insight.

He went on to introduce another Murrow emblem, the cigarette-smoking he had begun in college and had appreciably increased in the long days and bleak nights of European crisis.

"I don't know how you feel about people who smoke cigarettes, but I like them, especially at night in London. That small dull red glow is a very welcome sight. It prevents collisions, makes it unnecessary to heave to until you locate the exact position of those vague voices in the darkness.

"One night several years ago I walked bang into a cow, and since then I've had a desire for man and beast to carry running lights on dark nights. They can't do that in London these nights, but the cigarettes are a good substitute."

On the day Britain went to war Janet Murrow, apparently in need of some gesture of recognition, resolved to give up smoking "for the duration." This enabled Ed to smoke all the more, for he fell heir to her American embassy cigarette ration, necessary because the British varieties had become exceedingly scarce and their numerous substitutes unsmokable.

Janet never went back to the weed, but war reinforced Murrow's habit which at its peak would be going at the rate of sixty to eighty cigarettes a day. His career, in a sense, would be intertwined with cigarettes — as visible consumer, on camera as well as off; as financial beneficiary, through sponsorship; as question-raiser, in his television programs on smoking and cancer; finally, as presumed victim.

As Murrow had predicted on the first day of war, the RAF was long engaged in mere pamphleteering. After the sinking of the *Athenia* it appeared over Cuxhaven and Wilhelmshaven, but dropped no bombs. And on the ground, though sporadic shots were exchanged on the western front between the Maginot Line and the Westwalle, the first British army casualty, a corporal shot on patrol, was not recorded until December 9. The Allied strategy, if it could be called that, seemed to be to wait for the Nazi war machine to collapse of sheer overextension, and when some raised the cry for the bombing of the Krupp armament plant it was pointed out that this, after all, was private property. Moreover such a raid might bring reprisals to Allied private property.

The inactivity gave rise to rumors that, after his crushing of Poland, Hitler would propose peace to the West. Goering said as much in a speech appealing to Chamberlain to reconsider. Murrow, commenting that such a hope was vain, went on to a more touching matter.

"This particular aspect of the war didn't hit me with full force until this afternoon, Saturday afternoon. It's dull in London now that the children are gone. For six days I've not heard a child's voice, and that's a strange feeling. No youngsters shouting their way home from school. And that's the way it is in most of Europe's big cities now. One needs the eloquence of the ancients to convey the full meaning of it. There just aren't any more children."

The German troops reached and began to surround Warsaw. President Roosevelt reaffirmed American neutrality, though he was soon to call for its repeal. The reaffirmation confronted American radio with a dilemma. Some network executives held that the sinking of the *Athenia*, which had 240 Americans among her 1400 passengers, ended American neutrality.

They felt that strict neutrality would be contrary to public feeling, which was definitely anti-Nazi, and that observance of the neutrality policy would amount to censorship. Shirer, broadcasting from Berlin the official denial that a German submarine had sunk the *Athenia*, had to make it clear that he was only reporting the Nazi statement, not vouching for its truth.

Most of the broadcasting industry, however, believed that the President's declaration of a national emergency, to enforce neutrality, did impose obligations on what was, after all, a government-licensed activity. It was also feared that stimulation of anti-German sentiments might end by putting the United States itself into the war.

The networks took the self-righteous action of reducing their coverage of the war in Europe. Both NBC and Mutual actually halted all broadcasting from the Continent, though the former would soon resume from Berlin. NBC also dropped its unsponsored commentators and limited war bulletins to factual items at scheduled times, that is, with no interruption of other programs. CBS was left for a while as the only network broadcasting from the European mainland, though it too reduced the number of war bulletins and of Kaltenborn's commentaries. That veteran broadcaster soon left the network to which he had given luster in the Munich crisis, and joined the rival NBC for a more attractive commercial arrangement.

Fear of being accused of warmongering may have entered into its cutback decision, but the broadcasting industry as usual found sound fiscal reasons for it — the huge expense of day-long war coverage, the disruption of commercial programs, the "injury to regular listening habits." The

A damp day in London, in the background the BBC and All Souls Church, which somehow escaped the bombing

During the war, representatives of Europe's exiled governments in London broadcast to America. De Gaulle was not permitted to join them. Jan Masaryk at extreme right

action, especially the elimination of nonsponsored news commentaries, deprived American listeners of the full potential of public service by the networks, and presented European events under the auspices of breakfast food or shoe polish. It was a development that would mar radio, and later television, news ever afterward.

Still, the fact that the blitzkrieg soon ended in the East, while only the "phoney war" continued in the West, did provide a rationale for the reduction of European coverage. Moreover the novelty and excitement of the Anschluss, Munich and Polish crisis reporting had worn off. The technology of overseas broadcasting was taken for granted. Four- and five-way hookups had become ordinary. Like the war itself, radio settled down for the long pull.

In England, that first fall, after reporting universal belief that the long pull would amount to three years or more, Murrow toured the country, to witness RAF training of the young men who would soon be fighting the Luftwaffe and bombing Germany. In London, he noted, taxis no longer cruised but waited for passengers, to save fuel. Bond Street shops were all sandbagged. Tailor shop windows showed uniforms instead of tweeds or dinner jackets. Siren suits for women, one-piece coveralls, had made their appearance. Air-raid shelters were marked by black and red arrows. He was struck by the fact that London policemen were "not as impressive as they used to be. Bobbies wearing tin hats instead of their famous helmets, and their khaki haversacks contrasting with their blue uniforms," had "somehow lost all the dignified solemnity of peacetime." Admiral Nelson, atop his column in Trafalgar Square, seemed "almost out of place without a tin helmet and a gas mask." Shipping offices nearby no longer advertised sailing dates. The familiar statue of Eros at Piccadilly Circus had been removed for the duration.

Murrow never ceased to be impressed by the way in which democratic processes continued to function in Britain, even as the constrictions of war increased. The battleship *Royal Oak* had been sunk by a U-boat sneaking into the inner defenses at Scapa Flow. But Parliament had other matters on its mind.

"The Labor Party harasses the government's front benches with questions about allowances for soldiers' wives, profiteering, Indian policy and the qualifications of men appointed to handle a new department. There is a considerable number of Opposition members who maintain that Mr. Chamberlain is fighting a war on two fronts — against Hitlerism, and against changes in the social and economic structure of Britain. They profess to see a reflection of this policy in his ministerial appointments. They claim that too much of the supply and transport of Britain has been handed over to big business."

Despite the great debate that still went on in wartime, Murrow remarked one casualty. "Something is happening to conversation in London. There isn't much of it. You meet a friend, exchange guesses about the latest diplomatic move, inquire about a mutual friend who has been called up, and then fall silent. Nothing seems important, not even the weather. The experts — the political experts, not the weather experts — sound as though they were trying to convince themselves of their own expertness.

"Don't get the idea that these people are discouraged, or defeated. They are confident of winning this war somehow or other. They still exercise the Briton's right to complain. They haven't lost their sense of humor. But it seems that in this war courage and patience are the supreme virtues. Wit, happiness, manners and conversation sink gradually."

But war, even without the fighting, stirred up other activities. London nightlife was booming, Murrow reported. "There are more dance bands playing in London's West End now than in the months before peace went underground. Many establishments where one could eat without musical distraction in the old days have now engaged small orchestras. Customers want to dance. Places . . . are jammed nearly every night. People come early and stay late. Uniforms and civilian clothes are about evenly divided, but practically no one wears formal evening dress. That's a change.

"There is something of a speakeasy atmosphere about London's nightclubs. It seems that those who frequent restaurants and clubs are either more fatalistic or more careless than the average Londoner; anyway, few of them carry gas masks . . . But don't get the idea that all London sits about waiting for darkness and drink. Plenty of people here know nothing and care less about London's nightclubs and the nightclub life."

Cliveden, like other stately homes, had become an auxiliary hospital and a center for evacuated children from London's East End. But as the "phoney war" continued many of the evacuees came back from the country, and attendance in the air-raid shelters slackened off. In social circles the principal sacrifice of the war was giving up dressing for dinner.

On November 23, which was Thanksgiving Day in the United States, the first naval action of the war took place, the sinking in battle off Iceland of the armed merchant cruiser *Rawalpindi* by German warships. It was duly reported by the CBS correspondent. But Thanksgiving was also marked by the first radio broadcast of the CBS correspondent's wife, reflecting that while it was not a holiday in Britain it still had some meaning for Americans abroad in someone else's wartime. As the war continued, Janet would make many more broadcasts, on such subjects as food rationing, the scarcity of cosmetics, the dream of postwar nylons, the separation of parents from their children, and other "women's angles."

Murrow had reported that as the Battle of the Atlantic began to be joined, fishing trawlers were augmenting Britain's mine-sweeping fleet, and merchant sailors and fishermen were signing up at Grimsby for that service. Now he suggested to New York that he might profitably go out with the mine-sweepers, and was expressly forbidden to do so by Paul White. A day or two later he reported he was going to the country for a few days' rest, at the weekend cottage he and Janet had taken at Stanford Dingley in Berkshire.

The next time he broadcast he described the mine-sweeping expedition he had just returned from, an undramatic but nevertheless dangerous operation. "Mine-sweeping may not be magnificent but it's war," he concluded, reversing the judgment made of the Charge of the Light Brigade.

It was the first of many occasions when he disregarded safety for the sake of a story, contributing to Klauber's and White's gray hairs in New York.

The North Sea mine-sweeping venture was not a CBS exclusive. Also aboard was Murrow's NBC rival, Fred Bate. Indeed the BBC and other British organizations, to play fair with the American press and radio, insisted that there could be no exclusive story, under British auspices, for any newspaper or network, and the Americans went out in pairs, often in droves. So it was that Bate was with Murrow on many joint undertakings — visits to airfields and training camps, on bombing raids, and riding ambulances in the London Blitz. Each would then broadcast his own account, sitting together in a BBC underground studio, indeed often sharing the same circuit to New York, and nightly alternating the order of their speaking.

In the spirit of competition, NBC did virtually everything CBS did in the coverage of the war, and in the number of its broadcasts. "The difference," Fred Bate cheerfully confessed, "was that CBS had something we didn't have — Ed Murrow."

The Russian invasion of Finland and the bombing of Helsinki on November 30 began to end the phoney war period in Europe. Though it was remote from London, Finland was considered a part of western Europe and anti-Soviet feeling ran high in Britain. Also, the Nazi press had begun to talk about Britain's "aggressive designs in Scandinavia," an ominous augury for that peninsula despite its proclaimed neutrality.

From the Mannerheim Line in Finland, William L. White made some notable CBS broadcasts by an intricate arrangement. This took them by telephone to Helsinki, then submarine cable under the Baltic to Stockholm and Swedish landline to the south coast, more underwater transmission to Germany and across that country to Switzerland and the shortwave transmitter at Geneva. But NBC began to use Geneva whenever CBS wanted it.

Murrow solved the problem in London. He got the BBC to pick up the Swedish medium-wave transmitter, which in turn was receiving the CBS Helsinki broadcasts by telephone. They were piped by BBC to the shortwave transmitter at Rugby and relayed to New York. Their quality was accounted better than NBC's via Geneva, and they reawakened American interest in what had become for many a not entirely believable war.

From London, Murrow discoursed on "an interesting but unimportant war phenomenon." He reported that "all technical and documentary evidence about the so-called English climate has been suppressed. We aren't told what the weather is going to be, what it is, nor yet what it has been. Broadcasts don't mention the weather, nor do the papers. It must be two weeks old before it's considered a fit subject for public comment.

"Englishmen love to talk about their weather. Continentals have claimed that the Englishman's real home is in his barometer, that he is unable to forget it even during romantic unlit intervals. In prewar days Britain seemed to be a small island located halfway between a deep depression over Iceland and a high-pressure ridge near the Azores. Any Englishman could talk about his weather for fifteen minutes without repeating himself. But all that is changed. The weather is now dismissed with a few curt, but not always courteous, phrases. The weather prophets prepare their prognostications for the fighting forces, and the layman takes what comes. If it should rain soup the poor man would have no spoon, because he would have had no warning."

A few days later he discussed Britain's conscientious objectors, for three of every hundred called to military service asked for exemption — "the misfits, cowards, men of moral courage, call them what you will." He described the proceedings of a local board hearing cases, the exemptions on religious or other grounds, and the denials.

The most striking argument was that of an Oxford student. "He says that he is willing to defend Britain, but he doesn't believe that this is a defensive war. Rather than wreck the world, he would submit to German domination. He quotes Chamberlain as saying that the war is being fought in defense of small nations, and goes on to say that he is not interested in the small nations, and is prepared to go to jail rather than fight. His case takes twenty minutes before it is decided that he needn't fight."

There was also a young Welsh nationalist who refused to recognize the right of "England" to send him out to fight but said he would fight for Wales, provided the Welsh had the right to decide for themselves what they should and should not fight for. "The men on the bench tried to reason with him, pointing out that the Welsh members of Parliament voted for war, but he will have none of it. He refuses to recognize that a majority must be right. Decision has been reserved in his case and when the issue is settled an important precedent will be established."

Murrow thought that the men on the bench really tried to understand the objections. "I asked them for a definition of conscience and they couldn't give me one. But they all agreed that a British subject should have the right to say what his conscience dictates before he is forced to fight."

The first wartime Christmas was a doleful one in both London and Berlin, as Murrow and Shirer reported. An English newspaper cartoon showed Santa Claus's sleigh, an unidentified aircraft, being shot at by anti-aircraft guns.

On Christmas Day the Murrows were dining with Ivison Macadam, the head of Chatham House, as the Royal Institute for International Affairs was known. He had also become deputy director of the new wartime Ministry of Information under Sir John Reith. The normally cheerful Scotsman, whom Ed had known from the prewar days of student affairs, and his American wife were downcast by the absence of their two children, aged six and two, evacuated to the United States like so many others.

Murrow was also preoccupied. "I've got to broadcast and I have no story," he said. "I can't even talk about the weather [there was a London pea-soup fog on] because of military security." Then he was struck with an idea, and dispatched cables to America. A few hours later, in the middle of the night, in fact, the Macadamses found themselves in the BBC sub-basement talking to their children in Portland, Oregon. The conversation, heard throughout the United States on CBS, was the first of the six wartime Christmas broadcasts to which Murrow tried to impart a special Anglo-American flavor.

On New Year's Eve, when no horns were blown in London lest they be mistaken for air-raid warnings, Murrow broadcast a year-end report recalling the events of 1939, commenting on the disruptions, even without combat, caused by "a war which has confounded the experts," and foreseeing blockade, rather than bombardment or infantry action, as the Allied strategy for 1940. "The uncertainty remains, plus a large degree of boredom," he said.

To escape the boredom and the rationing, and to compare notes, Murrow and Shirer left their capitals briefly and met at the neutral halfway point, Amsterdam. Both were exuberant at the temporary release from what was more drudgery than danger. Coming back to the hotel from a large dinner, tramping between the canals in falling snow, they had a battle of their own with snowballs. They went ice skating, quaffed genever, visited the museum, and marveled at the Dutch store windows that were as fully stuffed as Dutch pillows.

They broadcast together to the United States, and Murrow showed that he was perturbed by British muddling and the belief in blockade as a decisive factor in the war. They also tried to tell the Dutch that their well-fed complacency was dangerous. Mijnheeren smiled and said they were neutral.

The Russo-Finnish War, at least, was real, and Murrow returned to London as the Russians attacked the Mannerheim Line. He was laid up for a week with respiratory trouble and a serious throat infection which he blamed on his frolicking in the Amsterdam snow, but his discomfort was more than physical.

"There is much discussion here of assistance to Finland," he broadcast, "but nothing new to report other than voluntary contributions. The military experts agree that assistance, if it's to be effective, must be immediate. But there's another consideration worth thinking about, and that is how long men's minds can retain the indignation caused by events in Finland.

"How many of us retain much of the sentiment or emotion felt over Austria, Abyssinia, Czechoslovakia or Albania? Those places just aren't talked about any more. There seems to be in certain quarters an almost academic interest in how long the Finns can hold out. The indignation and the urge to act resulting from the invasion of Finland appear to be evaporating, although British sympathy for the Finns is strong." In the United States, equally strong sympathy reduced itself in the end to the form of appropriations for "nonmilitary loans."

After Russia and Finland reached an armistice in March, Murrow remarked that American failure to help Finland had stirred a growing British feeling that "American statements about not selling small democracies down the river were just pious platitudes, and nothing else."

He also noted a tendency to point out that, under the cash-and-carry law which had replaced the strict arms embargo, American industries and investors would be making profits out of Britain's war, the more heinously because trade was also being carried on with the Soviet Union, reckoned to be on the other side.

It was a somber report on the suspicion-laden state of Anglo-American relations, and it centered about the person of the American ambassador to the Court of St. James's, Joseph P. Kennedy. He had just returned to London from a three-month visit to the United States — which he spent making isolationist speeches — with the remark that Americans "fail to understand this war."

Murrow quoted a British editorial suggestion that Mr. Kennedy ought to explain it to them, since he had had an opportunity to study it at first hand. He also cited the comment by Harold Nicolson, M.P., that the ambassador would be welcomed back to London only by the American business colony, which "still believed in appeasement," by "the bankers, the knights and baronets . . . the peace-pledge union, the friends of Herr von Ribbentrop, and the members of former pro-Nazi organizations."

"There is no doubt that a considerable number of people over here have resented Mr. Kennedy's utterances concerning the war," Murrow reported, leaving no doubt that he was one of them. "The British aren't accustomed to ambassadors expressing their frank opinions on international affairs in public. It isn't in the British tradition." Even worse, to Murrow's mind, was the fact that the ambassador's frank opinions were wrong ones.

The self-made multimillionaire from Boston, who had campaigned and raised funds for Roosevelt, had finally been rewarded with the ambassadorship at his own request, though diplomacy would seem the least likely of careers for a man not noted for circumspection.

He had arrived in London in 1938 in the midst of the Anschluss crisis, and it and the Munich pact six months later confirmed him in his isolationism, shared by many in the United States.

Kennedy's ambassadorship began in full tune with British appeasement. His British friends were indeed the bankers. His heart beat in time with Neville Chamberlain's and he called the prime minister by his first name. The Boston Irishman joined the "Cliveden Set," and danced at the Astors' town mansion in St. James Square. He believed with Lord and Lady Astor, and most of Chamberlain's cabinet, that nazism was preferable to war, for the result of war would be communism.

Meanwhile his son John, who had spent a summer at the London School of Economics two years before, under Harold Laski, was making his own notes on Europe at the London embassy, after visiting the Continent. "Have come to the decision that Fascism is the thing for Germany and Italy, Communism for Russia, and Democracy for America and England," he wrote down.

The elder Kennedy, a gregarious and injudicious man, was not only easily accessible to reporters at the embassy in Grosvenor Square, but freehanded with them. As he sat talking to them, with feet propped on the desk, he presented a peculiar problem to the American correspondents. They could not afford to ignore an important news source, and indeed could not help liking the breezy Bostonian personally, yet felt that the ambassador's dispatches — or as he preferred, his long transatlantic telephone conversations — did not constitute diplomatic reporting at its most perspicacious.

Murrow shunned the American colony of businessmen, oilmen and travel agents, who had their own reasons for wanting peace at any price, and the embassy was an uncomfortable port of call for him on his daily round of news sources.

These included Downing Street, the Foreign Office, the War Office, the Admiralty — where Winston Churchill was now ensconced — the pubs of Fleet Street and the clubs of Pall Mall. Foreign legations were also on a correspondent's itinerary, and later, as the war spread and deepened in Europe, various governments-in-exile would take up quarters in London, not to mention the American military and economic offices that would be set up when the United States entered the conflict.

The British government agencies included the cumbersome Ministry of Information, which was responsible neither for news nor for policy, and invidious to nearly everyone, for it was frankly the scapegoat for the separate cabinet ministries. American relations with the MOI were somewhat tempered by the presence there of Ivison Macadam. Complaints from the American press and radio were more seriously taken than those from the home press. "I speak your language," Macadam assured the Americans, affecting his wooliest Highland brogue and causing gales of laughter.

In war, even more than in peace, the place of American news correspondents in London was a special one. They were the primary channel to American interest and help. They were sought out by cabinet officers and society hostesses, lunched, dined and wined; talked to, and talked at. Most of them were not persuaded by Chamberlain and appeasement.

Before the fall of France, however, in the full bloom of the Kennedy ambassadorship, Murrow and other American reporters in London had their difficulties. On the one hand were British hopes, still somehow persisting, that Hitler had finally been satisfied with his conquests in eastern Europe and would not turn west. On the other were American fears, the perennial ones, of European entanglement, and mistrust of European, especially British, motives. Many Americans believed with Kennedy that Britain would expect the United States "to pull her chestnuts out of the fire."

During the Munich crisis Kennedy had taken it upon himself to assure Chamberlain of Roosevelt's unequivocal support, "whatever he did." He was reprimanded by the President for talking too much in public, and had to delete from a speech in Aberdeen the remark, "I can't for the life of me understand why anyone would want to go to war to save the Czechs." On Charles A. Lindbergh's say-so, after a visit to Germany, Kennedy assured the British that the Luftwaffe was truly invincible.

The ambassador was in the House of Commons diplomatic gallery when Chamberlain theatrically received Hitler's invitation to Munich, and smiled in approval. "Now I can spend Christmas in Palm Beach, as I planned," he said to Jan Masaryk of all people, and did so. At the Foreign Office's request he got the Hays film office in London to censor an American newsreel in which British editors criticized the appeasement policy.

Even after Hitler's seizure of Czechoslovakia Kennedy continued in favor of appeasement, though many Britons had become disillusioned with it. He made speeches in Britain calling for coexistence with the dictators, including one at a Trafalgar Day dinner which caused an uproar at home.

For it provoked both isolationists and interventionists, the latter because it proclaimed American disinterest in what Hitler did, the former because it identified American interests with the Chamberlain government. The speech especially aroused American Jews. And whatever else, it mirrored the ambiguity and uncertainty of American policies and feelings. Public opinion polls showed a majority of Americans favoring increased aid to Britain, but a similar majority opposed to American entry into the war.

As the war approached, Kennedy had continued to harbor faith in another Munich-like deal with Hitler to avert it, proposing to the President that the United States "put pressure" on the Poles. Even after war began, he urged the President to intervene as peacemaker. Both ideas were curtly refused by the White House.

When Ambassador Kennedy finally returned to London, in the spring of 1940, another Roosevelt envoy was on the same ship, the first of many private emissaries the President would dispatch on war missions. He was Bernard Baruch, an old friend of Churchill's, and he would consult with the First Lord of the Admiralty, leaving Chamberlain to the man who understood him so well, Joe Kennedy.

Murrow broadcast: "American talk of a negotiated peace sounds strange to many Englishmen, because they maintain that sincere and honest efforts were made to negotiate a peace before the war started." He continued on a note of foreboding. "American assistance and support, economic and moral, are welcomed in Britain, but advice as to how the war should be conducted or how the peace should be made is distinctly less welcome. So there are many people over here who foresee a certain amount of friction with the United States during the coming months."

He enlarged upon the theme in a letter to his parents. "The news from home is not encouraging. From here it appears that many people at home do not realize the lateness of the hour. This business is no child's game and we shall not come out of it without sacrifices far beyond anything so far experienced. At times it seems that our country has gone soft, as I once thought this country had. The price for soft living must be paid, and we may soon be paying that price.

"I remember you once wanted me to be a preacher, but I had no faith, except in myself. But now I am preaching from a powerful pulpit. Often I am wrong but I am trying to talk as I would have talked were I a preacher. One need not wear a reversed collar to be honest."

New events, however, were about to lessen tensions and bring the two English-speaking nations closer.

Hitler moved against Denmark and Norway. A British expeditionary force, originally prepared to go to Finland, failed in Norway. Chamberlain, exulting that Hitler had "missed the bus" by exposing himself to

British sea power, tried to portray the Norwegian retreat as a kind of victory and managed to eke out a vote of confidence, despite a large abstention within his own Conservative ranks.

The Norwegian campaign was the first test of British wartime information, and false and exaggerated news of the progress of British forces, put out by the armed services, reported Murrow, caused a great loss of public confidence in the government.

Nevertheless he saw no likelihood of a governmental change, because the required group of men ready and willing to take over from Chamberlain "had not yet been formed." He went on: "The future of this government rests largely in the rather pudgy hands of Winston Churchill. If he should openly blame the political leadership of the country for the reverse in Norway, Mr. Chamberlain's government might be forced to resign. So far, there is no indication that the First Lord contemplates such action."

Three days after the vote of confidence, however, the action was thrust upon him. For Hitler went on to invade Belgium, Holland and Luxembourg with ground forces and parachute troops, and his bombers blasted out the center of Rotterdam. The Chamberlain government resigned, after Labor refused to enter a coalition under the "Birmingham undertaker," as Churchill once called him, and Churchill himself became prime minister. Chamberlain remained as the president of the council, and Lord Halifax, another "man of Munich," remained as foreign secretary, though the anti-appeasement Anthony Eden became secretary for war.

The new government was confirmed by a Commons vote of 318–0 and Churchill made his declaration, "I have nothing to offer but blood, tears, toil and sweat."

Since he spoke within the confines of Parliament and did not repeat the speech later on the BBC, as he frequently did, his words were not heard outside Westminster. But so strong was their impact that after the war, when Murrow assembled a record album of Churchill speeches, he was told to be sure and include the message so vividly remembered by many that they could "hear it now." Churchill repeated the words in another speech after Alamein, more than two years later, and that version was recorded.

Murrow, speaking about the Churchill appeal, explained that the fallen Chamberlain had "made the mistake of asking too little rather than too much, of the people of this country." He noted that Churchill was sagaciously putting all the leading critics of various aspects of the war effort in charge of those same aspects.

The British army retreated through Belgium to the coast at Dunkerque, and he reported that "the British revolution — part of it, at least — occurred today." Clement Attlee, the Labor Party leader now in the Churchill war cabinet, had announced the government's intention of assuming "complete control of all persons and all property." In fact, under the Emergency Powers Defense Act, it could take over "everything except one's debts." As Attlee spoke barbed wire was being put around the Houses of Parliament, and sandbag and machine gun emplacements before the government buildings in Whitehall. German troops stood on the other side of the Channel.

"The revolution announced today by that small man in rather ill-fitting clothes and loose collar marked the course along which Britain will travel.

"This country has been ruled by men with extensive stakes in the profits of industry, by an oligarchy which has believed in its right to rule. Whether they have ruled well or ill is not at this moment important. The remote past has been blotted out by the news.

"Britain now places supreme control over the individual in the hands of the government. It's a new government. Had the old government recognized the lateness of the hour these new powers might not have been necessary, but this country is now united and it is important that a lifelong Socialist introduced the revolutionary bill today."

As always, Murrow was looking beyond military events and political personalities, including the Churchill personality, to the historical and social implications of the situation. He also foresaw another British move. "I believe Britain is about to increase her propaganda effort in the United States, and the attitude as I've heard it is this — the Americans think we're making propaganda anyway, so why shouldn't we do a better job of it? The British believe they have a good case and a good cause, and you can expect them to tell you more about it in the near future."

But the war itself made the most convincing propaganda in the United States. The "miracle" which Ambassador Kennedy said would be necessary to save the British expeditionary force in Belgium did occur at Dunkerque, and 335,000 men were saved. And ten days later German troops entered Paris. The fall of France left Britain alone, and set the stage for the Nazi air offensive designed to soften her up for invasion — unless she chose to surrender first.

During the Dunkerque evacuation Murrow spent his days along the Channel coast, usually at airfields with the pilots who were covering the movement, and at night drove back to London to broadcast. He saw the preparations for the expected German airborne operations — barricades, gun emplacements, trucks and tractors to be pushed onto runways, sentries with fixed bayonets, and the complete absence of road signs and place names. "The only thing to tell the traveller that Canterbury is Canterbury is the big cathedral rising out of the plain."

With Fred Bate, who knew General Alexander, he visited that commander, in charge of some of the coastal defenses, and was informed that the "miracle of Dunkerque" had been wrought only because of Hitler's anxiety to take Paris, and thus, as he thought, end the war in the West. German forces pursuing the BEF therefore veered off toward Paris, after merely making sure that the retreating columns had been pushed onto the beaches.

Murrow did not presume to call Dunkerque a victory, as some did, but said it was certainly a highly successful military operation, and noted that German losses in Flanders had been considerable. But the British force had been inadequately equipped. "The responsibility for this state of affairs rests squarely upon the men who led this country until a few weeks ago. They purchased a few months of normal living and normal working while assuring the country that all was well and that time was on the side of the Allies. But they bought that quiet and complacency in an expensive market."

At an airfield on the southeast coast he talked with fighter pilots who, though outnumbered, had engaged the Luftwaffe over Dunkerque. "A boy of twenty drove up in a station wagon. He weighed about 115 pounds. He asked the squadron leader if he could have someone to fly him back to his own field. His voice was loud and flat. His uniform was torn, had obviously been wet. He wore a pair of brown tennis shoes, three sizes too big. After he'd gone I asked one of the men who had been talking with him what was the matter with him. 'Oh,' he replied, 'he was shot down over Dunkerque on the first patrol this morning. Landed in the sea, swam to the beach, was bombed for a couple of hours, came home in a paddle steamer. His voice sounds like that because he can't hear himself. You get that way after you've been bombed a few hours,' he said."

Murrow was in the House of Commons the afternoon Churchill gave his report on Dunkerque, and described him as "Britain's tired old man of the sea."

As Churchill spoke of the RAF, which had bested the German air force, Ed noted that he "needed only wings and an engine to take off." But the prime minister did not conceal the fact that "a colossal disaster had occurred, and another blow must be expected almost immediately."

It was one of Churchill's greatest speeches. "I have heard Mr. Churchill in the House of Commons at intervals over the last ten years," Murrow said, going back to his first student visit to England. "I heard his speech on the Norwegian campaign and I have some knowledge of his writings. Today he was different. There was little oratory. He wasn't interested in being a showman. He spoke the language of Shakespeare, with a direct urgency such as I have never heard before in that House."

"We shall go on to the end," the prime minister had said. "We shall fight in France, we shall fight on the seas and oceans, we shall fight on the beaches, in the fields, in the streets, in the hills. We shall never surrender."

When Churchill repeated his speech that night over the BBC, it went beyond the Shakespearean. Those in the studio said that after his ringing words he put his hand over the microphone and added, "We'll hit them on the head with beer bottles, which is all we have to fight with."

With the evacuation of Dunkerque, Murrow reported, "there was a breathing space tonight, but no one here expects it to last long."

It lasted for a month. Then the Germans began to step up their air attacks on England and Scotland, and soon were sending over wave after wave of bombers. The Pétain regime was functioning in Vichy, but General de Gaulle was broadcasting from London as head of the Free French movement to whatever resistance forces there might be in France. "C'est moi, Général de Gaulle, qui parle."

In the United States the CBS network removed its ban on war songs, which had been regarded as unneutral. They were all, naturally, from the First World War, and its New York station played a medley of five of them — "Over There," "Tipperary," "Till We Meet Again," "K-k-k-katy," and "Pack Up Your Troubles."

Before the fall of France the network was spending thirty thousand dollars a month for war news, but Nazi conquest and Soviet encroachment had narrowed the European area of coverage. Helsinki was heard no more, nor Bucharest. Broadcasting was limited to London, Berlin and Rome. Though Shirer could report the progress of the Wehrmacht through Belgium and France, from various cities, he of course did so under German control. Sometimes he was able to evade it, as on the occasion of the armistice signing in the Compiègne Forest, a clear triumph for radio against all other media.

The fall of France stirred American apprehensions and increased anti-Nazi sentiments in the United States, often in extravagant ways. A local radio station in Milwaukee changed the name of its *German Hour* to the *Musical Sunshine Hour*. A band called Heinie and His Grenadiers was rechristened. Hitler's speech to the Reichstag, after the fall of France, was sponsored on CBS by a soap company in place of its regular program, *The Rise of the Goldbergs*. But a West Coast radio chain cut the Hitler speech off the air and announced it would not let its listeners hear the Fuehrer again "unless he mends his ways."

More pertinently, it was the fall of France that aroused the United States to more active support of Britain. Ambassador Kennedy was still prognosticating sure defeat for the British if they did not come to terms with Hitler, but President Roosevelt sent personal envoys to Britain to survey matters from another frame of reference, namely that of giving the British fifty overage destroyers in exchange for air and naval bases.

They reported that Britain could "take it," despite any amount of German bombing, and one of them, Lieutenant Colonel Carl Spaatz, of the Air Force, said flatly that Britain would not be invaded. The Germans would not attempt an invasion until they had beaten the Royal Air Force, and that, thought Spaatz, they would never do.

The British nevertheless were preparing for an invasion. Hitler had set mid-September as the time for Operation Sea Lion, as the invasion plan was called, and Churchill told Commons, "We await undismayed the impending assault." German dive bombers attacked Channel ports and shipping, and aerial dogfights were fought over the white cliffs of Dover. One of them made radio history, the first eyewitness account of such a battle, recorded by the BBC and broadcast in the United States despite the continuing network restriction on recordings.

On a tour of invasion preparations, Murrow visited a new-formed British battalion at Dungeness, and in spite of its lack of equipment and training, convinced its young recruits that they could repel any landings or airdrops. He talked to them like a cadet colonel at Washington State College, and also made an unforgettable impression on a young Eton schoolboy, John Grigg, who witnessed the scene with his father Sir Edward, an official in Anthony Eden's War Office. The American correspondent became fast friends with both father and son, the one to be given the title of Baron Altrincham, the other to become a "reluctant peer" who would renounce the title.

By mid-August Murrow, driving about the countryside, was reporting increasing German bombing attacks on airfields and shore installations. On one occasion he and Fred Bate had just left the Portland Naval Base when the bombers descended upon it, and the antiaircraft guns opened up. They witnessed the attack from a short distance on the road home.

All southern England had become an amphitheater for watching bombardments and aerial actions. "In some of the cities and larger towns people stand about in the streets, but the small villages take cover."

The king drove through one village and the two Americans followed the royal car back to London, wondering at the minimum amount of official protection accorded — one police car ahead and one motorcycle behind. As they reached the city air-raid sirens were sounding. With the all-clear, people resumed their box-office wait, sitting on their canvas chairs, for that night's concert at Queen's Hall, which was opposite the CBS office.

"I have come to the conclusion that bombs that fall some distance away seem very unreal. Queen's Hall is only about half an hour from Croydon airport, which in the British vernacular 'bought a packet' last night, but from the attitude of those people on the sidewalk, it might have been hundreds of miles away. One thing I do know. The bombs that drop close to you are real enough."

Not many weeks later, as the Germans turned their air might against London, the BBC would be hit and the CBS office bombed out, for the first of several times, while in another heavy attack Queen's Hall would be demolished.

With bombs beginning to fall on the London metropolitan area, Murrow reported on the nature of some of the explosions he witnessed. He was surprised by how little damage a bomb might do, unless by a direct hit. He noticed that window glass was blown out, not in. He gave the recommended position, "most undignified," that was assumed "without effort and without thinking" when a bomb hit nearby: "flat on the ground, face down, mouth slightly open, and hands covering ears."

He drove about London in an open car which he admitted was "not to be recommended" if only because of wet weather, but said it was helpful "to be able to look and listen as you drive along." Once he accelerated his little car through the darkness of the blackout, with an apprehensive Fred Bate beside him, and halted suddenly as an even blacker mass confronted them. He had stopped within inches of the barrel of a giant naval gun, being silently rolled through the streets on rubber tires.

He reported the air of unreality that bombings had for him. The planes usually could not be seen. The bombs "don't seem to make as much noise as they should." Anticipated reaction was not felt. "The sense of danger, death and disaster comes only when the familiar incidents occur, the things that one has associated with tragedy since childhood. The sight of half a dozen ambulances weighted down with an unseen cargo of human wreckage has jarred me more than the war of dive bombers or the sound of bombs. Another thing that has meaning is fire. Again, that's something we can understand.

"Last night as I stood on London Bridge with Vincent Sheean and watched that red glow in the sky, it's possible to understand that that's fire, as the result of an act of war. But the act itself, even the sound of the bomb that started the fire, was still unreal. What had happened was that three or four high-school boys with some special training had been flying about over London in about one hundred thousand dollars worth of machinery. One of them had pressed a button, and the fire and a number of casualties was the result.

"We could see the fire and hear the clanging of the fire-engine bells, but we hadn't seen the bomber, had barely heard him. Maybe the children who are now growing up will in future wars be able to associate the sound of bombs, the drone of engines, and the carrying sound of machine guns overhead, with human tragedy and disaster. But for me the ambulance and the red flare of fire in the night sky are the outward signs of death and destruction."

Between August 24 and September 6 the Luftwaffe flew more than a thousand sorties daily against the island, in what has come to be known as the Battle of Britain. This was distinguished from the Blitz on London, between September 7 and 18, and from the massive raids on provincial cities which followed it and continued intermittently through the winter. The Luftwaffe's efforts would reach a destructive climax the following spring, before Hitler turned his attention to the invasion of Russia instead.

During the Battle of Britain, fought in the air along the coast, and witnessed by residents of south England from their gardens — into which destroyed planes and parachuted pilots fell with some regularity — Murrow and other American correspondents had a front-seat view from the top of Shakespeare Cliff west of Dover, so-called because of its supposed association with King Lear.

The barrage balloons hung suspended over the Channel, and antiaircraft batteries near Dover Castle put lethal puffs into the sky against the attacking Heinkels and Junkers. British fighters tangled with Messerschmidts in the cloud-flecked blue, and Murrow ranged up and down the coast, from one airfield to another, talking to the British pilots who were "so few." Shirer, on the other side of the Channel, was meanwhile being forbidden to talk to returning German pilots, and Goering used several devices in order to conceal the extent of the Luftwaffe losses, like sending returned planes to fields other than those from which they had started.

As Murrow moved about southern England, he sometimes met Janet for a Saturday of rest at the Wilderness, a golf club near Sevenoaks in Kent. Dr. John Frew, of Guy's Hospital, a Scotsman, was his usual golfing partner and often the Frews and Murrows made a foursome. Sometimes Ed would take Dr. Frew back to London with him to broadcast, something he did with many of his English friends.

The two men, after dinner, would walk around the courtyard fountain sometimes until 3 A.M. — "both were great arguers," the others said — and talk not only about the war and what would come after, but debate such abstruse questions as whether animals went to heaven. Ed defended the thesis, though he was not sure humans went to heaven, either, and he would also have cheerfully taken the other side.

He would drive back to London to broadcast, the railway line being always bombed out, and sometimes after being up all night in the studio would drive back to Kent in the morning and return to London on Sunday evening, still without sleep. He "lived on coffee and cigarettes," Janet remembered, and of course on his nerves.

During the Blitz he wrote to his parents not to worry about him and Janet. "If the end comes it won't be too bad. I'm free of hatred, not too much ashamed of my life, convinced that individuals are not very important, convinced that I've done this job as honestly as I am able, done it in a way which you who are responsible for this life of mine need not be ashamed of."

While the Germans were intensifying their assault against Britain, preparatory to the scheduled invasion, the British made their first big air raid on Berlin. They inflicted no casualties, but panicked a population which did not believe such a thing could happen. It had been told by Goebbels that the RAF had been wiped out.

Two days later Berlin was hit again and this time Germans were killed. Shirer, at the radio transmitter as the bombs fell, was forbidden to report that an air raid was in progress, though Murrow would freely describe, within the limits of military security, those which took place while he was broadcasting.

The Germans used the raids on Berlin as their official excuse for bombing London, though they had already been doing so sporadically for two weeks.

During that time Murrow visited London air-raid shelters and talked to people gathered underground. He stood on the rooftops watching bombers strike other rooftops. He himself was a fire warden in his neighborhood — in his "spare time," he wryly said — and on several occasions handled nearby hits of incendiaries by smothering them in sand.

"Have reached point where hands shake so much, can't even read my own writing," he said in a note to his brother Lacey, then an Air Force lieutenant colonel. "Hasten to say that overwork and no sleep is responsible, not fright. If I had an idea you'd do anything about it, I'd ask you to pull a few wires and see if my commission could be restored. Think I could earn my pay in someone's intelligence corps. May pull out of here some day and go to Washington and see what I can do about it.

"Tis pleasant surprise to find out am not frightened when bombed, shelled and machine-gunned. Have had experience under all three now. Nearest bomb about 150 yards away, which close enough. Shelling definitely worst of the three. Have hunch today may stop one before this thing is over.

"Am going to Dover again tomorrow. No particular reason for going but just can't stay away. Maybe it's because that shelling shakes me up a bit and I want to find out why. The place is fascinating, like Madrid and Vienna. The shells make no noise, maybe that's why they seem harder to take.

"Janet is grand, good nerves, maybe because she's part Swede? Spending all her time evacuating children to the States, a proceeding which seems to me misguided. This business can't be faced by running away."

Much the same conclusion was being reached in Washington. Though it was somewhat late to help against the expected invasion, President Roosevelt had announced the exchange of destroyers for bases, thus ending American neutrality. The date was September 3, the first anniversary of the start of the European war, and on it the Luftwaffe struck in force three times at the British coast. The next day Hitler, speaking in the Berlin Sportpalast, vowed to destroy Britain from the air.

On the afternoon of Saturday, September 7, as Goering watched from the cliff at Cape Gris Nez on the French Channel coast, the mass air attacks on London began. At 4 P.M. the Luftwaffe took off, and over a period of ten hours three hundred bombers and six hundred fighters flew against the city, ravaging the Thames River docks and the East End and killing a thousand persons and injuring several thousand. After an early evening attack, which set oil installations ablaze and hit Woolwich Arsenal, the night bombers came, and used the raging fires to guide them to new targets. The thickly populated dockside boroughs of Poplar, West Ham, Stepney and Bermondsey were devastated by blast and flame.

Murrow and two other American correspondents witnessed the onslaught against London from the mouth of the Thames estuary. He had driven down the river that afternoon with Vincent Sheean and Ben Robertson, looking for a story. They could have no foreknowledge that it was Der Tag.

After they had crossed by ferry from Tilbury to Gravesend they were told that a Dornier bomber had crashed nearby and tried to locate it. Before they could, more Dorniers were overhead. They saw British Spitfires and Hurricanes climbing up in pursuit of the first wave of the bombers, then returning to their fields for refueling and ammunition.

As the raid began they put on their tin hats and decided to spend some time in the ditch, with passengers from a local bus that had also halted. They could see the flames from the burning oil tanks of Thameshaven, and the thick black clouds rising from the London docks. After two hours the all-clear sounded and the trio sought "a pie and a pint" at a pub nearby.

"Before eight the sirens sounded again," Murrow said as he broadcast the next day. "We went back to a haystack near the airdrome. The fires up the river had turned the moon blood-red. The smoke had drifted down till it formed a canopy over the Thames. The guns were working all around us, the bursts looking like fireflies in a Southern summer night.

"The Germans were sending in two or three planes at a time, sometimes only one, in relays. They would pass overhead. The guns and lights would follow them, and in about five minutes we could hear the hollow grunt of the bombs. Huge pear-shaped bursts of flame would rise up into the smoke and disappear. The world was upside down. Vincent Sheean lay on one side of me and cursed in five languages; he'd talk about the war in Spain. Ben Robertson lay on the other side and kept saying over and over in that slow South Carolina drawl, 'London is burning, London is burning . . .'

"It was like a shuttle service, the way the German planes came up the Thames, the fires acting as a flare path. Often they were above the smoke.

The searchlights bored into that black roof but couldn't penetrate it. They looked like long pillars supporting a black canopy. Suddenly all the lights dashed off and a blackness fell right to the ground. It grew cold. We covered ourselves with hay. The shrapnel clicked as it hit the concrete road nearby. And still the German bombers came."

At 3 A.M., as the attack tapered off, they went back to Gravesend, under the occasional fall of shrapnel. At first Murrow drove slowly and with some care, but he soon decided it was less dangerous to speed up, and certainly it was more natural for him. Their inn shook all the rest of the night, but they were too tired to be kept awake, and next morning they drove back to London, through the still-burning East End.

The scenes they saw — whole blocks destroyed, streets roped off, houses and stores smashed, mounds of glass being shoveled into trucks, firemen and first-aid squads raking through rubble looking for survivors, ambulances lined up, buses taking away the homeless with their dull eyes — were repeated every day, in varying degree, for fifty-seven consecutive days, between September 7 and November 3. The Luftwaffe attacked London even after it was evident that the city would not submit, after the invasion had been canceled, and when any military reason for the bombing had been replaced by open and admitted terror.

Every night, sometimes from rooftops — after all, he was a fire warden — sometimes from the deep underground BBC studio with its sandbagged entrance, Murrow gave eyewitness accounts of the life and agony of a great city. Haggard himself, a kind of walking wounded, suffering from chronic fatigue and lack of sleep — even when he slept he ground his teeth, so gratingly that his colleagues complained — he created with his words and voice a spoken Goya etching of suffering and courage. When he said "This . . . is London," he established the same kind of rapport with the American nation as Franklin D. Roosevelt did with his fireside chat.

He was helped in this relationship by comments and critiques on his broadcasts from the viewpoint of an American conservative, Wells Church, who had helped him arrange "talks" from Washington in the prewar days. Shirer disagreed with almost everything Church wrote, about the nature of the war and the American attitude toward it, but the very conflict of ideas helped keep Murrow's balance.

Just as intently listened to in Britain as Murrow's in the United States were the broadcasts of Raymond Swing from New York to the BBC. Swing explained America and American policies to the British as Murrow explained Britain to the Americans. Swing's Saturday evening broadcasts were waited for by British officialdom, as well as ordinary listeners. He even got a request from King George VI for an autographed photo, though, as he noted, he never received one in return.

Murrow lived every moment of the Blitz. His principal broadcasts, made after midnight — he was also on the air in the early mornings and frequently the late afternoon — came during the raids. Usually they began before he went to the studio, while he was still at home or at the office, and often on the way to or from dinner in Charlotte Street.

The small French and Greek Cypriot restaurants there, indignant that they could be suspected of black-marketeering, did profoundly better with the cheaper parts, called by the British "offal," than standard English cookery could. But Murrow was an indifferent eater at best, not much interested in what was set before him, and the point was that Charlotte Street was also the gathering place for BBC people and those from the Ministry of Information, at the nearby University of London. The only time any other correspondent saw Murrow actually enjoying food was during the Battle of Britain, when he and Fred Bate stumbled upon a small inn near the Channel and found the rarest of wartime delicacies, some Whitstable oysters. Murrow was seen actually smacking his lips.

During the Blitz, in London, as he walked along in his correspondent-about-town togs — gray flannel trousers, houndstooth sports jacket, khaki tin hat — or drove in his small open roadster, he had numerous narrow escapes from injury or death. Several times he was knocked down in the street by the concussion of bombs. Buildings around him were blown down. Once, walking back from Charlotte Street with Larry Le Sueur and Eric Sevareid, he suddenly stepped into a doorway, and they instinctively followed. A few seconds later a huge jagged piece of shell-casing hit the spot where they would have been.

Murrow would not go into an air-raid shelter except as a reporter to get a story. "Once you start going into shelters you lose your nerve," he explained to Le Sueur. Ed was regarded as fearless by other reporters, indeed foolhardy by some. One of them asked him why he took so many risks. "I have a peasant's mind," he said. "I can't write about anything I haven't seen."

Some of his colleagues chaffed him about the cult of masculinity, as they saw it, and some thought he was exhibiting a "death wish," but those who knew him well knew he was not particularly trying to prove anything, not even to himself. He was doing what he considered a reporter's job, finding out as much about a story at first hand as it was possible to do, and in a larger sense, sharing the experience of his time. His courage came, not from any lack of sensitivity to or awareness of danger, but from the deliberate clinical ignoring of it. As danger increased, he became grimmer of visage and drier of comment.

During the Blitz, Murrow and Fred Bate sought to make live broadcasts from a rooftop while a raid was in progress. The Air Ministry refused permission. Such eyewitness accounts, spontaneous and without a script, obviously could not be censored and might give something away of military usefulness.

To demonstrate that it could be done with impunity, Murrow put on his tin hat and went up to the BBC roof with a sound technician. They made a recorded broadcast describing a raid, which could not be transmitted to America because of the network prohibition against recordings.

The Air Ministry said it sounded fine, and was unobjectionable from a security standpoint. Moreover it had advanced the practice of wartime broadcasting a step or two. Until then the BBC, by opening a microphone on the roof, had provided "punctuation" for American broadcasts, in the form of ack-ack fire and sirens, though the broadcasts themselves were made from the safety of the sub-basement. Murrow and Bate thought this was deceptive, and now it was proved that the "real thing" was possible.

The Air Ministry still refused permission. It was taking no chances. Murrow made six more recordings and all were listened to with admiration, but the answer was still No. Finally Churchill himself was appealed to by the American, and he approved heartily.

A live rooftop broadcast was made, but Murrow's words were drowned out by the sounds of gunfire and plane engines. "I must have spoken too softly, so as not to be heard by the planes," he said.

Finally came the night when American listeners were able to hear the first of the air-raid broadcasts which one of them described as "metallic poetry."

"I'm standing on a rooftop looking out over London. At the moment everything is quiet. For reasons of national as well as personal security, I'm unable to tell you the exact location from which I'm speaking. Off to my left, far away in the distance, I can see just that faint red angry snap of antiaircraft bursts against the steel-blue sky, but the guns are so far away that it's impossible to hear them from this location.

"About five minutes ago the guns in the immediate vicinity were working. I can look across just at a building not far away and see something that looks like a flash of white paint down the side, and I know from daylight observation that about a quarter of that building has disappeared, hit by a bomb the other night."

Searchlights sprang up around him. "I think probably in a minute we shall have the sound of guns in the immediate vicinity. The lights are swinging over in this general direction now. You'll hear two explosions. There they are! That was the explosion overhead, not the guns themselves. I should think in a few minutes there may be a bit of shrapnel around here. Coming in, moving a little closer all the while.

"The plane's still very high. Earlier this evening we could hear occasional — again, those were explosions overhead. Earlier this evening we heard a number of bombs go sliding and slithering across, to fall several blocks away. Just overhead now the burst of the antiaircraft fire. Still the nearby guns are not working. The searchlights now are feeling almost directly overhead. Now you'll hear two bursts a little nearer in a moment.

"There they are! That hard stony sound."

He was speaking from the roof of the BBC, a prime military target, and from it he could see the dome of St. Paul's, the spire of Westminster Abbey, and the London University tower. In the damaged building across the street the portion that had disappeared were the two floors directly above the fourth-floor offices of CBS.

On his way to the office earlier that night, to write the broadcast he was to make at 3:45 A.M., he had had to throw himself flat five times, to escape bomb splinters. "It's pleasant to pick yourself up out of the gutter without the aid of a searcher party," he decided. When he got to 14 Langham Place, the top of the building stood agape, with bricks and plaster pouring down from it.

His broadcast that night, as it was heard in New York, was made in "a hoarse tremulous voice that broke into sobbing at one point, under the burden of emotion, fatigue and nerve-wracking strain."

He spoke of the bombing of downtown London night after night. "This is a race, the bomb squad trying to take away the bombs that have already fallen, before the next consignment comes down . . . But the milk and morning papers continue to arrive."

As he himself evaluated his broadcast, in a note written to Janet while the all-night bombing was still going on: "Have been doing some fair talking last few nights. Pulled out all the stops and let them have it. Now I think is the time. A thousand years of history and civilization are being smashed. Maybe the stuff I am doing is falling flat. Would be better if you could look at it, but have spent three years trying to make people believe me and am now using that for all tis worth."

He wrote his parents in the same vein. "They tell me from New York that I have acquired something of a reputation, but a reputation doesn't interest me much.

"Am more interested in being able to live with my own conscience during the coming years. As this thing goes on, and as America becomes more hysterical, you may read and hear some pretty hard things about your overgrown baby, for I propose to report this thing, not preach about it. There will be hate enough to spare without my adding to it. So whatever happens just remember that I am calling them as I see them . . ."

In New York the newspaper *PM*, which printed his broadcasts as news dispatches, carried the headline "Murrow Ducks Bombs in London."

During the next few months CBS would be bombed out of two more offices in the BBC neighborhood, in Portland Place and in Duchess Street, and then what was left of furniture and files was finally moved into an apartment house at 49 Hallam Street, not far from the Murrow flat at 84. The first night of occupancy in the new "deluxe" office was disrupted by a bomb which shattered the Central City synagogue a few yards down the street.

Despite all the damage and dislocation to offices, however, every scheduled CBS broadcast was made, though in the third bombing Murrow lost the journal he had been keeping and never returned to it.

During some of the most intensive bombing, Janet was in rural Somerset recuperating from "Blitz fatigue,". and he admonished her. "God's sake, keep your chin up," he wrote. "Your two letters arrived this A.M. What if you were home [in America] — think of those English women who've been separated from children and husbands for whole years. I'll be down to see you before long.

"Under no circumstances return to London till I say so. Corner of Langham Hotel hit by small bomb last night . . . I was dining with Dick Marriott at Langham when bomb fell — plenty glass blown in and pillars staggered but no damage to us. Also started couple fires lower Hallam and Great Portland Street, but no damage to flat. West End took pretty heavy hammering last night.

"Good luck, honey . . . the Murrow luck will hold and we shall come thru this all right."

Another letter followed. "Ordered new suit today. Tailors damaged but not ruined. Dropped a big one near Queen Anne Street tonight . . . shook the BBC, but all's well. Oh yes, also bought some wool socks and paid Betty [the maid]. Getting very domestic. Hard to find eggs, I'm told.

"Some of these big land mines they are dropping are no fun. Come down on parachute and you can't hear them coming."

Though the CBS offices were hit and much other damage was done to other buildings, the Murrow apartment at 84 Hallam Street somehow escaped. The red-brick building with stone facing, to which they had moved after a year in the red-brick building with iron railings in Queen Anne Street, was often shaken by blast, and the long carpet in the hallway of the flat would rattle and curl as the bombs fell. Neither Ed nor Janet ever went to the shelter in the mews behind the apartment house. Ed believed the oak table in his study was protection enough, and they would sit beneath that.

The other CBS correspondents in London, dossed down in another Hallam Street flat, had been told to get under their beds in case of bombing attacks. Unfortunately their beds were pallets or sleeping bags, stretched on the floor.

One correspondent of another American network always threw himself prone, as instructed, whenever the alert sounded, even though the action might be miles away. He would do so at mealtime in crowded restaurants, and in private homes, including the Murrow home, to the annoyance of his hungry companions. Whether at home or in restaurants, Ed and Janet always went on with their meal and paid no attention to the sirens.

One night the two of them, with their tin helmets, were walking back to Hallam Street after dinner in Charlotte Street. There was bombing a short distance off, and shrapnel pattered down. Murrow still had some time before his broadcast and thought he might drop in, as he often did, at the Devonshire Arms — or Announcer's Arms, as the BBC people who frequented it called it — where he was a proficient dart player. Janet asked to be taken home first.

As they came to 84 there was another hit nearby. They ran into their building and up to the roof. Ed believed it could have been the office, in Duchess Street, and knew that Kay Campbell was still there, as she always was until air time, with the news tickers running. "See you later," he said as he left.

On the way he passed the pub, which he would have entered five minutes before if he had gone directly there instead of taking Janet home. It had been demolished and several persons were killed inside and outside it, including one of Ed's closest BBC friends, Allan Wells, and his wife. The Wellses were neighborhood fire wardens, also, and they were outside with their sand buckets when the bomb fell.

The CBS office, as feared, had also been battered. Miss Campbell was hurled across the room and showered with dust and debris, but escaped serious harm. She was tidying up, with her customary cigarette drooping from her mouth, British wartime fashion, when Murrow arrived.

The BBC's Broadcasting House, the major target in an otherwise residential area, was shaken and scarred several times by bombs falling close by. Then on October 4 it "bought" its own "packet," and six persons were killed.

The nine o'clock news was on when the bomb hit. Cedric Belfrage, the BBC news reader, paused momentarily as the explosion was heard. Someone in the studio could be heard saying "It's all right." Belfrage gave a slight cough. "I beg your pardon," he said, as BBC announcers do, and continued reading the war news.

Because it was a military target, Broadcasting House was heavily guarded. A sentry with rifle and bayonet commanded its sandbagged entrance. Inside, the foyer was divided by heavy iron screening, with guards behind it. To broadcast it was necessary to descend three flights to the sub-basement, through a gas-tight door on each floor. Also on each floor there were sleeping figures in the corridors, in blankets, on mattresses, propped up in corners. The BBC concert hall on the lower ground floor, its seats ripped out, had been converted into a giant bomb shelter, its floor and stage also filled with sleeping people.

The various departments of BBC had been dispersed by the war, and the orchestra, drama and variety broadcasts now came from Bristol, which would have its own bombing nightmare, while Broadcasting House was used for news, public affairs broadcasts and speeches. It was thus the principal center for British "propaganda," as the Germans saw it.

In the sub-basement, the subway trains of the Bakerloo line could be heard directly underneath, and the corridors reeked with the cabbage that was cooked all day and night in the canteen. More sentries stood outside the studios, civilians with armbands and shotguns. Passes were examined at every stage of a broadcaster's progress. Down the dark hallway was the first-aid room, from which iodine odors emanated.

The small studio allotted to the three American networks was regarded by its occupants as the last redoubt, or at least the last point to be evacuated when the Germans came.

It was divided by a curtain into workroom and broadcasting booth, and was shared with three censors, who worked eight-hour shifts and were, respectively, a college professor, an antique dealer, and a musical arranger and composer. The crowded ménage also kept a mouse, fed on scraps.

Sometimes the tiny studio was further congested by radio engineers sleeping on mattresses. During one Murrow broadcast he counted nine bodies, all of which slept through it.

The censors were actually much more than that. They constituted BBC's American liaison unit, which provided the American broadcasters with all news facilities and arranged their trips to air bases, military camps, dockyards and factories. The relationship was not only a close one professionally but became a warm one personally. Not for Janet, who attended services regularly every Sunday at St. James's in Great Portland Street, but for Eric Warr, his censor, would Murrow deign to enter a church when in 1943 he stood as godfather to Warr's son Hilary. He would confess he was impressed by the Episcopalian ceremony and thought "there might be something to it."

The censors sat through the American broadcasts with their fingers on the switch, ready to turn the microphone off if the correspondent departed from the approved script. There was never such an occasion during the entire war, so far as the network broadcasters were concerned — it happened only once with a man from a small local American station — but one censor confessed he was so often entranced with Murrow's words that he would have probably reacted too late to any lapse.

At first the censors worried that Murrow might broadcast news he got from Churchill or from Lord Cranborne, who was the general utility man of the Churchill government — the censors felt "they told Murrow every-thing" including what was not covered by the evening's news directives. But he never violated a confidence or embarrassed them.

The censors welcomed Murrow's studio guests, especially exiled mon-archs and Allied politicians, because the BBC would then offer its famous though war-stinted "hospitality." This was about the only strong-drink supply they could get at the time, and they especially appreciated General de Gaulle. He would raise his hand, palm forward, and say imperiously, "Non, non, not a drop," which meant they could have more for them-selves, perhaps even the bottle.

On the night of the bombing Murrow and Fred Bate knew that Broad-casting House had been hit when the glass window between their studio and the control room cracked, even before the blast was felt. A medium-sized bomb had come into a window six stories up, smashed through one floor, hit another and lay still. Its original impact was virtually unno-ticed, but as an emergency bomb squad got a rope around it, it went off. The blast from the upper floor came down the elevator shafts and ventila-tors, and scattered dust and soot, as well as broken glass, through the studios. The precious BBC library on the fifth floor was wrecked, thou-sands of records and transcriptions were destroyed, and the telephone switchboard knocked out.

Dead and injured were being carried down to the sub-basement, past the studio toward the first-aid room, when Murrow began broadcasting. He spoke of the iodine smell and the stretchers in the corridor outside with "good friends" upon them.

Two months later, on December 8, Broadcasting House was even more extensively damaged, and with it the CBS offices once again. On this occasion it was a magnetic mine which went off in Langham Place, tear-ing a gigantic hole in the street, devastating the Langham Hotel opposite the BBC, and opening up the granite front of Broadcasting House and flooding the basements.

The mines, which Murrow had described as "no fun" and which the censors permitted no mention of — for they were British, captured at Amiens — had been used by the Germans in the Channel, but a new Ger-man model made them surplus, and they were being disposed of over London. Coming down by parachute, they were not only destructive but terrifying, for they landed without a sound, each carrying a ton of dyna-mite set to go off.

A policeman was killed in the Langham Place blast and twenty-four per-sons were injured, including not only BBC staff members, but Fred Bate, the NBC correspondent who was in his office nearby. He was badly hurt. The tendons of his leg were severed, and both legs burned. Gravel was imbedded in his head like shrapnel. His left ear was virtually torn off. He was taken to nearby Middlesex Hospital in an ambulance and later sent to the United States to convalesce.

Murrow was not in London on the night of that bombing. He had gone to Lisbon to say farewell to Shirer, who was leaving for home, and to snatch a brief respite from the war. Larry Le Sueur had left the CBS office in Portland Place just before the land mine fell, and no one was there, but once again the "f. and f.," as the British called the furniture and fittings, were demolished.

Three months later, in Bate's absence, the new NBC offices were hit. This time Murrow was on his home rooftop, as usual, during the raid, after leaving the studio, and saw the bomb fall. He ran to the NBC office and was first on the scene, even before the fire wardens. The occupants of the building had been shaken, but not injured.

Although the CBS offices, at their various locations, were useful during the Blitz — to receive mail, make telephone calls, and assuage thirst, with either tea or something more fortifying — the broadcasting correspondents, when they were not making their rounds in search of news, spent most of their time at the BBC, as their newspaper colleagues did in Fleet Street.

The BBC newsrooms received the agency reports from all parts of the world, and the BBC's own monitoring service provided radio news from enemy and neutral stations, while British governmental departments, from the prime minister's office and Buckingham Palace down to the clerk's office in Fulham town hall, kept the BBC abreast of developments of every variety.

The BBC broadcasting services were worldwide and in many languages, though during the war continental Europe was the principal target. The war, besides ending the convention that BBC announcers had to wear evening dress in order to read, unseen, the news, also sharpened the development of "outside broadcasts," or on-the-spot reporting.

Thus Murrow's August 24 broadcast from Trafalgar Square, with its nine live microphones, was something that the BBC was able to take in stride. In the following weeks and months every phase of war activity in the British Isles was thus graphically reported to American listeners.

On the fifteenth night of the London Blitz, for example, a notable Murrow rooftop broadcast was actually part of a full half-hour program, in the *London After Dark* series, which moved from him to Vaughn Thomas, in the Strand near Charing Cross railway station; then to Wilfred Pelletier, of the Canadian Broadcasting Company, interviewing people in the crypt of St. Martin-in-the-Fields, and ended with hundreds in that shelter singing "Pack Up Your Troubles."

During the Battle of Britain, BBC made possible a CBS news roundup which included live broadcasts from London, Manchester, Birmingham, Cardiff, Glasgow and Belfast.

When BBC realized the importance of American audiences, as Britain stood alone against Hitler, it sought an American adviser for its North American service, and Murrow, remembering Wells Church's helpful observations on the American scene and mood, recommended him for the post. It was Church's turn to be grateful.

During the many hours spent at the BBC, Murrow found a close understanding with R. T. Clarke, the quiet man who was the senior news editor, and who saw to it that BBC news was "written for the voice." More accurately, BBC bulletins were not written at all, but dictated directly to typists, so that they would be in the spoken language, more informal and yet clearer than much journalistic writing. Clarke had been struck by the thought that a spoken paragraph, unlike a written one, provided no chance for a rereading when the meaning was uncertain.

Murrow, as a proficient debater, also preferred the spoken word. Never having been a writing journalist, and therefore never finding it necessary to change his style for radio, he took naturally to the BBC method of dictating and followed it thereafter, with Kay Campbell as the faithful transcriber who accompanied him everywhere.

But Murrow's friendship with Clarke was more than a professional one. The Scotsman practically lived in Broadcasting House during the war, in a partitioned section of a basement room about half the size of a ship's cabin. It had two sleeping bunks, a table with a typewriter on it, two wooden chairs, and shelves filled with books in English, French, Latin and Greek. Clarke, besides being a journalist, was a Classical scholar. Part of his library was devoted to the American Civil War, in which he was an expert, and Murrow spent long hours talking with him about battles and generals of that other war. After all, his grandfather had been in it and had told him about it.

On the numerous visits he made to England later, when he was at the height of his career, though he might come to London to interview Harold Macmillan or Field Marshal Montgomery or to talk with Churchill, he would never fail to spend some time with Clarke, usually in a leather-cushioned recess at the Reform Club, and talk some more about British politics and Shiloh.

Another BBC intimate, during the Blitz, was J. B. Priestley the novelist, whose weekly radio *Postscripts* after the Sunday night news were listened to by an enthralled nation. As the two sat waiting for their microphones the socially conscious Priestley spoke, as he did in his broadcasts, less of the war itself than of its meaning and consequences. His very British theme was, "I'm no hero, but . . ." and he then listed the things that had to be done to make Britain over. Murrow was naturally inclined toward such thoughts also, and Priestley's strong convictions and the undoubted appeal he had to his large unseen audience helped to keep the American always mindful of the class conflict in Britain that the military conflict never quite obliterated.

Murrow's own BBC studio, despite its limited size, frequently accommodated visiting American correspondents, for the transatlantic radio circuit was the quickest way of sending a free personal message home. Ernie Pyle, the chronicler of G.I. Joe, came in to see Murrow broadcast and described him at work — gesturing with his right hand as he spoke; folding up his fist, then opening it as if tossing something away. He would make his points by nodding his head strongly. He perspired profusely. He looked at the clock. And he could hardly wait for the next cigarette. By now he had become a chain smoker, discarding the pipe he had occasionally used when he first came to London — it made him look older — and consuming cigarettes in a country which, because of climate and industrial pollution, had the world's highest rate of rheumatic and respiratory ailments.

After the night's work, and sometimes between the broadcasts at 12:45 and 3:45 A.M., Murrow and his visitors would grope their way up Hallam Street through the blackout, for the measured five hundred paces to the second-floor five-room flat at Number 84.

Sometimes Janet had coffee and sandwiches ready at London's only wartime "all-night stall," but usually she was asleep and remained so, for she had a daytime job of her own at the Ministry of Information and seldom saw Ed. Often other correspondents would arrive from Fleet Street, after filing their dispatches for the morning papers at home, and sometimes Foreign Office or House of Commons friends. A frequent guest was Jan Masaryk, now the foreign minister of the Czech exiled government. But usually, night after night, Murrow came home from the BBC with R. T. Clarke and Allan Wells, and they would sit up the rest of the night talking.

The visitors to 84 admired the sole Navajo Indian rug and blanket in London, and dipped into the whiskey. The fire was customarily going, for the autumn nights were chilly. Murrow, who had a small gift for mimicry, told dialect stories and anecdotes about the great he had met, and more often than not, as London awakened to another gray morning, a poker game would be in progress around the oak table in the study. Murrow was and continued to be a reckless player, and he frequently lost heavily because the courage of his convictions did not match his cards.

If he had to go back to the studio in the middle of the night, for programs heard at 11 P.M. or midnight in New York, Murrow had no compunction about calling friends and acquaintances to the BBC even at that hour, to take part in his broadcasts. They did not seem to mind even if, as sometimes happened, the signal failed.

Betty Matthews, the young Welsh girl who was the Murrows' maid, marveled at the people who visited the flat at all hours. They included Mrs. Churchill, who came to tea; Lady Mountbatten, and Lady Violet Milner, relict of one of Britain's famous proconsuls. Gilbert Winant, the American ambassador who succeeded Joe Kennedy, would come, and once his lateness at dinner ruined a plump pheasant from Norfolk.

Whatever American dignitaries might be visiting in London came, like Eleanor Roosevelt; American officers, including an occasional movie star like Clark Gable — whom Janet at first mistook for Ed's brother Lacey — British diplomats like Ronald Tree, and prominent Laborites, Ernest Bevin and Harold Laski.

But Betty remembered that her own father, a Welsh miner, and her brother, "a bit of a radical in those days," were also invited into the dining room by Murrow whenever they visited her, and were engaged in lengthy conversation about Britain. He always talked intently with all the Britons he met.

On one occasion Murrow had to drive to Cardiff for a broadcast, and he took Betty home to her small mining village, with its slag heaps. He quickly became acquainted with everyone there and visited the local workingmen's club which, with the chapel, constituted the true life of Wales.

Since Betty's husband Reg came from Norfolk, he managed an occasional turkey or chicken from the family farm, though often they were so tough that Murrow remarked they must have walked all the way. American food parcels helped, but the Murrows normally did what the British did, saved up their ration coupons to get a roast, then invited several people for dinner. Though Ed was an unenthusiastic eater, Betty could make him "come to life" with her steak and kidney pie. He thought eating at home was better than the Savoy Grill or the Ritz Hotel.

Jan Masaryk, regarded as one of the family, dropped in without invitation and took potluck. When Murrow disdainfully left his brussels sprouts, as he usually did, the foreign minister of Czechoslovakia said, "You can't do that," and reached over and speared them on his own fork, whether from hunger or a sense of virtue.

Sometimes between broadcasts Murrow went around to Masaryk's little apartment in Westminster Gardens for a few hours conversation. Once a bomb rocked the building. "Uncivilized swine, the Germans. They have ruined my soufflé," said the foreign minister.

At home one evening Murrow was describing to a new arrival from America the sound made by incendiary bombs. "Swish-swash, and then a plunk. And then another swish-swash and plunk," he said. His words had an immediate echo. Swish-swash and plunk. Swish-swash and plunk. Real incendiaries were hitting the roof. They ran upstairs and shoveled sand over them.

On a dark night Murrow was driving through Trafalgar Square during a heavy air raid, with the top down as usual. With him were Sheean and Quentin Reynolds, the big American who was doing with magazine writing what Ed was doing on radio, in describing the war.

Reynolds bet the others fifty dollars he could read a newspaper by the light of the flames. They stopped the car and Reynolds got out and won the bet, as bombs fell close at hand. Years later in a New York courtroom Murrow would describe the scene, appearing as a witness for Reynolds in the latter's libel suit against the columnist Westbrook Pegler, who had called him a "coward."

When the concentrated German attacks on London began, the first weekend in September, their purpose seemed evident. "This night bombing is serious and sensational," Murrow broadcast. "It makes headlines, kills people and smashes property, but it doesn't win wars. It may be safely presumed that the Germans know that, know that several days of terror bombing will not cause this country to collapse. Where then does this new phase of the air war fit? What happens next?

"The future must be viewed in relation to previous objectives. Those objectives were the western ports and convoys, the Midlands and Welsh industrial areas, and the southern airfields. And now we have the bombing of London. If this is the prelude to invasion we must expect much heavier raids against London.

"And we must expect a sudden renewal of the attacks against fighter dromes near the coast, an effort to drive the fighters farther inland. If the Germans continue to hammer London for a few nights more and then sweep successfully to blasting airdromes with their dive bombers, it will probably be the signal for the invasion. And the currently favored date for this invasion . . . is some time about September 18."

The date came and passed. The "few" of the RAF Fighter Command contained the Luftwaffe in the daytime battles in the sky. British bombers hit the German invasion fleet in Antwerp harbor. Operation Sea Lion was "postponed."

Yet the heavy pounding of London continued. September 15 brought two hundred bombers and seven hundred fighters over the city and sixty of the German planes were shot down that day, while the RAF lost twenty-six. Annually, since, Battle of Britain Day has been celebrated on September 15. Three days later the daylight bombing of London ended, but the night raids continued. It was evident Hitler's real aim was to break the will of the British people.

Churchill apostrophized Britain's "finest hour." Murrow reported to America: "The politicians who called this a 'people's war' were right, probably more right than they knew at the time. I've seen some horrible sights in this city during these days and nights, but not once have I heard man, woman or child suggest that Britain should throw in her hand."

As always, there were all sorts of people. "Like everything else in this world, the kind of protection you get from the bombs in London tonight depends on how much money you have. The most expensive dwelling places here do not necessarily provide the best shelter, but certainly they are the most comfortable."

He had visited both ends of the shelter spectrum that evening, and described the contrast. On the one hand there was the earthen trench that had been dug in Hyde Park, to make a cavern where people stretched out on hard wooden benches, or merely huddled together on the ground in overcoats and blankets.

"Dimmed electric lights glowed on the whitewashed walls, and the cannonade of antiaircraft and the reverberations of the big stuff the Germans were dropping rattled the dust boards underfoot at intervals. One woman was saying sleepily that it was funny how often you read about people being killed inside a shelter. Nobody seemed to listen."

Comparison was provided by the "upholstered sewers" where the affluent lived a gay underground nightlife during the blackout. Luxury hotels and restaurants had makeshift sleeping quarters and Murrow described "the famous cellar of a world-famous hotel," the Dorchester, which was directly across Park Lane from the Hyde Park trench shelter he had spoken of. The Dorchester, with heavy concrete between its floors, was believed the safest building in London. Foreign Secretary Lord Halifax had eight rooms and a private chapel, and other members of the government and the British peerage lived there.

Two flights underground, "on upholstered chairs and lounges, there was a cosmopolitan crowd," Murrow found. "But there wasn't any sparkling cocktail conversation. They sat, some of them with their mouths open. One of them snored. King Zog was over in a far corner on a chair. The woman sleeping on the only cot in the shelter was one of the many sisters of the former king of Albania."

In another Mayfair hotel Murrow observed "many old dowagers and retired colonels settling back on the overstuffed settees in the lobby. It wasn't the sort of protection I'd seek from a direct hit from a half-ton bomb, but if you were a retired colonel and his lady you might feel that the risk was worth it because you would at least be bombed with the right sort of people."

On successive evenings as the bombing continued the broadcaster presented some striking verbal vignettes. "Once I saw the *Damnation of Faust* presented in the open air at Salzburg. London reminds me of that tonight, only the stage is so much larger. Once tonight an antiaircraft battery opened fire just as I drove past it. It lifted me from the seat, and a hot wind swept over the car. It was impossible to see. When I drove on, the streets of London reminded me of a ghost town in Nevada — not a soul to be seen."

Again, describing an antiaircraft battery: "They're working in their shirtsleeves, laughing and cursing as they slam the shells into their guns. The spotters and detectors swing slowly around in their reclining carriage. The lens of the night glasses look like the eyes of an overgrown owl, in the orange-blue light that belches from the muzzle of the gun. They're working without searchlights tonight. The moon is so bright that the beam of the light is lost a few hundred feet off the ground. Someone should paint the chimney pots and gables of London as they're silhouetted in the flashing flame of the guns, when the world seems upside down."

Again: "There was a rainbow bending over the battered and smoking East End of London just when the all-clear sounded one afternoon. One night I stood in front of a smashed grocery store and heard a dripping inside. It was the only sound in all London. Two cans of peaches had been drilled clean through by flying glass, and the juice was dropping down onto the floor."

On another occasion he reported "on good authority, that the prime minister had a siren suit, one of those blue wool coverall affairs with a zipper. Someone said the prime minister must resemble a barrage balloon when attired in his siren suit. Things of that sort can still be said in this country."

Murrow would often tell of a taxi driver who left Liverpool Street station one night "when a couple of high-explosive bombs came whistling down. He hauled his ancient cab to the curb, where it was rocked by the blast of the bombs. He slid back his window and said, 'He'll do that once too often, once,' closed the window, and drove on. I have never understood exactly what he meant by that."

After the bombing of Buckingham Palace, a deliberate act by a single German plane sweeping along the Mall, Murrow reported that the incident "appears to have affected Americans more than Britons." For, he remarked, "there is nothing exclusive about being bombed these days. When there are houses down, in your street, when friends and relatives have been killed, when you've seen that red glow in the sky night after night, when you're tired and sleepy — there just isn't enough energy left to be outraged about the bombing of a palace. The king and queen have reaped the respect and admiration of the nation, but so have tens of thousands of humble folk who are much less well protected. If the palace had been the only place bombed, the reaction might have been different."

It was also true that if the East End had been the only place bombed, the reaction could have been different, perhaps indeed alarming. For the first German attacks on the populous impoverished areas along the docks had emphasized the difference between the rich and the poor, the bombed and the safe.

If continued, they might have caused mass psychosis in the East End and brought demands upon the government for negotiation. They could have threatened national unity. But if Britain needed sociologists to apply to the war, as Murrow had suggested, Hitler needed psychologists. The switch of bombing to London's West End and the middle-class suburbs equalized the terror, and constituted a German mistake.

Not all Londoners were brave in the Blitz. Many were frightened. Murrow saw them crying in the shelters, huddled miserably together, often angry or in despair. Many would have left the city, indeed the country, if they could. They simply endured. When the burden of endurance was shared, it was made lighter.

Though the broadcaster admired the British for their pristine virtues — kindness, common sense, competence and faith — as well as their courage, he also quoted a British question to him in the midst of a raid: "Do you think we're really brave, or just lacking in imagination?"

As he walked about the bruised and soiled streets he caught "glimpses of the London one knew in the distant days of peace. The big red buses roll through the streets. The tolling of Big Ben can be heard in the intervals of the gunfire. The little French and Italian restaurants in Soho bring out their whitest linens and polish their glass and silver for the two or three guests who brave the blackout, the bombs and the barrage. There are advertisements in the papers extolling the virtues of little rubber earplugs which prevent one from hearing the bombs and guns. In many buildings tonight people are sleeping on mattresses on the floor. I've seen dozens of them, looking like dolls thrown aside by a tired child."

At the peak of the Blitz, when fifteen thousand London buildings were damaged in a single week, he made an economics note. "To me one of the most impressive things about talking with Londoners these days is this — there's no mention of money.

"No one knows the dollar value of the damage done. Nobody talks about it. People who've had their homes or offices bombed will tell you about it, but they never think to tell you what the loss amounted to, whether it was so many tens or hundreds of pounds. The lead of any well-written news story dealing with fire, flood or hurricane should tell something of the total damage done in terms of dollars, but here it's much more important that the bomb missed you."

One evening a bomber pilot who had been over Berlin took part in Murrow's broadcast to America. As they waited for the microphone, a whistling noise was heard, followed by a series of three shattering thumps outside. "My God, what's that?" asked the twenty-one-year-old pilot. Ed said they were bombs. The pilot turned pale and shook his head. "I had no idea they were like that," he said. Though he himself had been bombing Germany for weeks, it was the first time he had ever heard a bomb come down.

They left the studio with the air raid still in progress. "A block of cheap little working-class houses had been set alight by the fire bombs. As we walked toward the blaze, gusts of hot air and sparks charged down the street. We began to meet women. One clutched a blanket, another carried a small baby in her arms, and another carried an aluminum cooking pot in her left hand. They were all looking back over their shoulders at that red glow that had driven them out into the streets. They were frightened.

"And that bomber pilot who had been over Germany so many times stopped and said, 'I've seen enough of this. I hope we haven't been doing the same thing in the Ruhr and Rhineland for the last three months.' "

Sometimes the tension under which he worked, augmented by broadcasting's precise timing, told on the broadcaster, and this evening provided one of the occasions. He wrote Janet about it.

"This business is sheer lunacy. If I crack, CBS will thank you very much, and in two months no one will think of the great Murrow. Which is probably as it should be."

New York had complained that he had exceeded his stipulated speaking time the evening before, which he noted he had done deliberately, and he flared up and "had at them with both hands" over the transatlantic circuit. "Found out later that they had quote distinguished guests unquote in the studio and were much distressed at my ill temper.

"Can't see why there is no time to tell greatest story of lifetime without being cluttered up with these ill-informed bastards in New York [a 'military analysis' had preceded his London broadcast] . . . Gunfire pretty heavy tonight, windows much shaken. I all right, think I have no nerves, but the letdown if I ever get out of this will be pretty bad.

"I am glad you are not here now. This is something no one should go thru if it can be avoided."

On another occasion he quarreled with New York after violating the network's sacred rule against recordings. He had made one of a German raid, and as he described it to Janet, "One of the bombs coming down is pretty strong meat. Am opening and closing show with a barrel organ playing 'A Soldier of the Queen.' Twill take the heart out of a few people, I think."

In a subsequent letter, "New York reported great response to records last night, many telephone calls, etc., but said I must have misunderstood as there was no relaxation of ban on recordings other than sound effects, and I should not have used music or talk. Opened and closed the thing with a barrel organ, also used one shot outside Coconut Grove where we had gunfire, music and drone of German plane overhead all at same time . . . twas best single piece of sound have ever heard.

"Afraid I blew up and said after this we would produce sounds in studio, that I didn't propose to risk my neck to get birds twittering in Regent's Park. Am tired of whole business and for tuppence would chuck the whole thing."

He was exaggerating, both about his ferocity on the circuit, which was regarded in New York as normal radio banter, and about his willingness to quit. But the incident was another example of his habit of doing what he thought had to be done, no matter at what risk and no matter what the network rules.

At the end of September, with the invasion no longer deemed possible, the British announced that the Germans had lost 2167 planes and 5418 pilots, gunners and bombardiers, over their island and its waters, in two months. But in the Battle of Britain two thousand British civilians had been killed and eight thousand injured. London took four-fifths of the casualties.

The American ambassador, Joseph P. Kennedy, left London after two years and nine months, in order to help the third-term campaign of the President who had not been listening to him. "I did not know London could take it," the departing envoy said. During the Blitz he had left London every evening for safer abode in Windsor Great Park. A parting salute to the island race, as Churchill called it, was given by Kennedy in an interview in Boston. "Democracy is finished in England. It may be here," he said, if the United States got into the war.

Murrow reported from London that democracy was not quite finished. Even in the midst of the battle, he found, the question of survival was no less important than others that were being raised. "What are the war aims of this country? What shall we do with victory when it's won? What sort of Europe will be built when and if this stress has passed?"

He never forgot that as the Blitz began the House of Commons calmly debated the conditions of internment for enemy aliens on the Isle of Man. Indeed the most striking fact about Britain's war for him was that — while bombing went on and the number of homeless multiplied and rations became tighter, as shipping losses mounted and battles were lost in Africa, as the United States moved away from neutrality to active support, and Roosevelt sent his envoys to London to work out the terms of aid — British parliamentary democracy continued in full play, and the House of Commons scrutinized and debated all emergency measures.

There were lapses. Churchill opposed any statement of war aims, in the belief that precise aims would be compromising and vague aims disappointing. The prime minister also found no relish in the contemplation of more socialism, which was freely being predicted for postwar Britain. J. B. Priestley found himself no longer broadcasting social commentary after the Sunday night news, and blamed Churchill for his quiet casting-away.

Also, while Churchill was underreacting to social change, British democracy may have overreacted to the peril of the "enemy alien" as the United States would to the "menace" of its Japanese-American citizens. The British were closer to the Fifth Columns and Quislings of Europe than the United States was to Japan, and Hitler had left no doubt that he would use every means at hand, including subversion, to bring Britain down. Certainly the possibility of invasion was a very real one.

But the seventy thousand "enemy aliens" interned by Britain were virtually all anti-Nazi refugees, who abhorred Hitler and indeed had opposed him before very many Britons had. After Dunkerque spy-fever spread through the island and resulted in the arrest of 1200 persons.

But most of them were soon released. As for the German attempt at radio propaganda, the Berlin broadcasts of William Joyce, or "Lord Haw-haw," caused amusement rather than alarm. Any Briton was free to listen to Berlin, if he wanted to, while Germans were forbidden foreign reception.

Broadcasting in October, Murrow cited the suggestion of Nicholas Murray Butler, president of Columbia University, that any faculty member not agreeing with his pro-British position, in the continuing American debate between isolationists and interventionists, should resign.

"That will make strange reading to British scholars," he said. "No university head in this country has made such a pronouncement. Even in wartime it's not customary for scholars to demand that their colleagues share their political and international views. It's still possible for British professors to pursue the search for truth without dictation. Maybe the British are too tolerant, but it must be remembered that that tolerance has produced a pretty high degree of national unity." And so, of course, had Hitler's bombs.

Murrow also noted that while military censorship was enforced — he called it "often stupid but seldom sinister" — and the American correspondents had protested its more erratic ways, "the expression of opinion is still free in this country. Material is published in the daily press and in news letters which would cause the author to lose his head in any other belligerent nation."

Civil liberties remained and civilian morale continued high, but British shipping losses were rising in the Battle of the Atlantic, and British resources were dwindling. The House of Commons could debate peace aims at some length, despite Churchill's displeasure, but it had become increasingly plain that victory could not be won without substantial American help.

Murrow reported the British opinion that "no adequate definition of democracy's objectives can be made until it comes from Washington, or in a joint declaration from Washington and London, and that presupposes American entry into the war."

But he added the view that "the British must be sure in their own minds, and be able to convince the Americans, that the new world order which America is asked to join in making is not merely a device to maintain the status quo for the benefit of the British Commonwealth." As Churchill would find out in the wartime conferences, this was also the view of President Roosevelt, who had been reelected to a third term in November. Not long before, the American draft machinery had been put into motion.

The theory that the United States could be of greater aid to Britain as a nonbelligerent than as a fullfledged ally "has perished," Murrow observed in December. The theory had been encouraged by the British, he said, to reassure those Americans who feared direct involvement in the war.

But "since the election we have heard nothing of this thesis. It's a dead and dynamited fish, and you would have difficulty in finding any responsible British official with a desire to revive it. It's possible that for a time certain Britishers believed that American aid on a neutral basis would be adequate and effective. If they thought so, their disillusionment has been rapid. Ask any Member of Parliament or any member of the Government whether he prefers a neutral America or a belligerent America, and you will get only one answer. Some would express a preference for winning the war without American aid, but most would admit that it can't be done."

When the worst of the Blitz was over, Murrow received a letter from his parents asking when he was coming home. He replied that he wasn't.

"I don't think you would want me to . . . This is the end of an age, the end of things I was taught to love and respect, and I must stay here and report it if it kills me. One life more or less means nothing. You know that and so do I. You raised a boy with a big voice. He worked hard and was lucky and has not yet used that voice to mislead the people who trust it. Some people, many of whom I don't know, trust me and they can't be let down."

He was able to leave the war for a few days, combining a breathing spell with farewells to Shirer, who had come to the end of his string in Berlin and was going home. They met in Lisbon, relaxed on the Estoril by visiting the Casino and enjoying the varied human types in the gaming rooms — spies, royal exiles, refugees, courtesans, and perhaps fewest of all gamblers — and they tried to broadcast a joint war report from neutral territory. But the Portuguese censor said that while he was held spellbound by their script, he would not be able to finish its translation for at least a week. They gave up the idea.

That Christmas Eve was celebrated in London largely in air-raid shelters, for it was not known that the city would not be bombed as usual that night, and Murrow signed off not with holiday greetings, which he thought "somehow ill-timed and out of place," but with "the current London phrase — so long and good luck." It was apparently the genesis of his familiar radio closing, when he returned home after the war, "Good night and good luck."

He and other CBS correspondents who came to London were able to take brief snatches out of the bombing with an occasional holiday at a CBS "rest camp" — a cottage at Bishop's Stortford in Hertfordshire. But it did not give much surcease. Once a swastika-marked bomber, flying very low, knocked out the railroad station, and bombs fell frequently in the neighborhood.

Two nights before the end of the year the old once-walled City of London, now the financial district, was set aflame by 1400 fires from incendiary bombs, but St. Paul's Cathedral somehow survived the holocaust of London's second Great Fire. On New Year's Eve Murrow told his American listeners, "There is no regretting the year that is dead, and little prophecy about the year that begins." He spoke with unusual intensity, even for him.

"Most of you are probably preparing to welcome the new year. May you have a pleasant evening. You will have no dawn raid, as we shall probably have if the weather is right. You may walk this night in the light. Your families are not scattered by the winds of war. You may drive your high-powered car as far as time and money will permit. Only those who have been undernourished for years are in danger of going hungry.

"You have not been promised blood and toil and tears and sweat, and yet it is the opinion of nearly every informed observer over here that the decision you take will overshadow all else during this year that opened a few hours ago in London."

Ten days later Harry Hopkins arrived, to become a "catalytic agent," as he put it, "between two prima donnas," Roosevelt and Churchill. He was sent to lay the foundations for the Lend-Lease agreement, for Britain was going bankrupt and could not pay for arms and supplies under the Cash-and-Carry law. Hopkins would find out what Britain needed, and the United States, in Roosevelt's words, would "get rid of the silly, foolish old dollar sign" and become "the arsenal of democracy."

The presidential emissary's train pulled in at Waterloo station one minute after a shower of incendiaries descended on the railway line between

Waterloo and Clapham Junction, blocking it for hours. There was no American ambassador in London when Hopkins arrived. Kennedy had resigned, but his successor had not yet been named.

Hopkins's first meeting in London was not with a member of the British Cabinet, nor even with officers of the American embassy. He had heard Murrow broadcasting from London at the outbreak of the war — he himself lay ill at the Mayo Clinic, believing he would soon die — and had continued to listen during the London Blitz. Now Murrow found himself summoned to Claridge's Hotel to see Hopkins. He believed he was being given an interview but the tables were turned. It was he who was questioned, about British political personalities and home-front morale.

Ed wrote his brother Lacey about the Hopkins conversation. "He announced his mission was so delicate that he couldn't spend any time with correspondents, who were old friends of his, then called me up an hour later and asked me to dinner. Had about five hours alone with him in which he spent some time telling me I should go home and talk with a few people. But am not coming home. After all I'm a reporter, without political ambition, and certainly don't propose to go home and do propaganda."

Casually he noted, "We were bombed again tonight but twas nothing serious." He added, "Sometimes am so damned tired can hardly make that mike bounce."

The mike continued to bounce, however, and he did not have to go home to do what could better be done in London. He was often tempted to return "immediately," he wrote to his student-days friend Chet Williams, "thinking perhaps I could do more good there than here," but had decided he could not. As for what he thought had to be done:

"I have no desire to use the studio as a privileged pulpit, but am convinced that some very plain talking is required in the immediate future, even if it be at the price of being labeled a 'warmonger.'

"With the Americans who have come over here recently, including the official representatives, I am convinced that if this country goes down, we at home will tear ourselves apart within five years, probably less. From what I know of the position here I am convinced that the hour is much later than most people at home appreciate."

But all American aid "short of war" had begun for Britain. Wendell Willkie, whom Roosevelt had defeated in the 1940 election, followed Hopkins to London, bearing the message to Churchill from Roosevelt (and Henry Wadsworth Longfellow) "Sail on, O Ship of State." Churchill, who could also quote, replied with the phrase, "Westward, look, the land is bright!"

In March the Lend-Lease Act was signed and a new and sympathetic

American ambassador, John G. Winant, replaced Joe Kennedy in London. On the same plane with Winant came Dr. James B. Conant, president of Harvard University, and Benjamin Cohen, a White House adviser. Cohen and Samuel Rosenman, a presidential confidante, set to work in London drafting the Lend-Lease agreement with Britain, and Averell Harriman would arrive to administer it. In steady stream, thereafter, came American scientists, technicians, legalists and businessmen, as well as all levels of diplomats, to work out not only intergovernmental but actually interdepartmental cooperation between the United States and Britain.

Many were men Murrow had known in the United States, when he was CBS director of talks, such as Conant, Vannevar Bush, now chairman of the National Defense Research Committee; Harriman and his assistant Philip Reed.

In London he became for them a prime source of information about, and interpretation of, the British scene, and they, conversely, discussed some of their problems with him. Men in the Government at home, like Felix Frankfurter, wrote to him.

Winant, who did not so much conduct diplomatic relations — since these were personally reserved to Roosevelt and Churchill, anyway — as run an Anglo-American governmental department store, always felt that though he was popular with the British, it was not he but Murrow who was the authentic American ambassador in London, representing the two countries to each other. This was the more so because, in addition to his broadcasts to Americans about life in wartime Britain, he had also begun broadcasting on the BBC to a British audience, explaining American politics and peculiarities.

For many top-drawer Britons, Murrow was the first American they had ever known well, and as European students had done in his younger days, some later confessed that he was not at all what they expected Americans to be like. Thus, to one who became a good friend, Lady Reading, Murrow possessed "the three qualities that every Englishman treasures above all others and wants for his son" — he was "absolutely fearless, had some ethical values, and was very generous."

It was a matter of perpetual amazement to visiting Americans, and to other American correspondents in London, not to mention British reporters, how wide an acquaintance Murrow had and how implicitly trusted he was, so that, as the censors at BBC explained it, "they told him everything."

As explained by one of "them," Viscount Cranborne, later the Marquess of Salisbury, with whom he used to go shooting — the scion of the Cecils and the North Carolina farmboy were equally good at bagging pheasant — Murrow was able to establish his unique position, not only because of his own personality but because of his courage. This "all

admired, especially Churchill. When Britons read or heard his broadcasts of bombing missions, they knew that he was no braver than a soldier, except that he didn't have to do what he did."

Moreover the war had produced in Britain a curious mixture of normality and abnormality. On the normal side, a bus caught in an air alert would wait for a red light to change to green before moving on. On the other hand, some of the class and occupational barriers had begun to come down, for the war itself was the only occupation, and a fulltime one. There came to be no division between working hours and social hours. One same small group of people — "informed" circles — would meet everywhere. "Informed circles" were not only small but concentric. It was at Ronald Tree's that Murrow met Lord Cranborne. It was at the latter's home, next door to the Ritz, that he met Cranborne's aunt, Lady Milner. It was through Violet Milner that he met those who, called after her late husband "Milner's young men," still believed in Britain's world destiny.

Since the wartime cabinet was a coalition, Labor ministers as well as Conservative were part of "informed circles." Ernest Bevin, the minister of labor, and Herbert Morrison, the home secretary, visited the Murrows at their flat, and the Murrows visited the insurgent Member for Ebbw Vale, Aneurin Bevan, and his wife Jennie Lee at their home near Sloane Square.

British friends who recalled him from the war days invariably remarked on Murrow's "long periods of silence." He would be voluble, talking about a subject he was interested in. Then suddenly, for many minutes, he would be "far away." Finally a smile would cross his face, and sometimes he would throw back his head and laugh, evidently expressing glee at the arrival of comprehension. He would explain the thought that had struck him and rejoin the interrupted conversation. Sometimes he laughed so hard that tears came into his eyes.

A British journalistic colleague described him as "no back slapper," in fact, "you might at first regard him as a hail fellow, fell met." When Murrow finally did smile, the act began at the back of his neck and crept around to the front, wrinkling his cheeks and brightening his eyes. The mouth was the last to succumb, but then it did so broadly.

After the Bombers' Winter of 1940–1941, when it was no longer a question whether London could "take it," but of how long it would go on and to what end, the American correspondents found tediousness replacing excitement. The city had changed that winter, not only physically but psychologically. Drudgery settled in. There were hardly any desperately gay all-night parties now. People went resignedly instead of defiantly to the shelters. Reporters no longer strolled around in air raids.

There was also a shortage of facts about the war. The armed services did not readily provide information, even if they possessed it, on grounds of military security. The new American ambassador, receiving many com-

Part of the CBS wartime staff in London: left to right: John Daly, Murrow, Paul Manning, Bob Trout

Bundles for Britain, during the war. Janet Murrow and other American volunteers with Mrs. Churchill

plaints from the correspondents, told Whitehall that "what the United States requires is not propaganda but the facts." For example, though Britain obviously needed American convoys to insure safe passage for the materials of war, Americans did not understand the urgency of the situation because the British refused to tell the full story of their shipping losses and deficiencies, lest it encourage the enemy.

During the winter, while Murrow was reporting the war from rooftops and air-raid shelters, Downing Street and the House of Commons, Janet had been going to the hospitals to gather news, and reporting on a home front that desperately needed emergency aid. One evening, after a broadcast, he told her that Paul White's wife Sue, in New York, was asking that Janet represent her American organization in London, to administer direct private aid. "It's called Bundles for Britain, or some such damned nonsense," he explained. Bundles for Britain would become a major interest of the correspondent's wife.

The organization was formed just before Christmas, and soon after the new year began a bomb scored a direct hit on the Royal Crest Hospital. From America, Bundles for Britain supplied its first major assistance, a ten-thousand-dollar donation to replace medical equipment.

Janet's first public function for the new organization was to present a mobile canteen to a London borough on behalf of the people of Spokane. "At least some Britons know how to pronounce it now," she wrote home.

Within six months American women, formed in 1100 branches, sent 250,000 knitted garments, 500,000 pieces of clothing, and seventy-two mobile feeding units to Britain, and contributed more than $2.5 million.

Bundles for Britain and British War Relief were rivals in the task of getting American comfort to the beleaguered island. Both were small compared to the Royal Women's Voluntary Services, the mass mobilization which had been through Dunkerque, the Battle of Britain and most of the Blitz before Bundles for Britain even appeared on the scene, and had engaged in evacuation, civil defense, clothing and food distribution, and "compassion." The largest part of the help from across the Atlantic for the British domestic front came through the American Red Cross, and was administered by the familiar green uniforms of the WVS.

Bundles for Britain, on the other hand, was a distinctly American presence in London, and the fact that American women, who did not have to be there, moved about in the bomb-damaged city and shared privation and danger was of immense psychological importance to Britons as the visible evidence of American support.

Nor was the United States unaware of the significance of such help. The wife of the CBS correspondent in London made broadcasts home about Bundles for Britain, and sometimes interviewed women M.P.'s. Gradually her scope widened to provide observations on British events in general, as they affected women. She also gave talks to British audiences on American themes, under the auspices of the embassy and the Ministry of Information, and found she had to read American history herself to answer the many questions.

At the Bundles for Britain offices in Dean's Yard, part of Westminster Abbey, other volunteers included the wives of the British prime minister and the American ambassador. With Mrs. Churchill, Janet established an immediate friendship that was to endure long past the war, when the Murrows returned to the United States but would send occasional food packages to the Churchills — their own small Bundles for Britain scheme — as rationing and austerity continued.

Because 10 Downing Street is the home of British prime ministers, as well as their office, Janet occasionally had lunch there with Mrs. Churchill, and once when Ed called to pick her up, the prime minister heard his voice and came ambling out of his study. "Good to see you, Mr. Murrow," he said. "Have you time for several whiskies?"

The American correspondent and the British statesman were cordially acquainted by then, and had a mutual respect for each other as practicing and successful broadcasters. Churchill was impressed by what other Amercans had told him about Murrow, and by the reports he got from his own embassy in Washington, about his effect on American opinion. Their relationship was on Murrow's part a deferential one, and on Churchill's perhaps more political than personal, for Marlborough's descendant was never really on personal terms with anyone. The widespread use of his first name by other politicians, reporters and the public was just as much British form as the use of last names in public schools.

On the other hand, Churchill did not call many by their first names, though sometimes he used nicknames, like "Prof" for his scientific adviser Lord Cherwell, and "Bobbity" for the Marquess of Salisbury, his close friend and associate. As for Mr. Murrow, Churchill always called him just that, and was probably the only leading Briton who did not refer to him as Ed, though Mrs. Churchill called Janet by her first name.

A friend who knew both of them ascribed the affinity between the prime minister and Murrow to the fact that both were "men of primary colors, with no pastels or shades." That was also, he believed, why Murrow liked other men "larger than life," such as President Roosevelt, General Marshall, Ernest Bevin and "Nye" Bevan.

Churchill had the habit of working late, thanks to his other habits of rising late and never missing his afternoon nap, and at times he called Murrow at two in the morning and invited him to a nightcap. Before the prime minister moved his quarters to the underground "Annex" nearby, Murrow would arrive at Number 10, where a single bobby provided the only security, and climb past the photographs of past cabinets decorating the wall along the staircase, to the living room on the top floor. After Churchill went "underground" he could still be visited at Number 10 in the daylight hours, but would be found in the Annex after dark.

It is fair to assume that Churchill learned something about American attitudes from Murrow, for it was only in public that, when he had to listen to others, he glowered "like a ferocious clam," as his critic Aneurin Bevan described it.

Murrow after the war characterized Churchill as "the most remarkable" man of the age. "In some ways and in some moods, he creates the impression of a precocious and indestructible juvenile. At other times Mr. Churchill appears to be a combination of an early eighteenth-century cavalry officer and a brilliant student of history . . . It requires but little imagination to picture him with ruffles at his wrist and cutlass at his belt, the embodiment of an Elizabethan pirate.

"He can be as emotional as a great artist, as hard and reckless as a great captain. He can produce a thunderous phrase with an impromptu air, although the phrase has obviously been well rehearsed and calculated.

"But his was the honor of marshaling and mobilizing the English language in such fashion as to sustain those upon whom the long dark night of tyranny had descended, and to inspire those who had yet time to arm themselves and beat it off," Murrow wrote, sounding like Churchill himself.

There was no question, at any rate, that the British prime minister had caught the imagination of most Americans and that this was an appreciable factor in obtaining American aid for the British war effort.

American radio, apart from its news broadcasts, made its own peculiar contribution. Transatlantic "people to people" programs became popular. One New York station broadcast a *Carnival for Britain*, in which Gertrude Lawrence spoke from Radio City Music Hall to Vivien Leigh, Laurence Olivier and the Lord Mayor of London, gathered in an air-raid shelter there.

On another New York station guest notables read "War Letters from Britain," a published collection, and the appeal was made, "Send one dollar to British War Relief for a Badge of Sympathy." NBC put on a coast-to-coast one-hour program, *We Shall Live Again*, with Princess Juliana of the Netherlands, Crown Prince Olaf of Norway, Prince Jean of Luxembourg, and Eve Curie, all from London; Ignace Paderewski from Florida; and other European exiles from the New York studios and Canada. Irving Berlin wrote a new song, beginning, "A little old church in England tumbled down."

Radio also furthered the continuing debate, "Does the American interest and future welfare demand a British victory?" Wendell Willkie said that if he believed the United States could survive a British defeat, he would not take a single risk of international entanglement. But instead he believed that if Britain collapsed, American democracy would be threatened, so whatever his other differences with Roosevelt, he favored granting the President the necessary power to help Britain.

Murrow reported from London that Willkie had been warmly received there as a presidential good-will envoy, on his "One World" air journey.

Another American visitor to London was Raymond Swing, who had been broadcasting to the BBC weekly, as, in effect, Murrow's opposite number. The two old friends exchanged observations. Swing, a modest man, was overwhelmed by the reception he received. At a lunch in his honor the two hundred guests included eighteen government ministers, in what was as much a tribute to radio as to Swing himself.

An Anglo-American radio bond was also forged by Elmer Davis, the former Rhodes Scholar who had replaced Kaltenborn as the CBS commentator. He came to London laden with gifts, a new watch for Murrow from Mr. Paley to replace the one he had broken in the blackout, nylon stockings, perfume, and rarest of all, some oranges and lemons.

The Indianian, whose motto was "Don't let them scare you," and Murrow were kindred spirits as well as fellow broadcasters. Davis did his commentaries from London in the middle of the night as calmly as if he were still in the studio in New York, and wandered about in the blackout without a pass, remarking that "nobody seemed to notice." He reported that during twenty-five days and nights he never heard or saw a bomb dropped. Murrow informed him that there had in fact been several night raids but that Davis had been too preoccupied with his broadcasts to notice.

Revisiting some of his London haunts, Davis took Murrow out to dinner one night and asked if any of his favorite Châteauneuf du Pape was still available. There were two bottles left, and "God knows when we'll get any more," said the restaurant owner. "The Germans are drinking it on the Rhone." The diners ordered one of the bottles.

Over it, Murrow told Davis he was sure Britain would hold out, and that the Germans would never come. Elmer looked at the empty bottle.

"Well, just in case they do," he said, "They certainly shouldn't have the privilege of drinking stuff like this. Let's have the other bottle."

After he had gone back to New York, Murrow wrote to Davis lauding his London commentaries. "I have hopes that broadcasting is to become an adult means of communication at last."

But at home broadcasting, as usual, was having self-doubts. CBS reiterated its rule, "There shall be no dramatization or emotionalization of the war," and barred Gracie Fields, the Lancashire lass, from singing five Shakespearean sonnets on the Bard's birthday, because they contained "prophetic passages" about the war.

A professional judgment on radio in the war was delivered in the columns of *Variety*. "While it does not create the tensions of the day, radio elongates the shadows of fear and frustration. We are scared by the mechanized columns of Hitler. We are twice-scared by the emotionalism of radio.

"Radio quickens the tempo of the alternating waves of confidence and defeatism which sweep the country and undermine judgment. Radio exposes nearly everybody in the country to a rapid, bewildering succession of emotional experiences. Our minds and our moral natures just cannot respond to the bombardment of contradiction and confusion."

As messengers bearing bad news were slain in ancient days, so the electronic medium was being blamed for what it reflected. The argument has multiplied, and become familiar and acrimonious in the television era.

So far as Murrow was concerned in the war, emotion might be unloosed but there did not seem much room for confusion about what was going on. When Harry Hopkins returned from London, he carried with him a full-length feature film, *This Is England*, with the commentary written and spoken by the broadcaster.

Shown in two hundred New York movie houses in a single week, with proceeds going to the RAF Spitfire Fund, it was the first extended pictorial account of Britain's purgatory, and it made a deep and widespread impression.

The Germans helped with the biggest single air raid of the war on London, on May 10. Bombers pounded the city all night, started more than two thousand fires, and killed or injured three thousand persons. The House of Commons was hit, Westminster Abbey and Big Ben, the British Museum, the church of St. Clement Danes and fashionable Bond Street. That was the night Queen's Hall, adjacent to the BBC, was destroyed, and the CBS offices hit for the third time.

British spirits were low, but though American aid was increasing, actual American entry into the war did not seem any more likely. Even the flight of Hitler's deputy Rudolf Hess to Scotland, to make a "peace proposal," was more mystifying than encouraging.

Hitler's invasion of Russia provided the first real change in the fortunes of war. Churchill, long a foe of the Bolsheviks, broadcast to his people that night, declaring that the Russian cause had become Britain's cause. Murrow then made his radio report to America. "Never before has he been so violent in his denunciation of Hitler, whom he termed a bloodthirsty guttersnipe," he remarked.

"The prime minister brought all his oratorical power to the appeal for aid to the Soviet Union, which he has always hated and still does. His plea was based on a combination of humanitarian principle and national self-interest." But while the British would give the Russians technical and economic assistance, there was no hint of military aid, Murrow explained, adding: "It is worth noting that the prime minister said nothing about the fighting qualities of the Russian army, and gave no optimistic forecast about the duration of this new German campaign."

Churchill and his military advisers, and even more particularly the military brass in the United States, headed by General Marshall, the Army Chief of Staff, believed that the Soviet army would not last long before a Nazi onslaught. Many Americans, like Senator Harry Truman, felt that the Nazis and the Communists should merely be permitted to destroy each other. In fact, said the man from Missouri, as the Wehrmacht advanced: "If we see that Germany is winning the war we ought to help Russia, and if Russia is winning we ought to help Germany, and in that way let them kill as many as possible."

Murrow subscribed to the theory of quick and inevitable Russian defeat. General Marshall said six weeks. The Germans said ten weeks. Some around Churchill were inclined to put it at a mere ten days. When Vincent Sheean appeared on a Murrow broadcast to do a report on the new turn in the war, the latter cautioned him to qualify his belief that the Red Army could hold out. But Sheean held to his opinion, and the CBS broadcast carried his prediction that when the war ended the Russian army would still be fighting, "even though it should retreat to Irkutsk."

Less than a month after the invasion began, Harry Hopkins was in London again. He, and this time Churchill, believed that the Red Army would hold after all. Churchill called Hitler's move a "grand climacteric" of the war, and Hopkins went on to Moscow to see what the United States could do about helping the Russians.

When even American military men were persuaded that perhaps Hitler had made a gigantic mistake, Roosevelt and Churchill held their Atlantic Charter meeting. It was something of an anticlimax to Britons, for they had expected it would end in America's entry into the war. Still the meeting was significant because it established Anglo-American cooperation on a personal and intimate basis, as well as a governmental one.

Yet, Murrow noted, while it had become easy for London and Washington to communicate in the physical sense, the quality and volume of the exchange of ideas and information were not remarkable. He called for more frankness, honesty and directness between the two Allies. He said Americans didn't have to advise Britons to be brave, while Britons should admit the Americans were not universally popular. He suggested more candor by the British in revealing more about the Battle of the Atlantic. Americans could not tell what was going on simply from a tonnage list of sunken shipping. More details would bring home to American workers the awareness that planes they had built had been destroyed by the Germans, and perhaps, he concluded, they would "want to do something about it."

An important contribution to the ambiguity of the war was General de Gaulle's presence in London as head of the Free French movement, while the United States not only maintained relations with the Pétain regime in Vichy, but tried to influence it. Murrow became involved in the delicate situation when he arranged a broadcast for the second anniversary of the start of the war, in which the heads of the exiled governments in London would read messages to their people.

There were problems enough having to do with protocol and the order of precedence, and it was finally decided the leaders would speak in the order in which their countries had been invaded. But more important, whatever the State Department said, Murrow did not recognize Vichy as the legitimate government of France. He had invited de Gaulle to take part in the program, and the general had accepted.

But now the British government stepped in, perhaps with some prodding from Washington, and refused to allow de Gaulle to speak because he was not a chief of state. Somewhat incensed, Murrow said that he could not be expected to tell that to de Gaulle. He had invited him in good faith and still wanted the general to take part in the broadcast. The Ministry of Information had to inform de Gaulle officially, thereby not adding to Anglo-French harmony.

The Atlantic Charter meeting, because it cemented Anglo-American cooperation, also increased by a few decibels the level of domestic debate in the United States. Senator Burton K. Wheeler, a leading isolationist, asked the Federal Communications Commission to investigate what he called the "muzzling" of the America First movement by radio. One American editor observed that never had an organization been offered so much free broadcasting time, yet yelled so lustily about being denied the air. He called the America First attacks on the industry "unmatched in all the history of broadcasting for arrogance and distortion."

The controversy had raged all year, during which time fifteen America First rallies had been broadcast by NBC alone, including Senator Wheeler himself eight times and Charles A. Lindbergh four times. It reached its climax in October, when an America First rally was held in New York's Madison Square Garden, with Lindbergh again as the speaker.

The program was not broadcast live by either network, and Senator Wheeler charged censorship. He had previously demanded a half-hour free time from both NBC and CBS between 9 and 10 P.M. but it had been

Back from the Blitz and five days before Pearl Harbor, Murrow is feted at the Waldorf. Archibald MacLeish, LEFT, *William S. Paley, CBS president,* RIGHT

refused, and CBS declared there was no reason why a private citizen like Lindbergh was entitled to a free nationwide audience every time he spoke.

The controversy over "censorship" by the networks would continue until the United States entered the war a few weeks later, and even after that would come other controversy over freedom of expression, between the networks and some of their own commentators.

Meanwhile, in November, after more than two years of what was still only a European war, Murrow went home on a three-month furlough, on the same ship, the *Excambion,* on which Shirer had sailed. Janet preceded him, to make an American lecture tour on behalf of Bundles for Britain.

Bob Trout, replacing Murrow during his leave, was delayed en route and arrived as the latter was leaving. "I'm sure you'll do better than I," Murrow told the studio veteran who had once instructed him how to use a microphone. "I don't really fancy myself as a broadcaster."

Murrow was to devote his leave to going about the United States and giving talks in various cities for CBS affiliate stations. He was welcomed home by the network with a large public dinner in New York — "the most celebrity-studded ever held for a radio employee," *Variety* said, in its down-to-earth way — at which he declared that victory over the Axis hinged on American participation in the war. If the United States did not enter, he said, Britain might perish. Or at best there would be a stalemated peace, "a delayed-action defeat."

The war would be decided, "not in front of Moscow, not on the sands of Libya, but along the banks of the Potomac," he declared. "General headquarters for the forces of decency is now on Pennsylvania Avenue." His remarks were broadcast throughout the United States and also short-waved to Britain. The date was December 2, five days before Pearl Harbor.

At the dinner Archibald MacLeish, regarded as the Roosevelt administration's poet laureate, introduced Murrow as a man who had "accomplished one of the great miracles of the world" and had destroyed "the most obstinate of all the superstitions — the superstition against which poetry and all the arts have fought for centuries, the superstition of distance and time." He had also expunged "the ignorant superstition that violence and lies and murder on another continent are not violence and lies and murder here . . . the black and stifling superstition that what we cannot see and hear and touch can have no meaning for us."

The poet was also conscious of politics. "There were some in this country, Murrow, who did not want the people of America to hear the things you had to say," MacLeish continued, a thought the broadcaster himself had frequently entertained.

"There were some who did not wish to remember that the freedom of speech of which this country is so proud is freedom also to hear . . . It is not to assure a man the delight of listening to his own voice that freedom of speech is guaranteed. It is to assure the people a chance to hear the truth, the unpleasant truth as well as the reassuring truth, the dangerous truth as well as the comforting truth."

Despite those "who do not want the American people to know what they are up against, the people themselves were not afraid to know. They were not afraid when you, Murrow, told them the truth about London in the terrible winter of '40–'41," the poet concluded. "So long as the American people are told, and told truly and told candidly, what they have to face, they will never be afraid. And they will face it."

The speeches made at the dinner were ordered printed and bound by Frank Stanton, and Murrow inscribed a copy to his mother. "For this and all else, you are responsible. You know all about the ideal. Love and luck, Ed."

On Sunday, December 7, Murrow and Janet were in Washington, invited to the White House for dinner that evening, to be asked by the President about Anglo-American relations and the war. It would be an informal occasion and a rare one, bringing together the two best-known voices on American radio.

Murrow was on the Burning Tree golf course that afternoon when the news from Pearl Harbor came. Janet called Mrs. Roosevelt, expecting that the evening's invitation would be canceled. "We all have to eat. Come anyway," she was told.

The President's chair was empty through dinner, as he worked in his oval study on the second floor, already transformed into the political GHQ of a world war. Mrs. Roosevelt left the table and came back several times, with messages from the President telling Murrow to stay on. At 11 P.M. Janet went home, but Ed remained. Cabinet members, Congressmen and military trooped up and down the stairs. Harry Hopkins passed by and waved. "If he said to wait, you'd better wait," he advised, as if Murrow would do anything else. The broadcaster also talked with the three principal Cabinet officers, Hull, Stimson and Knox.

After the others had gone, Under-Secretary of State Sumner Welles went over the war message the President had been drafting for Congress, and at midnight Welles also left. Though it was Sunday night, lights were burning in Government offices and armed sentries were already on guard outside some of them.

In Britain, that Sunday evening, Prime Minister Churchill had been entertaining at Chequers, his official country residence, at a birthday party for Harriman's daughter Katherine. All were at the table when Churchill as usual at 9 P.M., when the BBC broadcast the news, switched on the small portable radio set Harry Hopkins had given him. As the Pearl Harbor news was heard, and it was disclosed the Japanese had also attacked the Malay Straits and Hong Kong, Churchill jumped up to say that Britain was joining the United States against Japan "at once." He called the President by transatlantic telephone to tell him so. Roosevelt replied that they were "all in the same boat now."

At the White House it was a half-hour past midnight when Murrow was finally sent for. He found the President in his study, gray with fatigue.

He asked the reporter a few questions about the bombing of England, to which he probably already knew the answers, and then, when sandwiches and beer had been brought in, he told Murrow the full story, so far as it was then known, of America's own bombing, on its major naval base in the Pacific. The President gave facts and figures which would not be made public for many hours, if not weeks, and Ed noted that he did not put anything off the record.

Mr. Roosevelt left him in no doubt that the Japanese attack had been a complete surprise, contrary to the charges made by his opponents that he had provoked and expected it. Several times the President pounded his fist on the table, as he told of the American planes that had been destroyed "on the ground, by God, on the ground!"

Murrow declared after the war, and after Roosevelt's death, when a leading publication made again the familiar charge of deliberate provocation, that he had no doubt the attack on Pearl Harbor came as a surprise. And if Hull, Stimson and Knox were not surprised, he said, "then that group of elderly men were putting on a performance which would have excited the admiration of any experienced actor. I cannot believe that their expressions, bearing and conversation were designed merely to impress a correspondent who was sitting outside in the hallway."

Moreover as he left, he recalled, the President asked, "Did this surprise you?" Murrow answered yes, and the President said, "Maybe you think it didn't surprise us!"

"I believed him," he concluded.

In London, Bob Trout, whose planned three months' replacement of Murrow would extend to two years as the result of America's entry into the war, was asked by a BBC engineer that night about Pearl Harbor. "Did Mr. Murrow know this was going to happen? Is that why he went home?"

Murrow stopped at the CBS office in the middle of the night, on his way home from the White House, but gave no details of his meeting with the President. All the rest of the night in their hotel room, as Janet sat up with him, he paced the floor, smoking and smacking his fist. "The biggest story of my life," he kept saying. "I can't make up my mind whether it's my duty to tell it, or to forget it."

He did not tell it. He decided that the President had been using him as a sounding board, in full confidence, and thinking out loud. Though technically not bound by an off-the-record restriction, he felt that in conscience he was so bound, and waited for the details of Pearl Harbor to be made public in the routine official way. Next day he sat in the House of Representatives press gallery as the President called for a declaration of war.

Murrow continued his lecture tour, as Hitler followed the American declaration of war against Japan with his own against the United States, thus ending the debate and dissidence over American involvement in what Thomas Jefferson had called "entangling alliances," not only with Britain but with the Soviet Union.

On his journey around the country Murrow sounded the theme, perhaps grandiloquent, that "when this war is all over the entire world will be dominated either from Berlin or from Washington. We must see to it that we will win." When he arrived in Spokane, which was home ground, he was greeted by a huge crowd. "This . . . is Murrow," the chairman said, in introducing him. "This . . . is frightening," he began.

At his old college, Washington State, seven thousand people gathered in the men's gym to hear him. "It was the greatest event ever held in Pullman," reported the local newspaper. "Old friends came from points as distant as Walla Walla to shake his hand."

But though the United States was now at war, and tens of thousands of young men were enlisting even before their draft call came, Murrow found that many Americans were still viewing the conflict as a spectacle, and were "spectators with an inadequate understanding of our own responsibility." The United States had not yet become aware of its dominant position, "not yet acquired the habit of world leadership." And, he warned, "if we delay too long in winning the war, we will inherit nothing but a cold, starving, embittered world."

In response to a question after one of his lectures, he criticized the State Department for its condemnation of the Christmas Eve takeover of St. Pierre and Miquelon islands by "the so-called Free French." The State Department, he said, "has misjudged the nature of this war. It is a worldwide revolution, as well as a war."

Murrow's friend Elmer Davis after Pearl Harbor made a broadcast which Ed took to heart. "There are some patriotic citizens who sincerely hope that America will win the war, but they also hope that Russia will lose it; and there are some who hope that America will win the war, but that England will lose it; and there are some who hope that America will win the war, but that Roosevelt will lose it!"

During his home leave, as he saw America's youth being drafted, the former cadet commander again contemplated taking up his commission and going into the Army. He was told in Washington that he was performing at least equally important service as a broadcaster, and that in any event, he would not be given a combat commission, but rather something in public relations.

Instead, he signed a new contract with CBS for three more years, but insisted on a clause that would abrogate it if he did join the armed forces.

Winston Churchill came to the White House for Christmas, and on the first day of the new year 1942 the President, the prime minister, and the Soviet and Chinese ambassadors devised the declaration of the United Nations, twenty-six in number. They pledged a fight to the finish.

With American entry into the war, the broadcasting industry lost its anxiety neurosis about neutrality, objectivity and even emotionalism. The networks went on a twenty-four-hour schedule. Many local radio stations sent the White House messages of support. Some stations put armed guards around their control rooms and transmitter towers "to prevent sabotage." One network canceled a performance of Victor Herbert's *Babes in Toyland* as "too frivolous," and instead opera star Risë Stevens sang the National Anthem. Kate Smith sang it over and over. The new Office of Production Management took to the airwaves, the first of numerous Government agencies to do so, with a program called *Keep 'Em Rolling*.

On Pearl Harbor Day, the networks picked up news broadcasts from London, Buenos Aires, Singapore, Ankara, Santiago, Sydney, Rio de Janeiro, Mexico City, and Kuibyshev in Russia, where foreign diplomats and part of the Soviet government had moved from Moscow.

After Pearl Harbor, San Francisco became a major relay and listening post. CBS had correspondents in Honolulu and Manila, Sydney and Singapore, and even in Burma, Batavia and Chungking. But its reporter in Tokyo, W. R. Wills, was heard no more, and soon Singapore and Manila would also be silent.

At his new "piano" in Studio 9, a bank of push buttons, Paul White, the news director, was able to talk to his correspondents anywhere, or let them talk to each other.

Like the war itself, daily overseas radio news broadcasting was no longer concentrated in Europe. It had become global.

VII

"A kind of orchestrated hell"

D-Day in Europe was the day American news broadcasting may have been created for. American troops had been in action for nineteen months, in North Africa, Sicily and Italy, but Tuesday, June 6, 1944, was the bright and sunny day after the delaying storm when radio accompanied the invasion of the Continent in landing craft, underwent German aerial bombing and shelling, flew in bombing planes across the Channel, landed on the Normandy beaches, and joined as never before the American people at home with the men who in their name had opened the final chapter in Europe's liberation.

Just after 3:30 A.M., Eastern war time, awakening most of the nation which had not already been awakened by the first alarm from Germany, the United States Army Signal Corps radio channel from London, created for the occasion and feeding into all American networks, carried the first official bulletin that the invasion had begun.

Five minutes later, interrupting comment and analysis in the New York studios, from London again was heard a familiar voice, indeed by now the best-known and perhaps the most respected voice in broadcasting. Ed Murrow was reading General Eisenhower's order of the day to the troops in his vast command.

This was the beginning of the five-day "pool" operation in which the separate and normally competitive radio correspondents, spread out in numerous combat and observation assignments, broadcast not only for their own but for all the networks simultaneously.

The "kickoff" position on D-Day went by unanimous consent to the man who had not only been there the longest — seven years of crisis and combat — but was generally acknowledged the best. Only three months before he had been given the Peabody Award for 1943 for his reporting from Britain.

Murrow's assignment on D-Day was comment rather than combat, and even more than comment, it was coordination. He would much rather have gone across the Channel that day, in a landing craft like his colleagues Charles Collingwood, Larry Le Sueur and Bill Downs, or in a bombing plane like Dick Hottelet. Instead, in the dim basement of the Ministry of Information, at London University, while reporting on D-Day developments and reaction in London, he was also supervising the reception of the reports of others, and their safe relay or recording for the waiting coast-to-coast channels of America.

On that day radio as a news medium reached a never again equaled peak of cumulative and effective communication. In the twenty-four hours that followed the first word of the invasion — which came from the German Transocean News Agency two hours before Allied communiqué Number 1 — the CBS network devoted sixteen hours to invasion news and commentary, of which three solid hours came from London. People listened to radio who never listened before, if there were any such. In some periods during the day listening was statistically 200 percent of normal.

D-Day broke the audience size and concentration records previously set by the seventy-two hours after Pearl Harbor. There was this significant difference in addition. Virtually all the Pearl Harbor news was presented in regularly scheduled news periods, and on CBS only eight out of 137 commercial programs were preempted for war news, five of them for the Roosevelt and Churchill speeches on the day after the day of "infamy."

On D-Day alone seventeen commercially sponsored CBS programs were knocked off the air by war news, for a total of five hours. Before the invasion, indeed, sponsors and advertising agencies were warned they could be blacked out at any moment, and were even briefed by the network's military analyst, with the aid of a "secret" war map, to impress on them how patriotic their forbearance would be, and that anyway, their money would be refunded.

D-Day in Europe had been planned for ever since Pearl Harbor and Germany's subsequent declaration of war on the United States, and news preparations had kept pace with combat preparations. England had become the staging area that would reverse Hitler's never-consummated Operation Sea Lion. But there were numerous delays and diversions before the second front that Russia needed could actually be opened. For the United States was fighting a war in the broad reaches of the Pacific as well, and there were many in the country who believed it should concentrate on defeating Japan, while the two totalitarian monsters Germany and Russia tore each other apart.

During the period between Pearl Harbor and D-Day — as the United States assumed the major role in the war, as General Eisenhower moved to London to plan the continental invasion and its preliminary in North

American entry into the war converts the civilian of the London Blitz into a uniformed correspondent

Africa, and American correspondents there changed their English-cut tweeds for English-cut military uniforms and were finally permitted to ride on British bombing missions over Europe — Murrow left his London vantage point several times to report action, on the ground in North Africa or in the air, on gigantic raids against Berlin and Nazi-occupied Europe.

But basically his assignment was to continue the story of Britain at war, now joined by Allies, and as usual his reporting instincts were stirred by political and sociological considerations.

He had returned to London after Pearl Harbor, and after his American lecture tour, in the first dark wave of depression and doubt for the newly created United Nations, which then meant the Allied coalition against the Fascist Axis.

It was April 1942, and the United States had lost Wake and Guam, and suffered the indignities of Bataan. The British were plunged into gloom by the fall of Singapore with sixty thousand prisoners, after Churchill had said the fortress would be held, and they wondered about the fighting abilities of their men in the Far East and North Africa, where Bengazi also had fallen. Furthermore, shipping losses were mounting in the Battle of the Atlantic, and the German warships *Scharnhorst*, *Gneisenau* and *Prinz Eugen* had escaped in the Channel from Brest, under British guns.

In Europe the German attempt to take Moscow had failed and the Russians had made counterattacks in the Ukraine, but Hitler was about to open his drive for the Caucasus and the Volga River, and Leningrad was still under siege. At best, only a holding action was accounted possible on the eastern front.

Murrow returned to London to inaugurate a new series of Sunday afternoon fifteen-minute radio commentaries which he and his successors were to maintain on the CBS network for twenty-three years, one of the most seriously listened-to programs in radio history.

In these Sunday afternoon programs the Murrow style of broadcasting — temperate yet crisp, dignified yet informal, understated and never condescending, and always probing behind the news — set the pattern for what had become in effect a CBS style.

Murrow's instructions to the European staff that the war would make famous were simple. "Never sound excited. Imagine yourself at a dinner table back in the United States, with the local editor, a banker, and a professor, talking over the coffee. You try to tell what it was like, while the maid's boyfriend, a truck driver, listens from the kitchen. Talk to be understood by the truck driver while not insulting the professor's intelligence."

But it did not stop with telling what it was like. Murrow's broadcasts, in the war and ever after, dealt in editorial opinion in a noneditorial way. They might be called "subjectively objective."

As he took up the London round of reporting again — and it embraced such quasisocial enterprises as the Anglo-American Monday Evening Club, as well as formal and informal news briefings at British and American agencies — he told friends that the initial setbacks in the war had stirred up anti-British feeling in the United States, with the traditional Anglophobia and the normal scapegoat-seeking between Allies being added to by dismay over the British performance at Singapore. He also reported that the British ambassador, Lord Halifax, despite his hot dog-eating attempts to mingle with commoners, was not popular in the United States, though the Roosevelt administration esteemed him.

By something of a contrast, American entry into the war had brought an overwhelming desire in Britain for knowledge of the United States, and considerable thawing of the British reserve toward foreigners, especially those who spoke roughly the same language. American history was actually introduced into British schools, and in addition to Murrow's broadcasts on the BBC, Elmer Davis and Raymond Swing beamed American commentaries from the United States to the British home service.

Though the Japanese were rolling southward through Asia and the Pacific and most American eyes turned in that direction, Murrow kept his own steadily fixed on Europe, and not merely as a function of his assignment. He believed the true decision between democracy and dictatorship would be reached in Europe, not in the Far East, and that it would have to come by the massive Allied invasion of the Continent in the West, not by the bombing of Germany or by events on the eastern front. He endorsed the strategy of Roosevelt and Churchill who, at their White House meeting after Pearl Harbor, had set up a combined military command and determined that the war on Germany must take precedence over the war on Japan.

As a token that once again the Yanks would be coming, American troops were on the way to British North Ireland before the White House meeting had ended. Then Eisenhower, as chief of the War Plans Division, undertook to map out two operations for 1942, the invasion itself, later called OVERLORD, and the preliminary buildup in Britain, BOLERO, which would bring a million Americans to that already crowded island.

Four days before Murrow got back to London, Harry Hopkins and the American chief of staff, General Marshall, arrived there to present the two American plans to Churchill. But the prime minister was not so sure about a second front in Europe that year, despite Allied promises to Stalin. Churchill feared the cost in human life of an invasion, as well as the psychological effect of any failure, and favored a preliminary diversion in North Africa, leaving a second front until later.

The British by April were sending 350 bombers nightly over Germany, and on May 30 they made their first 1000-bomber raid, against Cologne. But as Churchill resisted the second front, he also resisted American desires to join the bombing of the Continent immediately, calling this "too ambitious." He said he frankly preferred that the RAF be given American planes for its own uses. But willy-nilly the American Eighth Air Force also began European strategic bombing from the United Kingdom that summer.

From London, Murrow, like Churchill, could view the entire panorama of widening global warfare, and he broadcast daily on its military aspects, in Burma, Madagascar, the Mediterranean, the Atlantic and North Africa — where Tobruk had now fallen, with thirty-three thousand prisoners — as well as its politics, principally the internal strains of the Anglo-American-Soviet alliance. But unlike Churchill, Murrow also gave some thought to internal British developments.

On a day when the RAF hit the Ruhr and the Rhineland, he spent most of his broadcasting time discussing old-age pensions. On the day when the Russians lost Rostov, he preferred to interview Sir Stafford Cripps about independence for India, to which Churchill was strongly opposed. Murrow noted the "considerable emotional allegiance" to Russia that had swept the British Isles, as a result of the Red Army's dogged fighting, and remarked that Russia was being more loudly cheered than the United States even though it was American and not Russian history that was being taught in the schools.

But while he did not foresee Britain going Communist after the war, as apparently some Americans feared, "anything approaching American economic imperialism would certainly drive this country into radical political and economic experiments, in concert with one or more European powers. Alliances are not always lasting, as this war and earlier wars have demonstrated."

The British ruling class was also thinking, somewhat dejectedly, of the future. One of its typical members, Murrow's friend Harold Nicolson, forecast "some sort of revolution" in Britain as a result of the war. "We may even have republicanism and a certain amount of persecution of the governing class. But that will die down, and we shall find some middle position between the extremes of the pendulum — a modified socialism, rather dependent upon America, rather impoverished, rather weak. But still existent, and with our independence and our honor maintained."

Murrow marked the end of three years of war for Britain with an expressive broadcast. "How long is three years? I don't know. It's long enough for people to marry and have children, long enough for a revolution, long enough for small boys to be able to put their elders to shame when it comes to identifying aircraft. And it's plenty of time for big English breakfasts, thick Devonshire cream, good cigarettes, and good wine to be lost in the mists of memory.

"Three years is long enough for you to forget what it was like to be able to buy and drive a new car, buy a new suit of clothes whenever you wanted it, and travel whenever you had the money and the inclination. Three years is long enough for schoolboys to grow up and become soldiers, but not long enough to permit you to forget the friends who have died. It's plenty of time for empires to change hands, for the reputation of generals to be made and unmade, for the social, economic and political fabric of nations to be ripped to shreds.

"More damage can be done in three years than can be measured in dollars. Millions of people can be made into slaves; hundreds of thousands may starve or be butchered. There's plenty of time for a civilization to die but not enough for a new one to be born.

"Three years, or three hours, is plenty of time to see timid, cautious, careful men and women turned into heroes. After all, it requires only a few months, or even a few weeks, for physical courage to become commonplace; war seems to become almost the normal existence."

As he reviewed the war which since the Battle of Britain had been "one disaster after another, each followed by a debate in the House of Commons, which in turn was followed by a vote of confidence," and mentioned the sacrifices made and the leveling social changes that had been forced into being, he arrived at this conclusion:

"The coming winter will be the worst that Europe has ever seen. There will be cold and famine and pestilence and despair and degradation. How many more such winters must pass depends to a large extent upon the United States. We are the only people fighting this war with plenty of food, clothing and shelter, with an undamaged productive system that can work in the light. We aren't tired and Europe is, all of it. We lack the incentive of the imminence of immediate danger. Our sacrifices must be made at long range and in cold blood."

But the range was getting closer and the blood becoming warmer. Harry Hopkins had made still another trip to London, to provide for action by American troops "somewhere" in 1942, so that there would not be another debilitating "phoney war" period. Against his own inclinations, which were still for invasion in Europe that year, Eisenhower was planning TORCH, the invasion of North Africa. At 20 Grosvenor Square, where he had set up headquarters diagonally opposite the American embassy; on the fourth floor of Claridge's Hotel, where sixteen rooms were under the command of the American Chiefs of Staff; at meetings at 10 Downing

Street and at Chequers, the complicated jigsaw puzzle involving men, munitions and movement — not to mention political motives — was being fitted together.

Eisenhower brought with him as his personal aide Captain Harry Butcher of the United States Naval Reserve, who only a month before had been the CBS vice president in Washington. The first person Butcher looked for in London was naturally Murrow, whom the commanding general of the European Theater of Operations would count on, it seemed, if not for military advice at least for social, such as who in London was "important," who "had" to be seen, and which invitations accepted.

Murrow was thought by Butcher and others at Number 20 to be on "intimate" terms with Churchill and Winant, but his social duties, besides playing poker and lending his left-handed golf clubs to Butcher and other southpaws, turned out to consist of steering Americans to the better restaurants, bravely functioning despite rationing and supposed price controls, where they usually nostalgically ordered hamburgers. After a few mouthfuls, he relished informing them that they were eating horsemeat.

Murrow's professional relationship with the commanding general of the ETO was that of reporter to news source, but he was also a member of the complaint board set up by the Association of American Correspondents to protest the amalgamation of the headquarters Public Relations Office with military censorship, the reporters feeling that these should be separate functions. Eisenhower not only agreed, but ended entirely the censorship of stories dealing with such questions as race relations in the armed forces — the policy was still "separate but equal" — in order that Americans at home might be aware of what the problems were.

In a broadcast on the BBC home service Murrow called Eisenhower a representative of "the great American middle class." Butcher reported that Ike chuckled when Murrow said, "I don't know whether Eisenhower is a good general or not." Within a few minutes, however, the commanding general was telephoning Murrow to tell him he could spend his radio time better than in providing personal publicity, since the war was not being "fought to make a hotshot out of Ike Eisenhower."

With the scene being set for action in Europe, and the Air Force beginning to be engaged, Murrow was impatient for some of it himself. "I'm fed up with this business of broadcasting," he wrote his Air Force brother Lacey.

"If the big boys in our Army and Air Force over here would let reporters go out and report some action, go to the only place where the story is, I wouldn't mind so much, but that isn't the system. If I'm a good boy maybe I can start flying with Spaatz's boys in another three months, but even that isn't certain. Meanwhile I'm going to do some flying with the British on submarine patrol.

"If I quit and come home and pass the medical, which I can, what are the chances of getting into a combat unit and staying there? Over here I'm told I can volunteer and get my training, and then sure as hell I'll be sent to Intelligence or be made a PRO, which is a fate worse than death. I'd rather fight the PRO than be one . . .

"Please don't think this outburst about what I'm to do with myself is dictated by any fear of what anyone else will say. After all, I was in and under this war three years before the brave boys who are now arriving over here. It's just the old Murrow conscience that's troubling me."

In another letter, after D-Day, to his parents, he would fancy himself as a combat officer. "I've seen men killed because their officers didn't know as much about military tactics as I do, and that sort of thing makes me mad," he wrote.

Meanwhile an American propaganda effort had been established, and it also began preparing for American military action "somewhere" in 1942. President Roosevelt created the Office of War Information and Murrow's Hoosier friend Elmer Davis was drafted away from CBS to run it. He was generally regarded as opposed to the spoon-feeding method of propaganda and Murrow lauded him for his straight talk. "He's one of the few Americans I have ever known to survive two years of Oxford with accent and outlook unimpaired," he said.

"He will, I am sure, share the hope of his friends on both sides of the Atlantic that someone may be found to criticize him and his activities as accurately, mercilessly and fearlessly as he has done to Government departments and offices."

OWI and its postwar successor, the United States Information Agency, were in for a continuum of merciless criticism, as Murrow would find out personally when he himself became the USIA director two decades later.

In 1942 OWI began its career in somewhat tenuous fashion by urging songwriters and music publishers to be more "tactful" and "constructive" in their war effort. It classified as "unsatisfactory" such popular songs as "Slap the Jap" and "Good-bye Mamma, I'm Off to Yokohama." On the other hand it found the "White Cliffs of Dover" genre "too peaceful," and "Don't Sit Under the Apple Tree" too sentimental. More in keeping with the war's high purpose, OWI thought, was "This Is Worth Fighting For." Under the spur, Tin Pan Alley produced a smash hit called "The Fuehrer's Face," and "Johnny Got a Zero" soon became another top tune.

At CBS the war was calling William S. Paley, the company president. He visited London that summer, met Eisenhower and Spaatz, and was introduced about town by Murrow. As always with Americans abroad, and especially in wartime England, professional and social relationships were not too carefully divided. The American correspondents knew the commanding general and his officers personally, as well as in line of duty. When Paley arrived, he not only found himself immediately lunching with Eisenhower, but visiting airfields and training camps with Murrow, attending briefing sessions, dining at the Connaught and Savoy with British officials, and increasingly impressed with the fact that, as so many had said, his correspondent was indeed "the most important American in London."

A short time later Paley was in uniform, joining Eisenhower in Algiers, in charge of the radio branch of psychological warfare. He had been most taken with the American commander. Murrow was more reserved in judgment.

Other CBS executives were also going into war service, and to prove of some significance to Murrow and his career in later days was the ascendancy of Frank Stanton, the young research and sales promotion head, to a vice presidency on his way up.

London became the scene of a major CBS war project, which would be called propaganda, as Norman Corwin, the radio medium's leading thoughtful dramatist, arrived there to write a series of shortwave programs called *An American in England*, dealing with various aspects of the military buildup. Murrow was the producer of the series, and appeared in it himself.

The two men, each dominant in his radio field, had met during Murrow's furlough home in the Pearl Harbor period. Corwin, a newcomer at CBS, had written, entirely in rhyme, a dramatic fantasy called "The Plot to Overthrow Christmas." It was broadcast on Christmas Day, and Murrow came to find Corwin and tell him he thought it worthy of W. S. Gilbert. It was the beginning of a sincere friendship and Corwin was overjoyed to find Murrow joined with him in a major radio project. Alas, the first program was never heard in New York. Corwin, "too clever by half," as he later realized, began it without announcement, with a scene in which an American in London, on the telephone, was complaining about being cut off. The New York engineers, listening, thought it was a case of crossed wires, and a real telephone misconnection. They pulled out all the plugs. Subsequent programs were luckier, and were provided with music by Benjamin Britten, but atmospherics usually interfered, so eventually *An American in England* was produced in New York. But for several weeks, Murrow and Corwin enjoyed putting the program together, and each other's company.

Murrow was also a participant in, and sometimes the chairman of, a BBC program called *Freedom Forum,* broadcast around the world. One of the other regulars on the program was his friend Harold J. Laski, of the London School of Economics, who had just dedicated to Murrow his book, *Reflections on the Revolution of Our Time,* a fact which Senator Joe McCarthy would try to make something of.

The dedication was not a casual one. Murrow was much influenced by the "gray eminence" of the Labor Party, the small, bespectacled and fluent storyteller, who looked like a bookkeeper but had the friendship and respect of three American Supreme Court Justices, Holmes, Brandeis and Frankfurter, and indeed of the American President.

Though McCarthy apparently did not know it, Laski was an opponent of communism. He accepted Marxist theory but the revolution he believed in was "revolution by consent." Laski's certainty that the war would bring a new social order to Britain, based on more equality, flavored much of Murrow's broadcasting during the war, and so did Laski's conviction that peace would to a large extent depend upon the responsibility of the United States. He had a deep attraction to America, had taught at Harvard, and written political science classics on American democracy and the presidency.

In his letters to Roosevelt, Laski had counted on the President to "teach" Churchill that it was not "the achievement of the past" but "the hopes of the future" that counted, and obviously the President tried to do so, often to Churchill's distaste.

The two great wartime rivals in Britain, in the arena of political ideology, were Churchill and Laski, and it is to be noted that Ed Murrow, the American, was friendly with both and represented each one fairly.

Another close friend of Murrow's, Jan Masaryk, sometimes appeared on *Freedom Forum* with him and Laski, to discuss European questions.

On one *Freedom Forum* program, dealing with the role of press and radio in war and after the war, Murrow said what he would often say again, as he critically appraised the industry of which he was a part. "The only thing that's important in broadcasting is what comes out of the loudspeaker, not the plans and schemes concocted in comfortable offices."

Radio was under some examination at home at that moment for its war reporting, and one critic assailed its profit motive which, he said, "results in broadcasting trivia on the same level as matters affecting human destiny." Moreover, he added, commercial sponsorship of news broadcasts was "prostitution of the decent impulses of the people."

In London, generals and diplomats were coming and going. The preparations for the North African invasion were in the final stage. At his Grosvenor Square office, Eisenhower's aide Harry Butcher hung a large detail map of Norway on the wall. Correspondents eyed it furtively, as they watched the packing-up process at headquarters. Eisenhower would move to Gibraltar to command the operations across the Mediterranean but some correspondents hinted to their editors that the invasion would come on the Scandinavian peninsula, which is what they were meant to think.

When Allied reporters received their travel orders, final destination unknown — among them was Charles Collingwood for CBS — some of them carried Arctic clothing. They did not need it in Algiers or Casablanca.

The political implications of the North African expedition were in some ways more important than the military, and Murrow was fully cognizant of them. The Sunday after the landing, and after the British victory at El Alamein, the church bells were rung throughout England by Churchill's order, though it was originally intended, when they were stilled at the outbreak of the war, that they would be heard next only to announce Hitler's invasion of the island. In his broadcast that day, Murrow noted that while the sound was pleasant after twenty-nine months' silence, "some of the bell ringers were sadly out of practice." He quoted one Briton as saying of the bells, "Tempting Providence, that's what it is!" and himself observed that it was "a long way from Bizerte to Berlin" and that the Allies had gone into North Africa "because we didn't have the stuff to go directly onto the continent of Europe."

He then turned to the deal General Eisenhower had made for the co-operation of Admiral Darlan, the Vichy commander-in-chief in North Africa. Looking at Darlan's political record, and being unwilling to "take the line that for the time, military considerations dominate," he wondered if this explanation would impress the Fighting French "who died trying to stop Rommel's advance at Bir Hacheim," and "whether or not we may stand dishonored in the eyes of the conquered peoples on the Continent."

He declared: "This is a matter of high principle in which we carry a moral burden we cannot escape. Wherever American forces go, they will carry with them food and money and power, and the quislings will rally to our side if we permit it."

Military necessity or not, he said, "there is nothing in the strategic position of the Allies to indicate that we are either so strong or so weak that we can afford to ignore the principles for which this war is being fought."

The shaft found its mark. There was a good deal of controversy in Washington about the Darlan deal, and Murrow's cautionary remarks were heard by Secretary of the Treasury Henry Morgenthau. He raised the question with Secretary of War Stimson, and Morgenthau and Supreme Court Justice Felix Frankfurter, a staunch admirer of Murrow, called on the President for a clarification of policy. They succeeded in toning down the White House's propensity for unstinted praise of Darlan, and the arrangement emerged as a cynical, somewhat shabby expedient, or as a British observer described it, a "disgraceful and most profitable episode."

The combination of the El Alamein desert victory, the North African landings, the Russian offensive at Stalingrad — which Murrow, echoing Churchill, had thought the Germans would take — and American progress on Guadalcanal created what some saw as a turning point in the war, though Churchill minimized it as "perhaps the end of the beginning." The Casablanca Conference in January 1943 produced the Allied watchword of "unconditional surrender."

Murrow did not go to Casablanca but he interviewed one of the American pilots who had flown Churchill there, as well to Moscow and other meeting places. The flyer was conscious of the heavy responsibility imposed upon him. "This fellow is Mr. England. If we dunk him into the drink, nobody knows what will happen," he said.

The end of what Murrow styled "the first year of global war" found Britain, temporarily free of bombs but still under blackout, a bit more cheerful despite austerity and fatigue. "Curiosity about America has grown by leaps and bounds," he reported.

"Any American over here could spend his whole time lecturing about home. American expressions are becoming part of the common currency of English speech. A year ago you seldom saw an English girl chewing gum. Now if you visit a town where American troops are stationed, the girls seem to be chewing as though to make up for lost years. The first year of global war brought the Americans to Britain, and the place will never be the same again."

One British upper-class reaction to the new order of events was set down by Harold Nicolson in his wartime diary. The M.P., who was attached to the Ministry of Information, was to conduct a group of American soldiers on a tour of Westminster. "In they slouched, chewing gum, conscious of their inferiority in training, equipment, breeding, culture, experience and history, determined in no circumstances to be either interested or impressed."

Murrow, who did not chew gum himself, saw it otherwise. "I believe that any American who watched the first year of global war from London would have at the end of it one dominant impression, and that would be the power and responsibility of his own country. It is fashionable, and probably true, to speak of this war as a revolution. When the French made their revolution more than a hundred years ago they hoped to regulate the destiny of nations and found the liberty of the world. That is the task that now confronts America and her Allies."

One of the means of producing a better British understanding of the United States was books. Murrow's old friend Chester Williams was "on loan" to the Ministry of Information from the United States Office of Education with the idea of opening an American library in London. Ambassador Winant asked Murrow if he favored such a plan. "If you believe the pen is mightier than the sword, how can you doubt it?" he replied. The London library, an immediate success, was the first of the two hundred such overseas reading rooms Murrow himself would administer as USIA director twenty years later.

The "war as a revolution" kindled the Labor Party's only wartime parliamentary revolt, over the Beveridge Report on social security, on the ground that the Churchill government's proposed implementation of it did not go far enough. Some even felt that Labor should leave the coalition and, while continuing to support the war effort, become an active voting opposition again in domestic matters. Murrow spent as much broadcasting time on the Beveridge Plan and on British manpower problems as on military operations, and he predicted rationing would continue long after the war's end.

But the unexpected setback encountered by the green American troops in the battle for Tunisia, with Anglo-American recriminations in London — each ally accusing the other of not doing well enough — and his own never-stilled desire to be at the scene of the action, made Murrow a battlefield reporter in the spring of 1943. He flew to North Africa, while John Charles Daly, fresh from New York, and Bob Trout manned the microphone in London.

"There were American troops on the move," he broadcast from Tunisia. "The men were brown, dusty and tough . . . the skin on their bare arms and throats seemed tight-stretched. Not many of them will be able to wear their civilian clothes when they get home.

"There were two privates beside the road. One came from Delaware, the other from the Texas Panhandle. One said he thought this country was worth fighting for . . . maybe. The other confided he had just received two valentines, one mailed last year, the other one this year. He thought that very funny. Neither one of them had quite figured out what this war is all about. One said, 'I'm one of those handcuffed volunteers. I got a letter saying my "friends and neighbors" had selected me to do some fighting. And here I am.'

"Finally you reach the point of the ridge. The guns are well behind you. Off to the right, six hundred feet below, is the floor of the valley. At first there seems to be blue smoke floating knee-high in one of the little side valleys about three miles away. Finally you realize that little valley is knee-deep with morning glories, and the breeze makes them look like drifting blue smoke.

"There must be men somewhere in Morning Glory Valley, for the mortar bursts begin appearing there. No trenches. No long line of bayonets glinting in the sun. Just that peaceful valley and the explosions on the hill beyond.

"You meet a captain who has just written a new song. It's called, 'There's a New World over the Skyline.' But as you watch shells bursting along those hills you know there won't be any new world over that skyline — just more hills, more land mines, and more Germans who have lost their freedom of maneuver and must be expected to fight for every hill and gun position."

The rugged North African terrain reminded him of his own Cascade Mountains, or the Blue Ridge. On one occasion he was up front, behind British guns, as a barrage opened a British infantry attack, and the Germans responded with their own artillery. It was not yet dawn, and his close, sharp, intimate reporting required no camera.

"The road winds white before you. The edge of the rising sun touches the fields and the ambulances going toward the front. There are dead and wounded men in the valley behind you. To get down to the other part of the front you drive through country that pleases neither the mind nor the eye, a country fit only for fighting . . .

"There is a cold cutting wind. When the clouds hit the mountaintops you expect them to make a noise. There is dust and cactus and thorn bushes and bad roads. It is a cold country with a hot sun.

"Tanks and trucks have cut through the dust and left bare rocks exposed. A dispatch rider is thrown from his motorcycle and its wheels spin in the air. Everything is covered with that white tired dust. Men's red-rimmed eyes look like smoldering holes in a gray blanket. The dust blows from right to left. You begin to meet ambulances coming back. They are taking the dust, as drivers nurse them carefully over those terrible roads. You can see them lift on the wheel, trying to ease the shock for the wounded back behind.

"If you had gone into the little town of Pichon, a few hours after it had been retaken, there are a few things you would have noticed. A fairly good road leading down to a stream. It is pockmarked with holes, where the sappers have removed land mines. A batch of Austrian prisoners being herded along. They are obviously well-fed, but their shoes are not good. They don't look particularly sullen, just tired.

"Where the road cuts down to meet the stream there is a knocked-out tank, two men beside it and two men digging a grave. A little farther along a German soldier sits smiling against the bank. He is covered with dust, and he is dead. On the rising ground beyond a young British lieutenant lies with his head on his arms, as though shielding himself from the wind. He is dead, too. Near him is a German antitank gun, its muzzle pointing at the sky.

"Pichon itself is a miserable dirty little town with a few whitewashed houses, their sides scarred and chipped with machine-gun bullets. Much of the firing was high. The Germans seem to have taken with them every piece of removable metal, including doorknobs."

The battles in North Africa were soon to end in Allied victory, followed by the invasion of Sicily and the fall of Mussolini.

But the Russians, the victors of Stalingrad, now on their way back toward Europe, were occupying a large and even an ominous role in many Western minds. Foreign Secretary Eden returned from the United States and reported to Murrow's Monday Evening Club the rising American suspicions of the Soviet Union.

Murrow had narrated a British-Soviet film on the siege of Leningrad. In a magazine symposium, *After the War, What*? he forecast that "the triumph of Allied arms in Europe will not bring peace, but revolutions. And the course of the revolutions will be determined by whose armies are where.

"Confusion and conflict will color politics in the liberated territories for a long time to come. Armies of occupation will have to control transport, food, health and other essential services. In most countries there will be two or more competing factions. The governments-in-exile may seek to ride back into power on Allied food trains."

He developed the theme in a broadcast marking Stalin's dissolution of the Comintern, the passing of which, he said, "won't make communism on the Continent either more or less likely, and it won't reduce the chances of revolution when it is over." Victory, he thought, would not settle the old problems of Europe, but merely furnish an opportunity to settle them.

"But what happens to Europe, whether it moves to the right or left, will be determined by Allied adherence to principles, not by whether the Comintern is liquidated. Communism is an item for export; so is democracy. The two are bound to compete. The realization of that fact is the basis of German propaganda, and it is also the basis of the Allied efforts to reach agreement with Russia about matters other than those directly connected with killing Germans.

"People who have had much talk with Stalin [by that time Churchill and Eden had visited the Kremlin, as well as Hopkins and Harriman] tell me that he isn't interested in acquiring more territory, or in the spread of his version of communism. But Russia's neighbor nations aren't so sure about that. They would like to learn that Britain and America had come to some agreement with Russia which would insure them that they could, in fact, count on the blessings promised in the Atlantic Charter."

Such an agreement, even when made, was not destined to be carried out. When a British friend, reflecting Churchill's views, spoke of anticipated Soviet-American problems over a postwar settlement, Murrow told him that he appreciated such "soul-satisfying pessimism."

The day after his broadcast anticipating the cold war, Murrow flew home for a month's stay, to discuss reassignments for his now sizable CBS news staff, and to enter the hospital for the first of what would be many physical checkups. He returned to his post on the crowded troopship that the luxury liner *Queen Elizabeth* had become for the war's duration.

At embarkation it was "like one of those old movies where twenty men emerge from a single taxicab. It seems that the ship must burst her sides, or the men must spill into the harbor . . . Someone must have made a mistake, forgot to give the order to stop that long twisting line of boys coming aboard, bent double under field packs and barracks bags." As the ship sailed there was "no cheering, no singing, no bands, and no crowds to see the boys off."

About fifteen thousand soldiers were aboard in accommodations designed for less than one-fifth that number. "A warrant officer remarks he thinks he'll go and see the dentist. Someone says, 'Trouble with your teeth?' and he says 'Not a bit, but they tell me the dentist's chair is the only place on this boat where you can sit down.'

"You stand on one deck looking down at another. The men are standing closer than the pickets on a fence. The soldier beside you says, 'Anybody who gets a sunburn on this ship will have to be bald-headed. There isn't room to turn your face up.' "

When they disembarked in England, "the men looked more confident than when they had come aboard. After all, they had crossed the big ocean, hadn't been seasick, and the big adventure was beginning. . . . I heard one say, 'I'm going to write my mother and tell her I crossed the ocean standing in line.' "

The troop train moved off. "Every window was filled with brown grinning faces. It seemed to me that the whole of America was on that train. The faces were from the mountains of West Virginia, from the Far West Coast. There were Negroes and Indians, Swedes, Poles and Italians. As the train gathered speed the windows were filled with a blur of brown faces, white teeth and close-cropped hair."

About the big liner, "I hope never again to cross in that ship," Murrow said. "Some day, if she lives, she will be luxurious. There will be thick carpets, richly decorated staterooms, soft music and good service. There will be men in evening clothes and women in elaborate dresses. But for me that ship will always carry the ghosts of men who slept on the floor, ate out of mess tins twice a day, carried their lifebelts with them night and day — the ghosts of men and boys who crossed the ocean to risk their lives as casually as they would cross the street at home."

Murrow arrived in London as the invasion of Sicily began, followed by the landing on the Italian mainland, and the Italian turnabout against Germany.

All this while the big American B-17 bombers were increasing the air offensive against Hitler's Europe, from Normandy to the Balkans, and engaging in daylight bombardments of Germany, while the British struck at night.

Murrow flew on several bomber missions over western Europe, and as the Allied leaders Roosevelt, Churchill and Stalin met in Teheran, he was in a British Lancaster attacking Berlin itself. His broadcast about the night mission of D-for-Dog, about the pilot Jock and the navigator Dave, was one of the most vividly remembered of the war. Many listeners thought it was the best of his career.

In it he described the German capital as "a kind of orchestrated hell, a terrible symphony of light and flame." D-Dog by skillful maneuver managed to elude both flak and fighters, though transfixed by German searchlights. Two of the four Allied reporters on the mission failed to return, though one of them, Lowell Bennett, parachuted from his damaged craft, was taken prisoner and later freed.

From takeoff to return, Murrow's account of the Lancaster's aerial odyssey gripped the listener in 1943. It still does, when heard as a phonograph record.

"D-for-Dog eased around the perimeter track to the end of the runway. We sat there for a moment. The green light flashed and we were rolling, ten seconds ahead of schedule. The takeoff was smooth as silk. The wheels came up, and D-Dog started the long climb. As we came up through the clouds I looked right and left and counted fourteen black Lancasters climbing for the place where men must burn oxygen to live. The sun was going down, and its red glow made rivers and lakes of fire on tops of the clouds. Down to the southward clouds piled up to form castles, battlements and whole cities, all tinged with red."

On the way to Berlin, under a quarter-moon, D-for-Dog saw the red tracer jets of an aerial battle and the burst of yellow flame that was a fighter going down — "interesting but remote."

Then "the dirty gray clouds turned white. We were over the outer searchlight defenses. The clouds below us were white and we were black. D-Dog seemed like a black bug on a white sheet."

Dead on time, D-Dog arrived over the target. "The sky ahead was lit up by bright yellow flares. Off to starboard another kite went down in flames. The flares were sprouting all over the sky, reds and greens and yellows, and we were flying straight for the center of the fireworks. D-Dog seemed to be standing still, the four propellors thrashing the air. But we didn't seem to be closing in.

"The clouds had cleared, and off to the starboard a Lanc was caught by at least fourteen searchlight beams. We could see him twist and turn, and finally break out. No one seemed to be shooting at us, but it was getting lighter all the time. Suddenly a tremendous big blob of yellow light appeared dead ahead, another to the right and another to the left. We were flying straight for them." The plane to the right was "coned," and attacked by fighters.

It was D-Dog's turn next. "With no warning at all, D-Dog was filled with an unhealthy white light. I was standing just behind Jock and could see all the seams on the wings. His quiet Scots voice beat into my ears. 'Steady, lads, we've been coned.' His slender body lifted half out of his seat as he jammed the control column forward and to the left. We were going down.

"Jock was wearing woolen gloves with the fingers cut off. I could see his fingernails turn white as he gripped the wheel. And then I was on my knees flat on the deck, for he had whipped the Dog back into a climbing turn. The knees should have been strong enough to support me, but they weren't, and the stomach seemed in some danger of letting me down, too.

"I picked myself up and looked out again. It seemed that one big searchlight, instead of being twenty thousand feet below, was mounted right on our wing tip. D-Dog was corkscrewing. As we rolled down on the other side I began to see what was happening to Berlin.

"The clouds were gone, and the sticks of incendiaries from the preceding waves made the place look like a badly laid out city with the streetlights on. The small incendiaries were going down like a fistful of white rice thrown on a piece of black velvet.

"As Jock hauled the Dog up again, I was thrown to the other side of the cockpit, and there below were more incendiaries, glowing white and then turning red. The cookies, the four-thousand-pound high explosives, were bursting below like great sunflowers gone mad. And then as we started down again, still held in the lights, I remembered that the Dog still had one of the cookies and a whole basket of incendiaries in his belly, and the lights still held us. And I was very frightened."

A German fighter made a pass at the Dog, but the big plane flew out of the cone, dropped its bombs, and Murrow "began to breathe and to reflect again — that all men would be braver if only they could leave their stomachs at home. Then there was a tremendous whoomp, an unintelligible shout from the tail gunner, and D-Dog shivered and lost altitude. I looked at the port side and there was a Lancaster that seemed close enough to touch. He had whipped straight under us, missed us by twenty-five, fifty feet, no one knew how much."

On the way home D-Dog saw more air battles and flew through an anti-aircraft barrage. Then it landed, welcomed by "the calm, clear voice of an English girl" in the control tower. At the debriefing, some of the airmen Ed had seen at the briefing were missing.

He summed up. "It isn't a pleasant kind of war, the men doing it speak of it as a job. Yesterday afternoon, when the tapes were stretched out on the big map all the way to Berlin and back again, a young pilot with old eyes said to me, 'I see we're working again tonight.' That's the frame of mind in which the job is being done. The job isn't pleasant; it's terribly tiring. Men die in the sky, while others are roasted alive in their cellars.

"Berlin last night wasn't a pretty sight. In about thirty-five minutes it was hit with about three times the amount of stuff that ever came down on London in a night-long blitz. This is a calculated, remorseless campaign of destruction. Right now the mechanics are probably working on D-Dog, getting him ready to fly again."

Murrow's description of the bombing raid on Berlin was printed by newspapers across the United States, and rebroadcast by the BBC. Paul White wrote him from New York, enclosing some of the clippings and admonishing him. "I hope now you are cured. Please, please, don't do it again."

A few days after the flight the BBC was marking its twenty-first birthday with a dinner at the Savoy, and Minister of Information Brendan Bracken as the speaker. The occasion began as an encomium for the public corporation's reputation for truth and its influence in war, but quickly became a demonstration for Murrow, who was present. Bracken called him "one of the finest broadcasters in the world [Hear! Hear!] and what is more, he has been the most faithful friend of Britain, and like all good Americans, has served his country with fidelity and loyalty, and made friends here who will never forget what he did for us."

Then Churchill's protégé spoke of Murrow's flight over Berlin. "If I had been president of CBS, Mr. Murrow wouldn't have been allowed to go on that journey. But it produced one of the finest pieces of writing I've seen for many a long day." ("Hear! Hear!")

As it happened, the president of CBS had in person forbidden Murrow to go on bombing missions. Bill Paley, a colonel now, was in London on a mission for Eisenhower's headquarters in Algiers, and he was appalled to find his correspondent going off periodically in a flak suit to take part in sometimes intensive action. "I don't want you to do it any more," he told Murrow sternly. "You may be right," Ed replied. "Consider me grounded." The next day he was on D-for-Dog over Berlin.

Paley was strongly impressed, not for the first or the last time, by the inner complexity of the broadcaster, and by the apparently irrepressible drive that made him do things, some of which might very well be contradictory to others.

Despite Paley's specific orders and his own stated submission to them, Murrow continued to fly, in both British and American planes. A few days before D-Day he actually made a live broadcast, the first such, from a Flying Fortress bombing occupied France. The mission was successful, but he somehow plugged in his flying suit, with its heating unit, into the transmitter circuit, and for once the beads of perspiration which were a part of every broadcast were not self-induced. When his hookup continued to generate heat, instead of sound, he used the pilot's transmitter, and the broadcast was heard loud and clear in New York.

Paul White continued to forbid Murrow's wartime flights, but finally gave up. "There was no way to make him stop short of firing him," he said.

Again, some of Murrow's colleagues thought he had a martyr complex, or was trying to prove he was not a coward. Some years later he himself tried to explain. "Partly it was being a Boy Scout, I guess. Partly, I like flyers. Partly it was a dromomania I have; I even have it when I drive a car. Partly it was vanity. I would hear the BBC playing back things I said, and nothing has ever made me feel as good as that. I can't be logical about it. Like in 1950, when I decided to spend my vacation in Korea, I couldn't think of any reason that made sense. It was just something I had to do."

He did like flyers. He made his 1943 Christmas broadcast, with Larry Le Sueur, from the hangar of an American bomber group "somewhere in England."

When he got back to the city it was to hear of General Eisenhower's appointment as Supreme Allied Commander for the invasion of Europe. Murrow recalled the general's arrival in London nearly two years before, and the snappy saluting that was expected from him by the British majors and colonels who mistook his three stars for a British captain's three pips. Ike's comment was, "I'd trade these three stars for a captain's rank any day, if I could trade years as well."

Aware of the politics, Allied and European, involved in the invasion planning, and remembering the furor aroused by the Darlan deal in North Africa, Murrow commented that Eisenhower "is about as nonpolitical as a general could possibly be. He doesn't know anything about European politics and he would be the first to admit it. Europe to him is a place where the German army must be defeated, and one is entitled to hope that he will not be given the official responsibility for decisions that may be taken in Washington or London." But it would be Eisenhower who would be criticized by many for the political decision to let the Russians alone take Berlin and Prague.

Murrow finished his appreciation of the supreme commander. "It just happens that Eisenhower has a certain genius when it comes to reconciling points of view. He is a chairman, a coordinator, one who has the ability to weld a fighting organization together."

The D-Day preparations in London, the spread of the war to the European continent by way of the Italian boot, and the imminence of the much larger action on the northwest coast of France, were accompanied by a small civil war within the American radio establishment at home. The issue was the hardy perennial, "Freedom of speech," and CBS was the focal point. Since the controversy was at the core of the contradictions of commercial broadcasting, and has had its repercussions up to the present time, affecting careers as well as opinions, not to mention the whole concept of public service, it deserves some attention. Murrow was only indirectly involved in the 1943 dispute, but would be more directly concerned later.

It began on a Wednesday night in late August when Cecil Brown, who had been banned by the Germans in the Balkans and by the British in Singapore, ran into what he considered censorship by the Americans in New York. In his CBS news analysis that night, following the Sicilian campaign and the Roosevelt-Churchill conference in Quebec, he opined that "any reasonably accurate observer of the American scene at this moment knows that a good deal of enthusiasm for this war is evaporating into thin air."

Paul White sharply rebuked Brown for views "under the guise of news analysis" which the CBS director said could not be justified as "factual reporting," and in addition were "dangerous to public morale." White charged the commentator with "defeatist talk that would be of immense pleasure to Dr. Goebbels and his boys," and reminded him of the long-standing CBS policy of "no editorializing."

The issue quickly became muddled. Although White took his stand against the expression of any editorial opinion, it was plain that what he really objected to was what Brown had said. Just as an American President can be praised but does not expect to be rebuked from a church pulpit, so, if the commentator had reported Americans to be in a frenzy of patriotism over the war, as others were doing, his remarks would patently have escaped censure.

It was not to be forgotten that radio stations were licensed by the Federal Government, as newspapers were not, and free speech or no free speech broadcast doubts about the war were not regarded in Washington as being in the public interest. In point of fact, radio had been marshaled and willingly served as the major propaganda arm of the Government. One of the commoner ways of personalizing the war, and later and truly unpopular wars and interventions, was for a broadcaster to say "we," when he meant the American Government, or American troops, or administration policy.

The Brown case, leading to the broadcaster's resignation, aroused his colleagues on all the networks, the more so when White publicly declared that CBS would stop commentators from the expression of any opinions, and confided that "we have got rid of the last one."

H. V. Kaltenborn led those who believed the issue was one of free speech. He recalled his own broadcasts during the Munich crisis, when with the encouragement and enthusiasm of the same Paul White he had extemporized 120 broadcasts without any hint of editorial control. He wondered how the American radio public would have fared if the crisis of 1938 had had to be reported under the rules of 1943. The veteran broadcaster said that CBS was trying to prevent the discussion of controversial topics.

But White restated the CBS purpose of "letting the radio listener make up his mind rather than allowing news broadcasters to make it up for him."

The network, he said, took no editorial positions — and therefore its commentators should not — because it would be "a tragic distortion of radio's function if individual station and network managements should attempt to control democratic public opinion." How the question became one of controlling public opinion rather than informing it was not stated.

The rebuttal of Kaltenborn and most other commentators was that no news analyst could possibly be completely neutral or objective, and moreover, contrary to White's evident belief, not all analysts agreed on all questions. Since they did differ, their broadcasts offered a spectrum of views. Indeed while CBS was trying to erase all editorial opinion, the other networks were presenting just such divergences of opinion by various men.

Kaltenborn also pointed out that broadcasters like Murrow, Shirer, and the CBS military analyst Major George Fielding Eliot expressed opinions, however circuitously they might be couched, in all their news reports.

White adhered to his position that the function of the news analyst is "to marshal the facts and present them so as to inform, not persuade, his listeners. In the case of controversial issues, the audience should be left with no impression as to which side the analyst himself actually favors."

Dorothy Thompson, broadcaster and columnist, held that CBS had instituted censorship by telling its commentators, like Murrow, that they must never say what they thought, though they had been chosen for their "background, knowledge, insight, clarity of thought, and special ability to make themselves understood."

The chairman of the Federal Communications Commission, James L. Fly, joined the fray, disagreeing with CBS and saying that opinion could be aired by individuals provided it was labeled as such. "It's strange to reach the conclusion that all Americans are to enjoy free speech except radio commentators, the very men who have presumably been chosen for their competence in this field." Why should radio commentators be limited to quoting the opinions of other reporters, and newspapers and magazines, without being able to give their own? "The listeners can get all these views from those newspapers and magazines. But where, under the new dispensation, can they get the opinions of Bill Shirer and Ed Murrow?" But the FCC chairman made it plain that the problem was not one for the Government, but for the industry.

Beyond all the questions raised in the heated debate was the larger and more fundamental consideration: who owns the air, the networks and local stations, or the people? That consideration is still with us.

At the time, in the midst of war, Representative Karl Mundt of South Dakota, who would become one of the leading investigators of "un-American activities," praised the CBS news policy of "no opinions" and warned other networks they might be taken over by the Government unless they mended their ways.

When Eric Sevareid returned to New York at the end of the year, after an enforced parachute jump into the Burma jungle and some months of reporting from Chungking, Paul White assailed the "stupid censorship" which had prevented the CBS correspondent from saying very much about events in China and giving his opinion of them. The executives of other networks at the luncheon seemed amused.

Though the controversy over editorializing had raised the issue whether true objectivity was possible, that remained the target of the CBS D-Day invasion "primer" issued by Paul White.

"Keep an informative, unexcited demeanor at the microphone," it commanded. "Give sources for all reports. Don't risk accuracy for the sake of a beat. Use care in your choice of words. Don't say 'German defenses were pulverized'; say 'German defenses were hard hit.' When you don't know, say so . . . Exaggeration and immoderate language breed dangerous optimism."

Eisenhower, back in London after more than a year in Algiers, had a new office at 47 Grosvenor Square, and Supreme Headquarters of the Allied Expeditionary Force or SHAEF had been installed at Bushey Park outside the city, with advance headquarters near Portsmouth, in the embarkation zone.

Also back in London was Eisenhower's deputy director of psychological warfare, Bill Paley. A radio offensive against Hitler's European Fortress was being planned, to accompany the military one, and one phase of it was the prerecording of D-Day messages by Allied rulers and prime ministers in exile to their people. King Haakon of Norway broke down several times as he made his recording for Paley. General de Gaulle, brought from North Africa on the day before the invasion, refused to take part in the program because he had not been informed of the D-Day plans. Churchill had to threaten to send him back to Algiers immediately, and de Gaulle's message was recorded too late to be included with the others and had to be broadcast later in the day.

With the approach of H-Hour on D-Day, American, British and Canadian invasion troops were deployed along the British coast all the way from Portsmouth to Plymouth. American armored divisions were drilling in the English meadows. The American generals Bradley and Patton had arrived to join the British general Montgomery, who was at the head of the expeditionary force. The Anglo-American air offensive against Germany had reached a new peak.

By the end of May there were nineteen American ground divisions in Britain, plus two airborne, and the British had seventeen divisions on the ground and two airborne. The Germans were listed with fifty-eight divisions in France and the Low Countries, and twenty-four in Scandinavia. But the significant fact was that 199 German divisions were being hard-pressed in Russia and East Europe.

To illustrate the extent of the preinvasion buildup, Murrow and the other CBS correspondents assigned to D-Day broadcast a special program which moved from him in London to Charles Shaw in a northern port, to Larry Le Sueur at a materiel center, to Dick Hottelet at a southern airfield, to Charles Collingwood at a Channel embarkation point.

"The planning of this operation is complex beyond description," Murrow reported. "Nothing like it has ever been seen. It is not just a matter of coordinating land, sea and air forces. It involves the loading of ships so that the things that are needed first will be the first to be unloaded. It means careful calculation of weather and tides, constant reconnaissance of enemy dispositions. And it means security, thousands of people knowing small bits of the plan but only a very few having knowledge of how the whole thing fits together.

"At no time in this war have I seen the planning officers talk less or work harder. As a matter of fact there is less loose talk among civilians than ever before. It's as though everyone realized the importance of guarding the plans, even when most of the movements must be carried out within sight of the enemy's air reconnaissance. But in the end of the day all the plans, all the preparations, must depend upon the men who will execute them, and personal boasting by British or American generals will not alter that fact."

After some impressions of "Americans in Britain as they wait for D-Day" — their tough training, their homesickness, their mechanical aptitude, their analytical approach to problems, their belief in solutions, above all their unlimited curiosity — Murrow concluded that they are "more interested in things than in ideas.

"Most of them believe that Europe is a much simpler place than it is. They are courteous, many of them are shy. They haven't much respect for things that are old. The Army, what I have seen of it, doesn't talk very

much about politics; it wastes a lot of food; it spreads the habit of chewing gum wherever it goes. It isn't much of a singing army, preferring
the tunes it danced to in peacetime to the so-called war songs.

"There doesn't seem to be much sentiment about small nations, except
the old-fashioned American attitude that big bullies should pick on somebody their own size. The feeling seems to be that the chip has been knocked
off our shoulder, and that we are sizable enough and just about ready, to
make the proper response."

On May 28 Eisenhower recorded his D-Day message to the people of
Europe, for Colonel Paley — it had to be redone, to the commander's
visible annoyance, because of the ambiguous phrase, "Do not needlessly
endanger your lives until I give you the signal" — and on the morning of
June 6, after the postponement caused by bad weather, and a day after
the capture of Rome, the message was broadcast, advising Europeans
that "the hour of your liberation is approaching." Ten minutes earlier,
Murrow had read Eisenhower's order of the day to his troops, over all
American domestic networks and the new Army Broadcasting Service in
Europe.

Murrow, with the other Allied correspondents not accompanying the
first wave of the invasion — there were five hundred American correspondents in London and twenty-eight of them had been chosen — was
locked in the Ministry of Information basement for the briefings that confirmed and explained the invasion.

Four thousand ships and eight thousand planes were taking part in the
gigantic effort. Collingwood was aboard an LST. Le Sueur was heading
for Utah Beach. Hottelet was in the first squadron of American Marauder
bombers striking across the Channel. Bill Downs, recently arrived in London from Moscow, was with a British unit splashing toward France.

Ever afterward, these men and the others he knew in London during
the Blitz and in Europe after the invasion would be the closest to Murrow, personally and professionally. They were his Roosevelt-before-
Chicago group, his Kennedy PT-109 club.

Having deployed his own forces, Murrow was now in the broadcasting
studio waiting for them and the other networks' correspondents to report.
Some would come back to London to broadcast. Others would send back
recordings made on the beaches. And when mobile transmitters could
finally be set up across the Channel, those on the beachhead could broadcast directly from there, their dispatches relayed by London.

Murrow had been talking to New York on the open circuit, during the
two hours of uncertainty between the German news agency's first invasion
bulletin and the official SHAEF announcement. Then, as the battle reports began to come in, he fed them to the waiting nation at home.

Wright Bryan, of Station WSB Atlanta, described the paratrooper drop into France that he had seen from an accompanying plane. Dick Hottelet of CBS and James Wellard of NBC described the bombing attacks on the French coast. Charles Shaw of CBS reported the invasion reaction of London's people — "That's good!" — "Thank God!" — and Stanley Richardson of NBC returned from a torpedo boat which had escorted the landing craft. The first account from an LST itself, as it prepared to shove off, was by Collingwood. Above all was the calm, yet throbbing and colorful account by George Hicks of ABC, aboard the USS *Ancon*, eyewitness to the full D-Day panorama on the Normandy shore.

The firsthand reports from London by radio's own correspondents crested the torrent of press agency bulletins, military analysis and home-front commentary that took over the American networks, as all commercial commitments were discarded and full facilities used. Many of the reports, including the best ones, were recordings, for the rigid rule of "nothing but live broadcasts" had been abrogated by the war, to provide front-line authenticity, even if slightly delayed.

Murrow, with the headphones clamped on, made several brief reports of his own on D-Day, but not until nearly twenty-four hours after he had opened the microphone to stand by for the invasion did he give his first substantive broadcast. He followed President Roosevelt, who had led the American nation in prayer that night.

It was nearly dawn on D-Day-plus-one in London, and the radio signal to New York had begun to crack up. The familiar voice had to cut through thick static as it began in the familiar way, "This . . . is London.

"Early this morning we heard the bombers going out," he said. "It was the sound of a giant factory in the sky. It seemed to shake the old gray stone buildings in this bruised and battered city beside the Thames. The sound was heavier, more triumphant than ever before. Those who knew what was coming could imagine that they heard great guns and strains of the 'Battle Hymn of the Republic' well above the roar of the motors . . .

"Here in London the steadiness of the civilian populace is one of the most remarkable things I've ever seen. People go about their business calmly. There was no excitement. Walking along the streets of London, you almost wanted to shout at them and say, 'Don't you know that history is being made this day?' They realized it, all right, but their emotions were under complete control . . .

"A great race against time has been started. We are attempting to consolidate our positions, to withstand the inevitable German counterattack, while the Germans are attempting to regroup their forces and prepare to strike before we are well established."

The war, like everything else, soon became a routine news operation for radio. With three hundred thousand men ashore by then, an Army transmitter was set up on the Normandy beachhead on D-Day-plus-four, able to reach the BBC in London, and by relay to carry direct reports to America. When the Allied armies began to move out of the beachhead the transmitter went with them, and press camps accompanied the various headquarters as they advanced. But the war theater was large and transportation was uncertain. Murrow reported to New York, in his capacity as coordinator, that after D-Day getting the story was no longer the hardest part of an assignment; what was difficult was getting it through. Atmospherics, circuit trouble, power failures were always occupational hazards in overseas radio. Now they were multiplied.

Radio men had to get to a transmitter in person, unlike newspaper correspondents who could send their dispatches by messenger. But as the mobile transmitters got deeper into Europe, they were less able to reach the BBC and the United States Signal Corps relay units in London. Moreover, the news media were assigned the poorer frequencies, the good ones being reserved for tactical use by the armies, and for psychological warfare.

In the latter branch of combat, Radio Luxembourg, the most powerful transmitter in Europe, would become an important factor. It was run by Colonel Paley and not only broadcast programs to Allied troops, but also masqueraded as an underground German anti-Nazi station, "Sender 1212" supposedly located in the Rhine Valley. It broadcast the remarks of German war prisoners, "thankful" to be caught by the kindly Americans, read the letters from captured German field post offices to addresses in the Reich, and told anti-Nazi jokes.

When Eisenhower moved SHAEF from Britain to France, and the press and radio corps was established at the Hotel Scribe in Paris, the power failures were frequent and the French telephone system could not be depended on. Murrow reported that a great many broadcasts were not getting through. "And those that don't reach the American living room don't count," he said.

So London remained the principal wartime communications center in Europe. And because each of the CBS correspondents in France could be aware of only his part of the whole military operation, it was Murrow in London who had to present the larger war picture, and not only in military terms but in political.

The first major political problem created by the invasion was the future civilian control of France. The United States intended a military administration until elections could be held, while General de Gaulle in London insisted that his Committee of National Liberation was the de facto government. Somehow President Roosevelt still seemed to believe that most Frenchmen favored Pétain, and Eisenhower's D-Day message to France had deliberately made no mention of de Gaulle. Murrow, in his broadcasts, did not minimize the importance of the continuing American mis-understanding with the French leader.

But in addition to being the communications center, London had be-come once again a zone of German military action of a particularly fear-ful kind. Six days after D-Day the first Nazi "secret weapon" — the V-1 or pilotless plane — landed in London's crowded Stepney area, the still desolate scene of the Luftwaffe's first big Blitz four years before, and de-stroyed a hundred homes, killing many people. The V-1's were called "buzz bombs" because they actually did buzz. As one neared, it produced a high pitch of noise overhead. Then the motor stopped. Five to fifteen seconds later the bomb exploded, spreading a thick, white, smokelike dust.

The V-1's, carrying a ton of explosives each, flying at four hundred miles per hour at a height of three thousand feet, caused ten thousand casualties in the first week, including a direct hit on the Guards Chapel in Whitehall during church services, which killed two hundred persons. Eight thousand V-1's in all were launched, with a toll of six thousand civilian dead and eighteen thousand seriously injured, before their launch-ing sites were overrun in late August. But two weeks later, in September, the first V-2, the rocket bomb, was fired against London from pads in Holland two hundred miles away. It too carried a one-ton warhead, but it arrived without buzz or any other warning. Besides their serious psy-chological effect, the 1300 V-2's that were fired between September and the following March killed 2700 persons and injured 6500.

The widening of the war in Europe widened the activities of the staff of CBS correspondents Murrow had put together and was now directing. Though each could report directly to New York from whatever combat zone he was in, they all regarded London as their base and moved in and out of the city as occasion demanded, sometimes for a brief rest — "some rest, under the buzz bombs," one of them remarked — sometimes to spell a colleague, or in a change of assignment.

Collingwood came back to London briefly from Normandy, before returning for the liberation of Paris. Le Sueur was with the United States First Army, also heading for Paris, but he too came back to London regu-larly. Shirer had checked in from New York and was broadcasting his commentaries from London. Sevareid was on the Italian front and would soon join in the landing in the south of France. Winston Burdett was in Rome with American forces. Ned Calmer also came to London from New York, while Dick Hottelet moved out to join the Allied advance through Belgium. Howard K. Smith, who had been on the "last train from Berlin," was with the Ninth Army in Holland after his long internment in Switzer-land.

There were always enough CBS correspondents to be found in London, it was said, for at least a small poker game. But though there was poker aplenty, and though he was dodging bombs again, gathering and reporting news, attending to the care and feeding of the staff, and serving as president of the Association of American Correspondents, Murrow decided that all this was not action enough for him. He flew again in bombing missions over France. And nothing could stop him from joining the war's largest airborne operation in September, when planes and gliders landed thirty-five thousand American and British troops behind the German lines in Holland. He rode in a C-47 carrying paratroopers, and he made a recording which he broadcast on his return to London.

Much of the Dutch countryside was under water, reminding him of the Mississippi in flood, as the troop-carrying planes moved toward the drop zone, with British gliders to their right and heavy bombers to their left, while fighters swirled protectively around them.

"There go the para-packs of a formation ahead of us — yellow, brown, red, drifting down gently, dropping the containers. I can't see — they're a little too far away — I can't see the bodies of the men. Yes, I can! I look back at the door, and the pilot gives me the clenched-hand salute, like a boxer about to jump. The ships ahead of us are still going on. There's a burst of flak. You can see it right from the side. It's coming from the port side, just across our nose, but a little bit low . . .

"More ships ahead of us are now dropping. Nine ships ahead of us have just dropped, and you can see the men swinging down. In just about forty seconds now our ship will drop the men. The men will walk out onto Dutch soil. You can probably hear the snap as they check the lashing on the static line.

"There they go! Do you hear them shout? Three! four! five! six! seven! eight! nine! ten! eleven! twelve! thirteen! fourteen! fifteen! sixteen! Now every man is out. I can see their chutes going down now. Every man clear. They're dropping just beside a little windmill near a church, hanging there, very gracefully. They seem to be completely relaxed, like nothing so much as khaki dolls hanging beneath a green lampshade. I see the men go down just north of a little road. The whole sky is filled with parachutes. They're all going down so slowly, it seems as though they should get to the ground much faster. We're now swinging about, making a right-hand turn."

The tape ran out. "That's the way it was," he finished.

A few days later Murrow was in Paris. The city had been liberated shortly before, and not without attendant confusion on American radio. Collingwood had halted with the advancing American army at Rambouillet to allow the Fighting French the token honor of first arrival, but he also took the precaution of recording an account of the liberation before it happened, the radio equivalent of the kinds of news agency story which is written in advance of the event and marked "hold for release," in this case to coincide with Collingwood's own arrival in Paris. But the recording got to London unusually rapidly, and was broadcast to the United States, twenty-four hours before the actual liberation, being accepted as an authentic eyewitness account of a historic event and printed as such in several newspapers. Collingwood reached Paris and broadcast from there live, but it did not spare the network's embarrassment. Meanwhile Larry Le Sueur had also had some trouble. He got to Paris, too, but neglected to wait for the official transmitter and used French facilities, uncensored. He was suspended for a brief time.

Murrow's first wartime visit to Paris lasted only forty-eight hours. Unlike some other correspondents, he had no real affection for the French capital, at any rate by comparison with London, and particularly since the capitulation of France, which he attributed more to lack of morale and will than of military prowess.

He observed that Paris had suffered practically no physical damage, and that luxury goods were still available, though at fantastic prices. He found "those familiar, well-fed but still empty-looking faces around the fashionable bars and restaurants — the last four years seem to have changed them very little." He was surprised by the number of well-dressed women in Paris, and pointed out that not only had the French textile industry continued all during the war, but that even television was developed.

The contrast between Paris and London was the more marked in that the French were now safely out of the war, as they had been more or less safely in it, while the British, in an atmosphere of Dunkerque, were undergoing the new agony of Arnhem.

Their First Parachute Division had been cut off there, and would be overrun and captured. They were the men Murrow had accompanied on their ill-starred drop the week before. "All attention, much hope and many prayers" were centered on Arnhem, he said, which was "taking its place in British folklore." In the House of Commons Winston Churchill said, " 'Not in vain' is the boast of those who returned to us. 'Not in vain' is the epitaph of those who fell."

The American presidential elections of 1944, in which Roosevelt sought a fourth term, were of as much moment to the British as the plague of silent V-2 rocket bombs, which Murrow regarded as the harbingers of a new and frightful age of missiles.

"The significance of this demonstration of German skill and ingenuity lies in the fact that it makes complete nonsense out of strategic frontiers, mountain and river barriers . . . It means that within a few years present methods of aerial bombardment will be as obsolete as the Gatling gun. It seems to make more appalling the prospect or the possibility of another war."

As for the elections, he was called to 10 Downing Street for lunch one October day, to be asked by the prime minister his expectation of the result. Prudently he said he thought it would be close. Churchill wondered out loud what the effect would be if he spoke in the House of Commons or on the BBC, in support of Mr. Roosevelt. Murrow said it would not help the President, perhaps even help defeat him, not only because Americans did not like to be told how to vote, but also because of anti-British feeling which had been stirred up in the United States by General Montgomery's cautious tactics in Normandy.

Churchill's eyes filled with tears, as Murrow reported they so easily and so frequently did. "I find it intolerable to remain silent," he said. But at any rate, "history will render the verdict, if not your fellow Americans at the polls." Roosevelt, as it turned out, beat Thomas E. Dewey easily enough, but less than nine months later Churchill himself was swept out of office, by his fellow Britons, the verdict of history notwithstanding.

Roosevelt's reelection brought to Europe, as Murrow saw it, "an audible sigh of relief, and in many languages," for it insured the continuity of the Allied policy toward a defeated Germany. But, he added, "no one has yet produced a formula for ridding the German people of their appetite for war, their recurring desire to shoot people and to take their land and their homes.

"If the German Home Guard really fights, if it is necessary for the Allies to fight and kill all the way to Berlin, then it may be that Hitler and Himmler will have been the instruments for eliminating the German will to war . . .

"It is an appalling prospect, but it may be that the German decision to offer their old men and young boys for slaughter will cause them to conclude that making war on other people does not pay."

The Murrows were back in America themselves soon after the elections, the first visit for him in the eighteen months since he had left in the troop-laden *Queen Elizabeth*. Before he left London he broadcast the belief that "there is a dim light in Europe now. The blackout is gradually lifting." He said that the United States had helped to bring this about, and that it represented "the hope and the fear of an awful lot of little people in Europe."

On the way home, stopping off in Paris, he told Shirer he felt he had been overseas too long and was out of touch with the United States. He and Janet planned to return home as soon as the war ended, he said, unlike the many American correspondents who would stay on in Europe.

At home, he spent a month touring the country by car, and broadcast from Los Angeles in the new year. For eight years, he declared, he had been looking at America from the outside. Now, traveling in the United

States, "looking and listening," he found no comparison possible between the two continents in wartime.

"We live in the light, in relative comfort and complete security. We are the only nation engaged in this war which has raised its standard of living since the war began. We are not tired, as all Europe is tired."

He expressed no doubt about the outcome of the war, but decided doubt about what would come after, fearing a return to American isolationism and "a reluctance to accept the position of leadership our military and economic strength has thrust upon us." For Americans, he thought, were "quick to criticize our Allies and quicker to resent their criticism of us. There is still much suspicion of the designs and intentions of foreign nations."

But he saw some hopeful signs. "There is certainly more serious discussion of fundamental problems in this country than there was three years ago — housing and education, and racial and religious discrimination.

"This is the testing ground of democracy. No one can doubt that the test will be severe. It will require tolerance and patience, and high principle in dealing with foreign nations. It may even require some sacrifice of sovereignty. Viewed from Europe, American policy will be decisive in vast areas of which we know little."

But one of the severest tests of democracy for the United States would be on domestic, not foreign soil, and it was at that moment beginning. Before it was over it would shake the nation and sear and deaden American radio and television, while raising Murrow himself to broadcasting heights.

Westbrook Pegler, the columnist, and the Hearst newspapers had opened an attack on an NBC commentator, William Gailmor, charging him with pro-Communist leanings. The network defied the criticism and supported Gailmor, saying that "communism is an easy label to apply to a political liberal with whom you disagree," and explaining that it judged its commentator solely by the text of his broadcasts.

The Russians were still Allies, in fact they were deep inside Germany smashing their way toward Berlin. But Pegler and Hearst were only slightly premature. In the postwar climate of anticommunism the broadcasting industry would be less principled and courageous, and judgment by the text of a script, if judgment were to be applied at all, would be replaced by "guilt by association" and blacklists based on suspicion.

Murrow was back in Europe for the closing act of the great drama of war. In a sense, the conflict had come almost full circle for him, he meditated as he flew with a glider squadron landing troops across the Rhine, and saw a familiar symbol of the long ordeal.

"We came back over Dover, where nearly five years ago we sat and watched for the German airborne invasion of Britain. The cliffs were still white, and washed by a sea that might have been the Mediterranean. It was blue, and looked cool, and our minds were with a lot of brave men who were beyond the Rhine."

Among many other broadcasts in the closing days of the war he did two which in the view of many listeners vied for the title of "best" with his "orchestrated hell" account of the bombing raid over Berlin. One was about the Nazi death camp of Buchenwald, the other about the capture of Leipzig.

He had attached himself to Patton's Third Army as it rolled through western Germany, and then what would become East Germany. He advised his listeners to switch off the radio if they were at lunch, or had "no appetite to hear what Germans have done."

He entered the barbed-wire gate of Buchenwald with the liberating American troops, and "there surged around me an evil-smelling horde. Men and boys reached out to touch me; they were in rags and the remnants of uniforms. Death had already marked many of them, but they were smiling with their eyes. I looked out over that mass of men to the green fields beyond, where well-fed Germans were plowing."

One of the camp's barracks was occupied by Czechoslovaks, and Murrow described an unexpected meeting. "When I entered, men crowded around, tried to lift me to their shoulders. They were too weak. Many of them could not get out of bed. I was told that the building had once stabled eighty horses. There were 1200 men in it, five to a bunk. The stink was beyond all description.

"When I reached the center of the barracks, a man came up and said, 'You remember me. I'm Peter Zenkl, onetime mayor of Prague.' I remembered him, but did not recognize him. He asked me about Beneš and Jan Masaryk.

"I asked how many men had died in that building during the last month. They called the doctor. We inspected his records. There were only names in the little black book, nothing more — nothing of who these men were, what they had done or hoped. Behind the names of those who had died there was a cross. I counted them. They totaled 242, 242 out of 1200 in one month. As I walked down to the end of the barracks, there was applause from the men too weak to get out of bed. It sounded like the handclapping of babies, they were so weak . . . As we walked out into the courtyard, a man fell dead."

Murrow had known Peter Zenkl before the war, indeed before Munich, when he visited Prague to arrange musical programs and other broadcasts for America. He may even have known him while he was engaged in student exchange before joining CBS. What he did not report but what Zenkl later revealed was that Murrow saved his life at Buchenwald. For the former mayor, a member of the democratic and pro-Western Beneš party, and among the first to be arrested by the Nazis, was even in Buchenwald an opponent of the Czech Communists, as he had been as minister of social welfare in the Beneš government.

When they saw Murrow and Zenkl together, some of the Communists in Buchenwald, expecting to hold power in Prague because of the presence of the Red Army, took the American aside to "warn" him, and denounced Zenkl and said he would be "liquidated" as soon as the troops had left.

Murrow cautioned Zenkl, who managed to get out of the camp that night and escaped. He later returned to Prague as deputy premier, but after the Communist coup in 1948, when Murrow's friend Jan Masaryk mysteriously died, Zenkl and his wife would flee their country and come to the United States, leaving his brother and nephew this time in Communist, instead of Nazi, imprisonment. Murrow and Zenkl retained friendly ties and had discussions about European politics until the broadcaster's death.

There were other excruciating encounters that April day in Buchenwald for Murrow. "In another part of the camp they showed me the children, hundreds of them. Some were only six. One rolled up his sleeve, showed me his number. It was tattooed on his arm. D-6030, it was. The others showed me their numbers. They will carry them till they die.

"An elderly man standing beside me said, 'The children, enemies of the State.' I could see their ribs through their thin shirts. The old man said, 'I am Professor Charles Richer of the Sorbonne.' The children clung to my hands and stared. We crossed to the courtyard. Men kept coming up to speak to me and touch me, professors from Poland, doctors from Vienna, men from all Europe. Men from the countries that made America."

He saw the crowded hospital where two hundred men had died the day before. "Tuberculosis, starvation, fatigue, and there are many who have no desire to live," said the Czech doctor. In the kitchen the German Communist who was in charge displayed the daily ration, "one piece of brown bread about as thick as your thumb, on top of it a piece of margarine as big as three sticks of chewing gum. That, and a little stew, was what they received every twenty-four hours."

The doctor had a chart on the wall, "very complicated, it was. There were little red tabs scattered through it. He said that was to indicate each ten men who died. He had to account for the rations, and he added, 'We're very efficient here.' " The doctor was Paul Heller. As the result of Murrow's broadcast his brother and friends in America learned that he was still alive.

Several of the inmates told Murrow that Buchenwald was the best concentration camp in Germany — "they had had some experience of the others." The doctor told him that the crematorium was not working because the Germans had run out of coke. So they simply dumped the bodies into heaps.

"We proceeded to the small courtyard. The wall was about eight feet high; it adjoined what had been a stable or a garage. We entered. It was floored with concrete. There were two rows of bodies stacked up like cordwood. They were thin and very white. Some of the bodies were terribly bruised, though there seemed to be little flesh to bruise. Some had been shot through the head, but they bled but little. All except two were naked. I tried to count them as best as I could, and arrived at the conclusion that all that was mortal of more than five hundred men and boys lay there in two neat piles.

"There was a German trailer which must have contained another fifty, but it wasn't possible to count them. The clothing was piled in a heap against the wall. It appeared that most of the men and boys had died of starvation; they had not been executed. But the manner of death seemed unimportant. Murder had been done at Buchenwald. God alone knows how many men and boys have died there during the last twelve years. I was told there were more than twenty thousand in the camp. There had been as many as sixty thousand. Where are they now?"

Murrow's visit to Buchenwald occurred on the day of Franklin D. Roosevelt's death. In the camp, "many men in many tongues blessed the name of Roosevelt. For long years his name had meant the full measure of their hope. These men who had kept close company with death for many years did not know that Mr. Roosevelt would, within hours, join their comrades who had laid their lives on the scales of freedom . . . At Buchenwald they spoke of the President just before he died. If there be a better epitaph, history does not record it."

There had been other accounts of other Nazi death camps, like those of Maidanek and Auschwitz in Poland, liberated by the Russians. But none carried the force and cold fury of Murrow's story from Buchenwald.

Though it was told on his regular Sunday broadcast, three days after the reports filed by other Allied correspondents — and deliberately delayed by him so he could "acquire detachment" — it was used by the BBC instead of its own reporter's account, and was printed on the front page of the London newspapers. From it Pavla Zenkl, living in Britain, learned of the survival of her husband Peter, after six years' absence.

A BBC executive later explained that since the British were acutely sensitive to anything that sounded like an atrocity story, Murrow's broadcast was used because it was felt he could not be accused of exaggeration. Fleet Street printed the radio account, though the story was three days old, simply because it was better than any of the stories already printed.

Murrow never mentioned it, but others with him said he openly wept several times. Impulsively, he took off his money belt and left it for the inmates, with several thousand dollars in it. (It was thought he had won most of the money the night before, in a poker game.)

Many thought it was the best broadcast he ever made, but he thought it a failure because he was unable to describe fully everything he saw and felt. "One shoe, two shoes, a dozen shoes, yes. But how can you describe several thousand shoes?" he said, of the pathetic heap of footwear which the Nazis had taken from the dead, and carefully catalogued, together with clothing, suitcases, human hair and gold teeth.

As he explained it in his broadcast, "I pray you to believe what I have said about Buchenwald. I have reported what I saw and heard, but only part of it. For most of it I have no words."

A few days later he entered Leipzig with a tank unit, accompanying infantrymen of the 69th Division. "It was about a thousand yards to the city hall. There were 185 men on the outside of the tanks. They started down the main street. There were thirteen tanks and five tank-destroyers. They were in a column, moving down a single street.

"When they began to roll, they were hit with bazookas and machine guns. When they turned a corner, the wounded slipped off. The medium tanks were traveling about thirty miles an hour and no man turned back. Lieutenant Ken Wilder started with a total of thirty-nine men, and when they reached the city hall he had eight. They had a company of infantry riding on the tanks, 185 men. Sixty-eight reached the city hall. The tanks were marked with machine-gun fire, and they were splattered with blood.

"An hour after reaching the city hall, those boys were driving German cars and motorcycles about the streets. In the place where we were sitting, a sniper's bullet broke a pane of glass in a window. A doughboy said, 'My! My! Somebody done broke a window. Things are getting rough around here. Folks are destroying things.' The Germans had given up. A few had shot themselves. One said he couldn't be taken prisoner by the Americans. He must commit suicide. A young lieutenant said, 'Here's a gun.' The German took it and shot himself just under the right ear."

The Army censors refused to pass Murrow's script, for reasons known to themselves. He took it to General Omar Bradley. The general read it. "You were there? This is the way it happened?" the general asked. Murrow said yes. Bradley scrawled his initials on the copy.

Before Leipzig, Murrow had participated in the capture of Nuremberg. "For purely personal reasons," he reported, "I wanted to have a look at the great stadium where the Nazis used to hold their annual party festival. Twice we were given wrong directions by sullen Germans, and I remarked to the jeep driver, 'These people don't seem very happy to see us.' And the driver replied, 'What do you expect? How do you think we'd feel if we was in New York and a couple of Japs in a jeep was drivin' around askin' the way to the Yankee Stadium?' The driver's ability to put himself in the other fellow's place was much greater than mine.''

Murrow did not get to Berlin until after the war. But when the advance party of American troops entered the devastated city, to open a press camp in Zehlendorf, one Berliner asked a colonel whether Murrow and Richard Dimbleby of the BBC would be arriving. He and his neighbors always listened to them describing the air raids on Berlin, he said, and believed them rather than the German news broadcasts.

Murrow returned to London in time for V-E Day, and American radio saw the European war out in style, as it had ushered it in. CBS was on the air for three solid hours, with reports from Washington, the United Nations conference in San Francisco, New York's Times Square, SHAEF in Versailles, Paris, various United States Army headquarters in Europe, Guam, and Eisenhower's hometown of Abilene, Kansas.

From London the chimes of Big Ben were heard, and Churchill declared, "The evildoers now lie prostrate before us," concluding his victory message with "Advance, Britannia!" The crowds streamed toward Buckingham Palace, the Houses of Parliament, and Trafalgar Square, and Murrow reported:

"There are no words, just a sort of rumbling roar. London is celebrating today in a city which became a symbol. The scars of war are all about. There is no lack of serious, solemn faces. Their thoughts are all their own. Some people appear not to be part of the celebration. Their minds must be filled with memories of friends who died in the streets where they now walk, and of others who have died from Burma to the Elbe. There are a few men on crutches, as though to remind all that there is much human wreckage left at the end. Six years is a long time. I have observed today that people have very little to say. There are no words."

In another broadcast, later that day — when "in the midst of all the celebration there have been many men and women with tears in their eyes" — he had his own wartime memories, evoked by a walk through the familiar streets.

"The war that was seems more real than the peace that has come. You feel a depression in the wooden paving blocks, and remember that an incendiary burned itself out there. Your best friend was killed on the next corner. You pass a water-tank and recall, almost with a start, that there used to be a pub, hit with a two-thousand-pounder one night, thirty people killed.

"You're walking north. If you walk far enough you'll reach an airfield where you landed after leaving Vienna with the sounds of shots and the screams in the night still ringing in your ears, the same field where you saw Mr. Chamberlain step out of his plane from Munich, speaking of 'peace in our time.' You pass a pile of familiar rubble and recall Mr. Churchill's remark when he walked down that street the morning after a raid. When the people came out to cheer him, and he said, 'They act as though I had brought them a great victory.'

"There are little streets where you might meet anyone, and tonight it's easy to imagine that old friends are walking there. Some of the boys you watched jump at Remagen. Flyers you watched go down in flames over Berlin, or a dozen other targets. And you wonder what's happened to the American boys who used to stand on those street corners, far from home and rather lonesome. The soldiers who trained for D-Day, and who since demonstrated they were not living on the revolutions made by their grandfathers."

The price of victory, he took notice, had been high. Europe was devastated, its political structure unstable, millions of its people hungry, homeless and in despair. "Perhaps we should remember, even tonight in the midst of the celebration, that the suffering will continue for many years. And that unspeakable crimes are still unpunished, and above all else, that power carries with it great responsibility. We have the power."

A few days before V-E Day, he had written in another celebratory vein to Janet's parents in Middletown. "We are both happy, feel we have been very lucky during this war . . . and that whatever gods may be have been more than kind to us." They were going to have a baby — "I felt as though a bomb had fallen near me" — and they needed a few things hard to get in England, diapers, baby dresses, nightgowns, blankets, safety pins, baby oil.

Britain's wartime austerity and privation would continue for several years, but of one commodity there was no shortage as the fighting in Europe ended, and that was the desire for political change. The coalition dissolved for new elections, the first in ten years.

Murrow stated the issues. "There may be involved, as undoubtedly there is, personal pride, desire for power and profit and prestige. But there has developed a fundamental difference of opinion as to the relationship between the State and the individual."

The outcome "will be powerful proof that all this talk about democracy, the right of the individual to speak his mind and register his vote, was one of the things about which the war was fought. This political campaign may have been ill-timed, it may uncover mean motives. But it will demonstrate democracy in action, even though it be only in a small island off the coast of Europe."

Churchill wanted his coalition to continue, at least as long as the war with Japan, and indeed he hoped that whatever the election results, even if Labor won, a new coalition could be formed, to go on. But Labor stood opposed, after an internal fight in which Harold Laski, the party chairman, and Aneurin Bevan, the Welshman from Ebbw Vale, won out, over the party's parliamentary leaders, Deputy Prime Minister Attlee and the minister of labor, Ernest Bevin.

Laski had always believed the war would lay the foundations of a new social order in Britain — convincing Murrow of the same thing — and now he had no doubt that Labor would win and form its own government. As for Nye Bevan, Churchill's principal debating foe in Commons, even before D-Day he had estimated Churchill's popularity to be fading.

"This is merely the immortal tragedy of all public life," he remarked, "that the hero's need of the people outlasts their need of him. They obey the pressures of contemporary conditions, whilst he strives to perpetuate the situation where he stood supreme."

The election swapped British prime ministers in the middle of the Potsdam Conference. Among those who might be accused of the "mean motives" Murrow had mentioned was his particular hero, the man who had led the nation through its "finest" as well as some of its darkest hours. For with the election campaign, in which Laborites vowed to make Britain "a home fit for heroes" by implementing some of the war aims, Churchill ended his role as national leader to become merely chieftain of the Tories. As such he assailed personally the Laborites who had faithfully served under him in the war. He said the Socialists would introduce a police state and a Gestapo, and singled out Laski as his principal target, charging him with plotting a dictatorship. Yet he had known Laski since the latter's childhood in Manchester — where Churchill, then a Liberal, was a parliamentary candidate, and Laski's father was a principal Liberal — and he had styled Harold Laski "a friend who is not a follower."

Whatever else he might have been, Churchill was not a very good politician. At Downing Street he had needed no press officer or public relations adviser, but he allowed the 1945 campaign to be masterminded by the publisher who, though a Canadian, was regarded as more imperial than the imperialists. "The voice was the voice of Churchill but the mind the mind of Beaverbrook," Attlee remarked of the Gestapo charge in the campaign.

Murrow took an absorbing interest in the election, indeed what might be called an active one in the campaign of Paul Wright, a young major of the King's Royal Rifles, running as a Liberal candidate in the much-bombed proletarian constituency of Bethnal Green, in London's East End. Wright's American-born wife Barbara, widow of an RAF pilot and a former M.P. herself, had served with Janet Murrow during the Blitz at Bundles for Britain.

The broadcaster decided that in human interest terms the Bethnal Green campaign had "all the elements." It had a good deal of Murrow himself. He addressed envelopes in Wright's headquarters and received endless cups of tea as he accompanied the major on his house-to-house canvasing. At one small dwelling in Russia Lane the two young men were told by a pugnacious woman in a man's cap, "I'd advise you to bugger off. We've always been Labor in this house, and we're voting for old Churchill."

Wright's campaign manager was a local fishmonger, on whose van was mounted the official loudspeaker. Murrow, seated inside with fish scales on his hat, regulated the volume, not too successfully. It was a hot day in June, and the van exerted a distinct presence as it jounced along.

Despite muttered misgivings about his status as an American citizen, Murrow even took the platform at one election meeting and spoke for ten minutes. He did not support any specific candidate, though he stood by the side of the Liberal, but urged the East Enders who had suffered so much in the war to hold fast to American friendship in peacetime. The audience was small and those present did not know who he was, even if they might have heard him on the BBC during the war. Moreover Wright was defeated two-to-one by the Labor candidate.

In reporting the 1945 campaign to the United States, Murrow told one of Churchill's stories of the Blitz, about the old lady who said to him, "There is one thing about these 'ere bombs — they do help to take your mind off the war!"

In the same way, he thought that the bombardment of campaign oratory had done something to take the elector's mind off the fundamental issues. This was consonant with his views about all elections, including American ones. But the British were to prove that their minds had not wandered.

Final results were not known for three weeks, because of the military overseas vote. But the trend was unmistakable. On election day Herbert Morrison, whom many saw as the next leader of the Labor Party and a prime minister, came to the Murrow flat to take a bath, and stayed the night. The Cockney statesman, swathed in Murrow's much-too-big bathrobe, sat up until nearly dawn, speaking of the "new day" which socialism, and a good deal of pragmatic common sense, would bring. He had no doubt of a Labor victory.

Murrow did, because he thought Churchill's polemics had overshadowed the issues. He had predicted a Conservative victory "with a small but workable majority." But Labor won resoundingly, with a clear parliamentary majority of 146 seats, and now Murrow explored the reasons.

"Mr. Churchill has changed his mind about very few things in the last fifty years. He has not always been right, particularly in his assessment of British public opinion . . . As a wartime leader, Mr. Churchill was indomitable and inflexible. The British electorate concluded that in the changed conditions of peace he would be equally inflexible, and so they voted him out of office. But one day, some day, he still hopes to return."

Some time later, reviewing Churchill's history of the war, he expanded the theme. Despite the adoring crowds and the shouts of "Good old Winnie," he thought, Churchill "was scarcely aware of his fellow countrymen. For him the battle was everything. He drove himself so hard in the intoxicating atmosphere of high command that he failed to realize other millions of nameless Britons, without his heritage, ability or vision, were driving themselves as relentlessly."

These others, moreover, "had visions of a fuller measure of equality, milk and hot lunches for their children, decent houses and 'fair shares for all.'" He hazarded the guess that Churchill was more popular in the United States than in his own country, while Roosevelt had been more popular in Britain than in the United States.

After the election, as Churchill was moving out of Number 10, a sympathetic caller remarked, "But at least while you held the reins you managed to win the race." Churchill answered, "Yes, I won the race, and now they have warned me off the turf." But he would be back in Downing Street in six years time, and the hinge of fate had not yet closed.

Attlee and Ernest Bevin replaced Churchill and Eden in the final phase of the Potsdam Conference with Truman and Stalin, and agreement was reached to partition Germany for occupation purposes. Murrow accepted it as he acknowledged most Britons had, with relief but not without foreboding. Indeed the agreement was regarded as a somewhat "frightening document" in Britain.

"Performance undoubtedly will not measure up to some of the promises. There is still a residue of mistrust and suspicion. But a question which might have caused the Grand Alliance to come unstuck was solved, however imperfectly." He added that "most reporters will be impressed by the assurances of free access to eastern Europe when that happens."

The Potsdam meeting "gave no guarantee of lasting peace," he observed. "It is proof of the magnitude of the task that lies ahead. Most of the Americans who came over here to fight this war didn't want to come. We thought after the last war that we had secured a Europe that wouldn't bother us.

"Now it is clear that whether we like it or not, American power and American policy will be a major influence in the Europe that emerges.

"Those who believe that Russia got everything she wanted out of Potsdam while we got nothing might consider the possibility that perhaps we didn't know what we wanted." But American isolationism was over, he was sure. "It is hard to see how we are going to escape from Europe again."

More forebodings came with the end of the war in Asia, after the dropping of atomic bombs on Japan and thus the introduction of a new factor in international relations. "Seldom if ever has a war ended leaving the victors with such a sense of uncertainty and fear, with such a realization that the future is obscure and that survival is not assured.

"There is a widespread recognition that the agreement reached at San Francisco is obsolete, and that the Big Four will have to think again if they are to devise any system which has even a reasonable chance of maintaining peace. President Truman's declaration that Britain and America will not reveal the secret of the Bomb until means have been found for controlling it brought no great reassurance. It does for the moment alter the balance of power, but such a solution is only temporary. Other nations, by research and espionage, are likely to solve the problem before we have mastered the countermeasures . . .

"Science has presented statesmanship with a problem, and its successful solution implies a revolution in the relations between nations."

No such revolution was in sight. Though America's senior statesman, Henry L. Stimson, retiring as Secretary of War, proposed to President Truman that the United States share with the Soviet Union the control of nuclear weapons and the development of peaceful uses of atomic energy — a "partnership upon a basis of cooperation and trust" — the plea was ignored, despite majority sentiment in the Cabinet for it. Defense Secretary Forrestal was the chief dissident.

Desire to keep the "secret" of "the Bomb," which Murrow regarded as unachievable, would become one of the chief fuel components for McCarthyism.

The conversion from war to a suspicious peace had its inevitable effect on American radio. Murrow came home for a month, without Janet — she was "expecting" in London — to discuss postwar coverage in Europe, for the two big networks had decided to retain full overseas news staffs. CBS had established five permanent bureaus, in London, Paris, Rome, Moscow and Germany, and in addition Howard K. Smith would be on roving assignment on the Continent.

In the United States, Murrow was impressed anew with the wealth produced by the American economy, no less than by the voice of his own chosen medium, radio. He was accustomed to the noncommercial programs of the BBC and other European systems, and he confessed that "at first the commercial advertising came as a shock." He thought, however, that radio "was telling me what to buy but not what to think."

There followed the statement of belief in his profession which he sought to practice by, but which he was already aware might not be fulfilled by radio itself.

"There is something unique about the American system of broadcasting. I believe that what comes out of the loudspeaker is the most honest and accurate reflection of what goes on in a nation. Radio reflects the social, economic and cultural climate in which it lives and grows.

"Compare broadcasting and you are comparing countries. Our system is fast, experimental, technically slick. It is highly competitive and commercial. Often it is loud, occasionally vulgar, generally optimistic, and not always right. But the man who is wrong has his chance to be heard. There is much controversy and debate, and some special pleading, but frequently the phonies are found out.

"There is no conspiracy to keep the listener in ignorance, and government does not guide the listening or thinking of the people. There is much talk, and you may think that it only contributes to confusion.

"The presence of a microphone does not guarantee objectivity, often it endangers humility. A loud voice which reaches from coast to coast is not necessarily uttering truths more profound than those that may be heard in the classroom, bar or country store. But there they are. You can listen, or leave them alone. By turning the dial, you can be entertained, informed or irritated."

He was thirty-seven years old, and he was sounding the note on which he was about to enter the American national scene, no longer a faraway voice.

"I believe that radio in a democracy must be more than an industry, more than a medium of entertainment, more than a source of revenue for those who own the facilities. Radio, if it is to serve and survive, must hold a mirror behind the nation and the world. If the reflection shows racial intolerance, economic inequality, bigotry, unemployment, or anything else, let the people see it — or rather, hear it. The mirror must have no curves, and must be held with a steady hand."

But the mirror was already flawed. As American industry, unhobbled from the war, began to enter radio on an unprecedented commercial scale, to advertise the consumer goods now made available, the controversy over opinions and censorship, which had produced the Cecil Brown and William Gailmor cases, was widening.

The Dies Committee of the House of Representatives, investigating "un-American activities," opened an inquiry into radio commentary, and requested copies of scripts not only from Brown and Gailmor, but from six other broadcasters, covering the end-of-the-war period.

The committee, as usual, leaked its suspicions to the Hearst and McCormick press, and the commentators for their part called for support from their own profession. One skeptical Congressman charged the committee's action was motivated by the National Association of Manufacturers, and several labor organizations rallied behind the commentators in a "Mobilization Against Thought Police in the U.S.A."

The House committee's newest vigilantism followed the *Amerasia* case, in which six persons connected with a magazine devoted to Pacific affairs were arrested for publishing "restricted" material about American foreign

ABOVE: *The new arrival, Casey Murrow. Good voice, of broadcast quality.* BELOW: *With his parents at a Seattle microphone*

policy. Critics of the State Department saw this as an attempt to censor journalism and broadcasting, by intimidating news sources and punishing opponents of official policy.

At the same time the War Department vetoed the script of one of the CBS program series called *Assignment Home*, dealing with the readjustment problems of returning veterans. The problem in question was that of racial discrimination, and the Pentagon would not let it be said on a program in which it cooperated that the Negro had the "right" to fight and die for his country, but not the right to a job if he came back home.

Murrow returned to England for the birth of Charles Casey Murrow on November 9, 1945. "I now take trembling typewriter in fatherly hands," he wrote Janet's parents, to tell them that a boy weighing eight pounds, four ounces had arrived. "His head was much too big, being in the tradition of Murrow heads," and "he has plenty of volume but is lacking in modulation. There are two offers to sign him up as a broadcaster, but I have advised him against any long-range commitments."

The child brought the parents close together again, after a time when Murrow's intensive work schedule, his assignments away from home, and their separate interests and even separate friends had sometimes made them seem to be living separate lives.

Murrow never explained, even to Janet, why he had chosen the boy's middle name, which he always used as a first name. Indeed, he originally wanted Casey as a first name whether the child was boy or girl. It may have had some connection with his father's lumber railroading days, and the paragon of engineers, Casey Jones. One thing he was sure of. He wanted no Edward, Jr. "Junior" was a term he sometimes used in opprobrium, though less frequently than "Buster," which he snapped out at someone deserving of real scorn.

The postnatal stay in England was a brief one. The prosperity which radio had enjoyed during the war — its commercial revenues in 1944 had been $384 million — was widening its horizons for the advent of television, held back in wartime but now beginning to stir and even attract sponsors. Bill Paley, after helping establish the American occupation's communications empire in Germany, came back to Madison Avenue as chairman of the CBS board, and Frank Stanton was elevated to the presidency. Paley also wanted Murrow back, as vice president in charge of news and public affairs.

His star broadcaster was reluctant and said he had no taste for the executive, but Paley thought he had lost his listeners with the war's end, and that in any case he should devote himself to broader matters, such as developing new types of programs. Murrow was finally persuaded. Having put together a good staff of correspondents, he thought that any future inadequacies of CBS news coverage would be on the administrative side. If he were in charge of it, perhaps there would not be so many.

During the war, when the bombs were dropping on London, one of the correspondents at home wrote Ed that he was foolish to remain abroad and in danger, that "this is where the money is." Murrow never forgave the man, though they would be associated in New York and Washington through the succeeding years.

But now the shooting was over. Even the war against Japan had not lasted long enough for Murrow to get to the Pacific, as he planned to do, at least "for a look." It was time to answer the call to be expressed by the title of a novel by Bill Shirer, dealing with the politically repressive trend in the nation and the broadcasting industry, *Stranger Come Home.*

In Europe Murrow had come to believe, and said so at every opportunity, that the old world's future and America's were bound together, and that not altruism, but self-interest dictated a continuing policy of American involvement in Europe. By involvement he did not mean intervention.

In the United States, in the fifteen years that followed, as an influential public figure at work in the most persuasive of public media, this would remain his principal theme. Its corollary was that America could not exercise world leadership by military power alone, or even economic power, but only by force of democratic example. This meant that the nation's political and social life must be subject to constant scrutiny and criticism.

And whatever American commitments might be abroad, he declared in a broadcast, they "should not extend beyond the areas where we are prepared to sustain and support them by all means at our disposal. We cannot, powerful as we are, do it alone." With the beginning of the American occupation in Europe and Asia, he asked, "Isn't there some chance that we may pay more attention to the defeated enemies than to the cultivation of our friends?"

Murrow made his farewells in London. At the Foreign Office, where he had gone to introduce his successor, Howard K. Smith, the burly Ernie Bevin, trade unionist turned foreign secretary, rolled after him down the corridor with an autographed photo, shouting, "Ed, Ed, damned near forgot. Map of me face!"

The BBC, as a parting gesture, gave Murrow the old-fashioned square box microphone he had used in the basement for six years, "with such distinction," as the inscription said. He spoke into it for the last time in his broadcast home from London on March 10, 1946.

The important thing about the war for him, he said once again, had not been the courage demonstrated or the victories finally won, but that Britain "chose to win or lose the war under the established rules of parliamentary procedure." The British army, he said, "retreated from many places," but "there was no retreat from the principles for which our ancestors fight." He thanked the British for "tea, hospitality, and information. And on occasion, inspiration."

On the BBC itself, to the British audience which had come to regard him as one of its own, he delivered a sort of Farewell and Hail, reviewing his sixteen-year relationship with the fog-covered islands, which had moved from cool acquaintance to warm admiration. He recalled many of the incidents of the war, and remarked, "You were living a life, not an apology."

He turned his face to the United States, to see to it that he would do the same.

VIII

"The only thing that matters in radio is what comes out of the loudspeaker"

DESPITE some of the complexities, like the Darlan deal, relations with de Gaulle, and the Badoglio regime in Italy, the European war had been relatively simple in its political context. The object was to defeat the Germans as effectively and expeditiously as possible, even if it required cooperation with what was generally reckoned as the hostile ideology and separate motivation of the Soviet Union.

There were warnings from some American diplomats, Harriman and Kennan among them, that trouble lay ahead, and certainly the United Nations Organization came into being in inauspicious circumstances in San Francisco, as the war ended and the Russians arrested the Polish leaders whom they had called to Moscow for negotiations. The Red Army was firmly implanted as an occupation force in all of eastern Europe except Yugoslavia, which had a Red Army of its own, and even before Mao Tse-tung, the men in the Kremlin knew that political power sprang from the barrel of a gun. Some in Europe and America feared the Red Army might even reach the Channel, just as Hitler had done. All that could keep them from doing so, it was said, was a shortage of boots.

Still, the euphoria induced by the long war's ending, the eagerness to bring the boys home, and most of all the reality of American monopoly of the nuclear, or ultimate, weapon overcame immediate fears.

After all, American G.I.'s and Russian Ivans had met and embraced at the Elbe. Zhukov had played magnanimous host to American commanders in Berlin, and Eisenhower had signed the Quadripartite Agreement for the city with the bemedaled marshal. Defending the Yalta accords, no less a one than Churchill regarded a schism between the West and the Soviet Union as "the worst thing that could happen to the fortunes of mankind." He felt of the Russians that "their word is their bond," and said so in Commons.

But the Potsdam Declaration sounded an alarm, in the dispositions over Berlin, and marked the end of the wartime coalition even before the hostilities with Japan had ended. Soon Churchill was talking of the "iron curtain" that had fallen across Europe. Then, when the United States enunciated the unilateral Truman Doctrine, and established the North Atlantic Treaty Organization — all in the name of "containment" of the Russians — the cold war would be joined.

After the fighting in Europe, this was the new conflict that Murrow came home to. He had been developing a postwar policy of his own. While fully alive to the threat to future peace that lay in the mutually suspicious Soviet-American relationship — particularly when the Russians developed their own A-bomb, as they inevitably would — he was also conscious of the mortal danger that lay in the failure of accommodation. Like General Marshall, the American he most admired, he did not believe that irreconcilability was inevitable. He accepted that time brought change, even healing, and felt that the American democratic ideology had no reason to tremble in confrontation with any other.

The Murrows, bag, baggage and Casey, left England a few days after Winston Churchill's Fulton, Missouri, speech, which helped bring clanging down the very Iron Curtain it postulated.

For Churchill proposed that "the Anglo-Americans, outside the United Nations and with the support of atomic weapons . . . create a unity in Europe from which no nation in Europe should be permanently outcast," that is to say, retrieve and rescue East Europe by the threat of nuclear war. Three months after the Fulton speech Churchill's longtime American friend Bernard Baruch referred to the situation as "a cold war."

Churchill's remarks were the more offensive to the Russians in that he himself, as Britain's wartime leader, had gone to Moscow and consorted with Stalin in apportioning European spheres of influence. The Russians were given a free hand in eastern Europe, and the British the same in Greece, with influence in Yugoslavia to be shared equally. Stalin carried out his end of the bargain by letting Churchill unprotested break the Leftist movement in Athens at Christmas 1944, and install a right-wing regime — an action repudiated by American Secretary of State Stettinius as interference with democratic processes.

But Communist-led guerrillas, with sanctuary across the border in Yugoslavia, had come to threaten Greece again, and this would cause President Truman to enunciate the doctrine of aid to countries resisting armed insurrection or "outside pressures," a doctrine which was to carry the United States eventually into Vietnam.

The question has been raised by some recent younger historians of who was responding to whom in the cold war, their thesis being that American provocation, rather than Soviet "expansionism," was the underlying factor. That there was an urgency of challenge on both sides there could be no doubt. In fact, two months before Churchill's Fulton speech, President Truman declared, "Unless Russia is faced with an iron fist and strong language, another war is in the making."

In his last broadcast from London, Murrow, commenting on the Iron Curtain speech — "from Stettin in the Baltic to Trieste in the Adriatic" — pointed out that Churchill and his party had the year before been turned out by the ballots of the British people, who like other Europeans, Murrow thought, were seeking a middle way "between the conservatism of Mr. Churchill and the suppressive collectivism of Mr. Stalin."

Although many might have seen the East-West conflict as soluble only by creating a world in either of the two rival images, he believed its outcome would be determined "not by dollars, not by American battleships showing a flag in the Mediterranean, not by luxury or productivity at home," but by the degree to which Americans understood "the role in world affairs that has been thrust upon them. And the importance, not only of our decisions but of our examples."

But apart from foreign policy, Churchill's speech had made a distinct contribution to the postwar American domestic climate. Several months before Joseph R. McCarthy was even elected Senator from Wisconsin, the British leader warned that "throughout the world, Communist Fifth Columns are established, and work in absolute obedience to directions they receive from the Communist center."

Churchill excepted Britain and the United States, "where communism is in its infancy," but the exceptions were unheard. To many Americans the recent exposure of a Soviet spy ring in Canada was proof enough that "Communist conspiracy" was at work in the New World also.

Murrow had begun his nine years abroad as a cultural impresario and a novice broadcaster. By acute observation, sensitivity, conviction, and inborn powers of persuasion, he ended them as a leading symbol of a kind of dignified intellectual passion about what happened in the world, a frank spokesman for American responsible leadership, and one who had access to what has come to be called the power structure. It was the highest level an American reporter had ever attained abroad.

But he came home not as a reporter, but a corporation executive, at a salary of forty-five thousand dollars. Radio was a thriving marketplace, though less of ideas than of goods. For the war had made it even more commercial. Air time no longer remained unsold, and the unsponsored programs, in which most of the medium's public service was offered, were being replaced by sponsored programs devoted to entertainment. One of the assumptions on which postwar reconversion in radio was based was that commentators and news analysts were, in the wartime term, expendable.

Murrow returned as a network executive in the midst of a furor caused by the FCC's "blue book," demonstrating the widespread failure of local stations to live up to their public service obligations. The broadcasting industry's reply was that the Federal agency, by displaying any interest in the nature and content of radio programs, threatened the First Amendment.

The networks as such were not involved in the controversy. Many local stations simply did not broadcast network public service programs, preferring their own lucrative commercial fare. But Murrow's assumption of a key position, on the very firing line between public service and commercialism, was generally seen as some evidence of uneasy network consciences.

The broadcaster spent an uncomfortable eighteen months as vice president, though other company officers found he was not at all the poor administrator he believed he was. As he later explained things, "It's the big desk with the telephones, the In basket and the Out basket. Conferences, memos, budgets and firing people. Who am I to be firing people, the Almighty Himself?"

He was involved in two particularly unhappy firings, one inaugurating his vice presidency, the other hastening his desire to end it. Paul White, who had been his superior as director of news, was now his subordinate, and White took it hard. The two young men had begun as inescapable rivals, because of their original administrative jobs, but after events had made Murrow a broadcaster and reporter, Paul White recognized and encouraged his talent. However, something always seemed lacking between the two.

Now Murrow was back as boss. CBS News received the Peabody Award for 1945 for its outstanding war coverage, and the largest commercial contract for radio news followed, as the Campbell Soup Company put up $1.5 million a year to sponsor the fifteen-minute evening news program *The World Today*. On it Bob Trout, in New York, brought in CBS correspondents from Washington and overseas capitals, in the now familiar "news roundup" style.

Whatever strains White might be under, and they included the physical pain of acute arthritis, he eased them by indulged exuberance at the office. He insisted on introducing the new program on the air himself, and his remarks were blurred and confused. They brought Murrow storming down from his office, only to find that the hapless White had been aided in escaping. The news director left CBS, it was officially announced, as part of the "network reconversion program." Wells Church, who had been White's assistant, succeeded him, and in the years that followed Murrow's reliance on Church, and Church's confidence in Murrow, was at the core of the successful and often brilliant functioning of CBS News. As for White, who had pioneered in the teaching and practices of radio journalism, he found a new career on the West Coast in broadcasting management. But his departure from CBS was a distressing affair, and helped create Murrow's distaste for some aspects of executive authority.

The other case was even more disturbing, because it was made to seem to fit into radio's growing postwar tendency toward self-censorship. It involved Bill Shirer, the man with whom Murrow had pioneered CBS news coverage from Europe a decade before, and who had reached a peak of his own at home as a sagacious and sensitive news analyst, even though some network executives continued to feel that his slow, almost subdued voice lacked the "commercial" quality that a voice like Murrow's, for instance, possessed.

Shirer's sponsor, a company which made shaving cream, became dissatisfied with him and decided to drop his Sunday afternoon news commentary and replace him with another broadcaster. Shirer was reassigned by the network, meaning Murrow, to another time period, though without a sponsor, thus suffering a serious reduction of income. He resigned instead. The sponsor then rejected the commentator named in Shirer's place and said it had decided that news programs had "lost their appeal."

Shirer had eighteen months remaining of his CBS contract and Murrow tried to persuade him to stay, but his old confrere said he felt his usefulness had been ended, and charged that he had in effect been gagged. As the man in the middle of the controversy, Murrow publicly explained that the reassignment had been made to "improve Columbia's news analysis," and denied that any pressure had been exerted by the sponsors, though they had clearly expressed their displeasure at not selling more shaving cream. He particularly denied that any political or ideological considerations had entered the case.

Privately Murrow felt that Shirer was no longer doing his best work, that he was rehashing too many newspaper editorials, and had become "ivory towerish" enough to have lost his original impact.

He also believed that sponsors, while not entitled to decide what a man said on the air, did have the right to choose the kind of program they wanted to pay for, such as news, sports, or entertainment, that being the nature of commercial radio. Murrow was sure moreover that Shirer would soon find another sponsor and wanted him to remain on the air.

Things would work out in radio so that sponsors would come and go, and various forms of sponsorship would be invented, without prejudice to the presentation of news — except for the physical and quantitative restrictions imposed by commercial formats. But Murrow, who in his broadcasting had not been overly conscious about such things himself, also

Murrow and Shirer, before they became disputants in a "freedom of the air" controversy

The complete radio reporter. At a political convention, 1948

thought later he had been too indifferent to Shirer's professional pride in his possession of a regularly scheduled and well-paid program.

The Shirer case, however, was taken out of any purely professional, or even commercial, context and made a cause célèbre of free speech. The commentator's supporters pointed out that he was the only network broadcaster openly opposed to the Truman Doctrine. *Variety*, the trade journal, in its annual review of broadcasting noted that the more liberal commentators had dropped away, and those left were "not only conservative, but what's worse, not intelligent."

A "Voice of Freedom" committee — which he later disavowed because he thought it was exploiting him — protested Shirer's resignation by picketing the CBS building, and criticized Murrow. The CIO Political Action Committee called for an FCC investigation, while the Progressive Citizens of America opened a campaign to "give radio back to the people." On the other hand, the House Un-American Activities Committee enlarged its interest in radio, and subpoenaed the scripts for all thirteen CBS programs by Norman Corwin based on the "One World" theme of the late Wendell Willkie. Inspection of the radio medium had become a continuing congressional practice.

The two things, the Murrow-Shirer relationship and the postwar climate of congressional investigation of "subversive activities," provided Shirer some years later with a novel, *Stranger Come Home*. Whether a roman à clef — and his Senator O'Brien was clearly Joe McCarthy — or an imaginary account, as Shirer insisted, the book's antihero, Robert A. Fletcher, a wartime radio broadcaster turned network executive, played an ambiguous, indeed shabby role in permitting the inquisition of the liberal-minded broadcaster patterned on Shirer himself. But the book proved ill-timed. It would appear in 1954, just after Murrow had publicly challenged McCarthy.

Besides raising an ideological specter which would plague Murrow himself when he became a broadcaster again, the Shirer case stirred the controversy over commercial sponsorship of news programs. One influential critic, Jack Gould of the *New York Times,* proposed that it be entirely eliminated. As things stood, said Gould, a sponsor had the right to pick a specific news broadcaster, and he wondered what would be said if a newspaper advertiser could decide what reporter should cover what story. He cited another current CBS case, that of Quincy Howe, who had been broadcasting a 6 P.M. unsponsored news program. But now a large insurance company wanted to buy that time period, and it would choose between two other broadcasters, while Howe would no longer be heard. "Why shouldn't CBS keep Howe there without the sponsor's concurrence?" Gould asked.

Murrow replied that the sponsor could not name a broadcaster without CBS concurrence, and that only the network exercised control of news and analysis. It was not a full answer. It conceded that a sponsor could select the broadcaster he wanted, and to that extent did influence the tone and even content of a news program, for each broadcaster had his own way of looking at things and his own means of expression.

As vice president Murrow was also in the center of the perpetual internal CBS debate over editorializing. Company policy drew a sharp line between news and opinion, but the latter was then made vague by always being called something else — analysis, interpretation, comment, background, perspective. "Objectivity" was demanded, when all that was meant was fairness. Matters were further complicated by internal dispute over whether the network, as such, had the right to broadcast editorial opinions of its own. The whole situation remained unresolved, and still does. When Murrow resigned the vice presidency he said his major purpose had been to establish a clearcut network editorial policy, but "I failed."

He had argued that the network had every right to express its views on public questions, as newspapers and magazines did, and that not to do so was to be remiss in its responsibilities. But even when restrictions on editorializing were removed by the FCC two years later, the networks refused to avail themselves of the prerogative. David Sarnoff, the grand panjandrum of broadcasting, distinguished between "having the right" to editorialize and actually "exercising" it, a doleful commentary in itself.

Murrow's fretful eighteen months as a network executive were not entirely unproductive, however, in the further development of public affairs programs. He called on his overseas staff to provide more depth to their news reports. The day had passed, he said, when multiple pickups from world capitals impressed the listener for mere technological reasons. "It is not distance that should lend validity to a broadcast direct from London or Chungking, but the fact that the broadcaster has something to say and a way of saying it that cannot be conveyed by print."

Peacetime reporting, he told his staff, was more demanding than wartime reporting. Broadcasting about the Marshall Plan or the Taft-Hartley Bill would require more work and understanding than describing a military engagement.

It was no longer enough for foreign correspondents to report factual situations from any one country. They must be aware of common European interests and problems. Above all, as the United States became more conscious of its world role, they must undertake the most important kind of assignment, that of interpreting the rest of the world to this country. This would also demand a new degree of sophistication from the listener, and unfortunately, he observed, many Americans believed that a reporter trying to explain the problems or philosophy of a Communist state was thereby condoning communism.

He had come back from Europe taking it for granted that although "radio didn't make the war and it can't make the peace, it can offer a platform for those who wish to debate issues, the outcome of which will determine if there is to be another war, or peace."

He formed a news documentary unit and gave it as its first assignment the postwar role of Germany. He instituted *As Others See Us*, a program devoted to foreign comment on the United States. He put on the network the popular program, *CBS Was There* — later *You Are There* — in which historical occasions were re-created, with CBS reporters playing their knowledgeable selves in the lively manner of the present day. In addition to the morning *World News Roundup*, he began a similar fifteen-minute daily program, picking up American instead of European or Asian cities. For the first time, regions of the country could learn by radio what other regions were doing, or thinking.

But the new program in which he took the sharpest interest, and for which he had felt the greatest need, was the controversial *CBS Views the Press*. Since there were no national, only local, newspapers, it was a New York local program intended as "an objective, critical analysis of the press," not a mere summary of printed news or opinion.

"We believe freedom of the press and freedom of radio are inseparable, and that mutual criticism will help both," he explained.

Until then criticism had traveled a one-way street. American newspapers, especially the metropolitan press, regarded radio news as unfair competition from the days when they prevented the news agencies from selling their services to radio stations, and compelled the new medium to find its own resources. The competition between newspapers and radio as advertising media was also an obvious factor. Though the public prints had since Munich come to the acceptance of radio as a news medium in its own right — indeed many newspapers had acquired radio stations — a large number of journals remained wary of radio's offerings, and seldom missed a chance to point out its shortcomings or excesses.

And now radio, or at least Murrow, was prepared to demonstrate that the press also was not above criticism, and that the Fourth Estate was often less the public service it pretended to be, and more the repository of the private views and interests of individual publishers and their friends. In its opening program *CBS Views the Press* was sarcastic about the "crusading" of leading New York newspapers against a somewhat exaggerated "relief scandal." Don Hollenbeck, who broadcast the program, also examined the New York "gossip columns" as a morass of personal prejudices, press agentry, jingoism, and often complete invention.

The reaction of the press to the new program was predictable. The editor of the *New York Sun* charged CBS with "following the Communist Party line" and being destructive of American institutions, like popular belief in the integrity of journalism. Other editors complained that freedom of the press was being undermined, not upheld, by the freedom of radio. Murrow replied that he considered the program constructive, and that it would continue.

When it did, probing into not only the methods but the opinions of the New York press, that powerful amalgam of interests struck back. It used its influence with public officials, advertisers, and its own readers to imply subversion by CBS, Murrow and particularly Hollenbeck. Right-wing organizations took up the cry in their pamphlets. Postcard protest campaigns were organized. A member of the FCC revealed that the FBI had been sending him "unsolicited information" about people in radio. The Un-American Activities Committee was still digging away at the subject, and the American Federation of Radio Artists, the union of broadcast performers and announcers, denied any Communist sympathies. Some of its officers opened an anti-Communist campaign in their own ranks, which would become a long bloodletting. The Hearst newspapers, often singled out by *CBS Views the Press* for their journalistic practices, took the lead in impugning motives, and Hollenbeck was the target, day after day, of Hearst "gossip" columns.

CBS Views the Press and other public affairs programs gave Murrow some satisfaction in his desk job, and he was also able to travel about the country, giving talks on such subjects as "The Pursuit of Peace" and "Freedom of Communication," and to attend broadcasting conventions, and become widely acquainted in Washington with public figures on terms which went beyond the requirements of program ideas and arrangements.

At a dinner of the Radio Correspondents Association he met David Lilienthal, the chairman of the Tennessee Valley Authority, who had been named to head the new Atomic Energy Commission. Lilienthal was going through the Washington mill, facing congressional charges of having allowed Communists into TVA, being opposed as a New Dealer by Republicans, running the gauntlet of covert anti-Semitism.

He was also compelled unhappily to sit in judgment on security clearances in the "sensitive" atomic energy establishment, making decisions based on FBI hearsay without the presentation of any defense by those accused.

On this first meeting, which grew into a cordial friendship, Lilienthal deplored the lack of what he called "atomic education" in the United States, not only in the technical facts, shrouded in official secrecy, but also in the potential peaceful uses of nuclear energy, to counteract the fears created by the destructive power of the Bomb. Lilienthal thought such education should not be a function of government, but part of the traditional learning process in the schools and through the communications media. Murrow agreed to help, so far as radio was concerned.

But though it had had its compensations, he had by now come to realize the disparity between his executive job and what he really wanted to do, which was to broadcast again.

Bill Paley had also sensed that Murrow's heart was in the studio, and not in the vice president's suite, though the latter had never confessed to any unhappiness as an administrator. Paley believed Murrow had been an able corporate official, and even twenty years later was by no means certain, despite Murrow's effect upon the medium as a broadcaster, that he might not have had even more important and more fundamental effect upon the entire industry if he had remained on the executive side.

In any case, when the proposal was made by the advertising agency involved that Murrow go back on the air with the network's principal news program, the nightly 7:45 P.M. broadcast, Paley endorsed it. "I know you really want to, Ed," he said. Murrow very much may have wanted to, but his reply was typical. "Well, if you say so, Bill. You're the boss."

The exchange also typified their genial relations. But though Murrow exercised his personal prerogative to take matters to the chairman directly, thus avoiding his immediate superior Frank Stanton, as often as not he found that it inhibited normal business dealings. When Paley, for example, disagreed with Murrow about programming, or questioned costs, or otherwise took him to task, both men felt acutely embarrassed, as they would not have felt if they had not been such good friends.

This time Stanton, contractual terms in hand, interceded to assure both men that it was merely a routine shift of assignment, not a personal affair. He was not too happy about the change. He also thought Murrow had done well as an executive, and though he was now losing a vice president, he moved to make Murrow a member of the CBS board of directors.

The broadcaster returned to his microphone on September 29, 1947, after an absence of a year and a half. During the next twelve years he would make his program the most authoritative and effective news period on radio.

The sponsor, the Campbell company, had allocated three million dollars for CBS air time that year, including Murrow's news program and another by the explorer-broadcaster Lowell Thomas, who had come over from NBC. Bob Trout, who had helped introduce Murrow to the microphone, had worked with him in London during the war, and had now been abruptly replaced by him, was vexed and went over to NBC for a while. But the change did not affect Trout's own friendly relations with Murrow. For Campbell's had sponsored Murrow during the war, had wanted him to continue afterward, and had been disappointed when he turned administrator instead.

Variety saw Murrow's return as giving "impetus to the cause of the liberal commentator," because of the reputation for integrity he had won overseas, and incidentally it said, because since the war more than a dozen "left of center" commentators had been quietly effaced from the networks.

Murrow's return was not without its beneficial financial aspects as well. He received virtual carte blanche and a ten-year contract which began at $2500 a week, thus tripling his previous income. He was also to get traveling expenses of $20,000 a year, shared by CBS and the sponsor, to allow him to seek material at home and abroad.

Since the sponsor had chosen radio as the medium by which to sell his soup, the contract barred Murrow from commercial television appearances, a requirement he did not regard as a deprivation. He believed, and always would believe, that radio was a more useful and serious means of communication, and he frequently said that a commentator had no need to be seen, only to be heard.

Perhaps more pertinently, however, television was not yet a major province of either network or sponsor interest, and was only creeping into American homes. The first postwar receiving sets were small in size, expensive, and limited in number. Programming was still largely experimental, consisting primarily of sports and variety acts, while news broadcasting was limited to the on-camera reading of brief press bulletins, between a vocal solo and a softshoe dance.

For the busy and money-making radio executives and advertising agencies of Madison Avenue, television was a furtive business, carried out by CBS in the remote recesses of the Grand Central Terminal building, with its Kafka-like corridors, Wagnerian caverns of scenic props, and stories of lost people wandering about for years in the gloom.

Television, it was true, had made a great splash with the Louis-Conn heavyweight boxing match, the camera coverage being better than the fight itself, and it was pointed out that a seat in the living room in front of the seven-inch screen was better than a fifty-dollar seat at Yankee Stadium, even though complaints were made that the announcer had talked too much, apparently unaware that the audience could now see for itself.

But though there were ninety television stations in the country as 1948 began, and some popular radio programs, like the *Major Bowes Amateur Hour* and *Town Meeting of the Air*, had gone over to the new medium, radio was still the dominant vehicle for mass entertainment. On it, news and special events had acquired new prominence by the increasing use of tape recordings of speeches, congressional hearings, ceremonies and other "actualities."

On radio, the new Murrow news program was an immediate success. It was virtually autonomous of the network, though using CBS network facilities and correspondents. The broadcast opened with the word N-E-W-S tapped out in Morse code, and then, "This . . . is the news,"

Murrow began every evening, recalling his "This . . . is London" of wartime.

The program consisted of both "hard news" and Murrow's analysis, or what he called "think piece." The news, written for his brisk speaking style by a veteran editor, Jesse Zousmer, and then edited by Murrow, was based not only on wire-agency copy, as so many news broadcasts were. It also used cables from CBS correspondents abroad, and voice reports by them and their domestic colleagues. It gathered the grist from American and European newspapers, American and foreign governmental publications, the *Congressional Record*, and the output of labor unions, foundations, banks and even stock-exchange firms.

As during the war, Murrow's reports sought historical perspective while being at the same time couched in terms of common experience. He was always conscious of the "climate of opinion" in which events took place.

His seventeenth-floor corner office was filled with books — as was every place that he inhabited — while magazines were piled on a table, and newspapers from everywhere billowed over the stand-up desk which Murrow used for reading. His commentaries, however, were dictated sitting down, to Kay Campbell.

They were usually drawn from his own personal news sources, or from his "feel" for a particular story. There was hardly a personage in public life — government, business, labor, education, science or the arts — whom the broadcaster could not talk to by telephone, send one of his reporters to see, or have lunch with in New York or Washington, or for that matter, London or Tokyo. Instead of merely quoting what someone had said on the floor of the Senate that day, he would talk to the man himself on his program that evening. He brought diplomats, college presidents, politicians, philanthropists, and baseball managers to the microphone. He also brought his son Casey at Christmastime and circus-time, to give the small-fry view of such occasions.

Though he would often embark on a light or humorous subject, he deliberately excluded from the program the kind of news that so many papers and broadcasters relished, for instance, crime and divorce. He dedicated his broadcast to the proposition that life was real and earnest, not necessarily in the best of all possible worlds. He had an air of deep personal involvement in that world. His programs took on the somber tones of the disjointed times, and his appraisal of the daily crises of the cold war was regarded by some as "the voice of doom." He sounds "like an unfrocked bishop," said one listener.

His portentous miter had been bestowed on him by Cabell Greet, perhaps his most faithful listener, and not merely because the puckish professor of English at Barnard College was the CBS speech consultant and arbiter of pronunciation. Murrow's diction and articulation may have been exemplary, but his spelling was always suspect and his pronunciation of proper names a little shaky.

The intimation of episcopacy, he told Greet, "has damaged my professional standing and caused me to be held in ridicule by my friends." He threatened "civil action," which he thought would be supported by several real bishops.

When Murrow mispronounced a name, like that of Senator Kefauver, he explained that its bearer and his supporters knew well enough to whom he was referring. He engaged in a lexicographers' duel with Greet about the pronunciation of Moscow, which he gave a bovine second syllable, recalling, he said, the Moscow of his college days, the only one he knew. Greet found evidence that even in Idaho only Easterners and cattlemen were guilty of the mispronunciation. Murrow had an answer to end this and all other phonetic arguments. He threatened to use names from the Siwash and Klamath Indians, for which he, not Greet, would be the authority.

Murrow remarked frequently that "the only thing that matters in radio is what comes out of the loudspeaker." He began his new program with a statement of editorial position. It was "not a place where personal opinion should be mixed up with ascertainable facts." However, it was not "humanly possible for any reporter to be completely objective, for we are all to some degree prisoners of our education, travel, reading — the sum total of our experience."

He did not regard his "think piece" as an editorial, though many others did. Some thought he was substituting personal editorializing for the corporate editorialization he had unsuccessfully sought. He explained that he did not advocate action, or try to formulate policy, but instead argued for principles or goals. He might draw conclusions from a given set of facts, he said, but listeners might reach different conclusions from the same facts. He regarded himself as a reporter, rather than a commentator. "The difference is that I'm less sure that I'm right."

Yet though his purpose may not have been to recommend action, opinion was manifest, judgments were made, and action was implicit, in almost everything he said. His selection of the news that he deemed important in itself constituted a point of view.

Bill Paley was not altogether pleased by Murrow's position. He felt it deviated from the strict code of news objectivity that the latter, as vice president, had helped formulate. "They say that nobody can be 100 percent objective," the CBS chairman later observed, "but I thought if we really tried, we could be 90 percent." He also believed there was sufficient expression of opinion on the CBS network, and that it was properly identified as such, and should not intrude into the news.

In general, however, radio's latest and quickly its most esteemed news program was accepted as it was intended, opinions and all. "There is no pandering to the supposed adolescent mental level of the adult listener," a Catholic magazine said of it. "It is a pleasure to be given credit for some intelligence, for a sizable portion, in fact."

Though it functioned swiftly, efficiently, and on a level of sophisticated seriousness, the Murrow fiefdom in its seventeenth-floor corner of the CBS building had about it an air of informality which sometimes reached apparently total relaxation.

Murrow came in from his Park Avenue apartment in the late morning, or frequently after the lunch which he had devoted to the acquisition of news or views. He would have talked to the office by telephone during the morning, after he had gone through the New York and Washington papers. If he did not already have an idea what he wanted to broadcast about that evening, then he got one at lunch, or during the course of the afternoon, as the world's news rolled in.

A good deal of the time his subject matter was determined by the cablegrams from the CBS overseas correspondents: Howard K. Smith in London, David Schoenbrun in Paris, Bill Downs in Germany, Bill Costello in the Far East. They were responsible for a full range of duties to the network, but they regarded themselves as working primarily for the man who had chosen them, and for his program.

In return he gave them the fullest and most satisfying professional expression that any news staff has ever had. He used not only their voices and their cabled dispatches, but their ideas, appraisals and advice, and he publicly acknowledged his indebtedness. Though it might sound like a one-man show, because of Murrow's presence and personality, the evening news program was a true news cooperative. In contrast to the anonymous and homogenized "group journalism" of weekly news magazines, the Murrow collective was composed of identifiable individuals, who moreover possessed differing, sometimes discordant, points of view. It was in its diversity that the strength and appeal of the program lay.

Probably not one of the "Murrow boys" believed that genuine objectivity was possible, but the CBS broadcasters, it could fairly be said, were marked by a sense of responsibility and what one reviewer called "a humility before the fact." When some of them came under pressure for the independence or unorthodoxy of their interpretation of events, as frequently happened in the Blacklist Era, Murrow stood up for them stoutly, whatever their beliefs or personal traits. He above all entertained a respect for facts, though he was the first to acknowledge that no one knew all the facts, and that in any event all the facts did not necessarily constitute all the truth.

The relaxation behind the office door marked Mr. Murrow was deceptive. Ed would loll about in his shirtsleeves, with his feet on the desk, snapping his red suspenders, his collar opened and tie loosened, talking on the telephone, receiving callers — more often than not they were people seeking help of some sort, especially financial — chatting with his air guests until it grew late in the afternoon and they began to worry about what they were expected to say, since he hadn't mentioned it.

About 5 P.M. things began to fall into place. The guest would discover that the pleasant chatter had somehow produced the points for the scheduled discussion of atomic energy, the New Hampshire primary, universal military training, German nationalism, or the World Series.

If one of his foreign-based colleagues happened to be visiting New York, he would inevitably be asked to share Murrow's time, and Ed would delight in a classical case of entrapment. They might have been talking about several subjects, and the visiting correspondent would probably have made a mental file of what he would say. But when the aired dialogue finally began Murrow invariably asked questions without notice, or introduced a completely different subject — Yugoslavia, for instance, to the Central European correspondent who believed he would be talking about Czechoslovakia. Unlike a courtroom, it was not possible to plead surprise, and what followed spontaneously was usually a better broadcast than anything which might have been mentally labored over.

If, as was usually the case, Murrow was to broadcast a "think piece" of his own, he would cut off the flow of traffic into his office at five o'clock, with a final news consultation and a small libation — he drank what he called "sipping" whiskey, twenty-five-year-old Scotch — with his two aides Jesse Zousmer and John Aaron.

Then while Zousmer wrote the text of the day's "hard news," and Aaron found an appropriate quotation for the "word for the day" with which the program concluded, Murrow sat tensely in a chair with his body leaning forward, looking steadily at the floor, his head propped on the elbows which rested on his knees, and while chain-smoking cigarettes, dictated his six-minute commentary as it would be read on the air. Kay Campbell took it down directly on the typewriter.

He was what might be called a "bleeder," both writing and dictating being slow hard work. Since he spoke concisely as a matter of course, his pondering over his scripts made what he said even more to the point. He was mentally polishing his own copy as he dictated.

A few minutes before air time, his sleeves still rolled up, his collar and tie still askew, Murrow would step with measured tread down the hall to the studio, with all the yellow copy paper in his hand. He was always tense, and his furrowed brow and sometimes the blue shadow of a beard made his face look drawn. His entry into the studio has been likened to that of a condemned man entering the execution chamber, but his solemnity was merely confirmation that for him a broadcast was a grave occasion.

Despite many years of practice, in all manner of situations, Murrow never conquered his nervousness before the microphone. Like many other fine broadcasters, and it was one reason why they were so good, he could not acquire the casual, sometimes vacuous ease of announcers or disk jockeys. As he sat reading his script with complete concentration, the copy held in his left hand, his right hand punctuated his remarks with finger movements, while his right knee would keep jogging beneath the table, through the entire broadcast.

His radio delivery was not really conversational, though it often sounded so. It was studied and even mildly theatrical, with a tone of what might be called pained sincerity. He never addressed himself to some imagined or personalized figure or group in the audience, as others did, but only to the subject at hand, and to the microphone. He was always more concerned with what he had to say than to whom.

In his office Murrow had on the wall a photograph of his friend Carl Sandburg, inscribed "To Ed Murrow, reporter, historian, inquirer, actor, ponderer, seeker." In the studio, "perspirer" could be added. When he broadcast, the sweat rolled down his face, in spite of the air conditioning. When he finished he would lean back, and as his announcer Bob Dixon concluded with "Listen to Murrow tomorrow," and they went off the air, he would add, "Yeah, he wasn't so good today."

Whatever the style or subject of Murrow's broadcasts, however disputed any conclusions he might draw, in one respect, that of diction, they won general acclaim. An expert called his "the best all-round American speech extant," and said it "combines an excellent general American pronunciation free of artificial, vulgar or provincial patterns; a deep, rich, resonant voice free of all nasality; a precise articulation that permits rapid delivery without loss of clarity, and a splendidly controlled vocal range that can project any kind of emotion without distorting the pitch of the voice." He was indeed Ida Lou Anderson's "masterpiece."

But it was from Bob Dixon, a rangy New Englander, that Murrow received the supreme broadcasting honor — fascinated attention from an announcer. Before Dixon became the evening news program's regular announcer he had been the "hitchhike" announcer, the man who closed a program by calling on listeners to "stand by" for the next one, and giving the network's "signature." Normally a hitchhike announcer tiptoed into the studio a few minutes before the end of the program in progress. But Dixon was so enthralled by Murrow's broadcasts that he sat through the entire fifteen minutes each evening, and "learned a lot." They were both outdoor enthusiasts and their rapport naturally went beyond the studio walls. Dixon indeed soon became a neighbor of Murrow's at Pawling. They hunted there together, for deer, pheasant, woodcock and possum, and "communicated in long silences."

Since broadcasting was always a strain, despite his cultivated air of relaxation at the office, Murrow's only real relaxation was provided by a cedar log cabin atop a hill in upstate New York, for weekends and summer use. Janet did a modicum of entertaining at their Manhattan home, but Rumblewood, as Casey named it after the sounds he heard in the logs, was the seat of their affections. It was in historic Dutchess County, about seventy miles from the city, and Murrow lived there in his favorite clothes, dungarees, flannel shirts and boots.

Murrow had been attracted to Pawling by Lowell Thomas, who offered him the use of a small cottage on his own spacious grounds there. But Murrow, then vice president and organizationally Thomas's superior, thought that might be regarded as unethical. As soon as he went back to broadcasting, however, he tried out the Pawling golf course, and settled in the house on Quaker Hill, with its fourteen acres of land. As a former woodsman, he said, he could appreciate "good log work," and the house had been built by Finns who had come to New York with the World's Fair.

An estimated two million listeners heard Murrow every evening, when he began his program. The Truman Doctrine was under full steam, and with it emergency economic measures to keep Western Europe going. Soviet-American relations were at their bleakest point. The United Nations at Lake Success was embroiled over the Greek civil war, and ever-rising bloodshed in Palestine.

Murrow dealt not only with the cold war abroad, but with its manifestations at home. The Un-American Activities Committee was examining Hollywood for Communist infiltration, and the broadcaster did not defend the film capital's celluloid product — "I am not obliged to view it" — or condemn the congressional right to investigate acts of commission or omission.

But he felt that "movies should be judged by what appears upon the screen, newspapers by what appears in print, and radio by what comes out of the loudspeaker. The personal beliefs of the individuals involved would not seem to be a legitimate field of inquiry, either by government or by individuals."

He acknowledged the difficulty Government agencies like the State Department or Atomic Energy Commission could have in maintaining security without violating the civil liberties of their employees. But there was no such problem in mass communications, he said. "Either we believe in the intelligence, good judgment, balance and native shrewdness of the American people, or we believe that government should investigate, intimidate and finally legislate. The choice is as simple as that."

He paused for emphasis. "The right of dissent, or if you prefer, the right to be wrong, is surely fundamental to the existence of a democratic society. That's the right that went first in every nation that stumbled down the trail toward totalitarianism."

Murrow's mention of security in connection with the Atomic Energy Commission reflected David Lilienthal's continuing troubles. The commission chairman, like the broadcaster, regarded the inevitable Russian atom bomb — it would come in September 1949 — as cause, not for panic, but for better international organization. Meanwhile the American bomb had become one of the crucial focal points of the cold war, in the Soviet-American "dialogue of the deaf" over "control" versus "disarmament." In addition it was involved in the struggle between the American military and civilian branches for authority, and the potential of non-military atomic energy had also raised the question of private versus public interest.

Murrow, on the air, supported Lilienthal in his objections to FBI clearance of the scholarship winners in the AEC Fellowship program for the study of science, on the ground that this would constitute Government interference with education. He also arranged for the chairman to speak to the Radio Executives Club, and suggested that he be critical of the broadcasting industry for its failure to give the facts about atomic energy, instead of encouraging hysteria about it.

Lilienthal sent Murrow a draft of the remarks he intended to make, and got the reply that they did not criticize radio enough for its refusal to meet its obligations of public service.

"It surprised me," Lilienthal wrote in his journal. "If he feels that way from within the industry, it must be bad." He was further surprised when Murrow made his speech the subject of broadcast commentary that evening, though perhaps he should not have been, considering that Murrow had provided both the occasion and the theme. He might even have been accused of "making the news," instead of merely reporting it.

At the same time Murrow had taken up another issue which particularly perturbed him, and which he would also refer to many times in the future. This was the freedom to travel, and the restrictions imposed upon it by the Government. In this case a New York Congressman, Leo Isaacson, had been denied a passport because he proposed to attend a conference in Paris sympathetic to the guerrillas in the Greek civil war. Since American policy, under the Truman Doctrine, was supporting the Athens regime against the guerrillas, even to the extent of military training and equipment, the State Department ruled that the Congressman's journey "would not be in the best interest of this country."

It was an argument to be made on many future occasions, including legal tests up to the Supreme Court, and Murrow's answer to it was that the State Department had infringed upon the Congressman's personal liberty. As for the effect abroad, "it is doubtful whether any oratory or intrigue in which Mr. Isaacson might have engaged would have been more damaging to the interest of this country than the fact that he has been denied permission to leave." And perhaps the most important aspect of the case was that "it has produced so little controversy in Congress and in the country. It's surely a matter worth arguing about."

Broadcasts of this sort evoked enthusiastic response from many listeners, but they also brought the inevitable protests. Murrow received a large number of such, some saying "we are at war with Russia," some others calling his views "treason." His sponsor, the soup company, received threats that its products would be boycotted, and in answering one letter defended the broadcaster as "a thorough anti-Communist and a complete American, believing most whole-heartedly in our system of government and life," terms which Murrow found egregious.

A week in Italy in April 1948, to report the postwar period's most important Western European elections, which the Communists were given a good chance of winning, earned Murrow more letters of rebuke. He had dared to submit that the youthful mayor of Anzio, whom he interviewed, could be a Catholic as well as a Communist.

The Communists did not win the Italian elections — the CIA and the State Department engaged a good deal of money, activity and open pressure to that end — and Murrow replied to one of his critics that he had some knowledge of totalitarian regimes, that "some of his oldest and best friends" had just been "liquidated" in Czechoslovakia. "If the Communist menace is to be combatted effectively it must be done, not on the basis of exhortation, but by understanding the sources and conditions from which it draws its strength."

His reference was to the recent Communist coup in Prague, during which Jan Masaryk was found mysteriously dead beneath his balcony window. In a broadcast, Murrow recalled the postwar sadness that had come to possess the familiar burly and once amiable man, the son of Czechoslovakia's founder, as his country moved deeper into the Communist shadow. He doubted that Masaryk had committed suicide, as the new Communist government said. Most Czechs doubted it also.

Just before he flew to Rome, Murrow was notified from Bellingham that his father, who had suffered a paralytic stroke two years before, had been affected by a second stroke. It was one of many occasions when because of the demand of his broadcasting obligations, he was unable to take time out for his personal life.

But his fulfillment of obligations was recognized. In their first six months on the air, he and his program had won three of the nation's leading journalistic awards. His broadcasts had covered a range of subjects extending from the wedding of Princess Elizabeth — in which he was aided by

Janet — to Senate debate on the Marshall Plan, and a ride on the American airlift into blockaded Berlin, in a plane loaded with thirteen tons of coal. "The engine spluttered, and the crew chief said, 'If you run out of gas, I can throw in a shovelful of coal.' "

Janet received an honor of her own, not for broadcasting — though she had done several programs on such subjects as clothing, cosmetics and consumer rationing in postwar London — but the King's Medal for Service in the Cause of Freedom, for her wartime work with Bundles for Britain.

At the royal wedding in 1947 Murrow took part in the broadcast to America from Westminster Abbey, and after a year without British austerity, discovered at the formal wedding ball at Buckingham Palace that his tailcoat had become too tight, and might split at any moment. He left early.

For both Ed and Janet the brief visit to London furnished the opportunity for renewing old acquaintance, and for seeing again the still-broken urban and rural landscapes to which they had given an appreciable part of their lives. They called on the Churchills, and Mrs. Churchill, who had written to Janet regularly, thanked her for the small food parcels that came as manna even to the best-off in Britain, "the little luxuries which are so necessary to people like us," as Lady Cranborne called them.

Other Britons were doing without "little luxuries" and even bare necessities. Murrow saw his old BBC preceptor, R. T. Clarke, who had written him about widespread illness at that genteel institution, due to lack of food. Clarke himself had lost twenty-three pounds, in twenty-one months, but had refused any gifts. His complaint was not against "work and worry," but that "our rulers, who feed at the Grosvenor, never think in these terms." Clarke, a staunch Liberal, did not by "our rulers" mean the monarchy or even the aristocracy, but the men of the Labor government. He believed he was "witnessing the gradual extinction of the old middle class." Murrow pointed out that it was apparently being succeeded by an even larger new middle class, even under austerity.

His report on the royal wedding — "it meant stability, continuity and an opportunity for a very considerable emotional outburst before another hard winter grips this island" — dealt with one of the few noncontroversial subjects of the time.

Considerable controversy, for example, was stirred by the murder of George Polk, the highly personable CBS Middle East correspondent, whose trussed body was found in Salonika harbor after he had tried to arrange an interview with the Greek Communist guerrilla leader, General Markos.

The Athens government called the murder the work of Communists, though there would seem to have been every reason for the Communists to take Polk to Markos, as they took another American correspondent,

Homer Bigart, a few weeks later, to prove that he was no myth, and to let
him state his case.

Eventually a trial was held in Salonika of an ex-Communist Greek
newspaperman, charged with complicity in the Polk murder. It was attended by the wartime OSS chief, General William Donovan, as an American observer, and he approved the proceedings and the verdict of guilty.
But Murrow, and the CBS correspondents who investigated the case and
reported the trial, were skeptical. In a series of broadcasts, the network
concluded that while it could not say Greek Fascists had murdered Polk
to prevent him from reaching the Communist leader, neither had the Greek
government made its anti-Communist case. Since the United States, with a
military mission in Greece and a large program of economic aid, was
fully committed to the Athens cause, the Polk trial and Murrow's doubt
became one of the criteria by which he and other CBS correspondents
were to be judged, in the "guilt by association" accusations of the Fifties.

Anticipating the publication of *Red Channels*, the blacklist of broadcasting, one of the leading congressional patriots, Representative Hébert
of Louisiana, charged that "a sinister Red network" was being created
and that "Communist infiltration" had been taking place in the radio
industry.

When David Lilienthal visited Murrow at Pawling that summer, both
quickly became despondent about the state of affairs. The AEC head,
though he had won his fight for civilian custody of atomic weapons, was
in the midst of another of his interminable disputes with Congress, and
talked about being forced to resign. He thought he might take a trip around
the world, writing magazine articles on the way, and Murrow promised
help if needed.

"Ed said he doubted if he could continue broadcasting long; his contract was airtight but if he kept talking anything except 'hate Russia' he
would be branded a dirty Communist," Lilienthal wrote in his journal.
The question of forming a speakers' bureau had come up. "He'd like to
join in such an enterprise when he moves out of broadcasting."

Murrow was at his gloomiest. He had already started to work on an
"escape plan," which would include doing film documentaries, as well as
speeches and record albums, and had even consulted lawyers on the details.
He told Lilienthal he was sure of financing.

But too much was happening to chafe very long.

The "vital" Italian elections were followed by the perhaps less vital
American elections of 1948, for despite the tocsin sounded by the Un-
American Activities Committee, there was no appreciable danger that
they would be won by the Communists.

American radio had struck a motherlode of popularity with "giveaway" programs, which distributed large cash awards in "contests," such as naming a dog, or describing "the funniest person I know." With the same exuberance, and some critics thought in much the same category, it now embraced the presidential contest. There was no shortage of contenders, and Murrow made radio an element in campaign journalism, instead of merely the vehicle for campaign oratory. His attitude was one of impartial amusement at some of the practices of politics, but of profound concern about its principles and some of its results.

Urged by many listeners to "pin 'em down!" he interviewed six of the eight presumed candidates on his nightly news broadcast, either in person in the studio or by radio circuit from elsewhere. They were asked some questions sent in by the audience, including, "Why do you want to be President?"

The candidates interviewed were the four Republicans, Harold Stassen, Senator Robert A. Taft, Governor Earl Warren, and Governor Thomas E. Dewey; the Socialist, Norman Thomas, and the former Democratic Vice President, Henry A. Wallace, who would form his own third party. President Truman was invited, but explained that he could not appear on exclusive broadcasts. General Douglas MacArthur cabled from Tokyo that "it would be impracticable to accept," though presumably on political, not logistical grounds, for it would have been as easy to talk with him in Japan as with Stassen in Minnesota.

Governor Dewey, incidentally, was one of Murrow's Pawling neighbors, and the bright prospect of his election had touched off a real estate boom around Quaker Hill, where it was expected that his farm would become the summer White House and a tourist attraction. The Dewey satrapy on the Connecticut line was so staunchly Republican that when Franklin D. Roosevelt drove through it, on his way to or from Hyde Park, Pawling residents ran into their houses, it was said, and pulled down the blinds.

The presidential programs may not have contributed much to the world's wisdom or understanding, but this was not the fault of the medium, or the broadcaster. They also won Murrow more plaudits, followed by praise for his reporting on both radio and television from the national party conventions. Though dreary and longwinded, these were the first political assemblages to take conscious note of, and begin to adapt themselves to, the growing television audience. Visual coverage over eighteen East Coast stations was supplied by the networks at a large financial deficit. But coast-to-coast radio was still the prime instrument at the conventions, and the subsequent elections.

On election night, on one television network, ABC, there was less public interest in the progress of the vote count than in whether Walter Winchell, the Broadway columnist and broadcaster, should take off his hat or keep it on. He wore it habitually before the radio microphone, but when he did so on camera, TV stations received hundreds of complaints about his lack of manners. The network capitulated and ordered him to uncover, whereupon many complaints were received of the unaccustomed view of his bald spot.

After the unexpected result, Truman's reelection, Murrow took a sardonic view of the public opinion polls, which had been proved wrong. "This election result has freed us to a certain extent from the tyranny of those who tell us what we think, believe and will do, without consulting us."

He also had some thoughts about his own and other communications media. This was the fifth consecutive presidential election, he pointed out, in which the majority of the American press had supported the losing candidate, beginning with Roosevelt's first campaign in 1932. In 1948, he took notice, "radio officially remained neutral during the campaign, but in general the most and the best time went to the party with the most money, and that may not be the best way of conducting a national debate over the air."

The election upset "ought to lead to more critical reading of newspapers, more critical and skeptical listening to the radio, a decrease in the willingness to accept predigested opinions and conclusions . . . The experts and the pollsters have in fact restored to us an appreciation of the importance and the purely personal character of our own opinions. From here on, it will be easier to doubt the persuasive or hysterical voice that reaches us through the radio, or the columnist who writes with power or persuasiveness, but who divulges few facts."

Murrow's critique of radio in politics, delivered on radio itself, and of the shortcomings of public opinion polls and "market research" in general, seemed to have been taken as a personal affront by Frank Stanton, the CBS president, whose principal job was defending the unimpeachability of the medium. Wrathful memoranda were exchanged between the two men, in what was their first overt conflict, although at directors' meetings Murrow could frequently be heard muttering sarcastically about "computer mechanics." The broadcaster's entry into television would make the conflict between the two men even sharper and more painful, though perhaps, in the nature of things, inescapable.

In the wake of the 1948 election came a technico-economic revolution in radio. The ban on recordings had been partially lifted during the war, to aid the coverage of news, but now in the entertainment area it became widespread custom to prerecord entire programs, often weeks in advance, instead of broadcasting them live. Programs were also repeated in the summer months, from recordings. Scores of high-paid radio entertainers were freed for stage tours, Hollywood movies, even home life. Prerecording,

Before See It Now *there was* Hear It Now *on radio. Murrow and Friendly at the start of their partnership*

to be carried from radio into television and used universally there, came to be a distinct cultural convenience, like frozen food or prefabricated houses.

The acceptance of and interest in such "electrical transcriptions" inspired one of the most successful of all recording enterprises, and brought together Ed Murrow and Fred Friendly, the man who would be his close associate for the next fifteen years — the decade and a half that would come to be known, with their help, as the golden age of television. They began in radio, however.

Friendly, ebullient and inventive, had begun his radio career at a local station in Providence where, at the age of twenty-two, just out of business college, he wrote a series of five-minute "documentary" programs, *Footprints in the Sands of Time,* which earned him eight dollars each. After the war, in which he served as a sergeant of "information and education" in the China-Burma-India theater, he came to New York, as the sparks flew upward, and persuaded NBC of the merits of a television program he had thought up. It offered a panel of more or less well-known "personalities," as they were called in television, who tried to name the authors of quotations taken from the week's news. The program was a mere summer replacement for something less earnest, but it was found to be "refreshing," and the other network, CBS, asked Friendly for a radio version of it.

Neck-deep in quotations, and acquainted now with Murrow, Friendly combined the two assets and proposed a record album of what he described as "aural history," narrated by Murrow and made up of spoken words of the recent past, as recorded on radio. The result was not one, but eventually three Murrow-Friendly albums, *I Can Hear It Now.*

Friendly chose the historic excerpts and wrote the connective narration. But both men together edited the compendium, from five hundred hours of recordings down to a concise forty-five minutes per album. Murrow's accomplished and familiar voice may have put the gloss on the narration and infused their production with a sense of chronicle, but the even more important fruit of the occasion was the successful experience of working together over Joel Tall's tape-editing machine. They had become a partnership.

Murrow and Friendly were brought together by the "talent" agent J. G. "Jap" Gude, and from their first meeting at Louis' and Armand's, the favorite CBS restaurant, Friendly recalled, Murrow "overcame" him by displaying complete confidence in him, an exhilarating experience on cynical Madison Avenue.

The first album embraced the fateful period 1933–1945, many of the events of which were part of Murrow's own reporting experience. It included the voice of Will Rogers, the cowboy comedian, wisecracking about the depression; President Roosevelt on fearing "fear itself"; Senator Huey Long on "sharing the wealth"; John L. Lewis, the labor leader, talking about the Bible; New York's Mayor LaGuardia reading the Sunday comics during a newspaper strike; Edward VIII's abdication message; a ranting Adolf Hitler; a happy Neville Chamberlain returning from Munich; Lindbergh's America First opinions; famous remarks by Churchill, Eisenhower, even Stalin; and the sounds of D-Day, V-E Day and V-J Day, and of the new Atomic Age.

By the time the second volume, 1945–1949, appeared a year later, the first album of *I Can Hear It Now* had sold 250,000 copies, something of an achievement. Indeed it was the first nonmusical album to be a financial success. A third album, 1919–1932, was subsequently issued.

The albums led to the weekly Murrow-Friendly program *Hear It Now*, which was in turn succeeded by *See It Now* on television, both programs bringing new concepts and new dimensions to their respective media.

Yet though the political year of 1948, and his nightly news broadcast, had established Murrow as radio's most celebrated commentator, the matter-of-fact verdict of "show business" was that Arthur Godfrey, the easygoing "personality" who cracked jokes, discovered "talent," and sold commercial products, was the real "Mr. CBS," for he had three programs of his own and earned five hundred thousand dollars a year. *Variety* remembered 1948 as the year in which CBS "raided" NBC and took away such headline attractions as Jack Benny and Amos 'n' Andy, the two leading comedy programs. The lure devised by Bill Paley was a plan to buy the "corporations" that the individual performers had turned themselves into, thus enabling them to pay capital gains rather than income taxes. As a result CBS for the first time took the lead in radio ratings from NBC, and in advertising time sold.

Television was still regarded as radio's little brother, but gradually more of the big radio programs were appearing on the home screen, backed by sponsors. The seven-inch "peephole" was succeeded by twelve-inch and even fourteen-inch receivers. By the middle of 1949, 1.6 million American homes had TV sets and new ones were being installed at the rate of one hundred thousand a month. More than half the American people had as yet never seen television, but they were hearing and reading about it increasingly.

Whatever its potential for mass entertainment, television was not regarded by the broadcasting industry, however, as either practicable or very interesting — or perhaps just salable — in the presentation of world and national news on a regular basis, that is, apart from such photogenic "special events" as sports, political conventions and congressional hearings. TV news was regarded as at best a daily instead of a weekly newsreel, devoted to the purely pictorial. Television had begun by taking over radio methods and personnel, but now it faced the formidable problems of devising its own techniques for communicating news.

Basic and weighty questions were involved, and Murrow brooded about them. Just as in radio the mere selection of news was an editorial judgment, so in television, he thought, a kind of editorializing could be done by the choice of pictures, as well as of subjects. But in radio it was normally the reporter or writer who evaluated the news, while in television parties of the third part intruded, the cameraman and the producer. In radio, as he himself had demonstrated, the news correspondent was his own reporter, writer, producer and broadcaster, but in television these functions were too often separated. The man who read the news in front of a television camera was not the man who had written the news, much less gathered it himself, and he was certainly not the man who decided what the news was.

In addition to posing the problem of editorial control, or lack of it, Murrow believed television news also impinged on the issue of the invasion of privacy. Moreover, "most news is made up of what happens in men's minds, as reflected in what comes out of their mouths. And how do you put that in pictures?" he wondered.

His conclusion was that television must recognize the limitations of the medium, and exercise both restraint and responsibility. The consideration would loom ever larger as television in effect began making its own news, and political speeches, demonstrations and even riots and other violence were staged not only on camera, but for the camera.

Murrow held that the uncontrolled scope of cameras could be dangerous, in the wrong hands, and could produce distortion rather than the true reflection of "a mirror behind." The commanding need in television news was to "sift and sort it through the mind," he thought, to insure human instead of merely mechanical discernment. "We need to argue this out before the patterns become set and we all begin to see pictures of our country and the world that just aren't true," he said in 1949, more than a decade before such matters began to be generally argued.

He had some other questions about television, though not necessarily the answers. The audience would become more selective in its choice of programs as the novelty wore off, he thought, though in fact the opposite seems to have happened. He doubted that television would alter politics. Dewey was a better broadcaster than Truman but had lost anyway, he pointed out. Since then, the Kennedy-Nixon "debates" have suggested television's political effect, and the camera personality of President Johnson undoubtedly helped him achieve his widespread unpopularity over the Vietnam War.

"Will anyone turn on the TV set at 8 A.M.?" Murrow asked in 1949, innocently enough. And not so innocently, perhaps, "Will television regard news as anything more than a salable commodity? Will the broad-casters exercise control, or abdicate, as radio has done?" that is, abdicate to the time salesmen and the rating services.

The cold war, on the international front, continued with the creation of the North Atlantic Treaty Organization, which Murrow saw as discard-ing the American tradition against foreign commitments, since it pledged the United States to defend "more than a quarter of the world." But even if NATO succeeded in stabilizing the position in Western Europe, he thought, the competition between the United States and communism would continue elsewhere, notably in the "third world" of India, Pakistan, Southeast Asia and the Arab Middle East.

Publication of the NATO treaty brought to the United States one of the men who had conceived it, now leader of His Majesty's Opposition in Britain, to make another public oration. Janet Murrow gave a luncheon for Mrs. Churchill, and Murrow used the occasion of Churchill's appearance at the Massachusetts Institute of Technology to recall his wartime speeches.

He did this for a projected new radio program, reviewing the week's news, and incorporating the voices and sounds of actual events into a narrative with some perspective. The "pilot" program, entitled *Sunday With Mur-row*, was not broadcast but merely auditioned by executives, advertising agencies and prospective sponsors, and then laid aside for lack of their interest. The men who controlled broadcasting said there were "too many" news documentaries on the air, and the CBS president announced a reduc-tion in the number of informational broadcasts in favor of "broader en-tertainment" for the masses.

Sunday With Murrow would eventually reemerge as *Hear It Now*, when the times were more propitious. Apart from its Churchill appraisal, it was noteworthy because on it Murrow expressed the undisguised opinion, and did not pretend it was "analysis," that the cold war at home, in the form of a growing campaign against suspected subversive activities, must be contained within constitutional grounds, and based on evidence, not hearsay.

The death of his friend Laurence Duggan six months before was per-haps still in his mind when he attended sessions of the trial of Alger Hiss for perjury. "There are forces and factors involved in this conflict that have not yet been placed upon the record," he observed. He tried to be "careful and cool" about "the subject that has been assailing your eyes and your ears for the past several weeks — the whole area of espionage, treason and subversive activity."

He did not deny the possible danger of Communist espionage and infiltration, nor the need for "legal, constitutional methods of protection," but he recalled that espionage, propaganda and infiltration were, after all, not new in history, and he thought the climate was "less salubrious" for communism in the United States than anywhere else in the world. Despite headlines and sensations, he believed it was possible to "sweat out successfully this continuing crisis, without losing our liberties while trying to defend them.

"It is deplorable that we have come to suspect each other more than we did before," he went on. "It is regrettable that individuals and some organs of opinion are disposed to convict people by association, or before they have been tried. If this tendency is accelerated, it may induce widespread fear, and endanger the right of dissent.

"But so long as neither the State nor an individual can take punitive action against a citizen except through due process of law, we shall have in our hands the weapons to defend our personal liberty and our national security."

Some liberals thought Murrow might be assuming too much, or evading the issue, which had to do less with legal processes than with the moral opprobrium and economic sanctions, such as unemployment, imposed against many who were convicted by association and without a trial. On the other hand, many listeners thought he was going too far in defense of what they saw as "the Communist conspiracy."

When eleven leaders of the American Communist Party, after a nine months' trial, were convicted of conspiring to advocate the forcible overthrow of the Government, Murrow analyzed the verdict and concluded, "We can't legislate loyalty."

"There are some things that this verdict does not mean," he explained. "It does not mean that membership in the Communist Party as such is illegal. The party is not outlawed. The verdict does not mean that you must not read any specific books, talk as you will, or peacefully assemble for any purpose, other than to conspire to overthrow the Government by force or violence. It does not mean that you are subject to legal action for saying things favorable to the Communist Party. Nothing in this verdict limits the citizen's rights, by peaceful and lawful means, to advocate changes in the Constitution, to utter and publish praise of Russia, criticism of any of our political parties or personalities."

It was an exegesis that might properly have been offered to the American people by the White House, the Department of Justice, the Senate Internal Security Committee, or even the court that rendered the verdict. But it was not, by any of them.

When Alger Hiss, after a second trial, was found guilty of perjury and sentenced to five years in prison, Murrow reported that Secretary of State Acheson had refused to "turn my back" on Hiss, and that "Republican Senator McCarthy of Wisconsin asked if Acheson is also telling the world that he won't turn his back on the other Communists in the State Department." The broadcaster decided that "a vicious controversy is just beginning."

It was indeed. In a few weeks McCarthy would be standing up in Wheeling, West Virginia, and saying, "I have in my hand . . ." The broadcasting industry would be among the first to succumb to what Murrow called the "un-American doctrine" of "guilt by association," and he himself was not to be spared.

Three former FBI agents, encouraged by right-wingers in the American Federation of Radio Artists, had begun to publish *Counter-Attack*, a pamphlet which listed radio performers and directors suspected of subversive tendencies. One issue declared that CBS was "the most satisfying network for the Communists."

Thus blacklisting came into effect, as advertising agencies, sponsors, and above all the networks, which had special vice presidents for the task, began checking with the lists in *Counter-Attack* before engaging "talent." The "counter-attackers" then issued a directory called *Red Channels*, citing 151 persons in radio for suspect "affiliations," and this became the blacklisters' Bible, kept in the bottom drawer of each vice president's desk. "Resignations" from important radio programs began to be reported, and some of America's leading actors were denied employment.

The 151 names in *Red Channels* included many well-known in the entertainment world, though the majority of them — actors, playwrights, novelists, dancers, singers, conductors, producers, directors — were not primarily identified with radio or television, and in fact, some not at all.

It also contained the names of a half-dozen news broadcasters, among them two CBS overseas correspondents, and one former such. Murrow himself was not mentioned, but it was his news staff that was being impugned. He stood by his men, both inside the corporation and outside, — "if you're in trouble we're all in trouble," he told one of them — and successfully defied the blacklisters. Many others in radio and television were not able to do so.

Some of those in *Red Channels* were cited for appearing at functions honoring other artists, presumably regarded as suspect, though the latter were not listed. One writer was cited for a book deemed favorable to Yugoslavia, though a footnote admitted that Yugoslavia had soon thereafter rebelled against Moscow and been ousted from the Cominform. One man was in *Red Channels* for favoring a boycott of Japanese goods in 1938, making him a "premature anti-Fascist."

Though Murrow was not listed in *Red Channels*, he quickly became the subject of attack in right-wing leaflets and the Hearst "gossip" columns because the CBS correspondents had been, and obviously because of his own outspoken comments on the air.

After CBS had been maligned several times as a particularly "Red" network, it actually hired the ex-FBI agents of *Counter-Attack* to investigate its employees, though the polite term used was "research." Despite this abnegation, the assaults continued and CBS instituted its own loyalty oath, the only network to do so, citing "wartime conditions." The result was widespread dismay and loss of morale.

Other networks, as well as advertising agencies, gave the blacklisting function, usually called "clearance," to their legal departments, which then decided who should be seen and heard on American radio and television.

The criterion of "clearance" was not professional, political, legal or even moral, but purely a matter of "public relations." Neither guilt nor innocence was relevant, only "acceptability." The charges of "Communist" were enough, and *Counter-Attack* not only made citations based on the Attorney General's list of Communist fronts, but added many other organizations which it decided for itself "ought to have been listed."

CBS was the special target of the Red-hunters because of its chosen nature. It had entered broadcasting in 1927 against the two NBC chains, lacking their commercials and with many gaps in its programming. It filled them by introducing new types of programs, many highly imaginative, and attracted new and young people, creatively inclined. These were apt to be more liberal in their outlook and more unconventional than the professional veterans of the older networks.

After the war, when broadcasting stood on the brink of television, William S. Paley had made the daring decision that CBS would organize, create and broadcast its own programs, rather than transmitting the "packages" of the advertising agencies, sponsors and theatrical producers. More creative people swarmed to CBS, and more unconventionality, of the kind that was now proving vulnerable before the mania of "clearance."

Murrow was at the time a member of the CBS board of directors, an unusual and perhaps anomalous position for one who not only professed to abhor the executive function, but whose broadcasting role transcended, and indeed denied, corporate inhibitions. His rationalization was that the position would give him the chance to scan the corporate budget, and perhaps exercise some influence on behalf of more news programming, "the only aspect of broadcasting that I know or care about."

Years later, Frank Stanton, who had proposed Murrow's membership on the board, would conclude that on the whole it had been a bad idea.

The inner conflict between Murrow the broadcaster and Murrow the guardian of the corporate interest was an inevitable one, even though he tried to avoid it by taking directors' meetings lightly, telling anecdotes of the eminent people he had met, in the spirit of Judge John Bassett Moore, of the World Court. The latter's advice to him had been, "When you meet men of great reputation your judgment of them will be greatly improved if you view them as though they were in their underwear."

For Paley, Murrow's directorship was another example of Murrow's complexity, indeed his contradictoriness. He felt that while Murrow did not actually like being a member of the board, and avoided the practice, what he did like was the idea, in a sense the status, of membership.

In any event, the directorship placed him within the CBS decision-making apparatus that instituted the loyalty oath, engaged in blacklisting, and took the first steps toward the diversification of interests, that would dilute and deflect the original commitment to broadcasting pure and simple.

Murrow was obviously unhappy about developments like these. But he felt, and continued to feel until it was no longer possible to do so, that he could temper the course of events from within the ruling structure, even though the auguries may not have been too bright.

Sometimes he let his discouragement show, for David Sarnoff, the head of the rival network NBC, who had always wanted Murrow, offered to let him write his own terms for coming over. Murrow felt that the prospects for improvement were even less at Radio City, and that CBS was the only network "that has any real respect among the people who know anything about news" even though that tradition was apparently beginning to be honored in the breach rather than in the observance.

Murrow instituted what would become an important news program on radio, and later television, the annual round table of CBS overseas correspondents, who came home to discuss with him each of the "years of crisis." But there was no longer any regularly scheduled news documentary or news feature on the CBS network except the weekly *We the People*. In New York City, *CBS Views the Press* quietly faded away.

The prevailing atmosphere of suspicion was deepened by the outbreak of the Korean War, on a day that was three days after the publication of *Red Channels*. The United States entered the war ostensibly on behalf of the United Nations, but it soon became an American anti-Communist crusade, and General MacArthur, moving toward the Chinese border, was only carrying out the Truman Doctrine.

It had been five years since Murrow smelled gunpowder, and within three weeks of the North Korean incursion across the 38th Parallel he was in the land of Chosen, reporting the conflict. As it had done before, war made radio, with its instantaneity, the dominant news medium again, and Murrow was still its leading figure. But revived public interest in news came too late for the soup company that had sponsored the 7:45 P.M. program for three years, and then decided it was not selling enough soup.

The sponsor, Campbell's, asked for the same fifteen-minute evening

time period for a musical program instead. But CBS took the unusual
stand — since it had decided precisely the reverse in the controversial
Shirer case — that the time in question belonged to the broadcaster, not
the sponsor.

There was no financial risk involved. New sponsors were standing in line
with money in their hands, to become identified with the country's leading
news broadcast. The successful bidder was the American Oil Company,
which had been Murrow's wartime sponsor for "This . . . is London."

In the midst of the happy reunion, if any blush was brought to Murrow's
cheek by memory of the Shirer case, it was not noticed. Now, instead of the
clicking Morse code, the program would begin with a metronome ticking
away, as the announcer Bob Dixon spelled out the sponsor's name,
A-M-O-C-O.

Murrow had asked his friend Elmer Davis what he thought of the idea
of going to Korea. He replied that if it remained within Korea, the war
was not worth the attention of a reporter "responsible for all the world's
news," and if it expanded, Washington would be the place where there was
more news than anywhere else.

"Of course you may feel a compulsion to get shot at again, though I
should think you have had your quota of that," the Hoosier wrote. "But if
the war becomes general, you might possibly enjoy that privilege even
here, in view of the at least theoretical capabilities of the Russian Air
Force."

Murrow went to Korea because, as usual, he thought it was something
he had to do, since for better or worse the war had become a part of
American life and history. He was a little dubious about breaking the news
to Janet, however. As he drove to Pawling for the weekend, he went over
the "lovely speech" he had planned, explaining what he felt to be his
obligation. When he got to Quaker Hill there was a fire in the fireplace
and his wife poured him the welcoming Scotch-and-water-without-ice. He
began his speech, but had got out only a few words when she interrupted.
"Your uniforms came back from the cleaners yesterday," she said.

Murrow supported the Korean War, indeed regarded it as inevitable
given the state of the world and the confrontation between the United
States and communism, wherever it might be defined as aggressive.

As American naval and air units went into action, he suggested that
"this new policy commits us to much more than the defense of the southern
half of the Korean peninsula. We have commitments quite as binding,
obligations quite as great, to Indo-China, Iran and Turkey, as we have to
Korea.

"We have drawn a line, not across the peninsula but across the world.
We have concluded that communism has passed beyond the use of subversion to conquer independent nations, and will now use armed invasion

and war. And we for our part have demonstrated that we are prepared to calculate the risks and face the prospect of war, rather than let that happen."

American ground troops were flown to Korea, and the Air Force was given authority to bomb military targets north of the 38th Parallel. Murrow decided to go to Korea himself, instead of going on vacation that summer, and when he got there two weeks later he rolled back five years and was a battlefield reporter again.

"This is Korea," he broadcast. "The whole business of coming out to this war in Korea is filled with familiar faces and memories. When we took off for Korea this morning [from Japan] an elderly sergeant struggled into his parachute with the remark, 'I have to pull this handle, and on this thing sawdust will fall out. Maybe a few moths, too.'

"There were five big canisters of blood abroad, all neatly sealed with red tape. Some of the boys had their feet resting on them. A lieutenant said, 'Maybe that's some of my blood they're shipping over.'

"The pilot came in to land on a rough strip at Pusan. He bounced three times and couldn't make it. So he poured on the coal, and took off for another try. He made it the second time. And when the crew chief came back, he remarked, 'Next week they're going to let that rugged pilot solo.'

"When we took off again the crew chief went back to reading his magazine. It had to do with how to interpret dreams. It wasn't so different from the last war."

He described Korea. "On the ground, this country seems only a few years ahead of the invention of the wheel. And the odors! The stench is as old as the world. Aside from the American military transports, the oxcart seems the modern means of transportation. Humans are pack animals, and even the packs are made of forked sticks tied together with handmade ropes. The big bulldozers, tankers, even the little jeeps, and especially the aircraft, blasting great dust storms off the field, appear to have been sent down from another planet."

Up front, he saw action. "I spent most of the day with the First Cavalry. Going up, we stopped at a six-gun battery of 155's. They were firing about one round a minute, at sixteen thousand yards. That's maximum. A plane was spotting for them and correcting fire. They didn't know what they were shooting at, but they thought it was enemy artillery. The spotting pilot kept calling in their directions, but didn't tell them the exact target. I asked the captain of the battery when it had gone into action. He grinned and said he didn't know, but he remembered it was on a Sunday.

"We drove on up to the regimental C.P., passed a burning village that had been set afire by our M.P.'s as they pulled back. To the north, a force of Communists had crossed a river. South Koreans had surrounded them on a hilltop, and had asked for an air strike. A young hotshot jet pilot, attached to the ground forces, picked up his phone and literally grabbed off four aircraft bound on another mission. He described the hill, gave the map reading, and explained that the South Koreans would wave white flags when the fighters came in. The colonel said this would have to be a fairly tricky operation, sort of hair-cutting on the hill. He hoped they wouldn't clobber the South Koreans by mistake.

"In less than four minutes we heard the guns of the fighters working as they sprayed the hilltop. The jet pilot on the ground picked up four F–80's on the telephone and put them on the same target. After they had finished, word came through on the telephone from a Lieutenant Lee, commanding the South Koreans who were besieging the hill, and the message said, 'The forces of the Republic of Korea wish to express their thanks to the Air Force for their timely intervention.' "

On that trip up front Murrow and three other correspondents were "taken prisoner" by American Marines who had become jittery guarding against North Korean infiltration. The quartet, Murrow, Bill Lawrence of the *New York Times*, Bill Dunn of Mutual Broadcasting, and James Hicks of the *Afro-American*, had somehow escaped injury when their plane made a skidding landing at night, and nearly careened off the runway at Chinhae. The others wanted to sleep at the airfield, but Murrow insisted on finding a Marine bivouac area, where they could push off for combat in the morning.

They were walking on the road when a voice from the darkness ordered them to halt. "Who's there?" Murrow identified himself and the others, but all the sentry wanted was the password, which the reporters didn't know. "I have no orders to let correspondents through," said the Marine. "Put your hands over your heads and don't move, or I'll blow you apart."

Other sentries came up. The reporters were marched off, at rifle point, until they met a captain. He recognized Murrow's name and voice, if not his features — Korea was a radio, not a "television war" — and vouched for the reporters while berating them for walking into a unit which, expecting an attack, had orders to shoot anything that moved.

Even the captain's assurances were not enough. The reporters were taken under guard to a command post, and spent an unpleasant night under "condition red," though Murrow did an on-the-spot report into his tape recorder.

Their company managed to hold its fire, but there was shooting all around them in the darkness. Much of it was at shadows, and that night the trigger-happy Marines killed two of their own number and wounded several others.

The G.I. war was not the only one that interested Murrow. He also worried about the strategy and tactics of the conflict, and on his way back from Korea he sat down to a microphone in Tokyo and said: "This is a most difficult broadcast to do. I have never believed that correspondents who move in and out of the battle area, engage in privileged conversations with commanders and with troops, and who have access to public platforms, should engage in criticism of command decisions or of commanders, while the battle is in progress. However, it is now time to cast up an account of the past ten days. For the question now arises whether serious mistakes have been made."

Murrow's criticism was that a premature American offensive had been undertaken in the quest for meaningless "victories," instead of a strong line being held until a properly supported action could be mounted. The Americans had also underestimated the enemy forces, with the result that the North Koreans had compelled the evacuation of the last American airstrip at Pohang. Although "we can kill North Koreans as fast as they decide to appear," the tactical initiative had been lost.

"And yet correspondents here have received cables from their home offices indicating that air-conditioned sources in Washington think the thing can be wound up this fall. To paraphrase the G.I.'s in Korea, that ain't the way it looks from here.

"So far as this reporter is concerned, he doesn't see where or when this conflict will end. For this is not an isolated war, except in the purely geographic sense. It is isolated only for the men who are fighting it."

It was August 14, 1950, only seven weeks after the conflict had begun, and in words that could also be applied to the Vietnam War of the following decade, Murrow went on to say that though American forces would not be driven off the peninsula, "when we start moving up through dead valleys, through villages to which we have put the torch by retreating, what then of the people who live there? They have lived on the knife-edge of despair and disaster for centuries. Their pitiful possessions have been consumed in the flames of war. Will our reoccupation of that fleabitten land lessen, or increase, the attraction of communism?"

Murrow wrote the strong words and spoke them into a microphone, but they were never heard by the American radio audience. They were recorded in New York in the afternoon, for use on the evening news program, but the CBS news executives decided that the broadcast contravened General MacArthur's directive barring criticism of command decisions. In the suppressed broadcast, Murrow himself acknowledged he might be violating the directive. But since he had done so deliberately, he clearly thought the situation warranted plain speaking, and he just as obviously intended it to help, not hurt, the American war effort.

The corporate explanation was made that "there was a difference of interpretations in censorship regulations," and that because Murrow was en route home "it was impossible to clear with him." Ed was supremely indignant, but he made no public reference to the suppression. As a member of the CBS board of directors, however, he could register his protest in the highest places, and after the meeting he said grimly that such a thing would never happen again.

Bill Paley, the board chairman, who regarded Murrow's broadcast as an open violation of agreement with the Defense Department, took the blame for the suppression, in a fiery personal encounter which, many years later, he recalled as the most difficult experience he had ever had with Murrow — a considered judgment which took into account all the public controversies that the network would become engaged in as a result of the broadcaster's programs.

Murrow opened the new season of his 7:45 P.M. news broadcast as the first radio commentator able to talk about Korea from direct knowledge, and he warned against any undue optimism and spoke of the propaganda appeal communism might have to Asian peasants oppressed by landlords, and to Asian middle and upper classes resentful of foreign domination. He was applauded by listeners and reviewers for going directly to the news again, instead of pontificating from behind an office desk. And while he was assailed by right-wingers for refusing to subscribe to their anti-Communist extremism, he was also criticized by the "Voice of Freedom Committee" for "Red-baiting." Its position was that South Korea had attacked North Korea.

The war dragged on, instead of justifying Pentagon optimism of a speedy end, and the Chinese Communists intervened, despite MacArthur's confident predictions they would never do so. Murrow would go to Korea twice more, with television cameras, to provide an ever newer depth to war reporting. But he regarded the first trip as his most satisfying assignment.

"I was more frightened than at any time during the European war," he recalled later. "Maybe it was because I was older. In Europe I felt the same age and generation as those fighting, even if I wasn't. In Korea I didn't feel that way.

"A B-26 gunner asked me if I had to fly combat to hold my job. When I said no, he looked as if he thought I was daft. 'You're getting a little old for this nonsense,' he said."

However important he felt the Korean War to be, Murrow continued to believe that Europe was the main arena for American interest, and for the challenge to communism. Like Eisenhower and Bradley — who would, however, change their views during the Vietnam War — he felt that involvement in a major land war on the Asian continent would be "unthinkable."

He warned against any military collision with China and decried the demands being made for use of the Bomb in Korea. Such talk "just frightens our allies, it's fairly childish, and it wouldn't stop the Chinese anyway," he said. When President Truman indicated he was considering the employment of the atomic weapon once again in the Far East, Murrow, much perturbed, called David Lilienthal to report the CBS correspondents' findings there that Europe was terrorized by the fear the Russians would retaliate by using their atomic force on the Continent.

Korea would of necessity be a major recurring theme in the Murrow news program for the next three years, as the hot war in Asia intensified the cold war at home and abroad. And his new weekly radio program, *Hear It Now*, introduced in December as "a document for the ear," was very much a document of its troubled times. On the first broadcast, two Marine privates in Korea talked about the retreat from the Chongjin reservoir. Secretary of Defense Marshall warned the nation of more travail ahead in the war. A New York newsdealer explained why he refused to sell the Communist *Daily Worker*. A draft board in Montana was "on strike" because the United States would not use the atom bomb. Anna Rosenberg, former Assistant Secretary of Defense, replied to the increasingly familiar charge of "pro-communism." The Duchess of Windsor talked about love. Carl Sandburg read his poem, "The People Yes." Dewey and Baruch spoke about economic mobilization.

Hear It Now was proposed by Murrow and Friendly as a half-hour program, but as soon as Paley heard the idea he insisted on a full hour. War had served once more to stimulate the public interest in news, and the news broadcast, a document for the intellect as well as for the ear, caught the fancy as well as the attention of listeners. *Variety* described it as "almost breath-taking in scope and concept."

Hear It Now, marking the formal inauguration of the Murrow-Friendly partnership in broadcasting, recalled the significant events of each week by the use of recorded sound. One criticism of it was that it might indeed be trying to cover too much ground, creating a kaleidoscopic effect. John Crosby, the reviewer, saw it as not trenchant enough. It had a point of view but "tried not to offend people." It should "take off its gloves and swing," he thought.

What the program did demonstrate, and its television successor *See It Now* would make even more clear, was that a point of view, and not the recorded snippets of "actuality," provided the best understanding of events and issues.

In *Hear It Now,* as in all their work, Murrow made the principal decisions as to contents and order of precedence but the two men usually collaborated in the writing. Friendly was responsible for the close, meticulous editing of the program — wasting no words, playing upon ironic contrasts, and not suffering fools gladly, unless of course their foolishness made a point — and Murrow was the reporter, the practical cogitator, and the consummate narrator. He often felt that Friendly had more enthusiasm than discretion in his news judgments, but together the combination was regarded in broadcasting as unexcelled.

Hear It Now was naturally followed by similar programs on the other networks, and achieved an exceptional rating for a public affairs broadcast, going out on 173 stations at the "prime time" of 9 P.M. and winning a Peabody Award virtually immediately. Its format became the standard for what are now called "radio news specials."

Hear It Now reviewed the Korean War, almost week by week, and one of its broadcasts, tracing the history of a pint of blood from the United States to the faraway battlefield, brought five hundred thousand pints of blood from listeners in response to an appeal.

The entry of Communist China into the war caused widespread bewilderment and apprehension in the United States, accompanied by the usual senatorial demands for "dropping the Bomb." Murrow did not belittle the crisis or minimize the danger, but when the United States and the Peking regime entered into diplomatic exchanges, he pointed out that negotiation was not to be confused with appeasement — a term as widely used then as it would be in the Vietnam War — and concluded that the United States was trying to carry out a foreign policy based on strength without actually possessing the strength required for global policing. "Our major obligation is not to mistake slogans for solutions," he said in one broadcast.

In the controversy between President Truman and General MacArthur, which ended with the military commander's recall after his continued public opposition. to the administration's limited-war policy, Murrow saw not only confirmation of the undisputed authority of the President, but also concordance with the country's greater interest, as he saw it — giving priority to the defense of Western Europe rather than to a full-scale war in Asia.

Most of all, the fact "that in a time of increasing militarism, the subordination of the military to civilian authority has been reestablished," he declared, "may appear to some to be an academic point, but not to people who have witnessed what happens when the civilian authority abdicates to the military."

Years later, when both the principals in the Truman-MacArthur controversy were in retirement, Murrow had a television interview with the former President and among the subjects discussed was the general's dismissal. MacArthur was asked to sit in turn for a "camera biography" but declined, with an implied rebuke for his old antagonist. "One who has filled a public position but does so no longer can best serve the Republic by maintaining silence," he sternly wrote to Murrow. Moreover the passage of years did not necessarily contribute to objectivity. The general had found Truman's remarks about the dismissal "entirely incompatible" with the truth of things. On the personal side, moreover, the former President on television had to him "seemed almost like a clown . . . it was entertainment, but not history."

MacArthur then gave Murrow his considered version of the dispute. He denied that he had misled the President into believing China would not enter the war. "He has the cart before the horse. It was he who misled me. As a field commander, my intelligence was limited to my own front. I had no means of knowing what was the political policy of Peking. That was a responsibility of Washington, and its authorities assured me there was no indication of intervention."

The real reason for his dismissal, said MacArthur, "was that I believed victory to be essential. Truman did not . . . The truth is, he lost his nerve just when victory was within his grasp. At that time we had the Bomb, they did not. We would not have had to fight globally, the threat would have been sufficient to force the enemy to yield. His knowledge that we would not, was the very signal for his intervention."

Though Murrow had supported Truman in the MacArthur controversy, as he would have supported any President against any general, he was critical of him on several other counts.

He was especially condemnatory of the executive orders establishing "security" in the Government, by the appointment of security officers, the classification of documents, and the withholding of any information that "might be useful to a potential enemy." Murrow was opposed to "Operation Clamming Up," as he called it, because he believed that giving security officers authority to decide what was "secret" in all Government departments allowed the Government to bury its mistakes and avoid criticism. More than that he believed that, despite the President's denials, it encroached upon the freedom of speech and of the press.

The American climate of opinion in the Frightened Fifties, Murrow thought, was at once the cause and the result of "an increasing tendency, with individuals as with nations, to conclude that the dissenters, those who fail to agree with us, are evil, malicious and disloyal.

"We appear to have lost some of our belief in the power of persuasion and the right of the individual to be wrong . . . Many of us are inclined to use Russia as the catchall for all our troubles, disposed to overestimate Russian strength, cunning and planning, inclined to believe that no solution is available except through force."

Yet the rational observer himself was caught up in an enterprise which, ostensibly dedicated to averting another world war, believed that an increase in American military strength, indeed some degree of militarization at home, was necessary to deter the Russians.

The Committee on the Present Danger, in fact, seemed definitely "in-

clined to use Russia as the catchall for all our troubles." It was an organization of business and professional men, some of the leaders of which
were intent on obtaining the presidency for General Eisenhower, then in
Europe again as the NATO commander. The committee's declared purpose was to insure the defense of Europe and the strengthening of NATO,
but it regarded the Korean War as part of a worldwide Communist
threat.

Murrow made it a rule not to join organizations which might prejudice
his reputation for fair comment, but he broke the rule to identify himself
with the Committee on the Present Danger. He did so, certainly, because
it regarded Europe as America's top priority, and perhaps because of the
membership of such men as J. Robert Oppenheimer, Judge Samuel Rosenman, and Dr. James B. Conant, its chairman. The last-named, president of
Harvard University, had also been active on the side of American intervention before the Second World War, was prominent in bringing scientists and educators into the Anglo-American wartime cooperation, and
thus had become a personal friend of Murrow. It was no doubt possible
to regard Conant's new efforts as a continuation of his earlier ones, and
Murrow himself had long been talking about America's "responsibilities."

The committee advocated sending more American troops to Europe,
instituting universal military training in this country, reducing draft de-
ferments, and introducing ROTC into medical and dental schools. Most of
the committee's officers believed that Eisenhower was the man to maintain an American military posture in Europe. Since they also believed
that the "present danger" was due to Russia's military presence in Eastern
Europe, they seemed to be anticipating the "rollback of communism" policy later enunciated, if only as propaganda, by Eisenhower's Secretary of
State, John Foster Dulles.

Murrow was not a particularly active member of the committee, though
agreeing with its tenets, and whether he shared its predilections for an
Eisenhower presidency can be doubted. He saw the NATO commander in
Paris that fall, renewing an acquaintance that went back to London in
1942, and found him reluctant to enter a hectic political campaign under
civilian rules, and also unclear as to whether he was a Republican or a
Democrat.

"He can afford to wait," Murrow concluded. The general did not wait
very long before deciding that he was a Republican, and that the country
needed him.

Murrow's brief trip to Europe was primarily to report on the 1951
British elections, in which Winston Churchill was returned to power after
six years in the opposition. The British people voted "their apprehension
of the future and their memories of the past," the broadcaster found.

He talked with Churchill after the final speech of the campaign, and that "indestructible juvenile," far from being enfeebled at the age of seventy-six, as had been reported, was chafing at the bit while waiting for the polls to open. He still gave the impression "that this island is too small a stage for him to play on." His voice had lost some of its resonance, but "his mind retains its cutting edge." And he was "aware that in this election both parties are in a sense contesting for the crown of thorns. But he has less reluctance than some of his colleagues to wear it."

As the Korean truce talks trudged unhurriedly and unheroically on that year — and the fighting continued while the talks did — Murrow's radio audience for his nightly news broadcasts had increased to three million. Despite the inroads of television, radio listening in general had increased, in fact, according to the ratings, it increased more in homes with television than in homes without it, whatever that might mean.

But in March 1951, Korea, atomic spies, the United Nations, rent control and everything else had been overshadowed by the televised hearings of the Kefauver crime investigating committee in New York. The former mayor of the metropolis, William O'Dwyer, and the gambler Frank Costello were the star witnesses, and the reticent Costello won the right to have only his hands, not his features photographed, adding to the hypnotic quality of the occasion.

Murrow noted that "the television performance has been fascinating, the audience fantastic — perhaps because the midgets in the box have been real."

The results of the proceedings were not impressive in legislative terms, though Senator Kefauver was thereby made a presidential candidate the following year, but their true significance lay in the fact that they had stopped a good portion of the nation dead in its tracks to watch, and during daytime, presumably working hours. A new phenomenon had been created, and Murrow spoke of the massive effect of television as against "the old-fashioned instruments of radio and print."

On September 12, 1951, the conference on the Japanese Peace Treaty opened in San Francisco. With it, for the first time, came coast-to-coast television, by means of the new coaxial cable and microwave relays. President Truman's opening address was carried by ninety-four television stations in all sections of the country. The Korean War had halted the opening of new television stations, but the coast-to-coast hookup, an international event featuring Dulles and Soviet Foreign Minister Gromyko, signified that the new medium had begun to stretch toward its true mass potential.

CBS followed the noncommercial public affairs program from San Francisco with the first commercial coast-to-coast broadcast, from Hollywood to New York and all points between.

A few days before the coaxial cable was opened, Murrow had declined an offer from his alma mater, Washington State College, to become its president, succeeding Dr. Wilson Compton, who was retiring.

For in spite of occasional doubts and disappointments, and even of "escape plans," he was not only committed to broadcasting, but was about to open the most important and rewarding chapter of his career. He was moving from the "old-fashioned" medium radio, to the new one, television, equally to command it.

IX

"This is what TV is for"

TELEVISION programs, though fleeting, or blurred by what comes next in an evening's viewing, or a week or month of evenings, are nevertheless often remembered for some striking scene, personality or concept long after their showing.

In the late afternoon of Sunday, November 18, 1951, an American television program called *See It Now* was shown for the first time. It brought together the striking scene, the personality and the concept. Both in itself and in its effect on the medium, it was perhaps the most significant television half-hour presented on the home screen until then.

Millions of Americans are still able to say "I can see it now," as they remember the unique scene with which the broadcast opened. In the control room of CBS Studio 41, in New York's Grand Central Terminal building, two television monitors were in view. On one of them the Atlantic Ocean was brought in, on the other the Pacific; on one the Golden Gate Bridge, on the other Brooklyn Bridge; on one the profile of San Francisco, on the other the skyline of New York — Telegraph Hill and the Statue of Liberty.

For the first time the continental sweep, dramatic power and sheer magic of television were displayed in the simplest and most striking way.

The simultaneous look at two oceans was made possible by the new coast-to-coast system of coaxial cable and microwave relay opened two months before, and it demonstrated that this latest technical achievement need not be limited to bringing the live images of comedians and singers from Hollywood to New York or vice versa — as if it made any particular difference where such acts originated — but could be used to show an entire nation to itself.

The television personality introduced by *See It Now* belonged to Ed Murrow, perceivable now in face, features and figure. He stood there dark and serious in the control room. It was also the first time that such

Off-the-tube photos of first See It Now *program, November 18, 1951*

an actual working area, with monitors, tuning panels and the unmistakable feel of the very innards of television, had been used as a studio, adding to the interest and involvement of the viewer.

The smoke curled up from what would be the ever-present cigarette in his fingers, and he said, "Good evening. This is an old team trying to learn a new trade."

He still believed radio was the more direct and forceful medium. He was extremely uncomfortable beneath the hot lights of the television studio, for he perspired profusely even in air-conditioned radio studios, and he was annoyed by the necessity for facial makeup. In the two weeks of technical rehearsals in the tiny control room before *See It Now*'s debut, the heat and the intensity of the lights, and the general crowdedness, came close to causing the discarding of the whole novel idea, and retirement to a more conventional studio.

But when the program actually took the air, all the problems were dissipated by the excitement of new adventure, the sense of achievement, and the immediate success. *See It Now* began, as all news programs did, for a stated period of thirteen weeks. It would endure seven historic years.

Television ended Murrow's invisibility. He had been seen on the screen on various occasions, at political conventions and on election night. He had appeared on the public platform and was widely acquainted throughout the country. But for most listeners he was still a disembodied voice, heard from a loudspeaker five evenings a week, since 1949 each year end with the assembled CBS foreign correspondents, and recently on Sundays on *Hear It Now*. To the voice they fitted whatever appurtenances they would care to imagine.

Now he was to be seen in the flesh, and regularly. Words and visage were brought together and they matched, which is not always the case with radio broadcasters. Taking account of the new dimension, *Variety* explained that "Murrow brings to the TV cameras a sureness, naturalness, and deep understanding of what he's talking about, plus a videogenic demeanor that in itself gives . . . a definite plus value." In other words, welcome to Show Biz.

That intangible quality now described as the telegenic does not require, as is too often believed on news programs, handsome features, a well-scrubbed appearance, an attractive smile, or even what Madison Avenue calls sincerity. Television personality knows no rules, except that it must somehow strike a spark "somewhere out there."

But Murrow, as he was unveiled to three million viewers on that Sunday afternoon, did possess the optimum attributes of good features — his eyes were deep-set and grave, his mouth and chin purposeful — a baritone timbre of voice, straightforward address, and serious intent, with an occasional Mephistophelian smile. On the screen, as off it, he had a quality that seemed to mock at complacency or propriety, and projected polite skepticism in massive amounts. It was ideally suited to the nature of the program.

And by the reckoning of Murrow and Friendly, the coproducers, it was the program, not the personality, that was important. They had been engaged in its preparation for five months, since *Hear It Now* ended in June, and though they applied to it the same ingredients as those of the daily Murrow radio news broadcast — conviction, fairness, change of pace, adherence to the meaningful and disregard of the trivial — they also knew that radio could not simply be transmuted into effective television. It had been tried too often, in newscasts which merely showed being read on camera what had normally been read into a radio microphone, or supplied vocal captions for newsreel pictures.

Moreover *See It Now* was a weekly not a daily news program, and therefore presumed to be more deliberative. Its purpose was not only to report what had happened, but to tell what it meant and explain how and why; not merely explain, but actually show.

Murrow and Friendly called it "giving the little picture." Their emphasis was on human beings affected by events, rather than on the events themselves, or as Murrow said about their coverage of the Korean War, "We narrowed our reporting down to the smallest possible units, individuals."

With its first program *See It Now* brought the Korean War home to Americans in a way they had not before experienced. The second portion of the half-hour was devoted to a camera visit with Fox Company's Second Platoon, of the United States 19th Infantry. It contained no artillery, no bombers, and no clichés. It showed the men of the platoon eating, sleeping, grousing, joking and waiting, in the eternal drudgery of war. It went with them to the top of Hill 525, where they took up a position, and it left them there, having established them as individuals and identified television viewers with them, as each member of the platoon stepped before the camera and merely gave his name and hometown.

Since the film was made, Murrow then reported, the company had suffered fifty casualties. His searching eyes looked directly into the camera. "Some of the wounded might need blood. Can you spare a pint?" he asked.

Demonstrating other technical possibilities of the medium, the first *See It Now* also showed Murrow in New York talking on live cameras to Eric Sevareid in Washington about Korean War atrocities, and then a telephone conversation between Murrow and Howard K. Smith in Paris about the United Nations and disarmament. Both ends of this conversation were filmed simultaneously and then assembled in New York to look like "live" television, predating the communications satellites by a decade.

See It Now also put into effect another idea Murrow had to illustrate the difference between it and the conventional news programs. "Let the news cameras cover a speech that is being made," he suggested. "Let our cameras cover the reaction of McCarthy, say, to the speech." Not McCarthy — he would come later — but Senator Robert A. Taft was shown by *See It Now* cameras listening contentedly, indeed almost purring, as Senator Everett Dirksen praised him at a campaign dinner and proclaimed that the next President must be "first an American, then a Republican." The cameras remained on Taft all the while, with his look of rapt satisfaction. It was hilarious, perhaps devastating.

As he had done when he began his nightly radio program, Murrow launched *See It Now* with a statement of warranty. "The mechanics of television doesn't confer great wisdom on those using it. We will identify our sources. We'll try never to get too big for our britches."

Beyond that, *See It Now*'s purpose was to probe the meaning of news, including situations not yet generally regarded as news.

It therefore called for long-range planning, the accumulation of filmed material which could be held for an appropriate moment, and flexibility, meaning the readiness to undo or discard something already done, in favor of a later or better story. Though it was largely a filmed program, it included "live" pickups from all parts of the country, and was therefore frequently as up-to-date with the news as that particular moment.

See It Now could use the resources of CBS at home and abroad, but was autonomous from the CBS daily news operation, and had its own crews roaming the world for film footage. It was often in conflict with regular CBS news assignments, playing hob with CBS administration by demanding priority on the time of correspondents and bureaus. It was frequently called the CBS "third news department," for radio and television news were at the time separate. Its independent position, impossible in the present integrated structure of news, was possible in 1951 only because like Topsy, "it growed."

Bound by no precedents, *See It Now* created its own. It was the first program to shoot its own film for its own specific purposes, rather than use film already shot for the newsreels and for daily news programs, or taken from the archives. Unlike any other documentary, it sent its cameras out without a prepared script. It made all its pictures with a sound track, never dubbed, never used actors, never rehearsed an interview, and shot as high as a twenty-to-one ratio of film not used, to film used. It might be called extravagant. It often cost one hundred thousand dollars a program, although when it began its sponsor paid only twenty-three thousand dollars a week toward the cost, plus thirty-four thousand dollars for the purchase of the air time. CBS made up the difference and *See It Now*'s financial deficit was always a sore spot with the company accountants, despite the program's prestige.

Murrow's attitude was that the amount a sponsor wanted to spend could not be allowed to determine how much was actually spent on a program, because a first-rate program might cost more than a sponsor cared to spend, and he refused, he said, to do a second-rate program.

See It Now obviously provided new breadth for television news, but it also created work methods which through their misuse by others, came to plague and stultify it. One such dubious factor was the field producer. He was absolutely necessary to *See It Now*, not only to control and keep germane the tremendous amounts of film shot, but to battle his way through the barriers of bureaucracy, suspicion and technical difficulties attendant upon the production of news film abroad.

A *See It Now* story consisted of more than the required film, however. It also demanded facts and interpretations which could not be pictorial. CBS News correspondents with *See It Now* units frequently had differences with producers, since it was the resident reporter and not the new arrival from America who knew the politics, economics and personalities of Yugoslavia, say, or Israel, or Britain. In the firm hands of Murrow and Friendly, who knew what they wanted, accommodation was arrived at between pictures and words. Unstinted credit was given to both the correspondent and the producer, as well as to the cameramen, which was a departure in television journalism.

But when field producers later became attached to daily news programs also, sometimes "producing" as little as a one-minute segment on the Cronkite or Huntley-Brinkley broadcasts, too often what has resulted reflects a producer's preconceived notions, or his desire for "action" rather than meaning.

Even more perilous to television, because of misuse, came to be *See It Now*'s disposition, not only to cover or explain the news, but also to "make" it.

What this meant to Murrow and Friendly was to employ television as a primary news medium, rather than a secondary or derivative one. They sought to report situations, problems and relationships before the printed media did, and in a different way. They were not content with a mere picture version of a *New York Times* series on crime, highway safety or education. Nor did they want merely to put on camera the familiar radio formats, such as discussion panels.

See It Now was consistently ahead of the news, whether in its unoptimistic appraisal of the Supreme Court's 1954 school desegregation decision, its anticipation of the Twenty-fifth Amendment on the presidential succession, its two one-hour programs on the emerging nationalisms of the African continent, or its two programs on cigarettes and lung cancer, years before the Surgeon General's report on the subject.

It also "made" news by compelling the Air Force to reverse itself in the matter of Lieutenant Milo Radulovich. It "made" news of a different sort when it sent Senator Margaret Chase Smith around the world, attended by cameras, and when it accompanied the Negro contralto Marian Anderson on a tour of Asia. In both the latter cases something memorable was created which would not have come into being otherwise. This was doubly true of the Marian Anderson program, for Murrow and Friendly had to find a sponsor for it themselves, after the CBS sales department had failed, because of its presumed "controversial" nature in the South.

These licit methods of "making" news were compromised to the detriment of television when cameras came to be used not only to photograph urban rioting but often to encourage it; not to illuminate controversy but to exacerbate it, by their very presence contributing an element to the situation which altered its complexion and consequences.

But these were problems of the future. In 1951 it was enough that a new way of doing things on television had been wrought. *See It Now* was hailed by the competitors of CBS, as well as by its viewers. An NBC executive thanked Murrow for "a challenge, a target, and an example." Another figure in the industry told him that "for the first time on TV, what I heard was as important as what I saw." A viewer wrote him, "This is what TV is for."

See It Now acquired commercial sponsorship in its third week, a relationship with the Aluminum Company of America that would last four years. Considering the frequently abrasive nature of the program, it was a bold thing for a sedate American corporation to do. But ALCOA was courting prestige, and did not have to worry about its profits.

Though encouraged by commercial success, which made it possible for *See It Now* to go on — its fate without a sponsor would have been an uncertain one — Murrow was still uncomfortable with the new medium of television, though he recognized the inevitability of its dominance. He did not give up radio, nor would he ever. He still broadcast his radio news program five nights a week. He felt that in radio he alone was in charge of the microphone, whereas in television the medium might take charge of him, with its cameras, lights, settings, and other paraphernalia; its producers, directors, coordinators, and stagehands. He knew that many stories simply could not be told visually. "What seems to concern television isn't the horror of the atom bomb, but the unique picture it makes," he said.

He was able to avert the pitfalls primarily by being himself, and using the medium, for all its technological razzle-dazzle, in a matter-of-fact way, like radio, to go to the source of the news and let it speak for itself.

See It Now, for all its purposeful tone, was not without its ludicrous moments, which helped keep the coproducers from getting too big for their britches. On one program, when Murrow was reporting on the use of atomic energy in medicine, with his friend David Lilienthal sitting in the studio to take part, the projector broke down while the filmed portion of the broadcast was on the air. Murrow's resonant voice slowed down on the sound track, spluttered, and as Lilienthal put it, got sour. After a moment's dire pause the live cameras came on, showing Murrow in the control room.

"What's wrong, boys?" he was heard asking the technicians. From the depths of telecine, the film projection room, came the hollow reply, heard by the millions of viewers. "We don't know what the hell's the matter, but we're working like hell to fix it."

Telecine was hastily cut off, and Murrow ad-libbed for a while until the film came back. By that time a large section of it had gone by and even Lilienthal could not tell what it was about. Then the film failed again, and Murrow switched to Lilienthal in the studio for his summation. "You and I have just seen, through the magic of television, a dramatic demonstration," he read from the teleprompter.

The two men left the studio for a drink, hastily. Friendly stayed behind with the technicians and reported that after the fiasco, the projector worked without a flaw continuously for six hours.

Since Murrow was daily occupied with his radio news program and the myriad things that went with it, the day-to-day workings of *See It Now* were in Friendly's hands. He it was who made sure that the film stories they wanted were produced for them, wherever in the world they might occur.

He badgered the cameramen and producers and demanded "complete dedication," such as he himself gave, at the expense of personal and even family relationships. With world-circling alarms and communiqués, he turned night into day for Palmer Williams, the assistant who knew the whereabouts of all personnel and all film shipments, the schedules of all airlines, and the customs regulations of all countries.

Members of the *See It Now* unit recalled that he issued "impossible" orders, which they then carried out. He made sure to issue them in Murrow's name. Friendly "bullied, humiliated, inspired, drove, sickened, ennobled, glorified his staff, and they gave him what he wanted, which only made him demand more," one *See It Now* producer remembered. Another has remarked that Friendly, without knowing a single thing about atomic energy, would have produced the atom bomb faster than Oppenheimer did. As Roosevelt once said of Churchill, Friendly "had a thousand new ideas a day, at least four of which were good." One observer called him "a character out of a bad novel" about the television trade. Murrow once described him as the only man he knew who could "take off without warming his motors." He called Friendly his "electric cattle-prod."

After he left CBS News in 1966, Friendly became the first Edward R. Murrow Professor of Journalism at Columbia University. In their years together the two men achieved striking symbiosis, both as craftsmen and as personalities. Both believed implicitly in the edifying power of the medium. Murrow's "almost mystical integrity," as a professional viewer put it, was matched by Friendly's "dedicated driving perfectionism." If Murrow had a feeling for the right story at the right time, Friendly, with his mastery of film editing, knew how to tell it in the right way.

In the *See It Now* workrooms, as film-cutters with their white canvas gloves cranked the endless frames from all over the world through the moveola machines, Friendly stood over them, night after night, sometimes all night long, picking the right frames and sequences, having them spliced in the proper order, cutting back and forth for emphasis and contrast. And week after week *See It Now* flashed the proof of painstaking, indeed painful, devotion.

Both were big men physically but, except when he briefly "blew his top," Murrow was spare of emotion as well as of carriage, while Friendly was in constant movement, cerebral as well as physical. His basic quality of overstatement balanced Murrow's of understatement. They admired each other, but not to the point of familiarity. For a long time Murrow jokingly called Friendly "Fritzl," a Teutonic diminutive which Fred detested, but which he endured until he could stand it no longer. When he complained, Murrow was surprised at the vehemence of his protest, but stopped promptly.

Because Murrow was the "on-camera" member of the partnership and Friendly worked behind the scenes, the latter sometimes felt that he did not get enough recognition, beyond the formal credit lines, for his share in the proceedings. It was routine for Murrow, walking down the street with friends or colleagues, to be halted not once but several times by adulators who insisted on shaking hands. He would be embarrassed, the more because those with him would stand by, anonymously and a trifle impatiently. But on one occasion at least, a *See It Now* group was halted by someone who walked up with outstretched hand, ignored Murrow completely, and said, "Pardon me, aren't you Fred Friendly?" He was a former fellow sergeant, who apparently never looked at television, and the incident raised Friendly's self-esteem.

Under the Murrow-Friendly partnership *See It Now* came to be regarded, as the critic Gilbert Seldes saw it, as "the most important show on the air — not only for the solutions it found to some problems, but also for the problems it tackled without finding the right answers."

In its first season of seven months it ranged across the United States and the world, dealing with such matters as the Schuman Plan for Europe, safety in the coal mines, the American government budget, baseball spring training, economic recession, the nationwide steel strike, the Suez Canal, the new communism of Tito's Yugoslavia, the mock atomic bombing of New York City, the politics of a presidential election year, and again and again, Korea.

See It Now was a kind of living news magazine, and its weekly editions touched on three or four subjects within the allotted half-hour. Gradually, however, the number of subjects per program decreased and the time given to each one increased, so that eventually *See It Now* was devoting a full half-hour to Trieste, Lieutenant Radulovich, a Big Four foreign ministers' conference, the recognition of Communist China, and tariffs. It even made "talking heads" absorbing television — pictured speech from people about the things they knew best — thus violating the rule that it was "action" the medium demanded.

Not all the *See It Now* programs were controversial. The program spent three days with Carl Sandburg, with whom Murrow had formed a mutual admiration society. They talked about Lincoln and language and history, at the poet's home in Flat Rock, in Ed's native North Carolina. Sandburg sang what he called the favorite Confederate war song, "Eating Goober Peas."

Murrow recalled the greeting he received from his Uncle Edgar, when he visited Pole Cat Creek after a long absence. "Ed, if you had come as often as I thought of you, you wouldn't be such a stranger as you are."

See It Now spent a week in Hollywood with the veteran producer Samuel Goldwyn as he made the film *Hans Christian Andersen*, and demonstrated what an intricate and costly technical enterprise movie-making was, and how far removed from the fan magazines.

See It Now introduced Dr. Jonas Salk and his colleagues on the day of their vaccine breakthrough against poliomyelitis; it happened to be the anniversary of the death of Franklin D. Roosevelt, a notable polio patient. Murrow talked with General George Marshall when he won the Nobel Peace Prize, the only soldier ever to do so, and with another soldier, presidential candidate Dwight D. Eisenhower, who admitted that the election campaign "very markedly" interfered with his golf.

For *See It Now*, Murrow flew through the eye of a hurricane, and he watched the Missouri River crest between Omaha and Council Bluffs, in a historic flood disaster. About Hurricane Edna, into which he flew with the Air Weather Service, he observed in a radio broadcast: "The eye of a hurricane is an excellent place to reflect upon the puniness of man and his works. If an adequate definition of humility is ever written, it's likely to be done in the eye of a hurricane."

The proportion of one to twenty in which shot film was actually shown meant that miles of footage on which months of labor might have been expended never reached the screen, to the anguish of cameramen and re-

Native son, and an adopted one, at Flat Rock, North Carolina. Murrow and Carl Sandburg

porters. On one occasion a four-week journey on the famed Orient Express, Paris to Istanbul with stops in Milan, Trieste, Belgrade and Salonika, wound up as nine minutes thirty-four seconds on the screen.

But by the same token the vast amount of unused *See It Now* footage built up the largest, most valuable, and certainly most fascinating library of "filmed contemporary history" in the United States, a tremendous boon for future scholars.

See It Now would be controversial, and occasionally highly so, but its appearance was preceded by a controversy involving Murrow which was perhaps the most embarrassing of his career. It occurred, not in electronic journalism, but on the old-fashioned printed page. *Collier's* magazine, one of the nation's leading weeklies, in October 1951 published a special issue devoted to "Russia — Defeat and Occupation, 1952–1960." This preview of "the war we did not want" was the only known case of a fifteen-cent magazine serving an ultimatum on a Great Power, for, said *Collier's*, "the Soviet Government must change its outlook and its policies," otherwise it would "disappear from the face of the earth."

To accomplish the Eggnog Project, as it was called in the editorial planning, *Collier's* enlisted thirty-four well-known writers, including Robert E. Sherwood, Arthur Koestler, Stuart Chase, J. B. Priestley, Walter Reuther, Hanson W. Baldwin, and Allan Nevins. Each described some aspect of the war that was "not wanted," some of them in terms that seemed to relish the prospect.

Murrow was asked to write an account of the atomic bomb attack that "destroyed" Moscow "on July 22, 1953," and it was described as his "36th combat mission," taking into account those he had flown in the Second World War and Korea. The bombing mission against the Soviet Union was ostensibly in retaliation for Russian atomic attacks on Washington, New York, Detroit and London.

Murrow wrote as if he were aboard a B–36 bomber, one of fourteen which made the long transpolar journey, although only two of them carried bombs. The first of these was hit and brought down. That left matters to the plane he was aboard. It dropped its bombs — "a radar job and very impersonal," "the most professional, nerveless military operation I have ever seen."

The main account of the mythical war, which began with a Soviet invasion of Yugoslavia followed by NATO's intervention on behalf of the United Nations, was written by Sherwood, the playwright, former OWI official, and Roosevelt-Hopkins historian, and was read and personally approved by the Defense Department's public information chief. It was sent to Murrow for his guidance with a note from *Collier's* — "Juicy stuff, my boy" — and the instructions: "One point please bear in mind — that we only drop one A-bomb."

A separate article described the bombing of Washington. "The American capital is missing in action," it began. Thousands were killed, but happily the President and his family were led to safety in a secret redoubt.

Baldwin's military analysis reported that the atomic bomb was used "extensively" by both sides but in a "limited" way, the principal American weapon being atomic artillery. A conflict of truly global scope took place for years, Baldwin recorded, indeed it lasted seven years even after the destruction of Moscow. With a great deal of satisfaction the *New York Times* military expert described the crushing of the Soviet Union in 1960, after only forty-three years of political existence. The world that survived was badly damaged but it was "free and peaceful."

Collier's' nightmarish enterprise sold many copies of the magazine, but it was a publishing debacle of the first magnitude.

As it happened, Murrow was in Paris when the magazine appeared. He was reporting the United Nations General Assembly meeting there, and the list of names involved in the Eggnog Project, including his own, convinced many Europeans that the *Collier's* war had been inspired by the American Government. At the United Nations, Soviet Deputy Foreign Minister Vishinsky quoted from *Collier's* as an argument against the disarmament proposal which had been formally made by the United States.

Murrow in a Paris broadcast condemned "irresponsible magazines in the United States" which "aid Russian propaganda about American intentions," but his horrified friend David Lilienthal imparted to his journal, "He should not be permitted to forget that it was he who wrote the most grisly of the stories." Lilienthal, who knew something about atomic energy, was especially appalled by the reckless and impersonal way in which the *Collier's* writers, including Murrow, had tossed nuclear weapons about on both sides, and wiped out great cities with the assurance that this was still "limited" warfare.

Murrow received a flood of protest for his share in the *Collier's* war. An American sergeant in Korea wrote that it had given him "a feeling of revulsion" and described it as "a shabby endeavor." He said he believed the United States had more to offer the world than force, and asked for an explanation of Murrow's motives. This indeed was the prevailing note of the volume of criticism — "Say it ain't so, Ed." One letter writer reminded him that the viewpoint he had taken in *Collier's* was at variance with his often expressed radio sentiments, namely that the fear of another war was out of proportion to a rational estimate of the world situation.

Many reputable journals condemned *Collier's* in their editorials. Since most of those involved were regarded as "of progressive, nonbelligerent instincts," the incident was seen as a booby trap for liberals, and an example of how the cold war had affected the national psychology.

It turned out that while the Pentagon had approved of the Eggnog Project the State Department had not, refusing *Collier's'* request for assistance and suggesting the idea be dropped. After publication, the Department received numerous urgent messages from American embassies abroad, reporting damaging effects and asking an official disavowal of responsibility. State did not go so far, but let it be known that *Collier's* instead should have described how the United States "won" the cold war, and avoided atomic holocaust.

Unlike some of the other contributors who had second thoughts, Murrow made no public statement about his role in the controversy. He, Sherwood, and Reuther notified a New York publishing house they did not want their articles included in a hard-cover edition, and since these were the leading chapters, the book did not come out.

Privately Murrow wrote a friend that he offered no excuses, but "I expect it was a case where a number of reasonably responsible people were 'sold' individually on what turned out to be an irresponsible project." Those who had taken him to task "were of course entirely justified," he said. To another friend he explained that he did not know the full contents of the *Collier's* issue, "but that is no excuse, I should have. I was impressed with the responsibility of most of the contributors and reluctantly agreed to do the short piece. I now regret my participation in that effort exceedingly."

While helping demonstrate that collective irresponsibility was possible even from individuals regarded as responsible, the *Collier's* incident was equally symbolic of the cold war being waged on the American domestic scene. It coincided with the ascension of the star of Senator Joe McCarthy, and with a peak period of "anti-Communist" activity and blacklisting in radio and television.

CBS was receiving hundreds of letters, all apparently inspired from the same source — a supermarket proprietor turned vigilante in Syracuse, aided by the local American Legion post — threatening a boycott of sponsors' products unless actors and others listed as "Communist fronters" were removed from broadcasting. Several CBS employees turned to Murrow for help in their troubles with *Red Channels* and the "loyalty oath," and he was made increasingly unhappy by the company's purge of some of its best talents, extending, in one case at least, into the *See It Now* unit itself.

The CBS reply to the boycotters was that it would not knowingly employ anyone identified with "any philosophy not coincident with the best interests of the United States, its institutions and citizens." It was not explained who would define the "best interests," or how.

See It Now broadcast several programs about civil rights, but their viewing audience was limited, for only fifty-seven stations in the entire

CBS network carried them. The *See It Now* "ratings," by which things were judged in television, were insignificant compared with the costly entertainment programs and "spectaculars," and it would never reach more than seven million viewers, after starting with three million. But it prided itself on the fact that its audience was "90 percent adult," and that it had a large juvenile audience as well, for many of the programs were recorded on film kinescopes and distributed widely to classrooms, at the request of teachers.

Week after week the program exceeded its twenty-thousand-dollar production budget, sometimes quintupling that amount. But lack of popular "ratings" was compensated for by critical acclaim. In the few weeks between its debut and the end of the year, *See It Now* won the Peabody Award, and received a special citation from *Variety* and "show business" as "the most original, informative and entertaining type of journalism now riding the video waves."

Murrow and Friendly, said the citation, reported "news which most people had never even suspected," and were threatening the precept that television could never equal radio's potential as a news medium. Murrow was still not convinced of television's superiority. And television had intruded more and more upon his sense of privacy, now that he was recognized, hailed and back-slapped everywhere he went. "I have my fair share of vanity," he remarked, "but I would prefer to be unrecognized rather than suddenly being engaged in conversation by people I don't know. They're well-meaning and polite, but I'd rather be left alone."

This was wishful thinking. In January 1952 the Nielsen ratings showed that for the first time more television sets than radio sets were in use throughout the United States between 9 P.M. and midnight. Radio was still ahead of television in advertising revenue, but this was the point at which the visual medium began to take over the American public's evenings. It was aided by the fact that 1952 was an election year, that President Truman had said he would not run for a second full term, and that General Eisenhower had come back from the post of Supreme Commander in Europe to seek the post of commander-in-chief of the United States.

As he had done on his radio program in 1948, Murrow talked to the leading presidential contenders, Kefauver, Harriman and Taft, on camera for *See It Now*. They were photographed in their homes, answering questions by telephone, and though the political content was insignificant the idea of such electronic "visits" would reap a television harvest later in Murrow's *Person-to-Person* program.

Candidate Eisenhower, the center of attraction, received a visit from Murrow and *See It Now* in the Denver backyard of his in-laws. Though it displayed the general's "personality," television also confirmed at that early date, though perhaps the American public was not really watching, that the candidate did not have many stimulating thoughts or words about anything.

But the 1952 campaign confirmed television as the "maker" of news that Murrow and Friendly had found it to be. Statements were made by candidates on television alone, and answered by other statements on television alone, and there were television debates between Kefauver and Taft.

Television's activist political role began at what was called in broadcasting the Battle of Abilene. At his hometown in Kansas, where he was announcing his candidacy, Eisenhower held a news conference for the printed press and radio, but barred the television cameras waiting outside in the pouring rain. Jesse Zousmer, in charge of the *See It Now* cameras for Murrow — who was also present — insisted upon equal access, and pushed his tripods into the meeting, followed by other television crews.

The newspapers and wire services protested vehemently. They said that by filming their expert reporters asking questions, and getting the candidate's answers, television was misappropriating what did not belong to it. The controversy would go on in all public arenas, reaching into the White House. At Abilene, Candidate Eisenhower changed his no-television rule, and when he became President his news secretary James Hagerty quickly established the first televised news conferences. They were merely filmed, however. It would be left for the next President to introduce "live" news conferences.

The national political conventions of 1952, both held in Chicago, received the full TV treatment for the first time, and it was widely believed that without television, not Eisenhower but Senator Taft would have been the Republican nominee. For the two camps clashed over the seating of rival delegations from Texas, Georgia and Louisiana, and the Eisenhower forces made the most of their television exposure to denounce the Taft "steamroller," the smoke-filled room, and the "big steal."

Convention delegates received demands from their own states, from those watching the proceedings on television, and voted to change the Credentials Committee rules, thereby giving Eisenhower the victory in the seating dispute, and paving the way for his nomination. The new medium, flexing its electronic muscles in competition with the written and spoken media, fought so hard for its own prerogatives against the convention managers, who were Taft supporters, that by that very fact it sided with the Eisenhower faction. Thus television itself became a political force, and so did its self-endowed interest in projecting controversy, indeed if need be, manufacturing it.

There were as many television journalists and technicians at the Republican convention as there were delegates, twelve hundred, and Murrow, not recognized by a doorman who evidently did not watch *See It Now*, was barred from the floor for inadequate credentials as the sessions began.

At the Democratic convention all delegates and alternates received instructions. "You will be on television. TV will be watching you. There are to be no empty seats, no sleeping, and good behavior is urged." Again Murrow was a floor reporter, not an analyst, but the big star on television was Betty Furness, who opened and closed refrigerator doors in the "live" commercials directly from the convention hall.

The Democratic candidate proved to be Adlai Stevenson, governor of Illinois, and while Eisenhower was shaking hands around the country and grinning, Stevenson spoke to the American Legion convention, at the height of the McCarthy era, in defiance of the Legion's own dogmas.

"The anatomy of patriotism is complex," he said. "But surely intolerance and public irresponsibility cannot be cloaked in the shining armor of rectitude and righteousness. Nor can the denial of the right to hold ideas that are different.

"The tragedy of our day is the climate of fear in which we live, and fear always breeds repression. Too often, sinister threats to the Bill of Rights . . . are concealed under the patriotic cloak of anticommunism."

The Committee on the Present Danger, to which Murrow belonged, saw its candidate elected and some of its members, but apparently not he, met with the general before he took office. They urged more American troops for Europe, the increase of military production, and the discontinuance of "defense support" to other countries, except for "further assistance to Indo-China in a way which will also aid France," this being sixteen months before the French disaster at Dienbienphu.

Murrow did join other committee members in a signed statement upholding the President's right, without specific congressional approval, to send more troops abroad. The Senate Foreign Relations Committee declared its approval in advance of whatever the President might choose to do to "strengthen the defenses" of Western Europe, just as it would do with the Tonkin Gulf resolution thirteen years later.

But though the committee believed, as Murrow did, that any Communist threat was an external one, and that McCarthyism was divisive, its meeting with the President-elect was widely and perhaps inevitably construed as within the framework of anticommunism at home. According to the *New York Times*, it was "calculated to give anti-Communism in the United States the respectability and authority which it deserves, but sometimes lacks, because of abuses by well-meaning zealots, more or less cynical demagogues, and those who make anti-Communism a profession." Among these it named Senators McCarthy and McCarran.

The ways in and out of anti-Communism were confusing, and while Murrow on this occasion adhered to the committee's view that "the higher the moral and intellectual level on which communism is fought, the more chance there will be of defeating it," when the conflict with McCarthy came a year later, he would adopt the Stevenson view that "too often, sinister threats to the Bill of Rights . . . are concealed under the patriotic cloak."

In the 1952 campaign Murrow saw both candidates, Eisenhower and Stevenson, as above their parties in a sense, because each had been nominated "without any knowledge by most of the delegates of his stand on controversial issues." When Eisenhower, seeking to "unite" the nation, became conciliatory toward Senators McCarthy and Jenner, both of whom had called General Marshall a "traitor," the broadcaster concluded that "in politics, as in war, there is no substitute for victory." He described Stevenson as "a man who spoke often in the accents of greatness," but who was defeated "because too many people like Ike." Murrow himself would not be among them for very long. He had supported Eisenhower because of the "present danger," but his own leanings were Democratic, from the days of Franklin D. Roosevelt.

After the election Murrow undertook television's most ambitious assignment until then. With a camera task force of fifteen men, plus five reporters, he flew to America's distant battlefront to film *Christmas in Korea*. This was *See It Now*'s first full one-hour program, another milestone for television news, and was also the medium's first combat report. "Murrow's Korea: The New Journalism," was *Variety*'s headline. "Even a battlefront brought into the parlor."

The program, giving full camera range to the conflict — moving from Heartbreak Ridge to downtown Seoul, from a hospital ship to a barracks; showing not only American G.I.'s but French, British and Ethiopian soldiers of the United Nations force — made the point that not only did heroism, frustration, patriotism and fatalism characterize this war, as all others, but that in addition this particular war was stalemated.

The *See It Now* visit to Korea followed the one made by General Eisenhower that, with its implication of ending the war, had helped elect him. "What Ike saw in Korea is still a state secret," *Variety* wryly commented. "What Murrow and Co. saw, the American people saw."

On the way home the long days and frenetic drive of the Korean assignment, with its cold, fatigue and sleeplessness, exacted their toll. Murrow had planned to stop off for a few hours in Seattle, to see his parents in Bellingham — his father was now an invalid — but instead he himself was laid low with influenza and landed in the hospital at Renton.

Christmas in Korea, seen across the nation a few nights before, had spellbound its viewers, and hundreds of telegrams and telephone messages were received at the hospital when the news of his illness was reported. He had come to be regarded by the state of Washington as its most notable

Christmas in Korea, 1952. He preferred talking to soldiers, not officers

"native son," and his filial report, when he recovered enough to hold a bedside news conference, was that it looked like a "permanent" war in Korea, and that he had found no one there who "knew the answer."

Back in New York, he failed to throw off his fatigue and went into the hospital for another week, for tests and X-rays, fearing it might be something more than mere flu. He passed the tests, but it was evident that the pace and tension of his business had become increasingly important, even hazardous, factors in his life.

The spring was a crowded one, attendant upon the change of administration in Washington, Senator McCarthy's hearings on the Voice of America — he called it the Voice of Moscow — and in Moscow itself, the death of the old despot Stalin. The McCarthy hearings were televised, and they raised some questions about the medium's ability to communicate a full and fair story, since many of those named by witnesses, on camera, were never given a chance of reply. But this was only a difference in degree, not in kind, from the newspapers and magazines which also tended to regard McCarthy's unsupported charges as proved facts, or at least gave that impression.

As to Stalin's death and the uncertainty it brought in its wake, Murrow spoke in a radio broadcast of the satellite leaders who had been kept in power by the old man's terror. "Nothing may happen on this Russian fringe as a result of Stalin's death, at least for some time," he remarked. "But empires always begin to crumble away at their edges. And if there are to be changes in Stalin's empire, as a result of his death, the signs will first be seen in Prague, Budapest and Warsaw, rather than in Moscow." It was three years before the Polish rebellion and the Hungarian uprising.

But life was not all war and politics. After receiving an award for "nonconformist" thinking, together with Albert Einstein, Murrow and the cameras were off again, this time to London for the coronation of young Queen Elizabeth.

The historic pageant was the first of television's overseas "spectaculars" and network competition was at its fiercest. Communications satellites were still years away, but something called Stratovision was planned by NBC, whereby six large planes, circling in the air at forty-thousand feet, and spaced 450 miles apart across the ocean, would relay live pictures of the royal doings by microwaves, for instantaneous viewing in America. None of this happened — it still hasn't — and instead CBS and NBC prepared to race by air from London with the coronation film.

They assigned five hundred men and spent a million dollars each on the coverage, but the race went to neither of the swift. The NBC jet had to turn back and the CBS jet left late. Meanwhile the BBC had flown its first film by RAF bombers to Montreal for the Canadian Broadcasting

Corporation, and from there the third American network, ABC, which had made no plans at all and spent no money, fed the Canadian program to its stations across the border. It beat CBS and NBC to the air by several minutes, with the first pictures.

Each of the two bigger networks had also employed "flying laboratories" for the processing and editing of film en route, so it could be shown in special, heavily sponsored programs later in the day. Murrow, drenched to the skin in the royal downpour of Coronation Day, left his commentator's post opposite Buckingham Palace before the ceremony in Westminster Abbey took place. He boarded the "flying laboratory," wrote his way across the Atlantic, and narrated the coronation special from Boston.

His television day might have seemed excessively high-wrought. Radio, with reporters at every conceivable vantage point in London, had broadcast each stage of the ceremonial "live" from 4:30 A.M. while the first television films were not seen until twelve hours later. On the other hand there was no doubt that a rare and splendid occasion of this sort, essentially pictorial, was of the true nature of television.

But the commercial nature of the broadcasts offended the British, unconditioned as yet to advertising on the air, and offended many Americans as well. Automobile commercials rang with phrases like "queen of the road," and "royal carriage," and NBC's use of a chimpanzee, for some Barnumish reason, during one coronation program is believed to have set back the advent of commercial television in Britain by two years.

After the coronation, after the signing of a Korean truce and a quickly crushed anti-Communist revolt in East Berlin, another Murrow expeditionary force flew to the former German capital for a one-hour program on "the face of the cold war," inaugurating *See It Now*'s 1953–1954 season. He also did his nightly radio commentary from Berlin — "a city without a country" where "the contest between freedom and communism is divided by half the width of a street."

He was deeply immersed in the planning for a new weekly television program scheduled to begin two weeks later. This would mean that on two of the five weekday evenings he would be engaged in television as well as in radio, with his live presence demanded on all seven occasions. *See It Now*, which had begun on Sunday afternoons, was now shown on Tuesday evenings, and the new *Person-to-Person* would be on Friday evenings.

He was also regularly recording another daily radio feature called *This I Believe*, in which notable and "successful people," from Jackie Robinson, the Negro baseball player, to Mrs. Roosevelt, from Thomas Mann to Darryl Zanuck, the movie producer, expounded on what they regarded, or wanted regarded, as their private philosophies. The program to which Murrow gave his services free of charge had become one of the phenomena of mass communication. Its three-and-a-half-minute nuggets of wisdom and

On assignment in divided Berlin, 1953

On the flight line for a simulated atomic bomb run

piety were heard not once, but two or more times each day on 196 CBS radio stations, a total of 2200 times a week, by an audience of 39 million people. It was broadcast by the Voice of America in six languages and became "the most widely listened-to radio program in the world." It was carried in eighty-five daily newspapers in the United States, and made a record album and two printed volumes which together were exceeded only by the Bible, in nonfiction book sales. After two hundred living persons had been heard, Socrates, Confucius, Lincoln and other immortals, played by actors, told what they believed.

Seldom in those crowded days was Murrow able to get to Pawling, to golf on the adjoining course, go shooting with Bob Dixon, or teach Casey the manly arts. He tried to interest the eight-year-old in hunting and fishing, but though Casey tolerated his instructions to please him, he was never really enraptured. Moreover Janet was perturbed when Ed tried to teach the boy to handle a pistol. She thought the noise would cause deafness.

After his weeks of absence, it took a British friend to reestablish Murrow's status with the local shooting gentry. The Cranbornes were visiting — he had become the fifth Marquess of Salisbury and would be entering Churchill's new government as Secretary for Commonwealth Relations — and the mild and self-effacing peer, clad in blue jeans instead of the conventional knickers of the Scottish moors, wearing a frayed jacket with leather-covered elbows, easily outshot all the Dutchess County nimrods.

But weekends at Pawling were infrequent now for Murrow, and it was evident that the claims of broadcasting had become too much for one man, even a man with his appetite for work. This was the point at which Raymond Swing became closely associated with Murrow's radio broadcasts.

They had been friends from the time when Murrow had taken the job that Swing did not take as the CBS director of talks. The latter had become a preeminent broadcaster in his own right, especially during the war. He then joined the Voice of America as its principal commentator, and soon was as well known around the world as Murrow had become at home.

During Joe McCarthy's campaign against the Voice, Swing kept Murrow informed of the deleterious effect it was having on the effectiveness of Government broadcasting. After McCarthy had caused the resignation of Reed Harris, deputy administrator of the United States Information Agency — the Harris hearings provided *See It Now* with a program showing the Senator in action — Swing resigned from the Voice of America. He was protesting the State Department's failure to stand by its people who had been maligned by McCarthy, or to fight back.

Murrow at once asked his old friend to join him at CBS. On Tuesday and Friday evenings, Swing would write the "think pieces" for Murrow to read on his radio news program, and he would also take over the administrative functions for *This I Believe* from Edward P. Morgan, another Murrow friend and fellow Washingtonian, who wanted to broadcast himself.

Swing was not to be a mere ghostwriter for Murrow. The two men shared views about most issues in politics and foreign affairs, and trusted each other's judgment. Murrow, who did not always observe the thin line between "news analysis" and "editorial opinion," was on larger questions now frequently and frankly making "personal comment" or "one reporter's comment" on his nightly broadcasts. So Swing felt he was saying, through Murrow, what both of them thought. Murrow usually picked the subject to be dealt with, as it grew out of or fitted into the day's news, and the two men consulted on the broadcast, but Swing was left free to write in his own way. Murrow did the final editing.

In hindsight perhaps the most clairvoyant of the broadcasts of the time was the one made on the opening of the 1954 Geneva Conference. The French had been defeated at Dienbienphu, and Vice President Nixon had advocated the use of American troops in Vietnam if the French withdrew.

"No decision has been made to send American troops to Indo-China. But neither has a decision been made not to send troops under any circumstances. And the second statement may prove to be even more important than the first," Murrow read from the script.

He observed that if it "came down to the bare choice of losing Indo-China to the Communists or saving it, some form of intervention may prove inescapable." But such talk was premature, "and advocates of intervention are unrealistic if they assume that the problem of Indo-China is primarily military. Actually it is much more political . . . It is to be won first of all in the realm of convictions. Only if the people of Indo-China believe that the fight against communism is the fight for their own freedom will they turn the present tide of the conflict."

Fifteen years and hundreds of thousands of American troops later, that would still be the unresolved situation in Vietnam.

At the time of the formal Murrow-McCarthy confrontation and during the Army-McCarthy hearings that followed, Swing was responsible for some of the most forceful comments made on the air about the Wisconsin Senator's activities. For as Murrow's television duties took more and more of his time, because of their increased scope, Swing came to write more of the radio commentaries. He remained with Murrow as long as the nightly news broadcast lasted, and then in 1959 went back to the Voice of America, where the pall of McCarthyism had lifted.

As with so many things done because of the exigencies of radio and television, the question of ethics did not enter into the fact that Raymond Swing wrote many of the broadcasts attributed to Edward R. Murrow.

The practice has become a common one, though it was less common then. Murrow had always engaged in collective journalism, after the war, but he had always acknowledged the cooperative effort and given full credit to all the others. With Swing's commentaries it was different. They were unidentified as such. They not only passed for pure Murrow on the air, but remain so for historical purposes. It is as if Pepys's uncle wrote parts of his diary, or Gibbon's secretary some of his *Decline and Fall*.

In any case the situation seemed to support Fred Friendly's contention that *Person-to-Person*, diverting him from the realm of news and comment, was detrimental to this more important part of Murrow. The same view was held by Frank Stanton, who opposed Murrow's entry into the "show business" side of television because he believed it would detract from his serious work with *See It Now* and the nightly radio broadcast.

On Friday night, October 2, 1953, sandwiched in between two serious Tuesday night *See It Now* programs on Berlin and on India, Murrow made his first appearance — somewhat defiantly, as far as Stanton was concerned — in his new television role as electronic "guest."

Person-to-Person attracted a much larger and entirely different audience from the faithful followers of *See It Now* and the radio commentaries, and the only controversy it ever aroused was the one among Murrow's friends of why he had ever deigned to undertake it. Sitting in an easy chair, dignified but apparently relaxed, with the smoke eddying from a cigarette in his fingers, Murrow during that first half-hour "visited" in their homes, first Roy Campanella, the baseball player, and then Leopold Stokowski, the conductor, and his wife, the former Gloria Vanderbilt.

The program, completely live, was made possible by technology — not only the three cameras and ten miles of wire that linked each of the visited homes with the studio, but also wireless microphones. These enabled the "hosts" to move about from room to room, in Park Avenue apartment or small-town cottage, followed by cameras as they exhibited their paintings, played their pianos, held up their trophies, and engaged in their hobbies, before a presumably enchanted nation.

The long-distance conversation between Murrow and his subjects, during which he could see them on his studio monitor but they had to address themselves to his voice coming over a concealed loudspeaker, was on the inconsequential side. The Murrow who asked a "notable" about his wood carving or his child's marks in school was not the same Murrow who asked Nehru about neutralism and Communist China, or inquired of the new Chief Justice, Earl Warren, whether he was a liberal or a conservative; or even the Murrow who chatted with G.I.'s in Korea about the weather and their hometowns.

Most of the program's guests-hosts were intimidated by the mechanical contrivances, and by the necessity of remembering the conversational cues

At Independence Hall. See It Now *delves into American history*

Murrow and Friendly screen a See It Now *report*

which were to set them and the cameras in motion. In fact, some of the questions asked were not seeking information at all, but intended as cues.

There were often awkward pauses, and at the beginning at least, Murrow sometimes seemed ill at ease with the inanity of the talk, and the false bonhomie of the occasion. Since the subject knew the line of questioning, for cue purposes, but Murrow did not know what answers to expect, there were many non sequiturs.

But gradually he adjusted himself to the program, and came to like it. He felt it gave his work an added facet, and one associate thought he even became interested in some of the people he talked to. Though the debut received mixed notices — one reviewer said, "This Murrow is an interloper," and another that he "should have hung up" the electronic telephone — the celebrity-studded *Person-to-Person* quickly became a popular success and even broke into the "top ten" of all television programs, in terms of audience appeal.

It did so well financially that he was able to reject advertising he found distasteful, as he had done on radio. This was an unaccustomed luxury on television, and *See It Now* by contrast would soon be scraping about for commercials. It also stirred some resentments among CBS television executives, who plainly thought that he had now really become "bigger than the network."

Person-to-Person illustrated once again the tug-of-war inside television between its show business psychology and its impulses toward enlightenment. It was originated by Murrow with Jesse Zousmer and John Aaron, the two men who had worked with him on his radio programs for six years. They still continued with the radio program as well, but because of the demands for their time now made by television, Edward Bliss became Murrow's "hard news" writer, as Swing had become his "think piece" writer.

One unusual aspect of *Person-to-Person* was that it was not a CBS program but a "package" sold to the network by the three men concerned, Murrow, Zousmer and Aaron, who owned it themselves. Murrow held a 40 percent share of the enterprise, and he divided this into trust funds for Casey and for his and Janet's mothers. It was an economic bonanza and would eventually be sold for a large price to CBS.

Person-to-Person was openly resented by Murrow's other producer, Friendly, and the Friendly–*See It Now* side of Murrow's life was in a perpetual state of feud with the *Person-to-Person* side. Some of the Friendly establishment called the Zousmer-Aaron establishment "the buttonhole makers," and Murrow himself sometimes used that term. When asked why he had started *Person-to-Person* he once replied, "To let Jesse and Johnny pick up some change."

It also provided him with enough to trade in his log house with four-

Murrow and Casey walk away from a "hard" landing of their plane, near Yakima, Washington

Murrow and Casey, with bulldozer, at Pawling

teen acres on Quaker Hill for a 280-acre farm nearby called Glen Arden, with a two-hundred-year-old mansion and a herd of sixty dairy cows. The glen for which it was named became his beloved place of retreat. It was a working farm and Murrow rode a tractor and sawed down trees with Bob Dixon. An English friend who visited there described it as "very like the Scottish border country."

Person-to-Person, with its mass audience, also made Murrow one of America's cultural folk figures. There were cartoons in the *New Yorker* about it, jokes on comedy programs and in newspaper columns, and Murrow became a kind of generic noun, instead of a proper name — "he thinks he's a regular Murrow" — and was even used as a verb, "to Murrow," meaning to engage in social chitchat. He was seen at dinner with Marlene Dietrich and Tallulah Bankhead — the latter appeared on *Person-to-Person* but the former refused — and it was difficult to decide which attracted more attention.

As for the program itself, what was intended to convey the impression of a casual call by Murrow often became, as the *New York Times* called it, "a state visit." Each of the two homes, besides receiving the cameras, the lights and the miles of wire, was invaded by six men of the camera crew, six more for microwave relays, electricians, producers, directors, makeup artists and telephone company engineers, while twenty-six men were required at the studio to receive the incoming pictures.

Yet it was only the cumbersome technics that made the program possible. Electronic skill created the impression of actual physical presence in the homes Murrow visited. And when he warmed up to it, he was actually to be seen smiling, a new view of him for many *See It Now* followers. Amid the long stretches of desultory conversation, frequently a spark was struck, a pearl dropped, or a personality illuminated that evoked warm human emotions.

Murrow was an effective interviewer in a special sense. His questions, even on *See It Now*, were sometimes too vague and even trivial, and on *Person-to-Person* they were too often only cue conveniences. But he had the quality of patience, and would simply wait silently for his response. Even when it came he might not say anything, but continue to wait, whereupon the other person would talk on, amplifying, explaining or embroidering. The result was often fascinating, but if both interviewer and subject were reticent, as was known to happen, it could be disastrous.

Murrow was sometimes criticized for not pressing his subjects, especially the political ones, on matters of more substance than their hobbies, and thus "making" news. His answer was that he could not presume to cross-examine those who had been kind enough to ask him into their homes. The plain truth was that *Person-to-Person* was not intended to be a political, much less a controversial, program. He kept his two television selves apart.

Some thought the program too obviously uncurbed in its deliberate "celebrity hunting," and scoffed at its mixed bags. Zousmer and Aaron, seeking what they called box-office appeal, openly dealt in contrasts, between those who had achieved some recognition in belles lettres, law, statecraft, the sciences or humanities, and those from "show business" or sport. Murrow's preference was for the former. The preference of the "buttonhole makers" was distinctly for the latter. *Person-to-Person*, reaching into various strata of the American social and cultural structure and bringing them down to the level of the mass audience, might have been regarded by sociologists as a great equalizer, or perhaps even a great vulgarizer.

Over the years it produced some memorable moments. On one occasion Krishna Menon, the irascible Indian delegate at the United Nations, bridled at some inferred criticism of Indian policy, and said, "That is an improper question for you to ask me." Murrow corrected him. "Perhaps it is an improper question for you to answer."

On *Person-to-Person*, Senator John F. Kennedy, of Massachusetts, interviewed with his bride Jacqueline, read a poem of which he was particularly fond. It was Alan Seeger's "I Have a Rendezvous with Death." Asked about his wartime ordeal as commander of PT-109, Kennedy called it "an interesting experience."

"Interesting?" said Murrow. "I should think that would be one of the great understatements."

Zousmer and Aaron were long bemused with the idea of Marilyn Monroe, the blonde movie star, on *Person-to-Person*, and envisioned her bracketed with Bernard Baruch, or even better for their "dream show," with Dr. Albert Schweitzer. They could never persuade Baruch or Dr. Schweitzer, but after a campaign lasting two years, Miss Monroe finally appeared.

She had just been divorced again and was in a period of self-retreat, but her manager thought she needed the publicity. She took five hours to put on her makeup, and with her tousled hair, little-girl face, and tight sweater, she resembled one of her own movie posters. But neither she nor Murrow was at ease. Their conversation was painfully stilted, and though the broadcast received the highest audience ratings, "it was a relief," one reviewer wrote, "when in the second half of the program Sir Thomas Beecham, the conductor, rescued the evening with sparkling talk."

Again, it was on *Person-to-Person* that the Duke and Duchess of Windsor made their first television appearance, but despite the supposed aura of royalty, the conversation was accounted superficial even by *Person-to-Person* standards, artificially coy, and dull.

Person-to-Person
was heavy on
show business,
light on content.
Its most glamor-
ous guest —
Marilyn Monroe.
The conversation
proved to be
stilted

On another occasion Zizi Jeanmaire, the ballet dancer, was changing into costume behind a screen while talking to Murrow, when a loose cable hit the screen and it barely escaped falling. "If I had ended up with a naked French girl on camera," Murrow reflected soberly later, "I would have said 'Good night and good luck,' got up, and gone home."

Zsa Zsa Gabor, the husband- and gem-collecting actress, opened her refrigerator on *Person-to-Person* and revealed a Hungarian salami, apparently her true treasure. A prominent playwright-actor was interviewed, and a Connecticut couple, watching at home, recognized on his wall two unidentified eighteenth-century portraits they had sold off a few years before. They heard the celebrity explain, "Ed, those aren't my folks. They're my wife's ancestors."

In February 1959, a month after he took power, Murrow talked to Fidel Castro in Havana, and even his small son Fidelito. Castro promised to shave off his beard by the following July 26, the anniversary of his revolution. Apparently he changed his mind.

On *Person-to-Person,* A. C. Nielsen, who had developed the widely used ratings system, demonstrated the recording device by which he said he could estimate the size of television audiences. It failed to work.

Murrow always received a few letters a week cautioning him about smoking so much, but one *Person-to-Person* program brought the largest wave of antismoking mail he ever got, and that even before it was shown. It reflected concern not for his health, but for that of Billy Graham, the evangelist, whom he had announced as the following week's subject.

After voices were raised about *Person-to-Person*'s visits to "celebrities," instead of "just ordinary people," Zousmer and Aaron tried "ordinary people" a few times — one was a mailman, another a farmer — but received even more complaints from those who said that if they wanted to see ordinary people they could visit their own relatives.

Murrow once explained that the appeal of the program was the sight of "extraordinary people doing ordinary things," like whittling, or fiddling with a hi-fi set.

As his CBS colleagues had done for years — "Well, Ed," was the way they invariably began to answer his questions when they appeared on his programs, and it became an intramural joke — most of those he interviewed on *Person-to-Person* quickly took to calling him Ed, though Sophie Tucker, the veteran trouper, addressed him as Eddie, which he found repugnant.

The number of people who recognized him in public, because of *See It Now*, was multiplied several times over because of *Person-to-Person*. According to Nielsen, it was seen in eight million homes, and whatever else might be said about it, it gave Murrow such a broad basis of popular esteem and what television calls "acceptance" that in the coming conflict with Joe McCarthy it would serve as a shock absorber, providing him with an advantage over the Senator.

In its six years on the air with Murrow — it continued briefly after he left it — *Person-to-Person* brought into American homes glimpses of other American homes, and a list of guests that ran alphabetically from Adams, Cedric, journalist; Adams, Edith, singer; and Adams, Sherman, White House adviser; through Elman, Mischa, violinist; and Lee, Gypsy Rose, striptease artist; to Zorach, William, sculptor. Among its subjects were actors and actresses, Cabinet officers, an African and an Asian prime minister, fashion designers, diplomats and Supreme Court Justices, scientists, university presidents, musical virtuosi, opera stars, prizefighters, a Roman Catholic archbishop, generals and admirals, economists, folk singers, ex-Presidents, men-about-town, athletic coaches, prison wardens, a lighthouse keeper, British peers, eminent counsel, and restaurateurs. Even the dog film star Rin-Tin-Tin was seriously proposed as a subject by Zousmer and Aaron, but Murrow rejected the idea with a note that said, "Lassie might ask for equal time, and some of our other guests might suffer by comparison." However a one-thousand-pound prize steer did share the honors with one *Person-to-Person* guest, the millionaire "farmer" Cyrus Easton.

In the face of criticism that their guest list was too heavily weighted — or as some said, too light-weighted — on the show business side, the producers offered a breakdown showing a virtually fifty-fifty division between entertainment personalities and others. Still, the show business impression remained, and with reason. When the 1955–1956 season ended, for instance, Murrow suggested that in the next season he would like to have on the program people he felt he could talk more comfortably with, and to some point.

He listed Margaret Mead, the anthropologist; John Hersey and John Steinbeck, the novelists; David Cohn, essayist, and David Lawrence, columnist and publisher; Sam Rayburn and Joe Martin, the rival party leaders in the House of Representatives; Ben Shahn, the painter, and Burris Jenkins, the political cartoonist; Shirley Booth, the actress; Tom Dewey, twice presidential candidate; and Dr. Karl T. Compton, of MIT, and Robert Hutchins, of the University of Chicago.

Murrow proposed, but Zousmer and Aaron disposed. None of the people he wanted appeared that year, or ever, on *Person-to-Person*. The new season's guest list instead included such more "popular" figures as Faith Baldwin and Mary Roberts Rinehart, novelists; Constance Bennett, Bette Davis and Anita Ekberg, actresses; Blackstone, the magician, and Cantor, the comedian; Cugat, the band leader, and Tennessee Ernie Ford, the "country and Western" singer; Ralph Edwards, television game master, and the royal Windsors.

Murrow kept *Person-to-Person* apart from *See It Now*, and his interviews on the one were of considerably less substance than those on the other. But one *See It Now* appearance could easily have been shown on *Person-to-Person* without anyone being able to tell the difference, as Murrow interviewed Secretary of State Dulles at his Virginia home, instead of his Foggy Bottom office, and chatted with him and Mrs. Dulles in nonpolitical vein.

The Secretary's hobby, and it gave him great pleasure, he said, was polishing their copper cooking utensils, and he proceeded to do so on camera. This so unnerved the sponsors, who made aluminum cooking utensils, that they filed a formal protest note with Murrow, and he forwarded it to its proper diplomatic address. An accommodation was arrived at. The Secretary explained that he had spoken without an aide-mémoire, but now wished to make a more considered written protocol.

His praise of copper on an aluminum company program "must at least have served the purpose of proving to your audience that these interviews are unrehearsed," he made amende honorable. The sponsors sought to revise the status quo by sending the Dulleses a complete set of their ware, but the Secretary doubted, in the note which closed the intermetallic incident, that they would be able to "wean me away from my use of copper."

Normally *See It Now* was somewhat more relevant. And after two years of looking at the "little picture" around the world, it recognized that a large mural labeled McCarthyism had been painted, and was being exhibited in Washington. It had presented earlier reports of the Wisconsin Senator's activities, such as his hearings on the Voice of America, but the full-length broadcast devoted to the case of Lieutenant Milo Radulovich was a burning-of-the-bridges marking its full entry into the controversy.

The Radulovich story was followed by a pair of Murrow interviews on *See It Now*, one with General George Marshall when the latter received the Nobel Peace Prize; the other with former President Truman, who declared that "the person" impugning Marshall's loyalty, namely McCarthy, was "not fit to shine the general's shoes." Murrow said he agreed with Truman's appraisal.

Succeeding *See It Now* programs delved into the dispute over the loyalty of the former Assistant Secretary of the Treasury, Harry Dexter White; the altercation between the American Legion and the American Civil Liberties Union in Indianapolis, and then undertook the broadside against McCarthy himself, in what has sometimes been called the single "most important" television broadcast seen in this country.

After the Murrow-McCarthy clash of arms, *See It Now* cameras focused on other congressional investigators of the McCarthy stripe and presented a Catholic prelate's views on the subject. "In this day and age,

Between "takes" of a television "conversation" with former President Truman.
BELOW: *with Janet Murrow*

anticommunism is sometimes the scoundrel's first defense," declared Auxiliary Bishop Sheil of Chicago.

It also showed an entire program devoted to the Fifth Amendment, and reported California elections in which a State Un-American Activities Committee was the principal issue.

During the sequence of events leading up to the climax with McCarthy, Murrow also made his third trip to Korea, now in a condition of armed truce, and for Christmas spoke from "a hole in the ground surrounded by sandbags."

However controversial his anti-McCarthy stand was, as indicated by the many denunciatory letters received from McCarthy supporters, it was not the Senator from Wisconsin but the Senator from Ohio who made Murrow the principal object of displeasure from CBS, and indeed the entire broadcasting industry. Unlike McCarthy, John Bricker of Ohio, ranking Republican on the Senate Interstate Commerce Committee, held real legislative power in Washington, which could affect the Federal regulations governing radio and television, and even lead to an investigation of network practices.

Bricker, the Republican vice presidential candidate with Dewey in 1944, was sponsoring a proposed amendment to the Constitution, to diminish the presidential treaty-making power. His immediate target was the United Nations covenants the United States had entered upon, with respect to human rights, labor relations and similar social matters. His objection was that these had become the law of the land, under the Constitution, despite any domestic statutes or usages to the contrary. He proposed that such treaties and executive agreements be approved not only by both Houses of Congress, but also by the State legislatures.

See It Now's program on the Bricker Amendment, shown two months before the McCarthy broadcast, pitted Democratic Senator Estes Kefauver of Tennessee against the Ohio Republican.

On the program, moreover, the dean of the Harvard Law School, Erwin N. Griswold, called the proposed amendment "an attack upon the Union itself," and said it would make the President "a figurehead instead of the spearhead of our foreign policy." Former Supreme Court Justice Owen Roberts described it as a dangerous proposal, violating the principle of separation of powers, and cited the Constitution's specific barrier against treaty-making by the states.

Bricker also had legal counsel on the program, a law professor from Georgetown University, and Murrow took no side in the matter, calling merely for more public argument about the Bricker Amendment, "so there will be no regret, whatever the outcome."

Merely to publicize the amendment, however, was a Murrow-Friendly way of taking issue with it. The Senator from Ohio felt that the program was indeed hostile, and his supporters, with stopwatches in hand, pointed out that it had given eleven minutes two seconds to the antiamendment view, and only eight minutes fifty-three seconds to the movers of the amendment.

Bricker had already dictated the choice of his debating opponent on the program, rejecting *See It Now*'s original selection of Senator Hubert H. Humphrey of Minnesota. Murrow and Friendly ordinarily repelled any such attempts to decide who would appear on their broadcasts, but Bricker refused outright to appear with Humphrey. Since Kefauver was also a leading opponent of the amendment, Humphrey was dropped in order to get Bricker himself. Neither Senator was told that their debate would take up the entire half-hour, but that was their obvious expectation, and both were clearly annoyed that other voices were added.

Bricker's unhappiness was also CBS's corporate unhappiness. Particularly perturbed was Frank Stanton, who as the CBS public spokesman and its leading witness at Washington hearings was concerned, perhaps overconcerned, with Federal legislation and congressional relations.

See It Now's stirring of the Bricker Amendment affair led to the first major disaffection between the network and its leading broadcaster, the censorship of Murrow's Korean criticisms having come to be regarded as a mere misunderstanding, and "only on radio." To other members of the CBS board of directors Murrow's brush with Bricker apparently signified his unawareness of the really serious problems of broadcasting, such as congressional scrutiny. Murrow's formula for handling Congress: "Stand up to 'em and tell 'em to go to hell," was regarded as too simplistic. The licensing of radio and television stations was, after all, under Government control, and theoretically at least could be revoked. When it was suggested that such matters as the equal-time doctrine and censorship attempts by Congress or the FCC be tested in the courts, the broadcasting industry's leaders would reply that court decisions could be unfavorable, as well as favorable.

Two weeks after the first one, *See It Now* fought another round with the Bricker Amendment, and this time the Ohioan and another legislator spoke for it, with only one opponent, John W. Davis, the constitutional lawyer. Bricker supporters looked at their stopwatches again and reported that even so, taking both programs together, they had received fourteen minutes fifty-nine seconds of air time and their foes fifteen minutes fourteen seconds.

Then Bricker, justifying the fears of the networks, introduced a bill which would impose FCC regulation directly upon the networks as such, instead of limiting it to the individual stations. The man who believed in states' rights over treaties may have had a principle in mind as he advocated more Federal control over broadcasting, but it was generally assumed that he was venting his spleen on Murrow and CBS, blaming them for the fact that his amendment was defeated, by one vote, in the Senate.

Further to illuminate Bricker's apparent intentions, the FCC was regarded as pro-McCarthy, in the context of the times. The appointment of one of its members had been credited to the Wisconsin Senator, and the commission had just proposed loyalty oaths for all radio operators, amateur as well as commercial, a step which the communication trades union opposed as "paranoic hysteria." It had also refused to renew the broadcasting license of Edward O. Lamb, with stations in Toledo, Ohio, and Orlando, Florida, because of "left-wing associations" which put his loyalty "in doubt." It would take Lamb three years to clear himself and win relicensing. But the FCC had never refused to relicense any station which failed to live up to its pledge of public service. And there were many.

Four months after the Bricker encounter, *See It Now* was in hot water again.

Murrow and Friendly had presented a program on amphibious warfare, showing naval and Marine training exercises on the South Carolina coast. "A loyal American," as he signed himself, a former Naval Reserve information officer, wrote to the Secretary of Defense — with copies to the President, Secretary of the Treasury, the two New York Senators, FBI Director J. Edgar Hoover, and CBS Chairman Paley — protesting the program as "further evidence . . . of continuing leftist tendencies, if not egregious treasonable action." American landing tactics had been shown, with specifications of the craft used, and close-ups of new rockets. "What perfect training film the Red Army will now have," wrote the loyal American.

Murrow replied that of course every foot of the film had been screened by the Pentagon for security, and every word checked. He enclosed copies of letters of commendation from the Navy's top brass. The writer replied that he had meant well and that his reaction was "a very natural and necessary defense mechanism." It was certainly a sign of the times.

Whatever discomfort Murrow and *See It Now* might be bringing the network, as a result of the successive controversies in which they involved it, no public hint was given of anything amiss. Once more Murrow and the program won the leading broadcasting awards, and when Bill Paley was also honored for outstanding service by the National Association of Broadcasters, he summoned the industry to shoulder its full responsibilities in news and public affairs. "Our own timidity in the vital areas of public information is self-perpetuating," he said. "It breeds pressures, which in turn breed further timidity."

Murrow was engaged with McCarthyism that spring not only as a reporter but also as a witness, testifying for a radio actor who had been listed in *Red Channels* and had filed a $150,000 libel suit. Though many leading broadcasting figures appeared in his behalf, the suit failed. The jury evidently decided that a man who could command such important friends had not really been damaged by blacklisting, even if he had lost his job.

McCarthyism was even more closely brought home to Murrow by the suicide of his friend Don Hollenbeck, after incessant attack by the Hearst columnist Jack O'Brian. The hounding went on even beyond death. The following day O'Brian wrote: "Suicide does not remove from the record the peculiar history of leftist slanting of news indulged consistently by CBS. Hollenbeck was typical of CBS newsmen. He hewed to its incipient pink line without deviation." Murrow was one of the honorary pallbearers at Hollenbeck's funeral.

After the bout with McCarthy, Murrow was also made the victim of an entire issue of *Counter-Attack*, the weekly blacklist bulletin put out by *Red Channels*. It declared he had received "too much praise" from the "Communist press," condemned all his programs about civil rights, and found him guilty of "unsoundness on vital issues concerning Communism."

See It Now was singled out for this kind of scourging not only because it did and said the things it did, but also because it was the only television program to do so. The other networks had not yet dared, or did not care, to emulate it. Its weekly impact was the more pronounced by the stodginess, scantiness and above all the conformity of daily television news programs. These were still newsreels to a large extent. Newscasts, short and studio-bound, steered clear of interpretation, or even explanation, of news events. Not until 1955, at the Big Four meeting which produced the "spirit of Geneva," was overseas reporting on film successfully achieved, by the integration of scene, correspondent, story and meaning. Not until 1963, or twelve years after *See It Now* began, were CBS network daily news programs increased from fifteen minutes to a half-hour, followed by NBC.

As the daily newscasts became longer and more perceptive, some of the reasons for a weekly program like *See It Now* were removed, at least in the minds of television management.

For even *See It Now*'s regular examination of American problems and policies, and the medium's power for public information and even political influence, had of course remained incidental — perhaps accidental — to the true interests of the broadcasting industry. They lay in attracting ever larger audiences to ever more entertainment, to the tune of ever louder commercial advertising.

In the authentic, that is to say the fiscal, history of television, 1954 was not the Year of McCarthy but the Year of the Quiz Show. One by one, such programs had begun to crowd the broadcasting schedules of all the networks. They included *I've Got a Secret, Stop the Music, Place the Face, Name That Tune,* and *What's My Line?* Over the hill, under the rainbow, waited the real "money programs," *Twenty-One* and *The $64,000 Question.*

Marching to the sound of a different drummer, Murrow had meanwhile received the annual Freedom House Award with the citation: "Free men were heartened by his courage in exposing those who would divide us by exploiting our fears."

He won the award after first having been passed over because he was "identified with one viewpoint," and the recipient originally chosen was the West German Chancellor, Konrad Adenauer. Murrow's partisans at a Freedom House board meeting pointed out that Adenauer was even more strongly identified with "one viewpoint," and not necessarily a valid one in terms of Europe as a whole. Elmer Davis was then nominated, but he was regarded as "too indiscriminate" in his attacks on congressional investigations. Murrow, presumably regarded as less "indiscriminate," was then voted the award, and he accepted it in words that Elmer Davis must have relished.

"There is a false formula for personal security being peddled in our marketplace. It is this, although not so labeled: Don't join anything. Don't associate. Don't write. Don't take a chance on being wrong. Don't espouse unpopular causes. Button your lip and drift with the tide. Seek the ease and luxury of complete equanimity, by refusing to make up your minds about issues that wiser heads will one day decide.

"This product, if it be bought by enough people, leads to paralysis."

At a memorial service for Edward Klauber, the pioneer of radio news and the man who had sent him to Europe seventeen years before, Murrow supplemented his Freedom House remarks, as he paid tribute to one who had influenced him. "I do not know whether he believed in the essential goodness or badness of man. But I do know that he believed passionately that the communication of information, unslanted, untarnished and un-distorted, was the only means by which mankind would progress.

"He knew that just because injustice, indignity, and inhumanity was not happening to him — he knew that it was still happening." The epitaph was not Ed Klauber's alone.

Presumably Murrow regarded as injustice and indignity what had be-fallen J. Robert Oppenheimer, the brilliant physicist who directed the Los Alamos nuclear laboratories during the war. Oppenheimer had been de-prived of his security clearance on grounds of "Communist association" in the Thirties, but it was also implied that he had opposed the H-Bomb for "other than scientific reasons." His position had been that further appraisal of the American position in the world, particularly vis-à-vis the Soviet Union, should be made before any such momentous acceleration of American armed might.

When Joe McCarthy appeared on *See It Now* to answer Murrow, he charged that treachery lay behind the alleged delay in the H-bomb program, and the following week secret hearings in the Oppenheimer case began, as the scientist fought suspension. These resulted in the unanimous finding that he was both "loyal" and "discreet," but the special panel voted two-to-one to uphold the suspension. Reinstatement, it said, would be "inconsistent" with the "security interests of the United States."

Millions of Americans never knew the difference between a "security risk" and a "loyalty risk," if indeed there was intended to be a difference, so a cloud still hung over J. Robert Oppenheimer as 1954 ended and Murrow traveled to the Institute for Advanced Study at Princeton, where Oppenheimer had become the director. *See It Now* planned a program on the institute, the most celebrated of the American "think tanks," where important, if sometimes abstruse, things were being done to extend the frontiers of knowledge.

The *See It Now* cameras spent several days among the learned, at Princeton. Albert Einstein refused to be interviewed, even by Murrow, whom he had congratulated on the McCarthy broadcast. Murrow's conversation with Niels Bohr, the Danish physicist, emerged on film as completely unintelligible. Not only was there a problem of language and accent, but the content of Bohr's remarks was beyond the scope of any layman, indeed of many other scientists.

"Up there you find a Nobel Prize winner every time you open a door," Murrow recalled. "Most of them I was unable to understand, and I was becoming very discouraged when I went in and sat down with Professor Oppenheimer."

For two-and-a-half hours Oppenheimer stood before the blackboard talking, and his ability to generate and propel ideas — which had before Los Alamos made him one of the great teachers of his generation — was fully apparent. Murrow decided that the *See It Now* program about the institute would consist entirely of this conversation. But it had to be edited down to half-hour length, or more precisely twenty-five minutes, to allow for the commercials.

The editing of a discourse which combined passion with scientific detachment was a monumental task, done in stages which removed ten- and twenty-minute precious chunks of it at a time, with the last cut, from fifty minutes to twenty-five, being the most painful. Equally monumental was the objection of Oppenheimer to a program entirely devoted to himself, instead of the institute and its sensitive assortment of savants. An Oppenheimer half-hour instead of an institute half-hour, he feared, would create the greatest embarrassment in those parts since Washington's crossing of the Delaware. Innumerable telephone calls from Oppenheimer, and dialogues with lawyers and other intermediaries, accompanied Friendly's editing.

Since Oppenheimer himself objected to the program, the network and the sponsors would also assuredly feel better without it, the more so because the physicist was still regarded as "controversial," and some viewers might feel offended by seeing him on the screen at all. Murrow and Friendly could easily have forgotten the whole thing, and substituted another program.

But Murrow felt that it had to be shown, not only in justice to Oppenheimer as a teacher and human being, but for its own values, as a thought-provoking contribution of the kind that television had too few of. He cut short Oppenheimer's protests with the blunt announcement that it would be shown. The scientist who had explained the quantum theory so that even Friendly understood it need not be expected to know the difference between a superb and a humdrum television program.

One who did know the difference was the CBS chairman. Mr. Paley saw it the morning before it went on the air, and was so enthusiastic as to propose, rather impractically, that it be allowed to run past the sacred "station break" instead of losing a final two minutes. But once again CBS had refused to advertise the program, and again Murrow and Friendly had to pay out $1500 of their own money for that purpose.

The broadcast did not discuss the Oppenheimer "case" as such. It did not have to.

After describing some of the work done at the institute — where the scholars "can't run away" from their creative work "to attend to other people's business," since "most people depend on being interrupted to live" — Oppenheimer spoke of the relations between scientists and government. He criticized the Government's demand for applied, as against theoretical, science.

"When the Government behaves badly in a field you are working close to, and when decisions that look cowardly, or vindictive, or shortsighted, or mean, are made, and that's very close to your area, you get discouraged and you may recite George Herbert's poem, 'I Will Abroad.' But I think that's human, rather than scientific."

The physicist spoke about the "security" thought to be provided by the McCarran Act against "Communist ideas" from abroad, by means of strict immigration rules.

"This is just terrible, and seems a wholly fantastic and grotesque way to meet the threat of espionage; just an enormous apparatus, surely not well designed for that, and terrible for those of us who live with it.

"We are rightly shamed by the contempt that the Europeans have for us, and we are rightly embarrassed that we can't hold [scientific] congresses in this country — that we often don't let people go to congresses who are the most wanted. Year after year, we've met in Rochester to discuss basic physics . . . There is one man who is the world's greatest in this, and very, very good. Ah, well, he sends his deputies and his representatives, and so on, but he doesn't come. And that's not one situation; it's over and over again. This is a scandal."

Oppenheimer lifted what he called the voice of his profession, on behalf of "the integrity of communication."

"The trouble with secrecy isn't that it inhibits science," or "that it doesn't give the public a sense of participation. The trouble with secrecy is that it denies to the Government itself the wisdom and the resources of the whole community, of the whole country. And the only way you can do this is to let almost anyone say what he thinks — to try to give the best synopses, the best popularizations, the best mediations of technical things that you can, and to let men deny what they think is false, argue what they think is false.

"You have to have a free and uncorrupted communication. And this is so the heart of living in a complicated technological world, it is so the heart of freedom, that that is why we are all the time saying, 'Does this really have to be secret?' 'Couldn't you say more about that?' 'Are we really acting in a wise way?' Not because we enjoy chattering, not because we are not aware of the dangers of the world we live in, but because these dangers cannot be met in any other way."

Murrow drew a deep breath. "Well, if I may say so, I think you were speaking there not only for your profession but for mine — if it is a profession."

Oppenheimer would be vindicated, after a fashion. In 1962 he was invited by President Kennedy to a White House dinner for Nobel Prize winners. In 1963 President Johnson presented him with the fifty-thousand-dollar Fermi Award.

But on the night of January 4, 1955, he was still "controversial," indeed to many "that traitor." And Murrow, as he had been the man who "attacked" McCarthy, had now become the man who "defended" Oppenheimer. At a dinner in Louisville, after the Oppenheimer program, at the annual Junior Chamber of Commerce ceremony to honor the year's "ten outstanding young men," one of them walked out as Murrow, the principal speaker, rose. He was Robert F. Kennedy, who had served as counsel for several months to the senatorial committee of a family friend, Joe McCarthy. Indeed, McCarthy had been expected by Murrow to replace Roy Cohn with Kennedy, and to bring the broadcaster before his committee after the Army hearings. But the discredit those hearings brought upon him apparently ended that idea. In any case, if Kennedy had waited that night at Louisville, he would have heard Murrow say a few more words about McCarthyism. Some years later, when Murrow entered the Kennedy administration, the feelings of the Attorney-General, as Robert Kennedy became, toward the broadcaster were entirely different, cordial and appreciative. But some say he was a different "Bobby" Kennedy by then.

Variety found that in the Oppenheimer program "pertinent facts were presented of great value to people in search of the truth, and a service was rendered by TV in permitting the truth to be heard." *See It Now*, it said, "exemplifies democracy at work."

But the program also caused right-wing groups to intensify their public campaign against CBS, calling it "the Red network" again, and they strongly protested a longer version of the interview, forty-eight minutes instead of twenty-five, which Murrow and Friendly distributed to universities clamoring for it. The corporation remained silent, with bowed head, before the attacks.

Murrow was intensely discouraged by the virulence and extent of the criticism, and perhaps more by CBS's submission to it. It was then that he brooded over the "great power but no responsibility" of the networks, as he talked with David Lilienthal at Pawling.

It had snowed when Lilienthal came up, and as they walked through the rugged glen that gave the farm its name, Ed identified the various marks on the white surface — the trailing tail of a pheasant, the claw marks of a raccoon, a rabbit in a hurry, a deer. The outdoors lifted his spirits momentarily.

But back in the house he talked bitterly, not only of the McCarthy program, which he felt CBS should have undertaken as a deliberate and positive editorial decision, but also of the denigration of Oppenheimer, with whom Lilienthal had been closely associated and whose views about the H-bomb he had essentially shared.

Murrow's pessimism was dark, but not exaggerated, as a personal experience soon confirmed. *See It Now* had continued to venture into the civil liberties minefield after the Oppenheimer program, and another of its vivid reports was on "book-burning" in California, where local patriots were trying to purge high-school libraries of books they considered "un-American."

On the day this broadcast was made, Murrow had called at the United States Passport Agency in New York, where he had left his passport for renewal. He was told he would have to sign a non-Communist affidavit before receiving it. He asked whether this was a new procedure for all passports, and was told it was not. Nor was it intended only for journalists going abroad. Nor could any regulation be cited for the action. It was "administrative procedure," he was told.

Murrow refused to sign the affidavit, wrote to the Passport Division's director in Washington, Mrs. Ruth Shipley, and was informed that the State Department had requested the affidavit because of "certain derogatory information" it had received. The department, under John Foster Dulles, and especially its Passport Division, under Mrs. Shipley, had adopted a policy of nonresistance to McCarthy. In fact one of the Senator's men, Scott McLeod, was the department's security officer.

Murrow had to see the thing through. He flew to Washington, and although Mrs. Shipley refused to be bearded in her den, he was granted an audience by the assistant passport director. But it could not be called satisfactory. The official refused to reveal the nature of the "derogatory information" that had been received, which meant there was no way for Murrow to challenge it. He admitted that the information, like all FBI material, was "raw," or unevaluated, and contained anonymous accusations without proof. The State Department man, under prodding, finally acknowledged that a principal source was *Counter-Attack,* the blacklist sheet that had devoted an entire issue to Murrow and CBS after the McCarthy broadcast.

Murrow asked whether his file also included "affirmative" information, such as his clearance and accreditation by the Defense Department as a correspondent, the many letters of commendation he and his program had received from the armed services; and his designation by the Federal Government to broadcast news over the emergency channels in the event of an enemy attack.

The passport official seemed surprised. The file did not contain such information, but he would be glad to add it, he said. Murrow remarked that the man asked no questions himself, but appeared content to rest on the "derogatory" nature of the dossier. He did explain, however, that if there had been any "real doubt" of Murrow's loyalty, a passport would have been refused outright, instead of being made subject to the signing of an affidavit.

The broadcaster said he had wanted to be sure there was no alternative to signing. The next morning he sent an affidavit to the State Department with the stipulation that it was not in recognition of the validity or accuracy of the "derogatory information." He offered to answer all questions, privately or publicly, about his activities and associations. No such request came, though the passport did.

Murrow had always been critical of travel restrictions imposed by the State Department for political reasons, and his own case, by no means a rarity in the McCarthy-McCarran days, had much to do with his later support of journalists who encountered passport trouble and faced prosecution for going to Communist China.

The pressures applied to Murrow and to CBS because of *See It Now*'s provocativeness also extended to the program's sponsors, and the Oppenheimer broadcast and another one some weeks later apparently decided a question which had been growing in ALCOA's mind. The 1954–1955 season became the last one for *See It Now* as a weekly program under regular sponsorship.

The other program had to do with a small Texas newspaper which had won the Pulitzer Prize for exposing a land scandal. Instead of being pleased by the prize, state officials were outraged by what they regarded as an aspersion on the fair name of Texas. The aluminum company was in the process of increasing its installations in the Lone Star State, and they made their feelings known directly to it.

So ALCOA decided it now wanted "to sell pots and pans," instead of engaging in institutional advertising, which it considered national television to be. It announced it was dropping *See It Now*, after four turbulent years.

Instead of seeking another sponsor, CBS dealt the program the additional blow of ending it as a regular weekly half-hour. It would be replaced by "six or more" hour-long documentaries during the following year, but on no fixed schedule. Madison Avenue dubbed the program *See It Now and Then*.

The bad news shook the *See It Now* unit, but failed to lessen its purpose or zeal. Murrow and Friendly simply went ahead with their current plans, and these included two programs on cigarettes and cancer — controversial and highly sensitive to network television, because of the heavy tobacco advertising on which it depended — a program on immigration, as influenced by the anti-Communist McCarran Act; and another on subscription television, also a painful subject to the commercial networks.

Nearly nine years before the Surgeon General's Report, which would say cigarette-smoking is the major cause of lung cancer, *See It Now* was the first television program to discuss the matter. It was contentious not only because the tobacco industry challenged any causative connection as unproved, but because cigarette advertising figured so prominently in the evening programs of all the networks, providing major revenue.

See It Now drew no conclusions. In two successive programs, it presented the cigarette-cancer argument pro and con, from medical authorities. Murrow himself was inclined to the "not proven" viewpoint, and believed other environmental factors were also involved. On the programs he said there was "a wide area of ignorance" about the subject, but also a determination to acquire knowledge, "the only ground upon which opinion and action can be based."

But Arthur Morse, the field producer, who had been assigned by Murrow merely "to see if there's a story there" and decided there was, believed

that at the end of the two half-hours a question about the effects of smoking had been raised in the minds of millions who had never thought of it
before. It was another typical example of the Murrow method.

At any rate, *See It Now* was hailed for outstanding public service in
broaching the matter at all, and breaking a notable taboo.

The two programs showed Murrow, for the first time since he had gone
on television, without a cigarette between his fingers. Scores of letters
were received asking if he had given up smoking because of what he had
learned about it. Actually, he was either puffing away as usual, or between cigarettes, and it was only by coincidence that the camera angles
did not show it. Whatever the truth about the effects of the habit, he always said that it had become "too late" for him to stop smoking.

See It Now would continue, on its irregular schedule, with other memorable programs — two on Africa, forecasting "the winds of change" from
Cairo to Capetown; several on the Middle East and the Suez crisis, with
Murrow flying to Israel; others on automation, the farm problem, neutralism in the uncommitted world, Communist Poland, and Murrow's two
milestone interviews with Chinese Premier Chou En-lai and President Tito
of Yugoslavia.

But something had distinctly gone out of the Murrow-CBS relationship.
Not only had television's most honored program, the only one of its
kind, been in a sense sloughed off, but the reasons for it were indicative
of what was happening to broadcasting in general.

See It Now had been the answer to radio's swifter news facilities by
providing perspective as well as pictures.

But commercialism was making larger demands than ever upon both
media, and effecting change. More and more frequently, news broadcasters
were being compelled to read commercials also, and the Association of
Radio News Analysts voted that any member who did commercials had
to resign.

Because the mushrooming growth of television had created wider and
wider audiences, advertising revenue, which is based on the ratings, also
increased enormously. Commercial time cost more, commercials themselves became more elaborate and more expensive, and sponsorship of
entire programs was a formidable financial undertaking for even large corporations. Much more money had become involved in making television
programs, and the desire of sponsors to avoid "controversy" and merely
sell goods was increasingly appreciated by the networks.

The inevitable result, reflecting the nature of both an affluent and an
acquisitive society, was the quiz show. It would dominate broadcasting
for four years until, by corruption, it almost brought the walls of the
television temple down about its ears.

Several such programs had made their appearance in 1954, but in the spring of 1955 a broadcasting impresario, Louis G. Cowan, who had devised the popular radio program *Quiz Kids*, also acquired a radio program called *Take It or Leave It*. On it, the term "the sixty-four-dollar question" originated, that being the top prize paid for a series of correct answers. For television, which had its own inflated currency, Cowan raised the prize from sixty-four dollars to sixty-four thousand dollars, cumulative over a period of four weeks. The idea immediately attracted "big money" sponsorship.

On the same evening that *See It Now* presented the second of its cigarettes-and-cancer programs, in fact just preceding it, *The $64,000 Question* made its debut on CBS, with a learned professor of English to select the questions, a strongbox to guard them, a bank vice president to vouch for their inviolability, and an "isolation booth" for contestants trying to answer them.

Besides, of course, the program gave away free more money than ever before on television.

On the first evening a New Jersey housewife answered seven questions about Hollywood movies but failed on the eighth. She was awarded a Cadillac convertible as "consolation." A Staten Island policeman, successfully answering questions on Shakespeare, won eight thousand dollars and was held over for the following week, in the progression toward the sixty-four-thousand-dollar jackpot. The *New York Times* called the proceedings "outlandish."

Murrow, watching the dawn of a new era on his control-room monitor, was horrified by what he saw. The president of CBS, Frank Stanton, said of the new quiz show and the others to follow it: "A program in which a large part of the audience is interested is by that very fact . . . in the public interest."

X

"Evidence of decadence, escapism and insulation"

See It Now, in its final regularly scheduled season 1954–1955, had presented forty-four half-hour programs which not only opened windows
on the world, but blew in through them the strong winds of pertinence
and controversy. As against these twenty-two hours of air time, *See It Now
and Then*, as it was jocosely called, in 1955–1956 presented five one-hour
programs and two of ninety minutes each, for only eight hours of air
time. It was a 60 percent reduction in visibility.

Apart from sponsorship uncertainty, *See It Now* was suffering from
the waning attention of a television audience that was steadily becoming
larger and broader-based, and that the broadcasting industry therefore
fed entertainment fare on progressively lower levels. As summed up by
Variety, although some new writing talent had made its appearance, like
Chayefsky and Serling, the 1954–1955 season would be remembered primarily for the appearance of Mary Martin as Peter Pan, for the television
debut of Disneyland, for the new commercial formats offered by early-
morning and late-night "magazine" programs, and for the advertising El
Dorado of "rotating sponsorship." What this latter meant was that so
costly had program-making and sponsorship become that the networks had
begun a scheme of sponsor-sharing. This entailed the fragmentation of
commercial time and added to the strident hard-sell atmosphere of the
medium.

Murrow had flown to London for the British elections, which continued
the Conservatives in power with an increased majority, but also marked
the retirement of their colorful but visibly aging leader. Winston Churchill's eightieth birthday had been not only a parliamentary but virtually a
state occasion, rivaling that of the Duke of Wellington a century before.

Murrow saw Churchill as usual and reported that, as usual, he had
"cried easily." But worshipful sentiment was not the only reason for the
meeting. He wanted the old warrior for a CBS television interview, and had

Interviewing Pandit Nehru in London, 1955

been authorized by Bill Paley to offer him one hundred thousand dollars. Knowing his man, he proposed the idea as "a service to the English-speaking peoples," and urged it upon him in the name of history. "Consider the instruction and inspiration that might be drawn from similar visual documents of Lincoln, Pitt and Hadrian if such documents existed," he urged the departing Prime Minister.

But Churchill knew that the time for interviewing him was now past. He was suffering from what Lord Moran, his physician, described as "advancing decrepitude." He was satisfied to let history judge him by the dramatic past, and as a practicing historian himself, he knew that the verdict had already been returned. He was also more interested in selling his own works than in engaging in other people's enterprises, no matter how well-paid, and he told Murrow that he had already made "certain arrangements" with the British film producer Sir Alexander Korda. Apparently these were to make a movie, improbable as it might seem, of Churchill's new and final book, *A History of the English-speaking Peoples.*

Whatever the arrangements, they bore no fruit, and three years later Churchill would turn to Murrow for help in getting his history to the screen. Murrow canvased the situation with his friend Sam Goldwyn, and was told there was no interest in the idea. He let the old gentleman down gently. Those in Hollywood, he wrote, "seem to feel that they lack either the skill or the financial resources to turn it into a movie."

Eventually Churchill allowed the BBC and NBC to produce a television series based on his wartime memoirs, but it was made up of old film and he did not appear in it as the feeble retired statesman of eighty-five, but the very active "former naval person" who was his nation's inimitable leader.

Murrow and Friendly did put together a record album of Churchill speeches, however, and were amused when he requested that his twenty-five-thousand-dollar honorarium be deposited in the Bank of Monte Carlo for him.

The contributions of 1955 to history included not only Churchill's retirement in favor of Anthony Eden, but increasing American involvement in Southeast Asia, and in Europe the emergence of the new Khrushchev leadership of the Soviet Union and its first contact with the West, at the "spirit of Geneva" meeting with Eisenhower and Eden. But on American television these things were overshadowed by the tremendous success of the "big money" quiz programs.

The $64,000 Question, the debut of which had so dismayed Murrow, achieved the countrywide number-one audience rating in only six weeks, a meteoric rise not duplicated since Milton Berle had rocketed to stardom nearly a decade before. Presenting a policeman who quoted Shakespeare, experts on the Bible, a shoemaker who knew all the operas, the program received vast publicity throughout the nation, indeed around the world. The opera-loving cobbler became a public hero in his native Italy.

The program also brought Lou Cowan with it to CBS. He became the network's "director of creative programming." At the same time he remained head of the firm which supplied the program, and retained his 42 percent of its stock. While he was an executive of CBS, his "package" company embarked on another quiz enterprise, *The Big Surprise*, on the rival network NBC, with prizes going even beyond sixty-four thousand dollars and up to one hundred thousand dollars. No one in television saw any conflict of interest in these activities, since both networks benefited impartially, and handsomely, by them.

But NBC was not content with its share and tried to lure *The $64,000 Question* away from CBS, by offering the sponsor an even more favorable air time, and at less cost. Meanwhile the sponsors of other types of programs, suffering from the competition of the quiz shows, applied pressure on the networks through their advertising agencies to produce higher ratings for them also, at whatever cost. In the proverbial jiffy, the quiz programs were shaking the whole structure of television.

Nothing in it was more badly shaken than *See It Now*. Even if ALCOA had continued its sponsorship, or the program had found a regular new sponsor, *See It Now*'s survival as a weekly feature would have been put gravely in doubt by *The $64,000 Question*'s spectacular success. For the soaring ratings created pecuniary problems, as well as joy, for the CBS network. Television programming, whatever contrary impressions it might give, was carefully put together, evening by evening, with the hope of carrying over as large an audience as possible from one time period to the next — broadcasting's own "domino theory" — thus increasing the latter's rating and revenue also.

But the audience which watched *The $64,000 Question* was not the same audience which week after week waited loyally for *See It Now*. And even if some of the viewers of the quiz program stayed tuned to CBS and were carried over to the *See It Now* program — instead of seeking another quiz program on another network — the fact was that the great advertising value of *The $64,000 Question* half-hour had automatically increased the value of the succeeding half-hour to the point where *See It Now* was priced out of the market.

Why should *See It Now* continue to be sold for fifty thousand dollars air time, with its smaller audience, when the same half-hour could command the much larger audience already watching *The $64,000 Question*, and bring in one hundred thousand dollars or more advertising revenue — provided another quiz program replaced *See It Now*? This is what inevitably happened, and CBS presented two "big money" quizzes in succession, both with extremely high ratings.

Despite the disadvantages of irregular scheduling — the loss of its sense of historical continuity, as well as the large reduction in the number of subjects it could explore — the occasional hour-long *See It Now* did give the producers more time to prepare each broadcast, more money with which to work — the individual budgets were now one hundred thousand dollars — and presumably a more considered and less fleeting quality of perceptiveness. Even with a greater interval between programs, they did not lose their faculty for being ahead of the news. The first broadcast of the new season, for example, devoted to the "Great Lottery" of the American vice presidency, had been started months before and was virtually complete when President Eisenhower's heart attack and ileitis gave it the most immediate kind of significance.

Similarly, *See It Now*'s programs on the Middle East and Africa, though months in the making, were most timely when they were shown, for regional crisis, on the one hand, and decolonization on the other were enduring phenomena.

Nor did the new and more meditative programs seek to avoid controversy, thus vexing the network executives who had hoped that, virtually out of sight, *See It Now* would also be out of mind. The first program, on the vice presidency, actually provoked the new sponsor, General Motors, into peremptory cancellation of its contract for the entire year. It took the program as an attack on Vice President Nixon, though he had been consulted on it. But some television reviewers thought that the cancellation had taken place not because of controversy but, to the contrary, because the new *See It Now*, unlike the old, was as one described it "purely objective, informative, factual — but dull." It may be that in the Eisenhower years all public affairs had become a mite dull.

Whatever the reason, that CBS should have agreed to the cancellation of contract without demur was taken by Murrow as corroboration of the extent to which he and *See It Now* had fallen in the company's order of things.

The breach widened further when CBS, without consulting Murrow and Friendly, granted a free half-hour to Secretary of Agriculture Ezra Benson, to reply to a *See It Now* program, *Crisis of Abundance*, about the plight of the small farmer. Benson particularly objected to a sequence showing an Iowa farm auction, and he appeared on the original program to deny that the auction was typical. "Any attempt to persuade the American people that the small farmer is dying in Iowa or anywhere else is a perversion of the truth," he said, "and I think it's demagoguery at its worst."

It would seem rejoinder enough, but having had his say, the Secretary was then given a whole separate program four weeks later to make a frankly political broadcast, in a presidential election year, defending the

Eisenhower administration's farm policy. While not conceding that there was any "crisis of abundance," he acknowledged that his overriding purpose was "to get rid of surpluses."

Murrow and Friendly had flown to Israel two days after the first farm program was shown, and were still there when they got word of the network's decision to yield a second one, which again seemed to them to deny their competence, and even integrity. In Tel Aviv, tired and grimy after a day of filming in the desert, Murrow wrote out a cable to New York, resigning in protest. He was prevailed upon by Friendly not to send it. As it turned out, after giving "equal time" to the Republican administration, to reply to Murrow, CBS had to give more "equal time" to two Democratic Senators to reply to Benson.

After the Secretary's second appearance Murrow "congratulated" him on getting free time from the company for political purposes, but pointed out that he had been unable to dispute *See It Now*'s statistics, since they had all come from his own department. The acrimony of the exchange illustrated the difference between *See It Now* and *Person-to-Person*. Four months earlier Murrow had "visited" the Mormon household of the Bensons "in person," but there was no talk of farm policy, and the broadcast had ended with a rousing hymn-sing in the parlor.

See It Now, without a regular sponsor, went into its fifth year as Murrow also began his ninth consecutive year with his nightly radio news program. But on radio, observed *Variety*, "something seems missing — television." The visual medium had both broadened and deepened Murrow's broadcasting power, but the irony was that just as he had realized the full use of television in public affairs, as previously in radio, his achievement should have been vitiated by the increased commercialism and lowered standards of television.

As for radio, the loss of a great deal of advertising revenue to television had sharpened the commercial competition on what was now definitely the lesser medium. Though less at CBS than elsewhere, the cries of the pitchmen became louder. Advertising was accepted, in fact eagerly solicited, that formerly would not have been touched with a ten-foot antenna. Programs which once had large national sponsors were now sold piecemeal, to individual local sponsors in all the cities in which they were heard. Institutional and "good will" advertising was replaced by commercials for the corner drugstore's one-cent sales.

Huckstering was not allowed to sully the Murrow radio program. It opened the season with a network of 150 stations, 125 of which represented him under his national sponsorship, while twenty-five were on a local or "cooperative" basis.

The trend everywhere else was for more of the latter, but Murrow objected to having his name and program identified with the long list of bathroom products, the commercials for which had made local radio itself as offensive as some of the symptoms described. These products included laxatives, depilatories, deodorants, "articles of feminine hygiene," insecticides, reducing aids and patent medicines. Local radio also specialized in commercials for money lenders, savings and loan associations, nightclubs, and correspondence courses. All these things were struck off by Murrow.

But broadcasting's ailments transcended the crassly commercial. Its most celebrated blacklisting case had begun to unfold, and Murrow took sides in it, for like all who appeared on camera or at microphone, he was a member of the American Federation of Television and Radio Artists.

The cause célèbre was that of John Henry Faulk, a Texas-born humorist and an authentic one. He had for four years been doing what *Variety* termed a "music-and-gab" program on the CBS local radio station in New York, and had branched out into local television on another station. He was a member in good standing of AFTRA, indeed was elected one of its local vice presidents. Suddenly he lost the larger part of his livelihood, because his name had been listed by a professional anti-Communist "research" organization called Aware, Inc. He filed a libel suit, and churned the entire broadcasting world.

Stalin had died and it was obvious that things were different in the Soviet Union — though Khrushchev had not yet made his secret speech denouncing the tyrant and his era — but the "spirit of Geneva" failed to slacken the cold war, and if Joe McCarthy had lost his power, McCarthyism had not lost its grip.

David Sarnoff, head of RCA, had submitted to President Eisenhower a program for "a political offensive against world communism," proposing among other things that the United States "ring the Communist world with fixed and mobile broadcasting facilities," distribute free radio receivers by the millions, and drop cardboard records from the sky, also by the millions, behind the Iron Curtain. By happy circumstance RCA, the parent corporation of NBC, was in the radio-set and phonograph record business.

The long-threatened investigation of radio and television had finally erupted, at the end of the slow fuse which *Red Channels* had started burning five years before. The House Un-American Activities Committee held hearings in New York on charges, reiterated by the Hearst and Scripps-Howard press, that for all the blacklisting in effect, the broadcasting industry was still filled with Communist supporters.

Of twenty-three witnesses called, the first eight flatly refused to answer the committee's questions. Others took refuge in the Fifth Amendment. Only one admitted any Communist affiliation. The broadcasters' union, AFTRA, voted to suspend or expel all who would not "cooperate" with the committee, and since it was necessary to belong to the union in order to broadcast, this meant loss of employment. In short, the union which should have protected its members from blacklisting had itself turned blacklister.

Control of AFTRA was in the hands of those who agreed with *Red Channels* and Aware, Inc. that "Communists" presented a clear and present danger to broadcasting, and the case of Winston Burdett, a veteran CBS overseas correspondent and one of Murrow's wartime staff, further encouraged the anti-Communists. Burdett testified before the Senate Internal Security subcommittee that he had been a "Communist spy" in Finland and Turkey. But he had broken with the Communists in 1942 before he joined CBS, and had told the company and the FBI of his past connection.

Though Burdett had long recanted, the case helped stir up the "Communists in broadcasting" issue more agitatedly. But it also mobilized those opposing the blacklisters within the union. Repudiating the leadership, an AFTRA meeting voted 197 to 149 by secret ballot to condemn Aware, Inc. for its activities. These included receiving payment for "clearing" performers for various programs.

The union leaders demanded a referendum of the entire membership and lost by 982 to 514, thus increasing the extent of their defeat. The result was new elections, and a "middle-of-the-road" leadership was chosen by a large majority, opposing both blacklisting and communism. The new president was one of Murrow's best friends and oldest CBS associates, Charles Collingwood. As he took office he challenged the congressional charges of Communist infiltration, and indeed a member of the House committee itself dared say that broadcasting "clearance" lists had become a financial racket. Elected with Collingwood as a vice president was John Henry Faulk.

Vincent Hartnett, a former FBI agent who had become director of Aware, Inc., and Laurence A. Johnson, a supermarket grocer in Syracuse, New York — who with the backing of a local American Legion post was able to threaten television sponsors with a boycott of their products — soon hit back. Faulk had received the largest vote in the union elections, and Aware, Inc. put out a special bulletin, circulated to the networks, sponsors and agencies, listing cases of "Communist association" by him.

Murrow and Collingwood supported Faulk, and the Texan was still able to broadcast on the network's local New York radio station, WCBS, though he lost all his other employment.

But after a year in office Collingwood ceased being AFTRA president, and Murrow had meanwhile ceased being a CBS director, and Faulk was fired by WCBS as well, and lost all his income. He had filed a three-million-dollar damage suit against Aware, Inc. for libel and conspiracy to defame, but though his case had become the litmus paper of blacklisting in broadcasting, it took six years for it to reach trial. Meanwhile Faulk was supported by contributions from friends. One of them was Murrow.

As the Texan told the tale, he was sitting in his about-to-be-vacated CBS office, painfully aware that he had been able to raise only twenty-five hundred dollars of the ten-thousand-dollar retainer asked by the celebrated trial lawyer Louis Nizer for taking his case. Murrow phoned him from the seventeenth floor to say that he was pleased about the filing of the suit, and to report that their mutual friend Carl Sandburg had told him, "Whatever's the matter with America, Johnny ain't."

Faulk went up to see Murrow and told him he still needed seven thousand dollars. Murrow appeared surprised that the network itself was not paying the trial expenses, remembering how CBS, or at least Bill Paley, had supported him when he was under attack by Joe McCarthy. Faulk explained that the CBS executives were opposed to his suit. Murrow said that Nizer would get the money the next day.

When Faulk protested that he might not be able to repay the money, Murrow told him it was not a personal loan. "I am investing this money in America . . . These people must be brought into court. This blacklisting racket must be exposed. This is a very important suit. I don't know whether even you realize how important it is."

Eventually Faulk would win the case, and with it the largest libel verdict ever recorded, $3.5 million, though this was later reduced to $550,000 by a higher court. The eleven-week trial left no doubt of the widespread blacklisting in radio and television, but by the same token struck a heavy blow at it.

The testimony which held the most painful meaning for Murrow, as he watched the trial closely — though he was by then no longer in broadcasting but had become director of the United States Information Agency — was that of two WCBS executives, one of them a close friend of Faulk's. Instead of testifying to the blacklisting pressure and the boycott threats exerted against broadcasting, as they could very well have done, they appeared for the defense, that is, for the blacklisters. They solemnly asserted that Faulk had not been discharged by CBS for Communist sympathies, but because his audience ratings had decreased. In cross-examination they conceded that what in fact had happened was that the ratings of the CBS station itself had decreased in the highly competitive New York market, and that Faulk's loss was considerably less than the station's own.

But the fundamental question in the Faulk case was not answered by the verdict in 1962 any more than it had been by the union election in 1955. What if Faulk had had Communist sympathies, instead of being anti-Communist? Would blacklisting have been defensible, and the absence of due process?

As 1956 began, Murrow, on a speaking visit to Charlotte, was "appointed" by the president of the Senate of his native state "Ambassador of Good Will Throughout the World for North Carolina." He could not have been much impressed, for North Carolina's writ, indeed CBS's, did not seem to extend to the Soviet Union.

He had applied to the Soviet embassy for visas for himself, Friendly and a two-man camera crew, to film a *See It Now* program called *Main Street, U.S.S.R.*, probing a small Russian city in depth, visiting its schools, newspaper office, factories, local council, sports fields, parks and theaters.

He was not only ahead of the news, but ahead of the times. It would take nearly ten years for such a program to become possible on American television. Then, when the uncertainties caused by Stalin's death were translating themselves into difficulties with the satellite states, as Murrow had foreseen, the Russians rejected North Carolina's good-will ambassador out of hand. Indeed, in all his years of broadcasting and global travel, Murrow never got to Moscow.

If he had any regrets about the rejection, they did not linger long. For 1956 saw the beginning of his love affair with the state of Israel.

Secretary of State Dulles's truculent anti-Communist policy, which regarded neutrality as "immoral," had led to the American mistake of ignoring the first Afro-Asian conference at Bandung the year before. The CBS news department followed the State Department's example, but in a difference of news judgment with it Murrow had sent his friend and collaborator Raymond Swing to Indonesia as his own program's reporter, at considerable cost — another galling instance of his independence.

Then Dulles followed his Bandung mistake with the mistake of pushing Egyptian President Nasser into Soviet hands, by withdrawing American aid from the Aswan Dam. This would lead to Nasser's nationalization of the Suez Canal and the Suez War.

The new Soviet influence in the Arab world helped intensify the hatred for Israel, by which that world is fueled, and Egyptian-Israeli relations were moving to a crisis when at the end of January Murrow and his *See It Now* contingent arrived at their hotel in Jerusalem at 2:30 A.M. Five hours later they were at the Mandelbaum Gate, filming an interview with the United Nations truce chief of staff.

Murrow spent ten days in Israel, while across the Sinai Desert and the Suez Canal, Howard K. Smith was in Egypt with cameras, to tell the other side of the story.

There was as yet no television system in Israel, but the small country had an active radio service, and an alert and tenacious press turned toward the United States, whence came so much of Israel's help. So every Israeli knew of Murrow's interviews with J. Robert Oppenheimer and

The Israeli side of the Suez crisis, 1956. Ben-Gurion in his desert retreat

Murrow and Nasser. The Arab side of the Suez conflict, 1956

Pandit Nehru, of his combat with McCarthy and his programs about the Salk vaccine and apartheid in South Africa. Now they read about him in their own country, and being unwise to the ways of "the little picture" on television, they marveled that at Hebrew University, where new buildings were being erected, he did not interview the president, nor even a learned professor, but talked instead with one of the construction workers, an original settler who had come from Moscow in the Twenties.

From Jerusalem the *See It Now* journey led to a kibbutz at the Gaza frontier, where in a watchtower Murrow spoke with a twenty-year-old guard. He visited Beersheba and a settlement of Kurdistani Jews, the potash works on the Dead Sea, and in the desert retreat at Sde Bokar, he had frank and full conversation with the Israeli leader, David Ben-Gurion. On the Egyptian side, meanwhile, Howard Smith was similarly engaged with Gamal Abdel Nasser.

Typical of Murrow's way of work was his nighttime report from a fishermen's collective on the Sea of Galilee. It would be sufficient, thought the Israelis, to do the filming aboard a fishing vessel anchored a few yards off the jetty, with cables from the shore supplying the necessary strong lights, and without vibrations from the engines to trouble the cameras.

But that, said Murrow, when he saw the Israeli plan, "wouldn't be kosher." So the *See It Now* company, bag, baggage and floodlights, moved two miles out into the choppy lake in a police launch, took its power from a portable generator, tossed about on the high waves, and seasick itself, nearly brought the fishing party to grief in a maze of tangled nets.

The enterprise was a hazardous one, but it did establish authenticity.

At the Syrian border the *See It Now* crew was involved in an international incident of a kind which had become routine in Israel. Murrow and the cameras were at Haifa, ready to leave for home, when he heard that Arab infiltrators had crossed the border and taken 312 sheep from the kibbutz Dan, in the northeast corner of the country. If the Israelis had entered Syria to retrieve their property they would undoubtedly have been condemned by the United Nations Truce Commission, though the original Arab raid was not condemned.

See It Now, having made the biblical span of Israel from Beersheba to Dan, reported the sheep-stealing incident at the border as another actuality of Jewish life, and left for home. Three days later in New York Murrow received a congratulatory message from Moishe Pearlman, the former British army major who had become the prime minister's aide and had served as the *See It Now* guide. Most of the sheep had been returned. It was thought the Syrians had become alarmed by the cameras on their border, with telephoto lens, and believed that evidence of their rustling had somehow been provided.

Wherever he went in Israel, Murrow had been hailed as a friend, and the warmth of the greeting, the biblical setting, and the spectacle of a small nation subsisting on courage against great odds — it may have reminded him of wartime Britain — made him a friend.

Even before he visited the tiny country, there was no doubt where his sympathies lay. Once he told David Lilienthal that if he were prime minister, he would have moved on Egypt, taken Cairo, and negotiated a settlement from there.

But there were two sides to the *See It Now* story. When Murrow saw the film Howard Smith had taken in Egypt, he wired him that it was "the most effective presentation of the Egyptian case ever shown in this country. And," he added ruefully, "I don't have to tell you what that will mean in terms of criticism here."

He was not wrong. *See It Now*'s "introspectacular" produced a violent reaction from Zionist groups in the United States, who objected to stating the Egyptian case at all, and who subjected the network to running criticism. The State Department also expressed apprehension that the program might give one side or the other, or both, the occasion for anti-American propaganda which would not distinguish between a private television company and the United States Government.

The ninety-minute program was one of three done by *See It Now* on the Middle East that year. Seven months later was told the story of the Suez War. This time Murrow and Friendly flew to Cairo, where they were surprised to learn that the Egyptians, like the Israelis, took a more tolerant and matter-of-fact view of their earlier program than American Zionists or the State Department did. But this time, when Murrow interviewed him at great length and with sharp questioning, Nasser refused to discuss Israel at all.

In November, after the American elections, Murrow was in Israel again, interviewing a post-Suez Ben-Gurion, and the military commander General Dayan.

It was partly because 1956 was an election year that the State Department, reflecting the White House, was especially sensitive to the Middle East situation, not only in itself but as it was presented on American television, to American voters.

But whereas in 1952 *See It Now* had week after week been concerned with American politics and the election campaign, it was unable in the 1956 campaign to find anything worthy of its cameras. The proceedings were lackluster from beginning to end. It was obvious that both Eisenhower and Stevenson would be nominated again, and Eisenhower re-elected. At the political conventions, electronic gadgetry was employed to give the illusion on television of excitement and conflict that were not present.

Indeed in retrospect the presidential contest was notable only for the fact that Stevenson called for an end to nuclear testing, and was regarded by his opponents as not only "soft" on communism, but lunatic.

Though Murrow was officially neutral in the campaign, as always, he offered to be of service privately as the Democratic candidate's "television adviser," not so much because he favored Stevenson — apparently he had hoped the nomination would go to Hubert Humphrey — as because he believed that television's political capabilities were not being properly used. He suggested that on paid political broadcasts it was not enough for the candidate merely to be heard giving his opinions. He thought these should be left for the campaign speeches, which were reported in the daily news programs.

Instead, campaign advertising on television should use the documentary method to make the candidate's points. Thus, Murrow explained, Eisenhower had declared that American prestige in Europe was never higher. It would not be enough for Stevenson to express his doubts. But if a French peasant, a German miner and an Irish shepherd were shown expressing their doubts, then all Stevenson would have to do would be to express surprise that the President was not better informed. Murrow saw it as a kind of one-two punch. The civil rights issue, he thought, would lend itself admirably to such political documentary, and he also proposed that Stevenson use radio and television on a regional instead of national basis, touching on specific local problems. All these methods are now widely employed by the professional campaign promoters, but they were new in 1956.

The longer, broader, deeper, more occasional *See It Now*, however, as it entered its second year with ten programs planned, was far removed from everyday American politics, in the partisan sense of Republicans versus Democrats. It sounded more like a postgraduate seminar in national and international environmental, scientific and social problems.

The subjects Murrow outlined to Paley included "the new Navy," with nuclear power; automation, segregation, American scientific and engineering education — this was a whole year before the Soviet Sputnik — the early-warning radar system, increasing American traffic congestion, America's "senior citizens," a small city in the Soviet Union; anti-American propaganda abroad; Latin America, the "third world" of political non-alignment, and the story of a fifty-thousand-mile world tour by the actor Danny Kaye, on behalf of the United Nations International Children's Emergency Fund.

Though for one reason or another, including disapproval or lack of interest by the CBS hierarchy, these proposals were modified or eliminated, enough survived to keep *See It Now* in the public eye.

It did not make a very large mote. Once again *See It Now* had been moved to a different time, and had become part of what was known as the Sunday afternoon "cultural ghetto." And while in general Murrow and the program had the continued support and interest of Bill Paley, the strained relations caused by the Ezra Benson incident and the critical wear-and-tear of the Middle East programs had emphasized again the intrinsic unease which *See It Now* caused the CBS corporate entity.

Murrow resigned from the company directorship he had held for more than seven years. His stated reason, to avoid a conflict of interest, was a valid one. For one thing, CBS wanted to buy from him outright the *Person-to-Person* program he and Zousmer and Aaron had jointly owned, until he acquired their share four months before. He was also about to enter negotiations with CBS for a new long-term contract.

In both cases he could have abstained from participation in the corporate proceedings, as a Supreme Court Justice does, to escape any ethical questions and heed his own sense of propriety.

But it was also true that his concepts of public affairs broadcasting, and of the broadcasting industry's public responsibilities, were getting more and more out of tune with the corporate concepts. He was glad to be relieved of the increasingly awkward monthly board meetings, which for him had never been meetings of the minds.

But CBS was not yet to be rid of its embarrassments from him. Murrow returned from his third trip of the year to the Middle East to find that, through the good offices of Premier U Nu of Burma, who was taking part in the *See It Now* report on the neutral "third world," the Chinese premier, Chou En-lai, about to visit Rangoon, had also agreed to a CBS filmed interview there.

Murrow flew to Burma for what was undoubtedly a news coup of the first order — even though Chou insisted upon written questions submitted in advance, agreed to answer only ten of the forty questions Murrow drew up, spoke in Chinese (although he knew English), and used standard propaganda phrases in reply, shedding no light on the recent events in Budapest or in the Afro-Asian world.

Yet the stilted interview was in marked contrast with the off-camera affability that preceded it. Chou's young aides, some of them the products of American universities, seemed most eager to be talking to an American reporter, and readily discussed Chinese policies and problems. Even Chou was friendly in his preliminary conversations with Murrow. He had apparently decided to forgive the American for the way in which his Secretary of State had turned his back on the Chinese premier at the 1954 Geneva Conference on Indo-China.

For a time Murrow thought he might have become the instrument of a Chinese-American "thaw." But as soon as the cameras started whirring,

Chinese masks were put on, and a strict exercise in Maoist terminology followed.

As Murrow later remarked, Chou En-lai's answers "were right out of the book. And I had read the book." He regarded the interview as the most disappointing he had ever had.

The significance of the program, however, was that in spite of all official barriers on both sides, and the unwillingness of the State Department to validate news correspondents' passports for China, in spite of the bitter feeling between Washington and Peking since the Korean War, an American reporter had succeeded in reaching and talking with the chief of the hostile government, no matter how unsatisfactorily. To John Foster Dulles the sight of Chou's imperturbable face in American living rooms must have been a galling one.

To lessen the shock, CBS presented it at the untoward hour of 11:15 P.M. on a Sunday night which was also the night before New Year's Eve, thus insuring minimal viewing. To "take off the curse" further, it followed the interview with an "analysis" by two hostile notables from the United Nations, one representing Chiang Kai-shek's Nationalist Chinese regime.

The only gratification for Murrow in the whole skulking incident, in which as he saw it he had merely done his journalistic duty, was that in his absence in Rangoon, Janet had appeared in his place on *Person-to-Person*. "At the risk of starting a quarrel," *Variety* reported, "she may be more effective as an interviewer than Ed. She is a good conversationalist, has poise, charm and warmth," and it might have been added, was probably not so easily bored as Murrow sometimes appeared to be. Her subjects did not seem promising, a movie actor and a young model, but the program was called one of *Person-to-Person*'s best.

The new contract which Murrow left the CBS board of directors to negotiate was perhaps the most elaborate in the entire history of journalism, covering twenty-nine pages. It was unbreakable, and ran for four-and-a-half years, plus ten succeeding years as a "consultant."

It incorporated Murrow's refusal to accept sponsorship from a long list of medicine-cabinet commodities, though not from cigarettes or beer, which were indeed two of his principal sources of revenue. It set his *Person-to-Person* fee at $1750 per program for the first eight months, then $2500 a program for two years, and $2750 a program for twenty-two months. On *See It Now* he would receive $3000 for a half-hour program, $5000 for one hour, and $7000 for ninety minutes, all increased after thirty months. On radio he was to get $3000 a week for his five nightly news programs, plus additional fees for other commercial programs. Thus, in a single week in which he did both television programs, he earned approximately $10,000.

A six-month leave of absence was also included in the contract, in any year he wanted, though not before 1959. This provision would enable him, in 1959, to take the sabbatical year which marked the beginning of the end of his long association with CBS, and his career as a broadcaster.

The lucrative arrangement may have recalled to him his father's often-expressed wonderment. "Don't seem quite right, you gettin' paid all that money just for talkin' — especially since you don't sound any different than you did when you were talkin' and hangin' around the porch years ago."

And the memory might have been made more poignant by the fact that Roscoe Murrow had died a short while earlier, following nine years of paralysis during which Mrs. Murrow had tenderly waited upon him every hour of the day. He was seventy-seven years old, and had been buried near Blanchard, in the Odd Fellows Cemetery at Bow.

Murrow's parents had listened to the broadcaster's words on radio from his early days in Europe, and allowed nothing to prevent them from watching his television programs on the receiver he had given them, joined sometimes by Bellingham neighbors.

Now, after his father's funeral — from which she had returned, characteristically enough, to induce fatigue and forgetfulness by digging up the entire garden — his mother sat by the receiver alone. Besides her gardening, she devoted herself to her collection of pitchers — porcelain, glass, pewter and silver — to which every member of the family added, from all parts of the world. Whenever someone could drive her, she would look for antiques, on both sides of the Canadian border.

Once she bought a huge clock in Canada, nearly twice as tall as she was. The dealer came down to Bellingham to put it in place, and then reported to Murrow by letter that he was not happy. Mrs. Murrow had wanted it "angle-wise in the corner," without support at the top. Since she had to stand on a stool to wind it, the dealer was afraid that "if she had a fainting attack" she would pull it over on top of her. He wanted the clock placed against the wall, but she had told him that space was for the television set. What should he do?

Murrow replied gravely, "My mother is a very opinionated person," and "there is very little either one of us could do" to change the clock's position.

As Murrow entered upon his new contract, the first whiff of fraud was emanating from the television quiz shows. A Las Vegas chorus girl, who had also qualified as an "expert in astronomy," sued *The Big Surprise* because she had been dropped, she said, for flunking a question in rehearsal. The suit was settled out of court a long time later, but though there had been much innuendo on Madison Avenue, this was the first concrete intimation that the quiz programs were not as authentic as they pretended to be, but went through what was called a "pre-show warmup," and therefore could be rigged.

The Big Surprise was one of the quiz "packages" retailed by Entertainment Productions, Inc., whose principal figure Lou Cowan had joined CBS together with his most successful product, *The $64,000 Question.* NBC had also introduced a powerful rival to *The $64,000 Question* called *Twenty-One,* which even conquered *I Love Lucy* in the ratings, and around which the quiz-rigging scandal now began to swirl.

Twenty-One was one of five quiz programs NBC had purchased for $3 million. For public interest in programs of this nature was not only feverishly high, but became even higher as they competed among themselves. The climax came when Charles Van Doren, a Columbia University instructor who had won $129,000 on *Twenty-One,* was challenged to a kind of intellectual world series by the winner of *The $64,000 Challenge,* the CBS program devised by Cowan as a twin for *The $64,000 Question.*

Even in the reign of the quiz shows, some Americans still looked at *See It Now,* and Murrow continued to present world affairs as he saw them, despite new discouragement from CBS. One form it took was an executive decision to suppress a broadcast written by Eric Sevareid, the network's Washington correspondent, critical of the State Department for refusing to allow correspondents to go to Communist China. Murrow was reprimanded at the same time by the editorial board for similar remarks. The two broadcasters appealed directly to Paley without result. Frank Stanton, the CBS president, appeared on television to defend broadcasting freedom, but this turned out to mean, not the freedom of commentators to express their views, but the freedom of cameras to have access to congressional hearings.

Murrow flew to London again to report on *Britain After Suez,* and returned for a study of Puerto Rican immigrants in New York. Between these two programs came an "inside Communist Poland" report a year after the Poznan riots, done by Daniel Schorr and edited by Murrow and Friendly.

Person-to-Person also produced a notable program, from the standpoint of publicity, if not of sociology. Under heavy guard, the news release said, because the prisoners might use the occasion to stage a riot on television, or even worse, "agitate" before a national audience, Murrow "visited" the warden of Alcatraz Prison chez lui. The *Person-to-Person* technicians, it was soberly reported, had to move fast to adjust their lights without getting trapped by the system of interlocking doors.

Two days later a more serious Murrow received the Albert Einstein Award at Brandeis University, and thought it was time to make a few remarks about broadcasting and the duty of television to do more than entertain.

He knew that most of the money that paid for radio and television came from a small number of American corporations, and that therefore the thinking of their executives was bound to have an effect on the nation's thinking, in terms of the kinds of programs they sponsored. Murrow proposed that better broadcasting be induced through these men, from the top. However much it could be criticized, he felt that the commercial system of broadcasting was still the better alternative to state-operated and government-financed communication. This was his ingrained approach to the deficiencies of the medium, and here lay the thesis of his 1958 Chicago speech that would vibrate through the industry.

The Albert Einstein Award also gave Murrow the opportunity for another provocative statement about current affairs. He spoke of the Einstein College of Medicine of Yeshiva University, the first medical school under Jewish auspices established in the United States. He had found its admission application a unique document.

"I am not asked to state my race. No questions are asked about my religion or nationality. No photograph is requested. The college is not curious as to my parents' birthplace. I am not required to give my mother's maiden name. You will have difficulty in finding a similar application from any other institution of higher learning in this land.

"They are interested in what academic trails I have followed, and where I propose to go; interested in my qualifications, rather than my ancestors. This, I suggest, is the essence of that overworked and often distorted phrase, academic freedom, which doesn't apply only to professors, but means the right of scholars to pursue the truth wherever it may lead them."

The famous, or as the State Department regarded it, notorious CBS interview with Nikita Khrushchev in the Kremlin, illustrated once more the difficulty of reconciling broadcasting's responsibility to its viewers with its obligations, real or assumed, to the government which controlled station licenses.

The official dissatisfaction that had been covertly manifested with the Chou En-lai interview came out into the open when the man who had replaced Stalin appeared on home screens. Unlike the stage-managed appearance of the Chinese leader, the Russian faced the American nation ready to field all questions, "spontaneous and unrehearsed," as the standard phrase went. The interview was hailed by *Variety* as electronic journalism at its enterprising best, indeed "democracy at work." But the State Department and others in Washington criticized the network for giving its facilities to an undoubted enemy of the United States, the more so since the intimate close-up of the Soviet leader, showing him to be very much a human being, made an undoubted impression throughout the country.

Khrushchev said nothing that had not been said before — except perhaps significantly enough that there was a divergence in Marxist theory between Communist Russia and Communist China — but the mere fact that he was saying it at all, directly to Americans in their homes, was enough.

There was some editorial criticism that the three American correspondents in Moscow who interviewed Khrushchev had allowed him to engage in massive propaganda without rebuttal, a statement which could also be made about appearances of the American President or Secretary of State. Some war veterans' groups, as usual, demanded that the Khrushchev program be canceled, even before seeing it.

White House aides suggested that Eisenhower be allowed to appear on Soviet television to "answer" Khrushchev, and this idea was supported by the Senate Majority Leader, Lyndon B. Johnson. The President backed away from it, and indeed from "equal time" on the three American networks, but he expressed public displeasure that a "commercial enterprise" should presume to consider such an interview to be news, perhaps even as important as an Eisenhower press conference. Various Congressmen, labor leaders and political refugee groups also criticized CBS for the Khrushchev interview, and the Socialist Party demanded equal time "to answer the Communist Party."

In public CBS defended the interview. "I come from a commercial organization," the network president Frank Stanton told the National Press Club, with a grin toward the President's disparagement of free enterprise. "A major duty of that organization is to report the news." CBS garnered several awards for the program, and again emerged as a defender of press freedom. But some industry executives did not hide their belief that the interview had offended some sections of public opinion, thus confounding their dedicated purpose of offending nobody.

As Murrow stated it before the Radio and Television News Directors Association, "The President of the United States uttered a few ill-chosen, uninformed words on the subject, and the network practically apologized . . . Many newspapers defended CBS's right to produce the program, and commended it for initiative. But the other networks remained silent."

Face the Nation's controversial interview with Khrushchev was followed by *See It Now*'s interview with Marshal Tito, for which Murrow flew to the Adriatic island of Brioni. To avoid the kind of row caused by the program filmed inside the Kremlin, CBS appended to the one-hour Tito film a half-hour live panel discussion of it. The heat level was down, because Tito had years before asserted his independence of Moscow, and the panel agreed that American aid to Yugoslavia was therefore justified. But again there were many in Washington who regarded all Communists alike as part of a single "world conspiracy," and again protests were made. One Congressman introduced a bill requiring State Department approval for all broadcast interviews with Communist leaders. Even Eisenhower could not support that, and defended "free access to knowledge and opinion."

See It Now, like the rest of the United States, entered the age of the intercontinental ballistic missile with the launching of the Russian Sputnik in October 1957. Four months earlier Murrow and Friendly had done a ninety-minute program on automation without any reference to the Soviet Union's progress in that field, because eminent American scientists had scoffed at Soviet technical education and said it presented no particular challenge to the United States. In 1946 Dr. Vannevar Bush, the wartime mobilizer of American scientists and a member of the postwar Committee on the Present Danger, had declared it would take the Soviet Union twenty years to develop the atom bomb, a feat which it accomplished in three. Now in 1957 the same Dr. Bush said, "Are you out of your mind?" to Raymond Swing when the latter, for *See It Now*, wondered whether Soviet technology, including missilry, might not be more advanced than American scientists suspected.

After Sputnik — beginning with a program in which Dr. Edward Teller, the man who had triumphed over J. Robert Oppenheimer in the H-bomb argument, declared that with Sputnik the Russians had achieved a victory "more disastrous than Pearl Harbor" — Murrow and Friendly made atoms and missiles, nuclear testing and fallout, one of their prime program concerns.

They also had a *See It Now* project in mind to send young Senator John F. Kennedy and older Senator John Sherman Cooper to critical underdeveloped areas of the world, recalling the successful 1955 *See It Now* odyssey of Senator Margaret Chase Smith. Both legislators were willing, but Kennedy became ill and was unable to go. The planning of the program, however, renewed the Murrow-Kennedy acquaintance which had begun with their *Person-to-Person* interview in 1953.

Murrow himself was being siren-called to the United States Senate, but resisted it. New York State's Democrats, who were still treading in the footsteps of Roosevelt and Lehman and usually fighting New York City's Tammany Hall, had frequently mentioned him as a senatorial possibility, and now several leaders urged him to run against the Republican incumbent, Irving Ives.

Murrow was dubious about entering American politics, which he regarded with skeptical and sometimes horrified amusement, and he was aware of the growing influence of television in politics, as he had indicated to Adlai Stevenson. His idea of the legitimate use of the medium for political purposes was not in accord with the growing practice.

"They say future political candidates must be personable on television. Why?" he asked. "Are we reaching the ridiculous stage where we will be invited to taste a candidate, like toothpaste? I find it ominous, this reliance on advertising technique and catchphrases, instead of statesmanship and leadership.

"Some people say TV separates the phoney from the statesman. I don't think there's anything in this new medium that can do that, until we start accumulating kinescope libraries to allow us to recall the phoney's past statements," that is, as he had done with Joe McCarthy.

When the proposal was first made that he run for the Senate, Murrow said, "I am a reporter with no political affiliations of any kind," and explained he was not qualified to represent New York State because "I don't even know all its history," a reason politicians might regard as overfastidious. But the "boom" continued, and when United Nations Under-Secretary Ralph Bunche refused a draft, the Liberal Party, in coalition with the Democrats, called on Murrow to join the ticket of Governor Averell Harriman, who was seeking reelection. Legislative leaders in Albany and even Tammany Hall sachems were sounded out on the plan.

Harriman, though he had known Murrow since Lend-Lease days in wartime London, would have preferred a professional politician as the candidate, and if possible an Irish Catholic. But Eleanor Roosevelt and former State Supreme Court Justice Samuel Rosenman, who had been a Roosevelt adviser, convinced him Murrow was the man. The vice chairman of the Liberal Party, Alex Rose, a union leader, came back from Albany and said, "Ed Murrow articulates the principles of democracy and liberalism with a deep devotion. He would make a great U.S. Senator."

Murrow's boss at CBS, Bill Paley, whom he consulted about it, also favored the idea heartily, envisioning another Daniel Webster on the Senate floor. He tried to persuade Murrow that a Senator did not represent any state alone, but was a tribune of the American people. He never understood why Murrow refused.

One reason was that the broadcaster had taken the question to another good friend, Harry S Truman, and the former President strongly advised him not to run for the Senate, though he had been a Senator himself. Truman told him, in effect, "You are much more useful on camera than you would be in camera."

Also Wells Church had suggested that if Murrow did want to enter politics he should at least do so from his native state of North Carolina, or from the state of Washington, where he grew up. Murrow would remember the lesson, and in 1964 when he was asked to support Robert F. Kennedy for Senator in New York, he called the President's brother a "carpetbagger" and refused.

In his own case, in 1958, he told Rose, "I have neither the intention nor the appetitite to run for elective office," and later he added, "It's more fun to cover politicians than to be one." In any event the whole business turned out to be academic. It was a year in which the Republicans won heavily in New York State. Not only was Harriman defeated for re-election by Nelson Rockefeller, but Republican Congressman Kenneth Keating easily won the Senate seat against the man the Democrats chose in Murrow's stead, New York District Attorney Frank Hogan, the professional politician and Irish Catholic Harriman wanted. Murrow's candidacy would have made no apparent difference.

His refusal to run in New York did not prevent him from being mentioned even for the presidency, at least by one Los Angeles businessman who offered to run his campaign "entirely at my own expense," because Murrow's "contacts with the world's leaders make you the most qualified individual in the nation for the presidency."

Despite any aversion to the ways of politics, Murrow could not escape, nor would he want to escape, influencing politics, not only in his own country but even abroad. Harold Macmillan, who had succeeded to the British prime ministership after the Suez debacle toppled Anthony Eden, had been two years in his high office but was by no means a well-known public figure.

He was a curiously reserved man for a professional politician, who had resisted television and even hated radio, allowing neither hellish device into Number 10 Downing Street, except for a small portable radio in his press secretary's office. Macmillan read Trollope in bed, and was regarded as something of a Trollopean character himself.

After a long siege in the name of Anglo-American relations — which Macmillan had cultivated since the days when he was the British political representative at Eisenhower's headquarters in Algiers — he was persuaded to appear on American, not British, television, in a *See It Now* interview with Murrow.

It was only another public affairs program in the United States — at least it was not "controversial" — but in Britain, where it was quickly shown by the BBC, it made the prime minister a celebrated figure overnight, and what was more important, a familiar one. His personality, dry, modest and sagacious, with an Edwardian touch, became apparent to millions of his countrymen for the first time. Murrow did not "make" him, but certainly implanted him upon the public consciousness, and Macmillan later remarked that the interview was worth five victorious by-elections. Murrow, a favorite of the British since the days of the Blitz and seen frequently on the BBC in his *See It Now* programs, was given wide credit there for another worthy bit of journalism.

Acclaim from abroad could not compensate for the state of affairs at home, between the editorial and commercial millstones of television. *See It Now* continued to make news headlines nearly every time it appeared, but as a television "property" it was arriving at the end of its tether. Awards or no awards, it was "hard to sell," reported the CBS sales department, and as the spring season came to a close, it was regarded as unlikely to return to the air in the fall. If it came back at all, it would be even more infrequently, with only four programs instead of ten.

Sometimes it seemed as if *See It Now* held more respect among the executives of the other networks, who had been compelled to introduce similar programs of their own. As it began to fade away, Sylvester Weaver, former president of NBC, observed that television had "abdicated its role in a democratic society," and with specific reference to Murrow and *See It Now*, added, "You can't really have in your hands the power that television has in this time of crisis, and be agreeable to solving the problem by letting it become a jukebox in the corner of the room to keep the kids quiet, and just pile on one crime or Western or game show after another."

Though economics played its part in the decision to let *See It Now* slip down the drain, its last big controversy also had something to do with its demise. This was what should have been an instructive program on the question of statehood for Alaska and Hawaii. But some members of Congress firmly believed that legislators from the fiftieth state of Hawaii would be "Communist controlled" because of the undisguised Marxist beliefs of the islands' labor leader, Harry Bridges. When Bridges, on *See It Now*, called one of the Congressmen "crazy" for thinking so, the latter demanded, and as usual got, from CBS free time to answer. In his reply he called Hawaiian statehood "a major objective of the Soviet conspiracy."

The affair might seem ridiculous in retrospect, but in the small ideological world of John Foster Dulles and Pat McCarran it was real enough, and typical, and once again Murrow and Friendly, who had not been consulted on the "equal time" decision, felt they were in the public position of having been repudiated by CBS. Murrow told Sig Mickelson, the head of CBS News, that the action had undermined his relationship with the company, and that he could not continue with *See It Now* under such conditions.

What Murrow wanted was some arrangement for consultation on such matters in the future, but when he took the matter to Paley personally, as he was still able to do, it was obvious that the company had merely been waiting for some such opening, and that the alternative course of dropping *See It Now* had been chosen. Murrow's letter of protest was regarded by the company as tantamount to a letter of resignation, at least from *See It Now*.

"I don't want this constant stomachache," Paley was quoted as having said. "It goes with the job," Murrow replied.

Whether Murrow could have resigned, even if he wanted to, is not certain. His "unbreakable" contract still had three years to run. *Person-to-Person* would be back for another year in the fall. And the new Murrow-Friendly program *Small World* was scheduled to make its start also.

There was still radio, not only the 7:45 P.M. daily news broadcast, but some documentary programs which he was narrating.

To some extent the gap *See It Now* was leaving would be filled by what were called "instant specials," quickly produced and unsubtle programs presented when some news development warranted. But that still left a considerable vacuum in television news and public affairs.

See It Now died on July 9, 1958, after seven years, with a final program on the reemergence of Germany as a world power. CBS, which had balked at the cost of continuing it, two weeks later opened an eleven-million-dollar amusement park at Santa Monica, California, to compete with Disneyland. This was part of its new practice of seeking investments outside broadcasting in order to "diversify." It lost heavily on the amusement park venture.

The time was a distressing one for Murrow. Elmer Davis, a man he swore by, had just died after an agonizing illness. Murrow felt that Paley, who for twenty years had been as much understanding friend as trusting employer, was no longer the arbiter between him and the corporation, but entirely on the corporation's side.

See It Now was gone. And *Person-to-Person* had produced one of those ludicrous but lamentable situations that go into satiric novels by disillusioned advertising men. A cigarette company, enlisting as cosponsor of the program, suggested that since Murrow smoked so incessantly and so visibly anyway, on *Person-to-Person*, he identify himself directly with its product. Everybody's guest was willing to cooperate, up to a point. He had his own brand, but in an emergency he would smoke anything at hand, and he had no objection to regarding *Person-to-Person* as a weekly emergency and smoking the sponsor's cigarettes, even permitting the pack to be shown on camera.

But the sponsor wanted more. It wanted him to smoke its cigarettes off camera also, wherever he went, and to make them his brand. Murrow objected as an American citizen to being deprived of a choice, and refused to become a walking commercial. He did agree, when off camera, to hide his own brand in a plain case, in order to avoid "any undesirable publicity" as a man who wouldn't smoke the brand that fed him.

Also ludicrous and lamentable, though on a vaster, almost gargantuan scale, was the disaster that was on the point of overwhelming the television jukebox as "Pat" Weaver had called it. As *See It Now* shuffled off this mortal coil, the congressional probers examining the entertainment industry took two more scalps. For refusing to testify, two television producers were dismissed by their respective networks. But this time only one case had ideological, or *Red Channel,* connotations. The other man fired was a producer of the *Twenty-One* quiz program.

Murrow had gone to the West Coast that summer to visit home territory, and he and Casey went down the Rogue River in Oregon for a six-day boat camping and trout-fishing trip that reinvigorated him.

Shooting the rapids in flat-bottomed boats was part of Casey's initiation into the masculine arts, under Lord Chesterfield's formula, often quoted by Murrow. "All a gentleman can teach his son is to ride, to shoot, and tell the truth." Such pastimes had become the more important because Casey was not permitted to do much television viewing. He was even forbidden *Person-to-Person,* and not merely because of the lateness of the hour. Murrow wanted him to read instead.

While they were away, six new quiz programs had been put on television, five of them making their appearance on the same day. They were *For Love or Money, Play Your Hunch, Lucky Partners, Haggis Baggis, Anybody Can Play,* and *Bid 'n' Buy,* which awarded the Scottish island of Stroma as its first prize. For the 1958–1959 season it was calculated that $24 million was being spent on "time and talent" for the nighttime quiz shows, with several million dollars more for the lesser daytime programs.

Murrow got back East just as CBS, without explanation, abruptly canceled its quiz program called *Dotto.* The first of the seven veils enveloping the great scandal was thereby lifted. It soon became known that a contestant on the program, standing in the wings to take his turn on camera, had found a notebook dropped by the woman contestant preceding him. It contained the exact same questions she was then, on stage, in process of answering, for a prize of four thousand dollars.

He thereupon notified the successful contestant's defeated rival of what he had found, and this enabled her to obtain a similar four thousand dollars from the program's producers as "compensation." The informant himself was paid fifteen hundred dollars to let matters go no farther, but he thought the sum trifling and reported the incident to the Federal Communications Commission. It is not recorded whether he paid back the fifteen hundred dollars.

The *Dotto* incident occurred after CBS, faced with the rumors of 'fixing" that eddied about Madison Avenue, announced it had looked into all its quiz shows and had failed to find any "improper procedures." Two days after the cancellation, the company wrote to the FCC to acknowledge that suspected rigging was the reason, and asked that this fact not be made public. The Federal agency agreed, and the CBS admission remained unrevealed for fourteen months.

Journalistic inquiries were now being made about other quiz programs, and among the successful contestants approached by reporters was the young Columbia University instructor, Charles Van Doren. He ridiculed any thought of rigging. "I never got any kind of hint or help," he proclaimed, "and as far as I know, nobody else ever did on the program."

Almost immediately Herbert Stempel, a college student who had lost to Van Doren after accumulating forty-nine thousand dollars in prize money, was telling a New York newspaper that he had been ordered to lose, and that *Twenty-One* was indeed rigged. The remaining producers of the program said they would sue for libel. The NBC network declared the charge "utterly baseless and untrue," and announced complete faith in the integrity of producers and program. One of the producers then played a tape recording. Stempel, it appeared, had demanded fifty thousand dollars for not revealing that he had been given the questions in advance, but had settled for the promise of a television production job himself. The job failed to materialize, but he withdrew the charges.

It was clear there was something to investigate about the quiz programs, and District Attorney Frank Hogan began to do so.

By this time the Maecenas of the quiz shows, Lou Cowan, after three years as "director of creative programming," had become no less than president of the CBS television network.

Although all his broadcasting experience had been in the realm of entertainment, it was passably literate entertainment, quite a few cuts above the soap operas and forfeit games that made daytime television hideous. And as an intellectual, by comparison with some other broadcasting executives — a man who even liked poetry, it was said, and read philosophy — Cowan was most favorably disposed to more news and public affairs programming. In his new post he divested himself of his stock holdings in the firm which supplied *The $64,000 Question* and *The $64,000 Challenge* to CBS — programs which had increased the profits of the cosmetics company sponsoring them from $1.2 million to $7.7 million annually — but he was never able to divest himself, even as the network president, of his role as a symbol of the Quiz Age.

But so far as Murrow and Friendly were concerned, Cowan was a sympathetic face on the CBS executive floor, and when Murrow returned that fall — after recording his voice at Philadelphia's refurbished Independence Hall, telling the history of the Liberty Bell to a million-and-a-half visitors yearly — he initiated the new *Small World* program with zest and anticipation.

Its debut on an October Sunday evening was called "fascinating television" by *Variety*, as it brought together — by simultaneous filming which was then edited in proper sequence in New York — a global conversation between Pandit Nehru, in New Delhi; Aldous Huxley, in Turin, Italy; and Thomas E. Dewey in Portland, Maine. The talk ranged from nuclear weapons, to Formosa, to totalitarianism. Murrow acted as the moderator, catalytic agent and goad, and *Variety* envisioned future programs bringing together Konrad Adenauer and Tallulah Bankhead, or Sean O'Casey and Casey Stengel.

As the critic John Lardner saw it, *Small World* featured the Higher Murrow as against *Person-to-Person*'s Lower Murrow.

Its conversations were not only global in physical arrangements, but often global in their scope. They attacked such matters as overpopulation, statecraft, international relations, and Lincoln's political philosophy. They exhibited some of the world's leading minds, as well as some not so capital, and when the "chemistry was right," as Friendly put it, *Small World* did offer "fascinating television," if only by proving that words and thoughts could be more meaningful than pictures.

The program was not always intellectual — as Brendan Behan, Ireland's bibulous playwright, demonstrated when he became progressively more maudlin on camera and finally disappeared in midchannel — but it was always cerebral. It also showed what could be done by good editing. Art transcends nature when a two-hour conversation is cut to half that time, with all the bons mots retained and the false starts, awkward pauses and irrelevancies removed. Nehru, Huxley and Dewey made enough conversation for two whole programs, even after editing, and thus were able both to open and to close the season. Many viewers thought that Murrow as devil's advocate was far better suited than by *Person-to-Person*. He obviously enjoyed *Small World* much more.

Small World's audience was relatively small also, but it was as appreciative as *See It Now*'s audience had been. A minister in the Midwest wrote to Murrow to complain that the program could not be seen in his small city because the local station had sold the time to something with a higher rating. "I refuse to be surprised," Murrow replied. "If we were to do the Second Coming of Christ in color for a full hour, there would be a considerable number of stations which would decline to carry it, on the ground that a Western or a quiz show would be more profitable. Forgive the irreverence, but there are times when I think that the Lord is wholly indifferent to this business of television, and this is why."

The quiz shows, suffering from no lack of audience, were still under investigation in New York City, with District Attorney Hogan going through a list of two hundred witnesses summoned before a special Grand Jury, when Murrow, in Chicago, said "something I have wanted to say for a long time."

He had in fact been saying it for a long time, in various ways, most notably when he had received the Albert Einstein Award and declared that "if television and radio are to be used for the entertainment of all of the people all of the time, we have come perilously close to discovering the real opiate of the people."

In September 1958, in a letter to a friend, he reiterated his long-standing belief that radio and television had "an obligation to expose the listener and viewer to the realities of the world in which he lives, and if those realities are harsh and unpleasant, that is not the fault of the medium. Now . . . the viewer is insulated from the realities."

Three weeks later, on October 15, before the Radio and Television News Directors Association, the most attentive forum in the broadcasting industry, he delivered a full-scale indictment of what was taking place around him.

It was a moment when television, ending its first decade, had achieved a revenue of a billion dollars annually. There were more radio and television sets in the country than people. The third network, ABC, had created such an intense competition for the sponsor's dollar that the two larger networks, seeking ever larger audiences, were offering ever more retreats from reality in their programs. The quiz shows and big-name comedy were the principal ingredients, as Madison Avenue gave the public "what it wants." But Murrow thought it was rather a case of the public having "come to want what you get," as Bernard Shaw had once put it.

The mass media, reported the Civil Liberties Educational Foundation, were being turned to "less for opinion, still less for radical or liberal opinion, and almost not at all for many-sided discussion." It added: "One cannot slake one's thirst at a dry well."

So Murrow was completely aware of what he was doing when he rose to speak in Chicago. He sent copies of his text in advance to news agencies and television editors, and to the trade paper *Variety*. But he sent none to Paley or Stanton or other CBS executives. He clearly meant what he said as an open challenge to the broadcasting prelacy.

"This just might do nobody any good," he began. "At the end of this discourse, a few people may accuse this reporter of fouling his own comfortable nest, and your organization may be accused of having given hospitality to heretical and even dangerous thoughts."

But he had to talk "with some candor" about the course of radio and television "in this generous and capacious land." He believed that "potentially the commercial system of broadcasting, as practiced in this country, is the best and freest yet devised." He confessed that "these instruments have been good to me beyond my due. There exist in my mind no reasonable grounds for personal complaint. I have no feud, either with my employers, any sponsors, or with the professional critics of radio and television." But he had come to have "an abiding fear regarding what these two instruments are doing to our society, our culture and our heritage."

He minced no words. Future historians, he said, would find in the film records of television "evidence of decadence, escapism and insulation from the realities of the world in which we live. I invite your attention to the television schedules of all networks between the hours of 8 and 11 P.M. Eastern time. Here you will find only fleeting and spasmodic reference to the fact that this nation is in mortal danger."

The Russians had already tested intercontinental ballistic missiles, to which nuclear warheads could be attached, while the United States had not.

Two Russian satellites had been launched, and Russian rockets would soon be encircling the moon and even hitting it, while the United States trailed badly in space. The state of Soviet-American political relations remained tense and acrimonious, with no apparent hope of detente, and meanwhile the United States had undertaken vague new commitments against communism on the Asian mainland in Indo-China.

Despite television's belief that it "must at all costs shield the sensitive citizens from anything that is unpleasant," Murrow was "entirely persuaded that the American public is more reasonable, restrained, and more mature than most of our industry's program planners believe.

"I have reason to know, as do many of you, that when the evidence on a controversial subject is fairly and calmly presented, the public recognizes it for what it is — an effort to illuminate, rather than to agitate." He mentioned several *See It Now* programs which, despite their controversial nature, had been accepted as fair, such as those on the Egyptian-Israeli conflict, on cigarette-smoking and cancer, and on radioactive fallout and the danger of further nuclear testing.

Television's timidity toward controversy, he thought, went hand in hand with its lack of confidence in itself. "There have been cases where executives have refused to make even private comment on a program for which they were responsible, until they had read the reviews in print," a habit of some CBS News executives with regard to Murrow productions.

"The oldest excuse of the networks for their timidity is their youth. Their spokesmen say: 'We are young. We have not developed the traditions nor acquired the experience of the older media.' If they but knew it, they are building those traditions, creating those precedents every day.

"Each time they yield to a voice from Washington, or any political pressure, each time they eliminate something that might offend some section of the community, they are creating their own body of precedent and tradition."

While concerned primarily about television, he also feared for radio, for him still "that most satisfying and rewarding instrument." In its communication of news and information, "in order to progress, it need only go backward — to the time when singing commercials were not allowed on news reports, when there was no middle commercial in a fifteen-minute news report; when radio was rather proud, alert and fast," in short to days already forgotten, even though so recent.

"In this kind of complex and confusing world, you can't tell very much about the why of the news, in broadcasts where only three minutes is available for news. The only man who could do that was Elmer Davis, and his kind aren't about any more. If radio news is to be regarded as a commodity, only acceptable when salable, and only when packaged to fit the advertising appropriation of the sponsor, then I don't care what you call it — I say it isn't news."

He came to the heart of the matter, the development of the corporate mentality, and broadcasting's internal contradictions. Both radio and television had "grown up as an incompatible combination of show business, advertising and news . . . The top management of the networks, with a few notable exceptions, has been trained in advertising, research, sales, or show business. But by the nature of the corporate structure, they also make the final and crucial decisions having to do with news and public affairs. Frequently they have neither the time nor the competence to do this."

He could speak as a recent member of the CBS board of directors himself. "It is not easy for the same small group of men to decide whether to buy a new station for millions of dollars, build a new building, alter the rate card, buy a new Western, sell a soap opera, decide what defensive line to take in connection with the latest congressional inquiry, how much money to spend on promoting a new program, what additions or deletions should be made in the existing covey or clutch of vice presidents, and at the same time, frequently on the same long day, to give mature, thoughtful consideration to the manifold problems that confront those who are charged with the responsibility for news and public affairs."

This was at a time when "diversification" to nonbroadcasting investments by the networks, and mergers with other and extraneous corporate interests, had only begun. Before long boards of directors would also be considering the manifold problems of half-a-dozen other kinds of business, distracting them from their original broadcasting purposes and diluting their obligations toward news and public affairs.

Murrow continued. "Sometimes there is a clash between the public interest and the corporate interest. A telephone call or a letter from the proper quarter in Washington is treated more seriously than a communication from an irate, but not politically potent, viewer. It is tempting enough to give away a little air time for frequently irresponsible and unwarranted utterances, in an effort to temper the wind of criticism," as CBS had several times done with *See It Now*.

The free-enterprise system of broadcasting, Murrow admitted, was not always free or enterprising. He became sarcastic. "There is no suggestion here that networks or individual stations should operate as philanthropies. But I can find nothing in the Bill of Rights, or the Communications Act, which says that they must increase their net profits each year, lest the Republic collapse."

He did not mean that news broadcasts should be subsidized by foundations or public funds. He knew that the networks spent considerable sums on public affairs programs without commercial return. "I have had the privilege at CBS of presiding over a number of such programs."

But such sustaining programs, no matter how worthy, were simply not broadcast by many local stations because they had no revenue attached to them. Therefore the license-holders had "welshed" on their pledge of public service, under the influence of the "money-making machine," and the FCC had failed to punish them because "in the view of many, this would come perilously close to supervision of program content by a Federal agency."

In this predicament, he addressed himself to the big corporations "who pay the freight" for radio and television programs. Were they wise to use that time exclusively for the sale of goods and services? "Is it in their own interest, and that of the stockholders, so to do? The sponsor of an hour's television program is not buying merely the six minutes devoted to his commercial message. He is determining within broad limits the sum total of the impact of the entire hour. If he always invariably reaches for the largest possible audience, then this process of insulation, of escape from reality, will continue to be massively financed, and its apologists will continue to make winsome speeches about giving the public what it wants."

He refused to believe that the buyers of television time wanted their "corporate image" to "consist exclusively of a solemn voice in an echo chamber, or a pretty girl opening the door of a refrigerator, or a horse that talks." He appealed to television's patrons directly, and to television's better self.

"Let us have a little competition. Not only in selling soap, cigarettes or automobiles, but in informing a troubled, apprehensive but receptive public. Why should not each of the twenty or thirty big corporations which dominate radio and television decide that they will give up one or two of their regularly scheduled programs each year, turn the time over to the networks for public affairs programs, to indicate their belief in the importance of ideas?"

This would not blemish the corporate image, and the stockholders would not object. "For if the premise on which our pluralistic society rests — which as I understand it is that if the people are given sufficient undiluted information, they will then somehow, even after long, sober second thoughts, reach the right decision — if that premise is wrong, then not only the corporate image, but the corporations are done for."

Murrow's formula for utilizing radio and television "in the interests of a free society" — and he explained he did not advocate turning television "into a twenty-seven-inch Wailing Wall" — frankly rested, he said, on "big business, and on big television, and it rests at the top." He believed it held "its own reward — good business and good television."

But his call for "a most exciting adventure, exposure to ideas," was acclaimed only outside the industry he was talking to. The speech was reprinted widely, and copies distributed by colleges, journalism schools and foundations. But Frank Stanton quickly made it clear that what Murrow had to say "does not, of course, reflect the views of CBS management."

As for Bill Paley, the warm personal relations he had once enjoyed with his foremost broadcaster, and which had gradually been eroded by the controversies he had stirred, were further badly damaged by the speech. The CBS chairman felt he had been betrayed from within the bosom of his own family, and took Murrow's strictures as a personal attack upon him.

Paley was the more offended because Murrow had not talked the matter over with him, or indicated his intention. It was true that Ed had sometimes said the same things, to not much avail, around the CBS office, but now he had waved broadcasting's dirty linen in public.

To Eric Johnston, head of the Motion Picture Association of America, who had told him the speech was "magnificent, factual, informative, and above all courageous," Murrow ruefully replied: "Thanks for your kind words. As you can imagine, my superiors here were not overjoyed." He reported to another friend, who had read the speech in faraway Israel, that "what happened as a result was exactly what I predicted — nothing. Lots of requests for copies, but no action."

Some took the speech as another evidence that television was "the light that failed," on the ground that an institution is crumbling when its leaders join its detractors. There were cold looks and distant nods for Murrow in the CBS building and along Madison Avenue, and he felt constrained to explain further. "The speech has been misinterpreted. I believe that our system of commercial television is the best ever devised. I have no objection to the bread-and-butter programs. I think good Westerns are the best entertainment you can watch.

"But I am frightened at the imbalance in programming. Beyond the obvious, television isn't doing much to arouse the curiosity of viewers . . . There is nothing in television to remind us of what Carl Sandburg calls 'our root-holes.' You can't learn about them by watching a guy with a six-gun on a horse."

On the other hand, to a personal friend who asked him why he had made the speech, he answered: "I've always been on the side of the heretics against those who burned them, because the heretics so often proved to be right. Dead — but right!"

Bill Paley never discussed the Chicago speech with Murrow. Nor could the chairman really understand why he had taken such a step. In retrospect he felt that Murrow perhaps resented the way in which the corporation, so to speak, had come between them, even beyond the growing complexity and impersonality of the industry itself. But the corporate structure was no more complex, Paley always felt, than Murrow's own mind and nature.

The speech had at least one immediate positive result. At year-end time in 1958, CBS presented no fewer than five full-length news programs, one reviewing the year's events, another Soviet-American relations, a report on Communist China, and even two hours devoted to trends in the arts and sciences.

But in the longer view, all the networks felt deeply aggrieved by Murrow's criticisms. Not only had he arraigned them as the servants of Mammon instead of the public interest, but they believed he had given ammunition to the congressional forces which were always seeking to put them under some sort of Federal control.

A touch of guilty conscience may have been involved. The House Committee on Legislative Oversight had recently censured the FCC for "fraternizing" with the television industry it was supposed to be regulating, and revealed instances of lavish entertainment of commission members by station owners. It went so far as to recommend a code of ethics for the FCC.

Murrow's comment, in a letter to the publisher David Lawrence, was that the congressional committee's finding "was like catching the boys playing penny ante in the outer room, when, if they had gone into the back room, they would have found them playing for millions. This trafficking in licenses is one of the more unsavory aspects of the whole industry."

With his relations with CBS at a new low, after the Chicago speech, Murrow on election night found himself relegated to the minor television role of reporting returns from the Eastern seaboard, and *Variety* likened him to "a spunky copper banished to a Staten Island station house."

He also became involved in another embroilment with the Federal Government over the sore subject, to him, of passport control. The case of William Worthy, a correspondent who had gone to Communist China without State Department permission — and who reported for CBS News from Peking while there — had moved up in the courts, and Murrow, after supporting Worthy in several radio broadcasts, drafted a legal brief at the request of his attorney friend, Morris Ernst.

The Justice Department refused to consent to its admission, lest as it said, "every other reporter should file." But the contents of the brief became known anyway, and it did not spare the Federal authorities.

Murrow's argument was that not only had Secretary of State Dulles deprived Worthy of his rights as a citizen, but he had also deprived the American people of "their right to know," and without due process.

"The right to information is not an abstract right," he said. "Democratic governments cannot survive unless the electorate has at its disposal all available information on which to reach intelligent conclusions about the future of our country, and indeed our world. A leadership responsible only to an uninformed, or partially informed electorate, can bring nothing but disaster to our world.

"The problem facing the court . . . is whether the people of our Republic can be denied knowledge gathered by our citizens, in this case in China," and Murrow saw the issue "as not only an individual right of citizens to travel throughout the world, but more particularly as a right of our people to have the potential power to reflect public opinion so that the foreign policy of our nation, enunciated by the Secretary of State, rests at least in part on the reflexes and reactions and debates of the people of our Republic."

It was not only a criticism of passport policy, but also of the Eisenhower administration's China policy. The question of the moment was the defense of Formosa by the American Seventh Fleet, including the offshore islands of Quemoy and Matsu, at the risk of hostilities with mainland China. Murrow had told one friend that "my evaluation of the Formosa policy is too profane to commit to print. Unfortunately, the same people who made the decisions that got us into this mess are still making them."

At CBS too, another bone of contention had appeared. One evening in the new year Murrow sat before a radio microphone and narrated an hour-long documentary program called *The Business of Sex*, dealing with the use of "call girls" as perquisites offered by some business firms to their clients.

Not since the Joe McCarthy days had a program of his equaled the public impact this one made. The Bureau of Internal Revenue became interested in the subject. District Attorney Hogan asked for a transcript. The police wanted to know more about the girls, the madams, and the procurers heard anonymously on the program.

The program had struck a sensitive nerve. The Hearst newspaper in New York carried a headline asking "Was the Murrow Exposé a Hoax?" The *National Association of Manufacturers News*, in an editorial, called Murrow a "past master of innuendo, smear, snide implication, and unsupported accusation," and recalled that he had "pilloried" the late Senator McCarthy "unmercifully and unfairly."

The *NAM News* carried weight along Madison Avenue, and some of the advertising agencies, the purveyors of broadcasting revenue, felt that Murrow had cast aspersions upon them and their lavish entertainment of clients. CBS vice presidents shuddered at the storm of publicity and at the ruffled feelings of the men in the gray flannel suits.

Yet the entire incident had been brewed by the accepted radio-television way of doing things, and by the development of a "star system" under which leading broadcasting figures, to enhance the importance of a program, were called upon to read scripts written by other people.

The call-girl program would probably have aroused no particular sensation if it had been narrated by John Doe. But Ed Murrow was "controversial." His programs did not merely report, they laid bare. They had political and social significance. They made impressions on Congressmen and clergymen. This was no ordinary, in-one-ear documentary.

Murrow presumably did not quarrel with the purpose or methods of *The Business of Sex*, or he could have refused to narrate it. He relied upon the competence of the reporters and editors who had done the job, as he had relied over the years. But since he took no part in the reporting or research himself, he was unable, when the story "blew," to defend its facts or its craftsmanship. All he could do was to remark on the peril of voicing the lines and thoughts of others.

It was true that on many *See It Now* programs, and on his radio news broadcasts, he had done the same sort of thing. But he was always an integral part of *See It Now*, even if he appeared only to introduce it while the rest of the program was devoted to a colleague's report. It was still his program and his material, and he took the responsibility for it, as was the case with his radio news broadcasts.

The Business of Sex was simply something handed him to read, which he had never seen before, but it was regarded as "his" program by those who heard it. The affair emphasized again the growing importance of the producer, rather than the correspondent, in broadcast journalism. Since then, the situation has become worse rather than better.

Even *Person-to-Person* managed to become controversial in the 1958–1959 winter of Murrow's discontent. In February, a month after the triumph of the revolution in Havana, he interviewed a pajama-clad Fidel Castro, by remote control. The Cuban "came through as a warm, troubled leader with loads of responsibility on his young shoulders," one professional viewer thought.

That was the rub. Ten days before, CBS had done a half-hour program already calling Cuba "a totalitarian dictatorship" that was "rapidly becoming a Communist beachhead in the Caribbean." The description was, if nothing else, premature, and Murrow had been angered by it. His view was that the United States, by a hostile policy, was helping push Castro into communism. But the verdict had already been rendered by the American "intelligence establishment," and it did not help CBS in Washington that once again Murrow was at odds with the CIA and the State Department.

Despite all the vicissitudes, *Variety* reported as 1959 got under way that Murrow still ruled the broadcasting scene, and that the furor over *The Business of Sex* was merely a reflection of that fact. Even though *See It Now* had vanished, even though he might be undergoing "disenchantment," *Variety* said, Murrow was engaging in more worthwhile radio and television programs than anyone else in those media. "He has a knack for aligning himself with the right people at the right time, and with the right show."

In addition to *Small World* every Sunday evening and *Person-to-Person* every Friday night, in addition to nightly radio broadcasts, he was presenting such strong television fare as *The Missing Class of '59* — the story of the Norfolk, Virginia, action of shutting all schools rather than permitting seventeen Negro students to sit with ten thousand white — and on radio, a series of six programs, *The Hidden Revolution*, exploring the social consequences of scientific discoveries in the nuclear-space age.

Also, his broadcasts and the successive controversies had made him more than ever a public figure, instantly recognizable, unmistakably individualistic, undeniably well-acquainted, and perhaps even truly influential. Not only did everyone call him Ed, but notables also signed themselves to him familiarly. "Van" was General Hoyt Vandenberg. "Jim" was James A. Farley. "Bill" was Supreme Court Justice Douglas, and "Averell" was Governor Harriman.

As a sort of universal clearinghouse for human anxieties, desires and needs, he received a vast mail from job-seekers, do-gooders, whither-are-we-drifters, Red-fighters, Red-baiters, peace-lovers, autograph-collectors, curiosity-mongers, testimonial-hunters, world-planners, and critics. He was usually addressed in terms of "problems" — "please give me your opinion of this problem." People sent him book manuscripts, plays, world blueprints, solicitations for funds, horoscopes, requests for tickets to television programs on other networks, and requests for advice. He contributed to museums, schools, memorial funds, foreign missions, libraries, fraternities, hospitals, settlement houses, the National Association for the Advancement of Colored People, the Police Athletic League, and the American Civil Liberties Union; to churches, though he was no believer, and to individuals "fallen on bad times." Janet's interests swelled the contribution list even more.

Appointments were always being sought in order that proposals might be presented — "if the issue which I wish to discuss were not of the most vital concern, I would not intrude" — and people with proposals were always being passed on to him by friends, one of the more active passers being Mrs. Eleanor Roosevelt. But Murrow was usually "just off" to interview Nasser or Nehru, and his assignments and absences were the best excuse for not becoming involved in myriad causes. When he was interested in something himself, however, it was quite different, for he quickly involved other people.

It was unusually difficult to reach him by telephone, through the barrier of several secretaries. People he knew well, or who thought they knew him well, frequently wrote that they had tried to get through four or five times, and failed. The truth was, he did not really want to talk to them at that moment.

He was thought to have scores of "intimate friends" among important people, for they called him by his first name, but most of them were merely "business" acquaintances. His fondness was not for politicians, actors, or "personalities" — one exception was Louis "Satchmo" Armstrong, the jazz trumpeter — or even for "men of action," like explorers or engineers, though he enjoyed rubbing elbows with them. His true communion was with men who dealt in words and thoughts, like Sandburg, Oppenheimer, and Admiral Rickover. Underdogs also appealed to him.

Essentially a shy man, he winced at familiarity, and though he relished badinage, permitted no liberties. His only intimates, and with no great intimacy either, were those with whom he worked every day. Once they formed the "We Don't Think Murrow Is God" Club. Every member was a vice president, and the presidency was left open for Janet. When Ed heard about it, he applied for membership.

Even with these close associates he maintained a deep reserve, and often the relationship seemed a one-way arrangement. "We go to Murrow when we have problems," one of them explained. "If he has any, he solves them alone." When Murrow did have problems, was upset, displeased, or forced unwillingly into an unpleasant situation, he withdrew. "His body is still there, he still answers you, but from a great distance. His mind is miles away," Fred Friendly once said.

Nor was Murrow's standing as a public figure entirely a favorable one. He aroused violent resentments, as well as admiration. The followers of Joe McCarthy continued after him relentlessly, for contributing to the destruction of their hero. They wrote to him in abusive terms. One suggested a suitable inscription for the new Murrow-style "Statue of Liberty" — "Send me your Commies, pinkos and crackpots, and I will put them on television." Hostile newspaper critics called him "America's Number 1 Stuffed Shirt" and a "camera hog." His most persistent journalistic calumniator, Jack O'Brian, of the Hearst press, usually referred to him as "Egghead R. Murrow."

Like or dislike, however, there seemed no reason to doubt *Variety*'s conclusion that Murrow was "win, place and show" in American broadcasting. There was general surprise, even shock and some apprehension, therefore, when he suddenly asked CBS for a year's sabbatical leave, starting July 1. He wanted to travel around the world and study, he said.

He had been telling Friendly once or twice each year that he was going to take a leave, and perhaps even quit broadcasting entirely, and go to a college campus.

Now he explained, "It'll be the first time in thirteen years I'll be seeing the first act of a play." He wrote Frank Stanton that for twenty years he had believed a reporter should take a year off at fifty, if he could. "I am a reporter, and that is what I would like to do."

The request came as a complete surprise to the CBS management, and with considerable publicity, not entirely favorable to the company. The leave was granted, presumably not without some expressions of relief.

Several factors went into Morrow's decision. One undoubtedly was the "disenchantment" with the broadcasting industry that had led him to make the Chicago speech, and that had been compounded by the lack of any industry response to it.

Another reason was the fatigue induced by his backbreaking work schedule. A few weeks before, the doctor had detected a bronchospasm in his chest, and had expressed fears of pulmonary emphysema. Murrow went through a rigorous series of medical tests and emerged successfully. But he still felt perpetually tired.

He also had personal reasons for taking a year off. For a long while he had been so devoted to his career and public activity that his home life suffered. He was away for days and weeks at a time, leaving Janet and Casey on their own. Luckily, she had become accustomed to it during the war, and was unusually self-reliant anyway. But now Casey was twelve, and had finished the eighth grade at the Buckley School. Ed and Janet wanted to take the lively and impressionable boy to some of the places that made up the world.

A final good reason to get away for a while was the CBS corporate decision to put all informational programs under the direct control of management, vested in a twenty-eight-member Program Plans Board. "No more controversy without committee approval" was the new order of things at 485 Madison Avenue. Murrow had become the Non-Organization Man in the widening and increasingly sticky web of corporatism.

For years he had been free to do virtually what he pleased with *See It Now*, though often subject to retroactive disapproval by the hierarchy. He and Friendly chose the themes, provided the viewpoint, developed the techniques, spent the money, and stood answerable for the results. Some considered that they "were" CBS, and in the best sense, they were. But as a corporation, CBS had to pronounce them antithetical. The Murrow-Friendly team, a humorist friend remarked, had become the Murrow-Hostile team.

Corporate control of news programming did not necessarily mean a reduction in the air time given to such broadcasts, but would certainly mean a change in their character. It was felt on the executive floor that "not every controversy is a crisis." It was asked, why couldn't facts be "entertainment" as well? By coincidence, no doubt, CBS disclosed in its annual report that for the fifth consecutive year, it had been the world's largest advertising medium.

Murrow's leave-of-absence decision brought him hundreds of distressed letters. Many listeners believed he was being forced off the air for his opinions, and quite a few ascribed it to the call-girl program on radio. Some wrote, on the other hand, to cheer his going, declaring they hoped it would be permanent. They defended Joe McCarthy. One man wrote to ask whether Murrow would send him back picture postcards of national capital buildings around the world, for his collection.

An American correspondent abroad, a long-time friend, asked Murrow whether he was going about things the right way. "Seems everybody would be better off if CBS took a year's leave of absence, and you stayed on to run the network."

Actually he would not be entirely disengaged from CBS during his sabbatical. He planned to continue *Small World* from various overseas stopping places — the program had demonstrated he could do this as easily as from New York — and would take part in other public affairs programs as the occasion arose. But he wanted to give up *Person-to-Person*, and he would also like to be freed of his evening radio news broadcasts, and instead do a weekly "news background" program, when he returned in 1960.

There were also some duties before leaving. He flew to London, and with Charles Collingwood, then the CBS correspondent there, interviewed Field Marshal Lord Montgomery. The peppery "Monty" criticized American postwar leadership, meaning that of his wartime commander, General Eisenhower. But he also predicted that the Soviet Union could not and would not go to war with the West, because that would leave "a billion Chinese" on her eastern flank.

Murrow received confirmation of the Soviet-Chinese hostility from Chancellor Adenauer in Bonn, on the same trip abroad. The conversation was off the record, which may have been why Der Alte was so frank. He also felt certain, despite the alarm in America, that there was no danger of war over Berlin. Khrushchev, he thought, was intent not upon military conquest but only the peaceful "economic penetration" of Western Europe.

As for China, Adenauer recalled his visit to Moscow nearly four years before. Even then Khrushchev had made it plain that Mao Tse-tung's intentions darkly occupied his thoughts. Discounting the bitter Moscow propaganda line, Stalin's successor said he had no objection to Germany's membership in NATO, and asked for German help in raising Russian living standards. For the Chinese, he said, "suck us dry like leeches. Imagine six hundred million human beings, each year twelve million more. Where will it end? These are people who live on a handful of rice. Therefore, help us!"

When on June 26 Murrow said "Good night and good luck" to the *Person-to-Person* audience for the last time, he had presented 250 programs in the series. His 499th and 500th guests were Hugh Baillie, former head of the United Press, and Lee Remick, the actress. After six years, during which it had been among the ten highest-rated programs, it was the only program still on the air in its original form. All 250 programs had been live, and no reruns had been shown. *Person-to-Person* had a 140-station network, and had collected twenty million dollars for CBS. It had also made Murrow, sitting in his easy chair with knees crossed and a smoking cigarette in his fingers, one of the most familiar, imitated and caricatured human beings in the nation. "Nobody's brow furrows, like Edward R. Murrow's," a magazine versifier wrote. In the new season his place on *Person-to-Person* would be taken by the affable Collingwood. But another television era had ended.

The same was true on radio. Just before he came to the *Person-to-Person* studio for the last time that evening, Murrow had said his farewell to his nightly radio news broadcasts, after twelve years. To the very end, despite the increasing pressures of television, and its glamour, ratings and money, he had conscientiously every night given his measure of devotion to the medium he still liked most.

On radio he called his departure "overpublicized," and said, "I haven't been fired. I haven't quit. My health is all right," in reply to the rumors that had so swiftly made the rounds. He planned to spend the next year "receiving instead of transmitting," and "I will return with at least the illusion that I know what I'm talking about, being fully aware that some of you are of the opinion this reporter has suffered from an acute case of that illusion for many years. My thanks to those of you who have reminded me that an amplified voice does not increase the wisdom or understanding of the speaker."

The partnership of Murrow and Friendly was not quite concluded. Murrow filmed five *Small World* conversations before he left, and would continue to do them around the world, thirty-three in all. He completed work on an hour-long *Biography of a Missile*, to be shown the following fall, and had several other television programs to do on his journey, the first of them in Iran. "This is a sabbatical?" inquired *Variety*.

But Friendly, left behind, would for the first time be producing public affairs programs without Murrow. With the quiz scandal rapidly developing, CBS had decided to burnish its image by instituting a new series of public affairs documentaries. It may have been an admission of error in the killing-off of *See It Now*.

CBS executives made it clear, however, that the new *CBS Reports* series, though produced by Friendly and though it might use Murrow's services as reporter or narrator, would not be another Murrow-Friendly enterprise, but a corporate-controlled one.

Friendly would be executive producer of the new series. He was assured of "reasonable access" to the network heads, but the increasingly convoluted ways of the corporation made this more a hope than an assurance.

Murrow advised him to take the job, provided he received "reasonable access," but Friendly said later that if their positions had been reversed, he knew Ed would have rejected the new order of things.

When his final *Person-to-Person* program ended at 11 P.M. that Friday in June, Murrow came back to the CBS building for a last call on Frank Stanton. They reconfirmed the arrangements for the sabbatical and for the broadcaster's return. The two men sat up until the middle of the night, disposing of a bottle of whiskey and reminiscing about the long years.

Perhaps because Murrow was going away, that night saw the closest and most amicable approach to each other that they had had in nearly a quarter of a century at CBS. For once, Stanton recalled, "the chemistry was right."

It was the only time. Their careers had started along parallel lines. They had since crossed each other numerous times. Now they were fixed on a collision course.

XI

"I don't think anyone has proved that bad television is harmful"

THE Murrow family sailed from New York for Gothenburg, Sweden, in a thick cloud of cigarette smoke. It filled the stateroom Ed seldom left on the ten-day journey, so that Janet and Casey dreaded to enter. Fog on the way across added to the heavy atmosphere, and so, most of all, did Murrow himself. He was "nervous and jittery and despairing," Janet wrote home. "Just couldn't understand why he felt so miserable. I tried to tell him that he couldn't expect a miraculous change in a few days, but I don't think I helped much." The grinding of teeth in his fitful sleep, which those who had shared a room with him during the war or on assignments always remarked on with awe, sounded loud and distinct.

The American television scene he left behind him had arrived at its "sorriest hour," as *Variety* described it. The approaching new season was regarded as the worst in its history — a statement made regularly every year since then — and one of the reasons was that the control of most entertainment programs was no longer vested in the networks, so that what had been bad enough would undoubtedly be worse. Of the new season's two hundred "specials," 175 would originate with the big sponsors themselves, financing the making of Westerns, situation comedies and police melodramas, in Hollywood. The Warner Brothers film lot there had come to be called the greatest single force in television.

The quiz scandal magnified the ignominy of the hour. The Grand Jury in New York returned a finding that the "big money" shows had indeed been rigged, though numerous witnesses had denied it, and Charles Van Doren had testified that he had never been given questions and answers. But another contestant on the same *Twenty-One* program demonstrated otherwise to the press. He opened three letters addressed to himself, mailed in advance of his three appearances, and they proved to contain the questions that were asked him on camera.

NBC had finally dropped the suspect *Twenty-One*, but the head of the ABC network declared, "You can't kill the drives that are behind the appeal of the quizzes." Then one of the *Twenty-One* producers was indicted for fraud and perjury.

The Grand Jury's presentment was impounded by the court when the two CBS quiz programs, *The $64,000 Question* and *The $64,000 Challenge*, moved to suppress it. But in arguing for the release of the document, District Attorney Hogan finally made public the evidence of fraud and hoax. This set into motion congressional hearings by the same Harris Committee that had lately been looking into the sociable relations between the broadcasting industry and members of the FCC.

The Murrow forces had landed in Europe. The *Gripsholm* was a day late because of propeller trouble, and Ed had to drive ferociously more than three hundred miles to Stockholm and an official dinner of welcome, so rapidly indeed that Janet was unable to stop and view the countryside from which her grandparents Johnson had come.

In Stockholm, Murrow was caught up in a round of interviews, army and navy inspection tours, cocktail parties and dinners, with Swedish government and radio-television officials. At the end of the week Casey said to Janet, "Mom, is it going to be this way all around the world?" The putative answer was yes.

Ed's black Thunderbird sports car had accompanied them across the ocean, and they drove to Oslo and Copenhagen, where he telephoned Friendly and learned he had to go to Iran immediately, instead of two months later. It would be like that all around the world, also.

Murrow flew to Teheran from Copenhagen, after seeing Janet and Casey off by air for Switzerland. There the boy would spend three months in school, while his parents carried out engagements, professional and social, in London. Casey took French and Latin, mathematics and history, in an international school near Geneva, but what he liked most were the long bicycle rides into the Swiss mountains.

While Murrow was in Iran his New York office received from a college discussion club a request for information about "the mortal dangers always referred to by you, that the United States is in." A secretary replied, "I much regret that Mr. Murrow will be unable to give you a list of mortal dangers, as he is out of the country and does not plan to return until July of 1960."

In Teheran the problem proved to be one less of mortal danger than of imperial insensitiveness. For the first time in his long television career, Murrow suffered what he felt to be an indignity, and expressed indignation. He had accompanied the cameras to the royal palace, to see that they were properly installed and to get a "feel" of the elaborate surroundings, on the evening before his scheduled interview with the shah. His Majesty had been playing cards in a summer house in the garden, but the evening turned chilly, and he announced he would take his bridge game inside, indeed into the very room where the *CBS Reports* cameras had been set up.

This meant that Murrow, crew, and cameras were bundled out of the palace by the imperial servitors, and quite evidently with the approval of His Imperial Majesty, until the next day.

Since the shah of shahs was at the time flirting with the Russians, while also seeking American aid, Murrow presumed that his own undignified exit — the "bum's rush," he called it — was a political demonstration for the benefit of the Russians, rather than personal unfriendliness. But the incident established a chilliness between him and the shah which clearly carried itself into the interview. *Iran, Uncertain Ally* was not regarded by him, or by the critics, as one of his better programs.

In London, Janet, who had returned from Switzerland, waited for Ed to return from Iran. He was to give a lecture on television and politics at the Guildhall, before the British Association for the Advancement of Science. When he did get back, Janet was ill. Indeed, all through their around-the-world trip both of them would be plagued by colds, flu, bronchitis, bursitis, and insomnia.

The Guildhall appearance was something that Murrow relished. In the setting where British prime ministers made their traditional annual speeches at the Lord Mayor's Banquet — "in a city where this reporter left all of his youth and much of his heart," he began — he told his audience of scientists, educators and parliamentarians of the limited marvels of television.

He thought its invention "potentially more important than the invention of the zipper," though this might be "an unreasonably optimistic view."

In politics, it was television's duty to "define, illuminate and illustrate the nature of political conflict, to supply the voter with the raw material upon which informed opinion may be based — to operate a marketplace in which ideas may compete on an equal footing."

Unfortunately, the voter might mistake "a mobile countenance for an agile mind," or "vote for profile rather than for principle." Television offered "no guarantee that demagogues can be kept from political power," and the hope that it would enable the voter "to sort out the phoney from the statesman . . . is not proved." The point was germane in Britain, which had just held its first "television election." Until then, British television had not reported the progress of any election campaign, or even carried speeches by, or interviews with, the rival candidates for prime minister. All the political parties feared these might influence the election results.

Murrow believed television to be indispensable to a democracy, he said, but feared that what was being asked of it in the United States was exactly what the totalitarian states were using it for — to distract, entertain, and make the governed content not to govern themselves. But in the United States this was "not by imposition, but by free choice."

While Murrow was speaking before the British association, his CBS superior, Frank Stanton, had been speaking in New Orleans before the Radio and Television News Directors Association, the same group to which, a year and a day before, Ed had made his Chicago speech.

Now Stanton, the man who when they began had hailed the quiz shows as "in the public interest," was not so sure, despite the high ratings by which he gauged things. He blamed "independent producers," not under network control, for the quiz scandal in which, he said, the networks as well as the public had been "duped." He did admit some network remissness, however.

"We should have been more thoughtful and critical of the whole idea of exposing to millions of families games in which contestants can win large purses.

"We really did not face up to the broader implications, whether such programs could ever be an appropriate form of widespread entertainment; whether in their very nature they might contain the seeds of their own abuse and eventual destruction, however well-intentioned the original concept may have been."

He then assured American viewers that thenceforth "what they see and hear on CBS programs is exactly what it purports to be." He not only ruled out any more quiz programs, but promised a "fresh hard look" at all that appeared on the home screen. *Variety* thought the CBS president had "gone overboard on the honesty thing." The news directors gave him their first Distinguished Service Award.

As Stanton amplified his luncheon remarks to the *New York Times* that evening, the "honesty thing" would include elimination of dubbed laughter and "canned" applause from the soundtrack of comedy programs, and the ending of other "deceits." He mentioned *Person-to-Person* as an example of a program that was not all it purported to be, since it created the illusion of spontaneity, whereas guests knew in advance what questions would be asked them. Hereafter, Stanton said, audiences would be told such programs were "rehearsed."

The CBS president's words were printed the day before Charles Van Doren and thirteen other quiz contestants were arrested in New York for perjury. The Harris congressional committee had heard testimony from

Van Doren's defeated rival, Herbert Stempel, that not only had he, Stempel, received questions in advance, but that he had also been coached in facial expressions, lip-biting, brow-mopping and stuttering, to heighten the tension of the contest, as he pondered in the isolation booth. Moreover, he said, he was told that he must "take a dive," or lose, to Van Doren.

As a result, the engaging young college instructor, who had by now been given a television producer's job with NBC at fifty thousand dollars' salary, revised his former statements, withdrew his denials, and admitted participating in program "fixing" no fewer than fourteen times. But only, he insisted, after initial unwillingness. He disclosed that his three months of quiz supremacy — during which he amassed $129,000, got himself two cars, and bought back the family home — ended when it was arranged that he lose in turn, "in a dramatic manner." The new champion would be a woman lawyer, and he said he was relieved when it happened.

Van Doren told his story with tears and breast-beating, and the House committee, visibly touched, praised him for courage and candor. This did not save him from being indicted for perjury, the loss of his university post, and discharge by NBC.

After Van Doren's appearance the committee turned to the CBS program, *The $64,000 Challenge*, and heard from two witnesses about more fixing. This and its sister program, *The $64,000 Question*, had been dropped the year before because of the suspicion that had grown up around them, although their founder, Lou Cowan, was still president of the CBS television network.

All those indicted for perjury pleaded guilty, sought the mercy of the court, and received it. Their only punishment consisted of suspended sentences and sermons. It could not be decided who, exactly, had been wronged by what they did, or suffered therefrom.

Perhaps the most striking aspect of the quiz scandal, in truth, was that though President Eisenhower called the contest-fixing "a terrible thing to do to the American public," the American public did not seem to mind at all.

It regarded the corruption as "part of the act" and the programs as purely entertainment, which was what the producers had said in the first place. Surveys were made showing that almost any member of the viewing audience would have taken part in rigged contests for the money. One poll showed that 54 percent of the American public still approved of quiz shows, after the rigging disclosures, while 25 percent saw rigging as either "nothing very wrong" or "perfectly all right." It was pointed out that no quiz contestant ever objected to rigging while it was going on, and none refused to continue after learning of it.

But public acceptance could not conceal the fact that the scandal had delivered a terrible blow to the self-esteem of the television networks. It implicated not only individuals, but the industry as such, which was presented by its critics as resorting to moral squalor to sell more advertising at higher rates. Despite denials, it was evident that rigging had been done with the knowledge, consent and support of some sponsors, who thereby increased their sales and revenues.

Network executives feared renewed demands for Federal regulation, perhaps of sponsors and agencies as well as of themselves, and Walter Lippmann and others called for "Public Service Television" to compete with commercial broadcasting. Lippmann proposed a nonprofit network like the BBC, a public corporation governed by trustees, but run by professional broadcasters.

This was the supercharged background against which Frank Stanton, in New Orleans, pledged a cleanup of CBS practices, and in his telephone interview with the *New York Times*, equated the rigging of the quiz shows with the "rehearsals" he imputed to *Person-to-Person*.

In Britain, after the Guildhall speech, Murrow took the midnight train to Manchester to make a television version of it for Granada-TV and his friend Sidney Bernstein, whose Granada Foundation had cosponsored the lecture. His New York office finally reached him in Manchester, by transatlantic telephone, to read him the *New York Times* story.

His immediate reaction was the same as his considered one, that so far as *Person-to-Person* was concerned, Stanton did not know what he was talking about. But he made no public comment. For one thing, he was busy. In addition to the Granada program, he was appearing on BBC, and also doing a *Small World* broadcast with Senator John F. Kennedy and Krishna Menon. So it was not until four days later, after waiting vainly for some clarification from CBS, and under the pressure of telephone calls from the British and American press, that he finally answered Stanton.

His formal statement taxed the CBS president with "ignorance both of news and the requirements of television production." Cameras, lights and wires, and indeed the human subjects themselves, had to be moved about during the course of an interview, he explained, and the only way to do these things without "chaos" was by using agreed-on questions as the cues for such movements. Murrow could have added that although the cue questions might be known, the answers were not; also that *Person-to-Person* was a completely live show and there was nothing to prevent anyone from saying anything at all, even libelous or obscene. The wonder was that for six years the program had managed to escape any untoward incident.

"I am sorry Dr. Stanton feels that I have participated in perpetrating a fraud upon the public," Murrow concluded. "My conscience is clear. His seems to be bothering him." A former FCC official suggested a new CBS quiz show, *Who's Got the Conscience?* with Murrow and Stanton as the contestants.

The new "purity kick in television," as one observer styled it, that Stanton's speech signalized, would not last long. In a few months the Hollywood film producers who made so many television programs refused any longer to eliminate laugh tracks, because the sponsors wanted them. The new notices carried by some programs, "The audience reaction is technically augmented," were dropped forever, and canned laughter is still to be heard throughout the land.

"Does Mr. Stanton want me to believe that Rochester really works for Jack Benny? Will they use real bullets for Westerns?" asked Goodman Ace, the radio-television scriptwriter. A Los Angeles television reviewer inquired whether Stanton knew that sponsors shellacked their products and used spurious ingredients, to make them more alluring photographically. Commercials were ridden with unproved statements, he said. The CBS president's reply was that he was not talking about commercials, but about program content only.

"Deceits," as he called them, were and are a regular part of virtually all television programs, including news. The teleprompter is the greatest deceiver of all, giving the impression that the broadcaster has memorized his remarks, or is ad-libbing them. The deception is heightened by the trick of occasionally glancing down at a script on the table before the reader, without actually seeing it. In filmed interviews, unless two or more cameras are used, the technique of reversing the camera to film the questions after the answers have already been recorded, allows the questions to be reworded to show a sagacity or truculence that were not present in the original. Sometimes entirely different questions are filmed, to fit the answers or give an entirely different meaning to them. When the CBS chairman of the board was told about "reverse questions" by a correspondent, he had no idea what was meant, and this was months after Stanton's speech.

Film editing can make a wise man out of a fool, or a bore. As with radio tape, so with film, a man can be heard to say exactly the opposite of what he actually did say.

But above all else, when lights and cameras are turned on, any program or event on television becomes staged. The instinct to act, within the average human being, seems even more deep-seated than any instinct for aggression, and without fear of anthropologists' contradiction. "It's the nature of the beast," meaning both the human beast and the television medium, is how producers explain away the histrionic nature of "issues," "confrontations," urban riots, labor demonstrations, campus revolts and other televised events.

As Murrow vented his feelings about Stanton's remarks from across the ocean, the *Person-to-Person* producers Zousmer and Aaron, his close associates for twelve years, resigned from CBS. *Variety* speculated whether

Murrow, as it had so often rumored before, would this time really sever his relations with the network also.

In London, no longer waiting for CBS "clarification," he now waited for CBS reaction to his own riposte. It was the last October weekend. On Sunday he and Janet drove to Chartwell, in Kent, for lunch with the Churchills. Something of a family gathering was held in the cool, comfortable house with its book-filled rooms. A well-used copy of Chapman's Homer had a place of honor on the shelves. A large wall-painting of Blenheim, Churchill's birthplace, was over the fireplace in the study where they sat, and along the staircase was hung the document Sir Winston prized above others, his warrant as Warden of the Cinq Ports.

The old gentleman himself, in his eighty-fifth year, had become very deaf and spoke with difficulty. He did not do much more than watch the others play croquet on the green lawn, not being interested enough even to feed his Australian black swans.

He was still the Member of Parliament for Woodford, but he went to the House of Commons only occasionally, each time raising a sentimental cheer. Sometimes he had a night out in London with The Other Club, the informal group he had helped found in opposition to The Club, the generic name for any one of a half-dozen in London's Mayfair.

From Chartwell the Murrows drove to tea with Sidney Bernstein, where they met Charles Laughton in a long white beard — he was playing King Lear at Stratford-upon-Avon — and on their return to the Connaught in London found a message from one of Ed's colleagues in New York. When the transatlantic polemic with Stanton was joined, it reported, CBS vice presidents had "dropped from Connecticut like cockroaches from a dirty shelf."

But only the next evening, Monday, did Murrow receive any direct word from the company, a cable that a member of the board of directors, a personal friend of his, was en route to London.

Frank Stanton, who ten years later would confess "it should never have happened," had decided to fly to London himself to talk with Murrow, but was then persuaded that "the lawyers can handle it." He was apparently unaware of how deeply the incident had rankled and felt that the broadcaster had completely misunderstood his purpose. This was to make it clear that the network, and not the "package" producers, would again be responsible for what appeared on television. Stanton felt that Murrow, in his resentment at the slur cast upon *Person-to-Person*, had overlooked the larger consideration.

He also thought that Murrow, three thousand miles away, did not appreciate his problems in trying to fend off Government intervention by self-policing. In the back of Stanton's mind also lurked the thought that somehow his original opposition to *Person-to-Person* as a program for

Murrow may have played a part in Murrow's blazing reaction to his remarks.

On the other hand, while Stanton may not have intended to attribute deception to *Person-to-Person*, by citing it in his statement that there would be no further "deceits" on CBS he encouraged exactly such an inference to be drawn, in the fraud-filled atmosphere of the quiz scandal. At any rate, Murrow so took it.

What arises from the incident, marking the beginning of the end of Murrow's tolerated relations with CBS, is the irony that between two men so schooled in the art of communication, each in his own way, there had been a lamentable failure of communication. Years of failure by both to cultivate some sort of understanding had exacted their toll. Neither Murrow nor Stanton observed the rule of Thoreau. Whichever one spoke, the other did not hear.

That Monday, when he learned that the CBS representative was on the way, Murrow had written to Jim Seward, the company vice president who was his business adviser. "I sat still for three days after Stanton's self-righteous statement on *Person-to-Person*. The telephone rang night and day. No one from CBS management even bothered to call me or send me a cable, so I finally decided something had to be said, and said it. I am sorry the whole thing arose, but I had nothing to do with initiating it."

He wondered if the matter might go further. "I am not reluctant to answer questions, but if subpoenaed or invited before a congressional committee, the questioning may range far beyond *Person-to-Person* and involve answers under oath which might tend further to destroy the credibility of television. This I want to avoid, and I am sure the company would feel likewise.

"If Stanton and company choose to have a thoroughgoing row, I am of course quite willing. But it seems the better part of wisdom for me to quietly disappear in the countryside."

The next day was the Murrows' twenty-fifth wedding anniversary, and they had planned to spend it alone, quietly vanished in the countryside.

Instead the CBS spokesman, Ralph Colin, was at the hotel all day, trying to draft a statement acceptable to both Murrow and Stanton. A public row was definitely not wanted by the company. It had enough on its hands with congressional critics. Colin received frequent telephone calls from New York, the gist of which was that the company thought Murrow should apologize formally for his remarks about Stanton. Murrow, on the other hand, thought Stanton should express his regrets for having coupled *Person-to-Person* with the tarnished quiz shows.

Neither adversary could satisfy the other. Stanton agreed to say that he had not intimated *Person-to-Person* was deceitful, but Murrow held that just such a suggestion had been made, and should be recanted. Murrow also refused to acknowledge that he had spoken "without a full realization of the background facts, and in the mistaken belief that his integrity, and that of his colleagues and producers, had been attacked. In those circumstances, his remarks were perhaps unduly vitriolic." There was nothing mistaken about his belief, he held, and his reaction had not been unjustified.

Murrow refused to sign the legal document that was finally put before him, and Colin went back with it to New York. "A couple of long and inconclusive conversations with Frank" followed by telephone, Murrow reported to Seward, during which the country's best-known and most highly esteemed broadcaster was, in effect, fired by CBS. However Stanton, according to Murrow, did not quite know how to put the decision into effect, especially in the midst of the full-blown congressional inquiry into the iniquities of television. If Murrow had been discharged, he obviously would have been ordered before the Harris committee immediately, as a star witness.

To avoid further publicity, Murrow and Janet fled to the Cotswolds for several days, and he described himself as "completely relaxed." On their return to the city, they brought Jack Howard and his wife in from their Sussex chicken farm for dinner. Howard had been the tail gunner in the plane D-for-Dog, in the wartime bombing mission over Berlin that produced what many radio listeners thought was Murrow's finest broadcast. The tail gunner was one of only two members of the bomber's crew to survive the war. The evening in London was a long and nostalgic one.

But Murrow was by no means "completely relaxed." As he thought about what had happened, foreshadowing the end of his broadcasting career, he perceived that what was going on at home was, it might be said, a struggle for the soul of television, involving the Government, the commercial interests of the sponsors and advertising agencies, and the networks. But the American public, apparently indifferent though it might generally be, was the eventual winner or loser.

He wrote to Colin that "it is my purpose to have some part in this battle," and said he planned to make a public declaration of "what I believe future policies and practices must be, if radio and television are to survive with maximum freedom and usefulness."

He went on. "I cannot undertake to defend all past practices, but can, I think, deal realistically with the potentials of the present system, and the dangers inherent in increased Government control . . . I want to try to make my small contribution regardless of what my relationship with CBS may be."

The response of the lawyer was quick and sharp. He told Murrow he would be well advised to make no further public utterances and "avoid any further open breaks with the industry." It was not proper for Murrow, so long as he was employed in television, "to lend aid and comfort to its enemies."

It was evident to Murrow that the corporate hierarchy had really had no idea of what he was talking about in his Chicago speech, and that "loyalty" to the industry transcended public service. Yet he would also frequently say of his relations with Stanton and the company, and not facetiously, "If I were in charge of CBS and ran it my way, I am sure it would go broke."

Certainly more was encompassed than a personal antagonism between him and Stanton. They represented the two faces of broadcasting, the communicational and the commercial. Murrow was interested and active only in news and public affairs, which formed only a small part of the radio and television spectrum. Stanton had the entire gamut of radio and television problems confronting him — sales, research, programming, public relations, audience response, affiliates, real estate, labor relations, and of course congressional committees.

It was true that Stanton did not know how *Person-to-Person* operated, or for that matter any other news or public affairs program. He had too many other things to think about, and as the corporation became a "conglomerate" of corporations, and nonbroadcasting interests intruded, news and public affairs programming would become even more remote.

But in all these other facets of broadcasting and nonbroadcasting, only the normal commercial customs and disciplines operated, though often exaggeratedly so. Most problems of competition, prices, contracts, wages, and congressional and public relations required only application to be resolved. Very few television programs caused more than small public ripples, for the vast majority were devoted to mere pastime.

But *See It Now* had made great waves in its time, and now *Person-to-Person* had become part of a ninth wave, and in each case Murrow was the reason.

While Murrow had been having his exchange with Stanton, the first of the *CBS Reports* news documentaries was shown on the network, and in its own way it represented the kind of painful integrity that television executives were only talking about. Many months before, when they began *Biography of a Missile*, Murrow and Friendly had decided that every stage of its progress from drawing board to launching pad would be recorded, including the things that went wrong.

They adhered to their plan. The launching was a failure. The rocket blew up. In six seconds, five million dollars and eighteen months' work were lost, and the two producers and their camera crew narrowly escaped being hit by flaming debris. *Biography of a Missile* was therefore not a success story, except in the only way that mattered, as an honest presentation of harsh facts.

In London, Murrow appeared in the first of a series of BBC television programs called *After the Battle,* in which correspondents who had reported the war surveyed the fourteen years since it had ended. He sharpened the pangs of memory for British viewers who, with him, recalled the London Blitz.

While Murrow was appearing on BBC, Frank Stanton was appearing before the Harris committee in Washington. He declared: "We have to find a way to live within this commercial system we have because I don't see any better one outside this room." He testified that he had been unaware of any program rigging, and had accepted the assurances of "our television people" that there was nothing wrong. "This has been a bitter pill for us to swallow," he said, promising to exercise more responsibility for the programs that went out over CBS.

The principal one of "our television people" was the network head, Lou Cowan, who was hospitalized when the hearings began, and who soon resigned at Stanton's repeated suggestion. He was generally regarded as a scapegoat, and Murrow and Friendly had lost one of their few friends at the CBS court.

Under Cowan it had actually become occasionally possible to preempt commercial programs for important public affairs in prime evening time. Even Cowan's own program, *The $64,000 Question,* had once been "bumped" for an hour-long report on China. Moreover the CBS News Department had achieved record sales of news and public affairs programs, and as Cowan was being summarily dismissed, it had registered thirty-eight million dollars in such "billings" for the 1959–1960 season, as compared with only six million dollars for 1956–1957, when *See It Now* was still alive.

After Cowan left some fifteen quiz programs remained on the air, in reduced financial circumstances, but the "big money" shows had faded away, blighted by scandal. But television had found a new way of minting money, while playing the old game of follow-the-leader. For 1960 would be the Year of the Western. ABC had eleven such programs scheduled, totaling seven-and-a-half hours of viewing time weekly; CBS had eight, for four-and-a-half hours; NBC had nine, for six-and-a-half hours.

Murrow's quarrel with Stanton was never settled, and it hung like a black cloud over the rest of the journey around the world. Ed and Janet flew across the Channel by air-ferry with their black sports car, and drove for ten days through France. Being at the wheel eased his tensions, and for the first time in years, alone together, "we belonged to ourselves," she noted. But fog and snow enveloped them for three days at Grenoble, and Murrow became restless again. He telephoned the London bureau, and it, naturally, had more *Small World* filming assignments for him from Friendly. He was to proceed to Geneva.

They picked up Casey on the way, after his brief term at school. "Left him there two months ago, rather pudgy thirteen-year-old; found him lean, fit, more self-reliant, still no great scholar, but the experience obviously paid off," Murrow wrote Friendly.

He also mentioned his strained relations with CBS. When he returned he would like to do a new radio program, he said, as well as *CBS Reports*. But "who knows, next year may never come."

Murrow also wrote his mother a filial letter of explanation from Geneva. "They panicked over the quiz show business, and thought to throw me to the lions. I wasn't standing still for that, and said so. My record, financial and otherwise, will stand the most careful scrutiny. I have not always been right but I have been honest. There is nothing to worry about. They may fire me or I may quit, but my record will stand up to inspection by one and all.

"Over the years I have become what is known as a controversial individual. That means I must expect to be attacked, and when that happens I must answer. Please don't let it bother you. It doesn't bother me at all.

"In the essentials of honesty I was pretty well trained, and if CBS wants a public showdown they shall have it. Lots of people and corporations will be hurt but I won't be one of them. In this business over the years you collect enemies, because you occasionally hurt people. I am rather proud of my enemies."

In a later letter home he further explained, "Stanton . . . doesn't like people who are not afraid of him, and he knows it."

The incident that didn't "bother me at all" gnawed away at him. "I seek no public row with my employers," he wrote Seward. "I feel rather like Clive in the House of Commons when he said to the Speaker, 'By God, sir, in retrospect I am amazed at my restraint.' I hope Stanton will not persist in his provocation about interview shows, or I shall have to come back and have it out in public.

"The next move is up to them. I am determined that if there is a break, they must fire me. After all, they hired my services, not my silence."

He was reading Macaulay on the trip, and continued to do so at St. Moritz, where they spent Christmas. Although Casey learned to ski, Murrow did not like the resort because of the "high-altitude parasites" there. He had also read *The Bible as History* and was "all steamed up" about doing "a Biblical series in modern dress, shot on the ground," an idea which the BBC finally carried out eight years later. He mentioned the Bible program to his mother, and added, "It would be strange, after your hoping but never saying that I should be a preacher, if I were to use television to bring the Bible to millions of people."

From St. Moritz he drove three times to Zurich to do *Small World* programs. When they left Switzerland in January for Rome, sleet and snow dogged them again along the way, and though at Pisa Ed accompanied Casey to the top of the Leaning Tower with schoolboy gaiety, despondency had settled upon him again. From Rome he wrote Seward, "This leave just isn't working out. I can neither sleep nor relax. The complete exhaustion is worse than when we left. It's rather discouraging. Maybe things will improve with a bit of sunshine."

They would get the sunshine in Israel. They drove to Naples to embark, and on the way he showed Casey the Anzio beachhead and the ruins of Pompeii, while at NATO southern headquarters Ed took a physical examination. He had applied for, and would receive, a lieutenant commander's commission in the Naval Reserve, as, of all the things he abhorred, a public information officer. He may have been thinking of leaving CBS, or perhaps, in his fatigue, he merely wanted the solace of a satisfactory health checkup.

But Janet had become ill again, as she had been in Switzerland, and when they landed at Haifa she was laid up there with rheumatic bursitis. This came close to being the end of their round-the-world journey, for the doctor ordered her to stop traveling. But she decided she would go on.

The ship to Israel was crowded with Jewish immigrants from Morocco, who gathered on deck and sang as they came in view of the Holy Land. The sight rekindled in Ed the deep feeling for the small state that he had been swept by on his first trip there four years before. At Haifa they were warmly welcomed by an old friend, formerly at the Israeli embassy in Washington, Teddy Kollek, who would soon become the mayor of Jewish Jerusalem, and indeed in time the mayor of the reunited city.

All doors were open to the Murrows in Israel, and though Janet had to remain in bed in Haifa and then at Lake Tiberias, Ed and Casey roamed the whole country from Dan to Beersheba, or as the new geography had it, from Acre to Elat. They had their difficulties. The sleek and powerful sports car, though a magnet for all Israelis — it was only the second of its kind seen in the country — suffered from a lack of proper fuel. The American embassy refused to yield any of its precious hightest, but a congenial major of the Israeli air force put them in the way of some aviation fuel. They mixed and diluted it themselves at small wayside stations.

Under armed escort they visited the Syrian border, where hostile incidents had again taken place. The Israelis had retaliated by crossing the boundary line, blowing up Syrian buildings, and capturing Soviet-supplied weapons. From Tel Aviv, Murrow even did a radio broadcast to New York about the latest armed exchange. At Tiberias, he and Casey went out on a fishing trawler with the same crew from the Ein Gev kibbutz that had appeared on *See It Now* in 1956. Without camera gear and generators for floodlights, it was a much more pleasurable Galilee excursion.

Murrow was working all the while in Israel, taking part in a *Small World* conversation with General Moshe Dayan in Jerusalem and General Maxwell Taylor in Washington; interviewing Foreign Minister Golda Meir. He also flew back to Rome for *Small World* recordings, and to make the pilot film for a new program Friendly called *Mid-Atlantic Parliament*, which never came to anything.

As he persisted in his work habits, his insomnia, teeth-grinding and coughing also persisted. If anything, they seemed worse, Janet thought, or was that merely because she was seeing more of him. "I have been reading Plato, which doesn't contribute to peace of mind," Ed wrote Seward.

In America 1959 had been inscribed by *Variety* as the Year of the Scandal, with the comment that "the breast-beating and soul-searching that followed emphasized the lack of standards, the lack of horizons, of purpose, or public service. The need for improvement was universally recognized. But apart from the technology, nothing improved."

Scandal continued in 1960. Before the Harris committee, Dick Clark, the favored disk jockey of teen-age America, was revealed as having preferred to play records in which he had a personal financial interest. Other performers were also accused of "payola," and then the chairman of the FCC itself, a champion within the Government of self-regulation by the industry as against Federal controls, was found to have received payola "at the summit," in the form of lucullan hospitality from a broadcasting tycoon, on the latter's yacht. The chairman, John C. Doerfer, resigned and was mentioned by some for the presidency of the National Association of Broadcasters, the watchdog of industry interests.

Testifying before the committee on the quiz scandals, Doerfer had conceded that rigging was "a kind of deceit" and "reprehensible," but pointed out that nobody had been harmed, after all, and that to do anything about it would "tamper with our cherished freedom of speech."

He went on to say, however, that if the book *Lady Chatterley's Lover* had been dramatized for radio or television — a Federal court had just ruled it was not obscene — "I would risk going to jail getting that off the air."

The Murrows were halfway around the world when the congressional hearings drew to a close. They had flown from Israel to India, after shipping home their American symbol the black sports car, and from New Delhi, Krishna Menon, now minister of defense, took Ed and Casey to Jodhpur to visit the maharajah and the Air Training College, "inspect" troops, and even go partridge-shooting from jeeps.

The maharajah kept firing away at the birds but Murrow, though a good marksman, did not even aim. "Why don't you fire?" urged His Highness. Said the American sportsman, "I wouldn't shoot anything on the ground from a car." "Why don't you just try it?" he was asked.

Murrow tried, and tried, and tried, and missed, and missed, and missed. The birds were evasive to begin with, and the double motion of birds and jeeps made shooting almost impossibly difficult. The virtuous sportsman finally bagged a pair. The maharajah got sixteen birds.

In New Delhi, Murrow met and talked with Paul Hoffman, who had been in and out of government and politics since the New Deal. Hoffman "wanted to talk about the future of television. I wasn't talking much," Murrow wrote Friendly. "He avowed the whole thing was far from finished. There would be 'basic changes . . . public was aroused . . . abuses could not continue,' etc. I listened. Emerged he had been talking to Nixon — you'll recall that Hoffman was largely responsible for his getting V.P. nomination in '52.

"Curious kind of talk. Hoffman sounded like Friendly. The Nixon reference intrigued me. Probably nothing to it, but Lyndon Johnson and others are vulnerable on this issue, and so far as I know, Nixon isn't.

"Curious thing, as viewed from where I have been for past few months, what happens to television at home seems more, rather than less important than it did before."

Nixon, after two terms as Eisenhower's Vice President, was seeking the presidency on his own, and Lyndon Johnson, Senate Majority Leader, who had become wealthy from a television station in Texas, would be the vice presidential running mate of Nixon's victorious opponent, John F. Kennedy.

Despite his uncertain relations with CBS, and his fatigue, Murrow was still a journalistic firehorse. When Prime Minister Nehru promised him personal assistance in getting into Communist China, he alerted Friendly to have "camera crew stand by." It was "most confidential, mentioned to no one. May be necessary to go without State Department validation of passport, which I have agreed to do. Sorry to be cloak-and-dagger but advised not to put foregoing in cable. In present condition not sure whether I hope this one comes off, but I hear bells ringing faintly in the distance. Not sure we deserve Indian help on this one, but we are going to get a major assist from them, and if they can't bring it off, no one can." But they could not. The Chinese refused.

In India, Janet again spent most of the time ailing at the hotel, but did manage to get to the Taj Mahal. And when they resumed their journey to Bangkok and Hong Kong, all three visited the ruins of Angkor Wat in Cambodia, and Janet could even climb to the terrace below the top one.

Murrow was the complete tourist for once, but his reaction was typical.

"Perhaps when I get home and sort out impressions, this trip will have been worth what it cost, but right now I suffer from a great sense of frustration and loss of time," he told Seward.

"Maybe because it's hard to break with habit, and I suffer from a curious sense of guilt when not working. There is also the fact that so far I haven't found a place where I am not recognized. Too many British and American tourists."

By the time they got to Hong Kong, Janet felt, despite some apprehension, that they had to make definite plans for the return home. "Ed needs to have another physical examination," she wrote, adding plaintively, "if only we could come home and not have anyone know."

Murrow himself wrote Seward from Hong Kong, "I am simply too tired to breathe properly. There seems to be no way to get away from people. The whole expedition just hasn't worked out. Have spent much of the past few days dodging reporters, old friends, who want to know what I do when I get back to the States. It will be worse in Tokyo.

"Unless I hear from someone in authority at CBS I am likely to say that the last contact I had was when they sent a man to London to tell me I was fired, and later I was told on the phone that they couldn't quite figure out a way to do it. And that's where it stands.

"As you know, I am in basic agreement with what Stanton is trying to do, but his last speech made me want to vomit."

By the time they got to Japan — where they visited the shrines at Kyoto, and Ed did another *Small World*, staved off persistent inquiries about his future, and contracted violent stomachache from a geisha dinner given for United Nations Under-Secretary Ralph Bunche — he was still uncertain about his future with CBS, but more certain about his own feelings.

Seward had suggested a conciliatory gesture of some sort toward Stanton. Murrow replied: "I have no desire to prolong a controversy with him, but under no circumstances will I say that my belated comment was extreme or unwarranted. What I shall say is, I go back to a regular schedule on July 1.

"I can think of nothing less important than what Dr. Stanton thinks of me, unless it's what I think of him. The only thing that matters in this business is what comes out of the loudspeaker, and what appears on the end of that tube. Having read his speeches, I gather a concerted effort is being made to improve what appears there. It will be a pleasure to try to contribute in some small degree to that improvement."

He refused to say that the dispute had occurred "as a result of misunderstanding on my part, or that I agree wholeheartedly with what he is trying to do, because after reading the speeches I am not quite sure what that is.

"I think I know what corporate loyalty is. I shall come back to work with good will. But if my conscience summons me to make public com-

A **CBS Reports** *program with Louis "Satchmo" Armstrong*

Every year-end Murrow and the CBS correspondents discussed the "Years of Crisis"

ment on the state of television or radio, I shall certainly do so, and be prepared to suffer the consequences."

From Tokyo the Murrows flew to Honolulu, where Casey at least learned surfboarding, and then to Seattle, from where Janet visited Ed's widowed mother at Bellingham. She was nearly blind, at the age of eighty-three, but insisted she needed no help, and was still strong in spirit and cheerful, though visibly enfeebled.

The travellers were back in the States many weeks before the official end of Murrow's sabbatical. But CBS had already announced the termination of *Small World*, which had in a sense kept him going during the otherwise unhappy and, it often seemed, pointless global hegira.

Once more it was a matter of sponsor's choice. The advertiser who had been paying for *Small World* preferred to switch over to the new *CBS Reports*, which would have more scheduled programs in the next season. As with *See It Now*, CBS could have been presumed to be able to find another sponsor for *Small World*. But it chose not to do so, and the Collingwood version of *Person-to-Person* would be taking over *Small World*'s Sunday evening time.

All there was left for Murrow to do, therefore, when he returned from his sabbatical, was an occasional *CBS Reports* — no longer "with" Friendly but this time "for" him — and a Sunday afternoon half-hour radio program to be called *Background*. It was a major, and perhaps traumatic, curtailment for a man who gloried in his work, and it represented his new standing, or lack of standing, with the company.

Adjustments are quickly made in broadcasting, and the plain fact was that during his absence everyone else at CBS, including Friendly, had become accustomed to it. Moreover, improved technology — videotape, for example, was now replacing film — had made the mechanics of television even more preponderant than its content. More money was being spent for news and public affairs programs, but their nature was changing. Blandness was replacing boldness, and entertainment took over from enlightenment, as committee rule prevailed.

In reaction to the criticism aroused by the quiz scandal, the industry had announced many more news and public affairs programs, but their number was stressed over their quality and purpose. Some would be controversial, like NBC's program on the U–2 spy plane, and CBS's *Harvest of Shame,* but for most of them the producers, including Friendly, would do "controversial subjects in a noncontroversial manner."

In the event, not even the promise of more news programming was carried out. For the 1960–1961 season only six of 108 scheduled programs on all networks could be called public affairs, news specials and documentaries, as against twenty-three Westerns, twenty-two crime dramas, and twenty-three of the newest genre, "situation comedy." David Sarnoff, the board chairman of RCA, said about all the pledges of reform, "I'm not sure that I know what it is that has to be reformed," and again, "I don't think anyone has proved that bad television is harmful."

This was the broadcasting climate to which Murrow had returned.

It was indicative of the national mood which had been brought on by the Eisenhower years — a mood of surfeit after the exhaustions of McCarthyism at home and Dullesism abroad, of credit-card affluence, suburban comfort, and complacent spectatorship. The Democratic candidate would base his campaign on the promise to "get this country moving again."

In the new climate CBS had lost the command in news and public affairs broadcasting which it had held for so many years, and which had been bestowed on it by the work of Murrow and the men around him.

The loss became clear at the Democratic National Convention in Los Angeles. Murrow appeared on television as a roving reporter, rather than a commentator, but when the rival NBC News team of Chet Huntley and David Brinkley easily won all the ratings, he was brought into the broadcasting booth and shared that position with the CBS "anchor man," Walter Cronkite. Other news assignments and broadcasters were also shuffled about, but no matter what it did, CBS was unable to regain the popular preference which had passed to NBC.

"A new cycle in television commentary [has] opened," the *New York Times* reported. "The passing of the Voice of Authority . . . also ended an era." The NBC version of the convention, as a kind of quaint American folk festival instead of a serious political event, entailed informal and often irreverent observation, rather than the sober didactic kind of reporting Murrow exemplified.

Jack Gould, the *New York Times* critic, accepted the new order of things but apparently preferred the old. He thought, despite what happened at the conventions, that CBS was still far superior to NBC in its news documentaries. But he wondered if the new concept of *CBS Reports* as a kind of corporate good-will venture would not blur the distinctive character of CBS News, founded on the responsible reporting of respected individuals, like Murrow, with whom the viewer could feel rapport.

Murrow's own dissatisfaction with the 1960 scene went beyond the corporation, or the political conventions. He was unhappy about the electoral choice offered to Americans. He had small regard for Vice President Nixon, the Republican nominee. He never forgot the role Nixon played in the hounding to death of his friend Larry Duggan in 1948, nor the senatorial campaign in California two years later, in which Nixon defeated Helen Gahagan Douglas by *Red Channel* methods.

But Murrow also shook his head at the nomination of John F. Kennedy by the Democrats. He was disturbed by the large amounts of money spent in the Kennedy campaign, but even more by the grim and unrelenting drive to win the nomination. He was acquainted with the Senator from Massachusetts, and did not deny his charm. But he saw him as a ruthless young man. "He frightens me," he remarked once, during the primaries, and on another occasion he told Arthur Schlesinger, Jr., one of Kennedy's advisers, that Kennedy would become a McCarthyite "overnight," if it seemed to his advantage. The young man from Massachusetts had never taken seriously or as a threat anything that a good friend of the family's like Joe McCarthy might ever do. Undoubtedly Murrow's unfond memories of Kennedy's father as ambassador in London during the Munich days may also have influenced his feelings toward the Democratic nominee.

Apparently Murrow would have preferred to see the nomination go to Hubert Humphrey, whom he had also favored in 1956, but Humphrey was overwhelmed in West Virginia by Kennedy wealth and organization.

Murrow thought it would be hard to vote for Nixon, considering his record, but that as a "poor boy" Nixon might be in closer touch with the realities of life than Joe Kennedy's gifted son. This might even be a "temptation" to support Nixon.

The Nixon-Kennedy television "debates," which partially redeemed the medium after the quiz scandal, helped change Murrow's mind, and he soon came to appreciate the Democratic candidate, not only with one stylist's admiration for another, but for his skill and courage. Kennedy had grown a great deal, politically and personally, since he was interviewed on *Person-to-Person* seven years before, and Murrow evidently saw him as capable of continuing growth.

As things happened, it would be Kennedy as President who would offer him the way out of the dilemma presented by the changed nature of television, and his own constantly deteriorating relations with CBS.

These were reemphasized when on his new Sunday radio program, *Background* — which had brought him a warm response from many listeners as well as a postcard from Dallas addressing him as "Dear Gloom and Doom" — he took his own network and NBC to task for having "remained mute," in the face of State Department suggestions to minimize the visit of the Soviet leader Khrushchev to the United States.

"This is dangerous business," Murrow remarked, made "more dangerous" because CBS and NBC, unlike the two smaller radio networks, ABC and Mutual, failed to challenge or dispute the State Department's intervention. He was not implying that the networks had actually been influenced by the Government, but they "should have reminded it, with just a little intestinal fortitude, that a man named Adolf Hitler once said, 'The great strength of the totalitarian state is that it will force those who fear it to imitate it.'

"It would appear the State Department was fearful the American citizenry would be exposed to dangerous thoughts. The danger lies, not in Khrushchev's propaganda, or the State Department's improper attempt to bring pressure, but in that the networks did not seize the opportunity to defend not only their limited independence, but one of the basic principles of a free society."

He could not help rubbing it in. "I would like to make it clear this does not necessarily represent the opinion of this network, merely the opinion of one reporter who had seen freedom of communications and the free traffic in ideas nibbled away in various countries."

The new season of *CBS Reports*, with Murrow as only one of its reporters, brought the network problems which, since they affected revenue, may have been regarded as more important than any sarcastic scoldings about mere principle.

Murrow and Friendly persuaded it to retain at least one principle, that in news and public affairs, a sponsor cannot be permitted to influence the content, viewpoint or tone of a program. It was a principle which came to be frequently ignored later in the broadcasting industry, when defense contractors and aerospace manufacturers sponsored programs, supposedly objective, dealing with Government policy and action in the fields of defense and space.

The battle in which at least temporary victory was won was fought over *Year of the Polaris*, a television report which was widely acclaimed, not least because it marked Murrow's return to the screen after his absence. "It pinpointed the essence of the unique Murrow talent, a keen, sifting, analytical mind," said *Variety*.

But the sponsor, a cigarette company, was less interested in Murrow's mind than in the sale of its latest brand. It sought to identify its new pack with the Polaris missile itself, using a model of the missile as part of its commercial, and somehow implying that its development was due to smoking. Murrow, with a cigarette constantly in his own hand, refused to allow that kind of copy.

It was an affront to the entrenched authority of Madison Avenue. The sponsor threatened to withdraw from *CBS Reports* entirely, and insisted on seeing in advance the next program, which had to do with the high cost of presidential campaigning in that election year of 1960.

Murrow and Friendly flatly refused to allow the cigarette company to preview the program, and were supported by the CBS executives, in this instance, who ruled that sponsors were entitled to know only the subject of any news program they paid for. The ruling was based on the "prestige, reputations and integrity" of Murrow, Friendly, and CBS.

The network's action was evidently occasioned by the increasing number of conditions and taboos being imposed on television by the sponsors and advertising agencies, who had taken control of so much air time away from the networks theoretically possessing it.

One cigarette sponsor, for example, dictated that on none of its entertainment programs, whether drama or studio panel game, could any actor or other participant smoke a pipe or cigar, or chew tobacco, or even chew gum that might be mistaken for tobacco. Only cigarettes could be smoked, and only king-sized, but no program could show untidy ashtrays, filled with cigarette butts. When public places like restaurants, office-building lobbies, or railroad or bus stations were seen, they had to have cigarette vending machines in full view.

A manufacturer of candy bars similarly forbade the use, or even sight, of ice cream, soft drinks, cookies, or any other product that "might be considered competitive to candy."

Another very large advertiser had program views which embraced socio-political as well as mere commercial packaging. Its twenty-two-point "policy code" stated: "Ministers, priests, and similar representatives of positive social forces shall not be cast as villains, or in an unsympathetic or anti-social role.

"No material shall give offense, even by inference, to any organized minority group, lodge or other organizations, institutions, residents of any state or section of the country, or a commercial organization of any sort.

"This will be taken to include political organizations, fraternal organizations, college and school groups, labor groups; industrial, business and professional organizations; religious orders, civic clubs, memorial and patriotic societies, philanthropic and reform societies, athletic organizations, women's groups, etc., which are in good standing.

"There will be no material for or against sharply-drawn national or regional controversial issues." The "code" did not seem to leave very much room for television-in-depth.

In Washington, meanwhile, the quiz scandal had produced legislation, on the basis of the Harris committee hearings, seeking to prevent any recurrence of rigging and "payola." The bill as proposed included a provision for the licensing of networks, and not merely the individual local stations. It also called for the temporary suspension of station licenses for continued indifference to public service. The first of these proposals was killed in committee in the House. The second was killed by a Senate sub-committee. Its chairman, Senator John O. Pastore of Rhode Island, opposed any license suspension because "the kids wouldn't be able to see *Howdy-Doody*. The station owners could go to Bermuda for ten days, but it is the kiddies who would do the suffering."

The presidential campaign that cost so much money — and future campaigns would cost much more, most of it spent on television and radio — came to an end on election night 1960, with Murrow missing for the first time from the CBS screen, on such an occasion. He had been stricken with pneumonia on the preceding weekend. It was not a diplomatic illness, as some thought, for he never walked away from an assignment, but the fact was that once again he had been relegated to a minor role.

It turned out to be just as well to be absent. The CBS computers projected a Nixon victory. A half-hour later they went just as wrong in the other direction, predicting a two-to-one victory for Kennedy, in what would actually be the closest finish in many years.

Machinery cowed men on this television occasion. Reporters and their observations were superfluous before the tide of statistics. It was, in a way, television gone mad, but election night 1960 was also the medium's biggest single event until then, viewed by eighty million people in thirty-three million American homes.

Soon after the election, members of Kennedy's personal staff were telephoning Murrow and seeking luncheon appointments. The new President wanted to know whether he would be interested in taking the directorship of the United States Information Agency. This was the Government's worldwide communicator of the "American image," which had not fully recovered from the traumatic blows delivered to it by Joe McCarthy.

Murrow had first been suggested to Kennedy by mutual friends, such as Theodore H. White, for the ambassadorship to London, a post which they regarded as a "natural," considering his reputation there, and which he himself would probably have relished. By a coincidence, Bill Paley was also being proposed for the Court of St. James's, to succeed his brother-in-law, John Hay Whitney. But the ambassadorship had already been promised to David K. Bruce.

The USIA directorship offer to Murrow was therefore a second thought of the new President. The broadcaster was not keen to join the Government, indeed any government, which meant to him not only bureaucracy but meant giving up his "purple cow" thesis that it was "more fun to cover politicians than to be one."

On the other hand, apart from its intrinsic challenge, apart from furnishing an answer to the President's call "Ask what you can do for your country," the job seemed the only way out of his difficulties with CBS and Frank Stanton that would not provoke a public row.

These difficulties had just been reconfirmed, by the management's rejection of a request by Friendly that Murrow should again become the "anchor man" and sole narrator, as well as coeditor, of *CBS Reports* and its biweekly alternate, *Face the Nation*.

After their collision over *Person-to-Person*, Murrow and Stanton, though in the same positions as before of broadcaster and executive superior, had carried on no visible communication. And now, as they began to disengage from the long years of incompatibility, it became known that they

The Murrows welcomed to the Washington New Frontier

Even as government official, he preferred shirt-sleeves

had remained rivals to the very end. For Stanton, too, was being considered for the USIA appointment by the President-elect.

Kennedy brought the matter up with a Harvard classmate, Blair Clark, who also happened to be one of Murrow's personal friends, and a colleague at CBS News. At Palm Beach, where he had gone to talk about a prospective ambassadorship — he would become the CBS News general manager instead — Clark was asked at the Kennedy swimming pool about the two men, and which would make the better USIA director. His answer was that if the job was considered to be primarily a matter of dealing with Congress about appropriations, as it so often seemed to be, then Stanton was the ideal appointee. But if Kennedy wanted someone to "tell the American story," as the phrase went, with some hope of making it credible, then Murrow was the man.

Thomas Sorensen, USIA adviser and brother of Kennedy's adviser, had listed the qualifications required. "Experience in world affairs and knowledge of foreign peoples . . . Should comprehend the 'revolution of rising expectations' throughout the world, and its impact on U.S. foreign policy . . . Pragmatic, open-minded, and sensitive to international political currents, without being naïve. Understand the potentialities of propaganda while being aware of its limitations."

It was an excellent, almost a hand-tooled description of Edward R. Murrow.

Outside the President-elect's calculations, Stanton was not a serious candidate for the USIA post. Unlike Murrow, he did not want to leave CBS. When he was also called to Palm Beach, and asked his suggestions about several Cabinet appointments, and then about the USIA, he gave Kennedy a list of several names for the latter job, including Murrow's. He then had no idea that he also was being considered.

The Kennedy consultation process, between election and inauguration, was a perfectly normal one but it had a special flavor where Stanton was concerned. During the campaign the CBS News election unit, among various surveys, had made one based on the Democratic candidate's religion, Catholicism. The results were broadcast, to no startling end. But first Kennedy's brother and campaign manager Robert telephoned Stanton, to complain bitterly that so much attention had been drawn to a matter he thought better left alone. Then the candidate himself telephoned, demanding, "What are you doing to me?" When Stanton pointed out that CBS had done nothing more than many newspapers, Kennedy replied, not very cryptically, "Yes, but they're not licensed by the Federal Government."

Relations were somewhat strained for a while, but when Stanton took over the arrangement of the first of the four Nixon-Kennedy television debates as the climax of the campaign — and many believed it was then that Kennedy won the election — the climate changed.

Now it was the Republicans who assailed CBS, accusing the network of skulduggery with its camera work, lighting and even Nixon's facial makeup, to emphasize his "five o'clock shadow." It turned out that the makeup and lighting were supervised by Nixon's own men, and that the camera technique of occasionally filming Nixon's reaction while Kennedy spoke was at least as old as *See It Now*.

The Kennedys were highly pleased by the effect of the first and crucial debate, and became affable. They telephoned Stanton frequently and asked him to Palm Beach and Georgetown. He had suggested several persons as possible USIA directors, but finally it was he himself who was first offered the position, by the President-elect. When he refused, Murrow became the choice.

But the broadcaster attached a condition to his acceptance of the job. He had asked Bill Paley for counsel, and the board chairman said it was not a matter on which advice could be given. He did not think Murrow should accept the Kennedy offer, but if he did, he should insist on full participation in Government decision-making. "Get it in writing, even if it has to be written in blood," Paley recommended. Murrow had the same idea.

He was not to leave CBS without a final flaming controversy, in fact one that would be sharpened and lead to embarrassment even after he joined the Government. On the Friday after a bountiful Thanksgiving Day, and designedly so, *CBS Reports* brought into American living rooms a 1960 *Grapes of Wrath*. It was described by one reviewer as "searing and searching," and "a needed indictment of a blight on the American scene."

Harvest of Shame was a report on the plight of the migratory farm workers, Negro and white, who as virtual peons kept the nation's larders stocked. The public reaction to it was one of surprised horror at the conditions portrayed. Farm organizations were horrified for other reasons, charging "highly colored propaganda" and "deceit." Farmers' spokesmen demanded "equal time," and shopkeepers at the Florida winter camp of the migratory workers, protesting the program — though the workers themselves obviously did not — threatened to boycott the sponsor's cigarette brand.

The controversy over *Harvest of Shame* coincided with a kind of phasing-out of CBS public affairs programs — "because they cost too much" — by James Aubrey, the television network president who had succeeded Lou Cowan, and who had dedicated himself to making more money than ever for CBS.

One of his first moves was to subvert *CBS Reports*. It had been shown irregularly for several months and was doing relatively well when Aubrey, faced with an unexpected situation in the week's programming, decided to give it regular biweekly scheduling. This was not the accolade it might have seemed.

For the unexpected situation was the phenomenal success, on Thursday evenings, of an ABC network program called *The Untouchables*, a series of melodramatic episodes purporting to be based on the Chicago gang wars of the Prohibition era. *The Untouchables* was truly untouchable, so far as Thursday night audience ratings went, no matter what the other networks presented in competition with it. Since any program scheduled for the same time as *The Untouchables* would automatically be machine-gunned to death by it, that was where Aubrey chose to put *CBS Reports*. Matters were made even worse by management's rejection of the idea that Murrow should become the program's principal reporter, narrator and coeditor.

The closing days of 1960 were the Twilight of the Gods at CBS. Murrow was preparing to leave. *CBS Reports* was before the firing squad. The Aubrey regime, which was contemptuous of news and public affairs, was solidly installed with such new popular entertainment favorites as *Beverly Hillbillies*.

To formalize the reduced role of *CBS Reports*, and for that matter the entire CBS News division, a News Executive Committee was created to decide news policy and supervise news programming. This may have been the straw that broke the back of Murrow's relationship with the network. The committee included the antinews Jim Aubrey, and its chairman was a company lawyer and congressional relations man, Richard Salant, who was soon to be given the title of president of CBS News. The editorial decisions were made by Bill Paley, as before, but to outside observers it might have seemed that they became more muffled than ever.

The network of *The Beverly Hillbillies* was not as likely to be suspected of harboring subversives as the network of *See It Now*, and Joe McCarthy was dead, so the actress Jean Muir, listed ten years before in *Red Channels* and unemployable in radio and television since then, was finally given a dramatic role by CBS. The long-delayed libel suit of John Henry Faulk against Aware, Inc. was in the pretrial stage and moving toward the courtroom. Blacklisting had eased in broadcasting, though it was by no means ended. Another seven years would be required for the folk singer Pete Seeger to appear on a commercial television network again, after his blacklisting in the McCarthy period.

The new administration was preparing to take over in Washington, and Murrow had become involved in its plans for the more effective use of the United States Information Agency even before his appointment as its director. Among the several task forces put to work by the President-elect, to deal with the problems lying ahead, one was studying the obvious inadequacies of the Government's propaganda around the world.

These inadequacies had come about partly because of the drubbing given the International Information Administration, as it was then known, in Senator McCarthy's investigation of it. As a result, it had concentrated on the negative propaganda line of anticommunism, instead of developing a positive program to support the American "image."

As the task force discovered, the United States, while generally "liked" abroad, was not highly respected, or regarded with much confidence as a leader. Doubts were expressed in many countries about American wisdom, perspective, understanding, and disinterestedness. Even American technology, which had commanded admiration where little else American did, had suffered in reputation from the successes of Soviet space and nuclear science.

The USIA, absorbed in its anticommunism, was found by the Kennedy task force to be ineffectual in identifying the United States with the "revolution of aspirations." It stood for the political and economic status quo, and had failed to come to terms with nationalism, perhaps the most powerful political and emotional force in large areas of the world.

On the working level, American information offices abroad had not established any rapport with the new elites of the world, whether middle-class or military, much less with organized labor and the intellectuals. They were found to be lacking in any clear objectives, in their cultural and informational programs.

Above all, the USIA had carried little or no weight in the formulation of policy by the American Government. It was not consulted by the White House or State Department about the possible effect of intended American actions abroad. It was told merely to rationalize and justify such actions, after they had been taken.

On the Kennedy New Frontier, it was said, all this would be changed. The USIA would bring applied psychology to bear on international relations. The task force recommended that a Psychological Requirements Board be created within the National Security Council, to concern itself with American prestige, define American objectives, and coordinate American programs with those of other countries of "the free world." It would also press psychological warfare behind the Iron Curtain.

In the new order of things, while the USIA would remain under the policy direction of the Secretary of State, its director would become the chief adviser to both the President and the Secretary on the psychological aspects of international problems. As such he would be a member of the National Security Council which, under Eisenhower, had been the Government's decision-making body.

Murrow, consulted by the task force, was firm in his belief that the

USIA director should have Cabinet rank and should administer an independent agency, kept out of the clutches of the State Department. He remembered that the department had failed to stand up for the agency in
its hour of direst need.

He was not enthusiastic about other aspects of the New Frontier's
propaganda concept. He thought undue emphasis was being placed on
psychological considerations, and not enough on the practical realities of
American interests overseas. The United States, he said, was "engaged
not in battle for men's minds, but for their bellies," and freedom and
justice were "meaningless below a certain caloric intake."

Even more important, the USIA could not define its objectives without
knowing what America's international objectives were. He cited as a prime
example of an American propaganda failure the hostile reaction in Britain
to the establishment of the Holy Loch base for Polaris submarines. This
was because Polaris, he thought, had been regarded in Washington as
simply another weapon, instead of an acute and sensitive political and
diplomatic problem.

As Murrow saw it, the important thing was not that the USIA director,
as a member of the National Security Council, should argue for or
against policy on psychological grounds. It was that he should be informed in advance of policies in the making, and take part in their formulation. As he frequently stated it, the USIA should be "in on the take-
offs, and not just the crash landings," like that of the U–2 spy plane shot
down in Siberia.

He believed that no matter how technically efficient a propaganda machine the United States could fashion, it would not be successful in making ill-advised or erroneous American policy decisions "intelligible and
palatable to the nations likely to be affected."

What he wanted, in short, was to influence American policy-making
into paths he did not consider wrong or unwarranted. It was only on such
terms that he accepted the USIA directorship when it was formally offered. That the President readily agreed was presumably a mark of the
esteem in which he held Murrow, but also an obvious token of the importance to be placed on USIA's new role.

John F. Kennedy was inaugurated on January 20, 1961, and a week
later Murrow resigned from CBS, after twenty-five years in broadcasting,
to become the head of the information agency, or as some put it, the
nation's Minister of Propaganda. He certainly was the most widely known
USIA director until then, or since, and the most lauded. He held all the
prizes and medals that broadcasting offered. He could put fourteen honorary degrees after his name, and was an honorary member of the Order
of the British Empire, a Chevalier of the French Legion of Honor, and
an officer in the Belgian Order of Leopold.

But he was also giving up an income of at least two hundred thousand dollars for a Government salary of twenty-one thousand dollars. "From champagne to lager beer," *Variety* said.

Having been given assurances of participation in policy-making, he looked forward to new satisfactions, to replace those he no longer felt at CBS. He believed it his duty to go to Washington and experience "the pleasure and pain of serving one's country" — "I have been criticizing bureaucrats all my adult life, and it was my turn to try," he explained — but he had some misgivings about it. One had to do with purely administrative functions, which he professed to dislike. Another had to do with the partisan politics he knew he would now be involved in, if only in crossfire between the White House and Capitol Hill, or at budget hearings before congressional committees. As the Government's official apologist, the USIA was an inevitable butt when American policies abroad misfired or backfired.

Murrow was no longer to have the privilege, indeed luxury, of politician-watching. "Are congratulations in order?" he was asked by a *CBS Reports* producer when the USIA appointment was announced. "No, condolences," he replied.

One of the television critics who had always appreciated Murrow, Jack Gould of the *New York Times*, thought he was accepting a thankless job, and deplored the end of the broadcasting career of "a man whose contribution can scarcely be exaggerated," in the form of "conscience, purpose and integrity." But he believed that Murrow's "tough individualism" would carry him through the anticipated battles with Congressmen and other self-appointed propaganda experts, and that his prestige and ability would rub off on the USIA, and rescue it from its accustomed depreciation.

At the Senate Foreign Relations Committee hearing on his confirmation, Murrow, a tense and nervous witness — made more nervous by not smoking at all in his two-hour appearance — was sharply questioned on the two television programs which had stirred up the potent agricultural lobby, *Crisis of Abundance* and *Harvest of Shame*. One committee member from Iowa expressed concern lest, in the name of objectivity, the new USIA director would minimize or ignore the more cheerful aspects of American life, and "stress the seamy side."

A Senator from Indiana suggested to the new director that "selling" the United States to the world was like selling a car, or radio or television set. "You don't advertise the weaknesses."

"You must tell the bad with the good, maintain editorial balance," Murrow answered, hands tightly clasped in self-restraint. "We cannot be effective in telling the American story abroad if we tell it only in superlatives."

The USIA would be accurate and truthful, and not try to conceal American failings. "If the bad news is significant, it's going to be reported abroad anyway. We should report it accurately."

As for the American image, "we shall try to make it clear that we as a nation are not allergic to change, and have no desire to sanctify the status quo. This nation not only has a birth certificate, it holds the patent rights on change and revolution by consent."

However, he would try to persuade television executives and motion picture distributors to keep "harmful product" at home, he said, while confessing there was no legal way to do so.

In no time at all he was involved at USIA in controversy of the kind that had become familiar at CBS. He ran into a storm of criticism in Hollywood, where he discovered it was not easy to discourage the export of the movies most likely to make money abroad, whatever the American image they presented. Indeed, the more garish and violent the image, it seemed, the more money they made.

Murrow also shocked a great many of his admirers, and incurred the only rebuke he ever received from the American Civil Liberties Union, for attempting as USIA director to keep the BBC from showing the *Harvest of Shame* program he himself had made as broadcaster, and shown the previous Thanksgiving.

The man who a few months before was disparaging his own network for not protesting attempted Government intervention in the field of news, now attempted Government intervention of his own. He telephoned the BBC director general, Hugh Carlton Greene — an old friend who was in charge of BBC broadcasting to Germany when Murrow was broadcasting to the United States, during the war — and asked that *Harvest of Shame* be canceled, as a "personal favor."

The request was refused, as it assuredly would have been by Murrow if he were in Carlton Greene's place, and the USIA director realized it should never have been made. It recalled the McCarthy era attempts to take from USIA shelves abroad books deemed "harmful" to the United States. It negated too much of Murrow's past, and was too high a price to be paid to be confirmed. For it was generally understood that a Florida Senator had asked him to make the request to the BBC, with the implied threat of an unfavorable committee vote otherwise.

Pierre Salinger, Kennedy's press secretary, later admitted that the President had also played a role in trying to keep *Harvest of Shame* off the BBC, fearing that Murrow's new position in the Government would make it seem some sort of administration reproach of farm interests.

Murrow at the time denied that any pressure had been applied from any source, and said the request to BBC had been his own decision. He believed the viewer abroad would not have the knowledge to realize that the abuses of migratory farm labor did not tell the full story of American agriculture.

"I yield to no one in my opposition to Government efforts to censor the free and complete flow of news," he said. "There is not enough pressure in Washington to have caused me to do it. I would much rather be accused of a lack of careful consideration, or stupidity, than of having done it as a result of pressure." Some friends, attributing Machiavellian cunning to him, preferred to believe he had done it deliberately in order to arouse a furor, and thus convince Senators and other would-be censors of the futility of attempted suppression.

Still, it was a serious mistake — the more so since, when shown in Britain, the program produced only praise of the United States for allowing its "shame" to be so publicly disclosed — and he never made it again.

At any rate, as one compensation in the thankless job, he had the pleasure of bringing back to the Voice of America the man whose courage he had admired for defying Joe McCarthy in 1953. He took him to a staff meeting and said, "Gentlemen, I just want to welcome Reed Harris back after eight years' leave." He made Harris his executive assistant, a kind of anonymous extension of himself.

Murrow also brought to the Voice of America William N. Robson, who had been one of CBS's luminaries in directing and writing, responsible for numerous triumphs in radio drama before and during the war. He had brought the network many honors, but when his name appeared in *Red Channels,* he was discharged. After ten difficult years, Murrow restored his dignity.

Though he had ended all connections with CBS, the new USIA director would be seen on three more *CBS Reports* programs, videotaped earlier for future presentation. But *CBS Reports* was in dire straits, and not all the local affiliates were unhappy that this was so, or that Murrow was leaving. The program had no sponsor, and it and *Face the Nation* were said to be losing the network $250,000 a month.

Harvest of Shame, which had wounded the American Farm Bureau, and *The Business of Health,* which had nettled the American Medical Association — it simply reported on proposed medical care plans, classified as "creeping socialism" by the doctors — resulted in pressures by these strong lobbies upon Senators and Representatives. These in turn used their influence with their local television stations against *CBS Reports.* Apparently not too much persuasion was required.

On Thursday nights, against *The Untouchables, CBS Reports* had been almost blacked out, as anticipated, and there was talk of relegating it again to the Sunday afternoon "intellectual ghetto."

The 1960–1961 season was regarded, though perhaps not by its vast audiences, as the worst and most sterile in the thirteen-year history of the television medium — at least until then. *Variety*, surveying the wholesale replacement of creativity and purpose by "mediocrity and even less," and finding the sole intention of programming to be "ratings and ratings alone," concluded that nobody in television seemed to care enough, or believe in it enough, to fight for a medium "as good as it could or should be."

But even in what many thought to be CBS's darkest hour, in terms of lost prestige — the leadership in television news was now firmly established with the rival NBC — there was the kind of balm which, for corporation executives and probably for stockholders, had become more important than prestige.

The network's profits for 1960 reached the thirty-million-dollar mark. CBS had six of the nation's ten most popular evening programs, and eight of the ten most popular in the daytime, by the Nielsen ratings. It had twenty-four programs in the top fifty, as against seventeen for ABC and nine for NBC.

But it no longer had Ed Murrow.

XII

"Not to capture but to free men's minds"

THE Bay of Pigs, the first venture into international relations of the new Kennedy administration, was a "crash landing" of American policy, after which Murrow and the USIA, the nation's propaganda arm, helped to pick up the wreckage. Contrary to the promise made by the President, Murrow was not in on the "takeoff."

If there was any consolation, it was that other members of the Cabinet, even of the National Security Council, were also not informed of the American plan to carry out an invasion of the revolutionary island ninety miles away, using a force of Cuban exiles and refugees — though truth to tell, any thoughtful newspaper reader in the spring of 1961 need not have been any less surprised by the event than Fidel Castro, who had been publicly predicting it. But Sorensen and Salinger, who had all-day access to the President's office, were apparently not aware of the invasion plot that had been hatched, nor was Adlai Stevenson, the American ambassador to the United Nations, who had his reputation destroyed by it.

The "takeoff" for the Bay of Pigs was Kennedy's, but the "flight plan" was the decision made by his predecessor President Eisenhower, a whole year before, to begin the training in Guatemala, as well as the United States, of what was first intended as a guerrilla unit, but soon became a landing force called Brigade 2506.

The new President inherited the scheme, and while he was evidently surprised by its existence and its extent, he had himself, after all, during the 1960 election campaign, called for strong action against Cuba. The fourth Nixon-Kennedy debate was in a sense a hoax, for it saw the Vice President, who not only knew but thoroughly approved of the invasion, chiding Kennedy for entertaining such "dangerously irresponsible" and "shockingly reckless" thoughts as giving American aid to Cuban "freedom fighters." Nixon later explained that his remarks were part of the necessary cover-up.

Though President Kennedy did give his USIA director a full seat in the National Security Council, the plain fact was that that organization itself, the linchpin of the Eisenhower's administration's governmental processes, was relegated by Kennedy to a much inferior role. He did not care for the Eisenhower "staff command" method of doing things, with interdepartmental differences smoothed over before they ever got to the commander-in-chief. Kennedy preferred to be in on the original discussions and hear the arguments, pro and con, which Eisenhower never cared to hear. Kennedy arrived at his decisions with the aid of "task forces" created to ponder a specific problem. The cumbersome National Security Council, which under Eisenhower had as many as sixty persons present at meetings, was reduced in size by Kennedy and made first a biweekly, then a triweekly occasion, and finally one convoked only when it had to be, for an ad hoc purpose.

Murrow's appointment had not yet been confirmed in the Senate when the Pentagon reported Brigade 2506's combat readiness. On March 11 the National Security Council, considering the invasion plan, modified various of its details, including the proposed landing site.

The CIA, which was mounting the invasion, said it had to be carried out speedily, for Castro was receiving new arms from the Soviet Union and would not long remain vulnerable, as he was then judged to be.

Any alternative to invasion, or its cancellation, was not seriously entertained. The young President, though he had expressed his doubts, was convinced by the CIA of the plan's sure success, and feared that a pullback would mar his administration, at least in the eyes of Cuban refugees, and encourage Castro's insults, and more pertinently, closer Soviet-Cuban relations.

The Bay of Pigs landing was set for April 5, then for April 10, eventually for Monday, April 17. Murrow was confirmed by the Senate committee March 15 and sworn into office March 21. He was thus qualified to take his place in the National Security Council, but when that body met again on April 4 he was not invited to attend. Those present did include Senator J. William Fulbright, chairman of the Foreign Relations Committee, and Arthur Schlesinger, Jr., the White House adviser whose *White Paper on Cuba*, denying any thought of armed intervention, had been issued by the State Department only the day before. Fulbright was alone in expressing open qualms about the Bay of Pigs, but in the end he did not vote against the invasion, and the President ordered the plan carried through.

If Kennedy had consulted Murrow at that point, there seems no doubt that his USIA director would have forcefully stated unqualified opposition to the Bay of Pigs plan. For whether it succeeded or failed, it would establish the New Frontier as a mere military demarcation line, and no propaganda would have an easy time persuading the rest of the world of the genuineness of high American pretensions. In fact, though the President must have thought otherwise, success for the Bay of Pigs venture would have been even worse than failure, from the propaganda point of view.

Moreover the USIA knew of a survey made in Cuba by an American research organization giving evidence of Castro's growing popularity, and in effect ruling out the possibility of any significant anti-Castro uprising. This was contrary to the CIA "scenario." USIA did not send this information to the White House since the White House had neglected to inform it of the Bay of Pigs plan. Five days before the invasion Kennedy publicly, though somewhat ambiguously, was still ruling out any Cuban intervention by "the United States armed forces," and declaring that the United States would adhere to the position that the issues in Cuba were "between the Cubans themselves."

Murrow's opposition to the Bay of Pigs, forthrightly expressed, could have reinforced Kennedy's own initial doubts, and perhaps have brought him second thoughts. But the CIA's overlordship of the project included the CIA "classification" rule that knowledge of it be limited to those having "the need to know." So far as the Bay of Pigs was concerned, the nation's information chief was deemed to have no such need.

It was not until the day before the invasion that Murrow learned anything about it officially, though New York and Miami newspapers were full of hints of imminent action — at least until the President prevailed upon the *New York Times* to suppress the story, an action which he later confessed compounded his error, and made it inevitable. A *New York Times* correspondent, unable to get the story of invasion preparations printed, told it to Murrow's deputy Don Wilson, with the suggestion that a USIA briefing center be set up for correspondents in Miami.

Murrow confronted Allen Dulles, the CIA director, with what he had learned about the invasion. The latter talked volubly of Cuba in general, but let out nothing about the plan, and it was evident he was pledged to secrecy.

But Dulles let the White House know that Murrow had been inquiring, and later in the day the President's adviser on national security matters, McGeorge Bundy, called the USIA director to his basement office. When Murrow joined the Government, Bundy had proposed himself as the USIA's White House "channel," but it had begun to look as if that would be a one-way thoroughfare.

Murrow made known to Bundy his strong opposition to the Bay of Pigs plan, but the first bombing strike against Castro's air force had already been made, and the die was cast.

Some who were privy to the invasion and voted for it later avowed that they had really been against it. But Murrow never said anything subsequently about his ingrained opposition. All he could do was try to repair some of the political damage done to the United States by the fiasco, in which Castro overwhelmed Brigade 2506 in three days and captured twelve hundred of its members.

For the invasion was a violation not only of treaties with Latin American states, but of the American Neutrality Act. This provided punishment for anyone "who knowingly begins, or sets on foot, or takes part in" any military or naval expedition against a country with which the United States is "at peace." However Attorney General Robert Kennedy, who had objected to an "American" invasion but not an American-engineered one, absolved the CIA of any violation of the neutrality act, explaining that the legislation was "not designed for the kind of situation which exists in the world today."

The Bay of Pigs introduced a kind of virus strain into the Kennedy administration. It led to the Cuban missile crisis eighteen months later. It may have prevented the President from intervening in Laos, as proposed by the same advisers, but it set into motion his program for global "counterinsurgency" against "wars of national liberation."

This was linked in the President's mind with Vietnam, as he made clear at the National Security Council meeting on April 22, after the Bay of Pigs failure, the first one which Murrow attended. Even Kennedy's assassination may have had some sort of Cuban context, judging from the ostensible pro-Castro activities of Lee Harvey Oswald.

At any rate, the Bay of Pigs brought Murrow into the administration with both feet. He was named by the President to an inner committee to formulate the new counterinsurgency program, with General Maxwell Taylor, chairman of the Joint Chiefs of Staff, and the President's brother, the Attorney General. The latter has recorded that the President had learned an important lesson, and that thereafter all viewpoints and all forms of opposition would be encouraged in the White House, in arriving at policy.

The Bay of Pigs also brought a change in the nature and functions of the USIA. George V. Allen, the career diplomat Murrow succeeded as its director, had under the Eisenhower "people to people" slogan, and from his own strong convictions, emphasized long-term cultural relations as the key to international understanding. The USIA's mission, as Allen saw it, was to diffuse "good will" in all directions. This was something, though perhaps not so vaguely, that Murrow had also long believed in.

But as a professional communicator, he also had long set the message above the medium. Since he had taken the USIA directorship not as an administrator but, as he hoped, a participant in policy-making, he endorsed the Kennedy view of the USIA as a direct policy tool. Instead of seeking general good will, the information machine would seek for

United States influence abroad leading to political action, with specific objectives.

Kennedy's experience during the 1960 election campaign may have helped shape his view.

He had made a campaign issue of a "missile gap" between the United States and the Soviet Union, only to discover when he took office what he perhaps should have known as a Senator, that nuclear superiority was in fact held by the United States. What actually existed, he then concluded, was a "propaganda gap," as the United States Advisory Commission on Information had styled it, and he sought to utilize the USIA to bridge it.

The USIA task force, which like other Kennedy task forces had collated facts and drawn up recommendations for the new administration, cited specific experiences in India — a country which the New Frontier regarded as perhaps the most important in the world in the cold war — to support the thesis that a propaganda which merely pursued good will was not enough.

In India, as elsewhere, American propaganda had been aimed at the top strata of the society, and was then expected to trickle down, like syrup, to lower levels. Communist propaganda was directed toward the vast masses who constituted bottom dogs. American propaganda, it was found, had little bearing on the realities of Indian life. Information distributed about movie stars, American colleges, technology, architecture, history and political institutions was readable, but remote, while the Communists made highly successful propaganda based on the "imperialism" and "nuclear threat" of the United States. The number of column inches printed in Indian newspapers about the pleasures and affluence of American life might impress a congressional appropriations committee, but in India it was unable to counter prejudices against capitalism, materialism, and racism.

The USIA's new role under Murrow, to make a direct connection between "product" and policy, had its risks as well as its presumed rewards.

The official jargon may have amused him. His Public Affairs Officers abroad, part of the Country Teams, had to reach Target Audiences (including Opinion Leaders and Mass Audience) with Psychological Objectives, as outlined in Program Memoranda, while keeping their activities within the PPBS, or Planning, Programming, Budgeting System.

But both purpose and pitfalls were serious enough. As future events would show, the skillful propagation of poor policy would merely intensify error. Also, short-term objectives were liable to change — for policy does not operate unilaterally or in a vacuum — and propaganda overcommitment to any of them could make them difficult to discard when it became necessary to do so. Short-term actions were likely to be reactions, following the newspaper headlines. Too many crises demanding "operational" response, as in Cuba, Berlin and especially Southeast Asia, might have been blunted by more preconsideration of the long-term implications of short-term "targeting."

On the other hand, "operational" response, while it might entail specific differences with the Soviet Union on specific issues, could also mean the end of the lengthy, automatic and largely sterile anti-Communist orientation of American propaganda. Pragmatism rather than dogma became the USIA watchword.

The new director, part of a new administration dedicated to making things "move," was embarking on a mission to bring some sort of clarity and cohesion to an area of government long marked by confusion.

Even before he took over USIA, and while still at CBS, Murrow had written and narrated for the Defense Department an entirely new kind of troop indoctrination film.

The Challenge of Ideas, a half-hour documentary, for the first time put the "evils of communism" into political and economic rather than emotional terms, and for the first time disdained the usual official sentimentality about "the American way of life," to show strikes and portray racial and other problems. The new film, distributed to military installations after Murrow took the USIA post, replaced two of the conventional types of anti-Communist propaganda, which had stirred some controversy. One was produced by the House Un-American Activities Committee, showing students rioting at its San Francisco hearings in May 1960. The other, produced by a member of the John Birch Society for a fundamentalist college in Arkansas, made the Birchite charge of Communist influences in the American Government.

Such primitivism, which he might have found laughable if it were not so repugnant, raised the question for Murrow of how Americans, suspicious of propaganda themselves, could every day and matter-of-factly carry out effective propaganda, conveying their country's policies and purposes to a skeptical and fearful world.

"To be persuasive, we must be believable. To be believable, we must be credible. To be credible, we must be truthful. It is as simple as that," was his answer.

It was not that simple. The substance of propaganda is information, but information is not necessarily either factual or truthful. It is selective, and that is what makes it propaganda. How can a Government information service provide "objectivity" when it is an arm of the Government? At his confirmation hearing, Senator Fulbright cautioned Murrow. "It is very easy to say we are going to speak the truth, but I predict you will have a very difficult time finding out what the truth is." Jesting Pilate had also made the point. The supreme test arrives when lying is deemed vital to the national security, or prestige, or face-saving.

Though persuasion, in terms of American policy, was Murrow's proclaimed goal, he faced the fact that the more propaganda was openly identified with a policy, the less persuasive was it likely to be. USIA might stress its own overt character, as against the covert nature of the CIA, but too often its method had to be to generate American propaganda without the USIA label, a kind of infiltration of communications. Thus it was not always too different from the CIA, though it might try to set itself apart spiritually. Some of the USIA foreign opinion surveys, or its analyses of Communist propaganda and even of presumed Communist intentions, could not be told from CIA appraisals, or the kind of "sociological" projects the Pentagon engaged in, like Project Camelot in Chile.

The double face of American propaganda, "black" and "white," covert and overt, had existed from the days of World War II, when the Office of War Information, the forerunner of USIA, was not always sure of its functions vis-à-vis the Office of Strategic Services, the forerunner of the CIA. It was difficult for the OWI, for instance, to rationalize the OSS policy of supporting Admiral Darlan in North Africa. Murrow as a broadcaster was opposed to the Darlan policy, and some of his criticisms had a tempering effect on the White House's exercise of it. Elmer Davis also presumably opposed the Darlan policy personally, but the OWI which he headed had to propagandize it. "Military considerations" were in control.

As in 1942 so in 1961 American propaganda was an uncertain trumpet. As Murrow assumed command of an agency with twelve thousand people in it, he had no illusions about the difficulties of his task. This was to try to make the USIA not all things, but one thing, to all men; not merely the voice of the American Government, but the reflecting mirror of a pluralistic, complex, sensitive American society.

He proposed to let policies speak for themselves, after having some share in forming them, but he echoed Kennedy's sentiments that "it is a dangerous illusion to believe that the policies of the United States . . . can be encompassed in one slogan or adjective, hard, or soft, or otherwise."

After the Bay of Pigs, perhaps partly because of Murrow's opposition to it, the relationship between the President and his USIA director was quickly established as a cordial one, based on mutual respect, though in their private characters both men had an instinctive reserve and a kind of scrutiny that precluded any real openhandedness. There may have been kinship in the fact that neither was a theorist, diviner, missionary or zealot. They were alike, perhaps most of all, in their search for meaning. For Kennedy, as for Murrow, the usual question was "Why?"

When Murrow took it over, the USIA in its quest for long-term "good will" was still sending around the world economic commentaries based on the golden legends of American free enterprise. From the New Frontier in India, Ambassador John K. Galbraith, irked by a USIA study of "people's

In diplomatic uniform, on a USIA mission abroad

The President speaks, but his USIA director is not enchanted

capitalism" which portrayed the President as chairman of the board and the American people as stockholders, sent it to the White House with the observation that the wrong Kennedy had obviously been elected — it should have been the President's father, old Joe. The President was delighted, and read the USIA fairy-tale to Murrow over the telephone, section by section, chortling after each one, "Is that what you really believe, Ed?"

In Kennedy's "ministry of talent" Murrow was certainly the best-known figure next to the President himself, and perhaps Adlai Stevenson. At the same time, again except for Stevenson, he was the oldest member of the administration, and though in broadcasting he was accustomed to seeing younger men move up rapidly, and to work with them, it was different, at the age of fifty-three, to begin a new career.

He was nine years older than the President, and perhaps overly conscious of the fact. He called himself the Satchel Paige of the administration, identifying himself with the Negro baseball player who was fifty when he got to the big leagues. It was touchingly ironic that the man who had been so conscious of his youth as to add years to his age should now be so aware of seniority.

Still the perennial critic of bureaucrats settled less painfully than might have been expected into a status and functions that were heavily larded with bureaucratism.

The reservations with which he took the appointment had more to do with this aspect of it than with the obvious challenge offered by the reshaping of American propaganda. It was no more confining to his restless nature to spend a nine-to-six day in a fourth-floor office at 1776 Pennsylvania Avenue — the address was covert American propaganda — than an eleven-to-eight day in a seventeenth-floor office at 485 Madison Avenue. It was no less comfortable to live in a house in Manning Place than in a Park Avenue apartment. There was more green grass and open air in Washington than in New York, and Pawling was not very much farther away. There were several good golf courses near Washington. There was still overseas travel to be done, and Cabinet members, Senators, diplomats, educators, correspondents and old friends to lunch with, though at the Cosmos Club instead of the Century.

But the difference was that he was no longer Murrow, the outside observer visiting Washington for a day or two for news-gathering purposes, but Murrow, a permanent resident and an integral part of the huge Government machine. When he lunched with Senators now, it was to reassure them that USIA opinion polls of American prestige made in foreign countries were not intended for domestic political purposes, even though the President sometimes used them that way when they were favorable.

When he saw Congressmen now it was to impress on them the need for more operating funds. When he had a drink with newspapermen friends, he could no longer talk frankly about policy problems — his ability to do so had made him what he was — because he himself was now involved in them. He freely admitted his change in perspective. "When you're sitting at a meeting in the State Department or the National Security Council you are jarred a little by the accuracy of some of the reporting of allegedly top-secret meetings."

Governmental red tape gave him hard going. Often, in his relations with the Washington bureaucracy, he found himself "talking into a dead mike." Interdepartmental frictions existed. Whatever support USIA received from the President was not matched elsewhere in the executive branch. Secretary of State Rusk, like his predecessor Dulles, did not much care about overseas opinion and had no real interest in the USIA's activities. Agencies like the Peace Corps deliberately shunned any close liaison with it, because they did not want to be identified with American propaganda in their activities abroad.

When the United States finally put its first astronaut into orbit, Murrow suggested to the director of the National Aeronautics and Space Administration that it might be effective propaganda to send the Mercury capsule around the world. Nonsense, the NASA man said, he had already promised it to the Seattle Fair, where Americans could see it. A few days later Murrow saw the President and repeated his world-tour suggestion. Next morning the NASA director, a battle-scarred veteran of the bureaucratic wars, telephoned Murrow. "I've been thinking it over, and I think it's a good idea. Let's send it around the world," he said. No other USIA director could have taken the matter to the President, and the orbit made by John Glenn's *Friendship*-7, this time on the earth's surface, was one of USIA's greatest successes.

Murrow found the agency so handicapped by bureaucracy and the civil service that he once suggested, not in fun, that 80 percent of USIA be transferred to an isolated, though comfortable, camp in the Utah desert, on retirement pay. The other 20 percent would do the necessary work.

He tried to bring to the USIA some of his CBS colleagues, those whom he had depended on over the years for their professional skills as well as their comradeship. He was able to comprehend, perhaps better than they knew, their reluctance to go into government service.

At 1776 Pennsylvania Avenue, a governmental beehive where, unlike 485 Madison Avenue, he had to tell the elevator operator what floor he wanted, he carried his CBS informality into the USIA. He received visitors, even distinguished ones, in shirtsleeves in a room that, like a radio studio, was kept air-conditioned in winter as well as in summer. As at CBS, he had a draftsman's table of wood and steel in one corner, at which he stood while reading. It was always covered with newspapers and magazines. The walls were occupied by filled bookshelves.

As always, he let others talk. He shunned Washington cocktail parties, and preferred a Scotch-and-water with one or two acquaintances, usually at home.

He worked late, bringing papers back with him at night, something he had rarely done at CBS. He had never slept well but now friends from London, visiting the Murrows, heard him coughing heavily and unceasingly in the night, and were perturbed. Janet said that the latest X-rays were clear, but they could not help wondering about his health. In spirit, however, they had never known him better, though he confessed to them that he did not mix easily with the young Washington intellectuals. He called these the "fluent society."

Some members of Congress, and even some members of the Kennedy administration, clearly rubbed him the wrong way, for he never tolerated fools, much less the self-righteous. He undoubtedly held some grudges. But as in his broadcasting career, it was rarely evident in his manner toward such people, or his basic judgment of them. Regardless of his own feelings, he seemed able to evaluate people and events on the evidence. He was therefore a welcome, indeed highly unusual, addition to government councils.

Some of his oldest friends, such as Sam Rosenman, who had once vigorously tried to persuade him to run for the Senate, thought Murrow's entry into Government service was a waste of talent, and would only bring him frustration and disappointment, as it had to Elmer Davis at OWI. But many others, especially in Washington, where they could see him, believed Murrow found himself again in USIA, after his long frustration and disappointment at CBS. He was no longer the gloomy "wraith" that one member of the Kennedy entourage remembered from New York dinner parties. With a new sense of purpose and a feeling of participation, he seemed to have become cheerful, cool, and committed again. The "professional doubter," Arthur Schlesinger thought, had at last "found someone since Churchill in whose intelligence and purpose he could believe."

1776 Pennsylvania Avenue was only two blocks from the White House, but under Murrow USIA was in mood even closer than that. Apart from President Kennedy's keen interest in how America was regarded abroad; apart from his intention of making policy use of the agency, and his high regard for Murrow, there was the fact that Don Wilson, the deputy director, on leave from *Life* magazine, had taken part in the Kennedy presidential campaign as a press aide, and was a "touch-football friend" of Robert Kennedy.

The number-three man at USIA, in charge of policy, was Tom Sorensen, the brother of Kennedy's principal adviser and speechwriter.

By statute both Wilson and Tom Sorensen were direct presidential appointees also, instead of being chosen by the new director, as might have been expected. They were already in place when Murrow arrived and there was an initial uncertainty about the relationship. It was then Murrow tried to persuade several CBS friends to join him. He soon found, however, that he, Wilson and Sorensen constituted a smooth-working "troika," as he called it, after the then-current Russian proposal for running the United Nations.

Murrow even overcame his original uneasiness with Robert Kennedy, the "young man of the year" who had once walked out on him. He attended the Attorney General's "Hickory Hill seminar" of Cabinet officials, and as he worked more closely with the younger Kennedy in counterinsurgency planning and other matters, he came to respect him more. But when Kennedy sought his endorsement in 1964 for the same Senate seat which Murrow had refused to seek in 1958, he would call him a "carpetbagger" and deny it. Janet did sign a public statement on behalf of Kennedy's candidacy. But Murrow wrote a friend explaining his rejection of it, and recalling his own refusal to run. "I am at least consistent in refusing to have anything to do with New York State politics. You will find somewhere in the records that about 1768 a new Governor-General was sent out from London. He was briefed intensively for three days on politics in the Colony of New York, and promptly committed suicide."

Murrow not only sat in the National Security Council but, more important in the Kennedy administration, in some of the smaller inner committees that really grappled with policy, like those on counterinsurgency and the Berlin crisis of 1961.

He did not speak much or often, and could go through an entire meeting without uttering a word, but when he did, he was listened to. "He never fought a problem. He never tried to impose himself on it," recalled one of Kennedy's closest advisers.

But Murrow could in no way be called an intimate of the President, and though the "blow torch" was frequently used, meaning the direct White House telephone, invariably it was the President who called him, as he called other agency heads, merely to "heat 'em up, and get 'em moving."

And as the administration faced serious new problems, and policy-making became more complex, delicate and even devious — while at the same time Murrow's physical activity was lessened by illness — the White House connection became a more tenuous one. Once again, as in the past, the USIA would be not consulted so much as informed, and told to propagandize.

In addition to White House task force meetings, Murrow attended the Monday, Wednesday and Friday morning briefings given to the Secretary of State by the Pentagon, the CIA and other agencies. He then held USIA troika meetings to discuss them. He also introduced his own Wednesday afternoon "think-ins" for USIA planners and program-makers. These collegelike bull sessions were devoted to give-and-take on any subject that came up, and were regarded as the most stimulating part of the work week by those present.

It was marveled at 1776 that the director himself should attend the staff Christmas party, the first ever to do so. In honor of the event, a special edition of *Amerika,* the USIA's magazine for Eastern Europe, was printed for party distribution, devoted entirely to pro-Murrow propaganda. None of these innovations, denoting cameraderie, survived his directorship.

As he turned American propaganda toward positive political ends, rather than mere "good will," Murrow took the line on Cuba that the United States was not counterrevolutionary, as Fidel Castro charged, but that approval of social change did not mean approval of authoritarianism, or attempted subversion of other countries.

He also increased American efforts to influence the so-called third world between the American and Soviet blocs, the nonaligned nations which John Foster Dulles had regarded as "immoral" for their neutrality. The USIA began to stress American pluralism rather than free enterprise, and the Voice of America, one witness remarked, "became the voice, not of American self-righteousness, but of American democracy."

Murrow described his kind of propaganda as an attempt "not to capture, but to free, men's minds."

Nonetheless it was policy that had to define propaganda, and the administration that had taken office partly on the foundation of a nonexistent "missile gap" faced the fact that five days before the Bay of Pigs, the Soviet Union had put the first man in orbit around the earth, Yuri Gagarin, with important implications for space and missile technology.

Kennedy therefore ordained an increase in American missile strength, accepting a "counterforce" rather than a "countercity" strategy. Evidently in fear of charges of appeasement from the Republican opposition, and always aware that he had won his mandate by the narrowest of margins, he challenged the Russians by a massive defense buildup. This in turn provoked similar action by them.

Such was the background for the Kennedy-Khrushchev meeting in Vienna, where the Soviet leader, overreacting to the American setback at the Bay of Pigs — Kennedy told him it was a mistake — probed to see how far he could go on Berlin, and threatened to make a separate peace with East Germany before the end of the year.

The grim meeting visibly shook the young President, and fearing the possibility of a nuclear clash over Berlin — his brother Robert declared he would use nuclear weapons to "save" that city — he recommended a shelter program at home, and further increased the American missile program.

It was not over Berlin but over Cuba that the nuclear confrontation would actually come. But meanwhile, after a moratorium of thirty-four months, the world was again made aware of the ultimate peril when Khrushchev announced that the Soviet Union would resume atmospheric testing.

The reaction to the announcement was something of a defeat for the USIA's new policy of trying to influence the third world, for the sixty-one nonaligned nations, meeting in Belgrade, did not condemn so much as regret the Soviet decision. They called on both sides to disarm, and indeed blamed the Soviet action on the United States.

Khrushchev's declaration of intention brought sharp reaction in Washington, however. The Joint Chiefs of Staff, the CIA, the Atomic Energy Commission, Congressmen, and many scientists, led by Edward Teller, urged the President to reciprocate, and order the resumption of American atmospheric testing immediately. The firmest voice raised against such a course was Murrow's.

At the National Security Council meeting where Secretary Rusk had prepared a statement announcing American resumption, Murrow argued his brief from the viewpoint of a propaganda chief who saw an opponent making bad propaganda for himself, and thought he should be left to continue to do so. He urged that as much time as possible be allowed to elapse, before American testing was resumed, in order to get the full psychological advantage of the undoubted pall the Russians had thrown upon the world.

Against the formidable array of those urging immediate testing — "who . . . will tomorrow contend that the decision to do so was merely another belated reaction to Soviet action," Murrow told the President, in passing criticism of the very rationale of the cold war — Kennedy decided merely to announce "preparations" for the resumption, while reiterating his hope for a treaty to ban further nuclear detonations and fallout.

The United States did not begin atmospheric tests again for eight months, by which time the Russians had made several, and over and over again USIA made the propaganda point that Moscow had unilaterally broken the moratorium. This was emphasized by playing back to the Russian people, in Voice of America broadcasts, the words of their leaders and of Radio Moscow, opposing any renewal of nuclear experiments.

The USIA also adopted new tactics toward the sensitive domestic racial problem, which had blemished the American image abroad. Instead of skirting the question, as it had at the time of the Little Rock school crisis, it faced it head-on. The new candor of its reporting and interpretation exposed it to the wrath of Southern Congressmen, and when the agency made a forceful film of the 1962 "March on Washington" to send around the world, congressional demands were raised for its suppression. Murrow overrode them. The *Harvest of Shame* incident had taught its lesson.

Despite inevitable friction with Congress — another dispute arose when the USIA gave domestic distribution to films of Mrs. Jacqueline Kennedy visiting India and Pakistan — Murrow's relations with the legislators were generally good, and he was accepted on Capitol Hill as plainspoken and even guileless.

He had difficult moments at budget hearings, where USIA was constantly on the defensive. Its results, if any, were intangible, though its costs were not, and no correlation could be made between its activities and the rise and fall of American "popularity" abroad.

As he sweated before congressional committees, he may have remembered the offhand way in which as a member of the CBS board of directors he had solved the network's problems with Congressmen by saying "Tell 'em to go to hell." Now, unlike other department heads who merely made opening statements and departed, he sat through all hearings, to support the testimony of other witnesses and bear the brunt of cross-examination.

But informally he was popular even with members of the Appropriations subcommittee. He had breakfast discussions with congressional groups, gave talks to senatorial secretaries, lunched with key legislators, and made radio and television appearances with Congressmen, for the "reports" to their constituents that were seen and heard in their own districts, a role which, naturally enough, no other USIA director had fitted.

Commercial radio and television had by this time become somewhat remote to the former broadcaster, but it was not without its grim interest, beyond his governmental association with it, as a user of film and sound material for USIA and Voice of America programs.

The commercial television scene had altered only for the worse since his departure. A former law partner of Adlai Stevenson, Newton Minow, had been appointed chairman of the FCC, and he stood up before the National Association of Broadcasters in Washington, and became as "controversial" to the industry as Murrow had been with his Chicago speech nearly three years before, and with much the same bill of indictment.

"When television is good, nothing is better. But when television is bad, nothing is worse. I invite you to sit down in front of your TV set and keep your eyes glued to that set until the station signs off. I can assure you that you will observe a vast wasteland," Minow declared.

"You will see a procession of game shows, violence, audience participation shows, formula comedies about totally unbelievable families, blood and thunder, mayhem, violence, sadism, murder, Western badmen, Western good men, private eyes, gangsters, more violence, and cartoons. And endlessly, commercials, many screaming, cajoling, and offending. And most of all, boredom. True, you will see a few things you will enjoy. But they will be very, very few. And if you think I exaggerate, try it."

The new FCC chairman's plea was for "more wide-open spaces between Westerns, and more public affairs than private eyes." As he took office a Senate committee began an investigation of television violence, crime and sex, but its chairman, Thomas Dodd of Connecticut — whose senatorial ethics were later to be put in question by his colleagues — shut off the hearings when they began to come too close to the bone of network responsibility. He even accused his committee staff of "persecuting" a network president, Robert Kintner of NBC.

Similarly, a three-year FCC investigation of the networks' allegedly monopolistic practices was ending inconclusively. The commission had tried to establish whether the networks denied American viewers the largest possible range and variety of television programming, in violation of the Communications Act. Minow's "vast wasteland" speech, with its implication of more Federal supervision, had spurred the networks once again to the temporary introduction of more public affairs broadcasts. But the industry's leaders still professed to believe that they were providing precisely "what the public wants." Frank Stanton, of CBS, foresaw no popular uprising against television. "One man's mediocrity is another man's good program," he told the commission, and it would be "antidemocratic" for anyone but the public to "choose."

Spokesmen for all three networks complained to the commission of the high cost of news and public affairs programs. Jim Aubrey, the president of CBS television, describing the medium as a "vast wonderland," reported that his network had "lost" five million dollars on such programs in 1961, even though more public affairs programs had become "commercial" and, whatever their subject, were accepted without the kind of commotion *See It Now* used to cause.

This very "acceptance," and the lack of public excitement or sponsor anguish, epitomized the changed character of such programs. A typical Murrowless *CBS Reports, Thunder on the Right*, presented the views and activities of the Minute Men, the John Birch Society, and other political extremists, in a detached sort of way, without conclusions. It might even have constituted free advertising for the right-wingers. It was produced by the same Fred Friendly who, with Murrow, had produced *See It Now*'s McCarthy program, with its very definite conclusions.

The new conformity of television news had by now also resulted in the resignation of Howard K. Smith as the CBS Washington correspondent, the man who after Murrow's departure had become the network's principal news figure. The issue was the hoary one of "editorializing." Smith had concluded a *CBS Reports* program on the racial conflict in Birmingham, Alabama, with some trenchant comments — for one thing, he compared some Southern white supremacists to Nazi storm troopers — but Friendly, the producer, eliminated them as "too editorial." Smith asked that the CBS policy for commentators be made as permissive as it had been during the Murrow period, or that it be changed to permit carefully labeled editorial opinion, as in newspapers. Both suggestions were rejected, and he left for ABC where, unfortunately, he did not fare much better.

Coincident with the decline in its standards of public affairs programming — and with a new high level of public complaints received by the FCC about misleading advertising and offensive commercials, as well as violence and crime — television was increasingly prosperous. It found ever new ways of being so. It was, for instance, utilizing forty-second instead of thirty-second "station breaks." These are the half-hourly intervals for local stations to cut in and identify themselves during network programs, under FCC regulations. But station breaks had come to be sold for local "spot" commercials, often of the shoddiest sort. An added ten seconds of station break seemed a trifling matter, but ABC, which pioneered the new advertising Golconda, expected to increase its annual revenue by $2.5 million, from its five owned-and-operated local stations. Similar treasure came the way of all network affiliates, as the "fifty-four-minute hour" on television became ten seconds shorter.

Yet vast and barren as the television wasteland may have been in 1961, it still provided 15 percent more network public service programming than the 1964–1965 season would do, as another FCC commissioner later noted. As for Minow, when he left the commission to return to law, he became counsel for CBS in Chicago, paid to defend the same practices he had latterly been criticizing.

Murrow had not quite escaped from the commercial television world in his government office. USIA's propaganda activities to some extent depended on material obtained from the medium. But when he tried to create a new kind of relationship between the Government and private broadcasting, the industry, so vulnerable for so many shortcomings, took pride in administering him a rebuff. It may not have been undeserved, illustrating as it did the altered perspective of the poacher turned game-keeper.

Murrow had made his suggestion in a letter to David Sarnoff, the broadcasting industry's first consul. He disavowed any desire to "influence or control" the export of American television films and programs, but he felt "if we in this agency could define more clearly than we have in the past what would be useful for showing abroad, particularly in the field of documentaries, we might persuade the networks to produce them for initial showing in this country, so that we might then make secondary use of them abroad."

USIA's role in inspiring, or "planting," such films would be kept secret.

A similar system already prevailed in its commissioning of books, without revealing subsidy payments to authors and publishers. The Book Development Program, financing works written "to our own specifications, books that would not otherwise be put out, especially those books that have strong anti-Communist content," was started long before Murrow came to USIA. It would come to grief in 1966 when a congressional committee called into question, not the books, but the secrecy enveloping them.

Any planting of television documentaries by the Government was scotched, however, at least in the form proposed by Murrow. The USIA director, whose indignation might have been presumed if such a suggestion had been broached to him while he was making *See It Now* and *CBS Reports* documentaries, had explained that the agency did not have men or money enough to produce its own propaganda films, and therefore sought to serve "the national purpose" through the networks.

Sarnoff, with apparently no deep feelings about such a covert relationship, turned the matter over without comment to his network president, Bob Kintner. The latter took time out from his defense of the medium against charges of displaying undue violence in its programs, and assumed the mantle once worn by Edward R. Murrow.

He chose to distinguish between "the national interest" and what USIA thought "would best serve its purpose."

Kintner called Murrow's idea not only wrong in principle — because it would mean government influence on the subject matter of television programs — but deceptive. While the USIA might secondarily show such films abroad, he pointed out, their primary use would be inside the United States, on network programs. Therefore, contrary to USIA statute, the Government would be engaging in domestic propaganda.

Murrow answered that he had been merely "thinking aloud" and had no desire to influence network programming. He hoped it would not be taken amiss if he suggested program ideas "informally" to "old friends" in the industry. Some time later, after Murrow had resigned from USIA, Kintner would leave NBC and join, as White House aide and speechwriter, the Johnson administration, widely regarded as having brought "news management" to its most diligent peak.

Following his brush with Kintner, Murrow also got into hot water with Hollywood again for similar reasons, proposing "consultation" with USIA on feature motion pictures. He had returned from a trip to Europe and Latin America decrying American movies for fostering an "undesirable and exaggerated" American image abroad. In an address to the Academy of Motion Picture Arts and Sciences, for which he received no Oscar, he declared that foreigners saw America through "fun-house mirrors."

He was especially troubled by the impact of American films in the underdeveloped areas, such as Africa, because "they not only present a false picture of America, which the Africans don't know about, but also false pictures of Africa, which they do know about."

Nearly everyone in Hollywood disagreed with Murrow's remarks, which were taken, logically enough, as an attempt at censorship. Eric Johnston, who had praised him for telling what was wrong with television, attacked him for hinting that there might be anything wrong with the movies.

Variety, one of the most ardent admirers of Murrow the broadcaster, did not care for Murrow the government publicist. "As a bureaucrat, he has assumed a propaganda perspective that is the opposite of his long-time career as a prime news interpreter." Even Hollywood labor unions assailed the USIA director. Propaganda, it was clear, would never be a polite word in America.

To Murrow's public troubles was added private grief. His mother died, eighty-five years old, after a final Christmas reunion with her three sons at Lacey's home in Arizona. They remembered the holiday occasion as entirely characteristic of Ethel Lamb Murrow. The trip was her first by air. At the airport, when she saw the machine which dispensed travel insurance, she insisted that Dewey take out the maximum. "It would be nice to leave something for the grandchildren," she said, anticipating disaster, as usual. When they arrived safely and landed, she said, "We certainly wasted our money on that insurance."

She did not feel well during the Christmas visit, and died a few days after her return to Bellingham, two days before the new year. She was buried beside Roscoe at Bow, beneath three elm trees.

Back in Washington again, the USIA director learned from field reports that American propaganda was having difficulties abroad, as well as at home. On a tour of ten African countries, to see for himself and with the hope of increasing information activities there, he discovered "a simple formula which would earn me an hour's rest at any time. I would just turn to a group and say, 'Tell me, what is the United States doing that is wrong?'"

In Leopoldville, over Radio Congo, he made his first broadcast since he had left CBS, and became acquainted with Ambassador Edmund Gullion, one of the New Frontier's battery of able young envoys on the no-longer Dark Continent, and a personal friend of Kennedy since his congressional days.

Murrow and Gullion also hit it off well, and after the former's death the diplomat would become the dean of Tufts University's Fletcher School, where was established the Murrow Center of Public Diplomacy.

In Guinea, where the Kennedy administration was cultivating the left-wing regime of Sekou Touré, the USIA director learned once again, as he had when nuclear tests were resumed, that anti-Soviet propaganda by the Americans was never as effective as anti-Soviet propaganda by the

Russians themselves. He arrived in Conakry just after the Soviet ambassador had been "expelled" for being too undiplomatic in his attempts to win friends for communism. The African coolness extended to a Soviet trade exhibition opened by the veteran revolutionary Anastas Mikoyan. Murrow was pointedly given a much larger and more cordial official reception than the man from Moscow. Then at the fair, Mikoyan did Murrow's work for him. He bragged to a nonaligned nation of the triumphs of communism, attacked the West, and told French-speaking Guinea, in Russian, to cooperate with the Kremlin, "or else."

Murrow arrived in Paris from his African tour, to help arrange a television "exchange" between President Kennedy and Soviet Premier Khrushchev, each leader to speak to the other's domestic audience. It was an enterprise conceived by the energetic White House press secretary Pierre Salinger, who had established a Moscow beachhead with the premier's son-in-law, while rumors of another Kennedy-Khrushchev "summit" floated in the air.

In Paris, Murrow and Salinger agreed with Kharlamov, the Kremlin press chief, on March 18, 1962, as the date for the twin television programs. Kharlamov also took the occasion to complain about the Voice of America's broadcasts to the Soviet Union, and to gibe at Murrow as a "master propagandist."

The USIA director, in return, said he wished Kharlamov could appear before the House Appropriations subcommittee. "With your testimonial to our effectiveness, I think they might give me twice as much money," he explained.

Apparently it did not enter Murrow's mind, though critics in the broadcasting industry were quick to point it out, that the United States Government had committed the American networks to carry a program without any consultation. The Murrow of *See It Now* and of the 7:45 P.M. radio program might have had something to say about such a situation.

However, the Kennedy-Khrushchev television exchange was canceled by the American resumption of atmospheric nuclear testing, eight months after the Russians had broken the moratorium. And a far more ominous Kennedy-Khrushchev confrontation lay directly ahead.

The state of Soviet-American relations was recorded in numerous ways, some peripheral, one of which was the amount of jamming done of the Voice of America's Russian-language broadcasts. During the Stalin ice age, two thousand jamming transmitters were used, and more money was spent by the Soviet Union in keeping out American propaganda than was spent by the United States in creating and disseminating it.

After Stalin's death and during the internal Soviet "thaw," the blackout became selective. Jamming was intensified on specific critical occasions

— the U-2 incident, the collapse of the Eisenhower-Khrushchev "summit" in Paris, and the tense situation between East and West Berlin before the Wall was built in 1961. But often there was no jamming at all, especially of musical or nonpolitical Voice of America programs.

When the BBC, also engaged in Iron Curtain broadcasting on a large scale, made a survey in 1961, it was not at all sure of the effectiveness of Western propaganda.

It found out that what Communist audiences wanted most was straight news and objective background information — the things they did not get from their own governments. After that came cultural affairs, science and technology, and Western music. What Communist listeners definitely did not want was anything ideological. They were as suspicious of counterdogma as of dogma.

However influential the Voice of America's broadcasts might be with Communist audiences could never really be known. But the sporadic jamming, and Kharlamov's complaint to Murrow, indicated that they at least had made some impress on the Soviet leadership.

When the United States resumed atmospheric testing, the Soviet jamming of American broadcasts increased sharply. It was one of the signs of strained relations, and perhaps even of impending crisis. For Khrushchev had made a fateful decision.

Just as the United States had put intermediate ballistic missiles on the European continent after Sputnik, to offset what it believed to be Russian intercontinental capability, so the Russians in 1962 put medium and intermediate missiles into Cuba, to offset what they believed to be increased American nuclear potential.

Historians have argued whether the Russians were trying to upset the nuclear balance of power, as American military men said, or simply trying to restore it. But in addition to any military implications it might have, Khrushchev's Cuban move was also political, signifying the entry of Soviet power into the Western Hemisphere, and it assuredly was psychological. It brought nuclear weapons within ninety miles of a nation that, for all the destructive force of intercontinental missiles from great distances, still had somehow felt protected by its two oceans.

Accepting the Cuban missile crisis as a confrontation in which the entire prestige of the nation was involved, Kennedy was apparently ready and willing to risk nuclear war to maintain that prestige.

The Cuban missile crisis began to unfold when Raoul Castro visited Moscow in July 1962, and was persuaded by Khrushchev to let Soviet nuclear weapons be introduced on the island.

Murrow, receiving the Distinguished Alumnus Award from his alma mater, Washington State University, and appearing as commencement speaker there, had declared that while the United States was "engaged in a great confrontation with an implacable foe," he did not regard a Soviet-American war as inevitable, but foresaw rather a Soviet-American "decision" by political means. He was not talking about Cuba, but about Soviet-American relations in general.

That summer, also, he fought off another attempt to recruit him to elective politics. Again, New York Democrats wanted him to run for the Senate, this time against the Republican incumbent, Jacob Javits, and President Kennedy, at a White House dinner, alternatively suggested that he seek to wrest the governorship from Nelson Rockefeller. Murrow was not seized with either proposal. The only political activity he would be interested in, he would remark grimly after a session with the congressional Appropriations subcommittee, would be to run in Brooklyn against its hectoring chairman, Representative John J. Rooney.

After the summer, the USIA director was on another far-flung trip, inspecting information libraries and other operations abroad, when in October, in Teheran, he was stricken with pleurisy, collapsed, and was hospitalized. Pneumonia developed, not for the first time.

He joked about it later. Speaking of the oasislike city where he had been so unceremoniously treated by the shah on his last visit, he said, "If you ever get pneumonia, that's the place to get it — the nurses are so comely."

But it was a serious illness, and the harbinger of worse. After a week in the hospital in Teheran — visited by his wartime British friend and BBC censor Lanham Titchener, now in the Foreign Service — he was flown home for recuperation, and arrived in Pawling on October 12, two days before a U-2 spy plane spotted the Soviet missile sites in Cuba.

Murrow was in bed during the two weeks of nuclear crisis that followed, and he must have wondered whether his optimistic commencement forecast that there could be no Soviet-American war was about to be mocked by catastrophic reality.

However, even if he had not been ill, he evidently would not have been included in the "takeoff" of this crisis any more than in that of the Bay of Pigs. President Kennedy and a small coterie of advisers — including some now outside the Government, like former Secretary of State Dean Acheson, former Defense Secretary Robert Lovett, and former United States Commissioner in Germany John McCloy, a Kennedy family friend — enveloped the situation in secrecy until it was unveiled as a full-blown emergency. Indeed the administration's "management" of news in the missile crisis, and especially its heavy-handed use of the Voice of America, brought protest from the professional broadcasters of that agency, and had congressional and other public repercussions.

By 1961, after it had become obvious that there could be no conciliation between his regime and the United States, Fidel Castro was proclaiming his Marxism-Leninism, and Soviet technicians had arrived on the island, after Cuba's expulsion from the Organization of American States in 1962, for Communist activity in the hemisphere.

Soviet surface-to-air missiles, the antiaircraft SAM's, were installed in August, but the Kremlin assured the State Department that they were purely defensive weapons. The Soviet news agency in September charged the United States with preparing aggression against Cuba, and threatened a "crushing retaliatory blow."

Murrow had taken the unusual step of himself writing USIA's reply to TASS. "The Soviet statement reflects a lust for power, and disregard for truth. The Government of the United States threatens no nation and no people." But after all, there had been a Cuban invasion, even though an abortive one.

Most Americans, including military men, accepted the Soviet SAM's for the antiaircraft rockets they were, but the CIA thought they might more specifically be intended to protect the sites of nuclear missiles. The truth was that the Russians had already secretly shipped medium-range missiles to Cuba and had begun to build their launching pads. When the U-2 plane photographed the sites, they were said to be within two weeks of operational readiness.

The President, inspecting the photographs and realizing that the testing time of his administration had arrived, called for absolute secrecy, and named a fourteen-member executive committee of the National Security Council to "manage" the crisis. Murrow's name was not among them, nor was Adlai Stevenson's, though the United Nations ambassador was told of the missiles by the President after ExCom held its first meeting. At this time, according to his brother Robert, the President, having profited from the Bay of Pigs experience, had widened the range and diversity of his advisers. But it was still a select group, a kind of separate State Department in the White House, that was engaged in decision-making.

Two days later, at a routine meeting of the Cabinet, at which Cuba was not even mentioned, the Attorney General noted that Murrow was not present. Murrow's deputy Don Wilson reported that he was still ill, at Pawling. The younger Kennedy suggested that Wilson remain in Washington that weekend, though without telling his touch-football friend why.

ExCom held two meetings on the same day as the Cabinet session and engaged in substantive discussion of two vital matters.

These were whether the American response should be invasion, air strike, or merely naval blockade, and the obvious corollary, whether the United States should eliminate only the missiles, or eliminate the Castro regime as well. This time Senator Fulbright, who had spoken against the

Bay of Pigs invasion but not voted against it, favored invasion rather than blockade, on the ground that the latter was more likely to lead to war with the Soviet Union.

When the ExCom decision had been made, to institute a naval blockade of Cuba rather than bomb or invade, Murrow's deputy was given USIA's "crisis assignment." This was to ensure that the President's radio and television speech revealing the situation and announcing the blockade was heard over every square inch of Castro's island. The Voice of America, which ordinarily did shortwave broadcasting, quickly set up mobile medium-wave transmitters in Florida, and with the cooperation of nine commercial radio stations, sent out the President's remarks in English and Spanish, and other American Government statements, over a twenty-four-hour period.

It was a highly efficient broadcasting operation, but it concentrated so much on the technological achievement of "loud and clear" reception everywhere that the USIA may have overlooked the deeper significance of the occasion.

For the missile crisis was deliberate brinkmanship, brought to the absolute, almost apocalyptic level. USIA, by radio, television, film, news releases and photographs, convinced much of the world that the Russians were entirely responsible for the deadly encounter, that the danger to the continued existence of the world was real, and that an American response, whatever it might turn out to be, was necessary. Its principal argument to European audiences was that the Soviet missiles in Cuba in no way resembled the American missiles in Europe. For, said USIA, Europeans continued to believe in a Soviet threat, while there was no American threat anywhere.

USIA followed the Kennedy administration directive that policy was what decided public opinion, in the propaganda game. But it also had to admit the existence of another factor. John F. Kennedy, besides being his own Secretary of State, was in a sense his own United States Information Agency. There was no credibility gap. Khrushchev believed.

The missile crisis was resolved, and Murrow from his sickbed praised USIA's performance. But his predecessor, George V. Allen, declared that the agency had abused its function, and had even, by its strong anti-Castro tone, made Castro more popular than ever in Cuba.

Similar doubts were expressed within USIA itself. The Voice of America's director, Henry Loomis, protested to Murrow against the "monolithic tone" which he said the Voice had been compelled to adopt in its broadcasts. He charged that it had been made to "distort" the situation and had thereby "failed to sound convincing."

If a news analysis, Loomis explained — drawing a parallel with the kind of "analysis" Radio Moscow was known for — "restricts itself to merely repeating in different words what the President or Secretary of State says, it becomes as time passes increasingly dull, and it reveals increasingly a propaganda motivation."

The Voice of America's plaint underlined its anomalous position in the propaganda machinery. Though organizationally a part of USIA, which was in turn bound to State Department policies, it had become accustomed to a free-wheeling procedure, in the direct and uninhibited way of commercial radio. It sought worldwide credibility, not as the voice of any particular American administration, but as the voice of an open American society, with disparate trends of thought, proclivity for discussion, and acceptance of dissension.

In the face of the Kennedy-Murrow desire to relate "product" directly to policy, many of the Voice's broadcasters and writers believed they could further American interests without directly speaking for American policy objectives. Their model was not Radio Moscow but the BBC, a public corporation above partisan, and even governmental, influence.

The trouble was that however the Voice of America might regard itself, foreign governments regarded it as an official mouthpiece of the American Government. The Cuban missile dispute between the Voice of America and its parent USIA was only the newest manifestation of a running skirmish, and Murrow found himself torn between the two sides. Unlike any other USIA director, he was a broadcaster himself, and one who had frequently been at odds with his management. He had tended to support the Voice against his own USIA Office of Policy and Research, and often against the evaluations of his public affairs officers abroad, who could be prejudiced by local frustrations, especially in the Soviet Union.

Nine years before, when the USIA was being taken out of the State Department — though remaining under the department's policy guidance — Murrow had been asked as a leading broadcaster to testify before a congressional committee on the information program.

He thought then that a Government news service like the Voice of America had to be staffed by competent newsmen, not advertising executives or psychological warriors, much less career diplomats. He went so far as to believe that its employees should not be protected by civil service, but should be part of the open market for talent in broadcasting, subject to its ups and downs and dependent on merit. Nor should the Voice of America have Congressmen looking over one shoulder, and the State Department over the other. Congressional inspection should concern itself with the Voice's intentions, not its personnel or methods of operation.

This testimony was given at the height of the McCarthy period, when the vogue was to oppose communism while using its methods. "I do not believe we can or should slant or angle the news broadcasts from this country. We are not operating a controlled society. There are too many alternative sources of information to permit successful slanting. We should above all else attempt to achieve credibility, for the measure of our success will be the degree to which we are believed."

If the Voice of America sounded confused at times, "reporting dissension in Congress or in country, I should not be disturbed. We should remember that dissent, division, and criticism are rare commodities in many countries we address."

Murrow's testimony was based on discussions with Raymond Swing, the Voice of America's former principal commentator, who believed the Government broadcasting service was failing because it paid little attention to its audience, and too much to State Department policy aims. Under State Department control it was pervaded by diplomatic caution. Instead of being courageous, positive, explicit, it was often timid and hesitant, and at some critical moments silent altogether.

What the State Department forgot, Murrow told the Congressmen, was that the listener was the real master. He could turn his radio set on or off.

The words he uttered in 1953 he still presumably believed in 1962, except that, as he had ruefully confessed, he no longer thought the elimination of civil service status was attainable. In those nine years the Voice of America had to a large extent become the kind of broadcasting service he thought it should be. Now he was faced with its accusation that it had been betrayed and forced to become again, in the missile crisis, the clumsy and ineffectual instrument he himself had ridiculed.

Even though he had been ill and away from the scene during the crisis, he was still responsible for USIA. And in the "moment of truth," his USIA had told only as much of the truth as would serve its purpose and make the United States "look good." As Chairman Rooney of the House Appropriations subcommittee often put it, the only function of the USIA and the Voice of America had been "to promote our way of thinking."

The situation was a painful one, and he could do little to mitigate it, except to set about repairing the damage done to the Voice of America by insuring that in the future it would speak for American opinion as well as American policy. The test would be the Vietnam War.

A few months after the Cuban missile crisis Murrow watched the start of construction on the new Voice of America transmitter, at Greenville, in his native North Carolina. When it was named in his honor, after his death, it was called "the most powerful voice of the free world." But he was always less interested in its radius and loudness than in what it would have to say.

Among its other consequences, the Cuban missile crisis of 1962 clearly emphasized the need for some sort of Big Two agreement on nuclear matters. It thus contributed as much to the education of John F. Kennedy as to that of Nikita Khrushchev, and there was now set in train the negotiation which would lead the following year to the treaty ending all atmospheric nuclear testing.

For the first time in its anti-Communist history, the USIA was able to stress the common interest, rather than the antagonism, of the United States and the Soviet Union. It was a propaganda line Murrow was only too pleased to follow, not only for its political implications, but also because it ended Moscow's jamming of the Voice of America. Not until the Soviet invasion of Czechoslovakia in 1968 would the jamming be resumed.

The possibilities of news broadcasting and propaganda had by now taken on a larger dimension, as "world television" came into being. The technical promise of communications satellites was plain to see — instantaneous transmission of "live" events or film across oceans and between continents — but the political prospect was somewhat more murky.

The first Telstar exchange between American television networks and the eighteen-nation Eurovision system showed to Europeans a "live" baseball game, the Statue of Liberty, the Mormon Tabernacle Choir, for some reason singing outdoors at Mount Rushmore, and a presidential news conference. It was a kind of Voice of America feature program, with pictures added to the sound. Was it news, or was it propaganda? Since communications satellites could not be launched by private enterprise, Telstar was a Government undertaking. The original plan was to make the USIA responsible for the American content of the program. But the networks protested any such Federal invasion of their sacrosanct domain. Instead of Murrow, representing USIA, the American producer became Friendly, representing commercial television. It hardly seemed to matter, not only as between producers, but as between Government propaganda and private programming.

After Telstar's premiere an assistant to FCC Chairman Minow recommended to the White House that more American investment be made in television systems in other countries, and more cooperation take place between the United States and other governments in television. It was proposed that an Office of International Television be created within USIA. But the networks regarded this as an up-to-date version of Murrow's earlier plan for USIA "sponsorship" of programs. The FCC assistant quietly departed.

But in one respect at least, Murrow was able to help widen the horizons of American television viewers, and free them from the economic nexus of the networks.

If anything had emerged from the FCC's three-year inquiry into network practices, it was the need for more television channels, to cater to minority and diversified tastes. This had been made possible by the development of television sets able to receive programs on ultra high frequencies, as well as the very high frequencies of the standard broadcast band. Even the networks were enthusiastic supporters of more channels for minority viewers, so that they could be more free to devote themselves to the mass audiences sought by the sponsors.

A "fourth network" became the goal of those who thought the three commercial networks were not living up to their full responsibilities, and two American philanthropic institutions, the Ford Foundation and the Carnegie Corporation, began looking into the possibility of endowing such a venture.

For the Ford Foundation, Murrow wrote a draft proposal for a fourth network. He saw it as a "competitive alternative" to the three commercial systems, and proposed that men like Fred Friendly and Irving Gitlin — who had started on his old *Hear It Now* radio program and then had directed public affairs for CBS and later NBC — be lured from the networks. Other writing and producing talent should be acquired, especially from among those "who had become disillusioned with network practices, but remain in their employ due to the absence of any alternative."

The fourth network's news and public affairs programs, Murrow believed, could take advantage of the commercial networks' "obvious" weakness — their failure to provide adequate news background, or "to deal with the conditions that produced the event, and the consequences that might be expected to flow from a given policy."

Caustically he proposed that the fourth network should, above all, not be called an educational network, for "anything tagged educational in this country is handicapped at the outset. The American people don't really believe in education. We had to pass laws to force parents to send their children to school."

Murrow foresaw the fourth network as not only fulfilling its own purpose — "to satisfy curiosity, to expand areas of interest, to stretch the mind" — but as becoming "the mature, discerning gadfly to all the mass media in this country." He thought that "with a little courage, and lots of judgment, it could become the conscience of communications in this country."

Thus he had apparently given up his long-standing conviction that American television could be qualitatively improved within the context of commercial broadcasting alone, whether by the doctrine of noblesse oblige, or in some other fashion.

Some of his associates at USIA saw a fourth network, which they hoped would be financed by Government as well as by foundation money, as an ideal opportunity to win domestic support for administration policies. They proposed that the network be used for "talks to the people" by Secretary of State Rusk, Adlai Stevenson, Arthur Goldberg, and other officials. They held that the Government could give the new network "prestige" by thus using it.

Murrow had by then learned some pros and cons of governmental news "management," and he replied that the exact opposite would be true, and that such a use of the network would be clear and blatant propaganda, in the most invidious sense of that word.

When the Ford Foundation decided that a fourth network was feasible, Murrow's old friend Morris Ernst appeared on the scene as fairy godfather, or at least foundation consultant, and offered Murrow himself the job of "uninhibited editor-in-chief of a great network."

The commitment, he said, would be for "a substantial number of years." But as 1962 ended, Murrow rejected the offer. He could not be "seduced" into leaving USIA at that time, he said, but he "wouldn't want to prophesy."

By then the country's sixty-eighth educational television station had been opened in New York City — the commercial networks contributed $1.5 million to it, generally regarded as conscience money — and eventually the Ford Foundation's interest took the form in the 1967–1968 season of the Public Broadcast Laboratory, a weekly experimental program that followed the original Murrow specifications. By no coincidence, PBL was begun by Fred Friendly, who after his resignation as president of CBS News had joined the foundation as its television consultant.

Risking the obloquy, as Murrow saw it, of being identified with educational television, PBL was followed at the start of 1969 by an actual fourth network, serving 150 educational stations from coast to coast. It was partly financed by the Corporation for Public Broadcasting, chartered by Congress to support the cause of noncommercial television. But its future remained in doubt. So long as Congress controls the purse strings, the assumption can be made that it will also try to control the content, and it has directed the fourth network to be "impartial" in "controversial" matters. The question of financing is the ultimate one for any form of noncommercial television, foredooming it in this country.

Murrow's refusal to "prophesy" about the future when he rejected the offer to head a fourth network set afoot the inevitable rumors that he might not much longer remain a civil servant. These were accentuated after a particularly trying bout with Congress in 1963, and concurrently, by the beginning of controversy over what was then a small war in Vietnam. The information agency had become a focal point of the Vietnam debate.

When Murrow appeared before the House Appropriations subcommittee, Chairman Rooney berated USIA for spending taxpayers' money "foolishly." The House then proceeded to cut the agency's budget from $157.9 million to $142.7 million with the principal reduction in the very two areas Murrow had tried so assiduously to cultivate, Africa and Latin America.

The USIA director did what a good civil servant never does. He took his case over the head of Congress to the people. In speech after speech, he attacked the committee's attitude. "Either the House of Representatives believes in the potency of ideas and the importance of information, or it does not," he declared in Atlanta. "On the record, it does not so believe."

The budget reduction would also affect USIA's film program, and would mean dropping documentaries on racial discrimination and other aspects of contemporary American life which had diminished the national reputation abroad.

Murrow explained why USIA had received little understanding in Congress. "Our concern is with the idea. We cannot judge our success by sales. No profit-and-loss statement sums up our operations at the end of each year. No cash register rings when a man changes his mind. No totals are rung up on people impressed with an idea. There is no market history of the rise or fall in the going rate of belief in an ideal.

"Often one's best work may be merely to introduce doubt into a mind already firmly committed. There are no tallies to total, or sums to surmise, when you've finished a day of explaining disarmament, or discussing with the disenchanted the hope of an Alliance for Progress." He called the House's budgetary reduction a "vote of no confidence." But he had no success in changing matters.

USIA was also receiving a vote of no confidence in Vietnam. For the war in Vietnam, in which American military "advisers" had begun to take part, had made it more than merely an information agency.

For the first time it was engaged not only in disseminating propaganda, or articulating it, but in manufacturing it, as part of the actual hostilities. It sought to provide "motivation" to the Vietnamese for their own war. It sent out drama troupes, sponsored "citizens' committees," scattered leaflets, and showed films all through South Vietnam. It engaged in direct psychological warfare with the "faceless" Viet Cong.

It was also engaged in shaping the attitude of Americans at home toward the war. It was the official spokesman in Vietnam for the increasing American presence there. It issued the news, both military and political, which American and other correspondents received in Saigon, or on the other hand, it withheld the news.

The agency could not have a monopoly in news, for correspondents were free to find out for themselves what was happening in Vietnam, and did. Nor could the agency exercise military censorship, for a formal state of war did not exist. The result was a bitter battle of cross purposes.

The USIA's brand of news in Vietnam, mirroring the optimism, simplicity and, as it turned out, the unreliability of the official assessment, brought it into violent conflict with the small corps of young American correspondents who did not believe the official "handouts" on the popularity of President Ngo Dinh Diem, the lack of support for the Viet Cong, or the success of the "strategic hamlets" program. In its news briefings, the USIA concealed the fact of actual combat by American "advisers." The correspondents knew better, though Senator Fulbright, who would become a principal opponent of Vietnam policy, confessed, "I didn't think it was a war at all. I thought it was an aid program."

Murrow was involved in the administration's Vietnam problems from the beginning, because of the special nature of the USIA mission there and because he was a member of the President's counterinsurgency task-force.

In 1961 the head of that group, General Taylor, returned from a visit to Saigon with Walt W. Rostow, McGeorge Bundy's deputy at the White House, to report that a military victory could be won. They recommended the open use of American combat troops, in fact an expeditionary force of up to three hundred thousand men. The President demurred, but did increase the number of armed "advisers" from eight thousand to sixteen thousand, while still professing to believe that American troops should not be engaged in combat on the Asian mainland, and more than that, as he told an interviewer, that the United States could not interfere in "civil disturbances created by guerrillas."

Another White House emissary sent to Saigon was Vice President Lyndon Johnson, who declared President Diem to be "the Churchill of today." He recommended "a major effort" in Vietnam. The President's brother, Attorney General Kennedy, visiting Saigon in February 1962, had declared explicitly, "We are going to win in Vietnam. We will remain here until we do."

Diem, who had lived for some years in the United States, was chosen to head an "independent" South Vietnam after the 1954 Geneva Agreement, which he had repudiated by refusing to carry out elections. His dictatorial regime had brought disunity instead of the hoped-for national unity in South Vietnam, and to those Americans who saw the Vietnam conflict as the result of "communist world conspiracy," Diem was nullifying their theory by making it all too plainly a civil war.

Thus there were in 1963 two currents of thought about Vietnam in the Kennedy administration. Lyndon Johnson might think Diem the new Churchill, and the CIA was supporting Diem to the end, and helping train his police. But State Department policy-makers, to some extent, and White House consultants were not sure that professedly democratic ends could be served by repressive, and even worse to the New Frontier pragmatists, unproductive means. Diem, it was felt, was at least guilty of poor public relations in his subjection of the Buddhists.

USIA was torn between the contrary views. Its representative in Vietnam, John Mecklin, felt there was no alternative to Diem. The American

Library in Saigon submissively weeded out books which displeased the
Diem regime, while the United States Cultural Affairs Office allowed
the regime to pick the students for American scholarships, with educational qualifications playing a lesser role in the choice than their political
reliability.

In Washington, on the other hand, USIA was influenced not only by
the anti-Diem views within the administration, but by the printed accounts
of the correspondents who were at odds with its mission in Saigon. Murrow
said about Diem, "This is certainly no democrat we're nurturing. Can there
be any way to make him look like one?" Diem and his sister-in-law,
Madam Nhu, saw to it that there was not.

Murrow several times went out of his way to commend the appraisals
of the State Department's young Research and Intelligence chief, Roger
Hilsman. Hilsman was one of those who saw the war in political, not
military, terms, and argued against "overmilitarizing," and above all,
"over-Americanizing" it.

The "doves," as they came to be called, also included Averell Harriman, Assistant Secretary of State for Far Eastern Affairs, whom Hilsman
would succeed, and some members of the Foreign Service. But Secretary
of State Rusk, Vice President Johnson, Walt Rostow, and the Joint Chiefs
of Staff favored a "head-on" policy, and believed in military victory.

Murrow once told the maverick Hilsman that a report of his, critical
of the "strategic hamlets" program, was "like a long mint julep at the end
of a hot day."

As for the Voice of America, which had recovered some of its amour
propre after the Cuban missile crisis, it was daily beaming to the Vietnamese people reports on the war and the internal political situation,
based on American news accounts, which their own government had suppressed or distorted.

It thus contributed directly to Diem's unpopularity, and encouraged
the Buddhists, students, and others opposed to the dictator. One notable
Voice broadcast, by Roger Hilsman, derided Diem's assertion to the American embassy that his war against the Buddhists had had no deleterious
effect on the war against the Viet Cong.

Diem complained to the embassy about this state of affairs, and the
controlled press in Saigon, spurred on by Diem's evil genius of a brother,
Ngo Dinh Nhu, daily attacked the USIA equally with the CIA, charging
they were trying to provoke a coup. Objectively speaking, Nhu was not far
from the truth.

As the feud between the USIA and the American correspondents in Saigon continued, Kennedy went to the extent of asking the *New York
Times* why its skeptical young man, David Halberstam, could not be transferred somewhere else. He seemed to have forgotten the ill service he later

decided the *Times* had performed, in acquiescing to his request to suppress the story of the Bay of Pigs invasion preparations.

Assistant Secretary of State Robert Manning, in whose province USIA lay, journeyed to Saigon as a mediator, without much success. John Mecklin was called to Washington to take part in the emergency discussions which went on for days about the Vietnam situation. The normal confusion had been increased by conflicting reports from the military and civilian troubleshooters sent to the scene — "Are you sure both of you were visiting the same country?" the President asked two of them sarcastically, at a National Security Council meeting — and by the fact that though an American green light had been given, some of the Saigon generals still hesitated before the finality of an anti-Diem coup.

Mecklin by now did not believe in the inevitability of Diem, and he recommended American pressure to force a change in the regime. He also urged the National Security Council to sanction the introduction of American combat troops. This suggestion was loudly ridiculed as impossible.

Despite the firm assurance of the Attorney General that "the American people will see Vietnam through," his brother in the White House was persistently uncertain. When Canadian prime minister Lester Pearson advised him to "get out," Kennedy said, "That's a stupid answer. Everybody knows that. The question is: How do we get out?"

Diem was not the only fly in USIA's Vietnam propaganda ointment. The American effort suffered from the fact that it was based on such Western political concepts as freedom, democracy, communism, and imperialism, all of which were meaningless to the great mass of Vietnamese. The basic problem was not that the South Vietnamese peasant was unable to identify himself with the Diem regime, or the later Minh or Khan or Ky or Thieu regimes, but that, from centuries of oppressive experience, he could not identify himself with any Saigon regime.

The frail reeds at which the United States was clutching in Vietnam, surrounding the quagmire, and the open difficulties of the USIA in its own war with the American correspondents, may have fed new rumors in mid-1963 that Murrow would be leaving the Government.

Variety, speculating on his possible return to broadcasting, reported that he was not really amenable to the Washington bureaucracy, was not happy making propaganda, was tired of fighting Congress, and had never become part of the White House inner circle. This was denied by the visible evidence of Murrow's public satisfaction in his job, and the conviction of friends and associates that he was as happy at USIA as Ed Murrow could be anywhere.

However, added *Variety*, it was undeniable that CBS needed him. The network's vital spark had gone. It had lost its news leadership to NBC, despite Fred Friendly's "flair." It may have been Friendly's reiterated assurance that Murrow would "definitely" come back to CBS that kept the rumors going.

There was considerable substance to them, however. At CBS, Frank Stanton, always au courant with developments in Washington, had proposed to Bill Paley that Murrow be asked to come back to the network. Plans were being made to extend the nightly fifteen-minute television news broadcast to a half-hour in the fall, and Stanton, recalling Murrow's preeminence with his nightly radio program for so many years, was confident he could duplicate it in television, to the discomfort of the rival Huntley-Brinkley program on NBC. The latter, following the CBS example, also intended to go to a half-hour in the fall.

Stanton's only doubt about his idea was whether Murrow, after nearly three years as the administration's propaganda chief, could regain his previous reputation for fairness and candor.

There is no evidence that, even if he had left the Government at that time, Murrow would have rejoined CBS, especially since he had been offered the fourth network. Too much muddy water had flowed over the dam of commercial television to provide him a comfortable return to Madison Avenue, and a whole new "generation" of practitioners, methods, and above all, corporate procedures had become entrenched in the short time since his departure.

In the end it was not dissatisfaction, disagreement over policies, personal pique, or the hope of redemption that ended Murrow's term of service to the Government. It was the illness that had for so many years nagged at and intruded upon him, and that now insisted on complete possession.

He and Janet had gone to Europe, for a USIA inspection tour combined with a pleasurable visit to remembered places. One of them was Vienna, where he had begun his news broadcasting career twenty-five years before. In Britain he attended a conference on North Atlantic problems at Ditchley, a "stately home" near Oxford — the English still, and especially in the Kennedy administration, believed they had a "special relationship" with the United States — and on what was to be his last meeting with them, saw again his friends from wartime. He looked well and remarkably untroubled. Some who had not seen him for years thought they had never seen him so lighthearted.

Back in Washington, in June, he was progressively aware that Government policy-making was not quite the limpid pool of idealism of the civics textbooks. The dichotomy within the administration over Vietnam was prolonged. The President's visits to Germany, Italy, Ireland and Britain in the summer of 1963 caused other questions to be propounded.

How could the President on June 10, in his American University speech, raise the prospect of detente with the Russians, and in effect wish for an end to the cold war, and two weeks later, carried away by the frenzied excitement of German crowds, proclaim, "Ich bin ein Berliner!" and deride those "who say we can work with the Communists"? How could the President on the one hand initiate talks with the Russians on the ending of nuclear testing, and on the other advocate a multilateral nuclear force in Europe, which the Russians regarded as a means of giving the Germans a finger on the nuclear trigger?

How could the President, declaring himself "opposed to coups," recall ambassadors and American aid from the tiny Dominican Republic and Honduras, after democratic regimes had been overthrown there, but accept and gloss over the military coup in large and important Argentina, which had toppled the most pro-American government in that country's history?

How could the United States supply arms to both India and Pakistan, in the name of friendship for both, when it was obvious they would use those arms against each other at the first opportunity?

For Murrow the question may not have been how the President could engage in such contradictions — he knew that diplomacy was a many-splendored thing — but how the USIA could be expected to make credible propaganda out of them. He took the problem to the White House basement, and McGeorge Bundy. The latter's function was to present all the options to the President, and not question their validity after one or more had been chosen. But he apparently recognized that USIA was more and more being given accomplished facts to make propaganda of, and again he offered to serve as Murrow's channel to the inner recesses of the White House. The offer seems to have brought no result.

Bill Paley, who came to Washington occasionally to lunch with Murrow, found him disturbed that the Kennedy administration, and his position within it, had not lived up to his expectations. The USIA director was critical of some administration foreign policy. To other friends, he had frequently made it plain that he did not take to Secretary of State Rusk's rigid view of the world, or what he considered the Secretary's lack of imagination. Rusk still spoke of Peiping, instead of Peking, thus refusing to concede that the Communists, who had renamed it, were in control there. Rusk had always regarded Chinese communism as merely a Soviet extension, and still did so, one of the major American misassessments.

In September, Murrow had to cancel a speaking engagement because of "laryngitis," and entered Washington Hospital Center for observation and tests. X-rays showed a spot on the left lung, and in a three-hour operation, the lung was removed on October 6. His brother Lacey had also lost

Convalescing from one of his bouts of illness

a lung some years before, and had managed to lead a reasonably normal life. There were many cases of long survival, the doctors said. The prognosis was optimistic.

But the removed lung was cancerous, and now massive doses of cobalt radiation were ordered. Whatever their therapeutic effect, they were grievously debilitating. Sometimes, in his slow recuperation, he was barely able to move.

It was only after the operation that Murrow gave up smoking, and he found it difficult to do so. As he had explained after smoking through the two *See It Now* programs about cigarettes and cancer, he was addicted. "Since I have been in this business I have smoked sixty to seventy cigarettes a day. I doubt very much that I could spend a half-hour without a cigarette, with any comfort or ease." But now he had to do so.

His incapacity removed him from the Vietnam dilemma. By September the President finally joined those, like Harriman and Hilsman, who believed in American measures, such as the suspension of aid, to bring Diem to his senses and end the anti-Buddhist campaign. After the Bay of Pigs, Kennedy had vowed that he would never again make the mistake of "listening to the experts," and apparently he was beginning to doubt the Vietnam experts, like Taylor and Rostow.

The coup which literally disposed of Diem on November 1, though not unexpected, shook Washington. The young President may have sensed the disaster that lay ahead unless a Vietnam solution could be found, and peace restored. Some of his advisers believed that the murder of Diem was the turning point of the civil war, and that it could make possible some sort of reconciliation between Saigon and the Viet Cong. Kennedy himself may have been aware of such a possibility.

But there was to be no solution. Murrow returned to his office, on an occasional basis, two weeks after Diem's assassination. Seven days later there was another assassination, and the Kennedy era abruptly and shockingly ended, in a few agonized moments, in Dallas. Any bright promises it held would not be fulfilled.

The USIA had to tell the story of the assassination and the succession, with the burden upon it of reassuring the world of the peaceful continuity of the American democratic process, despite its bruising by violence. But it also had to become overnight a Johnson, not a Kennedy, transmission belt.

The new President saw things differently. A man without the kind of "style" attributed to Kennedy, he expected a style could be created by manipulation of the instruments of image-making. Instead of basing propaganda on policy, his inclination would be to substitute propaganda for the carrying-out of policy. He preferred consensus to convincement. He seemed to regard government as a personal possession, and power as justified by itself, not by the uses to which it could be put, let alone the restraints it required.

Lyndon Johnson would look at the USIA as a public relations outfit. He certainly would want no counsel from it on substantive affairs of state. And though Kennedy might have envisioned an alternative in Vietnam, to the policy of seeking a military solution, Johnson discerned none.

On the afternoon of November 22, the maid in the Murrow home in Washington, watching a television soap opera, heard the first fragmented news of the attack on the President in Dallas. Murrow, too slowly convalescing from his operation, was so weak that day that Janet wondered whether she should tell him, fearing the effect of shock. She made sure he got back into bed before she did.

He shook his head. "A lot of people have been shot who came out all right," he said. She knew he was trying to cheer her.

When the news came that the President had died, Murrow fell silent. He was wondering, he told Janet, about the character and mold of the new President. He was less deeply shaken, it seemed, by Kennedy's passing than by the thought of Lyndon B. Johnson as his successor.

At the 1960 Democratic convention Murrow had not been convinced of the political expediency which demanded that the politico from Texas should become the young Kennedy's running mate, though he must have acknowledged later that Johnson had helped Kennedy to win.

As Vice President, Johnson's relations with USIA had been none too cordial. On his trips abroad his bursts of rage at embassy aides and public affairs officers, followed by salving attempts — the kind of "Johnson treatment" that would later drive White House assistants to distraction — became legendary. The loud demands he made for stage management to the deputy Assistant Secretaries of State who accompanied him often embarrassed them, and foreign dignitaries who were present, but did not seem to embarrass Johnson. He blamed USIA representatives abroad for not getting him more press coverage and larger receptions. He insisted on the exclusive personal use of USIA's chief photographer, who knew which his better profile was, and he took umbrage at Murrow's refusal to accede.

Now Johnson was President, and one of his first actions was to bring the USIA chief photographer into the White House as his own. As always with a new administration, the members of the old had submitted pro forma resignations, Murrow among them. But Johnson wanted all the New Frontiersmen to stay on, to provide the public appearance of continuity, and they agreed to do so for a while.

On the rainy Saturday when the body of John Fitzgerald Kennedy lay in state in the White House East Room, Murrow and Janet joined those of the administration who had come to pay their last respects. Murrow, drawn and weak, sought to avoid the cameramen and reporters, and insisted on walking up the back stairs, after having arrived at a side entrance.

But he could not escape the attention he did not want. He stumbled as he slowly worked his way upward, felt faint, and had to be revived with smelling salts. Somehow he managed, haltingly, to make his way past the bier.

The heights which television reached in the days after the Kennedy assassination, including its on-camera recording of Oswald's murder by Jack Ruby, and the somber panoply of the State funeral, led Murrow as USIA director to say that "the real promise of the medium was fulfilled." And only by television could the entire nation have plumbed the depths of the tragedy, and at the same time so fully appreciated that life and democratic institutions still went on.

But many voices were raised in doubt. For television itself may have contributed to the nurture of the national streak of violence, and its complete absorption in the assassination, with the vast technical resources at its command, created a national hypnotic neurosis, many thought, contributing to Ruby's act of vengeance and exhibitionism.

Could Murrow have remained with the Johnson administration any more than Sorensen, Salinger, and Schlesinger were able to? It seems certain he would not have stayed. The continuity rites were not intended to last long. But unlike the other members of the New Frontier, Murrow's decision lay not entirely in his own hands, but in the doctors'. Continuing illness necessitated a formal letter of resignation, for the urgent medical advice he received was to leave the damp winter climate of Washington.

The resignation, dated December 19 and effective in mid-January, cited the lung operation and reported Murrow's recovery to date as "normal," though he could not resume full-time duty for months.

"Shortly before he died, I spoke to President Kennedy and told him I might feel obliged to resign. After his tragic death, it had been my hope to continue to serve my country under your leadership. My inability to do so is deeply disappointing."

Before Johnson returned to the Texas ranch for his first Christmas there as President, he called Murrow to the White House and again urged him to stay. The USIA head replied that he would try to remain another month, but that he might be able to give the President only three or four days' notice in case of any medical emergency. A photograph taken that day by Yoichi Okamoto, the USIA camera chief who had been transferred to the White House, showed the tall gaunt frame of Murrow, walking slowly away in the dark December mist, with head bent low in despondency and submission.

The emergency came quickly. His health faded further, and he was warned by the doctors to leave Washington as soon as he could after New Year's. As he had promised, he called the White House to tender his notice and seek a farewell appointment with the President.

He was unable to get one. Every day, for seven days, he asked for and was not given a White House appointment, nor was he even allowed to talk to Johnson by telephone. The President was clearly unwilling to accept, illness or not, what might be regarded as the first defection from his administration, and that by a man so widely known and respected.

The White House remained silent. Murrow, disquieted and pained, booked a California flight for himself and Janet. Six hours before they left for the airport the President telephoned and brusquely read to him the statement he would issue about the resignation, effective four days later.

It was fulsome, and under the circumstances somewhat overly familiar, and therefore typically Johnsonian.

"You have done a magnificent job at your post. Your entire life, your eloquence and idealism and sound judgment, your determined drive and sparkling personality, all combine to make you superbly qualified for the task of conveying the true picture and purpose of this country to the world. You will be sorely missed.

"You leave with the thanks of a grateful President and a grateful nation. I close, Ed, with a paraphrase of the words you made forever famous on radio and television, 'Good-bye and good luck!' "

But the President ignored Murrow's recommendation that Don Wilson, the deputy who had served indefatigably during some critical days, be appointed his successor. He had his own man in mind, and Wilson was a personal friend of Robert Kennedy.

Some months later Murrow summed up his impressions of the two Presidents he had served as USIA director, in a frank letter to J. Robert Oppenheimer. As to Kennedy, "I have had great difficulty in trying to reach some judgment regarding that young man's relation to his time. I saw him at fairly close range under a variety of circumstances, and there remains for me a considerable element of mystery — and maybe that is good. I always knew where his mind was, but I was not always sure where his heart was.

"My experience with Lyndon Johnson was rather the reverse. I was never in doubt where his heart was, as he was generally beating me over the head with it."

Murrow's resignation because of lung cancer coincided with the Surgeon General's Report postulating a definite connection between that disease and cigarette smoking.

Three days after it had been accepted, though not yet made public, Roger Hilsman also resigned. Ted Sorensen left the Johnson administra-

The President accepts the resignation of his USIA director, who cannot conceal his illness

Leaving the White House after resigning as USIA director, on a bleak December day

tion six weeks later, and the exodus of other Kennedy men followed. The transition was over.

As Murrow's successor the President chose Carl T. Rowan, once deputy Assistant Secretary of State who, traveling with the Vice President, had given satisfaction with his deference, and the success of his publicity arrangements. Rowan had become ambassador to Finland, and his USIA appointment made him the highest-ranking Negro in the Government.

Ordered by the President "to tell the truth . . . to tell the good and bad," Rowan adopted a Johnsonian formula. "The best propaganda is the wisest use of the truth," he instructed. While in the State Department Rowan had expressed himself in favor of news "direction." If there had been news management by the Kennedy administration — and after the Cuban missile crisis Arthur Sylvester, assistant Secretary of Defense for Public Affairs, had declared, "It's in the Government's right, if necessary, to lie to save itself" — there would be news management multiplied by the Johnson administration.

Johnson entered the 1964 election campaign publicly presenting himself as a man resolved not to send "American boys to do what Asian boys should be doing," but even then he was evidently planning escalation in Vietnam. Safely reelected by a landslide majority against a Republican candidate whose vision seemed to be that of all-out war in Vietnam, Johnson himself began to increase the scope and tempo of the conflict.

Murrow's parting words as USIA director were remembered by those who remained in the agency under Johnson. He had said them before, but the change in administrations gave them added meaning.

"Communications systems are neutral. They have neither conscience nor morality, only a history. They will broadcast truth or falsehood with equal facility. Man communicating with man poses not the problem of how to say it, but more fundamentally, what is he to say?"

He received some parting words also, when Cabinet members and other governmental associates put together an album of remarks of tribute.

"With full respect for the utter seriousness of large affairs, you sensed that each of us has an unlimited capacity to be a little ridiculous," wrote Secretary of State Rusk.

"You leave a lot of your friends wiser than you found them, grateful for advice they took and rueful over some they didn't," said McGeorge Bundy, the "win the war" advocate who later would ruefully change his views on the possibility of victory in Vietnam.

"You were always the Voice of America, long before President Kennedy brought you down to Washington and made it official," wrote Arthur Schlesinger, Jr.

"When many of us were caught up in the collective excitement of the moment, pontificating around the table in the Cabinet Room, you were always the barrister with a brief for sanity," recalled Under-Secretary of State George Ball.

"At times when it seemed talk might be replacing thought, you usually spoke last but with most effect," said Under-Secretary Alexis Johnson.

Tom Sorensen, Murrow's aide at USIA, summed up the broadcaster's entire career. "I can hear it now: the unwavering idealism and the healthy cynicism."

Murrow had served thirty-four months as USIA director, and as one Washington observer viewed it, had brought the agency "from the doghouse to the White House."

On Capitol Hill, USIA was no longer the congressional whipping boy, and even though its budgets were still pared, the agency had increased its overseas posts from 199 in 89 countries, to 298 in 107 countries. The new giant Voice of America transmitter had been erected in North Carolina, broadcasting had been increased from 617 to 796 hours weekly, and new television studios were opened in Washington. The overseas distribution of American books was up to eleven million copies a year.

Despite its ups and downs, Murrow's participation in the National Security Council and other White House planning had helped boost the prestige of USIA and elevate the morale of its personnel. Despite its ins and outs, American propaganda had acquired not only a new respectability but, many believed, a new competence.

Under Johnson, USIA would soon lose its excitement and sense of purpose, not to mention its participation in government, as it strove to rationalize an unpopular war in Vietnam. Nor could it find much image-building material in urban rioting and civil disobedience, much less suggest a connection between them and the war.

The Voice of America also had a hard time with administration attempts to convince Europeans, who of all people knew better, of the similarity between Southeast Asia in 1968 and the Munich appeasement of 1938.

The new President did not seem to care much about USIA's difficulties. In his first budget in January, as Murrow was leaving, Johnson himself had cut the agency's budget by three million dollars below the Kennedy estimate.

When the Murrows flew to California it was at Dr. Jonas Salk's invitation, to seek the sunshine of La Jolla in aiding recovery. Since the two *See It Now* broadcasts in 1955 which had introduced the developer of the polio vaccine to America-at-large, Murrow had been one of the very few newsmen Salk trusted.

At La Jolla, adjoining the San Diego campus of the University of California, the scientist had established his Institute for Biological Studies, an orange-juice version of Oppenheimer's Institute for Advanced Study at

Princeton. To it he had attracted the talents of Leo Szilard, the pioneer in nuclear physics, and Francis H. C. Crick, codiscoverer of the molecular structure of the basic genetic material DNA, among others. He also wanted the talents of Ed Murrow. The center for ratiocination sought to bring together, as by an acetylene torch, all the elements concerned with the biological sciences, but to relate them to the humanities, creative arts, esthetics, and philosophy.

Murrow was invited by Salk to do his convalescing in the environs of the institute, receiving not only sunshine but a measure of scholastic communion. The California sun shone as promised, for a week. Then steady rainfall began.

Janet wrote home that Ed looked better, but was extremely nervous and did not sleep well. He needed physical exercise, and not, as Jonas Salk thought, intellectual stimulus. She suspected Salk would like Murrow to help him with the institute, and said "he kept after Ed in somewhat the Friendly manner." Murrow was finally prevailed upon to become a member of the board of trustees.

They took a house on a cliff for three months, overlooking the Pacific, with two golf courses nearby and a beach. But Murrow was unable to golf as yet, and he caught cold on the damp beach, and again succumbed to pneumonia. Soon, however, he was able to walk for an hour a day, and equally encouraging, he redeveloped his voracious interest in reading. She thought his progress was good.

Bill Paley flew all the way from New York to spend a day with him, and Murrow, against orders, insisted on driving to the airport to meet him, to show that he could.

Ed was weak, but eager to talk, and he showed a keen interest in CBS affairs. One of these was Fred Friendly's appointment as president of CBS News, a move which he frankly opposed. He valued his close long-time associate as a producer without peer, but was not so sure that his restless temperament would be compatible with the demands of administration or of corporate conformity, as indeed later proved to be the case.

The conversation led Paley to suggest that even if inactive, Murrow could serve as a consultant for CBS, telling it "what was wrong." Just such a role was specified in his contract, under which he still drew some income deferred from his active years. Paley felt encouraged that even though he was so manifestly ill, Murrow was so mindful of his métier, and even of CBS.

Murrow himself was less hopeful of the prospects. "I hear from friends in Washington that Stanton is passing the word I am definitely coming back to CBS," he wrote Seward. "Right now I feel I ain't goin' anywhere."

He revealed that publishers wanted a book from him, "which I am not about to do," and that once again he had been offered the job of "running an educational TV network." He asked, "Could I do it under present CBS contract? I think not." However he had been interested enough in the idea to ask his old friend Chet Williams, who had a research service in New York, for data on the financial and programming problems of noncommercial television. Williams received the clear intimation that he was going into that field, and considered it an important force in urban affairs.

He was less interested in other proposals. These included offers from both other networks, and from a newspaper syndicate eager for a weekly column. Robert Kennedy had asked him to do interviews with former Prime Minister Macmillan, Nikita Khrushchev, and others.

He had in mind the *Oral History of John F. Kennedy*. "I put him off," Murrow told Seward.

During his convalescence he also received many letters, from friends, colleagues and even former listeners, but those he liked best were from USIA people around the world remarking on the improvement in purpose and prestige, as well as in their own morale, which his tenure of office had accomplished. He went so far as to apply for a new passport, and this time he did not have to sign an affidavit to get it. The director, Frances G. Knight, conferred upon him what she regarded as a lucky number, E–000007.

Fred Friendly, newly appointed president of CBS News, visited La Jolla, "glowed with optimism, and did most of the talking." Friendly had been assuring all that Ed would soon be returning to CBS, and now assured Ed, too. But Murrow was not encouraged, and felt "pretty lousy," Janet reported.

One bout of pneumonia was succeeded by another, and in trying to play golf he tore some muscles and was in severe pain. As their three months on the coast came to an end, he was having sputum tests made, and the recurrence of the cancer was feared. He was unable to be much interested in the announcement that he had won still another Peabody Award, this time not as a broadcaster but as the director of USIA, for "the best radio contribution to international understanding," through the Voice of America.

The Murrows were back in Washington in May, with the 1964 election campaign under way, and soon Janet wrote of "an exciting day." Ed had gone to Burning Tree golf club for lunch, "and rode in a cart, while his cronies played. Everyone came over to say hello. It is exhausting."

Friendly in a speech said again that Murrow would be back at CBS soon, but when a reporter sought confirmation Ed replied that he was not well enough to make up his mind about anything.

But he did seem definitely better for a while, "back where he was when he got pneumonia," Janet explained. They planned to spend the summer in Pawling, and Ed looked forward to attending Casey's graduation from Milton Academy though Janet was afraid he might not be able to.

But he did. He could not deliver the commencement speech, as had been advertised — his former CBS associate Howard K. Smith stepped into the breach — but he saw Casey graduated with four honors, including the Lovering Medal for "outstanding integrity." Some on the campus thought he was carrying integrity to extremes to balk at counting the vote, as head monitor, when he was one of those being voted on. Casey, who was sounding more and more like Ed though he favored Janet in looks, was going to Yale in September, and his father said he enjoyed the Milton ceremonies because for once he didn't have to sit through an award speech addressed to himself.

He had frequent visitors at Pawling, and Fred Friendly was always on the telephone, in ferment with new ideas. One was to do a documentary report on that year's British elections, a task Murrow was obviously unable to carry out. But he did make suggestions for television programs, one on poverty in the United States, another on the landmark Supreme Court civil rights decision, having to do with the rights of accused persons, *Gideon versus Wainwright*. Both became highly successful CBS News presentations.

He telephoned Friendly one day and asked that his favorite *See It Now* cameraman, the veteran Charlie Mack, be sent up to Pawling "just to see how I might do on camera." Bad weather canceled the plan, and it was never carried through. But he seemed clearly to be thinking of going back to CBS. He told Janet that when they returned to the city in the fall, to be sure and get an apartment on the West Side so he would not have to "fight all that traffic" on his way to CBS News, now on West 57th Street. They bought a cooperative apartment on the west side of Central Park.

During the summer, meanwhile, Bob Dixon, the announcer of his broadcasting days who had also been his shooting companion at Pawling, came over to Glen Arden several times weekly. Dixon was qualified in physical therapy, and he eased Ed's pain with massages, and strengthened the tissue over the chest vacancy where the left lung had been.

In a CBS radio program at the end of July, *Farewell to Studio 9*, marking the moving of CBS News from Madison Avenue to its new quarters, Murrow made what proved to be his own farewell broadcast. He was not able to be present in Studio 9, where so many famous news broadcasts originated or were received from overseas, including all his own. He made his last contribution to radio from Lowell Thomas's studio in Pawling. His voice had lost its well-remembered resonance, and sounded exhausted. He was definitely not recovering his health.

But he did not lose his interest in the nation's affairs. During his time at USIA he had evidently shared in the Kennedy administration's division of feeling and confusion of policy about Vietnam. But with the Tonkin Gulf incident of August 1964, which gave President Johnson the means to carry out what would be continuing escalation, Murrow apparently believed that a step had been taken changing the entire nature of things, and was disturbed.

After the President's fifteen-minute television appearance late in the evening, sounding the Tonkin Gulf alarm, the CBS network allowed its White House correspondent to sum up for two minutes, and then gave the air back to its panting affiliates, so they could show their antiquated but lucrative movies. NBC allotted as much time as the President had used for comment and analysis of an obviously significant occasion.

As soon as the CBS program ended, an indignant Murrow was on the telephone to Friendly. "What do you mean by going off the air?" he demanded. "Even NBC did better." He berated the CBS News president for failing to live up to his responsibilities by not presenting a full and critical report. It was the sole major occasion of their entire association that Murrow had so angrily passed sentence on him.

Friendly later conceded that television's failure to grasp the full meaning of the Tonkin Gulf incident and the President's intentions, as evidenced by the carte blanche Tonkin Gulf resolution, and to report them to the American people, was evidence of the medium's deterioration as a true public service. Nor was its failure mitigated by the failure of Senators like Fulbright to appreciate what was happening.

In September, Murrow was awarded the presidential Medal of Freedom, the highest civilian honor in peacetime, with the citation: "He has brought to all his endeavors the conviction that truth and personal integrity are the ultimate persuaders of men and nations."

In October he made his last public appearance, at the Family of Man Award dinner of the Protestant Council of New York, one of several recipients of honors, including Adlai Stevenson, former President Eisenhower, and Chief Albert Luthuli of South Africa.

To the end, he did not doubt that his country had something worth saying to the rest of the world. But to the end, he wondered whether it was really doing so. Despite its vast technological achievements, he observed at the ceremony, the United States too often was unable to get its message "the last few feet" from the loudspeaker to the mind of the foreign listener.

At this last appearance his own ability to communicate had also begun to diminish. His speech was a faltering one, with slurred phrases and blurred meaning, and those present looked at one another in trepidation.

After the dinner a friend complimented him on his courage. "I was trying to fill a minute-and-a-half," he replied, referring to the average length of radio news reports, "and I found I couldn't."

At Pawling the next weekend he was walking slowly through the glen at his home with Jonas Salk and Sander Vanocur, an NBC broadcaster, when suddenly, as he talked, all was gibberish as it came from his mouth. His eyes showed that he knew what had happened, and Jonas Salk looked as if he had been struck.

Three weeks later Murrow was back in the hospital. The cancer had spread. A second operation was necessary. A tumor was removed near the brain, but several other areas of infection were found. It had become hopeless.

He left the hospital on Christmas Day, but instead of returning to Pawling he stayed in New York City through the worst of the winter. He was visited by many friends, when his health permitted, including Jacqueline Kennedy, the acting couple Alfred Lunt and Lynn Fontanne, and Bill Paley. The latter sensed that Ed, whom he had known for so many years, both professionally and personally, felt that there was something demeaning about what was happening to him. Perhaps he had envisioned a heroic death for himself, Paley thought, if not with his boots on, at least in a context of some meaning. But the wasting incursion of his illness was a humiliation to such an active and bespoken man. He had already worn out. Now he was rusting out also.

One of those who called frequently was Teddy White, the chronicler of presidential elections, whom Murrow had known through the years. After the operation he found Ed with his head swathed in bandages. Absent-mindedly, he kept tapping his skull with his finger. One day, Fred Friendly thought, he looked "like someone in Buchenwald."

But the uncertainty of his speech had been cleared up. He spoke again with clear articulation, though with little vigor. His visitors gave him political and professional gossip, and did their best to get him interested. But he knew he was dying.

The television world, at that point, had been overtaken by a new phenomenon. In their desperate battle for mass audiences, the three networks were virtually tied in the Nielsen ratings. "It was inevitable," remarked the *New Yorker*. "It shines with the clarity of a mathematical law." The three networks had arrived at the same answer in their search for the lowest common denominator of American attention.

"All have achieved complete homogenization of comedy, drama, variety, news, sports, public affairs, that will produce exactly the same mild tangy taste. No foreign ingredients — undue spontaneity, excessive dullness — have been allowed to intrude. Now that the identical formula has been found, the companies can dismiss their chemists and replace them with accountants, to keep track of the identical profits."

In order to arrive at this equipoise, CBS had lost 11 percent in its ratings over the preceding year, NBC had gained 11 percent, and ABC gained 18 percent. In the desperate reshuffling of programs that followed at CBS, news and public affairs were further denigrated in an attempt to regain ratings.

CBS Reports was withdrawn from sponsorship entirely, thus being eliminated from the commercial ratings, and it was shifted from Wednesdays to Mondays because on Wednesdays it was thought to be adversely affecting the rating of the comedy program which followed it, *Beverly Hillbillies*. It was replaced by comedy programs about a talking horse and a living doll.

For Murrow, that winter, the death of Winston Churchill, the man who symbolized a historical epoch, undoubtedly heightened his awareness of the imminence of his own passing, as another symbol of the same epoch. His hair had gone thin. His face was haggard. His frame was bent. The body which he had so often driven to fatigue and beyond was no longer his to command, though he still had the spirit to be impatient of it.

He reentered the hospital for the last time on March 3, 1965. As he did, the man who had been the Voice of America's director for seven years, including the three with Murrow, resigned. Henry Loomis's parting words to those who made the Voice speak was a call to adhere to truth and honesty, and ₁ot serve as the mouthpiece of a political administration.

The freedom of expression the Voice of America had gained under Murrow, after the Cuban missile crisis, had been abridged. The bombing of North Vietnam, which the President had begun the month before, had evoked sharp dissent within the United States and much critical comment from around the world. But adverse editorial judgments, from newspapers like the *New York Times*, *Le Monde*, and most of the British press, were deleted from Voice of America broadcasts, and only the favorable allowed to remain. Seldom had truth been so selective as it proved to be in the Johnson administration.

"To acknowledge the existence of forces and views in disagreement with those of the policy-makers, to take these specially into account in the formulation of output, is a sign of strength, and is good persuasive propaganda. The United States derives strength, not weakness, from diversity," Loomis said in his farewell remarks.

Lyndon Johnson did not think so. Even Carl Rowan, disaffected by the drastic alteration in USIA purpose and methods, could not serve his presidential patron any longer, and was on the point of departure. He would be succeeded by Leonard Marks, a close personal friend of the

The place and the shirt he liked best. At Pawling

Johnsons, indeed the family lawyer for the broadcasting interests which had made them rich. To the President, this constituted experience and dedication enough in the field of political communication. When Marks some time later was asked to sum up USIA's greatest achievement during his term of office, his reply was, "We stayed out of trouble."

As Murrow reentered the hospital he received a royal notification. In recognition of outstanding services in furthering Anglo-American friendship and understanding, Her Majesty had conferred upon him an honorary K.C.B.E., Knight Commander of the British Empire. Previously George VI had awarded him an honorary O.B.E., membership in the Order of the British Empire.

For Janet the pleasure of the occasion was mingled with despair over the terminal stage of his illness. In Britain, where the honor was called a "K," the commonest reaction was, "About time, too!" One London friend, who had little time for the monarchy anyway, thought it typical that the American film actor Douglas Fairbanks, Jr., had received an honorary knighthood many years before, while "she," meaning the queen, "barely made it with Ed before he died."

After two weeks in the hospital, "further complications" were reported in Murrow's condition, and he was sent home. The cancer had reached his brain.

More strictly speaking, he insisted on going home. Janet had telephoned Bob Dixon to say that Ed was frantically demanding him. At the hospital Dixon found Casey, perplexed by his father's brusque and agitated manner.

From the bed, Murrow seized Dixon by the arm with both hands, a desperate look on his face, and said, "You've got to get me out of here. If they won't let you, I want you to pick me up and carry me out." The announcer agreed. Then he told Casey his father wanted to go home to die.

Janet took him out of the hospital the next day. At Glen Arden, Bob and Ardeth Dixon had assembled nurses and made preparations to receive him. He lived three weeks, and died two days after his fifty-seventh birthday.

In those last days he kept saying to his wife, patting her on the hand, "Well, Jan, we were lucky at that." He gave Dixon his favorite pistol and an etching of a bucking bronco, which had survived the London Blitz.

He did not die of cancer of the lung, for his remaining lung was in good condition, but of a brain tumor, in fact several tumors were found. The hemastasis was obscure. Whether malignancy had gone from his lost lung to the brain, and how, could not be determined.

Murrow was no churchgoer himself. During his illness he had simply refused to see a clergyman who called to offer him solace. But Janet adhered to the Protestant Episcopal Church, and he was given a full church funeral. Inside the Madison Avenue church sat those who had known him on that symbolic thoroughfare. Large crowds gathered outside to watch for "celebrities."

His ashes were scattered through the shady glen of the farm which he loved, and where he had so often found needed retreat. A commemorative plaque was placed by Janet upon a huge boulder in the glen. Nearby, perhaps symbolically, six feet beneath his farmland ran the cable for Telstar, the first communications satellite.

He was mourned as "a giant of the bold generation of broadcast journalism . . . [who] brought the medium to maturity," as *Variety* stated it.

The tributes ranged from the presidential, through the congressional and professional, to the personal, and nearly all remarked upon his "unrelenting search for truth," and his belief in the proposition that "free men and free inquiry are inseparable." His radio and television obituaries were the occasion for widespread retransmission, at home and abroad, of the broadcasts which had made him famous. The most memorable of them, it was generally agreed, was the one on Senator Joe McCarthy in March 1954.

Janet Murrow received hundreds of letters and telegrams of sympathy, alike from those who had known Ed and from the listeners who felt they also knew him, through his broadcasts. Among them was a card from Milo and Nancy Radulovich, living in Sacramento. "Wherever men cherish human freedom and dignity, Ed Murrow's spirit will forever stand. To him, we owe what life and freedom is ours."

Murrow's death was deeply felt in Britain, where Prime Minister Wilson called him "a unique friend of this country." The Marquess of Salisbury, who had known them both exceedingly well, compared Murrow with Churchill for "such rare courage of all kinds." *The Times* of London's lengthy obituary was headed simply, "Mr. Ed Murrow."

The evening of the funeral was also the occasion for the annual Overseas Press Club dinner, and as might have been expected, it was turned into a memorial occasion for the only man who had ever won six OPC awards.

Shortly before Murrow died, CBS had undergone one of its periodic corporate upheavals. James T. Aubrey, Jr., who at the age of forty-six had dominated American television programming for five years, was summarily removed as president of the television network, though his principal contribution to American culture, *Beverly Hillbillies,* remained prominently in the broadcasting schedule.

"I thought I was doing just what you wanted," he wept to his superiors when he was fired. And indeed he had been. For Aubrey's exodus did not mean that the network was turning its back on the commercial rating system by which he lived. There were some personal factors involved in his dismissal, but it came after the large drop in ratings which had brought CBS down to the level of the two other networks, and necessitated the frantic rearrangement and displacement of CBS programs in midseason. Aubrey had lived by the ratings, and he died by them. His departure merely signified that someone else would continue the ratings game for the network.

Murrow may have received all the encomia for his contributions to broadcasting, but it is the Aubrey stamp on American television that endures.

Under Aubrey, CBS Television attained the biggest profits in the medium's history, until then. They went up from twenty-five million dollars in 1959, when he took over, to forty-nine million dollars in 1964, his last year. Every Wednesday evening fifty-seven million Americans watched *Beverly Hillbillies*, the most popular program on the air.

Aubrey believed that what the public craved was rural comedy, detective dramas, and sex symbols. No old people were wanted on his programs; the accent was on youth, to attract youthful audiences. No serious problems were ever considered, no thinking was required. The name Aubrey gave his pastime was Action. Its real name was Escapism.

In the quest for audiences, Aubrey not only moved *CBS Reports* out of the way of *Beverly Hillbillies,* but reduced news programming on the CBS schedule. He was aghast at the amount of broadcast time and money devoted to the 1964 presidential campaign — though the escalation of the Vietnam War was the principal Johnson-Goldwater issue, real or pretended — and believed that a fifteen-minute summation of the proceedings at 11 P.M. would have been sufficient coverage of the two national political conventions.

Once again, as so often before, a chairman of the FCC told the National Association of Broadcasters in 1965 that television projected a "distorted, inadequate, and unreal" picture of the nation.

An opinion survey found "growing disenchantment with television on the part of the affluent, better-educated section of the adult American public." It was made by Louis Harris, who also conducted election polls for CBS but now had his methods impugned by it. The corporation instead cited the Nielsen ratings to show that more of the "leadership community" than ever still loved Lucy.

But the Harris findings were confirmed by a *Variety* poll among the professional classes in the New York metropolitan area. It showed a distinct preference for news, public affairs, and socially conscious drama. Some of the terms applied to Aubrey's prime-time programs were "supermarket," "pulp-grind," "comic-strip," and "garbage."

It seemed to have become demonstrable that the qualitative improvement of television no longer lay intrinsically within the commercial broadcasting system, no matter how its component parts might be contrived.

The need for public television, at least as an adjunct and a leaven, was becoming more inescapable, though doubts about its practicability remained.

The 1965–1966 television season was an inglorious one. Viewers and reviewers denounced the networks for the banality and tawdriness of their programs. But network profits reached a new high. Larger and larger audiences were delivered to the sponsors as captives.

Year after year, it would be a familiar story.

Ed Murrow was dead. The Beverly Hillbillies lived on.

Acknowledgments

B ROADCASTING is oral, and so is much of its history still. "The golden age" of radio and television, which Ed Murrow exemplified, has passed, but so recently that its documentation is as much "biological" as bibliographical.

The living witnesses of a notable career played a major role in the preparation of this book, and grateful acknowledgment is made to them.

In North Carolina those who contributed recollections, all members of the Murrow family, were J. Edgar Murrow, Mrs. J. Harvey Dick, Mrs. John Claherda, and Mrs. Louise Dennis. Thanks is also given to Hal Sieber, of Greensboro, for his help in numerous ways.

In Washington State acknowledgment is made to Murrow's college friends, Edward Lehan and Asa Clarke; to his relatives, George and Alice Lawson, and George and Tilly Coble, and to Dennis Morrison, of Washington State University.

Among Murrow's friends who recalled phases of his early career were Chester S. Williams and Martha Biehle.

In London those to whom the author is indebted are Sir Ivison Macadam, Paul H. G. Wright, John Grigg, Ernestine Carter, Marjorie von Harten, Reginald and Betty Matthews, May Hermes, Mr. and Mrs. Eric Warr, Mrs. Katherine Frew, the Dowager Marchioness of Reading, and the Marquess of Salisbury.

In broadcasting, professional associates of Murrow who shared their recollections with the author were William S. Paley, Dr. Frank Stanton, Fred W. Friendly, Louis G. Cowan, Joseph Wershba, Blair Clark, Arthur Morse, Wells Church, Robert Trout, Bob Dixon, Katherine Campbell, William K. McClure, Edward Bliss, Jr., Theodore H. White, Dr. Cabell Greet, Norman Corwin, Leonard Miall, and Fred Bate.

Special acknowledgment is made for their kindness as well as their memories to Mr. and Mrs. Dewey Murrow, to Mrs. Lacey V. Murrow, and above all to Mrs. Edward R. Murrow and Charles Casey Murrow, who provided free access to their thoughts as well as their papers.

Thanks are profusely given to James M. Seward, who had much to do with this volume, in a variety of ways, and to the Columbia Broadcasting

System for permission to use the texts of Ed Murrow's notable broadcasts.

Thanks are also owed to Lawrence H. Odell, who read the manuscript and made numerous helpful suggestions.

The author's own twenty years in broadcasting and his association with Ed Murrow provided the background against which this book was written, and any errors in fact or faults in memory are entirely his.

Bibliography

Abel, Elie. *The Missile Crisis*. Philadelphia and New York, J. B. Lippincott, 1966.

Attwood, William. *The Reds and the Blacks*. New York, Harper & Row, 1967.

Barnouw, Eric. *A Tower in Babel*. New York, Oxford University Press, 1966.

————. *The Golden Web*. New York, Oxford University Press, 1968.

Bird, Caroline. *The Invisible Scar*. Philadelphia, David McKay, 1966.

Bliss, Edward, Jr., ed. *In Search of Light: The Broadcasts of Edward R. Murrow*. New York, Knopf, 1967.

Bluem, A. William. *Documentary in American Television*. New York, Hastings House, 1965.

Brown, John Mason. *Through These Men*. New York, Harper & Bros., 1956.

Burlingame, Roger. *Don't Let Them Scare You: The Life and Times of Elmer Davis*. Philadelphia and New York, J. B. Lippincott, 1961.

Butcher, Captain Harry C. *My Three Years with Eisenhower*. New York, Simon and Schuster, 1946.

Carter, Richard. *Breakthrough: The Saga of Jonas Salk*. New York, Trident Press, 1966.

Cater, Douglass. *Power in Washington*. New York, Vintage Books, 1964.

Chambers, Whittaker. *Witness*. New York, Random House, 1952.

Cogley, John. *Report on Blacklisting*. New York, The Fund for the Republic, Inc., 1956.

Cook, Fred J. *The Corrupted Land*. New York, Macmillan, 1966.

Crosby, John. *Out of the Blue*. New York, Simon and Schuster, 1952.

de Toledano, Ralph. *R.F.K. The Man Who Would Be President*. New York, Putnam, 1967.

Douglas, William O. *My Wilderness*. New York, Doubleday, 1960.

Elder, Robert E. *The Information Machine*. Syracuse University Press, 1968.

Fermi, Laura. *Illustrious Immigrants*. University of Chicago Press, 1968.

Friendly, Fred W. *Due to Circumstances Beyond Our Control*. New York, Random House, 1967.

Gedye, G. E. R. *Betrayal in Central Europe*. New York, Harper & Bros., 1939.

Goodfriend, Arthur. *The Twisted Image*. New York, St. Martin's Press, 1963.

Goodman, Walter. *All Honourable Men*. London, Longmans, Green, 1963.

Hibberd, Stuart. *This — Is London . . .* London, Macdonald & Evans, 1950.

Higgins, Marguerite. *Our Vietnam Nightmare*. New York, Harper & Row, 1965.

Hilsman, Roger. *To Move a Nation*. New York, Doubleday, 1967.

Horowitz, David. *From Yalta to Vietnam*. London, MacGibbon & Kee, 1965.

Johnston, Haynes. *The Bay of Pigs*. New York, Norton, 1964.

Kaltenborn, H. V. *I Broadcast the Crisis*. New York, Random House, 1938.

Kennedy, John F. *Why England Slept*. London, Hutchinson, 1940.

Lang, Kurt and Gladys E. *Politics and Television*. Chicago, Quadrangle, 1968.

Lilienthal, David E. *Journals*. New York, Harper & Row, Vol. 2, 1964; Vol. 3, 1966.

Lord, Walter. *The Good Years*. New York, Harper & Bros., 1960.

MacNeill, Robert. *The People Machine*. New York, Harper & Row, 1968.

Mecklin, John. *Mission in Torment*. New York, Doubleday, 1965.

Mehling, Harold. *The Great Time-Killer*. Cleveland, World, 1962.

Miall, Leonard, ed. *Richard Dimbleby, Broadcaster*. London, British Broadcasting Corp., 1966.

Middleton, Drew. *The Sky Suspended*. New York, Longmans, Green, 1960.

Murrow, Edward R. *This Is London*. New York, Simon and Schuster, 1941.

Nicolson, Nigel, ed. *Diaries and Letters of Harold Nicolson*. New York, Atheneum, Vol. 1, 1966; Vol. 2, 1967; Vol. 3, 1968.

Priestley, J. B. *All England Listened*. New York, Chilmark Press, 1967.

Renshaw, Patrick. *The Wobblies*. New York, Doubleday, 1967.

Rovere, Richard H. *Senator Joe McCarthy*. New York, Harcourt, Brace, 1959.

Saerchinger, Cesar. *Hello America*. Boston, Houghton, Mifflin, 1938.

Salinger, Pierre. *With Kennedy*. New York, Doubleday, 1966.

Schlesinger, Arthur M., Jr. *A Thousand Days*. Boston, Houghton, Mifflin, 1965.

Seldes, Gilbert. *The Public Arts*. New York, Simon and Schuster, 1956.

Sevareid, Eric. *Not So Wild a Dream*. New York, Knopf, 1946.

Sheean, Vincent. *Between the Thunder and the Sun*. New York, Random House, 1943.

Sherwood, Robert L. *Roosevelt and Hopkins*. New York, Harper & Bros., 1948.

Shirer, William L. *Berlin Diary*. New York, Knopf, 1941.

Smith, Walker C. *The Everett Massacre*. Chicago, IWW Publishing Bureau, 1917 (?)

Sorensen, Theodore C. *Kennedy*. New York, Harper & Row, 1965.

Sorensen, Thomas C. *The Word War*. New York, Harper & Row, 1968.

Swing, Raymond. *Good Evening!* New York, Harcourt, Brace-World, 1964.

Thompson, Laurence. *1940*. New York, Morrow, 1966.

Turner, E. S. *The Phoney War*. New York, St. Martin's Press, 1962.

Weinberg, Meyer. *TV in America*. New York, Ballantine Books, 1962.

Whalen, Richard J. *The Founding Father*. New York, New American Library, 1964.

White, Paul W. *News on the Air*. New York, Harcourt, Brace, 1947.

Woolley, Thomas Russell, Jr. *A Rhetorical Study: The Radio Speaking of Edward R. Murrow*. Northwestern University, 1957. A Ph.D. dissertation.

Wylie, Max. *Clear Channels*. New York, Funk & Wagnalls, 1955.

INDEX